Eros,
Wisdom,
and
Silence

Eric Voegelin Institute Series in Political Philosophy

EROS, WISDOM, AND SILENCE

Plato's Erotic Dialogues

James M. Rhodes

UNIVERSITY OF MISSOURI PRESS
COLUMBIA AND LONDON

Library of Congress Cataloging-in-Publication Data

Rhodes, James M.
Eros, wisdom, and silence : Plato's
erotic dialogues / James M. Rhodes.
p.   cm. — (Eric Voegelin Institute
series in political philosophy)
Includes bibliographical references (p.) and indexes.
ISBN 0-8262-1459-2 (alk. paper)
1. Love.   2. Plato.   3. Silence (Philosophy).
I. Title.   II. Series.
B398.L9.R46 2003
177'.7—dc21   2002043029

⊚™   This paper meets the requirements of the
American National Standard for Permanence of Paper
for Printed Library Materials, Z39.48, 1984.

Text Designer: Stephanie Foley
Jacket Designer: Susan Ferber
Typesetter: Bookcomp, Inc.
Printer and Binder: Thomson-Shore, Inc.
Typeface: Palatino

The University of Missouri Press offers its
grateful acknowledgment for a generous
contribution from the Eric Voegelin Institute
in support of the publication of this volume.

Chapter 3, "Mystic Philosophy in the Seventh Letter,"
reprinted from *Politics, Philosophy, Writing: Plato's Art of
Caring for Souls*, edited by Zdravko Planinc, by
permission of the University of Missouri Press. Copyright
© 2001 by the Curators of the University of Missouri.

To Anne Marie

Contents

PREFACE

This book about love is addressed to lovers. It tries to help lovers learn to sing Plato's hymns of love to the Essence Really Being that draws our souls up through love of beloveds, love of virtue, and love of the good, the beautiful, and the true to love of itself. It sings too of the love that stirs lovers to love, in hopes that we might know better what lies at the ground of ourselves. It also invites lovers to participate in conversations that move our souls to love—first and foremost in the beautifully intricate and endlessly fascinating conversations that Plato holds with his readers through the media of his letters and dramatic dialogues, but then also in the extended discussions of several of Plato's best interlocutors. Inescapably, it also invites one and all to take part in my own dialogues with Plato and his commentators. However, I hope to fade quietly into the background, allowing Plato himself to practice his dialectical care of souls.

Conceived as a conversation, this book is meant to be read side by side with Plato's works and those of his worthy interlocutors, several texts always open on the desk, dialogue going on with and among them. Small bits of the book should be perused along with the relevant parts of Plato, at leisure. If readers proceed casually in this way, letting the beauty of Plato's images and reasoning draw them into the discussion, they will fall in love with the realities that Plato envisages. Then, although the task of reading will be long, the burden will prove light. The reader will realize that it was not I who conducted the conversation but, rather, that it was the conversation that seized me and compelled me to utter it completely.

Writing a book such as this is a lesson in humility. One discovers how ignorant he was at the beginning of the inquiry and how little progress he could have made without the inspiration and aid of others. I am greatly indebted to many people: to Gerhart Niemeyer and Eric Voegelin, who guided me to the love of Plato and taught me how to understand him; to Zdravko Planinc, who read later drafts of my manuscript, pushed me to improve many of my arguments by resisting some and contributing significant insights to others, and liberally gave me necessary hermeneutic keys

xi

to Plato's dialogues; to the late Dante Germino, who also read later drafts of several of my chapters and obliged me to refine them by arguing with me about everything; to Oona Eisenstadt, whose comments on my introduction helped me to make it better; to Hajime Watanabe, who usefully criticized my earlier drafts; to Kevin Miller and Rodrigo Sánchez, who carefully read large portions of my manuscripts while they were students at Marquette University and responded by calling my attention to several things in Plato and other thinkers that had escaped my attention; to many other Marquette students who had the philosophic eros and helped me to see more by conversing with me intelligently, most especially Bernard Kearny, Amy Brabender, John Kovari, Mischa Beckett, Tim Dale, Kyle Strupp, Matt Reynolds, and Marguerite Meyer; and to two members of the Marquette Foreign Language Department (classics), Patricia Marquardt and Francis M. Lazarus, who frequently and generously gave of their time to discuss difficult Greek passages with me. My anonymous reviewers also contributed some excellent suggestions. None of these friends are responsible for my errors.

Surprisingly, I also have a huge debt to scholars with whom I profoundly disagree, particularly to Leo Strauss, his students, and their students. They are superb thinkers and not easily refuted, if at all. They forced me to learn how to read and showed me things that I never would have noticed had I not had to take their arguments seriously. They have my respect but not my assent.

I am grateful to the Eric Voegelin Institute for its generous support of the publication of this book.

Note on Citations, Transliterations, and Translations

In this book, I practice the usual method of citing Platonic works by embedding Stephanus numbers in parentheses in my text. References are to the Oxford series *Platonis Opera*. I have also consulted the Loeb Classical Library series *Plato*. When summarizing Platonic passages, I cite Stephanus page numbers. When quoting verbatim, I cite Stephanus line numbers as well.

Citations to Aristotle embed Bekker numbers in parentheses in my text. References are to the Oxford versions of the philosopher's works. I have also used the Loeb Classical Library series for Aristotle's works.

Citations to Homer, Hesiod, Aristophanes, Plutarch, and Xenophon are to the most recent Loeb Classical Library editions of their works. Homer is cited by poem, chapter, and line; Hesiod by poem and line; Aristophanes by play and line; Plutarch by treatise, section, and line; and Xenophon by treatise, book, chapter, and line. When quoting these authors, I embed the citations in the text. I relegate oblique references to them to my notes. On rare occasions, a few other well-known primary sources will be cited in text, as is customary.

When I employ a Greek word as a technical concept, I first give the Greek and then transliterate it into the Latin alphabet. I define the transliterated word when it first appears. I also try to transliterate properly. However, some Greek words—for example, Ἔρως and δημος—have long histories of transliteration without diacritical marks. In these cases, I bow to traditional usage, writing, for example, Eros and demos.

A word about my policy concerning translations is also necessary. For the purposes of philosophy, I prefer the most literal possible renderings of the Greek that are consistent with good English syntax, even though the most literal translations lack poetic beauty. There is a catch in this statement. Perfectly literal translation of Greek into English is impossible, for Greek has numerous expressions that lack English equivalents. The proper aim, therefore, is "as close to literal as is reasonable." I also prefer the most consistent possible renderings of technical philosophic concepts. By this, I mean that there are Platonic terms that should not be translated one way on a given page and in a different way some pages later. (On the other hand, there are times when nothing is lost by doing this. For example, it would be oppressive to translate *anthrōpoi* as "human beings" in every instance. Sometimes "people" or "persons" will do.) Nor should two technical terms be rendered in the same English (although this is sometimes impossible to avoid, for example, as in the case of the three Greek words for "love"). Violation of these rules causes readers to fail to realize that the same concept is being discussed from page to page or to miss the fact that different Platonic concepts have been confounded.

My preferences have required me to furnish my own translations of Greek texts, all laboriously elaborated, for I am no expert classicist or philologist. Still, I have tried not to stray too far from the best literal translations available or from the standard Loeb translations. All translations of German passages in primary sources are also my own.

EROS,
WISDOM,
AND
SILENCE

1

Eros, Wisdom, and Silence in Plato

The Platonic Socrates is renowned for proclaiming his ignorance. His reputation owes primarily to several statements that he makes in Plato's *Apology of Socrates*. For example, he denies that he is a clever speaker (17a–b). He argues that his enemies have said "nothing true" (οὐδὲν ἀληθές, 18b6) in their snide accounts of him, one of which is that he is a "wise man" (σοφὸς ἀνήρ, 18b7). He disclaims any share of wisdom about "the things under the earth and in the heavens" (19b–d). He insists that he has no knowledge of the virtue of the human being and the citizen (20b–c). He remembers that he was profoundly shocked when the priestess at Delphi, the Pythia, pronounced him the wisest man, "For I am aware that I am not wise at all, not much, not little" (21b4–5). He relates that the prophecy began to make sense when he questioned a politician who falsely judged himself wise. Then he thought to himself: "I am wiser than this person. For probably neither of us knows anything beautiful and good, but he assumes that he knows something when he does not, whereas I neither know nor suppose that I know" (21d2–6). He reacted in much the same way after he questioned some poets. Then, when he also interrogated some artisans, conscious that he "knew nothing, so to speak" (22c9–d1), he learned that they knew their trades, but not "the greatest things" (22d7–e1). He decided that he was wise in his understanding of his ignorance, and that "it is likely, men, that actually the god is wise, and that in this oracle he is stating that human wisdom has little or no worth" (23a5–7). Therefore, he concludes that the god has announced that Socrates "is worthless with regard to wisdom" (23b2–3). Socrates deprecates his wisdom and knowledge in other Platonic dialogues, too. Perhaps the most famous instance follows the demand of Thrasymachus in the *Republic* that Socrates present his own definition of justice. The philosopher replies that he neither knows nor claims to know (337e4–5). We take it, then, that Socrates asserts that he has no wisdom and knows nothing. However, this concept of a modest Socrates

1

dissolves when we read further. Later in the *Apology*, just after Socrates has denied that he has any information about Hades, he startles us by declaring: "But that to do injustice and to disobey one's better, whether god or human being, is evil and shameful, that I do know (οἶδα)" (29b6–7). Apparently, he claims some grasp of the virtue of the human being and the citizen after all. Socrates surprises us even more in the *Symposium*. He states there that he cannot oppose an agenda of speeches praising the god Eros, given that: "I say that I know (ἐπίστασθαι) nothing but the things of eros (τὰ ἐρωτικά)" (177d7–8). This use of ἐπίστασθαι constitutes an indirect but fairly strong claim to a more scientific (but not perfectly scientific) knowledge of erotics, as compared with his use of οἶδα in the *Apology*, which is a weaker affirmation of a general grasp of the bad and shameful. Next, the seemingly diffident Socrates floors us in the *Theages* by asserting an extremely powerful claim to some sort of science of erotics (even though it seems to be an incomplete one): "Rather I always say, you know, that I happen, so to speak, to know (ἐπιστάμενος) nothing except a certain small subject of learning, the things of eros (τῶν ἐρωτικῶν). As regards this subject of learning, I claim to be more clever than any human beings living previously or now" (128b2–4).

The contrast between Socrates' protests of his ignorance and his claims to a science of erotics makes us wonder: What, if anything, does Socrates know about eros? Why is eros so important or interesting that it is the only subject that Socrates elects to master? Is acquiring a science of the things of eros difficult? Or is eros such a trivial matter that an ignoramus could master it easily? Is Socrates' science of eros the foundation of his unscientific awareness of the virtue, or proper excellence, of the human being and the citizen? Are his flat assertions of his ignorance consistent with his claims to be amazingly clever beyond anyone with regard to the things of eros? Is Socrates ignorant, wise, or, somehow, both?[1] This book attempts to answer these questions.

EROS AND WISDOM

To ascertain whether Socrates knows anything about eros, we must study the relevant texts. Having yet to do that, we begin in ignorance. However, scholars will think it right to ask for a preliminary Socratic definition of eros, one that delineates the subject of inquiry.

---

1. Allan Bloom delivers himself of a tantalizingly paradoxical remark: "Socrates' knowledge of ignorance is identical with his perfect knowledge of erotics" (*The Closing of the American Mind: How Higher Education Has Failed Democracy and Impoverished the Souls of Today's Students*, 133).

Unfortunately, an initial survey leaves us somewhat confused, both as to what Socrates and Plato believe eros is in itself and as to what they deem its object to be. Regarding the essence of eros, Socrates formally defines what it is and what power it possesses in his first speech in the *Phaedrus*. He states: "It is clear to all that eros is a certain desire (ἐπιθυμία, *epithymia*)" (237d2).[2] In the *Symposium*, Aristophanes also says that eros is an *epithymia* (192e10–193a1). This seems simple enough. However, then, in his second speech in the *Phaedrus*, Socrates starts to call eros a "yearning" (ἵμερος, *himeros*, 251d4, e2), and one wonders whether he has merely deployed a synonym or changed his mind. The switch might be more than semantic, for the "charioteer" of the soul, upon experiencing *himeros*, beholds "the erotic vision" (τὸ ἐρωτικὸν ὄμμα, 253e5) and then remembers "the nature of beauty" (254b5–6), a reality encountered in a previous existence. Eros is evidently becoming a *himeros* activated by a mystical anamnesis, or recollection. Again, in the *Symposium*, all of the characters except Socrates refer to Eros as a god. Under the influence of Diotima, Socrates maintains that Eros is not a god, but a daimon. However, in the *Phaedrus*, Socrates contends that Eros is "a god or something divine" (242e2). This suffices to baffle us. We are compelled to conclude that eros is a desire or yearning that surfaces as human passion (which might not be well understood itself) and shades into a mysterious anamnesis and an ambiguous suprahuman reality. For now, that is all we can say.

With respect to the object of eros, the case is equally complex. English-speaking people automatically think of eros as desire for sexual intercourse. In the *Symposium*, Diotima tells Socrates that Greek speakers also restrict their concept of eros to sexual craving (205b). In the *Laws*, the Athenian Stranger comments that sexual desire is the eros that is sharpest and most maddening (783a). This explains the conventional usage. However, Diotima tells Socrates that eros is generically "desire of all good things and of being happy" (205d1–2). The Athenian Stranger, apparently upholding the same view, mentions that there is eros for food and drink (782e), for what one must do to be perfect in one's occupation (643d), for fishing and hunting sea animals (823e), for moderate and just practices (711d), for riches (831c), for ignoble gain (727e), and for insatiable, unlimited acquisition (870a). In the *Alcibiades I*, Socrates fears that Alcibiades will become a *dēmerastēs*, one who has eros for the demos (132a). This is not all. Diotima thinks that eros aims at the varieties of immortality that mankind can achieve (208a). The Athenian Stranger adds: "Nature makes everyone

---

2. "Desire" is the usual translation of *epithymia*, although this rendering might be a little too tame, for the concept contains the idea of *thymos*, the "spirited element" of the soul. "Spirited desire" might be more appropriate. However, I shall use the traditional "desire."

avidly desire immortality in every way" (721b7–c1). It appears that we have many loves, and that all want eternity.[3] Eros is not trivial, but vast. Its multiplicity in unity is dazzling. It is much more than genital sexuality. We cannot delimit it.

Although our little survey has not enabled us to settle on one intelligible definition of eros or to assign it a single object, it has shown why eros is so important to Socrates. If eros is "all desire of good things and of being happy," it initiates everything that we do throughout our lives. If our responses to eros can have outcomes as diverse as tendencies to moderate and just practices, on the one hand, and inclinations to ignoble, insatiable, and infinite acquisition, on the other, these reactions have everything to do with what kinds of people we are. Hence, they are also the chief causes of our felicity and misery. In our seemingly mundane pastimes, they govern how we use food and drink; how we love spouses, children, friends, and sexually attractive beauties; how well we perform our jobs; and how much we involve ourselves in the great scramble to gratify the acquisitive instinct. In our striving for immortality in every way, they aid or impede our progress toward the eternal. In the mythical language of Stesichorus in the *Phaedrus*, which should be understood poetically, they determine whether we will exist in the next cycles of our souls as animals and insects on this earth or take wing into the heavens, ascending toward the hyperuranian realities (in other words, the realities above the heavens). Socrates finds eros such an all-absorbing subject because this mystery spurs or draws him toward every aspect of his destiny. Eros is so bound up with everything about ourselves that matters that Socrates might equate his science of eros with obedience to the bidding of the Delphic Oracle, γνῶθι σαυτόν (Know thyself), although eros is not merely the self. It might be fair to call a scientific knowledge of eros wisdom.

Although it aims at self-knowing, Socrates' preoccupation with eros is not simply self-serving. Socrates' love of beautiful human beings apparently makes him care deeply about the qualities of their souls, for the sake of their happiness as well as his own. For example, in the *Alcibiades I*, Socrates professes his eros for Alcibiades' soul (131d) and then spends the rest of the dialogue educating the young man to the virtues, urging him to adorn his soul with their splendor. He "agonizes" for his love when Alcibiades shows signs of rejecting schooling in the virtues, a choice that will certainly ruin him both personally and politically (119c). In the *Symposium*, Diotima convinces Socrates that the lover undertakes his beloved's education, discussing virtue and the good man's character and pursuits (209b–c). In the *Phaedrus*, Socrates reiterates this, adding that the worthy lover sees to

---

3. I am grateful to Zdravko Planinc for this insight, and for calling my attention to the passage in the *Laws* that suggests it.

it that both he and his beloved ultimately take wing to the heavenly realm (256b). Erotic wisdom wants to communicate itself because it loves.

Socrates actively pursues those whom he will love and teach. At the beginning of the *Phaedrus*, he virtually tackles Phaedrus on the street, asking him: "O dear Phaedrus, where are you going, and from where do you come?" (Ὦ φίλε Φαῖδρε, ποῖ δὴ καὶ πόθεν, 227a1). He conceives this question sub specie aeternitatis, hinting to Phaedrus that he should consider his spiritual destiny and the adequacy of his motives for his actions. When Socrates discovers that Phaedrus is enamored of a vile, sophisticated speech designed to seduce a gullible lad, he does everything in his power to elevate his companion's form of love, finally addressing a heartfelt prayer to Eros that Phaedrus will redirect his life to Eros and philosophic discourses (257a–b). Although he cannot lavish the same care on every last Athenian as he does on his intellectual comrades, Socrates is also concerned for the condition of the souls of the many. Speaking to his jury of five hundred plus, he contends in the *Apology* that he has consistently urged "you" (plural, ὑμῶν, 30a8) to strive for the best possible souls. He has examined people and engaged them in dialectical discussions when they have proved deficient (30a–b). Some commentators doubt that Socrates has spent much time with the many, for Plato's dialogues never show him in conversation with common men.[4] Although it is true that all the interlocutors in the dialogues are aristocratic, this is not sufficient reason to distrust Socrates' word in the *Apology*. We also hear in the *Cleitophon* that Socrates has often chided "the human beings" (not the gentlemen, but the ordinary people, τοῖς ἀνθρώποις, 407a8) asking: "Where are you being carried, O human beings" (407b1), and urging them to educate the young to virtue. If Socrates could, he would compel his entire society to confront his "whither" question.[5]

If the eros that Socrates thinks he knows is real, inquiry into eros is just as necessary to our time as to his, and mastering his science of erotics is just as indispensable to our personal happiness as to his. Again, if that eros is real, Socrates' praxis is the appropriate model for the teachers of our age. If contemporary instructors manage to recapture Socrates' science of eros, they too should be impelled to beautiful young people by eros, look into the students' souls, examine the nature of their eros and virtue, do what they can to repair or at least diagnose defects in these areas, and offer this service to as many people in their societies as possible.

4. All these scholars follow Leo Strauss, *The City and Man*, 57.
5. Zdravko Planinc, "Homeric Imagery in the *Phaedrus*," chap. 5 in *Politics, Philosophy, Writing: Plato's Art of Caring for Souls*, holds that the Platonic dialogues refigure scenes in Homer. This implies that Socrates' interlocutors are aristocrats not because Plato has an animus against commoners, but because their models are the comrades of Odysseus, all of whom were aristocrats. I think that Planinc is right.

   Insofar as he gazed deeply into students' souls—which is not to say in every possible respect—Allan Bloom was perhaps the most Socratic teacher of the twentieth century. In his controversial book, *The Closing of the American Mind*, which he offered as "a meditation on the state of our souls, particularly those of the young," Bloom spells out the responsibilities of the Socratic praxis admirably. The teacher, he maintains "is, willy-nilly, guided by the awareness, or the divination, that there is a human nature, and that assisting its fulfillment is his task." Then he argues:

> The teacher, particularly the teacher dedicated to liberal education, must constantly try to look toward the goal of human completeness and back at the natures of his students here and now, ever seeking to understand the former and to assess the capacities of the latter to approach it. Attention to the young, knowing what their hungers are and what they can digest, is the essence of the craft. One must spy out and elicit those hungers. For there is no real education that does not respond to felt need; anything else acquired is trifling display.[6]

   Having spied out and elicited his students' hungers tirelessly for three decades, Bloom gives this depressing report of the state of their souls: American students believe that truth is relative. They are astonished by anyone who does not accept this proposition as self-evident. Consequently, they lack intellectual seriousness and learn little. Their relativistic families are also spiritually dreary, colorless, devoid of inspiring visions of mankind's meaning and good, intellectually moribund, bourgeois, and incapable of transmitting ethical principles effectively because their relativism has robbed them of moral authority. The students do not read great books anymore, thanks to relativism and the successful feminist assault on the Western canon. Instead, they are addicted to rock music. This music has "one appeal only, a barbaric appeal, to sexual desire—not love, not *eros*, but sexual desire undeveloped and untutored. . . . Young people know that rock has the beat of sexual intercourse." Like severe drug addiction, this "gutter phenomenon . . . ruins the imagination of young people and makes it very difficult for them to have a passionate relationship to the art and thought that are the substance of liberal education." The sexual frenzy of the rock music is part of a broader phenomenon. Sex has become "the national project." The students have joined this enterprise. They have abolished sexual limits and modesty and now engage in multiple "relationships," not promiscuously, but serially. The sex is so easy that it has become "no big deal." The result is that "sexual passion no longer includes the illusion of eternity." Young people, and not only they, "have studied

6. Bloom, *Closing American Mind*, 19, 20.

and practiced a crippled *eros* that can no longer take wing, and does not contain within it the longing for eternity and the divination of one's relatedness to being." This eroticism is sated, sterile, lame, and "is not the divine madness that Socrates praised." Casual relationships have also fostered the habit of approaching marriage with egocentric attitudes that lack constancy. This has contributed to the runaway divorce rate that "is surely America's most urgent social problem." The children of divorced parents are irreparably harmed. It does not matter that armies of psychologists are hired to persuade them that their parents love them and will spend "quality time" with them. The children feel grievously wronged, come to mistrust love, and develop a slight deformity of the spirit that closes them to the serious study of philosophy and literature. In addition to all this, the students are self-centered, that is, more interested in their careers and enjoyments than in other human beings or in great spiritual or political issues. In the vast majority of cases, they arrive at their universities seeking vocational training, without the sense that they are embarking upon grand intellectual adventures that might yield answers to the question, "What is man?" Thus, a defective American eros, not only in its sexual forms but also in all its branches, has prevented our students from waxing in wisdom and grace. By and large, American students become "flat souled."[7]

I myself am a professor of more than thirty-five years standing. I, too, have attempted to model my praxis on that of Socrates. I suppose, with Bloom, that the teacher's function is to assist the fulfillment of human nature and that one must study the students to do that work well. Like Bloom, I have gotten to know many of my students. I do not need to claim that I have done this as well as Bloom did. He devoted a great deal of time to soliciting his students' opinions, much more than I. However, I have had ample occasion to see and hear a lot. The students are talking when one enters classrooms and cafeterias; they acknowledge one's arrival with a nod and continue their conversations without embarrassment. At other times, students come to see one because they desperately need help, not with their studies, but with problems in their personal lives. These youngsters have cheerful, confident, public personas. Privately, they are wretched. They say why. The numbers of such unhappy youths never approach half of one's enrollment in a given year, but they might come to a fifth or a third when those who choose other advisers are counted. At any rate, a professor does get to know what is going on generally, if not in every particular.

Having seen what I have seen, I have the distinct impression that Bloom has diagnosed genuine dangers and trends in the United States but that

---

7. Ibid., 73, 79, 106, 122, 132, 119, 134. These quotations summarize and paraphrase pt. 1 of Bloom's book.

our youth are not as far gone as he thinks.[8] It may be that my perceptions differ from his because I teach at a Catholic university. America's social currents course through every institution in the land, but, in Catholic culture, they still meet some resistance, flow less strongly, and can occasionally be redirected. Whether this or somebody's keener or duller eye explains my partial disagreement with Bloom, I believe that our situation around the turn of the new millennium is as follows.

First, it is true that the great majority of American students believe that truth is relative. So do most of their professors. The propositions that there is a human nature and that happiness depends on fulfilling it inspire suspicion, if not mockery. However, the students' relativism is received rather than systematically deduced. Hence, it is soft rather than hard.[9] A Socratic professor can interest perhaps half of his or her students in ceasing to regard relativism as self-evident and in weighing questions about its validity self-consciously. Both intellectual honesty and prudence prohibit attempts to impose truth and natural right on the students as dogmas. The Socratic teacher must make whatever headway is possible by conceding the legitimacy of relativism provisionally and then starting the philosophic enterprise of careful, open-minded inquiry from scratch with every student who responds. If the educator does begin every quest sincerely convinced that the relativists might turn out to be right, the students become excited about the investigation and fruitful conversations ensue. This process requires self-discipline and endless hard work of the teacher, but there is no other way. It also keeps the instructor in the thick of the philosophic life, so it is a happy labor.

Second, it is true that relativism, bankrupt education, popular culture, and the immaturity that is natural to the undergraduate age group deprive students of intellectual ambition.[10] Thus, professors face appalling ignorance every day. However, I also think that college teachers are subject to amnesia and optical illusions. We forget how frivolous we were and how little we knew when we were eighteen or twenty. Soon, we imagine that we were always as well read and well informed as we are now. We owe the students the same chance to develop that we had. We must remember that it is not for nothing that Socrates requires his apprentices to reach their

8. In what follows, I am not attempting to provide an original critique of Bloom. Everything that I shall say has already been said more comprehensively and eloquently by one or another of the authors in Robert L. Stone, ed., *Essays on "The Closing of the American Mind."* My primary interest here is to provide an accurate description of the phenomena as I see them shortly before and after the turn of our new millennium.

9. As Eva Brann remarks, "[S]hallow opinions are most shallowly rooted" ("The Spirit Lives in the Sticks," in *Essays on "Closing Mind,"* ed. Stone, 185).

10. I agree with George Anastaplo that it is surprising that Bloom ignores the role of television in the miseducation of the United States ("In re Allan Bloom: A Respectful Dissent," in *Essays on "Closing Mind,"* ed. Stone, 270–71).

fifties before they take up philosophy. Socratic professors might be able to inspire half of their students to diligent study by awakening their wonder about the great questions. Stimulating wonder is our job. We ought not to complain because no one has done this work for us.

Third, it is not clear whether Bloom drew his conclusions about the families of his students from face-to-face contact, inferred them from the maxim "by their fruits shall ye know them," or generalized from the character of his own family, with which he is widely reported to have been at odds. I meet some of the families of my students annually. They are not as uniformly relativistic and vulgar as Bloom leads one to expect. True, they are almost never philosophic, and they cannot always avoid being influenced by mass opinion. However, they are generally thoughtful, interesting, committed to the ethical good as they understand it, and dedicated to the welfare of their children. If they have not always made their offspring as virtuous as they wished, their difficulties have often been the same as those noted by Socrates in the *Republic,* where he comments that it is virtually impossible for a human education to counter the effects of mass culture (492d–493a). We should sympathize with such parents rather than denounce them. The Socratic professor must build on the good work that parents have done and try to support them in cases in which they have been overwhelmed by the prevailing forces. On the other hand, divorce really is a grave problem. It scars children permanently. Still, the plights of these youths are not hopeless. As often as not, I have seen young victims of divorce driven toward the philosophic life by their injuries rather than away from it.

Fourth, Bloom is certainly right to contend that our college youth culture consists mostly of rock music.[11] One must grant that a lot of rock appeals to sexual desire and has a sexual beat. Further, much rock music (and also much of rap) is sheer alienation and unbridled aggression. A great deal more is revolting kitsch, chock-full of maudlin, artificial feeling, not unlike most of the popular music of earlier generations. However, if I may pervert Hamlet to a good end, there is much more in rock music, and intelligent students see much more in it, than is dreamed of in Bloom's philosophy. Some rock celebrates sexuality in a wholesome way that makes it a welcome addition to the education of the young. Some is not sexual at all, but has a happy-go-lucky bounce that expresses sheer joy of living. It is pure fun. Some is what the students call "social commentary." Although oftentimes naive, it has some beginnings of thoughtfulness. The exceptional rock piece might capture glimpses of beauty or otherwise depict

---

11. I am speaking of university students. There is another large segment of the U.S. population, including adults and young people, that is devoted to country music, which is not so popular among the students with whom I am familiar.

grave problems, ennobling human experiences, and profound insights differently from, but as authentically as, anything in classical music. Much as
Louis Armstrong was the starting point from which I naturally moved to
Bach, Mozart, and philosophy, in an era that seems Paleolithic to students
now, some good rock might propel our youths toward meditation on the
eternal realities. So, rather than tarring all rock music with the same brush,
as Bloom does, we should distinguish cases, differentiating the pernicious
from the healthful. To prevent needless disputes, and also to avoid cutting the ridiculous figure of a deluded, finger-snapping grandfather who
supposes that he could be up-to-date in the music of our young, I shall
not attempt to give examples of bad and good rock. It is more important
to observe that our students have been exposed to both kinds throughout
their lives. Accordingly, some will become casualties of rock and end up
sexually, erotically jaded, in the manner that Bloom so adroitly analyzes.
Others will fare better. The outcomes are not predetermined. Professors
can help decide which influences will win out by throwing invitations to
the philosophic life into the balance.

Fifth, it cannot be denied that sex has become the American national
project. A great many of our students have been swept up in this enterprise. Together with their countrymen, many have abolished sexual limits and modesty, as evidenced by their conversation and jokes, by the en-
tertainments that they enjoy (including steamy movies, MTV, and frankly
sexual dancing), and by their clothing. Many do have serial sexual relationships. Indeed, many young people feel tremendous pressure to establish
their credentials as liberated individualists by cohabiting with their sexual
partners ostentatiously. The recent annihilation of the great barrier to this
behavior, fear of pregnancy and childbirth, has probably made such casual
sex more common than it used to be. It seems likely that in the majority of
these cases, the students' sex has really become so easy that it is "no big
deal." In these instances, the eros has surely become sterile, devoid of Socratic divine madness, and incapable of taking wing into eternity, as Bloom
contends. Also, there is usually exploitation in these kinds of relationships.
Almost invariably, somebody gets hurt. Undoubtedly, there are exceptions.
There must be a number of cases in which there is perfect mutual giving
of self to other and a firm intention of permanence. These instances are
marriage in all but name and can be expected to eventuate in the Socratic
winged flights. The normal result, though, is heartbreak. Socratic teachers
cannot save students from these mistakes by prying into their private lives
or policing bedrooms. Neither can they prevent the errors by preaching
religious morality or the lessons of Plato's dialogues from their bully class-
room pulpits; words are mere abstractions to the young until the realities
of their self-inflicted injuries become manifest as pain. All the Socratic professors can do is to wait for the heartbroken students to crash-land in tears

in their offices and classrooms. When this occurs, the youths do not need pinch-faced authorities in tall, pointy hats to inform them that something has gone badly wrong with their love affairs. Rather, they need advice on how to heal their wounds and fulfill their erotic natures in true love. Here, Bloom seems mistaken if he supposes that the eros of the damaged souls can never take wing. Sometimes, it is disaster that opens unhappy souls to philosophy. The teacher must be prepared to lead the students to a more philosophic eros when it is needed and wanted. In this role, the Socratic professor can help some of the sorrowing youngsters.

Finally, it is true that a majority of the students are self-centered. To illustrate this problem, I can contribute a story of my own to Bloom's report. In Plato's *Republic*, Glaucon speaks of a magic ring that makes its wearer invisible. A lowly man who found this ring, a shepherd, got himself appointed messenger to his king. Then he seduced the queen, with her help murdered the king, seized the throne, took whatever he wanted from the marketplace, snuck into houses and slept with anybody he pleased, killed whomever he wished, released prisoners from jail if the whim took him, and generally did as he desired, like a god among mortals (359c–360b). In the eyes of this man, the good things in life were sex, wealth, and power. For thirty-five years, I have been asking students in my introductory courses what they would do if they had the ring. I have administered this survey by secret ballot to some three thousand youths. The results have been remarkably consistent. Every term but one, around 55 percent of the respondents have answered that they would use the ring in the same manner that the shepherd did.[12] The 55 percent hastily assure me that they would not kill anyone. That would be too gruesome. However, they would make progress with the sexually attractive, empty vaults, peek at the answer keys of law school entrance exams, take steps to ensure corporate promotions or political victories, and, occasionally, play Robin Hood. These students charmingly exhibit the lower varieties of eroticism. They, too, perceive the greatest goods in human existence to be sex, wealth, and power. They plan to grab these greatest goods for themselves as comfortably as they can, again failing to see misery ahead. The 45 percent are scandalized but find themselves both incapable of persuading their peers to be more just and accused of lying to themselves about how they would react if they had the ring. One frequently voiced minority rebuttal is that the pursuit of the goods of life would be boring and insufficiently challenging if one employed the ring at every turn. What this means to me is that more than the 55 percent perceive the good as the shepherd did. To be sure, someone will object that my study is scientifically invalid because I have not taken a random sample of the U.S. population. I answer that this is exactly why

12. The odd semester had a 50–50 percent split.

my findings are dismaying. We are discussing the fantasies of political science majors in a Catholic university, where one hopes for more reassuring results. The Socratic teacher who loves the students must raise questions about the shepherd's actions, striving to change the numbers. This effort does not always go unrewarded. The students are not bad at heart. All of us begin life self-centered; all need to learn to recognize a higher good. That is the point of education. A Socratic teacher can help effect the transformation.

Let us assume, therefore, that Bloom identifies real threats to the United States but is a little too alarmist about our situation. Many Americans are erotically ailing, but none inevitably end as dead souls. A Socratic philosopher can minister to a sick eros. I have noted that Socrates' first step is to engage his beloveds and his fellow citizens in inquiry. Although we do not see why, Socrates holds that a recovery from erotic diseases requires the quest for wisdom. His dictum that "the unexamined life is not viable for a human being" (*Apology* 38a5–6) applies to the ill especially. People still need Socratic teachers to urge philosophic inquiry upon the erotically infirm. Where, then, should the examined life lead?

To determine this, we shall have to turn from Bloom back to the Platonic Socrates. As I reflect upon Bloom's critique of the souls of the young, I become rather anxious, both about the treatment that he might prescribe for them and about his fidelity to Socratic philosophy. Bloom seems to deliver his jeremiads with an aggressive confidence. Does he suppose that he already knows the nonrelativistic truth of natural right? If so, does he try to impose it on his charges, not in obviously doctrinaire fashion, but subtly? Is that what Socrates does? If the families of potentially philosophic students are impossibly bourgeois, does Bloom believe that we should break the families up in order to rescue the students, perhaps by setting the students against their parents? Would this be in keeping with Socrates' judgment in the *Republic* that radical changes of the family cannot be shown to be possible (472e)?[13] What is the healthy opposite of "sexual desire undeveloped and untutored"? Whatever one's sexual orientation might be, a point not germane to the concern that Bloom's language raises here, does his "love" involve an artful hedonism or an elevated sexuality?[14] Is it compatible with

---

13. This question arises out of Bloom's comments in *Love and Friendship*, 441.

14. This question is inspired by something odd noticed by Anastaplo in "In re Allan Bloom," in *Essays on "Closing Mind,"* ed. Stone, 269. Bloom says: "Aristotle said that man has two peaks, each accompanied by intense pleasure: sexual intercourse and thinking" (*Closing American Mind,* 137). However, it is doubtful that Aristotle said that. He classifies the hedonistic life as one fit for beasts (*Nicomachean Ethics* 1095b15–20), arguing that the good for human beings is an activity of the soul in accord with excellence (1098a15–20); saying that excellence, or virtue, is of two sorts, moral and intellectual (1103a10–25); and concluding that the activity of the intellect according to its proper

what we uncomprehendingly regard as "Platonic love"? And what is the completion of human nature? Is it the antithesis of "sexual passion that no longer includes the illusion of eternity"? Thus, is it a passion that does embrace the "illusion" of eternity? Are we to understand that the terminus of the philosophic quest is indulgence in a mere illusion? Perhaps it will be appreciated that Bloom's phraseology sometimes causes us to doubt that he was a Socratic teacher in every respect. To decide fairly, we would have to peruse his books more carefully. More to the point, we would also have to learn how Socrates himself might answer such questions.

First, though, we need to consider another preliminary matter. Socrates has suggested that eros and its relationship to wisdom are critical to mankind's happiness and the teacher's work. American experience appears to verify that. There is a third sphere to which Socrates thinks eros and its need for wisdom are vitally important: politics. Plato indicates this by integrating the same story line into at least six of his dialogues: the *Alcibiades I*, the *Protagoras* as read in combination with the *Symposium*, the *Theages*, the *Republic*, and the *Phaedrus*.

In the opening speech of the *Alcibiades I*, Socrates states that he is the first erotic lover, or *erastēs* (ἐραστής), of Alcibiades, and the only one who has not deserted him.[15] Socrates has been a weird *erastēs*, one who would have excited panicky calls to the police in the United States. For years, he has followed Alcibiades around town silently. Only now, with the recently granted permission of his daimon, has he spoken to an Alcibiades who has come of age and is about to attend the Assembly. Socrates knows Alcibiades' secret wish. Alcibiades wants to become the master of Athens, Hellas, and the world. Socrates ironically offers to help Alcibiades do this. However, he suggests that Alcibiades is not ready for his chosen career because he is ignorant of the fundamentals of politics: justice and injustice. Alcibiades inquires why he should not be assumed to have learned these things from his fellow citizens, just as all children have learned to speak Greek from them. Socrates proves to him that he cannot have acquired knowledge of justice and injustice from the many because they contradict themselves on the subject. He tries to persuade Alcibiades that he should accept an *erastēs* who loves his soul rather than his body, that he must study his soul, especially the part of it that is the seat of wisdom, and that he must become virtuous, learn how to impart virtue to other citizens, and repudiate tyranny. Alcibiades assents to this, not because he rationally accepts it,

---

excellence would be perfect happiness, such that the activity of perfect happiness is contemplative (1177a1–35).

15. In Greek homoeroticism, the *erastēs* (lover) was an older male, usually thought to be on the giving end of homosexual intercourse, and the *erōmenos* (beloved) was an adolescent boy or young man, ordinarily thought to be on the receiving end of this intercourse.

but because he is fascinated by Socrates' apparent ability to compel people to say the opposite of what they think. He starts to pursue Socrates, not for who or what Socrates actually is, but because he wants Socrates to teach him the politically useful trick of manipulating minds.[16] Therefore, Socrates fears that his beloved will end badly as a *dēmerastēs*. So, in the first iteration of the political drama that Plato incorporates in the six dialogues, the essence of the story is this: A young aristocrat who is blessed with abundant natural gifts feels a massive eros for tyrannical political power. This would-be master of his polis and world lacks the knowledge that a statesman needs. When he becomes aware of this, he immediately conceives an urgent desire for political wisdom. However, he misunderstands the nature of political wisdom, supposing that it must be the science or art by which he will be enabled to realize his despotic dreams. He needs correction, but his eros for power and popularity might prevent this. (In his real life, Alcibiades becomes pathologically addicted to sex, victory, and power.) Evidently, the sickest eros must change its objects before it can be cured by inquiry. Political wisdom is compatible only with a nontyrannical eros.

The dramatic date of the *Alcibiades I* is 432 B.C. The action of the *Protagoras* occurs in the same year, some weeks or months later. In this dialogue, the first exchanges bring our attention back to Socrates' eros for Alcibiades. A companion asks Socrates how his love affair with the now bearded Alcibiades is going. Socrates allows that the youth is well disposed to him. This may be so, but we see clearly that there is trouble in store, for Alcibiades is no longer pursuing Socrates. Instead, he is going around with the future tyrant Critias. Actually, says Socrates, deftly changing the subject, he has just seen a beauty who caused him to forget about Alcibiades, namely, the wisest man of the time, Protagoras. The praise of Protagoras is surely ironic, for Socrates made mincemeat of him not an hour earlier. However, Socrates' companion has no inkling of this. He is thrilled to hear that the great sophist is in town and asks Socrates for an account of the meeting.

It transpires that Protagoras has been in Athens for two days professing to teach a new political *technē*, or art (πολιτικὴν τέχνην, 319a4). Protagoras argues that the many possess virtue and transmit it to the young (322c–324d). He himself claims to excel the many. He is especially expert at making gentlemen good citizens (318a–319a). He teaches them to exercise sound judgment in their household economies. In the affairs of the polis, he shows them how to become the "most capable in action and speech"

16. It is quite easy to see in the drama of the dialogue that this is Alcibiades' motive. In real life, Alcibiades' purpose seems to have been the same. At least this is suggested by Xenophon (*Memorabilia* 1.2.39–40). Xenophon says that Alcibiades and his friend Critias were never in sympathy with Socrates when they associated with him, but desired political advancement. I am grateful to Zdravko Planinc for reminding me of these Xenophon passages.

(319a1–2). This is as much as to say that he purveys political wisdom. His positions give Socrates ample reason to doubt his wisdom, for Socrates found it easy to convince Alcibiades that a people that contradicts itself with regard to virtue is scarcely capable of improving the characters of the young. However, this difficulty will not bother anybody who hopes to become the master of his city and universe. A *technē* that makes a gentleman the "most capable in action and speech" in the polis is precisely the kind of political wisdom that an ambitious youth like Alcibiades voraciously covets.

Socrates gets involved with Protagoras because Alcibiades is not the only young man in Athens who wants despotic power. On the morning of his meeting with the sophist, Socrates is awakened by Hippocrates, son of Apollodorus. This scion of a rich, slave-owning aristocrat is all in a tizzy because Protagoras has come. He suggests, with a laugh that does not conceal his earnestness, that Protagoras has done him an injustice by being the only wise man and not making him one, too. Hippocrates has little appreciation of Socrates, for he does not imagine that Socrates might be wise. He supposes that being wise means being a clever speaker (312d). Socrates knows well that Hippocrates is actually a gifted youth who aspires to be held in high regard in the city (316b10–c1). Like Alcibiades, this lad is in danger of becoming a *dēmerastēs*, or he already is one. Hippocrates regards the *technē* that Protagoras teaches as the means to his end. Thus, he wants Socrates to fix him up with Protagoras. After attempting to sensitize Hippocrates to the dangers of sophistry, Socrates reluctantly accompanies him to the house of Callias, where Protagoras is holding forth. It is no surprise that Alcibiades and Critias appear at Callias's door shortly after Socrates and Hippocrates. The two would-be tyrants are seeking the same technical shortcuts to power that Hippocrates craves. If they can pay Protagoras for his *technē* and absorb it in a few easy lessons, they can ignore the Socrates whose harping on the statesman's need for virtue militates against their ambitions.

Before rehearsing his discussion with Protagoras, Socrates tells his companion who was present at the meeting. He starts with the words: " 'And next I observed,' as Homer says" (315b9).[17] He thereby casts himself in the role of Odysseus in Hades. He is indicating that he descended spiritually alive into hell when he entered Callias's abode and that he now will call the roll of the spiritually dead. He reports that the enchanting Protagoras was lecturing two groups of notables that included the sons of Pericles. Also present were the sophists Hippias and Prodicus. Hippias was speaking to the lovers Eryximachus and Phaedrus about the nature of heavenly bodies. Prodicus was instructing the lovers Pausanias and Agathon.

17. The quotation is from *Odyssey* 9.601.

After some prolegomena that will be examined in another context, Socrates begins his conversation with Protagoras by gainsaying the sophist's assumption that virtue is teachable. Socrates appeals to the authority of public opinion to cast doubt on his interlocutor's position: the many recognize no preeminent guides to virtue. He reasons this way because Protagoras himself frequently bases his calculations on the authority of public opinion. Socrates also says that a great politician such as Pericles cannot even teach virtue to his sons, who graze everywhere like sacred oxen, trying to pick up virtue wherever they find it. He wants to anger the sophist with this calculated, stinging insult, which suggests that Protagorean doctrines are the kinds of fodder upon which cattle might feast but are not good food for healthy human souls.[18] To tell the truth, Socrates hopes to provoke a fight with Protagoras because he needs an excuse to destroy the sophist's potential influence over Alcibiades, Hippocrates, and Critias.

Protagoras replies with a myth and an argument designed to prove that Socrates is much mistaken about the people's opinion of teachers of virtue.[19] Socrates reacts by shifting the grounds and method of the debate. He asks Protagoras to give an account of the nature of virtue, especially with regard to the question of whether virtue is one or many, and with the response based on dialectical logic. When the sophist complies, Socrates exposes his answer as self-contradictory. Protagoras defends himself by engaging in a filibuster, whereupon Socrates threatens to leave. Callias ineffectually urges him to stay. At this point, Alcibiades interrupts the proceedings, prolonging the dialogue by praising Socrates' dialectical skills and daring the proud Protagoras to compete by Socrates' rules. Protagoras agrees to accept the challenge but immediately reneges, demanding that the company consider a poem by Simonides. Socrates evades the snares that Protagoras lays for him in this byway and then insists that they return to the dialectical study of virtue. Alcibiades intervenes again, successfully coercing Protagoras to join in the dialectic. Playing somewhat unfairly by mixing appeals to logic with appeals to public opinion, Socrates then pushes the argument to a conclusion that is lame because he and Protagoras flip-flop their positions without solving the problems. Frustrated modern scholars wish that Socrates' doctrines on virtue were worked out more neatly. However, that has not been Socrates' purpose in the conversation. From Socrates' point of view, the vague result is a smashing success, for Protagoras's

18. Cf. 313a–314b. This is to say nothing of the contempt that Socrates expresses for Pericles and his sons with this insult.

19. The myth and the argument are extremely interesting. I am glossing over them, together with virtually all of the substantive debate between Protagoras and Socrates, because I wish to focus on the dramatic plot of the dialogue, and also because I do not want to get caught up in the reasoning, which would force me to write an entire book on the *Protagoras*.

claim to political wisdom has been undermined. The would-be autocrats Hippocrates, Alcibiades, and Critias think that political wisdom should be able to win eristic competitions. Thus, they have been shown that they cannot obtain the *technē* that they want from the dialectically inept "wisest man" of their age.

Then what is the path to political wisdom and virtue? Is it right for Socrates and Plato to destroy other people's views about this issue and then to leave the question hanging? Plato will not be guilty of this offense. It has already been observed that a nontyrannical eros is a prerequisite for political wisdom. Plato invites his readers to move from the *Protagoras* to the *Symposium*, one of his great works on eros, political wisdom, and virtue. He ties the two dialogues together by means of a number of interesting dramatic inversions.

First, in the *Protagoras*, Socrates meets the grand sophist, who boasts of teaching a political *technē* without ever speaking of eros. Socrates is dragged to this engagement by a rich young man who does not perceive his philosophic superiority. In the *Symposium*, Socrates encounters lesser sophists who glorify Eros while soft-pedaling their intentions to act on the political implications of their eroticism. He goes to dine with them eagerly, dragging along a hesitant student who adores the ground on which he walks.

Second, in the *Protagoras*, the eminent sophists Hippias and Prodicus also expound their nonerotic opinions at garrulous length, whereas the lovers, Eryximachus and Phaedrus, and Pausanias and Agathon, remain utterly silent. In the *Symposium*, the lovers find their voices, presenting four highly eroticized versions of the views of their teachers, Hippias and Prodicus, while their masters have become the absent and silent sources of their premises.

Third, as noted above, Socrates quotes Homer in the *Protagoras* to hint that he has entered hell as a spiritually living Odysseus and that he is consorting with the spiritually dead. In the *Symposium*, while he is en route to Agathon's dinner, he persuades his student Aristodemus to accompany him by stating: "When two go together, one precedes another in devising what we shall say" (174d2–3).[20] With this, he ironically takes the part of Diomedes and casts Aristodemus as Odysseus in the scene from the *Iliad* in which the two go to spy on the camp of the enemy. He is setting out to beard physically living adversaries, one or more of whom might like to see him physically dead in Hades.

Fourth, in the *Protagoras*, when Socrates and Hippocrates arrive uninvited at Callias's home, a eunuch accuses them of being sophists and bars the door. Socrates must gain entry by denying the charge. In the *Symposium*,

---

20. The inexact quotation is from *Iliad* 10.224.

when Socrates has an obligation to arrive on time at a sophist's house for dinner, he stops outside to meditate and refuses to budge when the servants are sent to fetch him.

Fifth, in the *Protagoras* (347b–348a), Socrates says that he prefers gatherings of "the beautiful and good" (καλοὶ κἀγαθοί, a term for Athenian gentlemen) in which flute girls do not play, the works of absent poets who cannot be questioned are not interpreted, the participants test each other in dialectical exchanges, and the conversation is orderly no matter how much wine is drunk. In the *Symposium,* a sophist suggests getting rid of the flute girl, Socrates takes her place as an alleged flautist, everyone present creates a poem, dialectical exchanges are rare, and the discussion degenerates into chaos when wine begins to flow and the many are admitted.

Sixth, in the *Protagoras,* Socrates prevents a sophist from making long speeches and forces him to converse dialectically. In the *Symposium,* Socrates is compelled by a vote of the entire company to give a long speech (along with everyone else), and he is commanded to cease and desist from a dialectical discussion when he starts one.

Finally, in the *Protagoras,* Alcibiades breaks into a debate that is ending prematurely because he wants to delight in the spectacle of an eristic brawl. He celebrates Socrates' dialectical skills because he wishes to goad an overconfident sophist into continuing a contest that he believes Socrates will win. In the *Symposium,* Alcibiades prolongs a program beyond its logical end because he fears that a sophist has already fallen under Socrates' spell. He applauds Socrates' rhetorical abilities in order to poison the minds of the company against this seductive speaker, imagining that this is how he can defeat Socrates, whom he perceives as his opponent.

All these inversions inspire a hunch. If budding young tyrants force Socrates into nonerotic conversations with sophists because they ignorantly want a spurious political wisdom, failing to get it because Socrates deliberately contrives ambiguous results, perhaps a discussion about eros with sophists that Socrates freely joins will offer real political wisdom to aspiring tyrants who intellectually reject it. This would fit the impression that one gains from reading the *Symposium.* Each of the four sophists who speak in that dialogue appears to be afflicted with his own sort of tyrannical eros. Aristophanes, another of the orators at Agathon's party, has a questionable eros, too. Alcibiades, the final speaker, has a raging eros for tyranny. One speculates that the *Symposium* must be therapy for a tyrannical eros and, thus, the completion of the *Protagoras* and a necessary beginning of political wisdom.

In the *Theages,* Demodocus, a rural landowner and a committed democrat, approaches Socrates with his son Theages in tow. Demodocus is fearful because his son wants to become wise (121c–d), and he knows what Theages means by that term. Theages craves knowledge of how to rule human beings (123a). In fact, Theages openly confesses to wishing to be a tyrant (124e). Socrates succeeds in shaming the youth and his father, whereupon Theages retracts his statements, declaring that he desires to rule over only those who are willing to be governed by him. He does not propose to become a tyrant or a god (125e–126a). Theages and Demodocus then implore Socrates to become the youth's tutor. Socrates begs off, insisting that he knows nothing about making people good citizens. All he knows are the things of eros, about which he is so astonishingly clever (127d–128b). Theages objects that he is aware of fellows who have made progress by studying with Socrates, becoming superior to their cohorts. At this stage of the conversation, it is no longer clear what Theages understands progress or superiority to be. Socrates attempts to scare Theages off. He points out that young men who have studied with him when his daimon has warned against it have perished. Theages replies that the daimon's opinion can be ascertained in due course, so Socrates agrees to take him on. (Theages actually dies a few years later.) As things stand, Theages will accept instruction in the only subject that Socrates knows, eros, as a means to becoming politically wise.

In the *Republic*, the recurring story that we are tracing begins in the prehistory of the dialogue, in the lives of the real people who are made into characters in the drama. According to Xenophon, Socrates took Glaucon under his wing for the sake of his brother Plato and his uncle Charmides. There was trouble afoot. Glaucon was intent upon becoming a demagogue and a leader in the city although he was not yet twenty. He was terribly ignorant and callow. If he acted, he was sure to be dragged off the dais and ridiculed. Only Socrates could restrain him. In a conversation that Xenophon reports, Socrates called Glaucon's attention to several problems of political policy making about which he knew nothing and warned that he would suffer a fall if he insisted upon going into politics before being educated (*Memorabilia* 3.6.1–18). Presumably, Glaucon took this counsel to heart. This would explain why he appears in both the *Symposium* and the *Republic*, seeking what he takes to be political wisdom.

So far in the tale, there is nothing blameworthy in Glaucon's behavior, except perhaps for bad judgment born of immaturity.[21] Plato, though, provides more insight into Glaucon's heart than Xenophon does. His dramatic character Glaucon is an extremely erotic young man in at least three senses. First, he totally lacks sexual control.[22] He is aroused by every boy he meets in the bloom of youth, being driven like a person suffering stings (*Republic*

---

21. In Xenophon's usage, the term "demagogue" does not have the same pejorative overtones that it has in English.

22. Here, the criticism of Glaucon is that his sexual appetites are incontinent, not that they are homosexual.

474c–475a). It is a little-noticed fact that Glaucon's pederasty is ultimately responsible for the entire conversation recorded in the *Republic*. It is Glaucon, not Socrates, who decides that the two will remain in the Piraeus that night. Glaucon makes this decision upon hearing that there will be numerous youths with whom he can speak at a torch race (328a–b). Second, Glaucon is φιλόνικός and φιλότιμος, victory loving and honor loving to an extraordinary degree (545a, 548d–e). Third, it is Glaucon who tells the story of the magic ring that made the shepherd invisible. He spins this yarn because he wants Socrates to explain why he should not behave as the shepherd did if he were to lay hands on the ring (357a–362c). Like the shepherd, and like the 55 percent of my students, Glaucon regards the good things in life as sex, wealth, and power. He cannot see why he should refrain from injustice if wrongdoing will procure the goods that make him happy. Inasmuch as Glaucon is seriously willing to commit murder, rape, and other crimes to gratify his lusts, we may infer that he has an enormous eros for tyranny. It is interesting that with his unrestrained eros for sex, his singular eros for victory and honor, and his mammoth eros for tyrannical power, he greatly resembles Alcibiades. Socrates tries to answer Glaucon. This is a more significant way in which Glaucon is responsible for the substantive theoretical content of the *Republic*. In his reply, Socrates administers therapy to Glaucon's three loves, going to sometimes farcical lengths to moderate the lad's sexual passion, render his dreams of glory through militaristic imperialism illegitimate (especially the fantasies that he might have about fighting Hellenes), and eliminate his desire for despotic power. In the process, he speaks about the relationships between eros and tyranny (bk. 9), and he portrays the tyrant's life as totally unhappy. The *Republic* is another therapy for tyrannical eros that assumes that the alteration of this love is the prerequisite for political wisdom.

The *Republic* is linked to the *Phaedrus* by more inversions. In the *Republic,* Socrates is asked to stay and chat as he is leaving the Piraeus and heading back to the city. In the *Phaedrus,* Socrates asks an admirer of the absent Lysias to speak as he is leaving the city. In the *Republic,* Lysias, the best sophistical orator, is present but does not speak, whereas he speaks without being personally present in the *Phaedrus*. In the *Republic,* the highest point of a philosophic ascent is reached, and a new descent is begun presumably around midnight. In the *Phaedrus,* the nadir of a philosophic descent is reached, and a new ascent is begun at noon. One could adduce more examples, but these are enough to make me think that the *Republic* is somehow completed by the *Phaedrus*. In the latter dialogue, the erotically ailing man who aspires to tyranny is Phaedrus himself. Phaedrus is not so young anymore, but he obsessively affects youth and loves to be called young. One can tell that Phaedrus craves despotic power because the first two speeches in the dialogue, in which he delights, are clearly metaphors on tyrannical rule by means of manipulative rhetoric. In the third speech, Socrates gives poetic therapy to Phaedrus's eros, attempting to change its object. The concluding section on rhetoric aims to demonstrate that the sophistical-tyrannical use of this powerful tool is improper. So, Plato's constant dramatic refrain is that the healing of a tyrannical eros is necessary to political wisdom. This implies that the study of eros is the study of politics, and vice versa. Thus, the Platonic dialogues that we perceive as erotic are also political, and the dialogues that we classify as political are also erotic. I believe that these connections will prove to be visible not only in the arguments but also in the dramatic actions and settings of the dialogues.

If U.S. experience confirms that an understanding of eros is critical to mankind's happiness and the teacher's work, does it also verify that a healthy eros is essential to political wisdom? To answer this question definitively, one would probably have to do a philosophic-political history of the United States. Such a digression would engulf my present enterprise. I must content myself with an appeal to incidents that establish plausibility rather than certain truth. One episode that appears theoretically useful is the crisis of William Jefferson Clinton. This president was impeached on December 19, 1998, for committing perjury in his grand jury testimony about a sexual liaison and for obstructing justice in a sexual harassment suit against him. I dislike speaking about this scandal because everything about it was so banal. However, I reluctantly choose it as an example, together with related troubles that Clinton experienced, because most Americans have reacted to these events by taking a position on one of the eternal questions. To inquire whether a healthy eros is necessary to political wisdom is to ask if good character is a prerequisite for good statesmanship. The opinion evidently held by the majority of Americans, and certainly held by the most influential analysts of the Clinton impeachment, is that good character in principle has nothing at all to do with good governance. The modern many have come to believe that a superb politician needs only to be technically competent at transacting public business. A variation on this theme is the notion that a politician's private morality is wholly irrelevant to his or her public ethics.

The proponents of these doctrines try to carry their general point by appealing to the sexual case. They contend that known, or rumored, adulterers such as John F. Kennedy have been good presidents, whereas several faithful husbands have been bad ones.[23] These results were reached, they say, either because the adulterous presidents were technically skillful administrators, and the monogamous ones were bunglers, or because

23. It is particularly disappointing that the otherwise sensible and admirable Jeffrey Toobin, in *A Vast Conspiracy: The Real Story of the Sex Scandal that Nearly Brought Down a President*, frequently repeats the assertion that character is irrelevant to the discharge of political duties.

the privately bad ones were publicly virtuous and the privately good ones were publicly immoral. This might be true of some or several cases. Neither version of this argument is persuasive as principle, though. A fatal defect of the first formulation is that technical ability cannot be measured except in relation to an end, or telos, and the selection of an end is an ethical act. If the concept of good administration has any meaning at all, some goodness of character is required to ensure the choice of a good telos, such as liberty and justice for all as opposed to, say, personal gain. The second version is self-contradictory. While proclaiming virtue irrelevant, it concedes that a certain variety of good character, that is, "public virtue," is needed for good governance. Also, both arguments breezily beg the question of how a good ruler should be defined. They blithely assume that a popular figure who presided over victorious wars or economically prosperous times was a good chief executive and that an unpopular man who presided over losing wars or economic slumps was bad. This might not be true. Further, if these objections could be met somehow, the Clinton incidents reveal that the arguments occasionally prove false in their central thesis. They show that the arguments grossly oversimplify the relations among eros, virtue, wisdom, and the public-private issue. The theoretical problems cannot be reduced to the question of whether adulterers have been competent administrators. Not only the sexual eros but also every other sort of eros must be considered, as follows.

First, it is clearly possible that an adulterous president could make good political decisions. We probably have several examples of this in our history. This can occur because it does not follow that those who commit adultery necessarily do other wrongs. It is a principle of every ethics that recognizes moral choice that no evil inevitably entails another evil. However, it is not true that the private sexual conduct of presidents has never affected the discharge of their public responsibilities. President Clinton's case itself disproves the claim. In this debacle, the sexual harassment suit was filed against Clinton in May 1994. It is known that Clinton always believed that the lawsuit was instituted at the behest of enemies who would stop at nothing to destroy him. Still, Clinton began a new sexual affair in November 1995, with a total stranger whose discretion had to be suspect and who proved to be extremely indiscreet. He did this in the knowledge that his enemies would use the liaison against him and that fully half of his society would find his behavior repugnant if it were discovered. Even Clinton's apologists admit that this was incredibly reckless. The consequences were that a year of Clinton's second term was consumed by the scandal and that his always imperiled ability to lead was annihilated, leaving him to do virtually nothing but mark time during his last two years in office. I think it fair to infer that, here, an unrestrained sexual eros blinded a president to political wisdom and, thus, had an extremely negative impact on the performance of his public duties. Private consensual sex proved indistinguishable from a politically foolish act that made the attainment of various noble goals impossible, thus collapsing the much touted difference between private and public morality. It might be lucky that the results of Clinton's folly were no worse than the political paroxysms and storms of hatred that it generated. Clinton could have made other harebrained decisions while his judgment was impaired by the sexual eros. To indulge a flight of fancy, we may recall that it was a sexual eros that destroyed Troy.

Second, in the sexual harassment suit against President Clinton, he was asked questions about his consensual sexual acts with third parties not involved in the case. His indubitably perjured answers led to the grand jury investigation of his conduct and the impeachment. The fishing expedition into his sexual activities was censured as an odious invasion of privacy not only by his supporters but also by most Americans, and rightly so. People were generally unaware of the ironic background of the fishing expedition. It was Clinton who signed the Violence against Women Act into law, and it was this statute that obliged the judge in the harassment case to compel discovery of his consensual sexual encounters. Clinton and the legislators who agreed to the law did so perhaps because they believed in it and definitely because they were courting the feminist vote. Thus, when Clinton and his partisans protested the invasion of his privacy, they were furious about being hoist with their own petard. They never honestly admitted that they had passed a bad law that ceded too much power to prurient curiosity. It appears just to conclude that an excessive eros for victory and power, on the part of Clinton, the legislators, and those who demanded enactment of the offensive legislation, made them obtuse to political wisdom, steering the politicians to an incompetent exercise of their public stewardship.

Third, the independent counsel who referred the evidence of impeachable acts by President Clinton to the House of Representatives was originally assigned to investigate crimes allegedly perpetrated by Clinton and his wife in a failed real estate venture while he was the governor of Arkansas. I have no idea whether the Clintons committed the crimes. Suppose just hypothetically that they did do that. (If they did not, it is clear that certain senators did so a few years previously.) Such felonies would be instances of an ignoble eros for wealth, that is, examples of a private vice, that infected politicians and grew into public immorality. Socrates would deny that this fleecing of the people was politically wise, as witness his debate with the sophist Thrasymachus. (The savings-and-loan scandal did grave harm to U.S. society.)

Fourth, the chairman of the House Judiciary Committee who sent articles of impeachment to the Senate briefly entertained the possibility of inquiring into President Clinton's supposed violations of federal campaign finance laws. One accusation against the president was that in order to acquire funds needed to win the 1996 election, he accepted large campaign donations (that is, bribes) from the Chinese government. In return, he allegedly skewed U.S. foreign policy in ways favorable to China and detrimental to the United States. Again, I do not know whether these charges were true. Circumstantial evidence (some witnesses wanted for questioning fled to China) created an aura of authenticity around the accusations. Again, let us assume only hypothetically that Clinton was guilty. This would be another example of an extreme eros for victory and power that clouded political judgment, producing acts that bordered on treason.

Fifth, five days after the Judiciary Committee approved the articles of impeachment, President Clinton ordered U.S. forces to bomb Iraq for violating the Gulf War armistice rules. It was charged that Clinton did this to distract attention from his problems at home. Although I think this accusation false, many believed it. Suppose once again for the sake of argument that it was true. This would mean that Clinton murdered Iraqis and risked American lives to keep his power. Thus, we would have an example of a monumental tyrannical eros that was totally inconsistent with political wisdom and caused public evil. Indeed, the Clinton being painted here bears an eerie similarity to Alcibiades. Each man, the hypothetical American and the real Greek, was a *dēmerastēs* who committed treason and tyrannical murder for the sake of power.

Finally, throughout President Clinton's ordeal, he and his supporters maintained that he was being persecuted by unscrupulous enemies who wanted only to humiliate him and bring him down for reasons of political jealousy and hatred. This was essentially true. Of course, there were exceptions. The independent counsel, the chairman of the House Judiciary Committee, and some other Republicans undoubtedly believed that they were doing God's work. In their opinion, they were defending the sanctity of the laws and the president's oath against the claim that a president should be allowed to commit perjury when ordinary mortals had to tell the truth in court. They had a point. Nonetheless, the integrity of their position was compromised by the hatred that created and drove the original sexual harassment suit, by their sanctimony, by their incessant wallowing in the salacious details of Clinton's sexual affairs, and by their insistence upon staying their course when it became obvious that their efforts were counterproductive. Their folly was greater than Clinton's, for they were plainly succeeding only in discrediting religion and convincing the American public that private immorality is irrelevant to good governance, a conclusion that the people were drawing as a non sequitur from their foul play. It seems fair to gather that the Republicans were driven by a massive eros for victory that devastated their prudence, or political wisdom, too. The result was that they debased the public morality that they purported to represent and senselessly convulsed the federal government for more than a year.

Their personal viciousness gravely affected their discharge of their public duties.

Although I am close in time to the incidents that I have described, they are fading from public memory rapidly. They were never worth remembering. Any set of facts that I selected to clarify the problems under discussion would have been subject to the same criticism. What matters is to rise to the eternal from the transient and the base. With respect to the enduring question of whether good character is indispensable to good government, I believe that I have made a prima facie case for the propositions that character matters and that the Socratic claim that an exceedingly diseased eros is incompatible with political wisdom deserves a hearing.

SILENCE

If eros bears upon individual happiness, the teacher's work, and politics, we should certainly wish to learn what Socrates knows about it. However, this requires us to come to grips with the apparent contradiction that Socrates simultaneously professes his ignorance while claiming to have a wonderfully intelligent science of erotics. Does Socrates know erotics? Can we glean the things of eros from him?

At first glance, a reexamination of Socrates' language in the *Apology* seems to offer an easy solution of this problem. Socrates' comments about the artisans indicate a way in which his apparent contradiction could be reconciled. When Socrates says that he was conscious that he "knew nothing, so to speak" (22c9–d1), and then dismisses the artisans because they knew their trades but not "the greatest things" (22d7–e1), he could be taken to mean that he, too, knows various things, but that none or too few of these things are the greatest things, so that knowing all the things that he knows is to know "nothing, so to speak," because it is as good as knowing nothing. Then, in the *Symposium* and the *Theages,* where Socrates declares that he knows "nothing but the things of eros" and "nothing, except a certain small subject of learning, the things of eros," he could be understood as confirming that he does know the things of eros and that he is willing to call what he knows knowledge because eros somehow is both a thing within human ken and one of the greatest things. This, in turn, would be consistent with his denial in the *Apology* that he is wise, for wisdom would demand insight into all the greatest things, notably the divine things, which alone are noble and good, and not just eros, the only partially human thing that ranks among the greatest things.

This reconciliation of the apparent contradiction has much to recommend it, not least that it looks like it could be the truth. Granted, Socrates' protests of his ignorance at his trial would not be the whole truth, for they do not refer to his knowledge of eros. However, these disavowals would contain as much of the whole truth as the jurors wanted to hear. The jurors were interested in Socrates' alleged wisdom about the things under the earth and the heavenly things, his views on gods, and the effect of his rhetoric on the young. They would have been outraged if Socrates had begun to speak about eros—unaccountably, as it would have seemed to them. Socrates could honestly disclaim knowledge of the things that concerned them.

I shall assume, then, that there is no genuine contradiction in Socrates' words and that Socrates does actually know one of the greatest things, eros, at least in its human dimensions. Regrettably, this makes our task hard rather than easy. It means that learning Socrates' science of erotics is not simply a matter of reading the relevant pages of Plato's dialogues. If eros is one of the greatest things, Socrates and Plato would not have expounded the erotic science, certainly not in writing and probably not orally, either. I deduce this from Plato's extant correspondence.

In his Seventh Letter, Plato abjures the notion that Dionysius II of Syracuse and other dubious persons could have known that about which he is serious (περί ὧν ἐγὼ σπουδάζω). They could not have apprehended anything of the matter (περί τοῦ πράγματος), "[f]or there is no writing of mine about these things (περί αὐτῶν), nor will there ever be. For it is in no way a spoken thing like other lessons (ῥητὸν γὰρ οὐδαμῶς ἐστιν ὡς ἄλλα μαθήματα)" (341c1–6). A few sentences later, Plato declares that an attempt to write or speak about these things to the many would not be good for human beings, "except for some few who are able to learn by themselves with a little guidance." As for the others, some would be filled "with a contempt that is not right and that is in no way harmonious, and others with lofty and empty hopes, as if they had learned some mysteries" (341e2–342a1). These disclaimers echo others in the *Phaedrus,* where Socrates says that a word, "once it is written, is tossed about, alike among those who understand and those who have no business with it, and it knows not to whom to speak or not to speak" (275d9–e3). He goes on to proclaim the superiority of oral to written teaching (276a–b), insisting that a person who knows the just, the beautiful, and the good will not write seriously (276c).

We may be certain that if eros is one of the greatest things, Plato and Socrates would have been serious about it. Hence, they would not have written about it and probably would not have spoken about it, at least not seriously. I shall call their policy of refraining from writing or speaking about serious things "silence." The phenomenon of Platonic silence raises a question: If Socrates does know the things of eros, can we learn his science if he will not write or speak about it? The only possible answers are that we cannot or that we still can, if knowledge of the serious things cannot be spoken but somehow is generated or communicated without being spoken. If the first answer were right, our inquiry would necessarily end here, with the conclusion that, in Plato's view, human beings are doomed to permanent disorder. If the second reply held, we would have to wonder what kind of understanding of serious things is unspeakable but obtainable or transmissible without being spoken. Let us hope for the best and take the optimistic path.

One can conceive of two ways in which serious knowledge might be unspeakable but still engendered or transmitted without being spoken. The first possibility is based on Plato's words in the Seventh Letter, to the effect that whatever is serious "is in no way a spoken thing like other lessons." This might imply that there are realities that can be known, but not in the same way other things are known, that is, by means of verbal propositions. Owing to the natures of the realities, knowledge of them would be ineffable. If we learned what Socrates knows, we would not be able to incorporate it in creeds, lectures, or handbooks, we would not be able to demonstrate it with what positivists call "intersubjectively transmissible" evidence, and, hence, we could not enjoy the same kind of confident control of it that we have of the propositional sciences. In a sense, Socrates and we would be wise and ignorant at once. As observed by Eric Voegelin, the outstanding theorist who explored this hypothesis, our condition would be one of "knowing questioning."[24] How the Socratic wisdom could be generated or communicated if it is nonpropositional is not immediately clear. One supposes that Platonic dialogues and Socratic teaching would somehow guide readers and auditors to conditions or vantage points that enabled them to gain or receive the knowledge without direct verbal instruction. We would have to discover how this process worked by experiencing it.

The other possibility is founded on descriptions of strategies attributed to sophists and "the original humans" (τῶν ἀρχαίων) in some Platonic texts. In the work bearing his name, Protagoras states that his ancient predecessors knew that teaching politics to young men was dangerous. It could provoke jealousy, hostility, and conspiracies. Fearing these reactions, the old-time sophists disguised their reasoning as poetry (for example, Homer, Hesiod, and Simonides), as mystery cults (as in Orpheus and Musaeus), as gymnastics (for instance, Iccus of Tarentum and Herodicus of either Selymbria or Megara), and as music (such as Agathocles of Athens and Pythocleides of Ceos). Protagoras adds that he does not practice such trickery himself because the able men of every city always see through it,

---

24. Voegelin, *Anamnesis: Zur Theorie der Geschichte und Politik*, 289; *Anamnesis*, trans. Gerhart Niemeyer, 148. Henceforth cited as *Anamnesis* twice, the first referring to the German edition, the second to the English translation of Niemeyer.

whereas the many grasp nothing (316c–317b).[25] In the *Theaetetus*, Socrates says that the original people hid their theories from the many by camouflaging them as poetry (180c–d). In the *Republic*, Thrasymachus charges that Socrates himself resorts to "irony," that is, he pretends not to know when he actually has a quite definite opinion (337a).

Over the centuries, some superb thinkers have accepted Thrasymachus's attribution of deceptive tactics to Socrates and, by extension, to Plato. Thus, they argue that Plato and other genuine philosophers practiced "irony," or what has also come to be classified as "esotericism." They suppose that Socrates' knowledge "is in no way a spoken thing like other lessons," not in the sense that it is ineffable, but insofar as there are compelling reasons to keep it secret. It can be transmitted in verbal form to trustworthy recipients of secrets at will. Irony or esotericism is the technique of speaking and writing in ways that hide a dangerous secret from the many while revealing it to the few who are reliable. It will be instructive to provide some examples of perspectives on the classical philosophers' understanding of this art, three dating from times close to the origin of the tradition of esoteric interpretation, and the fourth from our era.

First, in his *Alexander*, Plutarch says of Aristotle's education of the young prince: "It seems that Alexander received not only the ethical and political argument, but also shared in those forbidden and deeper teachings which the men call by the private terms 'acroamatic' and 'epoptic' and which they do not impart to many."[26] Plutarch continues by informing us that the conqueror later rebuked Aristotle for publishing his acroamatic teachings. The master answered that his arguments were "both given out and not given out." Plutarch embellishes Aristotle's reply by maintaining that "truly his study of metaphysics is useless for those who would either teach or learn but is written as an example for those who have already been taught" (7.3.5). Of course, Plato is believed to be one of the men to whom Plutarch refers.

Second, preparing to present theological arguments that do not concern us here, the Christian Church Father Clement of Alexandria declares that he will write like Plato, meaning that he will attempt to say something unobtrusively or to reveal it without uncovering it or to prove it without saying anything.[27]

---

25. This is a major contradiction in Protagoras's doctrines. It is hard to understand how the multitude could know and teach virtue while being so stupid. Inasmuch as I am not writing a book about the *Protagoras*, I cannot devote time and space to this problem here.

26. "Acroamatic" means "for oral communication only." "Epoptic" means "for the initiated only."

27. Clement of Alexandria, *Stromateis, Books I–III*. For Clement's entire discussion, see pp. 31–33.

Third, in *The City of God*, Saint Augustine refuses to expound Plato's teachings about the end of all action, the cause of all natural objects, and the light of all acts of reason. He excuses his decision by asserting of Plato: "Indeed, he makes a point of preserving the well-known manner of his master Socrates, whom he makes a disputant in his books, that of dissembling any knowledge or opinion of his own, and because he approved this, the result is that Plato's own views on important subjects are not easy to perceive."[28]

Finally, with respect to Plato, the great modern theorist and champion of irony Leo Strauss precisely says:

> Irony in the highest sense will then be the dissimulation of one's wisdom, *i.e.*, the dissimulation of one's wise thoughts. This can take two forms: either expressing on a "wise" subject such thoughts (*e.g.*, generally accepted thoughts) as are less wise than one's own thoughts or refraining from expressing any thoughts regarding a "wise" subject on the ground that one does not have any knowledge regarding it and therefore only can raise questions but cannot give any answers.[29]

It should be noted that Strauss's second form is identical to the subterfuge that Thrasymachus attributes to Socrates. In another place, Strauss comments: "Every decent modern reader is bound to be shocked by the mere suggestion that a great man might have deliberately deceived the large majority of his readers." Strauss does not rest after making the shocking suggestion, but consternates his readers further by indicating that "some great writers might have stated certain important truths quite openly by using as mouthpiece some disreputable character."[30]

It is an astonishing fact that most modern commentators on Plato are oblivious of his silence. They behave as if Plato wrote prosaic and not altogether competent essays containing logical, analytic, and other kinds of reflections on the validity of *p*. Although it is true that Plato does such chores only occasionally, it appears to me that the works that interpret them as his essential activities miss his thrust. It follows that the bulk of the Plato scholarship that has adopted this line will be useless in an investigation of Socrates' science of eros; we cannot treat Platonic dialogues as compendiums of publicly stated doctrines. To progress in this inquiry, we must start

28. Saint Augustine, *The City of God against the Pagans*, 8.4. In Latin, Augustine says: "Cum enim magistri sui Socratis, quem facit in suis voluminibus disputantem, notissimum morem dissimulandae scientiae vel opinionis suae servare adfectat, quia et illi ipse mos placuit, factum est ut etiam ipsius Platonis de rebus magnis sententiae non facile perspici possint." This passage is not easy to translate into idiomatic English. My translation is guided by, but also differs substantially from, that of Henry Bettenson in the Penguin edition of Augustine, *Concerning "The City of God against the Pagans."*
29. Strauss, *The City and Man*, 51.
30. Strauss, *Persecution and the Art of Writing*, 35, 36.

by recognizing that Platonic silence presents a serious hermeneutic issue. Then we must find appropriate grounds for choosing between the possible ways of comprehending it. Our understanding of the very nature of philosophy will turn on our verdict.

It would be wrong to prejudge this matter. However, I must confess at the outset that I am much inclined to favor the first account of Plato's silence rather than the second, for the following reasons: The first explanation seems more faithful to the meanings of Plato's and Socrates' words than the second. It also appears more adequate to the realities that Plato and Socrates discuss than the second. Further, it is unseemly that practices that Socrates attributes to sophists and poets in the Platonic dialogues, that one sophist imputes to all his predecessors, and that another sophist facilely projects onto Socrates (perhaps revealing more about himself than his exasperating opponent) should be imputed to Plato and Socrates in the latter account. This reading has a dangerous potential actually to turn Plato and Socrates into sophists. This appears to be the tendency of Strauss's open description of Socrates' public pronouncements as conventional bromides that are less wise than his real thoughts. It also appears to be the effect of Strauss's equation of Plato's truths with the assertions of his disreputable characters, such as Thrasymachus.[31] Plato and Socrates are thought to be known to teach piety toward just, wise gods; obedience to such gods; and the virtues of moderation, courage, justice, and wisdom. If these views are conventional notions that are less wise than the philosophers' real knowledge, which is contained in the statements of the unsavory characters, it would be easy to infer that the secret doctrine attributed to Plato and Socrates posits the absence of any ground of human order other than man's will. Plato would become an advocate of Protagoras's motto, "man is the measure," which the Athenian Stranger (ostensibly?) rejects, arguing that god would be the measure in Magnesia (Laws 716c4–6). We cannot settle the dispute between Protagoras and the Stranger by declaring dogmatically that Protagoras is wrong. Neither can we resolve it by alleging arbitrarily that Plato furtively sided with Protagoras. That claim would need strong proof.

It may be inquired, therefore, if I think Leo Strauss a sophist. I answer that it would be incautious to judge him without understanding him better. Below, I shall explain the rival views of Plato's silence more fully, adduce the reasons I believe that the first explanation of Plato's silence is right and why Strauss's account might be mistaken, and then let the chips fall where they may. Meanwhile, I can append another word about one of Strauss's students, Allan Bloom. A six-chapter section of an anthology of essays on

31. Cf. ibid., 16.

The Closing of the American Mind is devoted to the suspicion that Bloom was a "nihilist."[32] The idea is that although Bloom's book purports to be a critique of U.S. culture from the standpoint of traditional ethics, it is really a critique of U.S. culture from the vantage point of an undisguised atheism and radical alienation from traditional morality, a critique that feigns opposition to the "nihilism" (that is, hedonism) to which Bloom himself allegedly adhered. Whether he was guilty as charged or not, the fact that these suspicions could be raised exemplifies both the sophistical potential of irony that I distrust and irony's potential to backfire on its theorists, however unjustifiably. If the accusations proved to be well founded, then it would be an open question as to whether Strauss stood to Bloom as Socrates stood to Plato or as Socrates stood to Alcibiades.[33] Strauss and many of his students and admirers eloquently repudiate hedonism.

A Plan of Inquiry

The hermeneutic issue posed by Platonic silence needs a much fuller airing than I have given it. It requires a treatment that recounts the most important arguments on all sides of the debate and then opts for the best of them, or something even better, on the basis of Plato's and Socrates' own statements. Only a thorough consideration of the wisest opinions could make us sure that our tentative decisions about the matter were not taken in culpable ignorance of difficulties that better minds had already discerned.

It is too late to learn why the ancients thought Plato was silent. However, the three-cornered quarrel among those who ignore the phenomenon completely, those who perceive Socrates and Plato as spokesmen of wordless insights, and those who see the two philosophers as esotericists has stretched across the millennia. In the late modern era, beginning, let us say, with the nineteenth century, a few of the West's leading thinkers have debated the issues. The most talented parties to the dispute have been Friedrich Schleiermacher, G. W. F. Hegel, Søren Kierkegaard, Friedrich Nietzsche, Leo Strauss, Eric Voegelin, Paul Friedländer, and Stanley Rosen. Hegel may be counted as a leader of the camp that disregards silence. Schleiermacher, Kierkegaard, Voegelin, and, I think, Friedländer see it as a response to ineffable knowledge. Nietzsche, Strauss, and Rosen view it as esotericism. All of the thinkers on this list are either giants or men of caliber whose books tend to be required reading in many modern philosophy

---

32. Stone, *Essays on "Closing Mind,"* pt. 5.
33. Anastaplo suggests the Alcibiades comparison ("In re Allan Bloom," in *Essays on "Closing Mind,"* ed. Stone, 272).

courses. Arguably, a study of these writers should yield a good grasp of the most perceptive modern opinions about Plato's silence. The first substantive chapter of this book will survey these authors' views of Platonic speaking and writing.

Plato's own statements about his silence are contained in his Seventh Letter. There are scholars who believe that this epistle is a forgery. It will be necessary to deal with the issue of the letter's provenance. Also, to attempt to reach valid conclusions about Platonic silence by quoting a few snippets from the document, the ones cited above, is a dubious procedure. The relevant passages must be understood in context. The second substantive chapter of this work will discuss the Seventh Letter's provenance and then analyze its whole argument to see how it explains the practice of silence.

In the *Symposium*, Alcibiades portrays Socrates as a Silenus whose outside differs from his inside, that is, as a rhetorician whose ostensible doctrines cloak his real meanings. Alcibiades urges Socrates to refute him if he lies. Socrates apparently objects to nothing that Alcibiades says about him, so most commentators treat Alcibiades' characterization of his former teacher as Socrates' own interpretation of his silence. As recounted above, Socrates speaks for himself about this matter in the *Phaedrus*. Again, it would be improper to tear the pertinent passages out of their settings. This book will strive to understand the presentations of Socratic writing and speaking about serious things in the *Symposium* and *Phaedrus* while considering these works as wholes and, hence, in the contexts of their investigations of Socratic erotics.

At a minimum, a complete analysis of Socrates' science of erotics would undertake an intensive study of the *Symposium*, the *Republic*, and the *Phaedrus*. If the Athenian Stranger is Socrates in disguise, the *Laws* would have to be included, too. Considering that Socrates has a lot to say about noble lies in the *Republic*, and that noble lies seem relevant to the problem of silence, it appears that Socrates' discussions of this practice coincide with his most extensive reflections on the nature and management of eros. If the Athenian Stranger is Socrates, and if the Stranger's law against irony (908d–e) is a significant indirect hint about the character of his silence, the *Laws* strengthen this correlation. When we remember that the Seventh Letter is a testimonial to Plato's eros for Dion, we detect eros and silence associated in the same Platonic work again. It is also true that the Athenian Stranger's interlocutors in the *Laws* seek political wisdom, I think more intelligently than the men in the *Symposium*, *Republic*, and *Phaedrus*. Plato also urges political wisdom upon all or some of the recipients of the Seventh Letter. None of this can be accidental. Somehow, the subjects of eros, wisdom, and silence belong together in Platonic thought.

Now a methodological question arises. Is there an order in which Plato's erotic works should be treated? Modern commentators tend to believe that we should read the dialogues in the order that they say represents the progressive development of Plato's ideas—in other words, in the chronological order of their composition. This assumption is untenable. There is no evidence that there was a progressive development of Plato's ideas, and we do not really know when the dialogues were written. The most recent efforts to date Plato's dialogues, which generally use stylistic analysis (usually computerized), have been summarized by Leonard Brandwood.[34] If I were to accept the premises of the scholars whom Brandwood surveys, which I do not, our ideas of the order of the composition of the dialogues would still be extremely rough, with Plato's works dividing into the categories "early, middle, and late." I am not persuaded by these scholars' premises for reasons offered in cogent arguments by Kenneth Dorter, Zdravko Planinc, and Jacob Howland.[35] Their grounds for rejecting stylometric dating are essentially that the stylometric analyses are extremely arbitrary in their assumptions about what represents youthful, middle, and elderly Platonic styles, and they attempt to prove their cases self-referentially. What these studies establish, at the most, is that some Platonic dialogues resemble each other stylistically more than they resemble others. This really tells us nothing about the dates of composition or a progressive development of Plato's ideas. Hans-Georg Gadamer adds, "It is more or less fatal for this theory . . . that the ancient tradition never reports such a change in views in either Plato or Aristotle—aside from a single observation in the *Metaphysics,* Mu 4, 1078b10 which makes the number theory appear to be a late form of the doctrine of ideas."[36]

It might even be the case that each dialogue had several dates of composition, insofar as each may have been revised several times in order to be joined dramatically with all the other dialogues to which Plato wanted it to be connected. One could picture Plato's study in the Academy as a gigantic workshop in which there were dozens of drawing boards, with all the older and newer dialogues always on them, always being modified as they were fitted into a single whole that Plato was constructing. This might explain how Plato could have built so many dramatic links into so many works that were produced over a lifetime.

Even if we could be sure of the dates of composition of the dialogues, I do not see why people believe that this would reveal anything important. It seems to me to be a much more fruitful approach to understanding Plato to attempt to read his works in the manner that he wanted them to be read. We

34. Brandwood, *The Chronology of Plato's Dialogues.*

35. Dorter, *Form and Good in Plato's Eleatic Dialogues: The "Parmenides," "Theaetetus," "Sophist," and "Statesman,"* 5–6; Planinc, *Plato's Political Philosophy: Prudence in the "Republic" and the "Laws,"* 13, 19; Howland, "Re-Reading Plato: The Problem of Platonic Chronology."

36. Gadamer, *The Idea of the Good in Platonic-Aristotelian Philosophy,* 8.

have a plain indication of his wishes in this respect, namely, his dramatic dating of the dialogues.

Plato gives his works dramatic dates by having the speakers mention contemporaneous events that his Athenian audiences would have recognized. As seen above, he also links the dialogues by causing the same people to appear in them at different stages of their lives. The *Symposium*, *Republic*, and *Phaedrus* are joined in these ways. Thus, by paying close attention to Plato's dramatic clues, we can discern the fictitious chronological order in which he intends his stories to unfold. This, in turn, will inspire us to ask what Plato means by locking his plays together as he does. I shall assume that Plato intends his dialogues to be studied in their dramatic order and that there is no legitimate purpose to be served in speculating about the dates of their composition.

Some caveats are needed. The fact that Plato's dramatic dates would have been evident to Athenian audiences does not mean that they are plain to us. For example, Plato causes the action of the *Republic* to take place in conjunction with the first Bendideia (354a10–11). We are not sure when that occurred. Also, we must beware of deliberate anachronisms. Plato has Aspasia and Socrates (*Menexenus* 244d1–246a5) and Aristophanes (*Symposium* 193a2) mention wars that happened after their deaths. Eva Brann suggests that Plato edifies the Athenians by having Cephalus appear in the *Republic* as a ghost.[37] Such anomalies could make it difficult to get dramatic sequences right. However, when the anachronisms are taken into account, it still seems possible to be confident about the order of the plays that Plato envisaged.

Three of our stories, those of the *Symposium*, *Republic*, and *Phaedrus*, appear to end and begin in the *Symposium*. In this multilayered drama, the initial speaker, Apollodorus of Phalerum, complies with an unnamed comrade's request to narrate to him and others several speeches that were given at a banquet that Socrates attended some time ago. The dialogue opens with Apollodorus telling the companion that he believes himself not ill-prepared to do what he has been asked, for just the other day he did it for Glaucon. By making this Glaucon a young man in his twenties (173a5), Plato means us to understand that he is the same Glaucon who appears in the *Republic*, Plato's brother. Because Apollodorus is known to have been a late disciple of Socrates, and because Glaucon thinks of Alcibiades as still living (172c2–3), we must follow Martha Nussbaum in dating this conversation dramatically to 404 B.C., shortly before the assassination of Alcibiades.[38] The three-drama history ends here; its beginning then is narrated retrospectively.

37. Brann, "The Music of the *Republic*," 3.
38. Nussbaum, *The Fragility of Goodness: Luck and Ethics in Greek Tragedy and Philosophy*, 168–69.

For the sake of a reference point, we may allow the scene to shift from here backward in time to the occasion of the *Protagoras*. The action of this play transpires when people are noticing that the youthful Alcibiades has become bearded (hence, around 432, shortly before the outbreak of the Peloponnesian War). Socrates is a rising philosopher, perhaps thirty-eight years old. Alcibiades is a haughty youth of eighteen or nineteen. Agathon is fuzzy-cheeked, thus between fourteen and eighteen (see *Symposium* 181d), and Phaedrus is probably eighteen. Pausanias and Eryximachus must be in their early thirties. Both sets of lovers have begun the careers that will make them what they are in the *Symposium*. Phaedrus and Eryximachus are being taught by Hippias to affirm the ontological primacy of Earth. Agathon and Pausanias are being educated by Prodicus. This well-meaning but uninspiring sophist will not be able to offer Agathon enough sustenance to keep him from going over to Gorgias. As seen above, the *Protagoras* dramatically points ahead to the *Symposium*.

We now come forward in time, to the party described in the *Symposium*. The account of the feast that we shall hear is not original with Apollodorus, who is too young to have been there himself. Apollodorus will repeat the narrative of an older eyewitness, Aristodemus of Cydathenaeum. The banquet occurs shortly after Agathon's first tragedy wins the prize at the Lenaea, thus in 416. Obviously, the participants have aged sixteen years since the *Protagoras*. Agathon, for example, is no longer a youth but a thriving playwright of thirty to thirty-four. Alcibiades is not the brash stripling of nineteen but a greatly popular politician of thirty-five. Socrates is not the promising junior philosopher of thirty-eight who could be patronized by a celebrity such as Protagoras but a recognized cranky genius of fifty-four. The firestorm that Protagoras kindled in 432 by proclaiming man the measure and teaching his new political art of acquiring power is now raging out of control. It must be resisted by a wholesome Socratic eros. Socrates provides the needed counterweight in his *Symposium* speech. Then he carries this work further in the *Republic,* to which the *Symposium* is linked by Glaucon, and in the *Phaedrus,* to which the *Symposium* is connected by Phaedrus.

We move next, I judge, to the *Republic*. The dramatic date of this dialogue has always been disputed, owing chiefly to careless reading. For example, A. E. Taylor states that the date must fall during the Peace of Nicias, circa 421, because the battle of Megara in which Glaucon and Adeimantus are reported to have fought could have been that of 424, because the soldiers are home, and because Cephalus is still alive.[39] Taylor's reasons are not weighty. If Glaucon was only a boy in 416, as the *Symposium* (173a5) tells us, he could not have fought at Megara in 424. It must be the battle of 409 that

---

39. Taylor, *Plato: The Man and His Work*, 263.

is meant. Given the character of ancient warfare, the soldiers could have been home often. One ancient tradition has Cephalus dying in 439. Thus, his presence in the *Republic* does not favor 421 any more than the dates that most classicists choose, various years after 411, when Cephalus and his family, or at least the family, returned to Athens after having lived for a long time in Thurii. The authority who hitherto has been most influential in the selection of a post-411 date, August Boeckh, sets the dialogue in 406/405, contending that Cephalus must be assumed to have lived past 408, and that the first Bendideia must have also been later than that.[40] Boeckh's speculations are not decisive, but he can be proved to be close to the mark. In the *Theages,* Socrates states that Sannion is currently fighting with Thrasyllus against Ephesus and Ionia. This campaign took place in 409.[41] At the end of the *Theages,* Socrates accepts Theages as a probationary student. Theages is healthy and aspires to a political career. In the *Republic,* Socrates mentions that Theages is a comrade whose sickness prevents him from abandoning philosophy for politics (496b6–c2). If we allow Theages enough time to survive his probation, and more time to become too debilitated to go into politics, we infer that the *Republic* must occur at least a year or two after 409. Zdravko Planinc then narrows the date down much more precisely, to the week of the Plynteria in 407. He argues ingeniously and persuasively that, recent opinions to the contrary notwithstanding, the *Republic,* the *Timaeus,* and the *Critias* form a trilogy, that the conversations in the latter two dialogues follow the speeches of the *Republic* closely in dramatic time, that they all must be set during a brief period when Hermocrates, the tyrant of Syracuse, is likely to have visited Critias in Athens, and that the most plausible historical date of Hermocrates' presence in the *Timaeus* and *Critias* is that of Alcibiades' return to Athens, on the Plynteria in 407.[42] As for Cephalus, we can suppose him near death (328e6) or already dead. He would be more fun as a ghost. We may also view the first Bendideia as a symptom of the corruption of the Athenian aristocracy. The *Republic* is connected to the *Timaeus* and *Critias* by the fact that the temple of Bendis became a headquarters of the thirty tyrants by 404.[43]

This brings us to the *Phaedrus.* Probably, one reason Phaedrus must be Socrates' interlocutor in the dialogue that bears his name is that he is a crude, narcissistic, manipulative rhetorician and, thus, incarnates the lowest common denominator to which Lysias and other sophists have fallen in

40. Boeckh, *Gesammelte kleine Schriften,* 448–49.
41. The date is common knowledge, being available in classical dictionaries.
42. Planinc, *Plato through Homer: Poetry and Philosophy in the Cosmological Dialogues.* Before reading Planinc, I was persuaded that Eva Brann's denial of the connection between the *Republic* and the *Timaeus* ("Music of the *Republic,*" 20–21) was sound, but Planinc refutes her reasoning.
43. August Friedrich von Pauly and Georg Wissowa, *Real-Encyclopädie der classischen Altertumswissenschaft,* s.v. "Bendis."

the last days of the Athenian empire, or one to which they appeal. The eros of Phaedrus, Lysias, the other sophists, and the Athenian democrats and oligarchs whom they represent must be redirected if Athens is to be saved. The time remaining for this rescue of the city is growing short. We know that the conversations of the *Phaedrus* must be dated after the week of the Plynteria in 407 because a still-living Polemarchus is said in the dialogue to have turned to philosophy (257b3–4), and he could not have done this prior to his education in the *Republic*. We also know that the action of the *Phaedrus* must transpire before 403, the year of Polemarchus's murder. Indeed, given that Socrates and Phaedrus walk outside the walls of Athens in the dialogue, we perceive that the play must be set in a time when there were still walls, and when it was still safe to stroll outside them—in other words, before the battle of Aegospotami in fall 405. Thus, the *Phaedrus* must take place in the summer of 407, 406, or 405, quite close to the final catastrophe that touched off the Alcibiades hysteria of 405 and 404.

So, the *Symposium, Republic,* and *Phaedrus* form a trilogy that interlocks with other trilogies in the Platonic corpus. Their fictitious chronological order is Agathon's banquet in the *Symposium,* the *Republic,* the *Phaedrus,* and the opening scene of the *Symposium,* which closes the circle of the three dialogues and takes us back to Agathon's banquet. An adequate inquiry into Socrates' science of erotics would study the three dialogues in the order indicated and then move to the *Laws,* which I tentatively suggest is set after Socrates' death, so that the philosopher must appear as an unrecognizable shade, or, as Planinc indicates, as the Odysseus-Socrates of the concluding myth of the *Republic,* who returns to earth as an unknown private man.[44]

Unfortunately, this book cannot be the complete inquiry into Socrates' erotic science that I envisage. A sound treatment of all the dialogues enumerated would run into thousands of unwieldy pages. The study must be broken into parts. For reasons that are partly logistical and partly theoretical, the most manageable analysis would produce a trilogy of my own, the first book concentrating on the hermeneutic debate, the Seventh Letter, the *Symposium,* and the *Phaedrus;* the second on the *Republic;* and the third on the *Laws.* Logistically, it happens to be just possible to encompass the *Symposium* and *Phaedrus* in a single investigation, these dialogues being smaller than the other two. Theoretically, it is sensible to divide the *Symposium* and *Phaedrus* from the *Republic* because, in the former, Socrates urges a good, positive eros on his interlocutors, describing it at length, whereas, in the latter, he chiefly attempts to cure Glaucon of an evil, tyrannical eros, mentioning the good, positive eros only briefly. This book will be the first of my projected trilogy.

44. Cf. Planinc, *Plato's Political Philosophy* (the chaps. on the *Laws*) and *Plato through Homer.*

Both the *Symposium* and the *Phaedrus* are too large to analyze in single chapters. My treatment of them must also be broken into smaller pieces. Where should the cuts be? I think that the *Symposium, Republic,* and *Phaedrus* all have the same tripartite structure, this being another of the factors that links them as a trilogy. All three dialogues begin with movements that simultaneously ascend in the intelligence of their sophistical arguments while descending into the depths of evil. Then they turn to Socratic ascents to visions of the highest Beauty, or Good, or Being. Then they descend again into portraits and analyses of evil political phenomena. I shall follow Plato's divisions of the material. I shall devote three chapters each to the *Symposium* and the *Phaedrus.* The three *Symposium* chapters will cover the dialogue's two preludes through Agathon's speech (a descent), Socrates' oration (an ascent), and Alcibiades' speech through the last scene (a descent), respectively. The three *Phaedrus* chapters will look at the prelude through the first two speeches (a descent), Socrates' palinode (an ascent), and the discussion of rhetoric (a descent), respectively.

One last question must be addressed. The existence of the hermeneutic debate over the correct way to interpret Platonic silence means that we moderns do not really know how to read Plato. How can I read him without knowing how to read him? I answer, provisionally, that I must trust that Plato knew what he was doing when he wrote his dialogues and, hence, that he had solid grounds for everything that he did. Therefore, we must read Plato by paying attention to everything in his publications, including not only his reasoning, with its logically sound syllogisms, its contradictions, its digressions, its emphases, and its silences, but also his dramatic actions and settings and his uses of poetry. We should examine all these components of Plato's writing without preconceptions of their relative cognitive value. Only thus will we avoid anachronistic impositions of our ideas of what philosophy ought to be on a thinker who has an arguable claim to be the greatest of the philosophers. Of course, it would literally be humanly impossible to scrutinize "everything," down to the last word, in the texts selected for study. I, at least, lack the ability to do that. However, I have found a way to approximate the ideal discipline. I have discovered that if one meditates on the reasons for every major turn of a Platonic argument cum drama, one learns important things that escape notice entirely when one reads without pausing to inquire. So, I shall attempt to look into "everything" in Plato's writings in that sense.

Paying attention to everything in a Platonic work might be frustrating because it will require a more sustained and more serious effort than many people are willing to give. It will also result in exegesis that, in the language of a useful cliché, will often seem to lose sight of a forest because it has veered into happy contemplation of beautiful individual trees. Another source of irritation might be that Plato's silence will not let us indulge our usual lazy habit of swooping into a text, snatching a few dogmas that seem to capture the essence of the material, and congratulating ourselves on our new erudition. It will not even permit us to understand in advance what is supposed to happen to us when we read a Platonic dialogue. We must wait to find out, hoping that we will know it when we see it. So, the journey upon which we are about to embark will be long and arduous. My hope is that for lovers of Plato, the time and effort will fly by unnoticed, so that both writer and readers will be surprised that the study is finished so soon.

2

MODERN VIEWS OF PLATO'S SILENCE

Plato directly and indirectly cautions his students that he does not communicate with them straightforwardly. To repeat the warnings quoted previously, Plato fiercely denies in his Seventh Letter that Dionysius II and other dubious individuals could have known that about which he is serious (περί ὧν ἐγὼ σπουδάζω). They could not have understood it, "For there is no writing of mine about these things (περὶ αὐτῶν), nor will there ever be. For it is in no way a spoken thing like other lessons (ῥητὸν γὰρ οὐδαμῶς ἐστιν ὡς ἄλλα μαθήματα)" (341c1–6). He remarks further that an effort to write or speak about these things to the many would not be good for human beings, "except for some few who are able to learn (ἀνευρεῖν) by themselves with a little guidance." As for the rest, some would be filled "with a contempt that is not right and that is in no way harmonious, and others with lofty and empty hopes, as if they had learned some mysteries" (341e2–342a1). In the *Symposium*, Plato makes Alcibiades declare that Socrates is a Silenus figure, with an outer casing that conceals divine images inside (215a4–c3, 216c7–217a1). In the *Phaedrus*, he makes Socrates maintain that a word, "once it is written, is tossed about, alike among those who understand and those who have no business with it, and it knows not to whom to speak or not to speak" (275d9–e3). Socrates goes on to proclaim the superiority of oral to written teaching (276a–b), and to insist that one who knows the just, the beautiful, and the good will write only for amusement (276c). In the *Protagoras, Republic,* and *Theaetetus*, Plato also has Socrates indicate that he is perfectly aware of poetic and sophistical arts of ironic (or esoteric) speaking and writing, in which a thinker's real views are divulged to a few while simultaneously being concealed from many.

These indications have inspired a long tradition of cautious interpretation of Plato. It is not certain that the tradition dates to the Academy because the best evidence, Aristotle's use of Plato, is inconclusive. However, it clearly predates Plutarch, who took it for granted that the classical philosophers have "forbidden and deeper teachings" that they "do not impart to many," and that their publications are useful only to those who already know the materials therein (*Alexander* 7.3.5). It is strongly established by the time of the Christian Father Clement and by the era of Saint Augustine, whose Plato makes a point of "dissembling any knowledge or opinion of his own," with the result that his positions on important topics "are not easy to perceive."[1] Since Augustine, the best Western readers of Plato have been wary of handling his works as if they were easily accessible doctrinal treatises.[2]

To state that the tradition of cautious exegesis of Plato has been a long one is not to say that it has had many representatives. The best readers of Plato have been relatively few in number. Further, to speak of a single tradition is not to suggest that its bearers have agreed on the question of how to understand Platonic silence. In the nineteenth century, four of the West's foremost thinkers and some lesser lights engaged in an acrimonious dispute about the subject. The quarrel began when Friedrich Schleiermacher took issue with some earlier giants and some now obscure professors who held that Plato was an esoteric writer. Schleiermacher claimed, rather, that Plato tried to bring his companions and readers into contact with "inner" ineffable truths that they had to see spiritually for themselves. Next, G. W. F. Hegel spoke up. Hegel was aware of the texts that gave rise to the debate but criticized both sides, arguing that Plato disclosed all he knew. Søren Kierkegaard replied to Hegel in his doctoral dissertation on Socratic irony. Although a Hegelian, Kierkegaard sided with Schleiermacher, declaring that Socratic irony pertained to an ineffable good, one that no predicates could capture. After this, the controversy died down for a time, largely because nearly everyone had become a Hegelian. In 1888, however, Friedrich Nietzsche accused Socrates and Plato of an irony that marked not a superior will to hide the truth from the many but a base fear of facing it. He dissented from other esotericists about the proper reasons for irony but not about its existence.

Plato's warnings about his writing and the quarrel about their meaning were forgotten for the next sixty years, thanks to Hegel's influence. Unhappily for good education, students therefore were taught histories

---

1. Augustine, *City of God*, 8.4. Diogenes Laertius, whose competence as a reader of Plato seems doubtful to me, does not paint the same pictures as Plutarch, Clement, and Augustine. He is confident that he can give a concise summary of Plato's doctrines. However, even he observes that Plato deliberately uses a complicated vocabulary to make his writing less intelligible to the ignorant. See his "Plato," in *Lives of Eminent Philosophers*, 3.63.

2. One could also cite the Arabic tradition, which includes Al Fārābī, Averroes, and the great Jew who wrote in Arabic, Moses Maimonides. I shall ignore these thinkers in this book because they are represented adequately by Leo Strauss.

of ideas by academics such as George Sabine without ever hearing the faintest rumor of Plato's caveats. However, from the mid-1940s to his death in 1973, Leo Strauss revived the arguments of the esotericists, maintaining that Plato deliberately deceived, and kept profound secrets from, the many. His simultaneously open and veiled analyses of the irony of Socrates and other truly great philosophers are now inspiring strict intellectual discipline in a third generation of doctors of philosophy. This does not mean that Strauss ever persuaded or silenced Sabine and his Hegelian ilk completely. As Stanley Rosen reports, Strauss's efforts to rejuvenate the esoteric reading of the most admired philosophers produced "disbelief and ridicule." Indeed, they made Strauss "one of the most hated men in the English-speaking academic world." Although a self-acknowledged devotee of Strauss, Rosen himself accuses his master of not having gone far enough in his expositions of Platonic irony. Of all Strauss's students, Rosen gives the theory of philosophic esotericism the most surprising new slant, a "postmodernist" one. Meanwhile, Eric Voegelin wrote practically nothing about the particular issues in Plato's dialogues that caused Schleiermacher to propound his theory of the links between their dramatic form and inner truth. However, he did declare that the Platonic dialogue is "an exoteric literary work, accessible individually to everybody who wants to read it." He also held that Socratic statements symbolized not objective facts, but "experiences of transcendence" that language could capture only analogically. He thus arrived at an equivalent of Schleiermacher's view of a Plato who combined openness with respect for ineffable insight. Then he developed an explanation of Plato's philosophy that went far beyond anything that Schleiermacher had discovered. Paul Friedländer also realized that no one could understand Plato without taking his irony into account. He argued that Thrasymachus was wrong about its nature, that Socrates veils truths that he wants to show, and that the "ineffability of the highest Platonic vision" is symbolized by "the irony of Socratic ignorance."[3]

In this chapter, I shall summarize the opinions of the important modern thinkers who have been parties to the dispute over the nature of Platonic silence. As indicated previously, my preliminary hunch is that Plato really is silent with respect to the things about which he is serious, and that his silence has more to do with ineffable knowledge than with the irony or esotericism envisaged by Strauss. Despite this possible bias, I shall attempt to represent all the views fairly. Then, in both this and subsequent chapters, I shall compare the modern opinions with Socrates' and Plato's own statements, explaining why I judge that the Schleiermacher-Kierkegaard-

---

3. H. Sabine, *A History of Political Theory,* esp. chaps. 2–5; Strauss, *Persecution* and *City and Man;* Rosen, *Hermeneutics as Politics,* 114, 107; Voegelin, *Order and History,* 3:12; Friedländer, *Plato,* 1:chap. 7, esp. pp. 147–48.

Voegelin-Friedländer interpretations are more convincing—unless, in the event, I should reach the opposite conclusion.

While surveying the modern thinkers, we should keep some questions in mind: What, if anything, does Plato conceal? Why and how does he hide it? To inquire more fully: About what is Plato serious? Why must it be unspoken? Is it not a spoken thing simply, or is it not a spoken thing merely in the way that other lessons are spoken things? What is the function of Plato's dialogues if they do not talk about what is serious? Do they somehow communicate the serious, or move their more able readers to it, without speaking of it? Do they help only a few to learn the serious in this manner, namely, those who can progress with a little guidance, while simultaneously preventing the less talented from becoming contemptuous or conceiving delusions of grandeur? Why is Plato alarmed by the contempt and vain hopes that speaking of his serious thoughts would evoke in the many? What relationships subsist between the truths that Platonic dialogues do not broadcast and the arguments that their characters make? When the dramatis personae speak, does Plato's lack of seriousness render the words of Socrates and all the others false? Is Alcibiades right to say that Socrates is a Silenus, with an outer shell that hides his insides? If so, is there a method of penetrating this Silenus shell? Why does Socrates not write at all about what he knows? To know the answers to questions such as these would be to understand Platonic silence. My presentation of Hegel will, of course, attempt to ascertain his reasons for denying the existence of this phenomenon. My accounts of the other thinkers will aim to elicit their answers to the kinds of questions posed here.

Friedrich Schleiermacher

In 1804, Friedrich Schleiermacher published his first volume of German translations of the dialogues of Plato. He opened it with a general introduction of his series. Subsequently, he furnished each dialogue with its own introduction as well. In his general introduction, he indicates that his scholarship has three purposes: He proposes to make Plato accessible to the public (which already puts him at odds with esotericists). He wants to arrange the dialogues in the order that Plato intended, so that readers might grasp what is taught by their "natural" connections. Believing that the correct sequence of Plato's writings is identical with the order of their composition, he hopes to acquire rough notions of the relevant dates from clues found in the dialogues themselves.[4]

4. Schleiermacher died before he could do the *Timaeus, Critias,* and *Laws.* See the entire argument that Schleiermacher makes about Platonic silence in Platon, *Werke,* vol.

I am skeptical of Schleiermacher's third aim because it too often entails deductions from premises that are mere conjectures. For example, Schleiermacher considers the *Phaedrus* Plato's first dialogue, in part because he regards its style as youthful.[5] However, when we are dealing with a Plato who changes styles like a chameleon, who can be sure of this? I also think that Schleiermacher's brilliantly conceived and entirely valid second goal can be achieved only by following Plato's manifestly intended dramatic order. These criticisms notwithstanding, Schleiermacher's analyses are truly illuminating.

In the sections of his general introduction that pertain to our inquiry, Schleiermacher declares that Plato has a greater right than any other philosopher to complain of having been understood wrongly or not at all. Even the best interpreters are superficial. They speak with all too evident uncertainty. They treat the relationship between Plato's content and his form too casually. They advance premature claims to know Plato better than Plato knew himself, ignoring the great value that Plato attached to "consciousness of ignorance." They are blind to Plato's great premeditation in putting his dialogues together. Some of them are systematizers who want philosophy to be a structure of neatly partitioned sciences. Others are fragmentizers who treat particular works by taking from them what they like. The former are frustrated by their inability to derive a tidy, transparent system from Plato. They condemn his dialogue form as a hindrance to clarity, accuse him of self-contradictions, and dismiss him as a presumptuous dialectician who is more eager to refute others than to build a science. They are obtuse to his sense of the unity of knowledge, which prevents him from confining any of his writings to a single field. The latter tear lines out of context and see nothing in Plato's dramatic art form except a loose dress for loose talk. All such exegesis is little more than a confession of total inability to comprehend Plato.[6]

Having thus disposed of the worst Plato scholars, Schleiermacher turns his critical eye on others only slightly better. He argues that it has dawned on some that Plato's conclusions have been missed, and that this has led to another kind of error:

1:1, "Einleitung," 5–38. I refer to Schleiermacher's general introduction as "Einleitung." I cite his introductions to each dialogue as "Einleitung to [name of dialogue]." Partially adequate translations of all these essays are provided in *Schleiermacher's Introductions to the Dialogues of Plato*. The "General Introduction" to all the volumes is found on pp. 1–47.

5. Schleiermacher, "Einleitung to *Phaidros*," in *Werke*, by Platon, 1:1, 50–51. The idea that the *Phaedrus* has a youthful style is supported by Diogenes Laertius, *Lives of Eminent Philosophers*, 3.38. This is probably the only opinion that Diogenes Laertius and Schleiermacher share, for Schleiermacher thinks that Diogenes is "without all judgment" ("Einleitung," 5).

6. Schleiermacher, "Einleitung," 7–10.

Thence, others, for the most part with just as little correct insight but with more good will, now have formed the opinion, partially from isolated utterances of Plato himself, partially from a widespread tradition preserved from antiquity of an esoteric and exoteric in philosophy, that Plato's real wisdom is contained in his writings either not at all or only in secret, hard to detect indications. This idea, indeterminate in itself, has developed in the most manifold forms, and people have emptied Plato's writings of their content, now more, now less, and contrariwise have sought his true wisdom in secret teachings that he as well as never entrusted to these writings. Indeed, great debates were arranged to determine which of Plato's writings were exoteric and which esoteric, so as to know where at the most a trace of his true secret wisdom still might be sought.[7]

The isolated sayings of Plato to which Schleiermacher alludes are the lines cited above from the Seventh Letter, *Phaedrus*, and *Symposium*. The "tradition preserved from antiquity of an esoteric and exoteric in philosophy" extends most notably in Schleiermacher's lifetime into the work of lesser thinkers such as Wilhelm Gottlieb Tennemann and also into that of great men such as Gotthold Lessing. Schleiermacher probably regards Tennemann and Lessing as the culprits who use the long tradition as justification for emptying Plato's philosophy of its content.

Tennemann was a professor at Jena and Marburg, renowned in his day, who published the eleven-volume *History of Philosophy* from 1798 to 1819. (Hegel knew Tennemann and referred to him in his own *Lectures on the History of Philosophy*, with numerous expressions of contempt for his intelligence. Kierkegaard was also still reading Tennemann after 1841.) Tennemann declares that, offensive as the idea is to many, Plato had a "secret philosophy," that is, a "scientific philosophy," as distinct from a "popular" one. This probably was so because Plato, unlike Aristotle, was not protected by a powerful king. At first, Tennemann concludes of Plato: "If he had an esoteric philosophy, which cannot be denied, then we may not seek it in his still extant writings, and since these are for us the only valid sources for his philosophy, we really must renounce a complete and fundamental acquaintance with his system." Perhaps this loss is too much to bear, for Tennemann then begins to speculate that Plato must have allowed elements of "his system" (as if he had a "system") to creep into his writings here and there, interspersed with materials intended to throw people off the track, but still allowing intelligent readers to reconstruct "the system" by selecting the right pieces.[8]

7. Ibid., 11.
8. Tennemann, *Geschichte der Philosophie*, 2:220–22.

Lessing, an illustrious leader of the German Enlightenment, maintains that Leibniz, following "all ancient philosophers," had been a practitioner of the "exoteric lecture." That is, in his public works, Leibniz (and therefore all the ancient philosophers) had accommodated "his system" to "the ruling doctrines of all parties." He had pretended to adopt their opinions, giving these inadequate beliefs "a tolerable meaning," and setting his own convictions aside, for purposes that Lessing states ambiguously, if not ironically. Also, in dialogues titled *Ernst and Falk: Conversations for Free Masons*, Lessing makes Falk declare that Free Masonry is grounded in human nature, in something of which it is the case that "those who know it cannot say it," in the sense that the wise cannot say what better is left unsaid.[9] This means that Lessing thinks it possible to convey higher truths in plain words, but supposes that the wise must leave these verities unspoken while deceiving the many about their real convictions. As applied to "all ancient philosophers," this principle assumes that Plato had a "system" but empties his dialogues of their ostensible content.

In support of Tennemann and Lessing, the Platonic statements excerpted above could be interpreted as follows: Plato, on his own testimony, refuses to commit his deepest thoughts to writings that are accessible to the many because he is afraid that the many will misunderstand and become contemptuous or vain. Therefore, he writes nothing serious, except perhaps clandestinely to the few who can learn by themselves with a little guidance. Also, when lecturing, he carefully chooses to whom he will speak and not speak. This implies what Schleiermacher denies, that Plato's dialogues should be emptied of their content, that is, considered to present nothing in the way of published doctrines to which Plato is genuinely committed. Hence, it appears to mean that Plato's "real wisdom is contained in his writings either not at all or only in secret, hard to detect indications." A corollary would be that Plato has two doctrines, namely, the esoteric, the serious teaching that he discloses only to the wise, and the exoteric, the sham teaching that he propagates openly. When the idea of the "noble" lie is mixed into the calculus, Plato's words might even mean that the fraudulent precepts of the wise deceive the many by paying exoteric lip service to the "ruling doctrines" of all parties, thus keeping the many under control. The ancient tradition of the esoteric and exoteric, authenticated as it is by the likes of Plutarch and Augustine, reinforces this conclusion.

Schleiermacher answers Lessing, Tennemann, and their lesser allies with two kinds of arguments. He suggests some miscellaneous objections to his opponents that involve matters of method, history, logic, and probability.

---

9. Lessing, "Leibniz von den ewigen Strafen," in *Lessings Werke*, 11:18–19; Lessing, *Ernst und Falk: Gespräche für Freimaurer, Erstes Gespräch*, and *Zweites Gespräch*, in *Lessings Werke*, 12:6, 12–13.

Then he proceeds to a philosophically principled reflection on Plato's mode of teaching. The miscellaneous objections reduce to the following points.

First, we have seen that in his initial statement of the position that he is rejecting, Schleiermacher asserts that the esoteric-exoteric distinction is spun from "isolated utterances" of Plato. He evidently does not believe that people like Lessing are innocent of the fallacy of the "fragmentizers," the exegetes who quote Platonic lines out of context for use in promoting their pet ideas. He does not concede that an argument like Lessing's can be established on the foundation of a few excerpts, without reference to their functions in the wholes in which they are set, for the snippets might not mean what the fragmentizers think.

Second, Schleiermacher observes that the concepts of the esoteric and the exoteric need a critical sifting, inasmuch as the distinction between the terms pertains to different things in different times ranging from the Pythagoreans to the post-Aristotelian sophists. He contends that no technical definition that evolved during these times fits Plato.

Third, Schleiermacher maintains that no one ever has identified as esoteric a Platonic doctrine that is not openly explained or adumbrated in the extant dialogues. The existence of unwritten Platonic secrets has to be viewed as undemonstrated if nobody can point to one that is not already written.

Fourth, if the errant scholars intend to refer Plato's uses of the esoteric and exoteric to his struggle against polytheism and popular religion, this is totally unsuitable, for his assumptions about these subjects are plain to see in his writings. It is incredible that Plato's students needed other teachings about religion, or that they took a childish delight in shouting behind closed doors what was already being said publicly, only more softly.

Finally, Aristotle certainly would have known whether Plato had hidden his real opinions. However, Aristotle never mentions privately circulated Platonic works, or a secret meaning of the published dialogues. Instead, when he disagrees with Plato's public arguments, he attacks them with the most bitter reproaches that a genuine successor could muster. This is not the behavior of a man who knows that he is fencing with shadows.[10]

As justifiable as these objections may be, the fact remains that Plato warns that he has not written on that which he takes seriously. Why, then, should his works not be emptied of their ostensible content? It is this diffi-

---

10. For objections two through five, see Schleiermacher, "Einleitung," 11–13. Thomas Aquinas has a different explanation of Aristotle's attacks on Plato. He contends that Plato had a faulty method of teaching, one that employed misleading metaphors, and that Aristotle deliberately criticized the metaphorical meaning of a phrase, knowing full well that it was not Plato's real meaning, in order to prevent popular misunderstandings. See the commentary by Aquinas in Aristotle, *Aristotle's De Anima, in the Version of William of Moerbeke and the Commentary of St. Thomas Aquinas*, 107.

culty that makes Schleiermacher offer positive remarks about the nature of Plato's teaching—but not a summary of his doctrines. He declines to give a preliminary account of the substance of Plato's philosophy, expressing doubt that this would be possible in the first place, and pleading that his object is to allow readers to form their own judgments.[11]

Schleiermacher starts his positive meditation by declaring that it is desirable to render his opponents' mistakes and their causes perfectly transparent. To this end, he says ironically that it would be laudable to lay Plato's philosophy out analytically, piece by piece, stripped as much as possible of its context, relations, and form, leaving nothing but its bare yield, thereby proving to all that it is integral, with no lost wisdom that needs to be sought. However, this would lead only to an "imaginary" understanding of Plato's work, for "in it form and content are inseparable, and every sentence is understood correctly only in its place, and in the connections and boundaries in which Plato has set it." Also, Plato's intention is not only to present his *Sinn* (a difficult German concept that combines the English ideas of sense, understanding, intellect, consciousness, and meaning) to others in a living way, but also to stir up and elevate the *Sinn* of others in a living way. Hence, it is necessary to comprehend each of Plato's dialogues as a whole and in its relationships to all the others.[12]

If this is true, Schleiermacher could clarify his adversaries' errors and their causes only with an enormous commentary on the entire Platonic corpus. Because this would exceed his scope, he must advance his introductory argument by violating his own principles, that is, by interpreting a few isolated Platonic utterances. He opts for a brief exposition of the passages in the *Phaedrus* (especially at 275 ff) cited above. He notes that Socrates complains about the uncertainty of written communication: One cannot be sure that the reader's soul assimilates written thoughts through its own activity, so as to attain to truth. It is likely that such a soul attains to a merely apparent grasp of words and letters, and that it conceives an empty conceit *(leere Einbildung)*, as if it knew what it does not know. Therefore, it would be folly to build on writing, and it would be correct to rely only on living, oral teaching. Plato's writing is for the sake of the writer and for those who already know, not for the sake of those who do not yet know.[13]

Schleiermacher continues by raising the question of why oral instruction is preferable to writing. He answers that there could be no other explanation than this: When the teacher stands in a present and living reciprocal relationship with the learner, he sees at every moment what the student has and has not grasped, and can assist the activity of his understanding when

11. Schleiermacher, "Einleitung," 7.
12. Ibid., 13–14.
13. Ibid., 15.

it fails. This advantage can be realized only through the form of conversation. Further, as is maintained in the *Phaedrus*, the father of an oral statement can respond both to objections and to the hard-mindedness *(Hartsinnigkeit)* of the person who does not know yet, whereas writing cannot reply to questions that anybody might put to it. Schleiermacher adds incidentally that the interaction between teacher and student depicted here makes it unthinkable that Plato should have delivered long, esoteric lectures.[14]

If Plato favors oral instruction and distrusts writing, why does he write so much? To solve this puzzle, Schleiermacher follows up Plato's indication that writing is for the sake of the writer. He is referring to Socrates' comments *(Phaedrus* 276c–d) that writing is intended to remind the author of what he knows and to amuse him. Schleiermacher assumes that Plato must want a remembrance of the thinking done by himself and his students, one that imitates the conversations by which they have progressed toward knowledge. Thus, Plato presumably strives to make his writing resemble his oral teaching, and he almost certainly succeeds. Plato considers all thought "independent activity" *(Selbsttätigkeit),* so that any memento of his own instruction and learning would necessarily have to replicate their original forms. This alone would make dialogue indispensable to his written as well as to his oral communication.[15]

If Plato's dialogues replicate his oral teaching, as Schleiermacher says, it follows that the philosopher also writes to "bring the still unknowing reader to knowledge," or that he proposes "at least to be cautious with regard to him, so that he does not impart an empty conceit of knowledge." If Plato has these intentions, it could be true simultaneously that his dialogues must not be voided of their content and that he does not commit his serious thought to writing. For it is Plato's aim "to conduct every investigation from the beginning onwards, and thereupon to reckon, that the reader either will be impelled to his own inner begetting of the envisaged thought, or forced to surrender himself most decidedly to the feeling of having found and understood nothing." So, it must be true that whatever cognitive status Platonic statements have in themselves, they should be viewed as indispensable stepping-stones toward whatever Plato knows. At the same time, "it is requisite that the end of the investigation not be directly spoken and verbally laid down, which easily could snare many who gladly would rest content if only they had the end."[16]

To teach in his writings, Plato attempts to reduce the reader's soul to the necessity of seeking the end of the inquiry, and to set that soul on the correct path to it. He achieves the first of these purposes by bringing the

14. Ibid., 15.
15. Ibid., 16.
16. Ibid., 16.

soul to a clear consciousness of its ignorance, such that it could not in good will remain there. He accomplishes the second by propounding riddles and contradictions, the solution of which could be found only in the thought in prospect, or by dropping apparently irrelevant and accidental hints that will be appreciated only by those who actually search with independent activity. Or he might cloak his real investigation, not as it were with a veil, but with an adhesive skin that conceals only from the inattentive what ought to be observed and found, and that sharpens and clears the *Sinn* of the attentive for the inner connection. It is approximately by these arts that Plato attains what he desires or avoids what he fears with everyone. It is only in this sense that one may speak about the esoteric and exoteric in Plato, namely, that these terms refer to the conditions of a reader who does or does not become "a true auditor of the inner." Or, if one chooses to apply these concepts to Plato himself, the esoteric is his immediate teaching, and the exoteric is his writing. Plato is certainly capable of expressing his thoughts purely and completely to his immediate hearers whom he knows to have followed him.[17]

This last remark requires us to clarify what type of knowledge Schleiermacher imputes to Plato. Is it the doctrinal science that Lessing envisages, that is, the propositional information that the wise could transmit to the many if they wished, but which they keep secret because "those who know it cannot say it," in the sense that they cannot say what better is left unsaid? This is extremely dubious. On Schleiermacher's account, if anyone ventured to tell the many what Plato sees, the result would not be the cultivation of the same vision in the minds of the many, but the generation of empty conceits in their souls, as if they knew what they did not know. Only those who had exerted independent activity and, thus, had engaged in an "inner begetting" would ascend to Plato's knowledge. Only "the true auditors of the inner" would find Plato's verbally expressed highest thoughts intelligible. So, Plato's *Sinn* has more to do with independent activity and inner begetting than with spoken words. Why is that, though, and what kind of *Sinn* is that? Schleiermacher does not answer. Plato's readers must find out for themselves.

Søren Kierkegaard and G. W. F. Hegel

As a mercurial young genius, Søren Kierkegaard was a voracious reader, an inventive writer, and a slow student who spent ten years at the University of Copenhagen. Although it seemed improbable that he would ever

17. Ibid., 16–17.

finish his graduate studies, he presented and defended a brilliant disser-tation, "The Concept of Irony, with Continual Reference to Socrates," in 1841. As an older man, Kierkegaard repudiated his dissertation, the gist of his dissatisfaction with it being expressed in the lament that he had been a Hegelian fool.[18] I would soften Kierkegaard's self-criticism. Although his dissertation is Hegelian, it also resists Hegel in striving to be true to Plato's texts and by offering a plausible argument about Socratic and Pla-tonic irony.

To extract Kierkegaard's possibly tenable analysis from its recanted He-gelian matrix, one must begin with an excursus on Hegel's chapters on Socrates and Plato in his *Lectures on the History of Philosophy*. In this sum-mary, it will become evident that Hegel's treatment of these thinkers is a four-headed version of Schleiermacher's worst nightmare.

First, instead of viewing the Platonic dialogues as means to becoming "true auditors of the inner," as Schleiermacher suggests, Hegel construes them as admirable but partial and, hence, ultimately inadequate advances toward his own recently elaborated propositional doctrines.

Socrates is called "the great form" in whom "the subjectivity of thought was brought to consciousness in a more definite, more penetrating man-ner" (as only Hegel's intellect can know). "Infinite subjectivity, freedom of self-consciousness, has arisen in Socrates." Socrates' "principle" is that "the human being has to find what is his destiny, what his purpose, what the final purpose of the world, the true, that which is in and for itself—attain to the truth—through himself." Nonetheless, Socrates failed. He "did not come to the point of having a philosophy, of developing a science." His good "is the universal which determines itself in itself, realizes itself, and should be realized—the good as purpose of the world, of the individual." Sadly, this "is not yet presented in its concrete determination." It is "merely formal," and it is "in this abstract attitude that the defect of the Socratic principle lies. The affirmative does not let itself be specified." Although we can assert of Socrates that "the spirit of the world here begins a turnaround (*Umkehr*)," the spirit "carried it out completely later." It is "from this higher standpoint" that Socrates must be considered.[19]

---

18. As quoted by Howard V. Hong and Edna H. Hong, eds. and trans., in introduction to *The Concept of Irony: With Continual Reference to Socrates*, by Kierkegaard, xiv.

19. Hegel, *Vorlesungen über die Geschichte der Philosophie*, 39, 40–41, 54, 62–63; Hegel, *Lectures on the History of Philosophy*, 1:384, 386, 399, 407. One trusts that the ideas in this Marheineke edition do not differ greatly from those in the first edition that Kierkegaard knew, copies of which are hard to obtain. I have compared the *Werke* text with that of the *Jubiläumsausgabe* (see Bibliography) and have sometimes allowed the latter to guide my sense of the meanings of the former. Although the Hegel translations in this book are my own, they sometimes coincide with those of E. S. Haldane and Frances H. Simson in Hegel, *Lectures on the History of Philosophy*. In such cases, only one translation is possible. I cite Haldane and Simson as *Lectures on Philosophy* in this note and below.

Plato is the thinker who begins "philosophic science as science." It is Plato "who grasped Socrates' principle that being [or essence, *Wesen*] is in consciousness, in its truth, that the absolute is in thought, and all reality is thought." Unlike his unscientific predecessor, Plato does not mean by this "the one-sided thought. . . . Rather, it is the thought of reality as thinking as well as of a single unity, the concept and its reality in the movement of science, the idea of a scientific whole." Despite these praises of Plato, we must be attentive to "what the Platonic standpoint does not achieve, what his time generally could not achieve." We grant that "Plato's true speculative greatness" lies in "the closer determination of the idea," in which the absolute is grasped both as Parmenides' pure being—which, as universal, good, true, and beautiful, "rules, penetrates, and produces the particular, the manifold"—and as Heraclitus's void. However, in Plato, "this self-producing activity is not developed, so Plato often fell into an external teleology." His philosophy suffers from the defect that the determinate idea and the universal fall apart.[20]

Second, if, perchance, one should find it rather hard to recognize Socrates and Plato in these characterizations, it would be fair to examine the hermeneutics by which Hegel arrives at his unexpected remarks. One finds immediately that Hegel disagrees with Schleiermacher's belief that Plato's "form and content are inseparable." He wants to "separate the form . . . in which Plato has advanced his ideas . . . from philosophy as such in him." He forbids us to regard the dialogue as "the most perfect form in which to present philosophy." As Hegel maintains in several of his works, the most perfect form in which to present philosophy is the scientific system that exhibits the necessary progression of thought to its completion in the idea. The disadvantage of dialogue is that it moves arbitrarily rather than necessarily, or at least creates a misleading appearance of doing so in Plato.[21]

Another major problem with Plato's dialogue form is that it involves "a deficiency with regard to the concrete determination of the idea itself." This defect is that the art form mixes "simple [that is, cloddish] representations (*Vorstellungen*) of being and the comprehending recognition of the same." Consequently, it plunges straight into myth. However, "the myth belongs to the pedagogy of the human race." It causes people to occupy themselves with stories, detracts from purity of thought by focusing on sensuous forms, and cannot express what reason wants. When the concept is fully developed, it no longer needs the myth. Thus, "Plato's exalted spirit, which had a perception or conception of spirit, penetrated through this, his subject, with the concept, but he only began this penetration, did not comprehend the whole reality itself with the concept—or [one could

20. Hegel, *Vorlesungen,* 147, 155, 199, 202; *Lectures on Philosophy,* 2:1, 9, 53, 56.
21. Hegel, *Vorlesungen,* 160, 161–62; *Lectures on Philosophy,* 2:14, 16.

say that] the insight that manifested itself in Plato did not realize itself in him as a whole."[22]

Both of these critiques imply that as a matter of principle, Plato's philosophy must be distilled out of its dialogue form. Hegel suggests the possibility of this procedure by claiming that the protagonists in Plato's publications have "plastic" interlocutors who give simple yes and no answers rather than stating their own views. (I interject that this is a stunning notion; it makes a person who has examined the behavior of the interlocutors wonder how closely Hegel read Plato.) This permits the protagonists to unfold a "beautifully consistent dialectic process"—even though "we certainly do not find in Plato a complete consciousness of the nature of dialectic," an awareness that Hegel himself has. Accordingly, we must dispense with the Platonic dramas and their characters, and maintain, as Hegel does throughout his analysis, that "Plato" speaks through the persons of Socrates, Timaeus, Critias, and the two Strangers. One can and must also separate the popular fantasies in Plato's myths from his "philosophic idea." The latter is found in "Plato's *philosopheme* [philosophic propositions]," and *philosopheme* "are thoughts and must, in order to be pure, be presented as such."[23]

Third, far from concurring with Schleiermacher's judgment that Plato's sense of the unity of knowledge prevents him from confining any of his writings to a single "field," Hegel sees the problem "that the Platonic philosophy does not declare itself to be one specific field." This is a serious defect of Plato's thought. The trouble is, "[w]e cannot find a systematic exposition of philosophy in this way." Hegel rectifies Plato's error by giving an account of his view of the true natures of philosophy and knowledge and of "the particular parts of philosophy that become prominent in his work." He maintains that there is a "Platonic philosophy" divided into "three parts" and then proceeds to assemble it. In this revision, he demonstrates that he rejects Schleiermacher's rule that in Plato, "every sentence is understood correctly only in its place, and in the connections and boundaries in which Plato has set it." He culls passages that seem to apply to the same topics from different dialogues and freely recombines them into apparently coherent doctrines. He also corrects Plato's "unfortunate expressions," such

----

22. Hegel, *Vorlesungen*, 163, 165, 163; *Lectures on Philosophy*, 2:17–18, 20, 18.

23. Hegel, *Vorlesungen*, 162, 161, 195, 165, 164–65; *Lectures on Philosophy*, 2:16–17, 49, 20–21, 19–20. The term *"philosopheme"* is a non-Germanic compound of Greek words for "philosophy" and "sayings." If it is not Hegel's coinage, it certainly is an exceedingly rare usage. Hegel's notion that Plato philosophized through propositions that he put into the mouths of Socrates, Timaeus, Critias, and the Strangers was propagated by Diogenes Laertius, *Lives of Eminent Philosophers*, 3.52. Some say that this proves that Hegel was right; others retort that this dates the moment in antiquity when all understanding of Plato was already lost.

as "anamnesis." From time to time, he does not scruple to omit an entire section of dialogue because it is a "beginning, a childlike effort," that is "superficial and confused."[24]

Finally, in his remarks on esotericism in Socrates and Plato, Hegel differs from both Lessing and Tennemann on the one hand and Schleiermacher on the other.

Socrates was "just, true, sincere, not harsh, and honorable" toward others. Thus, he taught students with whom he associated "to know that they knew nothing; indeed, what is more, he himself said that he knew nothing, and therefore taught nothing." (We must observe here that Hegel apparently did not read Plato carefully enough to notice that Socrates said that he knew the things of eros scientifically.) Socrates was honest, for "it may actually be said that Socrates knew nothing." His celebrated irony consisted entirely in telling this truth. It was not "hypocrisy," the "greatest irony." Socrates and Plato are falsely charged with being the originators of hypocrisy. However, their irony was a "tragic irony" that was "a manner of speech, a chummy cheerfulness," that had as its aim "to lead to the true good, to the universal idea."[25] Accordingly, Lessing and others are wrong because they think that Socrates lies, and Schleiermacher errs in arguing that Socrates tells less than he knows, remaining silent about higher truths. In proclaiming his ignorance, Socrates says what he has to say—nothing.

Plato is distorted greatly by Tennemann's remark: "Plato availed himself of the right that every thinker has, that of sharing only so much of his discoveries as he found good, and of sharing only with those whom he thought receptive. Aristotle also had an esoteric and an exoteric philosophy, only with this difference, that with him the distinction was simply formal, while with Plato, on the contrary, it was also simultaneously material." Hegel retorts: "How absurd! That looks as if the philosopher possessed his thoughts like external things. But thoughts are something entirely different. It is quite the other way around: the philosophic idea possesses the human being. When philosophers explicate philosophic topics, they must judge according to their ideas; they cannot keep them in their pockets." To be sure, there actually is "something esoteric" in the communication of ideas. However, this is merely a matter of leaving it to speculation to bring thoughts together as unions of the different, as in the case of the identity of being and nonbeing. It is not as if Plato had two philosophies, one for the world, for the people, the other the inner, reserved for intimates. There is nothing cryptic about Plato, for "the esoteric is the speculative that is written and printed, and, yet, is hidden from those who are not interested in

24. Hegel, *Vorlesungen*, 162, 163, 166, 195, 179, 233; *Lectures on Philosophy*, 2:17, 21, 49, 34, 87.
25. Hegel, *Vorlesungen*, 50, 54, 56, 57; *Lectures on Philosophy*, 1:395, 399, 401, 402.

exerting themselves."[26] Once again, Lessing and Tennemann err in supposing that Plato is deceptive or secretive; Schleiermacher is wrong to imagine
that Plato says nothing of an ineffable truth that lies beyond his published
arguments. There is no Platonic silence.

Having read Schleiermacher, Hegel sneers at his philosophically "superfluous" literary concerns and thereafter takes no account of him.[27] It
is safe to surmise that Schleiermacher's answer to Hegel, if it were stated
bluntly, would run along the following lines: Hegel treats the relationship
between Plato's content and form too casually. He makes premature claims
to understand Plato better than Plato did, for his pictures of a sagacious
but primitive Socrates and a magnificent but still amateurish and bumbling Plato, who lacked historically advanced insight into the ends of their
thought, and into the proper methods of conducting it, cannot be credited.
He undervalues Plato's "consciousness of ignorance," which would preclude Hegel's perfect science. He is absolutely obtuse to the extraordinary
premeditation that Plato put into the construction of a dialogue. He is a
systematizer who attempts to convert philosophy into a structure of neatly
divided fields, despite Plato's sense of the unity of knowledge that forbids
this. Therefore, he tries to lay Plato's philosophy out analytically, piece by
piece, stripped as much as possible of its context, relations, and form, so
that nothing is left but its bare yield, never realizing that Plato's *Sinn* involves an unspoken true hearing of the inner. At the same time, he is a frag-
mentizer who mangles Plato by taking from him what fits his preconceived
scheme. In all this, he virtually confesses to a total inability to comprehend
Plato, and arrives at an imaginary knowledge of him.

Whatever the merits of the Hegel-Schleiermacher quarrel, the philosophy faculties of Europe were Hegelian when the young Kierkegaard was
a student, so it comes as no surprise that his doctoral work reflects this
fact. True, the dissertation does astutely suggest an original investigation:
"Now, everyone knows that the tradition has linked the existence of Socrates to the concept of irony; from that, it in no way follows that everyone
knows what irony is." Then, however, as a "Hegelian fool," Kierkegaard
undertakes an essentially Hegelian explanation of the essence of Socratic
irony. The Hegelian elements of his interpretation can be summed up in
the following propositions: History is, as Hegel avers, "the unfolding of
the idea." Socrates represents a stage of this process, for the meaning of

26. Tennemann, *Geschichte der Philosophie,* 2:220; Hegel, *Vorlesungen,* 157, 214; *Lectures
on Philosophy,* 2:11, 12, 68. The expression translated as "how absurd" is *wie einfältig,*
which connotes silly simplemindedness. Some writers view Hegel's concession that
there is "something esoteric" about the communication of ideas as a sign that even
he is committed to an esotericism of Lessing's type. This takes Hegel's remark out of
context. He explicitly denies the implication.

27. For example, see Hegel, *Vorlesungen,* 156; *Lectures on Philosophy,* 2:10.

his existence in the world is that of "a moment in the development of the world spirit." He is "the historical turning point at which subjectivity made its appearance for the first time." Thus, he has the strengths and weaknesses that Hegel attributes to him. His great accomplishment was "the negative determination that subjectivity determines itself in itself. Nevertheless, Socrates lacked the objectivity in which subjectivity is empowered, is free in its inner freedom, the objectivity that is not the narrowing but the broadening boundary of subjectivity." This is the same as to assert that "his position was infinite negativity." Kierkegaard infers that irony is "the first and most abstract determination of subjectivity," and also that it is "infinite absolute negativity."[28]

If we object that these conclusions are not instructive, because they appear to be mere anachronistic projections of Hegelian categories onto Socrates, we shall probably come close to the gist of the older Kierkegaard's self-denunciation. Now, however, it is time to make the case that the youthful Kierkegaard's appraisal of Socratic and Platonic irony is not simply that of a Hegelian epigone. The first step in this argument is to note that the young Kierkegaard's very attribution of irony to Socrates is an act of rebellion against the master, for Hegel, it will be recalled, denied that Socrates was ironic in any but a "cheerfully chummy" manner.

In his investigation of irony, the young Kierkegaard proceeds by attempting to discern the philosophical positions of the historical Socrates in an intuitively computed average of the portraits painted by Xenophon, Aristophanes, and Plato. This appears misguided to me. We are not sure whether each of the sketches is true to its model or misrepresents it, so averaging them proves nothing. However, if nothing else, Kierkegaard's quest for the historical Socrates again demonstrates some independence of Hegel, who argues that there is no need to ponder what in the Platonic dialogues belongs to Socrates, and what to Plato. Kierkegaard also sides with Schleiermacher against Hegel in the hermeneutic dispute. He applauds Schleiermacher's respect, and regrets Hegel's disrespect, for context. He courageously accuses Hegel of reading Plato uncritically.[29] Hence, he cannot follow Hegel in regarding Socrates as a mouthpiece for Plato in phony

---

28. Because I wished not to be utterly dependent upon an English translation of a treatise in Danish, a language of which I know little, my quotations of Kierkegaard in this book are translations of the German version of *The Concept of Irony*, titled *Über den Begriff der Ironie: Mit ständiger Rücksicht auf Sokrates*. I was surprised to discover that my translations sometimes coincided with the English renditions of Hong and Hong. I gather from this that both the German and the English translations must be exact. In both languages, Kierkegaard is cited by marginal numbers that refer to volumes and pages of the 1901–1906 Danish edition of *Søren Kierkegaards samlede Værker*. The citations for this first set of quotations are *Begriff, Concept*, 13:107, 107, 279, 337, 290, 295, 337, 329.

29. Hegel, *Vorlesungen*, 158; *Lectures on Philosophy*, 2:13; Kierkegaard, *Begriff, Concept*, 13:300–302.

dialogues that should have been written as prose treatises. He believes that we must describe Socrates as historically and dramatically distinct from Plato. On this basis, he attributes different kinds of irony to each of the classical masters.

In Kierkegaard's view, the dialogue that most accurately reflects the historical Socrates is the *Apology*. Kierkegaard accepts the story that Socrates is obsessed with the oracle's reply to Chaerephon. He contends that Socrates "understands it as his divine calling, his mission," to go around examining others, so that every time he encounters a dubious claim to wisdom, "he can be helpful to the deity and show that the person in question is not [wise]." His usual method of helping the god is to pose a question, "not for the sake of the answer but, rather, to use the question to suck out the apparent content . . . and thereby to leave an emptiness behind." Elsewhere, he adds: "Herewith, we see irony in all its divine infinitude, which simply lets nothing stand. Like Samson, Socrates seizes the pillars that support knowledge and hurls everything down into the void of ignorance." This is the irony that Hegel has attributed to Socrates, but with a difference: Socrates is insidious in this shaking of the pillars; unlike Samson, he feigns to hold them up even as he destroys them: "He lets what exists exist but for him it has no validity; meanwhile, he behaves as if it did have validity for him, and under this mask he leads it to its certain destruction." So, clearly, "what Socrates said meant something different. The external was not at all in harmonious unity with the inner but was rather its opposite."[30] Therefore, by starting with the assumption that the Platonic dialogue is more than a defective literary form, Kierkegaard discovers a Socrates who does not fit Hegel's idea of him as unreservedly "true" and "open" toward all.

The opinion that Socrates is called by a god to an ironic overthrow of knowledge might be deluded. However, a nonideological reader who is faithful to Plato could judge that Socrates is plausibly and perhaps even justifiably serious about a god. Socrates' posture would then be incompatible with the notion that he represents pure negativity and that he is an early expression of the subjective freedom of Hegel's world spirit, a stance that requires atheism.[31] This difficulty compels Kierkegaard to move away from Hegel decisively.

The youthful Kierkegaard begins to retract his analysis of Socrates' negativity and free subjectivity when he asks whether Socratic irony serves anything positive. "Infinite absolute negativity" might be too strong. Here, Kierkegaard originally accepted Hegel's comment that although aiming to

    30. Kierkegaard, *Begriff, Concept*, 13:134, 134, 131, 136, 337, 108.
    31. On the necessity of atheism in Hegel, no one thinks more clearly than Alexandre Kojève, *Introduction to the Reading of Hegel: Lectures on "The Phenomenology of Spirit,"* esp. 57, 67, 89–90, 97, 107, 120, 146–47, 258.

lead mankind to the true good, "Socrates came to the idea of the good, the beautiful, the true only as the boundary—i.e., came to ideal infinity as possibility." However, Kierkegaard finds that he cannot rest here, for such a good is divorced from the universal and is virtually empty. This is to say: "As much as Hegel in several places seems to want to attribute a positivity to Socrates, and even though he ascribes to him the idea of the good, it nevertheless proves that the individual becomes capriciously self-determining in relation to the goal, and that the good as such in no way has unconditional binding power." Further, "since we now have recognized that the positive side was not positive in the same sense as the other was negative, we see that Socrates has validated the universal only as the negative." This leads Kierkegaard to challenge Hegel again. He charges that Hegel argues like Appius Claudius Pulcher, that is, in a Procrustean manner. He remarks sarcastically that Hegel is "too hasty and too much feels the meaning of his position as commanding general of world history," so that he misses things that should be in a complete treatment. Kierkegaard is therefore drawn back to Schleiermacher, saying, "What Schleiermacher attributes to Socrates is the idea of knowledge, and this is the very positivity . . . that Schleiermacher thinks Socrates hides behind his ignorance."[32]

Kierkegaard asserts that Hegel's analysis is wrong in that "the main direction of the flow of Socrates' life is not portrayed with exactitude." Hegel does not realize that the "movement in Socrates is toward attaining to the good." Further, "His meaning in the world development is to get there. . . . His meaning for his contemporaries is that they got there." This happened constantly, for Socrates' life was "always forward, forward, to get there and to have others get there." At the same time, "he also arrived at the true, i.e, the true in- and for itself, at the beautiful, i.e., the beautiful in- and for itself, in general, at being in- and for itself as both thought and being." Then what was this good, this true, this beautiful, this being? Kierkegaard argues that Socrates firmly refused to say, for "it is essential for the ironist never to express the idea as such but only fleetingly to indicate it, to take with one hand what is given with the other, to possess the good as private property." Why this silence, though? At one point, Kierkegaard mentions that "Socrates attained to the idea, yet in such a way that no predicate made evident or betrayed what it actually was, much more were all the predicates witnesses that were silenced before its splendor." In another place, he

---

32. Kierkegaard, *Begriff, Concept,* 13:278, 302, 310, 301 (two quotations), 288–89. Pulcher commanded a Roman naval force. He had to consult priests to learn whether the auspices for his campaign were favorable. When he did not get the results he wanted, because the sacred chickens were refusing to eat, he threw the chickens overboard. Kierkegaard thus accuses Hegel of jettisoning evidence that contradicts his pet conclusions.

argues that Socrates "beautifully binds men firmly to the divine."[33] If this represents the "positivity that Schleiermacher thinks Socrates hides behind his ignorance," he thus offers a mystical explanation of Schleiermacher's proposition that Plato's knowledge must be won by an inner begetting, and of the reasons that the concepts that symbolize it will be intelligible only to others who have engaged in this independent activity.

As for Plato, Kierkegaard ascribes to him one type of irony "that is only a *stimulus* for thought, that spurs it when it becomes sleepy, disciplines it when it becomes licentious," and another sort that "is itself the performer of the operation and again is itself the end striven for." The first irony corresponds to a dialectic "that in relentless movement sees to it that the question does not become entrapped in a capricious understanding, that is never weary and is always ready to set the problem afloat if it runs aground." The second irony is combined with a dialectic that "takes the most abstract ideas as its point of departure, wants to let these unfold themselves in more concrete determinations, a dialectic that wants to construct actuality with the idea." Kierkegaard equates the first sort of Platonic irony with Socratic negativity.[34] The other looks like Socratic positivity. Hence, when the young Kierkegaard deviates from Hegel, he envisages an unspoken Platonic knowledge that is not so much secret as ineffable for the spiritually obtuse. In this, he emulates Schleiermacher, except that he tentatively moves in an openly mystical direction.

Friedrich Nietzsche

Friedrich Nietzsche is a self-proclaimed esotericist. In *Beyond Good and Evil*, he says that the hermit—and it is given that every philosopher was first of all a hermit—does not believe that any philosopher "ever expressed his genuine and final opinions in books." To this, he adds a rhetorical question: "Does not one write books precisely to conceal what is hidden in oneself?"[35]

To understand Nietzsche's esotericism, we must ask three questions: First, what form does it take? How does the philosopher hide what he harbors? Second, what does he conceal? Third, why does he hide it?

33. Ibid., 13:311 (five quotations), 143–44, 221.
34. Ibid., 13:207.
35. The collected works of Nietzsche, *Nietzsche Werke: Kritische Gesamtausgabe*, are organized by section (*Abteilung*), volume (*Band*), page, and line. I shall cite them as *NW* with all four numbers. Translations of Nietzsche in this book are mine. Walter Kaufmann also has good translations, and mine are often close to his. (Sometimes only one translation is possible.) Thus, I shall cite his work, too. Here, see Nietzsche, *Jenseits von Gut und Böse*, in *NW*, 6.2.244.12–17; and *Beyond Good and Evil*, in *Basic Writings of Nietzsche*, 419.

With regard to the form of his esotericism, Nietzsche tells us that when those who are not meant for his highest insights hear them without permission, the insights must and should sound like follies and crimes to the eavesdroppers. The exoteric and the esoteric are found wherever one believes in rank rather than equality, and the difference between them consists not in the fact that the exoteric tries to see and understand from the outside, but, rather, in the fact that the exoteric attempts to see from below, whereas the esoteric looks down from above.[36]

This little gem of self-revelation bears the following interpretation: There is abroad in our land an understanding of esotericism that explains it as a defense against persecution. The philosopher knows truths that the many would detest as follies and crimes. If the philosopher proclaimed these truths, the many might murder him for his outrages. Thus, the philosopher pretends both to endorse the views of the many and not to hold the despised truths in order to avoid being killed. Vulgarians who encounter his exoteric statements stand "outside," looking in but failing to catch the esoteric truths that are divulged only to "insiders." This distinction between the exoteric and the esoteric seems plausible, but Nietzsche denies that it is correct.

Epitomizing the right view, Nietzsche trumpets the truths that the many see as follies and crimes, not addressing the many but not preventing them from hearing, either. He flaunts his commitment to these verities, which is authentic rather than feigned, with an astonishing frankness. He wants his auditors to know that he embraces what the vulgar call follies and crimes. Thus, the many do not stand outside, but inside his confidence. However, they still do not grasp what more the philosopher thinks, for he stands on a height far above them, while they wallow in a depth far below. When the philosopher broadcasts his highest insights, which must and should sound like follies and crimes to the unqualified, these verities portend greater profundities that have not been bared yet, for "[e]very philosophy also *conceals* a philosophy; every opinion is also a hiding place, every word also a mask."[37] Hence, the esoteric is hidden by its inaccessibility to inferior minds and by Nietzsche's decision to stop explaining what he could still clarify. The unsuited have as much chance of unraveling the deeper truths as a dog has of grasping the ramifications of a book open under its paw. In the meantime, the philosopher cannot be troubled to care that the many hate him for shocking their sensibilities. His esotericism is one of superior intelligence, defiance, and strength, not one of secrecy and fearfulness.

---

36. Nietzsche, *Jenseits*, in *NW*, 6.2.44.11–22; *Beyond Good and Evil*, in *Basic Writings of Nietzsche*, 232.

37. Nietzsche, *Jenseits*, in *NW*, 6.2.244.26–28; *Beyond Good and Evil*, in *Basic Writings of Nietzsche*, 419.

If Nietzsche's truths are concealed in the sense that they are much too profound for the vulgar to understand, and also in the sense that Nietzsche stops articulating implications, our remaining puzzles about his esotericism become all the more interesting. What is it that could be so opaque to the many? Whatever it is, why does Nietzsche not simply announce it if the unqualified never could grasp it anyway? Why should he bother to write books to veil it?

We are not yet in a position to ascertain the content of the truths that Nietzsche hides, not least because Nietzsche himself suddenly, surprisingly creates a suspicion that such truths do not exist. "Indeed," he declares, the hermit "will doubt whether a philosopher even *could* have 'final and genuine' opinions, whether behind every one of his caves there does not lie, must lie, another deeper cave—a more comprehensive, stranger, richer world on the other side of the surface, an abyss behind every ground, under every 'grounding.' "[38] Thus, for the moment, we must leave the question of what Nietzsche hides in abeyance.

However, we should still like to know why Nietzsche troubles to conceal his ultimate views, whether they have to do with an infinite regress of abysses or some highest, real opinion. In either case, it does not appear to make sense to conceal something if it is intrinsically obscure to those from whom one proposes to hide it. Nietzsche supplies a motive for this curious behavior in one of his most famous passages. He says:

> All that is profound loves masks; the most profound things of all even hate image and parable. Should not just the *opposite* be the right disguise in which the shame of a god promenades? . . . To a person who has profundity in his shame, his fates and delicate decisions befall him on paths to which few ever attain, and the presence of which his nearest and most trusted may not know: his mortal danger hides itself from their eyes, as well as his reconquered security of life.

Nietzsche seems to elaborate on this later as he explains his concept of a "fundamental will of the spirit" (*Grundwillen des Geistes*). The spirit wills to be and to feel itself lord of itself and its surroundings. Its will expresses itself in various drives, one of which is "a suddenly erupting decision for ignorance, an arbitrary seclusion, a shutting of its windows, a sort of posture of defense against much that is knowable, a satisfaction with the dark." Here, Nietzsche admits, "belongs the occasional will of the spirit to let itself be deceived," and also the spirit's will to deceive others, in which "the spirit enjoys the multiplicity and subtlety of its masks; it enjoys in this also the

---

38. Nietzsche, *Jenseits*, in *NW*, 6.2.244.17–22; *Beyond Good and Evil*, in *Basic Writings of Nietzsche*, 419.

feeling of its security."[39] So, Nietzsche's esotericism seems to have more to do with his preoccupation with himself than with his worries about what the many might discover. It is motivated by his delight in masks, by his will to be lord, by his sense of the proper attire for the shame of a god, by his need to veil his mortal danger from his dearest friends and even from himself, and by his desire for a feeling of security behind his masks. All this generates more perplexities that require analysis. However, it is time to leave the topic of Nietzsche's esotericism for a while, letting it serve as background for his critique of Plato's irony. I shall return to the problem of why Nietzsche himself loves masks at the appropriate juncture.

As for Plato, Nietzsche's *Twilight of the Idols* wages war on "eternal idols" that block a revaluation of all values, a war in which Nietzsche sounds the idols with a "hammer." The book has an essay titled "What I Owe to the Ancients." Nietzsche says that the only Greek whom he venerates is Thucydides, who manifested "the unconditional will not to hoodwink oneself and to see reason in *reality*." Nietzsche also says of Thucydides that "there are few thinkers so rich in mental reservations (*Hintergedanken*)."[40] He gives Socrates and Plato the opposite kind of report, execrating them both as philosophers and as ironists.

In his exoteric remarks, at least, Nietzsche counts Socrates and Plato among the idols consigned to destruction by the hammer. Referring to the argument of his first book, *The Birth of Tragedy*, Nietzsche boasts: "I recognized Socrates and Plato to be symptoms of decadence, tools of the Greek dissolution." Socrates is "a cave of all bad lusts." Plato is no artist, but a decadent bore whose dialogues contain a "dreadfully self-satisfied and childish kind of dialectic." He is "aberrant from all the basic instincts of the Hellene," "moralistic," "pre-existently Christian," and, all in all, a "higher swindle." In contrast to Thucydides, he "is a coward in the face of reality, consequently he flees into the ideal."[41]

What inspires this outpouring of contempt on Socrates and Plato? To learn this, one must look where Nietzsche points, into *The Birth of Tragedy*. There, Nietzsche recounts the experience that causes him to disdain the classical philosophers. He relates the story of how Midas captured Silenus and asked him what is most desirable for man. The daimon answered: "What is best of all is entirely unattainable: not to be born, not to be, to be *nothing*. But the second best is for you—to die soon." Nietzsche comments:

39. Nietzsche, *Jenseits*, in *NW*, 6.2.53.26–29; 54.13–18; 173.14–15, 31–32; 174.1–4, 8–9, 16–18, 20–22; *Beyond Good and Evil*, in *Basic Writings of Nietzsche*, 240–41, 349–50.

40. Nietzsche, *Götzen-Dämmerung, oder, Wie man mit dem Hammer philosophiert*, in *NW*, 6.3.52.5–16; 150.10–13, 18–20; *Twilight of the Idols; or, How One Philosophizes with a Hammer*, in *The Portable Nietzsche*, 466, 558.

41. Nietzsche, *Götzen-Dämmerung*, in *NW*, 6.3.62.2–4, 30; 63–64, 65.22–23; 149.16–19, 24–25, 27, 28–32; 150.1, 3–4, 5–9, 28–30; *Twilight of Idols*, 474, 475, 476, 477, 557, 558–59.

"The Greek knew and felt the terror and dreadfulness of existence." He himself laments this painful horror. He regards anyone who believes in "reason in reality" as deceived because he himself finds being absurd.[42]

Nietzsche's Hellene displays his noblest instincts when he is confronted with the void. As Nietzsche indicates in his mature postscript to *The Birth of Tragedy*, this aristocrat reacts with a "pessimism of *strength*." This implies that he looks directly at the horrible truth of the absurdity of being and summons the fortitude to acknowledge his situation. However, it also means a great deal more. Instead of sinking into paralysis after facing the nature of his reality, the noble Greek demonstrates his accord with "the truly existing primal unity" (*das Wahrhaft-Seiende und Ur-Eine*) by seeking "redemption through appearance" (*Erlöstwerden durch den Schein*). In his quest, he turns to art: "Here, in this greatest danger of the will, *art* approaches as a rescuing sorceress, skilled in healing. She alone is able to bend these nauseous thoughts about the dreadfulness and absurdity of existence into conceptions with which one can live." The act of embracing poetic or artistic salvation is in itself a demonstration of tremendous strength. The poet, perfectly conscious that existence is meaningless and that no comfort avails, nevertheless devises tragedies filled with beautiful images, and consoles himself with them, not by deluding himself, but by delighting in appearance in a manner that defies the void. This comforts the artist because it proves that "life is at the ground of things, despite all changes of appearances, indestructibly mighty and pleasurable." Nietzsche explains further in his postscript, a self-analysis done after he has forsaken his youthful metaphysics of "the truly existing primal unity," that the poet actually rejoices in his ability to say: "This crown of the laughing one, the rose-wreath crown: I crowned myself with this crown; I myself pronounced holy my laughter. No others did I find today strong enough for that." Therefore, the artist saves himself by exercising his will to power. Instead of behaving as a coward before reality, he admits the absurdity of being but wills it into insignificance. It is chiefly in this sense that Nietzsche can say in *Twilight of the Idols*: "We have abolished the true world." Nietzsche's experience of absurdity and his "courage before reality" therefore are the source of the first "postmodern" deconstruction of being, which essentially is an act of defiant will.[43]

---

42. Nietzsche, *Die Geburt der Tragödie: Oder, Griechenthum und Pessimismus*, in *NW*, 3.1.31.21–24, 29–30; 52.33–34; 53.1, 12–18; *The Birth of Tragedy; or, Hellenism and Pessimism*, in *Basic Writings of Nietzsche*, 42, 60.

43. Nietzsche, *Geburt der Tragödie*, in *NW*, 3.1.6.12–13; 34.29–30, 27–28; 53.21–23, 12; 52.9–11; 16.17–19; *Birth of Tragey*, 17, 45, 60, 59, 26–27; *Götzen-Dämmerung*, in *NW*, 6.3.75.8; *Twilight of Idols*, 486. There is another sense in which Nietzsche denies that there was ever a true world to abolish. In *Götzen-Dämmerung*, he endorses the teaching of Heraclitus that all material reality is in flux. With the Platonic Socrates' intelligible realm

Addressing himself to the question of how the Hellenes discovered artistic redemption, the Nietzsche of *The Birth of Tragedy* conjectures that inasmuch as this salvation requires a victorious resistance to nature, the wisdom that discovers it must spring from "an enormous event opposed to nature" *(eine ungeheure Naturwidrigkeit)* that conquers nature "through the unnatural" *(durch das Unnatürliche)*. Indeed, Dionysian wisdom is "an antinatural horror" *(ein naturwidriger Greuel)* in which the knower "hurls nature into the abyss of annihilation" by virtue of having to suffer "the dissolution of nature in himself." This necessitates the Dionysian man's involvement in the most loathsome crimes (such as incest), sacrilege, and evil generally. Accordingly, the "Aryan" nations have embraced Prometheus and have generated "the sublime view of *active sin* as the genuinely Promethean virtue." This noble Aryan *"justification* of human evil" compares favorably with the "feminine" Semitic myth of the fall, which Nietzsche rejects for its moralism.[44]

What is wrong with the Semitic myth and even more with the Christian morality that flows from it is that they prevent people from crowning themselves with laughter. Christians decline into "life's nausea and disgust with life," and into "enmity to life." Christianity is "basically a craving for nothing." Furthermore, Christian morality causes people to despise the artistic means to salvation. It relegates art to the realm of lies and damns it. Resuming this critique in *Twilight of the Idols*, Nietzsche reminds his readers of "an insight that first was formulated by myself: that *there are no moral facts at all."* He renews his insistence that the philosopher should "situate himself beyond good and evil." Far from obeying this order, Christian priests have ruined noble peoples with their moral teaching. Particularly, they have made the Teuton "a caricature of a man." They have turned him into a "sinner" who is "sick, miserable, malevolent against himself; full of hatred of the impulses of life, full of suspicion against all that still was strong and happy. In brief, a Christian."[45]

Socrates and Plato played vile roles in this depravation of the species. Nietzsche asserts that Socrates "was denied the satisfaction of looking into the Dionysian abysses." He means, apparently, that Socrates never realized the hopelessness of searching for reason in reality, and never saw the necessity of an artistic salvation that celebrated the will's joy in life.

---

dismissed as imaginary, and his visible realm reduced to flux (a description of the visible realm with which Socrates or Plato might have agreed), "being" becomes a totally empty fiction.

44. Nietzsche, *Geburt der Tragödie*, in *NW*, 3.1.63.1, 5, 11, 14; 65.14, 29–30, 32, 27; 13.11–12; *Birth of Tragedy*, 68, 69, 70, 71, 24.

45. Nietzsche, *Geburt der Tragödie*, in *NW*, 3.1.12.23–24, 19, 28–29; *Birth of Tragedy*, 23; *Götzen-Dämmerung*, in *NW*, 6.3.92.6–8, 1–2; 93.10–16, 19–20, 22–23, 25–28; *Twilight of Idols*, 501, 502.

Therefore, Socrates promulgated his supreme law: "Everything must be understandable to be beautiful." In his judgment, the demands of this law were never satisfied: "Wherever Socratism directs its probing glance it sees lack of insight and the power of illusion and deduces from this lack the inner perversity and reprehensibility of what is there." Thus, Socratic reason "condemns existing art and existing ethics" and embarks upon a desperate mission to find intelligibility. Socrates' law and anathemas moved Euripides to kill classical tragedy. They led Socrates to "a profound crazy notion" *(tiefsinnige Wahnvorstellung)* that became the foundation of science, namely, "the unshakable belief that thought reaches along the leading thread of causality *(an dem Leitfaden der Causalität)* into the deepest abysses of being, and that thought not only is in a position to apprehend being, but to correct it." This, in turn, inspired Socrates to preach a new morality: "Virtue is knowledge; people sin only from ignorance; the virtuous person is the happy person." Plato "prostrated" himself before Socrates "with all the fervent resignation *(Hingebung)* of his enthusiast-charlatan soul *(Schwärmerseele)*" and then held Socrates up as an ideal. This development was the ruination of Western man. Nietzsche rhetorically suggests that Socrates resolved to be so scientific only out of cowardly fear of the truth. In *Twilight of the Idols,* he also charges that Socrates *"wanted* to die" after being "sick a long time," and that the "moralism of the Greek philosophers from Plato on is pathologically conditioned; so is their high regard for the dialectic." This is why he calls Socrates and Plato degenerates.[46]

It is within the framework of this history that Nietzsche takes up the topic of Socratic and Platonic irony. He offers a twofold analysis of these phenomena.

First, Nietzsche portrays Socrates' irony about knowledge as a self-protective measure. Expanding his condemnation of Socratic science, he inquires: "Is the resolve to be so scientific perhaps only a fear of, and escape from, pessimism? A subtle emergency defense against—the truth? And, morally speaking, a sort of cowardice and falseness? Amorally speaking, a crafty deceit *(Schlauheit)*? O Socrates, Socrates, was that perhaps *your* secret? O enigmatic ironist, was that perhaps your—irony?" The insinuation is that, unlike the tragic Hellene, Socrates could not face the absurdity of existence squarely and resorted to scientistic rationalism as an analgesic. As Nietzsche states later, Socrates fell into a "self-swindle" *(Selbstbetrug).* His irony consisted in a compulsive refusal to acknowledge the void and to stop his frantic search for intelligibility each time honesty demanded it. It was a psychological defense mechanism. Considering Nietzsche's

---

46. Nietzsche, *Geburt der Tragödie,* in *NW,* 3.1.88.5–6; 81.6–7; 85.27–32; 95.7–12; 90.25–30; 87.32–33; 6.34–35; 7.1–2; *Birth of Tragedy,* 89, 83–84, 87, 95, 91, 89, 18. *Götzen-Dämmerung,* in *NW,* 6.3.67.14, 17; 66.13–15; *Twilight of Idols,* 479, 478.

suggestions that Plato also lacked the resolve not to hoodwink himself (*sich Nichts vorzumachen*) in a search for reason in reality, that Plato's cowardice accounted for his idealism, and that Plato's "true world" was an "error" (*Irrthum*) that was a "comfort," he also sees Plato's esotericism as a psychological self-delusion.[47]

Second, in considering ethics, Nietzsche calculates that the nonexistence of moral facts implies that all claims to insight into good and evil must be either foolish or dishonest. Which explanation is the true one? In *Twilight of the Idols*, Nietzsche contends, "This is the great, the uncanny problem that I have been following the longest: the psychology of the 'improvers' of mankind." This is his result: "We may state it as the highest tenet that, to *make* morality, one must have the unconditional will to its opposite. . . . Neither Manu nor Plato nor Confucius nor the Jewish and Christian teachers have ever doubted their *right* to lie. . . . [A]ll means by which mankind was supposed to have been made moral were from the ground up immoral." How, though, can Nietzsche prove this? How can he be certain that ethics has not always been a terrible blunder? He defends his stance in one of his notebook entries that his sister collected under the title *The Will to Power*. "One errs," he says, "if one presupposes an *unconscious and naive* development here, a kind of self-swindle. . . . The fanatics are not the discoverers of such thought out systems of oppression. . . . Here the most cold-blooded circumspection was at work, as Plato had it when he thought out his *Republic*." Why should Socrates and Plato have fabricated such lies? In *Twilight of the Idols*, Nietzsche conjectures that "the irony of Socrates" is "an expression of revolt, of mob *ressentiment*." In light of Plato's "pre-existent Christianity," one must assume that he, too, was involved in the general revolt of the lowly that Nietzsche discusses in the *Genealogy of Morals*. However, Plato's case, which must be subsumed under that of all "priests," presents a strange twist. Worthless as they are, priests nevertheless believe themselves to be "the norm, the pinnacle, the highest expression of the type man," so they crave a rulership that befits their imaginary status. Then they figure out what they need to acquire and exercise power and concoct falsehoods about morality to satisfy these requirements. Thus, "the cause of the holy lie is the *will to power*."[48]

It now seems that Nietzsche sees Socratic and Platonic irony as one part

47. Nietzsche, *Geburt der Tragödie*, in *NW*, 3.1.6.34–35; 7.1–5; *Birth of Tragedy*, 18; *Götzen-Dämmerung*, in *NW*, 6.3.66.25; 150.12–13; 74.2, 14; *Twilight of Idols*, 478, 558, 485. There are further remarks in the same vein in the *Nachlass*.

48. Nietzsche, *Götzen-Dämmerung*, in *NW*, 6.3.96.11–13, 9–11, 17–22; *Twilight of Idols*, 505; *Nachgelassene Fragmente: Anfang 1888 bis Anfang Januar 1889*, in *NW*, 8.3, entry 15 (45), p. 234, ll. 1–7; entry 15 (42), pp. 227–30, all; *The Will to Power*, 92; 89–91; *Götzen-Dämmerung*, in *NW*, 6.3.64.20–21; 96.1–5; *Twilight of Idols*, 476, 505; *Nachgelassene Fragmente*, in *NW*, 8.3.233.15–20; *The Will to Power*, 92.

psychological self-deception that arises out of a cowardly inability to face the absurdity of being and one part swindle that emanates from the desires of inferior men for revenge upon their betters and power over the human race. Should one be satisfied with this, or are there reasons to suspect that Nietzsche has a deeper teaching about the classical philosophers that uses these censures as exoteric cover?

There are some difficulties attendant upon the summarized arguments that require one to tarry a while over this question. It has been seen that (1) Nietzsche calls Dionysian wisdom "an anti-natural horror" with which the knower "hurls nature into the abyss of destruction" by suffering "the dissolution of nature in himself," thus conquering nature "through the unnatural"; (2) he denies that there are any moral facts; and (3) he also denounces morality as the spiritual disease of hostility to life. However, in *Twilight of the Idols,* he also includes an essay on "morality as anti-nature" (*Moral als Widernatur*). In this work, he portrays nature as a measure of health, describes traditional moralities as antinatural, and holds out the possibility of a healthy, naturalistic morality ruled by an instinct of life.[49] Further, it was just noticed that Nietzsche associates the motives of the Platonic priest with the will to power. In *Thus Spoke Zarathustra* and several other major works by Nietzsche, the will to power is the highest, not to say the only, reality. Nietzsche apparently contradicts himself. How can his inconsistencies be reconciled?

It might be hypothesized that the difficulties should be fixed up by an esoteric reading. One could contend that Nietzsche silently indicates through his contradictions that (1) being actually is not absurd at all; (2) Dionysian wisdom does not plunge nature as such into the abyss of destruction but, rather, seeks to suppress only diseased natures and to nourish healthy ones, the achievement of natural vitality being the actual purpose of life; (3) Socrates and Plato secretly shared this agenda and deliberately created the illusion of an intelligible realm of reality different from the visible one to hide both the meaning of life and the necessarily cruel intentions of the strong from the weak, who must be crushed pitilessly; (4) Socrates and Plato therefore were excellent rather than poor artists; (5) there really are moral facts, but these truths are quite different from what the majority of human beings must be taught if they are to be dominated conveniently; (6) the true natural morality justifies the tyrannical rule of the healthy over the ill; and (7) Socratic irony and Platonic irony, like Nietzsche's irony, are disguises of these verities. One could also speculate that some such reasoning explains Leo Strauss's enigmatic remark that Nietzsche could "insist on the strictly esoteric character of the theoretical analysis of life—that is, restore

---

49. Nietzsche, *Götzen-Dämmerung,* in *NW,* 6.3.76.1; 79.16–18, 21–24; *Twilight of Idols,* 486, 489–90.

the Platonic notion of the noble delusion," as if Nietzsche were simply carrying on Plato's work.[50]

It seems to me that although this analysis of Nietzsche's contradictions is attractive at first blush, it cannot stand serious scrutiny for the following reasons.

First, the type of esotericism envisaged here is not the superior, defiant, strong kind that Nietzsche proclaims from above. Rather, it is a sneaky, manipulative, "priestly" variety imposed on outsiders by insiders. It simply is not Nietzsche's style to think like this.

Second, the account suggested here is less coherent than the incoherence that it purports to reconcile. Nietzsche's Zarathustra suggests openly that "peoples" should rule "herds," that is, that real men living according to his principles should have tyrannical power over the many.[51] Nietzsche lets everyone see that an overman likes power as much as priests do. It does not make sense that Nietzsche should protect Socrates' and Plato's metaphysical secrets and dissemble his own naturalistic assumptions when he trumpets their implications to every blockhead. It also seems illogical that if he himself wishes to govern by noble lies, a strategy that he condemns in discussing the case of the priests, he should torpedo the morality designed to keep the many in check, replacing it with doctrines that are likely to have the same effect on the masses that Ivan Karamazov's conversation had on Smerdyakov.

Third, Nietzsche's inconsistencies can be explained much more economically as functions of his publicly bewailed spiritual problem. Nietzsche claims to suffer because his reality is absurd. He wants to attain to another existence, or a different consciousness, in which the defect of his reality is repaired or neutralized. He also desires to communicate this intention to others. However, it is linguistically impossible to speak of a deficient reality being changed essentially yet persisting in some core of its original essence, where it can enjoy its essential change, without adopting paradoxical symbols. Nietzsche's original collision with this hard, unyielding obstacle results in his idea of "the truly existing primal unity, eternally suffering and contradictory" (das Wahrhaft-Seiende und Ur-Eine, als das ewig Leidende und Widerspruchsvolle).[52] This ontological oxymoron at once denotes a unity and a duality with a positive half that craves continuous redemption and a negative half, a being in the mode of defect, that torments its other half and that must be overcome to permit the deliverance of its whole self to a

50. Strauss, Natural Right and History, 26.

51. Nietzsche, Also sprach Zarathustra: Ein Buch für Alle und Keinen, in NW, 6.1.57.2–3; Thus Spoke Zarathustra: A Book for All and None, in The Portable Nietzsche, 160. This text is merely one example of many where Nietzsche or Zarathustra expresses such a sentiment; the argument does not rest on this passage alone.

52. Nietzsche, Geburt der Tragödie, in NW, 3.1.34.29–31; Birth of Tragedy, 45.

state of happy consciousness. Thus, Nietzsche's initial encounter with the linguistic impossibility produces a classic Manichaean symbol.

I think that a good book on Nietzsche would show that he creates another Manichaean symbol when he becomes an "antimetaphysician." Now the divided *Ur-Eine* is succeeded by the will to power as the core reality. The will to power itself is divested of all attributes of "being," "nature," and the Kantian *Ding-an-sich* insofar as it is conceived not as essence, but as action ("there is no 'being' behind the doing").[53] As a "doing" not supported by an ontological substrate, the will to power cannot help doing what it does; it simply does it. What it does is to express itself as the self-overcoming drive of the potential or realized overman and also to bend back upon itself in the sickly, self-destructive manner of the weaklings. It does this until the overman, as it were, "redeems" the "doing that is not being" (the will to power) in himself. So, humanity is still described with dualistic, albeit antimetaphysical, expressions, such as those in Zarathustra's dictum: "What is great in man is that he is a bridge and not a purpose: what can be loved in man is that he is a *going over* and a *going under*."[54]

Next, Nietzsche brings the expression "nature" back as a synonym for the primal unity and the will to power, *but not for Plato's intelligible realm of being*. His usages are equivocal. "Nature" variously connotes the primal unity's or the will's positive portion, the negative half, and the whole. This is why it is seemingly both salvific and destructive, and why it yields opposite moralities, the healthy one being creatively willed by the positive part to ensure its felicity, and the pathological one being imagined to be an ontological fixture and harming life. Nietzsche's "revaluation of all values" is entirely a product of his will, founded upon the willed utilities of the positive part.[55] Thus, Nietzsche's inconsistencies are not the artifices of a sneaky, manipulative esotericist but the unavoidable linguistic consequences of the modern version of the Manichaean experience of being.[56]

We must assume, then, that Nietzsche's attacks on Socrates and Plato are earnest. His charges that they were craven degenerates who destroyed an art that saved mankind through appearance, that they replaced it with a sterile philosophy of Ideas, and that they thus exposed the race to the disease of Christian morality are not esoteric tricks. Neither are his attacks

53. "Es giebt kein 'Sein' hinter dem Thun, Wirken, Werden; der 'Thäter' ist zum Thun bloss hinzugedichtet,—das Thun ist Alles."

54. Nietzsche, *Zur Genealogie der Moral*, in *NW*, 6.2.293.27–28; *On the Genealogy of Morals*, in *Basic Writings of Nietzsche*, 481; *Also sprach Zarathustra*, in *NW*, 6.1.11.2–3; *Thus Spoke Zarathustra*, in *The Portable Nietzsche*, 127.

55. See, for example, Nietzsche, *Also sprach Zarathustra*, in *NW*, 6.1.26.12–14, 25–27, 30–31; *Thus Spoke Zarathustra*, in *The Portable Nietzsche*, 138–39.

56. My analysis of Nietzsche's Manichaeanism disagrees with Peter Berkowitz, *Nietzsche: The Ethics of an Immoralist*. I think that Berkowitz underestimates the radicalism of Nietzsche's antimetaphysics.

on Socrates and Plato as thinkers who were ironic for reasons of cowardice and a sickly envy.

Nietzsche still claims to be an esotericist himself, however. It is time to return, briefly, to the reasons for Nietzsche's love of masks. We must begin by asking our remaining questions in a slightly different way: To whom, about what, and why is Nietzsche ironic?

Nietzsche himself confirms our inference, stated above, that his esotericism has more to do with his preoccupation with himself than with concerns about the many. Zarathustra says: "Whoever writes in blood and aphorisms does not want to be read but learned by heart. In the mountains the nearest way is from peak to peak: but for that you must have long legs. Aphorisms should be peaks, and those addressed great and tall-growing."[57] The great, tall-growing types whom Nietzsche addresses are not the many. Rather, Nietzsche aims his esotericism and his whole philosophy essentially at himself, at his own will, and at men like himself who live in the heights. One of the inadequacies of Plato's irony is that it is precisely not aimed at his own superior will and at lofty men, but concerns itself with worthless individuals whom Plato wants to rule by means of sneaky, "priestly" manipulation.

The subject matter of Nietzsche's esotericism is governed by the fact that as he speaks to his own will, Nietzsche is striving to facilitate the "fundamental will of the spirit," which wants to be and to feel itself lord of itself and its surroundings, that is, to be a god. The spirit cannot achieve this status simply by wishing it. It faces mortal dangers in its quest. The perils arise out of the fundamental truth that Nietzsche acknowledges, the basic truth of which all mankind should be conscious, that being is absurd. Once a thinker has confronted this truth honestly, he might find that all its consequences militate against the possibility and success of his project of self-deification. Therefore, Nietzsche makes these consequences the topic of all his philosophy and all his esotericism. It is another of the shortcomings of Plato's irony that he does not make the horror of being its first premise and does not devote all his energies to helping the spirit overcome the obstacles to its fundamental will. Instead, Plato worries about the opinions of last men and flea beatles.

So, why is Nietzsche esoteric toward himself and great men? The answer

---

57. Nietzsche, *Also sprach Zarathustra,* in *NW,* 6.1.44.13–17; *Thus Spoke Zarathustra,* in *The Portable Nietzsche,* 152. The German word rendered as "by heart" is "*auswendig.*" This word always receives this translation, but it does not literally mean "by heart." It means something like "out-turning," in the sense that something has been learned so thoroughly that it has been turned inside out. Zarathustra means that a writer does not want to be read for the details of his argument, which are meaningless, but for understanding of the absolute essence of what he has in mind.

rests upon the centerpiece of Nietzsche's philosophy from his youth to his death, his commitment to the necessity of "redemption through appearance." Whenever the spirit sees that yet another line of argument tends to end in the impossibility of self-deification in an absurd existence, it has to bolster its flagging divine will by yielding to "a suddenly erupting decision for ignorance, an arbitrary seclusion, a shutting of its windows, a sort of posture of defense against much that is knowable, a satisfaction with the dark," and also to "the occasional will of the spirit to let itself be deceived" and to deceive others like itself who might falter under the weight of the adverse conclusions. That is, it has to conceal the worst truths from itself and, then, overcome the shame caused by its consciousness of its own dishonesty. It does this by writing books to conceal from itself what it harbors, by slipping into one mask after another until it has given up its morbid attachment to the truculent truth. It then "enjoys the multiplicity and subtlety of its masks; it enjoys in this also the feeling of its security." The most crippling defect of Socratic-Platonic irony is that it is not directed toward the fully conscious, willfully playful self-deception of the self-deifying philosopher himself. By occupying itself with the opinions of cows, it misses the whole point of philosophy.

On these grounds, I think that Nietzsche would be surprised to hear that he could, and actually did, "insist on the strictly esoteric character of the theoretical analysis of life—that is, restore the Platonic notion of the noble delusion." He advocates the adoration of appearance and identifies his illusions not secretly, but publicly. His conscious, deliberate self-delusion is chosen freely and, hence, is completely different from Socratic science and Platonic idealism, which are the issues of minds that are unbalanced by fear, of minds that are hysterical and thus vulnerable to error. He thinks that his images are noble, whereas Socrates' and Plato's delusions are contemptible. Although he agrees that Socrates and Plato esoterically propagate illusions, he is far from hoping to repeat their pathological deeds. Further, his glorious "someplace" where "there are still peoples and herds," which I mentioned above, is a form of *antipolitical* order dictatorially ruled by overmen and their apprentices. This someplace has the language of good and evil that its citizens have willed, not our contemporary moral babble. Nietzsche has no interest in a Socratic or Platonic *political* order created and maintained by ethical chicanery.[58] So, although he concedes that Socrates and Plato lie about morality in their quest for power, he declines to

---

58. Nietzsche, *Also sprach Zarathustra,* in *NW,* 6.1.57.2, together with the whole of the chapters "Vom neuen Götzen," pp. 57–60; and "On the New Idol," pp. 160–63. Cf. "Zur Kritik des Manu-Gesetzbuchs," in *Nachgelassene Fragmente, in NW,* 8:3, entry 15 (45), pp. 233–34; and "Toward a Critique of the Law-Book of Manu," in *The Will to Power,* 91–92.

join them for the sake of preserving either bourgeois society or the Socratic way of life.[59]

What remains is the conclusion drawn earlier. Nietzsche pictures a Socratic irony and Platonic esotericism that are one part psychological self-deception stimulated by a fainthearted inability to face the absurdity of being and one part higher swindle conceived in the longings of failed men for revenge upon their betters, and for universal power. His attack upon them is not an esoteric disguise of agreement with them with respect to how we should respond to the terror of the void, but a charge that their irony proceeded from weakness rather than strength. Thus, he agrees with Lessing that they were esoteric, but denies that their motives were right.

LEO STRAUSS

Leo Strauss joins the debate about Platonic silence on the side of Gotthold Lessing.[60] Perhaps he also sides with Friedrich Nietzsche secretly. He opposes Friedrich Schleiermacher and G. W. F. Hegel. He treats Socratic and Platonic irony specifically in *The City and Man* and the esotericism of great philosophers generally in *Persecution and the Art of Writing*. At first, his analysis of irony seems straightforward. As one reads further into his work, however, one realizes that he writes esoterically about esotericism. Therefore, his account of its purposes is difficult to understand.

In *Persecution*, Strauss glances briefly at Schleiermacher, calls him a "great theologian," and credits him with "an unusually able argument."[61] One infers from both of his books just cited that he appreciates Schleiermacher for his hermeneutic principles, as follows.

First, Strauss strongly argues: "One cannot understand Plato's teaching as he meant it if one does not know what the Platonic dialogue is. One cannot separate the understanding of Plato's teaching from the understanding of the form in which it is presented. . . . At any rate to begin with one must pay even greater attention to the 'form' than to the 'substance,' since the meaning of the 'substance' depends on the form."[62] This rule tallies with

59. Thus, I respectfully disagree with the view that Nietzsche is a "postmodern Plato." Cf. Catherine H. Zuckert, *Postmodern Platos: Nietzsche, Heidegger, Gadamer, Strauss, Derrida*, chap. 1; and Stanley Rosen, *The Mask of Enlightenment: Nietzsche's "Zarathustra,"* xiv. I believe that Nietzsche would be dismayed to find himself at the center of Strauss, *Studies in Platonic Political Philosophy*, chap. 8, a placement that intimates that his essays were "Platonic."

60. Strauss said: "Lessing was always at my elbow. . . . As I came to see later, Lessing had said everything I had found out about the distinction between exoteric and esoteric speech and its grounds" (Leo Strauss and Jacob Klein, "A Giving of Accounts," 3).

61. Strauss, *Persecution*, 28.

62. Strauss, *The City and Man*, 52.

Schleiermacher's maxim that Plato's "form and content are inseparable," and it entirely rejects Hegel's dictum that it is necessary to "separate the form . . . in which Plato has propounded his ideas . . . from philosophy as such in him."

Second, Strauss declares: "What it means to read a good writing properly is intimated by Socrates in the *Phaedrus* when he describes the character of a good writing. A writing is good if it complies with 'logographic necessity,' with the necessity that ought to govern the writing of speeches: every part of the written speech must be necessary for the whole; the place where each part occurs is the place where it is necessary that it should occur." Strauss also maintains: "The context in which a statement occurs, and the literary character of the whole work as well as its plan, must be perfectly understood before an interpretation of the statement can reasonably claim to be adequate or even correct."[63] This recalls Schleiermacher's insight that one must respect Plato's great premeditation in composing his dialogues. It also implies assent to Schleiermacher's rule that in Plato, every sentence is understood correctly only in its place, and in the connections and boundaries in which Plato has set it. It abjures Hegel's method of culling *philosopheme* from different texts and recombining them into arguments of allegedly greater logical coherence.

Third, in keeping with Plato's awareness of the mysterious wholeness and heterogeneity of being, Strauss denies that a Platonic dialogue can be construed as "a chapter from an encyclopedia of the philosophic sciences or from a system of philosophy."[64] This reaffirms Schleiermacher's analysis of Plato's sense of the unity of knowledge. It pointedly rejects Hegel's effort to remake the Platonic corpus into a system.

Finally, Strauss notes that Plato never appears in his own dialogues. Thus, he affirms (at least provisionally): "In none of his dialogues does Plato ever say anything." To writers who believe that "Plato speaks through the mouths of his spokesmen," he replies that "we do not know what it means to be a spokesman for Plato; we do not even know whether there is such a thing as a spokesman for Plato." Elsewhere, he adds: "The views of the author of a drama or dialogue must not, without previous proof, be identified with the views expressed by one or more of his characters, or with those agreed upon by all his characters or by his attractive characters."[65] Thus, in his own way, Strauss reproduces another of Schleiermacher's conclusions, that we cannot tell from Plato's dialogues what Plato seriously thought. He contradicts Hegel's assurances that Plato puts his

---

63. Ibid., 53; *Persecution*, 30.
64. Strauss, *The City and Man*, 61–62.
65. Ibid., 52, 53; *Persecution*, 30; *The City and Man*, 50; *Persecution*, 30. This means that Plato's views *could* be identified with those of one of his characters *with previous proof.*

final judgments and settled doctrines into the speeches of Socrates, Timaeus, and the Strangers.

Strauss's sympathy with Schleiermacher's hermeneutics does not extend to the latter's interpretation of Platonic silence. Strauss differs from Schleiermacher—and also from Hegel—over the question of whether Plato has one teaching or two, the esoteric and the exoteric.[66]

In *The City and Man*, Strauss moves immediately to the crux of this disagreement. He renews Kierkegaard's question, remarking, "Very much, not to say everything, seems to depend on what Socratic irony is." Now, whereas Schleiermacher had analyzed esotericism as a matter of whether Plato's audiences could be true auditors of the inner, Strauss answers: "Irony is a kind of dissimulation, or of untruthfulness." Citing Aristotle's comment that the historical Socrates always understated his own merits (*Nicomachean Ethics* 1127b22–31), he continues by maintaining: "Irony is then the noble dissimulation of one's worth, of one's superiority." Because the highest form of superiority is wisdom,

> [i]rony in the highest sense will then be the dissimulation of one's wisdom, *i.e.*, the dissimulation of one's wise thoughts. This can assume two forms: either expressing on a "wise" subject such thoughts (*e.g.*, generally accepted thoughts) as are less wise than one's own thoughts or refraining from expressing any thoughts regarding a "wise" subject on the ground that one does not have knowledge regarding it and therefore can only raise questions but cannot give any answers.[67]

This definition of "irony in the highest sense" has another important feature: "If irony is essentially related to the fact that there is a natural order of rank among men, it follows that irony consists in speaking differently to different kinds of people." Strauss thinks that the "if" clause is satisfied. This leads him to the following argument: In the *Phaedrus*, Socrates states that writing is an invention of doubtful value. However, Plato wrote dialogues—a contradiction that would call Socrates' intuition or Plato's work into question unless it were reconciled. However, the contradiction can be reconciled:

> We may assume that the Platonic dialogue is a kind of writing which is free from the essential defect of writings. Writings are essentially defective because they are equally accessible to all who can read or because they do not know to whom to talk and to whom to be silent or because they say the same things to everyone. We may conclude that the Platonic dialogue says different things to different people . . . or that it is

66. Strauss, *Persecution*, 28.
67. Strauss, *The City and Man*, 51.

radically ironical. . . . The proper work of a writing is to talk to some readers and to be silent to others.[68]

Taking further instruction from Xenophon, Strauss learns the two different ways in which Socrates the speaker (and, hence, Plato the writer) was inclined to approach others: "It would not be strange if Socrates had tried to lead those who are able to think toward the truth and to lead the others toward agreement in salutary opinions or to confirm them in such opinions." Accordingly, "the proper work of a writing is truly to talk, or to reveal the truth, to some while leading others to salutary opinions; the proper work of a writing is to arouse to thinking those who are by nature fit for it."[69] We should note that Nietzsche preceded Strauss in the judgment that the real content of writing should be addressed only to the naturally fit.

It is now clear that for Strauss, Socratic irony is a form of untruthfulness in which the philosopher, a naturally superior man, (1) has "wise thoughts," and, indeed, even knows "the truth"; (2) has it in his power to "express" his wise thoughts, or to "reveal" the truth, to those who can think, by "truly talking"; (3) is silent about his wise thoughts, or refrains from telling the truth, to his natural inferiors who cannot think, although he definitely could transmit his knowledge to them by talking if he wished; (4) dissimulates his wisdom, either by expressing less wise, generally accepted thoughts or by pretending not to know the truth; (5) uses writing to reveal the truth to the thoughtful and to lead the thoughtless to untrue, salutary opinions; and (6) communicates with readers who can think by relying on them to "read a good writing properly," such people knowing that "the good writing achieves its end if the reader considers carefully the 'logographic necessity' of every part, however small or seemingly insignificant, of the writing."[70] Some things are not so plain, though. If we grant that the philosopher is already wise, which Socrates, as Strauss expects, denies, just why does the philosopher conceal his wise thoughts? Further, what is his truth? What is the character of the logographic necessity that should govern a good writing? Is this necessity scientific (that is, identical with the demands of inquiry or explanation) or is it rhetorical (in other words, identical with the aims and techniques of the program of simultaneous disclosure and deception)? How can one "consider" the logographic necessity of a writing to get at its teaching?

On the subject of why the philosopher dissimulates his wisdom, Strauss first offers a reason of gentility: the superior man "spares the feelings of his inferiors by not displaying his superiority."[71] One surmises that Strauss

68. Ibid., 51, 52–53.
69. Ibid., 53–54.
70. Ibid., 54.
71. This is clearly not a Nietzschean consideration.

himself is being ironic and that he has some ulterior motive for saying this, for he certainly knows from the *Apology* that whatever Socratic irony truly aimed to do, it shamed Socrates' inferiors, resulting in a murderous resentment of him. Strauss soon proposes another reason. He declares that "the literary question, the question of presentation, is concerned with a kind of communication. Communication may be a means for living together; in its highest form, communication *is* living together." So, the "literary question properly understood is the question of the relation between society and philosophy." One gathers that the wise man resorts to irony because it is the only form of communication that enables philosophers and the many to live together. Why is that? Strauss drops a hint not unrelated to the fate of Socrates: "Xenophon's Socrates engaged in his most blissful work only with his friends or rather his 'good friends.' For, as Plato's Socrates says, it is safe to say the truth among sensible friends."[72] One concludes that a superior man must be ironic to the many and tell the truth only to friends because revealing the truth to the many is dangerous for philosophers.[73] Why should that necessarily be so, though? Strauss seems to fall silent. Thus, *The City and Man* does not finish any direct explanation of why a philosopher hides his wise thoughts.

This guarded book is even less informative about the substance of the verities that the philosopher conceals. Strauss provides no obvious tantalizing clues, no ironic suggestions. He is equally laconic about the nature of the logographic necessity, the iron law that dictates the construction of a good writing. He does raise brief hopes that he will be helpful in the matter of how the logographic necessity should be considered. He declares that the Platonic dialogue reveals to us "in what manner the teaching conveyed through the work is adapted by the main speaker to his particular audience and therewith how that teaching would have to be restated in order to be valid beyond the particular situation of the conversation in question." He also remarks that "we must understand the 'speeches' of all Platonic characters in the light of their 'deeds,'" the "deeds" including such things as the settings of the particular dialogues, the traits of the participants, the manners in which their conversations arise, the intentions of the main speakers, their successes and failures in attaining to their ends, the silences of these characters with regard to the "facts" known to Socrates or Plato but not mentioned in the speeches, and casual remarks.[74] These observations are surely useful. However, upon close inspection, they turn out to be nothing more than excellent advice on how to read fine dramas with minimally adequate understanding, some of this counsel having also been

---

72. Ibid., 51, 52, 54.
73. This does not appear to be a Nietzschean consideration, either.
74. Ibid., 54, 59, 60.

given by Schleiermacher. They do not illuminate the problem of why Plato *necessarily* put these kinds of dramatis personae into his dialogues, why he *necessarily* assigned them precisely these speeches at the times when they are spoken, or why he *necessarily* made them perform these deeds at the junctures when they occur. Thus, Strauss avoids explicit explanations of everything about Socratic esotericism that he leaves unclear in his original delineation of it.

Perhaps Strauss implicitly clarifies these matters in *The City and Man*, in the relationships among his analyses of Aristotle, Plato, and Thucydides. Possibly, an acute study of the book would ascertain such an implicit teaching. However, this work would be prohibitively long. Here, it will be more practical to turn to *Persecution and the Art of Writing* in search of additional explicit enlightenment.

Not surprisingly, *Persecution* presents original prototypes of most of the arguments of *The City and Man*. There is the emphasis on untruthfulness: Strauss indicates that he will risk shocking decent modern readers with the suggestion that "a great man might have deliberately deceived the large majority of his readers." There are the philosophers who alone possess the "scientific truth." There is the capacity of the philosophers to communicate "the truth" to the "trustworthy," the "intelligent," the "thoughtful." There is the silence of the philosophers to the many, although they could reveal the truth to them if they wished. Indeed, Strauss goes out of his way to mention "that some great writers might have stated certain important truths quite openly by using as mouthpiece some disreputable character; they would thus show how much they disapproved of pronouncing the truths in question."[75] In such cases, the truths lie in the great writers' works like the purloined letter, unidentified, for the philosopher knows that he would "defeat his purpose if he indicated clearly which of his statements expressed a noble lie, and which the still more noble truth." In making "noble" truths utterable, Strauss plainly opposes Schleiermacher, whose verities require an unspoken hearing of the inner, and Kierkegaard, whose divine truths silence all predicates before their splendor. He clearly sides with Lessing, whom he describes as "one of the most profound humanists of all times, with an exceedingly rare combination of scholarship, taste, and philosophy," whose authority he cites for the precept that "there are truths which should not or cannot be pronounced," and whose rule he repeats, with a slight but significant variation of language, by remarking that "there are truths which would not be pronounced in public by any decent man." He agrees with Hegel, too, on the narrow issue of whether truth is ineffable.

Persecution also speaks of the dissimulation of philosophic wisdom in "popular teaching of an edifying character," which consists in the expres-

---

75. Perhaps there is such a thing as a spokesman for Plato after all.

sion of opinions "not . . . in all respects consonant with truth." It treats the use of writing to "perform the miracle of speaking in a publication to a minority, while being silent to the majority," a miracle in which "an author does not tire of asserting explicitly on every page of his book that *a* is *b*, but indicates between the lines that *a* is not *b*," such that the book offers "two teachings: a popular teaching of an edifying character, which is in the foreground, and a philosophic teaching concerning the most important subject, which is indicated only between the lines." Finally, it suggests the philosopher's reliance on "the very careful reader" to know how to ascertain the meaning of his book, thus grasping "the truth about all crucial things" that is "presented exclusively between the lines." Strauss does not maintain that this reader will consider logographic necessity, but he boldly imposes what might be an equivalent obligation on him, that he should "adapt the rules of certainty which guide his research to the nature of his subject."[76]

This prepares the ground for another try at the unanswered questions, which can be put into expanded form: Why does the philosopher hide and dissemble his wisdom? What is "the most important subject"? What are the "crucial things"? What is the philosopher's truth, or his teaching about the most important subject and the crucial things? What is the nature of the logographic necessity that ought to govern a good writing? Alternatively, what makes the hermeneutic "rules of certainty" certain, and what are these rules? How does one consider the logographic necessity of a writing? How does one adapt the rules of certainty to the nature of the philosopher's subject?

Addressing himself to the question of why the philosopher conceals and dissimulates his knowledge of the truth, Strauss opens *Persecution* with the theme of his second answer in *The City and Man*, namely, the topic of "the relation between society and philosophy." He asserts that the book will "supply material useful for a future sociology of philosophy." Such a sociology is needed because the contemporary sociology of knowledge "did not see a grave practical problem" in "the fundamental relation of thought as such to society as such." This is to say that the contemporary sociology of knowledge "failed to consider the possibility that all philosophers form a class by themselves, or that what unites all genuine philosophers is more important than what unites a given philosopher with a particular group of non-philosophers." Strauss means that the fundamental relation of thought as such to society as such is a relation of class struggle. Philosophers qua philosophers cannot live peacefully with the rest of society. As Fārābī realized, "there was no harmony between philosophy and society." Hence, Fārābī indicated "the most obvious and crudest reason" that "the

---

76. Strauss, *Persecution*, the quoted and paraphrased points being found on 35, 34, 25, 25, 25, 25, 36, 35, 28, 36, 36, 35, 25, 36, 25, and 30, respectively.

philosophic distinction between the exoteric and the esoteric teaching" was necessary: "Philosophy and the philosophers were in 'grave danger.' Society did not recognize philosophy or the right of philosophizing." Strauss states the case more bluntly in his own name: Philosophers adopt their "peculiar technique" of writing in response to "persecution" because it helps them avoid "the greatest disadvantage" of public communication, "capital punishment for the author."[77]

This argument leaves one theoretically unsatisfied. Everybody is aware that philosophers, prophets, and artists have occasionally been persecuted, that some have been killed, and that others have had to lie low in order to avoid trouble. Why, though, should we believe that, far from being chance meetings of truth or zealous opinion with evil or intolerance, these most lamentable troubles inhere in "the fundamental relation of thought as such to society as such," thus rendering irony "necessary" to philosophy? Why should revealing the truth to the many be unsafe for philosophers in principle?

Beginning his answer to this question, Strauss declares: "To realize the necessity of a sociology of philosophy, one must turn to other ages, if not to other climates." He then launches into an extremely enigmatic discussion of substantive theological, philosophical, and political matters. This suggests that in addition to "the most obvious and crudest reason" for irony and esotericism, there are subtle and refined ones. Indeed, one infers from this turn of the argument that class struggle between philosophers and the other members of society arises because the very natures of the "wise" subjects, the "most important" subjects, and the "crucial things," together with "the truth" about all these things, inevitably inspire deadly antagonism between the philosophers and the many. We shall learn the ultimate reason that philosophers dissimulate their wisdom as soon as we discover what their truth is.

So, the next logical step is to resume the inquiry into Strauss's most important subject, crucial things, and philosophic truth. However, we must now expect serious difficulties. If the causes of class hatred between philosophers and the multitude are "fundamental to thought as such," this implies that the philosopher's truths are intrinsically offensive to the many. It follows that they can *never* be pronounced in public "by a decent man," for this will *always* "do harm to many people who, having been hurt, would naturally be inclined to hurt in turn him who pronounces the unpleasant truths." Again, if the sources of the class antagonism are "fundamental to society as such," the many could *never* be fit to hear the truth. In this regard, Strauss approvingly reports the view of "earlier" writers who "believed that the gulf separating 'the wise' and 'the vulgar' was a basic fact

77. Ibid., 7–8, 17, 25.

of human nature which could not be influenced by any progress of popular education: philosophy, or science, was essentially a privilege of 'the few.' They were convinced that philosophy as such was suspect to, and hated by, the majority of men." Hence, even if they "had had nothing to fear from any particular political quarter," such thinkers "would have been driven to the conclusion that public communication of the philosophic or scientific truth was impossible or undesirable, not only for the time being but for all times."[78] This means that, Schleiermacher's objections notwithstanding, it is improper to demand that Aristotle, Strauss, or any other good reader of Plato prove that Plato dissembles his truths by disclosing the truths that Plato dissembles. Because persecution is more than an accident that happens during chance meetings of thought with evil, because persecution is a necessary consequence of every collision of genuine thought with society, no one may reveal the philosophic truth that alone would make it evident that this truth should not be revealed. This forces Strauss to allow his word about the fundamental relation of thought to society to be doubted. He asserts: "The truly exact historian will reconcile himself to the fact that there is a difference between winning an argument, or proving to practically everyone that he is right, and understanding the thought of the great writers of the past."[79]

We now appreciate that given the political (rather than ontological or epistemological) impossibility of public communication of the scientific truth, Strauss never will say explicitly what philosophers know or why they hide it. He will indicate these things only esoterically, obeying Maimonides' injunction to disclose "only the 'chapter headings' " of the truth.[80] Here, one is tempted to think that Strauss botches the job of hiding verities from the many, for two of his "secrets" are rather easy to see in *Persecution*. However, I believe that this is Strauss's variation on the trick of the mother quail.

The two secrets that are not so hard to discover are found in the abstruse discussion of theological, philosophical, and political matters that Strauss undertakes when he says that to realize the necessity of a sociology of philosophy, one must turn to other ages, if not to other climates. Undoubtedly because he is confining himself to a list of "chapter headings," Strauss serves up what looks like a jumble. He refers to different levels of contemporary understanding of "Christian scholasticism" and of "Islamic and Jewish medieval philosophy." He then moves freely among authors such as Plato, Fārābī, Maimonides, Halevi, Averroes, Avicenna, Islamic *falāsifa*, and Spinoza. He also freely blends several subjects, including

78. Ibid., 36, 34.
79. Ibid., 30.
80. Ibid., 46–47, 53. Cf. Moses Maimonides, *The Guide of the Perplexed*, introduction to pt. 1, cause 6.

Christian scholasticism and Islamic and Jewish medieval philosophy; the literary sources of these bodies of thought in Aristotle and Plato; the essential difference between Judaism and Islam on the one hand and Christianity on the other, that is, their diverse ideas of Revelation as Law and as Faith; philosopher-kings; Plato's *Laws;* the "Christian notion" of "the natural law"; Fārābī's *Plato* and his other important books; the purpose common to Plato and Aristotle; Fārābī's view of Plato's doctrine of the immortality of the soul; Plato's solution to the problem posed by the fate of Socrates, and the persistent grave danger to philosophy and philosophers, which is illustrated, in part, by "the issue of Jerusalem versus Athens" and philosophy's statuses under Judaism and Islam, on the one hand, and Christianity, on the other.[81] Next, Strauss interrupts these arcane reflections for a chapter ostensibly devoted to a straightforward explanation and defense of his thesis. Then he expands upon his original topics with abstruse monographs on Maimonides, Halevi, and Spinoza.

A close reading of Strauss's presentation of these "chapter headings" shows that besides assembling them, he combines them with comments that give them a plainly visible Averroist tendency. The following examples are typical of his drift.

First, for the "great man" Maimonides, Fārābī was the greatest philosophic authority after Aristotle. The book by Fārābī that Maimonides most recommended treated of God and the universe in part 1, and of the city in part 2. It was titled *The Political Governments.*[82]

Second, the *falāsifa* were "driven to interpret Revelation as the perfect political order which is perfect precisely because it lays upon all sufficiently equipped men the duty to devote their lives to philosophy." When they rejected rational commandments, "the *falāsifa* implied that the principles of morality are not rational, but 'probable,' or 'generally accepted.' "[83]

Third, Fārābī's primary human requirement for "the complete happiness of nations and of cities" is philosophy. When Fārābī comprehends that the philosopher and the king prove to be identical, it becomes clear that "philosophy by itself is not only necessary but sufficient for producing happiness: philosophy does not need to be supplemented by something else, or by something that is thought to be higher in rank than philosophy, in order to produce happiness." The praise of philosophy "is meant to rule out any claims of cognitive value which may be raised on behalf of religion." Through the mouth of Plato, Fārābī maintains that religious speculation, the religious investigation of the beings, and the religious syllogistic art "do not supply the science of the beings, in which man's highest perfec-

81. Strauss, *Persecution,* 7–8.
82. Ibid., 9.
83. Ibid., 10, 11.

tion consists, whereas philosophy does supply it." Fārābī "goes so far as to present religious knowledge as the lowest step on the ladder of cognitive pursuits, as inferior even to grammar and poetry."[84]

Fourth, Fārābī's esoteric investigation of Plato "silently rejects Plato's doctrine of a life after death." His commentary on Aristotle's *Nicomachean Ethics* "declares that there is only the happiness of this life, and that all divergent statements are based on 'ravings and old women's tales.' "[85]

Fifth, the status of philosophy was much more precarious under Judaism and Islam than it was under Christianity. However, this more precarious status of philosophy under Judaism and Islam was "not in every respect a misfortune" for philosophy. It guaranteed philosophy's private character and, thus, its inner freedom from ecclesiastical supervision. By implication, philosophy's relatively favored status under Christianity was a greater misfortune for it than its precarious status under Judaism and Islam. This reasoning forces us to notice that Strauss speaks of "Islamic and Jewish medieval philosophy" in his book repeatedly but of "Christian philosophy" never. He acknowledges that no one can be learned in Christian sacred doctrine without considerable philosophic "training." He does not thereby raise "Christian scholasticism" to the status of "philosophy."[86]

Sixth, Halevi and Maimonides were "great men," Jews of "philosophic competence." They "took it for granted that being a Jew and being a philosopher are mutually exclusive." Spinoza "bluntly said that the Jews despise philosophy."[87]

Seventh, "The issue of traditional Judaism versus philosophy is identical with that of Jerusalem versus Athens." In this regard, it is hard not to see the connections among "the depreciation of the primary object of philosophy—the heavens and the heavenly bodies" and the command not to eat from the tree of knowledge of good and evil in Genesis, the divine name in Exodus, the admonition that the Law is not in heaven nor beyond the sea, Micah's saying about what the Lord requires of man, and Talmudic utterances to the effect that one had better not study the primary object of philosophy.[88]

Eighth, to obtain examples of writing between the lines, we can "easily imagine" a historian living in a totalitarian country. One assumes that Strauss is thinking of Russia and Germany circa 1941. Thus, one would expect his historian to write a circumspect critique of something like the government's myth of the class struggle and the proletarian revolution, or

84. Ibid., 12–13.
85. Ibid., 13–14.
86. Ibid., 19, 21.
87. Ibid., 11, 19, 20.
88. Ibid., 20–21.

its myth of the fall of the Aryan race through miscegenation with "animal men" whose offspring were the Jews, and of the guilt of world Jewry in the *Dolchstoss* of the German army in 1918. Instead, with the prefatory comment that his illustration is "not so remote from reality as it might first seem," Strauss elects to fancy that his historian will "doubt the soundness of the government-sponsored interpretation of the history of religion." He pictures his fictitious scholar staging mock attacks on "the liberal view." These assaults employ "virulent expansions of the most virulent utterances in the holy book or books of the ruling party."[89]

Ninth, the great Halevi knew well that "a genuine philosopher can never become a genuine convert to Judaism or to any other revealed religion," for "a genuine philosopher is a man like Socrates who possesses 'human wisdom' and is invincibly ignorant of 'Divine wisdom.'" Also, Halevi's dialogue, the *Kuzari*, has a minor character named "the philosopher." This interesting man "denies as such the premises on which any demonstration of the truth of any revealed religion is based," ostensibly because he has not enjoyed the experience of Revelation. However, the "philosophers" whom Halevi knew "went so far as to deny the very possibility of the specific experiences of the believers as interpreted by the latter, or, more precisely, the very possibility of Divine revelation in the precise sense of the term. That denial was presented to them in the form of what claimed to be a demonstrative refutation." Moreover, the philosopher prefers prudence to an inflexible moral or natural law. Strauss comments: "It is hardly necessary to add that it is precisely this view of the non-categoric character of the rules of social conduct which permits the philosopher to hold that a man who has become a philosopher, may adhere in his deeds and speeches to a religion to which he does not adhere in his thoughts; it is this view, I say, which is underlying the exotericism of the philosophers."[90]

Finally, Spinoza's aim in the *Theologico-Political Treatise* was "to refute the claims which had been raised on behalf of revelation throughout the ages." Spinoza often contradicted himself about biblical faith, the second halves of the contradictions indicating that theology demands obedience, not truth, and that "the very foundation of theology is an untruth." This supports the hypothesis that "there is a fundamental antagonism between reason and faith." It should be observed that Strauss himself propounds this last thesis in depicting a basic conflict between the pillars of Western civilization.[91]

The general thrust of these pronouncements, and of many others like them, generates the suspicion that Strauss secretly—but not too secretly—propagates the following teaching. First, the "most important subject" is

89. Ibid., 24–25.
90. Ibid., 104–5, 107, 139.
91. Ibid., 142, 170, 171; Strauss, "The Mutual Influence of Theology and Philosophy," 111.

the relationship of philosophy to religion and politics, this being the reason that Strauss professes elsewhere that "the theological-political problem has remained *the* theme of my investigations."[92] Second, reason is the only means of human access to "the truth." Philosophy, which is reason's product, is the only body of human thought with a legitimate claim to be true. Third, "the truth" is that every religion, and every popular, categorical morality such as "natural law" doctrine that agrees with religion, especially by promising rewards and threatening punishments in an afterlife, is demonstrably bogus. Strauss publicly proclaims that philosophy and Revelation have "never" refuted one another.[93] However, that assuredly is one of Strauss's ironic, exoteric lies. The great Halevi understands that Revelation has been refuted. Fourth, Karl Marx's claim should be broadened. Religion and morality together are the opium of the people. Historically, priests have given this drug to the many to control them. Admittedly, this manipulation of the people has been salutary both for the people and for philosophers. It has prevented the people from destroying society, which is good for the people, who are society, and for the philosophers, who depend upon a stable, irenic society as a condition necessary to the life of philosophy. This is one reason that the philosophers keep their truth to themselves. Strauss comments:

> Philosophy or science, the highest activity of man, is the attempt to replace opinion about "all things" by knowledge of "all things;" but opinion is the element of society; philosophy or science is therefore the attempt to dissolve the element in which society breathes, and thus it endangers society. Hence philosophy or science must remain the preserve of a small minority, and philosophers or scientists must respect the opinions on which society rests. To respect opinions is something entirely different from accepting them as true.[94]

Fifth, all priests are dangerous to philosophy because they fanatically protect their fraudulent doctrines from public exposure. Christian priests, though, have threatened philosophy much more than Jewish or Islamic priests because they have imagined themselves competent to philosophize and to oversee philosophy. The Christian priests have eliminated philosophy from Christian culture. Sixth, the people are also dangerous to philosophers when they sense that their religions and moralities have been contradicted. The many even menace society itself when they get carried away by their beliefs. National Socialism grew out of the most virulent utterances in the Christian holy book. Last, accordingly, philosophers dissemble

92. Quoted by Pangle, in introduction to *Studies in Philosophy*, by Strauss, 19.
93. Strauss, "Mutual Influence," 117.
94. Strauss, *"What Is Political Philosophy?" and Other Studies*, 221–22.

their wisdom and pretend to be devout adherents of society's religions and moralities.

The suspicion that Strauss secretly—but not too secretly—maintains this doctrine cannot be proved at law because he slyly builds deniability into his words.[95] However, Strauss declares frequently that everyone must choose between philosophy and the Bible, and Rosen confidently comments: "No competent student of Leo Strauss was ever in doubt as to his teacher's choice."[96] By extension, one could suggest that no serious reader of Strauss ought to doubt that he subscribes to the Averroist tenets just enumerated. Nevertheless, no one should think that Strauss's esoteric teaching has now been laid completely bare.

There are three grounds for assuming that Strauss has more or deeper secrets. First, he has made his Averroist opinions quite easily visible. He must want many readers to see them, yet he does not want many to ascertain his principles. Second, if the antireligious creed were Strauss's whole teaching, we would have the unseemly spectacle of an intelligent man timidly uttering opinions that he knows "enlightened" Westerners have been stating frankly through much of the modern period with impunity. Strauss could not avoid grasping that the social reality contradicts his proposition that the philosophic truth "poses a grave practical problem in the fundamental relation of thought as such to society as such." Third, and most tellingly, Strauss mentions that examples of the most important sorts of persecution for his purposes are "found in the Athens of the fifth and fourth centuries B.C., in some Muslim countries of the early Middle Ages, in seventeenth-century Holland and England, and in eighteenth-century France and Germany—all of them comparatively liberal periods." He also remarks: "Spinoza attempted to appease not any orthodox theologians but those who were more or less inclined toward a liberal Christianity. He concealed his partial, but decisively important disagreement not with the orthodox theologians but with liberal believers of all shades."[97]

It would be fair to take Thomas Jefferson as an example of Strauss's idea of a worthy liberal. In a famous saying, Jefferson once insisted that "it does me no injury for my neighbor to say that there are twenty gods, or no God. It neither picks my pocket nor breaks my leg."[98] Thus, Strauss knows that in a comparatively liberal period, "liberal believers" would bat nary an eye over his stage whispers about Averroist atheism. They would find his "secrets" much too harmless to warrant persecution. This makes it plain that

95. Cf. Strauss, *Persecution*, 24, 14.
96. Rosen, *Hermeneutics as Politics*, 112.
97. Strauss, *"What Is Political Philosophy?"* 32–33, 226. This is why we do not need to turn to "other climates" to understand esotericism. Liberalism is *our* climate.
98. Jefferson, *Notes on the State of Virginia*, in *The Life and Selected Writings of Thomas Jefferson*, 275.

Strauss's seemingly clumsy efforts to hide his antireligious tendencies are a ruse to draw his most benighted readers away from his serious, real secrets. For the more sagacious, he clearly indicates that his verities are something much different, something that would disturb the liberals. It is not necessary, or even probable, that the undisclosed something would be a theological disagreement; liberals tolerate everything in that line. The "theological-political problem" proves not to be "the most important subject" after all. In Strauss's view, this disposes of Schleiermacher's objection to seeing religious irony in Plato, who would have also used it as a conspicuous decoy to bore Athenian liberals. The unrevealed something would not be an ethical disagreement, either. Strauss's ideas of "the non-categoric character of the rules of social conduct" and of the conventionality of ethics, which appear at first glance to justify our suspicions that he and his students such as Allan Bloom are sophists and "nihilists," distress "orthodox" believers but certainly not the positivistic liberals who have succeeded Jefferson. Strauss's apparently incompetent efforts to disguise his moral relativism are another ploy that induces liberals to view his "secrets" as tame old hat.

To continue our search for Strauss's genuine buried treasure, we turn to the second of his easily discernible secrets. In addition to imparting a clearly visible Averroist tendency to his "chapter headings," Strauss gives them a rather thinly veiled aristocratic-monarchical cast, as we shall see in the following examples.

First, as we have observed, Strauss introduces his doctrine of the "natural order of rank among men" offhandedly, as if he were trying to sneak it by his readers. His naturally superior men, the philosophers, have a sense of noblesse oblige that protects society by "respecting" opinion, "the element in which society breathes." Indeed, the philosophers encourage all opinion that is "salutary"—one supposes that this means "salutary for society"—whether or not it is true. Everybody can "discover" immediately that Strauss's premises are aristocratic. His claims will antagonize the demos, who acknowledge only equals and insist that they think for themselves. Incidentally, we must admit that the claims would not upset the most able liberals. Thomas Jefferson declared to John Adams: "I agree with you that there is a natural aristocracy among men. The grounds of this are virtue and talent. . . . The natural aristocracy I consider as the most precious gift of nature, for the instruction, the trusts, and government of society."[99] It happens, however, that the tactics urged by Strauss do anger liberals of a more recent vintage, who do not like talk of elitists who manipulate popular opinion.

Second, we have also noticed that Strauss maintains that philosophers

---

99. Jefferson to Adams, October 28, 1813, in *Life and Selected Writings,* by Jefferson, 632–33.

constitute a class by themselves. In *Persecution*, in his treatment of the eternal class struggle between philosophers and society, he asserts: "The philosophers . . . defended the interests of philosophy and of nothing else. In doing this, they believed indeed that they were defending the highest interests of mankind."[100] This looks like an inept attempt to prettify the arrogant idea that philosopher aristocrats are devoted solely to knowledge and, accordingly, alone understand what is best for the human race. Everybody can "unmask" such imperiousness immediately. The democratic many will be incensed. Again, their finest leaders will not share their outrage. Jefferson, who believed in a natural aristocracy of talent and virtue, would have been forced to concede that the philosophers are a class unto themselves, standing alone in their dedication to the rational discovery and defense of truth. It is possible that he would have been alarmed to hear that his aristocrats "defended the interests of philosophy and of nothing else." Then again, his fears on this score would have been allayed when Strauss explained that he meant that the philosophers "were defending the highest interests of mankind." Jefferson, an aristocratic liberal who was also a genuine democrat, a true lover of the less capable many whom he desired to serve, would have assumed that philosophy's exclusive interest in the truth led automatically to the advancement of the highest interests of all mankind, including the backward, sometimes balky demos who had to be guided to their own good. He would have continued to accept Strauss on this basis, though expressing concerns about some of Strauss's language. However, the more recent liberals are enraged by Strauss's snobbery. They wish to be the vanguard of the people while remaining men and women of the people.

Last, in his famous *Natural Right and History,* Strauss maintains that "the best regime, as presented by classical political philosophy, is the object of the wish or prayer of gentlemen as that object is interpreted by the philosopher." Actually, he continues, "wisdom appeared to the classics as that title to rule which is highest according to nature." Government by the wise would therefore be the best regime if it were practically possible. However, the many unwise cannot recognize the wise, and the few who are wise cannot rule the many who are unwise by force. Somehow, the requirement for government by the wise has to be reconciled with the need for the consent of the unwise to their governments. The solution of this problem is to institute the rule of law administered by leaders who will govern in the spirit of the wise, that is, the rule of law administered by gentlemen. The gentleman is not wise, but he is a "political reflection, or imitation, of the wise man." Hence, it is clear that "the practically best regime is the rule, under law, of gentlemen, or the mixed regime." In *Persecution,* Strauss also speaks highly

100. Strauss, *Persecution,* 17–18.

of the "alliance between philosophy and princes friendly to philosophy."[101] In all this, Strauss apparently tries to conceal not his oligarchic and monarchical inclinations, but the fact that his philosophers, who will be exercising influence on princes and gentlemen, will strive to disguise their dominance of society under the cloak of "consent of the governed." Nonetheless, this scheme is transparent. Democrats will condemn it angrily. As an aside, it is necessary to notice one last time that Thomas Jefferson would not have shared in the general consternation. He undoubtedly perceived John Locke as a wise man and himself as a gentleman, or even as a prince, who ruled in the spirit of the wise man, such that his presidency reflected "the alliance between philosophy and princes friendly to philosophy" in a manner consonant with the requirement for the consent of the governed. However, because it would have been inconsistent with his aims, Jefferson would have winced at the use of the terms "gentlemen" and "princes." He would have wished natural leaders who truly loved the demos to have democratic public labels. Strauss's apparent change of focus has infuriated the more recent liberals, who denounce him as a conservative for his oligarchic and monarchical machinations.[102]

The general drift of these arguments, with their natural elites who deftly shape public opinion, their aristocratic class consciousness that arrogates to philosophers the sole responsibility for advancing the highest interests of all mankind, and their government by gentlemen and princes who listen to philosophers, generates the suspicion that Strauss secretly—but not too secretly—longs for the realization of some vestige of Platonic philosopher-kingship. In Strauss's own words, he wants philosophers to have an impact on gentlemen and princes that amounts in some modest but meaningful way to "the secret kingship of the philosopher who, being 'a perfect man' precisely because he is an 'investigator,' lives privately as a member of an imperfect society which he tries to humanize within the limits of the possible."[103] Not even Jefferson would have tolerated this. The liberal president was strongly opposed both to Plato and to kings. The more recent liberals are apoplectic about Strauss's ambition; it is this, more than anything else in his advocacy of esotericism, that has made Strauss "one of the most hated men in the English-speaking academic world."

Strauss's muted call for the secret kingship of the philosopher, a dominion exercised by means of intellectual influence on gentlemen and princes,

---

101. Strauss, *Natural Right and History*, 139, 140, 141, 142–43; Strauss, *Persecution*, 15.

102. Cf. Shadia B. Drury, "The Esoteric Philosophy of Leo Strauss" and *The Political Ideas of Leo Strauss*. In some quarters, this book was greeted with outrage. Most of the anger was directed at Drury's tone. However, some was also aimed at her analysis of Strauss's politics as aristocratic. This is puzzling, for Drury only repeats what Strauss seems to have intimated more or less openly.

103. Strauss, *Persecution*, 15, 17.

satisfies one criterion for identifying his true esoteric doctrine: Although the call is, in the main, acceptable to Jefferson, in the end it is a decisive, important disagreement with liberal believers of all shades. However, I doubt that the hankering for a philosopher-king recast as a gray eminence is Strauss's real secret, for an obvious reason: It is shielded from the liberals approximately as well as a Christian mother hides a basket of Easter candy from her four-year-old child. Nothing is secret about a public proclamation of the call for a secret kingship, particularly not when the author bludgeons us with the proclamation. It is simply too hard to believe that Strauss, a surpassingly intelligent man, imagines that he can put liberals off the track of this "secret" by giving them a potent scent of "the truth" that is certain to attract their attention and kindle their hatred.

To be sure, Rosen seems to think that Strauss commits this "error." In an effort to account for the gaffe, Rosen speculates that "Strauss's apparent disregard of Socrates' advice in the *Phaedrus* to adjust one's speech to the audience is a part of his exoteric accommodation to the circumstances of his time."[104] If this is true, however, Strauss's tack is not an "error." Rather, it is a ruse devised to put liberals on the trail of the wrong doctrines, for Strauss knows that no classical philosopher ever went so far as to say, and he himself certainly could not think, that the gentleman is the political imitation of the wise man, or that the gentleman typically heeds the philosopher.[105] I infer that Strauss reckons that his greatest safety lies in adopting the pose of an oligarchical, monarchical crank, one that makes him the most hated man in liberal society. His calculation is that once the liberals have enjoyed venting their indignation at him, they will be amused at the fantasies of an obscure professor who, in his academic isolation, imagines himself a king. Having laughed, they will think no more of him and inquire no further into what he is doing. In this connection, I believe that if Strauss learned that a liberal would publish an attack on him titled "Sphinx without a Secret," he would smile happily.[106]

Well, then, are we at a dead end, or can we get some inkling of Strauss's truths? In this matter, it is impossible to be sure of anything. Still, I think that we can approach the secrets a little more closely. To do so, we must take seriously Strauss's comment that "some great writers might have stated certain important truths quite openly by using as mouthpiece some disreputable character." If a philosopher such as Plato has done this, his ultimate secrets will be lying around in his texts like the purloined letter, unlabeled and unrecognized.

So, the question now is whether Plato has a "disreputable character"

---

104. Rosen, *Hermeneutics as Politics*, 133.
105. On this point, I agree with ibid., 136.
106. Cf. M. F. Burnyeat, "Sphinx without a Secret."

whom he uses "as mouthpiece." Strauss appears to point to one. Immediately after speculating that great writers might put their important truths in the mouths of unsavory persons, Strauss adds: "There would then be good reason for finding in the greatest literature of the past so many interesting devils, madmen, beggars, sophists, drunkards, epicureans, and buffoons." "Sophists" appears in the middle of this list, thus indicating who might be the most significant of the "disreputable characters." It is possible that a sophist is the "mouthpiece" for Plato's "important truths." Which sophist? In *The City and Man*, Strauss discusses Thrasymachus extensively. He holds that "in a sense," Thrasymachus's intervention "forms the center of the *Republic* as a whole." He suggests that Socrates strikes up a "friendship" with Thrasymachus, one "never preceded by enmity." He says: "For all ordinary purposes we ought to loathe people who act and speak like Thrasymachus and never to imitate their deeds and never to act according to their speeches. But there are other purposes to be considered." He maintains that Thrasymachus's "principle remains victorious," neglecting to mention the possibility that this situation, which might be said by way of exaggeration to obtain at the end of book 1 of the *Republic*, is altered drastically by the remainder of the dialogue. Finally, in *Persecution*, Strauss cites Fārābī to the effect that Plato undertook "a correction of the Socratic way," so that the "Platonic way—as distinguished from the Socratic way, is a combination of the way of Socrates with the way of Thrasymachus."[107]

Which Thrasymachean principle "remains victorious"? Strauss is thinking of Thrasymachus's famous definition of justice as "the advantage of the stronger." What is "the way of Thrasymachus"? This expression is obscure, but it reminds one of Thrasymachus's argument that the rulers of cities tend to the good of their subjects in the same sense that shepherds tend to the good of their flocks, namely, in order to fleece them. Strauss declares that the definition of justice as "the advantage of the stronger," when it is cast in the form of legal positivism, "is the most obvious, the most natural, thesis regarding justice."[108] This is interesting. Thrasymachus himself does not assert that his thesis is the most natural. Thrasymachus never says anything about nature at all. We must inquire what Strauss means by calling Thrasymachus's thesis the most natural, for he might be doing more than embracing the sophist's doctrine; he might be adding something of his own to it. Of course, it appears that Strauss means merely that legal positivism is the explanation of justice that occurs most readily to anyone who wonders

107. Strauss, *Persecution*, 36. Cf. Strauss on the parable of the pious ascetic, in *"What Is Political Philosophy?"* 135–37. On the significance of the "middle," see Strauss, *Persecution*, 25, 185; and Strauss, *The City and Man*, 73, 74, 74, 84. ("Not yet refuted" at the end of an early book is not necessarily the same as "victorious" [*Persecution*, 16]. Strauss is intelligent enough to know this.)
108. Strauss, *The City and Man*, 75.

about it. If so, I doubt that he is right about this. Strauss also might mean that the proposition that justice is the advantage of the stronger is naturally correct. If so, and if Strauss is serious about this, the implication is that Strauss believes in the existence of an order of being in which the strong naturally rule the weak, for the advantage of the strong and against the interests of the weak. A further implication is that Strauss is committed to a "natural right" that demands the victory of the strong and the subjugation of the weak. An order of being in which the strong naturally exploit the weak would be terrifying to the weak. Belief in a natural right that calls for the oppression of the weak, which would be sufficient to associate Strauss with sophistry but not to convict him of "nihilism," would be absolutely loathsome to liberals. The "truth" of what we could call "Thrasymachean natural right" looks as if it satisfies both of the criteria that it would need to meet to be Strauss's real secret. It is buried more deeply than his other pseudosecrets. It is anathema in comparatively liberal periods.

Does Strauss actually subscribe to Thrasymachean natural right? His obvious belief in a natural order of rank among men is certainly consistent with such a commitment. Some other statements that he makes are compatible with it, too, as we learn in the following examples.

First, in the popular *Natural Right and History*, Strauss argues:

> In the common view the fact is overlooked that there is a class interest of the philosophers qua philosophers, and this oversight is ultimately due to the denial of the possibility of philosophy. Philosophers as philosophers do not go with their families. The selfish or class interest of the philosophers consists in being left alone, in being allowed to live the life of the blessed on earth by devoting themselves to investigation of the most important subjects.

Strauss also comments: "If striving for knowledge of the eternal truth is the ultimate end of man, justice and moral virtue in general can be fully legitimated only by the fact that they are required for the sake of that ultimate end or that they are conditions of the philosophic life." Once again, Strauss seems to think that the condition in the "if" clause is fulfilled. Accordingly, he asks "whether morality does not have two entirely different roots." Further, in *The City and Man*, Strauss says that according to Clitophon, one of Plato's characters (*Clitophon* 410a6–b1), the only opinion of justice that Socrates adopted was that "it consists in helping one's friends and harming one's enemies." (Strauss ignores the next sentence, in which the befuddled Clitophon protests that his conversation with Socrates soon made it appear that the just man never harms anyone, but strives to benefit all.)[109] It should

---

109. Strauss, *Natural Right and History*, 143, 151; Strauss, *The City and Man*, 70.

also be remembered that for the philosopher in Halevi's *Kuzari*, the rules of social conduct are "non-categoric." When added up, these remarks appear to imply that there are two moralities, or two kinds of justice, one for philosophers and one for the demos. Both serve the interests of philosophers, who are obliged to comply with the demotic ethics only when it contributes to their realization of man's ultimate end.

Second, it is necessary to repeat that in *Persecution,* in his treatment of the "class struggle," Strauss comments: "The philosophers were very far from being exponents of society or of parties. They defended the interests of philosophy and of nothing else. In doing this, they believed indeed that they were defending the highest interests of mankind."[110] In considering this remark for the first time, I interpreted it to mean that "defending the highest interests of mankind" was identical with "defending the highest interests of all men," an error that Strauss might have been glad to see because it soothed the anxious liberals. However, in the new light of Thrasymachean natural right, the phrase "defending the highest interests of mankind" would clearly mean "promoting the interests of the highest men."

Finally, in his treatment of the philosopher's practice of dispensing "salutary" opinions to the multitude, Strauss reflects: "Being a philosopher, that is, hating 'the lie in the soul' more than anything else, he would not deceive himself about the fact that such opinions are merely 'likely tales,' or 'noble lies,' or 'probable opinions.' " Nor would he need to worry about tricking those whom he wished to enlighten, for he could "leave it to his philosophic readers to disentangle the truth from its poetic or dialectic presentation. . . . For philosophic readers he would do almost more than enough by drawing their attention to the fact that he did not object to telling lies which were noble, or tales which were merely similar to the truth." Still, the philosopher's hatred of the lie in the soul would not deter him from inflicting this deadly falsehood on the many, because "he would defeat his purpose if he indicated clearly which of his statements expressed a noble lie, and which the still more noble truth." In this regard, one must realize that "lying nobly" is what "we" call "considering one's social responsibilities."[111] It may be that "salutary" opinions are salutary for the philosophers, not for society.

The general thrust of these examples gives rise to the suspicion that Strauss secretly—a lot more secretly than in the previous instances but still not altogether secretly—subscribes to the following teaching. First, the summum bonum is the philosophic life. Every other good is relative to this one. Thus, for philosophers who wage class warfare to preserve philosophy, everything is permitted. They may visit any expedient harm on non-

110. Strauss, *Persecution,* 17–18.
111. Ibid., 35, 36.

philosophers. Second, it is not true that philosophy is the highest good for all. Mankind is divided into higher, middle, and lower natural classes. The interests of the highest group, the philosophers, are simply "the highest interests of mankind" without being the interests of the other groups. Hence, among the injuries that philosophers may inflict upon *all* other classes is the human *summum malum*, the lie in the soul. The lies that the wise purvey to all others are "noble" not in the sense that they elevate the others to nobler conceptions of the truth, but in the sense that they advance the class interests of the nobility, this being the "social responsibility" of all noblemen. Last, in the *Republic*, Thrasymachus teaches the truth of natural right. Plato takes it into his "way." Thus, a second evil with which philosophers afflict all the others is to treat them as shepherds use sheep. If a nobleman revealed the truth to any of the lower classes, he would ask them the question that Nietzsche puts to Biedermann: "How does your life, the life of the individual, receive its highest value, its deepest meaning? How is it wasted least? Certainly only in that you live for the advantage of the rarest and most valuable specimens, but not for the advantage of the majority, i.e., those who, taken individually, are the most worthless specimens."[112] In short, it seems that Strauss does—not so secretly—side with Nietzsche in the debate over the purposes of irony. This would explain why he so oddly refers to Nietzsche as a Platonist, for he projects Nietzsche's aims onto Plato. He thinks that all great philosophers from Plato to the present strive for a secret kingship that exploits all the lower classes, including gentlemen and liberals.

If this assimilation of Strauss to Nietzsche is correct, it illuminates a question that has puzzled many: Why does Strauss appear to torpedo esotericism by disclosing its existence, its methods, and its first three layers of pseudo- and real secrets to any minimally capable person who can read? We now suspect that his fear of persecution is only a pose in which he playfully and ironically reproduces Nietzsche's practice of allowing the many into his confidence about his "follies and crimes" because he is sure that beings on a lower plane will still not understand the deeper things that he conceals. Strauss is almost more openly contemptuous of the many than Nietzsche because he makes it plain that he only pretends to believe that the many could comprehend his work if he told them plainly what he is doing.

This means, of course, that we have still not penetrated to the bottom of Strauss's well of secrets. Where do we go next to find out what he really thinks? There is a possibly important clue to the answer to this query

---

112. Nietzsche, *Unzeitgemässe Betrachtungen*, in *NW*, 3.1.380.30–35; 381.1–2 (there is no corresponding Kaufmann translation). Along with straightforward definitions, "Biedermann" has the ironic meaning of "Philistine."

in *Natural Right and History*. Strauss says there that philosophy consists in an ascent from opinions to truth that is guided by opinions. Opinions contradict one another. "Recognizing the contradiction, one is forced to go beyond opinions toward the consistent view of the nature of the thing concerned." In other contexts, Strauss makes self-contradiction a clue to the real meaning of a philosophic writer. Here, contradictions between opinions have a stronger role. Through them, "the opinions prove to be solicited by the self-subsisting truth, and the ascent to the truth proves to be guided by the self-subsistent truth which all men always divine."[113] Studying contradictions can (and apparently does) lead all human beings to the ultimate truth.

What does Strauss mean, though? How can it be the case that "all men always divine" the self-subsistent truth? How can Strauss argue this after having issued his dismal prognosis for the prospects of popular education? Further, what is this "self-subsistent truth" that all men supposedly recognize? Is it that the contradictions are contradictions? I doubt this, for I often find myself disagreeing with Strauss and his students when they claim to see a contradiction. What else could it be? Do all men always divine anything whatsoever? Furthermore, why is meditation on contradictions the path to truth at all? Why would reflection on the most recondite contradictions not lead to the discouraging inference that there is no way to an ultimate truth? Or is this precisely what a Nietzschean Strauss means, and do all men implicitly, unconsciously recognize the absurdity of being all the time, that is, every time they shrug their shoulders when they cannot resolve a contradiction? Is the recognition of the void the totality of a Nietzschean package that Strauss projects onto Plato, thus making Nietzsche Plato's legitimate successor?

If this is Strauss's intent, his esotericism is, like Nietzsche's, aimed finally at himself. It is a tool that he uses playfully to divert his attention from the abysses that regress eternally, thus perhaps preventing him from being a god. The aura of mystery that he maintains around his philosophy is the screen that he uses to veil what he is doing from himself. Stanley Rosen puts this another way: "We may also understand Strauss's reluctance to make too explicit his Nietzschean conception of philosophy as an act of the will."[114]

A last word on Strauss: In my analysis of this great thinker, I have attempted to elucidate the narrow topic of his concept of esotericism. I have not tried to speak to the thrust of his lifework, a project that would probably require several books. In my smaller undertaking, I have attempted to

---

113. On contradictions as clues, see much of chap. 2 of Strauss, *Persecution*. On contradictions as guides to self-subsistent truth, see Strauss, *Natural Right and History*, 124.
114. Rosen, *Hermeneutics as Politics*, 137.

move in a disciplined way from statements that Strauss wrote to inferences about the meaning of those remarks. I am not confident that I have done this correctly. If I have erred in my interpretation, and if I have been mistaken in thinking that Stanley Rosen understood Strauss better than some others, I greatly regret it. I have two additional things to say. First, considering the vitriolic debates about Strauss's intentions that have raged among his students, I clearly will not be the first to have gone astray. Second, if a brilliant man deliberately writes in order to prevent people from understanding him, there is an excellent chance that he will succeed in achieving this aim.

STANLEY ROSEN

Stanley Rosen himself is a grateful student of Leo Strauss who nevertheless announces: "I am in considerable disagreement with Strauss's general program."[115] His dissent from Strauss assimilates irony to postmodernism, pressing esotericism in rhetorical directions that Strauss does not wish to take.

Rosen agrees with his teacher about much. Like Strauss, he proclaims "recognition of irony as the central problem in the interpretation of Plato." Although he dislikes the "great theologian," he also accepts Schleiermacher's "canon of interpretation," especially with regard to the nexus between form and substance in Plato's works, and the importance of context. He echoes Strauss, and reaffirms Schleiermacher, in asserting that "those who extract what they take to be Plato's theoretical views or 'arguments' from their dialogical and poetic presentation are studying images of their own theoretical presuppositions, but not Plato." Again like Strauss, he disavows Schleiermacher by saying: "In sum, it is entirely clear that Plato practices 'esotericism.' "[116] How, then, does he differ from Strauss?

The answer is revealed in Rosen's choice of a word, when he states that he repudiates Strauss's "program." Apparently, a "program" has two parts, one for each of the two queries that Rosen puts to Strauss: "whether his intentions were sound and his rhetoric suitable to the task."[117] It is significant that a "program" is composed of "intentions and rhetoric," and not of other elements that one might have imagined to be characteristic of philosophy, such as wonder and a plan of inquiry. We may expect that Rosen will disapprove of Strauss's intentions and rhetoric.

---

115. Rosen, Plato's "Symposium," xiv.
116. Ibid., xlii, lvi; Rosen, The Quarrel between Philosophy and Poetry: Studies in Ancient Thought, 11.
117. Rosen, Hermeneutics as Politics, 125.

So, what were Strauss's intentions? How could we know whether they were sound? These questions are illuminated by what appears to be Rosen's idea of the intention of all genuine philosophers. Rosen makes several intriguing statements on this subject: "The ancient philosophers rejected the warnings of the poets, as exemplified in Pindar's admonition: 'do not strive to be a god.'" "The man of religious faith regards it as madness to attempt to become a god. The pagan philosophers, especially those of the Socratic school, thought otherwise." Socrates says in the *Philebus*, "[T]he wise all agree, thereby exalting themselves, that intellect [*nous*] is king for us of heaven and earth." The "philosophical question of the Platonic dialogues, and in particular of the *Phaedrus*," is "how can a human being become a god?" The political name of individuals "who aspire to be gods" is "philosopher-kings." Alexandre Kojève is "exactly like Plato" in that he tries "to become a god." Plato was a "seriously playful god." Aristotle says in the *Ethics* that the theoretical life is higher than human life, adding: "Not *qua* human will one live it, but he will achieve it by virtue of something divine in him. . . . If then the intellect is divine in comparison with man, so is the life of the intellect divine in comparison with human life." In announcing this fact, "Aristotle is even more explicit than Plato. . . . Aristotle's representation of himself as divine is a radical simplification of Plato's poetic evasiveness." Generally, "As Socrates puts it, the classical philosopher wills that the intellect be god." As for the moderns, "Kant acts not like a humble empirical scientist but like a world-maker or god." "On the Hegelian account, one denies the separation of the eternal from the temporal, or identifies the two as the structure of the Concept, that is, the philosophical speech about the totality or the whole. . . . As a consequence, . . . he who is able to repeat the totality of this discourse becomes a god." Nietzsche, "like all great philosophers, engages in the divine prerogative of willing a world into being and hence of creating a way of life." Generally, "from Descartes forward, the intellect resolves that the will be god." Rosen himself does not wish to risk "being excluded from the company of the gods." Does Strauss share the grand obsession? Rosen asserts: "Strauss and Kojève, and Strauss as much as Kojève (once we put aside Strauss's exoteric flirtation with Hebraic tradition) are atheists who wish to be gods."[118]

What does Rosen mean by "being a god"? In one place, Rosen replies that to be a god is to be *causa sui*. Is this, then, really Strauss's highest, most secret

118. Ibid., 16, 54, 44, 65, 71, 105, 106, 59, 180, 25, 96, 126, 180, 18, 17. It might be significant that Rosen omits the following comment by Kojève in *Introduction to Hegel*: "Now, if a being that *becomes* God in time can be called 'God' only provided that it uses this term as a metaphor (a correct metaphor, by the way), the being that has always *been* God is God in the proper and strict sense of the word" (120). He adds that to construe oneself as God in the proper and strict sense of the word is "absurd."

wish? Strauss never says this in so many words. However, as a student of Strauss, Rosen might know more than an outsider.

Let us assume for the sake of argument that Strauss's intentions might be "sound." Now Rosen sees a problem. The classical philosophers of the Socratic school "understand by praxis the construction of a cosmos in which there is an exoteric separation of *theoria* and *poiēsis*." Strauss follows them, but the moderns do not. Rosen observes further that the "quarrel between the ancients and the moderns . . . has its inner or esoteric meaning in the question *quid sit deus?*"[119] Evidently, one can fail to understand what it means to be a god and, thus, fail to become a god by taking the wrong stand on the issue of whether there should be an exoteric separation of *theoria* and *poiēsis*. Why is that?

The explanation of this mistake seems to depend on the difference between the ancient and modern positions on the necessity of thoroughly consistent esotericism, or on the relative merits of "strong" and "weak" irony. In *Persecution*, Strauss says that the earlier philosophers saw the gulf between the wise and the vulgar as "a basic fact of human nature which could not be influenced by any progress of popular education." These classical thinkers practiced strong esotericism by adhering to the rule that public communication of the philosophic or scientific truth was undesirable for all times. Strauss follows them by inveighing against the "heterodox philosophers" who "believed that suppression of free inquiry, and of publication of the results of free inquiry, was accidental, an outcome of the faulty construction of the body politic, and that the kingdom of general darkness could be replaced by the republic of universal light." In keeping with this notion, the apostates practiced weak irony: "[T]hey concealed their views only far enough to protect themselves as well as possible from persecution," and otherwise revealed their truths openly in order to "enlighten an ever-increasing number of people who were not potential philosophers." On Rosen's account, Kant was one of Strauss's worst heretics. He planned to "counter the pre-Enlightenment rhetoric of caution with a rhetoric of daring, that is to say, of frankness." In this, he meant "to produce a new kind of human being, one who is mature rather than immature." Further, Rosen stresses that Kant's transition from prudence to frankness is *"produced not simply by historical circumstances but by Kant's will to change those circumstances."*[120] One must ask whether a god is a being who acknowledges the necessity of strong esotericism or who opts for the weak variety. When the question is stated thus, it immediately becomes clear to Rosen

---

119. *Quid sit deus?* means "What is god?" Rosen, *Hermeneutics as Politics*, 16–17. Strauss himself calls *quid sit deus?* the "all-important question which is coeval with philosophy" (*The City and Man*, 241).

120. Strauss, *Persecution*, 33–34; Rosen, *Hermeneutics as Politics*, 30–31.

that Strauss's intentions, or at least his means of realizing them, are fatally defective. To admit the necessity of strong esotericism is to accept nature as a limitation on the divine will. It is to wish to be a god without affirming one's own omnipotence. Hence, it is to abandon the project of being *causa sui*. Similarly, to separate *theoria* (seeing) and *poiēsis* (making) is to confess publicly that nature constrains the divine will. Strauss wants to be a god but does not believe in the possibility of his divinity. Rosen must repudiate him and does so by proclaiming himself a postmodernist, that is, one who openly unifies *theoria* and *poiēsis*. (Rosen might be too hasty in rejecting Strauss for this reason; the possibility that Strauss only pretends to practice the strong irony while actually engaging in the weak might complicate the analysis.)

Well, then, what about Strauss's rhetoric? Although Strauss has gotten the aim wrong, can his rhetoric accidentally realize the right intention? This depends chiefly on the nature of the task. What must a god's rhetoric accomplish? Rosen has already specified a portion of the job, "to produce a new kind of human being, one who is mature rather than immature." This is only a part, though. One must recall the problem that moved Nietzsche's Zarathustra to come down from the mountain: "But at last a change came over his heart, and one morning he rose with the dawn, stepped before the sun, and spoke to it thus: 'You great star, what would your happiness be had you not those for whom you shine?'" As Rosen knows well, deities must have "worshipers (disciples)," and "the masters require servants."[121] So, the would-be god must establish his divinity by willing it, by preparing many other individuals to will their divinity, too, and by convincing all these potential gods, who will want to act like supreme beings, and whose passions therefore might be quite strong, nevertheless to adore and obey him—a self-contradictory enterprise.

On top of that, the self-made god must face the difficulty that gods need unlimited speculative freedom, but the many who are not yet divine remain to be enlightened, a process that "is impossible without the extirpation of ignorance and superstition." The eradication of ignorance requires "a restrictive political rule, or the employment of enforced purification, with or without force of the vulgar sort, but always by means of rhetorical polemic." It seems that Rosen has not dispensed with Rousseau's insight that people must be "forced to be free." It is not for nothing that he endorses Kojève's denunciation of modern liberal democracies as "the result of the *failure*, not the success of the Enlightenment," uses the expression "we Maoists," and ominously warns Richard Rorty that he "is making himself a candidate for the guillotine," this perhaps being a joke

---

121. Nietzsche, *Also sprach Zarathustra*, in *NW*, 6.1.5.5–9; *Thus Spoke Zarathustra*, in *The Portable Nietzsche*, 121; Rosen, *Hermeneutics as Politics*, 108, 181.

that loses its humor when one contemplates the West's long history of political murder.[122] These parts of Rosen's project seem self-contradictory, too.
His gods must devise a rhetoric that smooths out all the difficulties by directing an efficacious blend of weak esotericism, frankness, ad hominem
verbal attacks, and outright violence at the body politic—a hard job, if not
impossible. Is Strauss's public teaching adequate to the task?

Rosen does not believe that Strauss keeps all these requirements of divine rhetoric in balance. Obviously, when Strauss denies the possibility of
bridging the gulf between the wise and the vulgar, he renounces the aim of
creating a new race of mature men and gives rhetoric absolutely improper
purposes. Rosen says: "I take Strauss's error to be this: from the correct observation that there is always and of necessity a tension or indeed conflict
between philosophy and the city, Strauss draws the false inference that it is
always necessary for philosophers to accommodate to the city in the style
of Plato, Cicero, Al Farabi, and Maimonides." Strauss thus manifests an apparent disregard of Socrates' advice to adjust his speech to the audience.[123]

This Nietzschean critique is imprecise. If Strauss's observation of the "necessity" of the sort of conflict that he envisages—a war between philosophers and hopeless troglodytes—is "correct," his ideas about accommodation seem more strategically apt than Nietzsche's defiance. Rosen must
mean that there is always and necessarily a tension between philosophy
and polities of malleable people, the variability of human nature being
the relevant condition under which a demand for "adjusting to audiences"
would be intelligible. The conflict that Rosen supposes is necessary must
have to do with the gods' need for worshipers, both before and after the creation of the new world. If this is the matter about which Strauss has erred,
then does it make sense to claim that his rhetoric is cowardly? Is it right to
say accusingly that "were we to enact a 'city' rooted in Strauss's version
of the 'noble reserve' and the 'calm grandeur' of the classical thinkers, the
results would be restrictive and demeaning to the human spirit, and hence
base rather than noble"?[124]

Rosen reaches the same result with regard to Strauss's procurement of
worshipers. Strauss finds disciples who adore him, but he relegates them
to the degraded status of "a special race of academic administrators, themselves acting under the impression that they are wise men." With respect
to the task of bringing freedom into balance with enforced purification,
Strauss's rhetoric takes the form of "a generalized philosophical thesis according to which the gentleman, i.e., the rural aristocrat, is the practical
imitation of, and points toward, the philosopher." Rosen asserts that this

122. Rosen, *Hermeneutics as Politics*, 33, 139, 187.
123. Ibid., 133.
124. Ibid., 133.

"is philosophically mistaken, and it has bad political consequences for philosophy." The flaw in the philosophic reasoning is Strauss's suppression of "the Platonic teaching that philosophy is divine madness." The political folly lies in the irrelevance of Strauss's vision of gentlemanly rule to our time, which wants freedom.[125]

What do Rosen's disagreements with Strauss have to do with Platonic silence? Exactly this: We have already seen that Rosen attributes divinity to Plato. Rosen informs us further that "Plato practices esotericism . . . in the sense that he seeks to persuade us that philosophy has won, or can win, its quarrel with poetry." However, "the principles of Socrates', and of Plato's, conceptions of philosophy are indeed to be found within the dialogues." At a "deeper level" of Platonic esotericism, which is nevertheless perceptible because it rises up to the surfaces of the dialogues, it is suggested that "there is no quarrel between philosophy and poetry." So, Plato's exoteric separation of *theoria* and *poiēsis* is merely provisional, weak irony. Further, in the context of the choice between cautious and bold rhetoric, it "should never be forgotten that the publication by Plato of his dialogues, given the political circumstances of his day, was a revolutionary act of extreme fearlessness." Thus, to understand Plato's esotericism better than Kant or Strauss do, one must realize that Plato "was in fact a Kantian." That is, "Plato was a 'modern,' not an 'ancient.' "[126]

In another place, Rosen offers a different account of Platonic irony, or at least another perspective on the same explanation. He surprises us by asserting that "Strauss never accuses Plato of duplicity"—a claim that is incredible in the face of the argument of *Persecution and the Art of Writing*. Relying on Nietzsche, Rosen now declares that there are two kinds of esotericism, the first a deliberate concealment of one's views "for reasons of prudence, playfulness, or aristocratic pride" and the second a reflection of "the intrinsic deceptiveness of becoming." Both are "the inevitable consequence of our warranted suspicion of nature." This is to say with Nietzsche that being, at root, is a randomly shifting chaos. Thus, Rosen argues: "Honesty here stands for philosophy as an existential requirement of the higher human type: a frank perception of the fanciful or invented status of natural order is the basis of concealment. To exist is to conceal chaos." The "higher man, who alone is capable of self-knowledge," has a sense of social responsibility to the many who could not bear knowledge of the true facts, so he "conceals this concealment."[127]

If we wonder what this Hegelian and Nietzschean reasoning has to do with Plato, Rosen promptly replies by moving to unify the philosophies of

125. Ibid., 137, 136, 134–37.
126. Rosen, *Quarrel between Philosophy and Poetry*, 12, 26; Rosen, *Hermeneutics as Politics*, 137, 122, 140.
127. Rosen, *Metaphysics in Ordinary Language*, 62, 2, 3.

Nietzsche and Plato. He appeals to a passage in Nietzsche's *Nachlass* without quoting it fully. The passage reads as follows: "My philosophy *reversed Platonism:* the farther from the really being, ever more pure, more beautiful, better it is. Life in appearance as goal."[128] Rosen treats Nietzsche's understanding of his philosophy as "reversed Platonism" as if it meant "Platonism." It seems to me that one might wish to take Nietzsche at his word, as if he meant "reversed" Platonism, that is, he is conscious of Plato's affirmation of a being that really is being, and that he is also conscious of his own affirmation of a being that is merely a randomly changing chaos as a doctrine directly opposed to Plato's. However, Rosen does not see the matter this way. He proceeds to complete his unification of Nietzsche's and Plato's philosophies by assimilating early Greek poets, musicians, and sophists who are cited in Plato as practitioners of irony to Plato himself. He states, for example, that "Protagoras understands that Being is deceptive. Plato does not contest this." Therefore, the dispute between Protagoras and Socrates is "the quarrel between noble and base sophistry."[129] Plato, it seems, is an esoteric writer not only because he is a "Kantian" but also because he is a "noble sophist." Nonetheless, this term might apply more to Rosen than Plato.

Eric Voegelin and Paul Friedländer

Eric Voegelin, whose claim to be the twentieth century's greatest reader of Plato seems to me to excel that of Leo Strauss, pays no direct attention to the dispute about Platonic irony that I have been following throughout this chapter, except to assert that the Platonic dialogue is "an exoteric literary work, accessible individually to everybody who wants to read it."[130] However, his statements about the proper interpretation of Plato show that he is well aware of the most important issues and that he has serious opinions about them.

Like Strauss, Voegelin contends that one cannot understand a Platonic dialogue unless one knows what it is. He holds that "in the history of Hellenic symbolic forms," the Platonic dialogue was "the successor to Aeschylean tragedy" in a time when Athenians had closed their hearts to Aeschylus's "struggle for the order of Dike [Justice]." Socrates had become the new defender of right in Athens, with Plato succeeding him. With regard to the Platonic dialogue, Voegelin infers: "The drama of Socrates is a symbolic

---

128. Rosen quotes the recent paperback edition of the Nietzsche collection that I have been citing: Nietzsche, *Kritische Studienausgabe,* vol. 7, p. 199, 1870/71, passage 156.
129. Rosen, *Metaphysics in Ordinary Language,* 13.
130. Voegelin, *Order and History,* 3:12.

form created by Plato as the means for communicating, and expanding, the order of wisdom founded by its hero."[131] This means that if we wish to understand Voegelin's Plato, we need to learn what a "symbolic form" is.

Also like Strauss, but in his own way, Voegelin is sensitive to the Platonic distinction between the few and the many. His declaration that the dialogue is accessible to everybody who wants to read it does not imply that it is accessible to everybody simply, for there may be many who refuse to read it, some because they are too crushed by the exigencies of making a living to have time for it, others because they are too poorly educated to conceive the need to read it well, and others because they are too lazy or otherwise vicious to be amenable to it. In fact, looking at the actual history of Athens, Voegelin argues that "the question will arise to whom the new symbolic form is addressed, if the decisive public, the people of Athens, does not want to listen."[132] Besides having to discover what a symbolic form is, then, we need to find out who are the few to whom Plato finally speaks. Let us begin with the latter question and work back to the former gradually.

Appealing to "the Digression of the *Theaetetus*" (172c–177c), Voegelin holds that the Platonic dialogue is accessible *in principle* to everybody, even the most stubborn politician or sophist. Any such person who will not listen to a philosopher in public "is still man" and can be "stirred up in private." This is to argue that when it has become impossible to address "the decisive public" collectively, it remains possible to address each of its members individually. Socrates in person can force his attentions on many people severally, requiring them to face the questions that they manage to evade when addressed jointly. Voegelin thinks that a Platonic dialogue could have the same effect on "the decisive public" taken singly. True, a document does not have as much leverage on individuals as Socrates in the flesh has; it must wait to be picked up by a reader. A writing potentially can be addressed to the whole public, but it actually speaks only to the part of the public that is moved to examine it—which might turn out to be a larger proportion of the public than Socrates could reach in person. Voegelin believes that Plato intends to attempt such an approach to the public. Thus, he asserts, "The personal conversation between Socrates and the individual Athenian citizen is continued through the instrument of the dialogue."[133]

It is clear from this reply that Voegelin holds no truck with Strauss's irony. Voegelin's Plato does not intend to reserve the truth for the wise few and feed salutary lies to the foolish many. He does not have two doctrines, one esoteric and one exoteric. Like Schleiermacher's Plato, he makes his work

131. Ibid., 11, 10.
132. Ibid., 11–12.
133. Ibid., 12.

equally accessible to everybody, at least in the sense that he keeps no secrets and would like to convert everybody to philosophy.

In Voegelin's opinion, the fact that Plato is not an esoteric writer does not signify that he incorporates his most profound wisdom in his dialogues. Voegelin is cognizant of Plato's Seventh Letter and gives it an extensive analysis. He understands that Plato "himself has never written directly on the core of his philosophy, and never will, for it cannot be put into words like other knowledge."[134] Neither does Voegelin think that the indirect words that Plato uses will guide all people equally to the result Plato wants to achieve with them, or that everyone will understand these words in the same ways. The statements that the entire Athenian public taken severally is Plato's intended audience and that the Platonic dialogue is equally accessible to everybody who reads it are only one answer to the question about the identity of those to whom the work is addressed. The reply is correct as far as it goes, but it must be supplemented by another, an answer that takes into account what a "symbolic form" is.

The phrase "symbolic form" itself is a theoretical concept that Voegelin has formulated in response to his own experience of being. Voegelin's introspection does not reveal that man is "a self-contained spectator, in possession of and with knowledge of his faculties, at the center of a horizon of being." Rather, it shows that man is "an actor, playing a part in the drama of being and, through the brute fact of his existence, committed to play it without knowing what it is." Indeed, "at the center of his existence man is unknown to himself and must remain so, for the part of being that calls itself man could be known fully only if the community of being and its drama in time were known as a whole." Socrates and Plato grasped this. Accordingly, Voegelin argues that the "Socratic irony of ignorance has become the paradigmatic instance of awareness" of the "blind spot at the center" of man's self-knowledge.[135] Like Kierkegaard, Voegelin sees Platonic irony as a function of man's real inability to enjoy the highest wisdom. Unlike Strauss, he does not envisage it as a defense of a wisdom that naturally aristocratic men actually have while pretending to be unwise.

It is man's effort to penetrate his crucial self-ignorance that produces "symbolic forms." To say that we have a blind spot at the heart of our self-knowledge is not to say that we know nothing at all. Voegelin remarks: "Man can achieve considerable knowledge about the order of being, and not the least part of that knowledge is the distinction between the knowable and the unknowable." Our understanding of the things distant from the "core" of philosophy, or from the "center" of man's existence, consists in the kinds of information normally defined as knowledge, that is, empirical

---

134. Ibid., 19–20.
135. Ibid., 1:1–2.

and logical propositions about these mundane things. However, when we have those experiences upon which the "core" of philosophy touches, those at the "center" of our existence, namely, the experiences that we call "God," "man," "world," and "society," we encounter realities associated in a "community of being" that "is not given in the manner of an object of the external world but is knowable only from the perspective of participation in it." In these cases, our knowledge consists in symbolic representations rather than in propositional facts. As Voegelin declares, we are then engaged in "a process of symbolization" that must be depicted as "the attempt at making the essentially unknowable order of being intelligible as far as possible through the creation of symbols which interpret the unknown by analogy with the really, or supposedly, known."[136] "Symbolic forms" are the complex analogies thus generated.

It becomes necessary to resort to symbolic forms when we desire to communicate our experiences of the order of the reality that we inhabit and, particularly, our experiences of the ground of that order. In the early history of mankind, people generally symbolized "society and its order as an analogue of the cosmos and its order." Later, Israelite prophets, disciples of Jesus, and philosophers such as Plato symbolized "social order by analogy with the order of a human existence that is well attuned to being." In the transition from the first to the second type of symbolization, the experienced realities that are labeled with "God" words came to be represented as distinct from and superior to those classified as "man," "world," and "society" (or as "cosmos" when taken all together). Voegelin comments, at least in the works published around the middle of his career, that the prophets, followers of Christ, and philosophers had "experiences of transcendence." These experiences arose in conjunction with "the discovery of a true order of the human psyche." Thus, "Plato was engaged concretely in the exploration of the human soul, and the true order of the soul turned out to be dependent on philosophy in the strict sense of love of the divine *sophon* [wisdom]."[137]

According to Voegelin, the experiences of transcendence that occurred when sensitive observers looked into their souls became the sources of political theory and the standards for judging it. Theory, Voegelin says, "is not just any opining about human existence in society." Rather, it is "an attempt at formulating the meaning of existence by explicating the content of a definite class of experiences." Its argument is "not arbitrary but derives its validity from the aggregate of experiences to which it must permanently refer for empirical control." However, this means that although a Platonic dialogue is "an exoteric literary work, accessible to everybody individu-

---

136. Ibid., 1, 5, 6.
137. Ibid., 5; Voegelin, *The New Science of Politics*, 62–63.

ally who wants to read it," not just anyone could produce or understand one. On the problem of being or becoming an adequate theorist, Voegelin comments: "Theory cannot be developed under all conditions by everybody. The theorist need perhaps not be a paragon of virtue himself, but he must, at least, be capable of imaginative re-enactment of the experiences of which theory is an explication." As for the problem of understanding, he says: "Theory as an explication of certain experiences is intelligible only to those in whom the explication will stir up parallel experiences as the empirical basis for testing the truth of theory." This implies that a "theoretical debate can be conducted only among *spoudaioi* [serious, mature men] in the Aristotelian sense; theory has no argument against a man who feels, or pretends to feel, unable of re-enacting the experience."[138] This can be stated another way. Voegelin has come to the same conclusion as Schleiermacher: Although Plato had no secrets, his works can be understood only by the true auditors of the inner.

Voegelin's perceptions of the principles governing the reading of Plato would deserve a much more comprehensive summary if they were being studied for their own sake. However, enough has been related here to indicate Voegelin's position vis-à-vis the debate about Platonic irony. It is necessary to add just a few words about later developments of Voegelin's theories that will bear on our inquiry into Plato's *Symposium*. In *Anamnesis*, Voegelin declares: "The experience of concrete-human order . . . is not knowledge of an object but . . . a tension, insofar as man experiences himself as ordered through the tension toward the divine ground of his existence. Nor does any of the terms that emerge in the exegesis of this experience relate to an object. Neither the tension is an object, nor are its poles."[139] The analogical symbols at the core of philosophy refer to "nonobjective realities." This goes beyond Schleiermacher.

Paul Friedländer deserves to be honored as one of the few mid-twentieth-century scholars who recognized the problem of Platonic irony. He contributes some interesting ideas to the conversation. He observes that Thrasymachus, in the *Republic*, was wrong to interpret Socratic irony as hypocrisy: his error lay in demanding a single answer about justice from a man "for whom there is, as an answer, only continuous search." That is, Thrasymachus was wrong not to take Socrates' professions of ignorance seriously. Friedländer also argues that the irony of Socrates has to do with "the ineffability of the highest Platonic vision." The answer to a Socratic question "is only complete in the vision of the eternal forms and in the dawning realization of something that is beyond being." Thus,

---

138. Voegelin, *New Science*, 64–65.
139. Voegelin, *Anamnesis*, 287, 147.

Socratic, Platonic irony both veils what the philosopher sees and reveals it.[140] Voegelin could not have put it better.

PLATO AND HIS MODERN READERS

This survey of Plato's modern readers has identified several questions that are crucial to the proper interpretation of his texts: Is Plato's dramatic dialogue form an integral part of his philosophy or merely a charming artistic wrapping for his real substance? Does it have a necessary role in advancing our insight into reality, or is it a philosophically useless trifle that impedes communication and comprehension? Is Plato silent about his most profound truths, or does he put them into the mouths of Socrates, Timaeus, the Strangers, and, perhaps, others? Is every Platonic sentence understood correctly only in its place, and in the connections and boundaries in which Plato has set it, or may Platonic propositions be transported into various contexts? What is Socratic or Platonic irony? A manner of speech, a "pleasant rallying" that prods students toward the good, hiding nothing except what the readers are too lazy to work out for themselves (as Hegel believed)? Plato's principled refusal to speak about ineffable matters that are evident only to auditors of the inner, or *spoudaioi* (as Schleiermacher and Voegelin agreed)? A shaking of the pillars of knowledge that reduces human learning to the nothingness of ignorance because no predicates can speak to the divine splendor (as Kierkegaard said)? A pathological manifestation of cowardice before the terror and horror of absurd existence that is one part psychological self-deception and one part swindle perpetrated by inferior people who desire universal power and revenge upon their betters (as in Nietzsche's belief)? A mendacious dissembling of wisdom that conceals the truths of atheism, natural aristocracy, and Thrasymachean natural right from the demos; cleverly manipulates the many; and secretly reveals the most fundamental truths to those who can understand (as Strauss wrote)? A boldly honest dishonesty that deceives insofar as it maneuvers the multitude into the paradoxical position of free and mature gods who adore higher philosopher gods (as Rosen argued)? This range of questions and opinions proves that we do not automatically comprehend Platonic irony upon discovering its existence. Hegel and his followers might be right about it. Or Schleiermacher, Kierkegaard, and Voegelin might be right. Or Nietzsche, or Lessing and Strauss, or Rosen might be right. However, not all of these commentators can be right, for then we would have an absurdly self-contradictory Plato. So, which of the three major ways of considering a Platonic text, if any, is the correct one?

140. Friedländer, *Plato*, 1:143–44, 147–48, 153.

As stated in the previous chapter, it would be wrong to try to settle this issue a priori. We could not judge the matter without having read Plato himself, with a view toward seeing which of the three approaches appears to fit best. However, as I have indicated, I suspect that the interpretation developed by Schleiermacher, Kierkegaard, Voegelin, and Friedländer is the better one, both because it seems the most adequate to the realities under discussion and because it appears to be the most consistent with the thrust of the documents. I can elaborate a little more on the grounds of my preliminary impressions here.

Hegel, I think, must be rejected out of hand. We have already noticed that Hegel was not the most careful reader of Plato. There are two additional reasons for challenging Hegel's judgment. First, it clearly presumes that (1) Hegel could know Plato better than Plato knew himself, because his historical vantage point allowed him to see the relationship of all thought to ultimate knowledge, and (2) Plato was not intelligent or advanced enough to avoid the errors of a simpleminded conception of being and an unsystematic and, therefore, unscientific method of handling materials. If anyone still affirms Hegel's historicist claims on behalf of his science, we, at least, cannot accept them without assessing his suspect reasoning. Even less can we concede the proposition that poor Plato was too simple to know what he was doing. Plato deserves more intellectual respect than that. This requires us to operate provisionally on the basis of the hypothesis that in Plato's view, philosophy had to be a fusion of dialogical form with intellectual substance, that he wanted the form to permeate the meaning of the substance, that he therefore gave the statements of his characters strong relationships to their dialogical contexts, and that he wished to reason or teach through his dramas conceived as wholes rather than through isolated *philosopheme*. We may not assume that Plato wrapped his philosophic truths in darling theater pieces merely because he wanted to give expression to an artistic flair, or that he stupidly or carelessly failed to notice that an essentially meaningless dialogic form hindered science and pedagogy. Second, Hegel unwarrantedly and utterly ignores what Plato says in the Seventh Letter (341c–d), that he never has written anything on that about which he is serious. We may not presuppose the nonexistence of Platonic silence. If we want to get rid of it, we are obliged to offer proof that Plato's remarks in the Seventh Letter are inapposite.

Our inability to follow Hegel forces us to maintain a critical distance from some other famous commentators who accept his hermeneutic assumptions. Here, I do not mean that we should be especially skeptical of people who adhere to the Hegelian dialectic as a philosophic method or to Hegel's myths of the *Weltgeist*. Rather, I am still speaking of scholars who hold that Plato's philosophy consists in *philosopheme* that are found in the mouths of Socrates and other Platonic spokesmen, that there are no barriers to transporting these *philosopheme* from one context to another, that Plato's purposes and achievements can and should be judged by the standards of Hegel's systematic science (or by those of some even more "advanced" science in which the object of an exercise is always to ascertain the logical or empirical validity of *p*), and that Plato was insufficiently intelligent to see clearly what he should do. In our era, these presumptions have been taken in analytic and historicist directions. Gregory Vlastos exemplifies the former tendency and George Sabine the latter. The Platonic studies of Vlastos are shot through with the phrase "Plato says." In my own work, I shall not imagine that I know that "Plato" asserts anything. To speak more precisely, I shall not claim to know that Plato asserts anything about the highest things. Again, Vlastos typically tries to expose fallacious Platonic logic and then confidently talks about what might have been "if Plato had understood his own theory better." On the contrary, I shall suppose that we lack proof that Plato even had a "theory" in Vlastos's logical sense of the concept and that Plato deliberately could have had Socrates make a bad argument in a play. Vlastos also laments "Plato's" teaching of a utilitarian doctrine of love in the *Lysis* and then inserts that teaching into the *Republic*. In opposition to this procedure, I wonder what it means that Plato dramatically causes Socrates to say what he says to characters such as Lysis and Glaucon in the contexts in which the statements are set. The much less competent Sabine composes a "history of ideas" in which chronologically prior thoughts determine later ones. In doing so, he announces that "the main positions developed" by Plato "may be reduced to a few propositions," all of them "dominated by a single point of view," thus enabling us to speak facilely of "the fundamental idea of the *Republic*." I, on the other hand, do not take the fact that Plato's dialogues sometimes mention his predecessors as evidence that his "principles" evolved out of earlier ideas. Also, in view of the Seventh Letter, I doubt that these "principles" are within easy reach.[141]

It will be objected that this rejection of Hegel, Vlastos, and Sabine is wholly unjustifiable because it flies in the face of interpretations by the absolutely most authoritative reader of Plato, Aristotle. In the *Physics*, Aristotle states that it is "Plato" who says something "in the *Timaeus*" (209b11–12). A reasonable person would infer that Aristotle regards characters such as Timaeus, Socrates, and the Strangers as Plato's spokesmen. Also, Aristotle devotes several discussions to Platonic arguments that are theories in Vlastos's sense of the term.

This entirely welcome objection compels me to repeat some of Voegelin's remarks. By accepting the Schleiermacher-Kierkegaard-Voegelin-Friedländer opinion of Platonic silence, one approves of two statements that appear

---

141. Vlastos, *Platonic Studies*, 56, 8–11, 13; Sabine, *History of Political Theory*, 40–41.

contradictory to a superficial observer, but are actually perfectly compatible. Voegelin, it will be recalled, holds that the realities at the center of our existence are mysteries, propositions about them being analogical rather than factual. He adds that this does not mean that we know nothing at all. We have propositional science of what is not at the core of our being. This noncontradiction accurately reflects Socrates' simultaneous declarations of ignorance and knowledge. This is one reason that Schleiermacher declares that Platonic writings may not be emptied of their content. There are also ethical reasons that the comments of Socrates and other characters are pedagogically important. Socrates often accepts propositions provisionally because they are partially correct and can be pruned of their errors as they are pushed in the direction of the ultimately unknowable realities. Thus, Plato and his characters both do and do not say things in the dialogues—depending on whether one intends to refer to propositions about realities at the core of human existence or realities away from the center. Statements in Plato's dialogues must always be honored as the indispensable stepping-stones toward whatever Plato knows, even though they are not his serious insights. This would explain why Aristotle speaks as he does. All this assumes that Aristotle invariably reads his master rightly, a point on which there is some scholarly disagreement.

This leaves us to choose between the Lessing-Nietzsche-Strauss-Rosen understanding of Platonic silence and the Schleiermacher-Kierkegaard-Voegelin-Friedländer interpretation. I am inclined to eliminate all Nietzschean exegesis from this calculus, for it depends on the dogmatic premise that being is absurd. If it is not true that existence is meaningless, or if we cannot demonstrate this proposition even if it is true, Nietzschean readings become arbitrary. It would be a happy event if we could settle the dispute between the Strauss and Schleiermacher et al. line by comparing their analyses with the Platonic texts quoted at the beginning of this chapter, with the exegesis most closely matching the plain meanings of the words being judged best. The trouble with this idea is that it is precisely the passages cited that have given rise to the conflicting accounts. I think that careful analysis of these texts will show that they proclaim ineffable truths. When I have finished my careful exegesis, others might still disagree, thus substantiating the warning that Socrates gives about one of the drawbacks of writing: When we ask texts what they mean, they always repeat the same things, never explaining themselves (*Phaedrus* 275d4–9). If we resign ourselves to this outcome in advance, we still need not despair of a simple solution of our problem. At least we can inquire whether there are other Platonic statements that explicitly clear up the ambiguities.

We do need to recognize that "irony" is mentioned several times in Plato's dialogues. The word is used by four different kinds of characters, as follows.

First, Socrates. In the *Lovers*, Socrates encounters two rivals for the favors of a boy. One fancies himself a philosopher. At one point, Socrates relates that this self-satisfied rival "very ironically spoke doubly" (133d8). He told Socrates his real opinion, even though it contained admissions favorable to his opponent, but he conceded nothing in direct conversation with his enemy, wishing only to embarrass and defeat him (see 134c1–6). In the *Euthydemus* (302b3), Socrates mentions that a pompous proponent of eristic paused rather ironically, as if pondering some great matter. In the *Apology* (38a1), Socrates says that he fears to make a claim because he will be disbelieved "as one being ironic" (that is, as one dissembling).

Second, Hermogenes. Diogenes Laertius reports that Hermogenes and Cratylus were two of Plato's teachers.[142] In the *Cratylus* (384a1), Hermogenes complains that Cratylus is being ironic, refusing to explain what he means, and claiming to have private knowledge that would compel agreement if it were divulged.

Third, the Eleatic and Athenian Strangers. In the *Sophist*, the Eleatic Stranger attributes irony to sophists who pretend to know what they do not know (268a7, 268b3). This sense of irony is worked into the definition of the sophist with which the dialogue concludes (268c8). In the *Laws* (908e2), the Athenian Stranger decrees death penalties for the ironic crimes that atheistic sophists commit.

Fourth, persons unhappy with, or hostile to, Socrates. In the *Symposium* (218d6), Alcibiades confesses that he offered sexual favors to Socrates, and that Socrates reacted by assuming his characteristic ironic manner, mocking Alcibiades and disclaiming the virtues that Alcibiades saw in him. In the *Gorgias* (489e1), when Socrates makes an ostentatious show of having failed to understand Gorgias, Gorgias accuses Socrates of being ironic. Socrates replies that it is Gorgias who has been ironic, having failed to disclose his true meaning earlier. Finally, in the perhaps most often cited case, Thrasymachus exclaims in the *Republic:* "O Herakles! That is the usual irony of Socrates. I knew it, and I predicted to these people that you would be unwilling to answer, that you would be ironic and do anything other than answer if someone asked you something" (337a4–7).

We also need to observe that Platonic characters explicitly discuss the deception of the many and the avoidance of persecution. There are two especially noteworthy examples, discussed below.

In the *Theaetetus*, Socrates analyzes Protagoras's dictum that "[m]an is the measure of all things, of the things that are, as they are, of the things that are not, as they are not." He begins with this outburst: "By the Graces! I wonder if the all-wise Protagoras did not speak riddles to us, the vulgar many, and tell the truth secretly to his students" (152c8–10). Later, Socrates

---

142. Diogenes Laertius, *Lives of Eminent Philosophers*, 3.8.

offers to help Theaetetus search out the concealed truth of the great sophist, and mockingly exhorts the lad to look around to make sure that none of the uninitiated, that is, those who think that nothing exists save what they can touch with their hands, are listening (155d–e). With respect to a Homeric verse about the origins of all things, Socrates also matter-of-factly informs the mathematician Theodorus that the ancients hid their meaning from the many inside their poetry. With obvious sarcasm, he argues that those who came later, being wiser, were candid even with shoemakers (180d).

As reported previously, Protagoras declares in the dialogue that bears his name that the leading sophists of earlier times, such as Homer, Hesiod, Simonides, Orpheus, Musaeus, and a number of athletic trainers and musicians, disguised their art as poetry, mystic rites, and so on. He explains that they did this in order to avoid the odium and ill-will attendant upon teaching in great cities. However, he thinks that these poetic sophists failed in their purpose, for their real teachings did not escape the notice of the able men in any city. He also holds it unnecessary to take special measures to prevent the stupid multitude from seeing. Thus, he speaks openly (316c–317c). Later in the same dialogue, Socrates himself argues that the Cretans and Spartans have more ancient traditions of philosophy than the other Greeks and that they deliberately pretend to ignorance to conceal the fact that it is by virtue of their wisdom rather than their arms that they rule the rest of Hellas. He maintains further that Simonides attempted to make a name for himself by overthrowing this practice (341d–343c).

If we were to concede what we do not immediately grant, that such references to irony and deception add up to "Plato's" notion of esotericism, we could infer that "Plato's" concept bears a closer likeness to Strauss's picture than to those of his other interpreters. Plato clearly knows all about the practices of refraining from revealing what one thinks, dissembling one's opinions by pretending not to know or by endorsing creeds that are contrary to one's beliefs, concealing one's commitments from the multitude and divulging them only to a chosen few, speaking differently to different kinds of people, using lies to control enemies, and disguising atheism as reverence for the gods of the city to escape persecution. However, continuing on the premise that these allusions to irony and esotericism constitute "Plato's" idea of them, we would also have to concede that "Plato" strongly condemns them. Speaking through Socrates and the Strangers, "Plato" indicates that he and Socrates do not want to be thought ironic. He attributes irony only to pompous asses, poets whose works are forbidden in the just city, and sophists who richly deserve capital punishment. "Plato" also declares through Protagoras that irony is politically useless. It is particularly significant that irony is imputed to Socrates only by his enemies.

Responding to this last point, Strauss proclaims that "where there was so much smoke there must have been some fire or rather that avowed irony would be absurd."[143] This is quite a strange thing for Strauss, who represents nothing if not avowed irony, to say. That aside, it certainly is possible that "Plato's" denunciations of irony are exoteric propaganda designed to throw fools off the track of an esotericist. However, it is equally possible that Plato wanted irony to be understood as a vicious habit of poets and sophists who confused Socratic silence, which they could not understand on genuinely philosophic grounds, with their own mendacity. The snippets quoted above do not provide sufficient evidence to choose between these interpretations.

Plato's modern readers have served us well by alerting us to the possible explanations of his silence. However, it is now quite plain that to learn why Plato was silent about serious things, and what he really thought about the just, the beautiful, and the good, we must study his relevant writings as wholes. I shall read Plato's Seventh Letter and dialogues as documents in which everything is important. Heeding Schleiermacher and Strauss, I shall look carefully not only at plain arguments and actions, but also at devices that draw veils over the reasoning, making it hard for the inattentive to see. Heeding Voegelin, I shall also be sensitive to the symbolic character of Plato's images and their potential to represent ineffable experiences of the realities at the core of man's being. Now it is time to turn to a rigorous analysis of the Seventh Letter, to see if we can tell what it really says about the reasons for Platonic silence.

143. Strauss, *The City and Man*, 52.

3

MYSTIC PHILOSOPHY IN THE SEVENTH LETTER

The author of the Seventh Letter calls himself Plato. He discusses, among other things, a failed experiment. At the behest of his beloved, he tried but failed to educate a courageous, moderate, just, and philosophic ruler (336a9–b1) under conditions in which an entire society aspired to nothing but feasting, drinking, nightly amours, extravagant spending, and idleness (326b7–c1, 326c6–d2), thus forcing him to argue against such debauchery (326b5–d2). He also states that he never has written, and never will write, anything about that which he regards as serious (341b7–c2). He treats the philosophic reasons for his silence extensively. The Seventh Letter therefore seems to be the only extant work in which Plato, speaking in his own name, meditates on the practical attempt of a noble eros to cure an evil eros. It is also the only work in which he directly explains his mysterious silence.

I am interested in the Seventh Letter chiefly because I wish to understand its explanation of Plato's silence about the serious things. I shall devote the bulk of the present chapter to this topic. However, the epistle has a double bearing on our inquiry into eros. On the one hand, it is a testament to, and is suffused with, an eros that Plato undoubtedly considers noble and good. Although the Seventh Letter does not treat this beautiful eros formally as an object of investigation, it shows how such an eros drives a philosopher's choices and inspires some of his loftiest acts. On the other hand, the epistle wrestles with the extremely difficult problem of how the philosopher, his beloved, and their friends can surmount the political evils caused by an eros that Plato certainly considers depraved. Again, the letter does not inquire into this evil eros in itself but it demonstrates its pernicious effects to every discerning eye. In a book on Platonic eros, these relationships of the Seventh Letter to Socrates' erotic science cannot be ignored. This chapter will open with an introductory section on the roles of eros in the epistle.

With regard to the question of the grounds of Platonic silence, the fact that Plato tells us his motives in the Seventh Letter is genuinely exciting.

One is tempted to exclaim: "What a treasure," and to let the epistle govern all exegesis of Platonic texts, if only we can interpret it correctly. There is, however, a fly in the ointment. There are classicists—one cannot know exactly how many—who consider the letter a forgery. This chapter will need a second, introductory section on the provenance of the epistle.

EROS IN THE SEVENTH LETTER

To appreciate the roles of eros in the Seventh Letter, we must begin by harking back to our preliminary discussion of the objects of eros. We saw that in Plato, eros is not simply or only desire for sexual intercourse. Eros includes sexual craving, but it also involves desires for a broad range of other objects, such as food, drink, job skills, fishing, just and moderate practices, wealth, ignoble gain, and unlimited acquisition. This range has noble heights and base depths that I must now highlight.

On the noble side, we find in the *Symposium* that there is an eros that starts as sexual longing, as a man's desire for a lad. This sexual attraction— let us not bowdlerize the text by portraying it as something else—takes a form that Diotima calls "the right pederasty" (211b5–6). It ascends from the love of the beautiful youth through the love of all beautiful bodies, the love of beautiful souls, the love of moderation and justice or of beautiful customs in cities, the love of learning and the sciences, and the love of wisdom (that is, philosophy) to an ultimate vision of beauty and the acquisition and cultivation of real virtues (208e–212a, especially 211b–212a). In the *Phaedrus,* this sexual attraction rewings the souls of the lovers for their flights back to the eternal realm from whence they originally came (255b–256d).

On the shameful side, we see in the *Republic* that the ascent to the noble vision can be refused in favor of a descent to a base power. The first step on the ignoble path is not a sexual desire but, according to the playful Muse, a miscalculation of the perfect number that governs divine births, a mistake that results in the mixing of metals in souls and the generation of war and hatred. From there, the descent proceeds through the loves of honor, wealth, and license to tyranny. At the nadir, a youth's keepers—"dread magi and tyrant-makers"—plant "some eros" in his soul, an "eros" that is a "great winged drone" (572e4–573c2). The drone-eros becomes the ruler of the soul and takes madness as its palace guard, with the consequence that "eros from of old has been called a tyrant" (573b6–7). The tyrannical youth becomes drunken, erotic (now in the strictly sexual sense), and melancholic. His sexuality—an inclination with which his development has not originated, but terminated—runs in the direction of "feasts, revels, parties, prostitutes," just the style of hedonism that Plato faced in the city where he hoped to educate a philosopher-king. This tyrannical sexuality is compatible with beating a father or mother for the sake of a new girlfriend, concubine, or boyfriend. Therefore, in our anachronistic modern terms, the drone-eros and the tyrannical sexuality constitute an evil disposition that could arise equally in the soul of a heterosexual, a bisexual, or a homosexual, or gay. Finally, the drone-eros leads the tyrannical man beyond parent beating to many other terrible acts, including murder (546a–575b, especially 572e–575b).

The fact that eros can produce such contradictory results raises a question: Is there one eros, or are there two? If eros is one, it must have healthy and diseased states. If there are two erotes, we might say with Eric Voegelin that the *"Eros tyrannos* is the satanic double of the Socratic Eros."[1] In either case, both sides of the single eros or the two opposed erotes seem to affect the history that is related in the Seventh Letter strongly.

In this epistle, Plato reports that when he paid the first of his three visits to Syracuse, he was approximately forty years old and Dion was a "youth." Dion was probably twenty or thereabouts. Plato says nothing explicit about a sexual attraction to Dion that he might have had. However, Diogenes Laertius, the biographer who wrote a life of Plato early in the third century A.D., says that when Dion was murdered, Plato composed an epitaph for his grave:

> Tears for Hekabē and the women of Ilion
> The Fates wove as destiny at their births,
> And for you, O Dion, after earning praise for noble deeds,
> The *daimones* poured forth in waste fair-flowing hopes,
> You lie now in your spacious fatherland honored by townspeople
> After making my heart rage with eros, O Dion![2]

A more literal translation of the last line of the epitaph, ὦ ἐμὸν ἐκμήνας θυμὸν ἔρωτι Δίων, would speak of being driven mad with passionate eros for Dion. Diogenes thus suggests that Plato loved Dion with an intensity that was exquisite, graceful, beautiful, raging, and sexually ardent. Should we believe this suggestion? Should we go even further and assume that Plato was sexually intimate with Dion—thus entering the lists in a controversy that has broken out among scholars from time to time?

I think that we may take it as an established fact that Plato loved Dion. All the ancient sources attest to this. So does the Seventh Letter, insofar as it shows Plato going to extremely great lengths to help his friend, including

---

1. Voegelin, *Order and History*, 3:127. "Erotes" is the Greek plural of "eros."
2. Diogenes Laertius, "Plato," in *Lives of Eminent Philosophers*, 3.30. My thanks to Patricia Marquardt for the translation.

that of risking his life on more than one occasion. It is also obvious that every line of the epistle breathes Plato's love and his mourning for Dion. I speculate further that Plato was a man of gay sensitivity who was sexually attracted to Dion. I hasten to warn that this kind of supposition is anachronistic—Greeks simply did not think in our terms—and also that it ultimately does not matter, for all Platonic eroticism eventually ascends from bodies to souls, as did Plato's eros for Dion. However, for the sake of accuracy, we must observe that Platonic eroticism always seems to begin with bodies, a point that makes our anachronistic question about Plato's relationship with Dion more or less unavoidable.

The speculation that Plato was a gay man and sexually attracted to Dion is supported by probable conjectures rather than airtight logic: The ancient sources appear to take Plato's homoeroticism for granted. At the same time, they say nothing of Plato marrying a wife. Plato seems to write with personal experience of pederastic desire in several places, notably in the *Symposium*, with its heartfelt insistence on "right pederasty"; in the *Phaedrus* (250e–252b, 253c–256d); in the *Republic* (474c–475a); and in the *Charmides* (155d)—texts that will be analyzed or described more fully below. Let us grant, then, that Plato was drawn to Dion sexually, bearing in mind that this does not matter ultimately for the argument because Platonic eros soon ascends from bodies to souls. No ethical person will be distressed by the suggestion that Plato might have been or was a man of gay disposition. The Roman Catholic Church, which may be taken as fairly representative of contemporary religious opinion on the subject, counsels us that "the homosexual condition" is not chosen. It thereby acknowledges that gay predilections arise by some process that occurs in nature. This is why the church states that gay persons "must be accepted with respect, compassion, and sensitivity" and that "every sign of unjust discrimination in their direction should be avoided." Diotima also contributes an ethical word on the subject. When she speaks of "right pederasty," she envisages a type of boy-loving that must not only be "accepted" but also be admired because it is "right."[3]

So, then, was Plato sexually intimate with Dion? I should not be surprised if he were, for sexual attraction is powerful, and the physical consummation of true love must be thought to appeal irresistibly to people of every orientation. Also, there is an offhand remark in the Seventh Letter that almost appears to confirm that Plato and Dion were intimate. Plato says that Dion kept in mind ἐμὴν συνουσίαν (327d1–2), literally "our being together." The word συνουσίαν, translated as "being together," is the

---

3. *Catechism of the Catholic Church*, secs. 2358, 2359. The latter section faintly echoes this sentiment when it declares that gay orientation can be a springboard for an ascent to "Christian perfection."

standard Greek idiom for sexual intercourse. Nonetheless, the case is not absolutely certain, for συνουσία can also mean simply "being together." It does not necessarily refer to sexual coitus. There are also contrary indications. In texts that have given rise to the idea of "Platonic love," Socrates suggests that the drive to consummate pederastic love should be resisted (for example, in the *Phaedrus* 253d–254e, 255e–256d and the *Republic* 403a–c), and the Athenian Stranger hints that homoerotic intercourse is unnatural (*Laws* 836c). In these lines, it is almost as if Plato had anticipated the doctrine of the Catholic Church that "[h]omosexual persons are called to chastity."[4] However, on the contrary of the contrary, the *Phaedrus* contains passages (255a–e) that seem rich in homoerotic imagery. Furthermore, even where Socrates seems to discourage homoerotic union, he does not issue severe condemnations of it. Rather, he declares that the lovers who do have sexual intercourse attain to a second-best condition that provides no mean reward (*Phaedrus* 256d). When all this evidence is added up, we are baffled. We cannot prove either that Plato was intimate with Dion or that he forbade himself the consummation of his love.

Fortunately, we need not answer this question. If Plato is silent about any intimacy, we may assume that it is irrelevant to the business of the Seventh Letter, precisely because it is in the nature of all healthy Platonic eroticism to rise from bodies to souls. Thus, we may put off until later a complete treatment of the *Symposium, Phaedrus, Republic,* and *Laws* passages and concentrate now on other sorts of consequences of Plato's eros for Dion.

What is important here is that Diotima envisages a "right pederasty" that originates as sexual attraction to a young man and ascends from the love of the beautiful youth through the love of all beautiful bodies; the love of beautiful souls; the love of moderation and justice, or of beautiful customs in cities; the love of learning and the sciences, and philosophy (the love of wisdom), to an ultimate vision of beauty and the acquisition and cultivation of real virtues. It seems to me that Plato's love of Dion followed this course fairly closely. Soon after Plato met Dion, he was instructing him verbally in what was best for the human beings and urging him to realize it. Dion heeded him more than any other lad he had known, coming to value virtue more highly than pleasure (327a–b). Thus, there was an ascent from body to soul. Next, Dion began to believe that the excellences could be extended to Dionysius II and all the inhabitants of Syracuse (327c ff). Much of the Seventh Letter is devoted to the history of this project, for the sake of which Plato risked his life and Dion died. This represents an ascent from the love of souls to the love of beautiful customs in cities. Eventually, the time came when Dionysius II grew jealous of Dion. The tyrant demanded that Plato take him as his special friend instead of Dion and

4. Ibid., 2359.

praise him more highly than Dion. Plato comments that the best way to bring this result about was for Dionysius II to occupy himself with learning and philosophic discourses (330a–b). This means that in Plato's relationship with Dion, there clearly was an ascent from the love of beautiful laws to love of the sciences and philosophy. For reasons that will become plain as I follow the narrative of the Seventh Letter, it is doubtful that Dion rose higher than this. However, Plato discharges his ultimate duty to Dion by finishing his history with two accounts of his experience of a leaping flame that floods the soul with the light of wisdom and reason, perhaps an equivalent of the vision of beauty (341c–d, 344b–c). Hence, it appears that the "right pederasty" inspired every move that Plato made with regard to Dion and Syracuse, from his original befriending of Dion and his teaching of the lad to his perilous efforts to help reform the tyrant and his denials that Dionysius II could have known the things about which a philosopher was serious, denials that required the accounts of the leaping flame.

It is also important that Socrates says that the drone-eros drives tyranny. Given Plato's remarks about nearly universal feasting, drinking, nightly amours, extravagant spending, and idleness in Sicily, it seems that the winged drone must have been buzzing around everywhere on the island, causing most of the inhabitants to aspire to tyranny and to be receptive to it. If Socrates is right, the drone's domination of souls was decisive in the dashing of Plato's hopes for Dion and Syracuse.

The drone-eros defeated Plato's efforts first and foremost in the case of Dionysius II, the tyrant. Plato and Dion frequently advised Dionysius to order his life in such a way as to win self-mastery, or an internal harmony, in which he was surprisingly deficient (331d–e, 332d–e). This is to say that they wanted him to control his appetites and acquire the virtues. Thus, they wished to see him ascend from the things of the body to a lovable beauty of soul. The tyrant could not make the ascent. Others, probably dread magi and tyrant-makers, persuaded Dionysius that Plato and Dion were plotting against him, thus stimulating his drone-eros, that is, here, his lust for power, and his fears of losing it. This, undoubtedly together with Dionysius's jealousy of Dion's place in Plato's affections, prompted the tyrant to expel Dion, his brother-in-law, from Syracuse; to persecute Dion incessantly; and to contemplate having Plato killed, acts as heinous as parent beating, or more so. The tyrant ultimately arrived at a total refusal to do justice (335c–d). We must also suppose that the drone-eros motivated the deeds of Dion's assassin, Callippus, for Callippus aspired to tyranny, too.

These considerations suggest that the Seventh Letter could be interpreted as the saga of a great struggle between the Socratic eros ("right pederasty") and the tyrannical winged drone-eros in real life. However, Plato does not make this argument explicitly in the Seventh Letter. Therefore, I shall refrain from pushing this exegesis further here. I shall be content to permit its essential correctness to become evident in the reflected light of what we learn from Plato's other works. Meanwhile, we may turn to the charge that the Seventh Letter is a forgery.

The Provenance of the Epistle

The authenticity of the Seventh Letter has been questioned since higher criticism came into vogue in the nineteenth century. Some skeptics have doubted the epistle's bona fides for substantive reasons. Others have made stylistic critiques. I shall concentrate on the substantive objections, treating the less impressive stylistic ones briefly in passing.

Ludwig Edelstein has been the most influential twentieth-century critic of the Seventh Letter. Edelstein's book, *Plato's Seventh Letter,* presents 171 pages of relentless argument against the authenticity of the epistle. His myriads of objections to the document cannot be summarized with sufficient brevity. However, they can be categorized by type, and the most cogent examples of each variety can be adduced.

First, lack of attestation. Edelstein points out that the Seventh Letter is not mentioned by any ancient writers or compilers of catalogs of Plato's works before Cicero. He views this classical silence as extremely suspicious. He also characterizes sections of the epistle as Plato's "autobiography," or as his *"apologia pro vita sua,"* and finds fault with them as such. For example, he says that the "Plato" of the letter reports having wanted to go into politics as a young man, but Aristotle "implies that Plato chose philosophy as his career," and no ancient biographer relates that Plato had this youthful wish. Further, "there is nothing in the account of Plato's life that an outsider could not say as well as Plato. The epistle gives a typical rather than an individual picture of Plato's development, while the personal data that appear in the biographies of others—such as his literary interests and his study of philosophy with Cratylus and Socrates—are absent." Moreover, the letter clearly "is not a straightforward historical report written simply for the sake of giving the whole truth." Rather, "the omissions noted, the silence concerning essential data one wishes and is entitled to know and about which other sources provide information, suggest that the writer has aims that he does not state directly." In this respect, "it is fair to say that an autobiography which is concerned less with the facts than with a certain view of the facts can readily be imagined to be the work of someone who used the material at his disposal to conjure up Plato as he pictured him."[5]

Second, anachronisms. The "Plato" of the epistle declares that he and Dion recommended a foreign policy to the tyrant Dionysius II, that he

---

5. Edelstein, *Plato's Seventh Letter,* 1, 2, 9, 6, 108, 10, 14, 15.

should "re-people the devastated cities" of Sicily. This "Plato" also remarks that Dion, had he remained in power, "would next have colonized the whole of Sicily and made it free from the barbarians." However, the need to repeople Sicily "existed as little during the reign of Dionysius the younger as it had existed at the death of his father," because the country "was not depopulated" when the elder tyrant died. The devastation of Sicily occurred during the civil wars that followed the murder of Dion, and it was actually Timoleon of Corinth who undertook the repopulation of the island after he had pacified Syracuse in 344 B.C. As for Dion, he had secret dealings with the Carthaginians, and accepted their help in his campaign against Dionysius II. Once again, it was Timoleon who defeated the Carthaginians. "In short," says Edelstein, "it looks as if the author of the epistle were thinking, in both these instances, not of what happened in Plato's time, but of events that occurred much later, after Plato's death."[6]

Third, disagreements with Plato's teachings in the dialogues. Edelstein concedes that the "style of the letter resembles the style of the old Plato." However, this does not prove that the document is genuine: "There is always a chance that someone imitated Plato's art of writing even to perfection." Therefore, a decision about the authenticity of the epistle "must in the end rest on the interpretation of the content." As Edelstein proceeds with his exegesis, he discovers that "the further one reads, the more one meets with assertions which hardly can have been made by Plato," and this forces one to give up belief in the Platonic origin of the letter.[7] To illustrate, see the six examples that follow.

"Plato" refers to Socrates merely as his "aged friend" or his "associate." In fact, the missive "mentions no one with whom Plato studies," making him appear to be wholly self-taught. So, "while the dialogues suggest strongly that Plato's encounter with Socrates was crucial for his life," the "autobiography" would not permit one to "guess the significance his relation with Socrates had for him." Further, "It surely is hard to believe that Plato could at any time in his life have spoken of Socrates' death as caused 'by some chance' or 'ill-luck,' " as the letter does.[8]

"Plato's" judgment of the restored Athenian democracy "in comparison with that he passes on the regime of the Thirty seems more favorable than one would have supposed." Also, the epistle praises the concept of "just government with equal laws," and this "surely is not the principle embodied in the constitution of the Republic." Nor does it jibe with the Laws, which advocates a mixture of equality with inequality.[9]

6. Ibid., 32–34.
7. Ibid., 2, 4.
8. Ibid., 7, 8, 9, 10.
9. Ibid., 10, 12, 13.

"Plato" alleges that he went to Syracuse to try to found a state in accordance with his political theories because he did not want to think himself "a man of mere words." However, the Plato of the *Republic* says that it makes no difference whether his heavenly city ever comes into being on earth, and that the virtuous man does not get into politics willingly.[10]

"Plato" insists that he "never [*sic*] instructed Dionysius." However, he admits that he talked to the tyrant about politics, and "it is not easy to see how any real counseling could be done without initiating Dionysius into Platonism, since the rulership was to be in the hands of a philosopher-king."[11]

Lamenting the disastrous failure of all his plans, "Plato" declares that his downfall was caused by "some chance mightier than man." Plato's *Republic* acknowledges the role of fortune in human affairs. However, the lament is still un-Platonic, for the *Laws* teaches that "in addition to chance and opportunity and God, there is operating in human affairs the force of 'art' . . . , that is, reason." When one has seen how un-Platonic the letter's appeals to fortune are, the suspicions aroused by its historical anachronisms "have turned into certainty." The epistle "cannot be the work of Plato."[12]

Last, "Plato" claims that his serious insights are ineffable. The *Phaedrus* says "nothing" of this. Actually, the letter's "philosophical digression" is wholly un-Platonic.[13]

Fourth, evidence of a disciple's desire to whitewash Plato. Having attained to "certainty" about the letter's fraudulent character, one can corroborate this judgment by noticing that the document strives indefatigably to cover up Plato's guilt for the catastrophic outcome of his meddling in the politics of Syracuse. To cite just one instance, in the sorry matter of Dion's assassination, "It would be hard to guess from the account given that the Academy must have been blamed, and rightly so, for the crime perpetrated . . . [f]or the two men, whose names Plato does not deign to mention—Callippus and Philostratus—were themselves members of the Academy, or at least Platonists." Further, Aristotle, when discussing the frame of mind in which people do wrong, "includes in his long enumeration 'those against whom we have a complaint, or with whom we have had a previous difference, as Callippus acted in the matter of Dion, for in such cases it seems almost an act of justice.'" From this, Edelstein deduces: "Some people who were close to the Academy, then, felt that Dion was culpable and actually defended Callippus who, in their eyes, was not a vile criminal." This and similar examples constitute evidence of a disciple's

10. Ibid., 16.
11. Ibid., 23.
12. Ibid., 53–56.
13. Ibid., 83 and all of pt. 2.

ardent desire to defend his beloved, deceased master against accusations that were in the air of Hellas.[14]

On the basis of such reasoning, Edelstein infers that the Seventh Letter could not have been written "earlier than the end of Timoleon's career—in 336 B.C, approximately twelve years after Plato died," and that it was probably written "in the first decades after Plato's death." He confesses that the author "is quite an impressive writer," "a man of philosophical acumen" who is "especially well versed in Plato's later thought" and "thoroughly familiar with all the other writings," even though he "goes against the very essence of Platonism."[15] These reasons for pronouncing the Seventh Letter a forgery seem compelling. Yet, upon closer inspection, they turn out to be paper tigers.

First, attestation. Since the advent of higher criticism, Plato's authorship of many of the dialogues and all of the epistles traditionally ascribed to him has been called into question, precisely because there is no assuredly valid ancient catalog of his publications. The only canonical works that have escaped being classified as forgeries by one specialist or another are the ones to which Aristotle specifically attests. Scholars have attempted to prove that Plato did or did not write the others by employing stylometrics, or by preceding Edelstein in declarations that certain statements were or were not theoretically consistent with or worthy of a presumably known central core of Platonic doctrine. The result of all this sophisticated rumination has been an absolute lack of consensus about any of the disputed dialogues and epistles; higher criticism has answered none of the questions that it has raised.[16] Further, the failure of any author before Cicero to mention the Seventh Letter is scientifically meaningless. No definite conclusions can be drawn from it. This is only the weakest of several grounds for judging that all of Edelstein's arguments about attestation are contentious. Here are some stronger ones.

Edelstein is aggrieved that no one before Cicero vouches for the epistle. Nevertheless, he is perfectly willing to reject the letter's assertion that Dion's friendship with Callippus was "not based on philosophy" (οὐκ ἐκ φιλοσοφίας, 333e1–2), to ignore Plutarch's acceptance of that disavowal, and to embrace the only writers of antiquity who say that Callippus was Plato's student, Athenaeus and Diogenes Laertius[17]—even though he ea-

---

14. Ibid., 49.

15. Ibid., 38, 114, 111.

16. Cf. R. Hackforth, *The Authorship of the Platonic Epistles;* and W. K. C. Guthrie, *A History of Greek Philosophy,* esp. the table on 401. See also the critique of higher criticism by Thomas L. Pangle, "Editor's Introduction," in *The Roots of Political Philosophy: Ten Forgotten Socratic Dialogues,* by Plato.

17. Cf. Plutarch, *Dion* 54.1; Athenaeus of Naucratis, *The Deipnosophists* 11.508c; and Diogenes Laertius, "Plato," in *Lives of Eminent Philosophers,* 3.46. The title of the book

gerly pounces on all of Plutarch's apparent divergences from the epistle, and even though the later authors wrote in the third century A.D., some 550 years after Plato, and one and a half or two centuries after Plutarch. It seems that despite the discrepancies between the ancient sources, and despite the relative distances of these sources from the events, Athenaeus and Diogenes are cited about Callippus by nearly every modern commentator who has an ax to grind with the author of the Seventh Letter, or with Plato himself.

Furthermore, the epistle does not present itself as "Plato's autobiography," or as his *"apologia pro vita sua."* It purports to be Plato's reply to certain dubious persons who have demanded his assistance in a political conflict. To insist that the letter give unique or full autobiographical data is to act in blatant disregard of its literary character. Edelstein is not "entitled" to the data that he "wishes." He has a right only to that information which the author of the epistle believes relevant to his business with the bellicose men to whom he is writing. In a highly charged situation in which a real, or even a fictitious, Plato is explaining why he might well refuse to support a possibly misguided and illicit adventure, it might be quite understandable that he does not think to include material that would interest his later biographers, saying to people who are probably thugs: "Oh, by the way, when I was a young man, I wanted to be a poet, and I later studied with Cratylus." Similarly, it might be forgivable that he forgets to ascertain which facts about his life will be unknown to his biographers, so that he can authenticate his letter with a personal revelation, or that he does after all let such a revelation slip, disclosing to his correspondents a memory of his youthful political aspirations, of which he had unfortunately neglected to inform Aristotle. It is indicative of the biased nature of Edelstein's argument that he damns the author both for making and for not making such unique revelations. Another warning sign of prejudice is Edelstein's misuse of Aristotle to undermine the letter's description of Plato's youthful political ambitions. It is extremely hard to miss the fact that the text that Edelstein cites, *"Metaphysics* I, 6," neither says nor "implies" anything about the young Plato's choice of a career. Aristotle is busy here with a summary of different philosophies of being and their intellectual relationships; he is not writing biography.

Second, chronology. Dionysius I was a warlord who spent his entire life in a vain effort to expel the Carthaginians from the western part of Sicily,

---

by Athenaeus translates into English as *The Sophists at Dinner.* The book is filled with gossip. Athenaeus makes his character Pontianus deliver a scurrilous attack on Plato, one characterized by inconceivably stupid arguments, distortions, and bald-faced lies. Given the nature of this diatribe, one suspects that Athenaeus simply invented a vicious story about Plato's teaching of Callippus and that this falsehood became a tradition.

to keep the native Sicel population of the island subservient to Syracuse; to subjugate the Peloponnesian and Chalcidic Greek cities of the northern, eastern, and southern Sicilian seaboards to his imperial rule; and to extend his power into the Tyrrhenian, Ionian, and Adriatic Seas. In the desperate struggles that this first Dionysius precipitated in every campaigning season for thirty-eight years, aristocrats whom he had driven from Syracuse and the cities that cherished their liberties tenaciously opposed him. When Dionysius defeated his enemies (the nobility, cities that resisted him courageously and well, cities that were the oldest and staunchest allies of Carthage, and rebel Sicels), he did not treat them gently. In 402 B.C., he ousted the Syracusean aristocrats from Aetna, leaving the place empty until Carthage settled it with Campanian mercenaries. Between 402 and 400, he destroyed Naxos and Catane, and sold their citizens into slavery. In 397, he conquered the barbarian city of Motya, selling its population into slavery, except for Motyan Greeks who had helped Carthage, whom he crucified. In 387, he annihilated Rhegium, in the toe of Italy. When his sieges of free cities failed, he laid their countrysides waste, causing mass starvations that must have decimated their populations. This is to say nothing of his punishments of insurgent Sicels.[18] So, it is misleading to assert that at the death of Dionysius I, no cities in Sicily or in his wider theater of operations were depopulated. If the real Plato wrote the Seventh Letter, he might have been thinking of Naxos, Catane, Motya, Rhegium, and other places that were reeling from the effects of the tyrant's tender mercies. He need not have been showing an embarrassing foresight of the devastation that followed the fall of Dionysius II and the assassination of Dion. Even if we did not know these things, Edelstein would have to explain how an "impressive writer," and a person of "great philosophic acumen," who was working only twelve to twenty years after Plato's death, could have been ignorant of the historical situation in which he was setting his forgery. As for Dion, one suspects that he fancied himself an ethical but shrewd practitioner of realpolitik. The fact that he negotiated with the Carthaginians does not mean that he had no plan to ultimately get rid of them.

Third, doctrines. It is highly doubtful that Plato's dialogues purvey a core of his essential teachings from which a forger of the Seventh Letter could diverge, for his central insights are probably unspoken. However, if we grant Edelstein's premise for the sake of argument, his attacks on the epistle still appear to prove only that he comprehends neither what is said

18. For an interesting biography of the tyrant, see Brian Caven, *Dionysius I: Warlord of Sicily.* Caven seems to be so impressed by Dionysius that he cannot understand why any reasonable person would have objected to the warlord's tyranny. In his view, all the ancient criticisms, Plato's first and foremost, were unfair. The issues raised by Caven would be worth a scholarly article in another venue; they cannot be addressed here.

in the dialogues nor what is written by the allegedly false Plato, as seen in the following examples.

It is true that in the course of telling the story of the origin of Dion's views, the Plato of the letter calls Socrates his "aged friend" (φίλον πρεσβύτερον, 324d9–e1). Edelstein wants him to confess that Socrates was more, a teacher who taught him the doctrines that he later transmitted to Dion, rather than claiming to be entirely self-taught. Only in this manner could the author of the epistle testify to the "significance" that Plato's encounter with Socrates had for him. Edelstein thus reveals that he has no grasp of Socrates' concept of teaching, or that he fails to take it seriously. In the *Theaetetus* (149a–151c), the function that Socrates claims for himself is that of the midwife. He has no wisdom, and teaches nothing. However, by means of his art, all whom the god may have permitted (ἂν ὁ θεὸς παρείκῃ, 150d4) have found themselves pregnant with beautiful things and have brought them forth, the delivery being due to the god and himself (ὁ θεός τε καὶ ἐγὼ αἴτιος, 150d8–e1; see *Apology* 33a5–6). Accordingly, Socrates would have considered even the slave boy in the *Meno* to be "self-taught," that is, at least not taught the geometric demonstration by a human teacher. Moreover, in the *Republic*, Socrates declares that education consists in an art of "the turning around" (τῆς περιαγωγῆς, 518d3–4) of the soul, and he denies that it is a matter of putting vision (that is, knowledge) into the soul (518d5). These passages are inconsistent with Edelstein's idea of teaching as a transmission of doctrines.

Further, in calling Socrates his "friend," the Plato of the epistle might be paying him the highest honor and alluding to the great significance that Socrates had for him. Imagining how Dion might have reacted had Plato not traveled to the court of Dionysius II, the author has Dion addressing him as the one who above all is able "to exhort young people to the good and the just and thus to bring them on every occasion to friendship and comradeship toward one another" (328d6–e1). If this defines the work of a "friend," it also describes what Socrates did for the Plato of the letter, depicting Socratic midwifery in Dion's language.

An incomprehension of Socratic teaching is also evident in the assertion that Plato would have "initiated Dionysius into Platonism" if he had wanted to transform him into a philosopher-king. Once again leaving aside the question of whether there is such a thing as "Platonism," I should think that a Plato who believed with Socrates that education turns souls around rather than implanting vision in them would have tried to guide Dionysius through a turning ascent to philosophy, and that he would have stopped short of the highest studies if the tyrant's soul had shown itself incapable of negotiating lower stages of the turn. Thus, it is believable that Plato "never" spoke to Dionysius about serious things, or that he did so "only once" (345a2–3), as Plato actually says.

The Seventh Letter's surprisingly temperate treatment of the Athenian democracy might reflect implicit hints in the *Republic* that for all its faults, democracy is still the one defective regime that is usually willing to allow philosophy to thrive privately (557b–558c; see *Apology* 31e1–32a2). Indeed, a democracy might even let philosophy flourish publicly, despite the fact that a large proportion of its citizen body has been provoked by a voluble philosopher. Socrates would have been acquitted if he had happened to draw thirty more jurors who were favorably disposed to him (*Apology* 36a5–6)—this is the first and most obvious sense in which his death could legitimately be attributed to bad luck—and Plato himself lived and philosophized in the Athenian democracy unmolested, which could not have occurred under the rule of the Thirty. Further, it is not "equality" that Socrates rejects in the *Republic*, but "a certain equality" (ἰσότητά τινα) that democracy dispenses "to equals and unequals alike" (558c5–6). In the *Laws*, the Athenian Stranger, whose words Edelstein seems to catch only in snatches, praises a "truest and best equality" (ἀληθεστάτην καὶ ἀρίστην ἰσότητα) that distributes "more to the greater and less to the lesser," thus giving "to each according to its own nature measure" (757b6–c3). This also looks like a "principle" of the *Republic*. There is no reason the real Plato could not have been thinking of the "truest and best equality" in recommending "equal laws" to the epistle's recipients, who were likely to have been bent on something quite different.

Edelstein is right to quote Socrates as teaching in the *Republic* that it makes no difference whether the just city that has been founded in speech exists in heaven but not on earth (592b1–5). However, he conveniently misses what comes just before that, Socrates' comment that the man who has intelligence will not partake of the politics of his fatherland "unless some divine chance happens to occur" (ἐὰν μὴ θεία τις συμβῇ τύχη, 592a7–9). The author of the Seventh Letter reports that Dion enticed him to Syracuse by asking how he and Plato could want opportunities better than those now presented by "a certain divine chance" (θεία τινὶ τύχῃ, 327e4–5). Dion was arguing that Socrates' condition had been met. So, if Socrates spoke for Plato, it would have been reasonable for Plato to worry that refusing Dion would make him a man of "mere words," that is, that it would unmask him as a big talker who boasted bravely and nobly about what he would do if he had the opportunity but then failed to do it when the chance came. Further, the author of the epistle speaks of going to Syracuse to educate a ruler, not to get into politics himself. His intention thus bears at least a vague resemblance to what the Athenian Stranger does in the *Laws*.

The passage on chance cited by Edelstein (*Laws* 709a1–c4) says not that human art always overrides god and fortune, or that it can never be overridden by them, but that it "accompanies" (συγχωρῆσαι, 709c1) them, and that it is gentler than they. The Athenian Stranger's next speech makes it abundantly clear that a happy land needs *both* good luck and a legislator who knows the truth. Edelstein has misread the text again. Generally, we need to learn more about the Platonic concept of fortune.

Contrary to Edelstein's claim that the *Phaedrus* says "nothing" about the impossibility of verbal expression of Plato's serious insights, Stanley Rosen argues that in that dialogue, "philosophy, narrowly understood, is throughout a silent vision of beings, the hyperuranian beings."[19] Rosen is right. It will also be seen below that Edelstein's objections to the so-called philosophical digression are ill-conceived.

If this is not enough to show that Edelstein's doctrinal debunkings of the epistle are invalid, I would refer readers to Margherita Isnardi-Parente's comparison of the philosophic doctrines of the "philosophical digression" of the Seventh Letter with the teachings of certainly Platonic dialogues. Her meticulous analysis is vastly superior to anything offered by Edelstein or, for that matter, by anybody else. After much reflection, Isnardi-Parenti leans strongly in favor of judging the epistle authentic.[20]

Fourth, Plato's *Apology*. In antiquity, as in modernity, Plato undoubtedly had his share of accusers. It is right to observe that the Seventh Letter occasionally pauses to deny charges that Greek critics lodged against the philosopher. However, we are obliged to consider an obvious possibility: Perhaps Plato was entirely innocent and had a right to defend himself against unjust slander. It is difficult to guess what might have happened in Syracuse if Plato had not "meddled." However, let us imagine that Plato had never gone there and had never educated Dion. Dion was the brother of the Syracusean wife of Dionysius I and was later married to his sister's daughter. Dionysius II was the son of the tyrant's Locrian wife. Why should we not assume that a clever but un-Platonic Dion would have murdered both of the Dionysii at an opportune time, thus securing the tyranny for himself and his own or his sister's progeny, or thereby plunging Syracuse into civil war and destroying its empire a quarter century before this occurred? We must also recall that it is not proved that Callippus and his brother had any connection with the Academy or philosophy. Nonetheless, let us suppose that they were associated with the Academy. What of it? Do good teachers or good parents never have students or children who ignore their instructions?[21] Finally, Edelstein simply misrepresents Aristotle's analysis of Callippus. At *Rhetoric* 1373a19,[22] Aristotle is describing the

19. Rosen, *Hermeneutics as Politics*, 68–69.

20. Isnardi-Parente, *Filosofia e Politica nelle Lettere di Platone*, chap. 2. I am grateful to my generous friend and colleague Michael Fleet for translating this material from the Italian into English for my use.

21. There is an excellent discussion of the possible relationships between Callippus and the Academy in Kurt von Fritz, *Platon in Sizilien und das Problem der Philosophenherrschaft*, 133–34.

22. This is Edelstein's citation. See all of *Rhetoric* 1373a18–21. Speaking of the attitudes characteristic of the perpetrators of evil deeds, Aristotle says that in a case like that of Callippus, the act appears not unjust to him.

state of mind in which Callippus had Dion murdered. The assassin had met Dion in Athens and had attached himself to a rising star, becoming one of Dion's field commanders. By the time Dion toppled Dionysius II, Callippus had conceived some grievance against him—probably that Dion was not constructing a new tyranny in which Callippus would be the greatest minister—and he believed it just to have his leader killed.[23] Aristotle's remark does not even remotely imply that there were people who were "close to the Academy" and "actually defended Callippus."

These refutations of Edelstein do not establish that the real Plato writes the Seventh Letter. They merely reduce Edelstein's "certainty" about the provenance of the epistle to uncertainty. We should like a more substantial basis for a study that contemplates treating the letter as a key to the interpretation of Plato.

The best discussion of the problem of validating Platonic writings is Friedrich Schleiermacher's. Although Schleiermacher is fully aware of a difficulty in starting with Aristotle's attestations—who will certify that the certifier is really Aristotle?—he agrees to begin with the usual assumption that the dialogues mentioned by Aristotle are genuine, those in the "first rank" being the *Phaedrus, Protagoras, Parmenides, Theaetetus, Sophist, Statesman, Phaedo, Philebus, Republic* (to which I add the *Laws*), and—by affinity with the *Republic*—the *Timaeus* and *Critias*. To judge the remaining publications in the traditional corpus, Schleiermacher does not consult other ancient catalogs, for he regards them as unreliable. Rather, he says, each writing must authenticate itself by passing three tests. One of the tests is *not* agreement of a disputed piece with doctrines in the accepted works, for this would deny Plato a right that everybody else has, that of changing his mind. The first test examines the writing's language, applying stylometrics. Schleiermacher, whose Greek is excellent, doubts that any modern scholar knows enough Greek to render this measure decisive. The second test is that of characteristic subject matter, which suffers from the defect that Plato might have ventured into new areas from time to time. The third, and surely the best, test looks to the most important characteristics of Plato's unity of form and composition. The writing must spread charm and beauty over everything. It must also "compel the soul of the reader to its own conception of ideas," whether by frequent recommencements of investigations from other perspectives that are nevertheless led back to a common middle point, by apparently capricious lines of thought, by the concealment of the greater aim under a lesser one, or by a dialectical commerce in concepts.[24]

Whether the Seventh Letter meets the first criterion is much disputed. As

23. Cf. Plutarch's account of the plot of Callippus, in *Dion* 54, 50–57.5.
24. Schleiermacher, "Einleitung," 23–33; Schleiermacher, *Introductions to the Dialogues*, 26–40.

noted above, Edelstein thinks that the style of the Seventh Letter is Plato's. The contrary is argued by modern experts in stylometrics who do computer analyses. These scholars presuppose that classical Greeks had styles of which they were not conscious. The unconscious styles show up, for example, in the numbers of times that authors use *kai* and in the numbers of words that they tend to place between the definite article and the noun. A statistical investigation that measures such factors in the Seventh Letter, the *Apology*, later Platonic dialogues, and an epistle of Speusippus is said to prove that the letter could not have been written by Plato and that it was probably the work of Speusippus. It may be that this computer analysis has been more influential than Edelstein's book in persuading contemporary linguists that the Seventh Letter is fraudulent. However, one need not be awed by its reasoning. Let it be granted for the sake of argument that Plato was subject to some law of unconscious style. Why should we imagine that Plato had only one unconscious style? We all know perfectly well that without thinking, we speak differently to babies, children, adults, dull and bright students, foreigners, and experts and laymen in our fields. We also know that we write our scientific works one way and our personal letters another. Our styles in all these types of speaking and writing might be subject to subconscious urges yet different from each other. The authors also claim that their method proves that parts of the *Laws* and other dialogues were either written or revised by Speusippus. I cannot disprove this, but I would appeal to the considerations just adduced. I do not see why unconscious drives could not have dictated different styles in the same dialogues, the results perhaps depending on unaccountable factors such as how well Plato slept from night to night, or on his mood swings. I should also think that Aristotle would have known and mentioned the intervention of Speusippus in the *Laws* rather than treating the dialogue as a work by Plato.[25]

It also happens that there are strong adherents of computer analysis who believe that Plato could have written the Seventh Letter.[26] Stylometrics thus leaves us as uncertain about its proper conclusions as the original nineteenth-century higher criticism did. Therefore, I feel free to follow the lead of Schleiermacher, reject stylometrics as the decisive test of Platonic authenticity, and ask whether the Seventh Letter passes Schleiermacher's other tests.

Schleiermacher's second criterion is characteristic subject matter. The Seventh Letter clearly satisfies this measure. I believe that full analysis will

25. The skeptics are M. Levison, A. Q. Morton, and A. D. Winspear, "The Seventh Letter of Plato." These authors need to explain to their readers how they solve the well-known GIGO problem, if they do.

26. Philip Deane, "Stylometrics Do Not Exclude the Seventh Letter." See also the perceptive and amusing comment of von Fritz, *Platon in Sizilien*, 10–11.

prove that it also passes the third test. It does compel souls to bounteous new conceptions by means of fresh starts, seemingly erratic sallies, and concealments. Therefore, I think that I see Plato's hand in it. For me, this justifies putting the epistle at the head of my inquiry. Of course, I shall not be able to show that Plato certainly composed the document. Skeptics will object that Schleiermacher's tests are wrong, or too subjective in their application. There is no way to obtain stronger evidence. Accordingly, I shall end these reflections with a stipulation and a question. I judge that the letter was probably written by Plato, but I concede that it could have been produced by a first-generation disciple, probably Speusippus,[27] who had mastered Plato's philosophical art. If the letter is not authentic, should we not assume that its highly accomplished forger knows Plato better than we do, especially if he is Speusippus? In the study to which I now proceed, I shall avail myself of the convenience of calling the author of the epistle Plato.

THE LITERARY CHARACTER AND PLAN OF THE LETTER

Let us suppose that Plato's authorship of the Seventh Letter were attested beyond the shadow of a doubt by Speusippus, or Aristotle, or anyone we wished. This would still not tell us what kind of a writing the document is. As seen in the case of Edelstein, ignoring the nature of a Platonic publication can cause gross misrepresentations of its argument. We need to know what the epistle is. Meditation on the letter has led me to three hypotheses about its character and plan, which I shall declare at the outset.

First, it may be that in 353 B.C., there really were men who wrote to Plato demanding his help with a countercoup, and that Plato actually replied to them. It may also be that Dion's murder inspired Plato to concoct a fiction in which he invented his correspondents, and some or all of his anecdotes, as a pretext for reflecting on the events in Syracuse in an open or privately circulated letter. It does not matter which of these scenarios holds, for the crucial point is that the epistle is a poem deftly created to achieve its author's aims. Whether the letter is a historically factual or a fictitious poem, it is the poet's purposes that count. What are these ends? Plato's enemies allege that he is trying to cover up his guilt for the Syracusean disaster. Perhaps his friends would argue that a grief-stricken Plato is writing an elegy to his beloved Dion. Although the letter contains possible traces of such motives, both of these accounts disregard what it strives to do as a whole, namely, to make the relationships among politics, philosophy, and the highest realities and truths visible in the context of a practical effort to

---

27. Cf. Levison, Morton, and Winspear, "Seventh Letter of Plato," 321.

yoke philosophy with historically existing power. It is this intention that requires the *poiēsis*.[28] The story of Plato's experiment, whether it is factual or partially or entirely fictitious, must be told with great artistry if the souls of readers are to be enabled to see the relationships in question against the backdrop of an attempt to make power philosophic.

Given that the epistle has this character and design, one must submit to its poetry to learn what Plato hopes to convey. As an example of submitting to poetry, I would urge that nobody could profit from *A Midsummer Night's Dream* by caviling incessantly about the doubtful historicity of sprites and fairies. To be uplifted by Shakespeare, we must get into the spirit of his play, accept the existence of Puck and the others, and see to what noble heights we can be led from there.[29] Similarly, to be educated by the Seventh Letter, we must get into the spirit of the poem, allow the epistle to be what it purports to be, cheerfully grant the existence of Plato's correspondents and his trustworthy belief in the factuality of the narrative, and try to discover to what truths all this is meant to guide us. Then, when we come to decide whether Plato's teaching is beneficial for us, we shall praise or criticize not his story, which is only a mythical vehicle even if it is factual, but its moral. In doing this, we shall be according the letter the same treatment that we give to the Platonic dialogues.

Second, the plan of the Seventh Letter seems obscure, not only to classicists whose chief interests are linguistic, but to individuals of philosophic competence, too. Thus, the epistle bewilders and frustrates its readers. For example, R. G. Bury, the Loeb translator, contends that Plato repeatedly departs from the stated purpose of his letter, namely, "to offer 'counsel' to Dion's friends," in order to defend himself against Athenian accusations of misbehavior in Syracuse. Bury asserts that owing to this, the epistle is "somewhat confused" and "full of digressions," having "only one page . . . out of nearly thirty" devoted to its "professed object." More alarmingly, the letter has a long "philosophical digression" of which it is "difficult to see the relevance." There might be general scholarly agreement on this point, for it is easy to find learned essays on "the philosophical digression" that treat it as if it were separable from the rest of the epistle. Some also maintain that the excursus itself is muddled. One especially confident scholar feels moved to help its poor, struggling author by striking statements that do not make good logical sense from its text.[30]

---

28. *"Poiēsis"* means "the making of poetry."
29. I would make the same argument about all of the bard's historical plays. Shakespeare takes liberties with facts in order to present his profound questions and insights. So what?
30. Bury, "Epistle VII: Prefatory Note," 471, 463, 469, 473–74, 471–72; Nicholas P. White, *Plato on Knowledge and Reality*, chap. 8; Hans-Georg Gadamer, "Dialektik und Sophistik im siebenten Platonischen Brief," chap. 6 (see also the bibliography on 92–

Commentators have been protesting that Plato's plans are obscure and that his writings meander ever since Aristotle, surely with his tongue in his cheek, said that Plato had filled the *Republic* up with digressions (τοῖς ἔξωθεν λόγοις πεπλήρωκε, *Politics* 1264b39). The reason for this is obvious. As already noted in Schleiermacher's analysis, it is Plato's authentic trademark to write with frequent recommencements of investigations from other perspectives that are nevertheless led back to a common middle point, apparently capricious lines of thought, concealments of the greater aim under a lesser, and a dialectical commerce in concepts. I think that we shall find an apparent philosophical digressiveness that really is purposeful in the Seventh Letter, thus disposing us to believe that Plato composed it, or to applaud the admirable forger who saw that he had to imitate his teacher's playfulness.

If Friedrich Schleiermacher is right, Plato wrote this way in order to cloak his real investigation with an adhesive skin that hides what ought to be seen from the inattentive, and that sharpens and clears the *Sinn* of the attentive for the inner connection. If Leo Strauss or Stanley Rosen is correct, he does it in order to communicate esoterically with the wise and to befuddle the many, or to prepare them for their eventual enlightenment. In any of these cases, there are two possible responses to the epistle's crazy-quilt nature. One can say: "This is confused, full of digressions from the stated purpose, irrelevant, and illogically stupid," and then lay the document aside in perplexed disappointment, or even revise its text. This might be the reaction of the philosophically incompetent, whom Plato is glad to excuse from further conversation. Or, one can try to cooperate with the letter's poetry, recognizing that its *poiēsis* is calculated to compel closer attention to how the many new beginnings are led back to a common middle point, how its apparent caprice is wholly rational, and how lesser stated aims both conceal and reveal greater ones. I shall assume that this is the response that Plato hopes to evoke. Thus, I shall presuppose that the teaching of the letter has not been mastered by anyone who cannot show how all its parts fit together, or by someone who cannot explain why the "philosophical digression" is fully intelligible not in itself, but only as a part of the whole, so that it is not really a digression at all.[31]

In this setting, submitting to the Seventh Letter's poetry will mean starting with, and watching closely, the plan of the writing that Plato embeds in its surface, and moving from there to the real substance that he wants the

---

93 n. 8) (the Gadamer essay is translated into English in "Dialectic and Sophism in Plato's Seventh Letter," chap. 5); Andreas Graeser, *Philosophische Erkenntnis und begriffliche Darstellung: Bemerkungen zum erkenntnistheoretischen Exkurs des VII. Briefs,* 16.

31. In this, I must even disagree with Voegelin's comment that the larger part of the epistle has only a "loose" connection with the advice that Plato gives to his correspondents (*Order and History,* 3:15).

attentive to perceive. Plato supplies the superficial outline by announcing changes of subject matter. The titles and Stephanus pages of Plato's sections may be listed as follows: (1) "You Wrote to Me with Orders" (Ἐπεστείλατέ μοι, 323d6–324b4); (2) "The Manner of the Origin of Dion's Opinion" (δόξα, 324b5–330b7); (3) "Counsel" (330b8–337e4); and (4) "My Return to the Court of Dionysius II, and How It Was Most Probable and Just" (ὡς εἰκότα τε καὶ δίκαια, 337e5–end). Alternatively, the last section may be titled "The Later Journey by Sea to the Court of Dionysius II, and How It Occurred Most Probably and Harmoniously" (ὡς εἰκότως τε ἅμα καὶ ἐμμελῶς). (The two Greek phrases in the fourth titles come from 330c4 and 337e5, respectively.)

Third, how can one cooperate with the poetry of the Seventh Letter and move from the plan just given to Plato's real substance? I think that one does this by participating in the narrative imaginatively and actively. Two examples from Plato's outline will suffice. Plato's transition from the first to the second sections of his missive consists in the remark that now is an opportune time to tell the story of the origin of Dion's opinion. One must imagine that the rough soldiers whom Plato addresses will wonder what this topic has to do with their demand, and why the moment is right. Plato's jump from the third to the fourth parts of his letter is an invitation extended to anyone who might be interested in his story to listen to it. Again, one can picture those combatants who have persevered this far asking in amazement why they should be interested. "Active participation" means putting oneself in their place and mulling these problems over. Two outcomes of such imaginative reconstruction are possible. The irascible soldiers, and their modern academic counterparts, could exclaim in exasperation: "This man is a doddering old windbag who can't stick to the point!" Such individuals would lay the letter down, and that would be the end of their serious instruction by Plato. Others, after extending themselves beyond what they had believed to be their capacities, could begin to see excellent reasons that Plato's moves are the only ones that make rational sense at those junctures. Their education by the philosopher would continue. I think that those who follow the latter route will find themselves in absorbing conversation with Plato. This is another sense in which the Seventh Letter is a poem. The document really is a dialogue in which Plato himself is the protagonist and his capable readers are the interlocutors; the poet's art makes himself and the thoughtful members of his audiences into characters in his myth.

Although I have proclaimed these hypotheses about the literary character and plan of the letter in advance, I do not expect that they should be accepted on faith. This is an affair in which the proverb holds absolutely true: The proof of the pudding will be in the eating. We may now turn to a substantive analysis of each of the sections of the epistle.

"You Wrote to Me with Orders"

The epistle begins with Plato's formulaic wish of well-doing to "Dion's household associates and companions" (Δίωνος οἰκείοις τε καὶ ἑταίροις, 323d7–8). This greeting and the letter as a whole are not addressed to Dion's "friends," as they are made to do by careless translators and commentators. Ancient Greek household associates and companions might be "friends" in modern eyes, but not in Plato's estimation. The importance of this distinction will become apparent in due course.

My arbitrary heading for this section of the epistle quotes the first words of its opening sentence: "You wrote to me with orders to suppose that your intention (διάνοιαν) was the same as Dion's, and, further, you exhorted me to make common cause with it, as far as I can, both by deed and word" (323d9–324a1). Having summarized the demand made upon him, Plato answers that he will consent if his correspondents really have the same opinion and desire (δόξαν καὶ ἐπιθυμίαν, 324a2) as Dion, but, otherwise, he will have to think about it many times. Further, he will tell the addressees what Dion's intention and desire were, not from conjecture, but from certain knowledge. When Plato was about forty, he had made Dion's acquaintance in Syracuse, Dion then having been about the same age as Hipparinus (Dion's son) now.[32] Dion had then arrived at a conclusion from which he never deviated, that the Syracuseans should be free and live under the best laws. It would not be surprising if a certain one of the gods (τις θεῶν, 324b3) caused Hipparinus to adhere to the same view now. Plato concludes this introduction by giving notice that he will relate the manner of the origin of Dion's opinion, a story that is worth hearing for both young and old, because the moment is right (καιρὸν, 324b7).

Whether the addressees are real or fictitious, they surely must be annoyed by this opening. They have claimed to share Dion's intention, but Plato, with his conditional "if," has expressed doubt as to whether they really hold Dion's opinion and desire. He has also failed to tell them how they can persuade him, and he has passed up an apparently perfect opportunity to do so. That is, he has given them a concise (albeit vague) formulation

32. There is a major difficulty here. It is doubtful, but not altogether impossible, that Plato is referring to a Hipparinus who was Dion's nephew, the son of Dionysius I and Dion's sister, and who was briefly tyrant of Syracuse after the death of Callippus. It is more likely that Plato means a son of Dion. Yet, according to Plutarch, Dion's only son died shortly before Dion, hurling himself from a roof in a fit of childish displeasure (cf. *Dion* 55.4). It might be a mark of the authenticity of the epistle that Plato does not know that he is referring to a dead youth, the news of the lad's accident not having reached him. A forger such as Speusippus, writing ten or twenty years after the event, would certainly be aware that Dion no longer had a son as of the pretended date of the letter (cf. Bury, "Epistle VIII: Prefatory Note," 569–70).

of Dion's intention, and he could have gone on to write, "Just furnish me with evidence that you agree, and then I shall help you," but he has neglected this courtesy. Further, they have insisted upon his aid, but he has been very evasive. Having hinted that a difference between their intention and Dion's opinion would cause him to think about their demand indefinitely, he has left the contingency hanging, and has not gotten around to promising or refusing help here or anywhere else in the letter. Instead, he has apparently become distracted and hazy. He has paid a pious compliment to Hipparinus without extending it to all the household associates and companions, without indicating why it is pertinent, and without explaining why it would not be surprising if a god has blessed the young man with devotion to freedom and the best laws. Then he has heralded the story of the genesis of Dion's opinion, without saying what his purpose in telling the tale is, or why it will be valuable for young and old, or why the time for it is right. Compounding this ambiguity, he has not stated what his aim in writing the epistle is. Particularly, he has not mentioned that the purpose of the letter is to give advice to its addressees. Everyone must wonder what his intention is, if he has one.

It is obvious here that one has already come to Plato's first digressions and that his real argument is beginning to vanish behind them. As I have suggested above, Plato now wants his good readers to articulate and pursue the questions that he dramatically raises. So, just why does Plato distrust the affirmation of the associates and companions that they cleave to Dion's intention? Why does he not invite them to prove that they want freedom under the best laws? Why does he give no definite answer to their demand? Why does he single Hipparinus out for the pious compliment? What thinking does this accolade reflect? Why does he meander off into the story about the origin of Dion's opinion? What is his general aim?

An adequate analysis of the problems should start with what is perfectly plain. The household associates and companions have maintained that they share Dion's intention and have demanded Plato's assistance. Plato has unexplained doubts about their claim to adhere to Dion's opinion and desire, but has promised to help them by deed and word if it is true. Let it be granted that Plato would really be happy to render aid to his correspondents if they had Dion's intention. It follows that Plato would have to determine whether they do have Dion's opinion and desire and that he must put off giving a definite yes or no until this issue has been resolved. Then why does he not request evidence that his addressees do share Dion's intention?

This question will be answered with another: How should the household associates and companions demonstrate that they hold Dion's opinion? Should they swear oaths that they are committed to freedom and the best laws? Should they provide affidavits that they have frequently been heard praising freedom and the best laws in the past, and that they have served in Dion's entourage and fought in his army for so many years? Should they offer to sit examinations on the natures of, and philosophic proofs about, freedom and the best laws? Let us assume that Plato is open to the possibility that they could do all this in a manner that convinced him of their sincerity and their ability to bandy definitions and syllogisms. If, nevertheless, he decides not to ask for these kinds of credentials, it seems proper to deduce that he doubts such evidence would demonstrate that his correspondents are dedicated to Dion's intention. There could be three obstacles to such a judgment.

First, Plato might not admit that human beings acquire true opinions by hearing their verbal formulations and experiencing positive feelings about them, or by learning a few logical arguments about them and then proclaiming their validity. One recalls that in the *Republic,* Socrates urges Glaucon and Adeimantus to give the soldiers of the just city a musical education to true opinion. In doing so, they must understand that long imitation settles "into habit and nature" (εἰς ἔθη τε καὶ φύσιν, 395d2); they must strive to regulate imitation and thus to inculcate "beautiful habit in the soul" (τῇ ψυχῇ καλὰ ἔθη, 402d1–2). If Plato agrees with Socrates on this point, he might be worried that people who entertain opinions by virtue of emotional agreement with a speech or facile manipulation of logical terms have not genuinely appropriated them. A peek ahead in the letter seems to confirm that Plato has some such concern. One finds that he disapproves of certain pests in Syracuse who are "stuffed with some things heard incidentally from philosophy" (παρακουσμάτων τινῶν ἔμμεστοι τῶν κατὰ φιλοσοφίαν, 338d3–4). He also fears that Dionysius II might be "stuffed with things heard incidentally" (τοῖς τῶν παρακουσμάτων μεστοῖς, 340b6). It appears that in the pathological state envisaged, people have filled their heads with phrases caught from here and there and repeat them without having any real grounding for them in their souls, such as might be found, perhaps, in long habituation. In this diseased condition, they do not hold the opinions that they fervently mouth, or have an inner attachment to the realities behind their words, any more than talking parrots do, no matter how sincere or logically skillful they are. The hypothesis that Plato insists upon habituation to true opinion seems to be supported further by his expression of the negative concern that no one could become wise (φρόνιμος, 326c2) by practicing the hedonistic Italian-Sicilian way of life "from youth" (ἐκ νέου, 326c3). Thus, Plato might doubt that Dion's associates really adhere to Dion's opinion and desire because he wonders whether their convictions about freedom and the best laws are rooted in passion and the intellectual pretensions of logicians or in solid habit. Plato's correspondents might only be "stuffed."

Second, in giving his correspondents a capsule statement of Dion's intention and desire, Plato has included the observation that Dion held his views unchangingly. This suggests that Plato looks upon sharing in an intention not only as a matter of acquiring an opinion by habituation, but also as one in which strength of character stabilizes the soul's commitment to the corresponding desire. This account would recall that in the *Republic*, Socrates believes that Glaucon and Adeimantus resist the sophistic view of justice because he trusts their characters (368b1–3). It would also be reminiscent of Socrates' great fear in the *Republic* that the guardians might lose the opinion that they should always do what is best for the city, and of his plan for tests of the guardians' ability to remain steadfast against forgetting, argument, pain, and pleasure (412e–414a). Another glance ahead in the epistle appears to verify that Plato has something like this in mind. Plato reports that when he was debating with himself the question of whether he should undertake his first visit to the court of Dionysius II, he was anxious about the volatility of the desires of the young. If desires depend upon opinions, this implies that he was also worried about the fluidity of youthful opinions. His decision to go to Syracuse hinged upon his knowledge that the nature of Dion's soul was stable, Dion now being sufficiently measured (μετρίως, 328b2–6). However, the souls of Plato's addressees might not be stable.

Third, in declaring that it would not be surprising if a god has caused Hipparinus to adopt his father's opinion, Plato might be disguising the most important point as a chance offhand remark. That is, he might be indicating that divine intervention is a prerequisite for receiving the habituation that makes an inner attachment to the opined realities of true opinion possible, for possessing the strength of character needed to have a stable matching desire, and perhaps also for being able to envisage and believe the truth.

As in the previous two cases, this interpretation would be reminiscent of statements in the *Republic*. There, Socrates ponders the chances of educating the young to virtue in the face of the corrupting pressure exerted on them by the many. He comments: "For there is not, has not been, and will not be a different character with regard to virtue receiving an education against theirs, not humanly, O comrade; for the divine case, according to the proverb, we make an exception to the argument. For you should know well that, if anything is saved and becomes what it should in this condition of regimes, you will not speak badly by saying that a god's dispensation (θεοῦ μοῖραν) saved it" (492e2–493a2). Also, Socrates trusts the natures and characters of Glaucon and Adeimantus because they seem to be "affected by the divine" (θεῖον πεπόνθατε, 368a5–6).

Another look ahead in the letter finds Plato frequently making remarks that echo this Socratic view of the chances for right education, and of the prospects for extending its truth into right order. For example: (1) Repeating his praise of the right philosophy that he had made years earlier, Plato contends that there will be no end of evil until philosophy and power are joined through some dispensation of a god (ἔκ τινος μοίρας θείας, 326b3), thus quoting the phrase of *Republic* 493a1–2 almost verbatim, and conflating it with the call for the philosopher-king of *Republic* 473c2–e6. (2) Dion thought that perhaps Dionysius II could be converted to his intention with the assistance of the gods (ξυλλαμβανόντων θεῶν, 327c4), and Plato counts this as one of Dion's "right intentions" (327d7). (3) Even small measures of right opinion are bestowed by a certain divine fortune (θεία τις τύχη, 336e3). (4) Dion's friends must now carry out his and Plato's policy with the help of a divine dispensation and fortune (μοίρᾳ καὶ θείᾳ τινὶ τύχῃ, 337e2). (5) The alternative to being stuffed with some things heard incidentally from philosophy is to be "really philosophic, being familiar with and worthy of the matter by divine agency" (ὄντως ἦ φιλόσοφος οἰκεῖός τε καὶ ἄξιος τοῦ πράγματος θεῖος ὤν, 340c2–3). All this argues for the inferences that Plato attributes his philosophic character to divine dispensation, and that Dion had to thank the same divine agency for the true opinion that he had. If Dion had the god's favor, it might be reasonable to suppose that his son Hipparinus is also loved by the god. Then, one could expect him to have received from the god Dion's habituation to true opinion, his strong character, and his ability to envisage and believe truth. However, Plato has no grounds for assuming that his addressees are similarly graced.

One is inclined to think that Plato singles Hipparinus out for the pious compliment because he wants to signal the lad that he alone is likely to share Dion's intention, and that he alone is likely to grasp the argument of the letter. One also supposes that Plato jumps to the story of the origin of Dion's opinion because he hopes to ascertain whether the youth meets these expectations. Dion's household associates and companions will probably discard the epistle in disgust and storm out to their wars. If Hipparinus is divinely favored, he will pick it up, study it privately, become captivated by the account of the origin of his father's opinion because he recognizes his own experience in it, and reply to Plato with a thoughtful reflection on how he acquired his own views and how that process has formed his soul. This will be evidence that he shares in Dion's opinion and desire. Plato will help him, but not the other correspondents, if he sees such signs. Now is the opportune moment for Plato to tell the tale of the rise of Dion's opinion because his need to administer this test is immediate.

We may conclude that the opening of the Seventh Letter is not rambling and vague, as it appears, but concise and clear to the thoughtful. It suggests to the household associates and companions that sharing Dion's intention is a matter not of emotional or logical affirmation, but of arriving at his opinion and desire in the appropriate manner. It then implies a conditional offer to the possibly favored Hipparinus. The proposal will be veiled in order to avoid exposing Hipparinus to the risk of suffering Dion's fate.[33]

"The Manner of the Origin of Dion's Opinion"

Plato promises to narrate this story from the beginning. He relates that as a youth, he had planned to go into politics. When the Thirty Tyrants seized power, some of them were his relatives. They invited Plato to join them. Plato expected the Thirty to lead the city out of its unjust way of life into a just way (ἔκ τινος ἀδίκου βίου ἐπὶ δίκαιον τρόπον, 324d4–5). However, they were worse than their predecessors. Plato saw how they treated his "man-friend" (φίλον ἄνδρα, 324d9–e1), Socrates, the most just of men then living, when they attempted to force him to do an unholy deed. Plato therefore withdrew from public affairs. When the Thirty were overthrown, he felt the desire to get into politics again, but less strongly than before. The democrats committed atrocities, too, but they were relatively moderate. Yet by some chance (κατὰ δέ τινα τύχην, 325b5–6), certain democrats executed Plato's companion (ἑταῖρον, 325b6), Socrates, on an unholy charge of impiety that he, of all men, least deserved. Upon reflection, Plato concluded that it is difficult to manage the affairs of cities rightly, and impossible to act politically without men who are friends and trustworthy companions (ἄνευ φίλων ἀνδρῶν καὶ ἑταίρων πιστῶν, 325d1). Such individuals were not available. The prospects for finding new ones were bleak, for Athens was no longer governed according to the customs and practices of the city's fathers, and everything was being corrupted. Although Plato had been eager to participate in public affairs, and although he had continued to think about how things could be improved, looking for an opportunity to act, he eventually realized that all cities were badly governed and almost incurable without a prodigious preparation mixed with some fortune (τινὸς μετὰ τύχης, 326a5). So, he was compelled to declare (λέγειν τε ἠναγκάσθην) when praising the right philosophy (τὴν ὀρθὴν φιλοσοφίαν, 326a5–6) that by it one is enabled to discern (κατιδεῖν, 326a7) all forms of justice both political and private, and that there will be no end of evils in human affairs until right and true philosophers acquire power, or until rulers of cities become real philosophers through some divine dispensation (ἔκ τινος μοίρας θείας, 326b3).

Although this exposition of the rise of Dion's opinion has only begun, Plato has already said enough to raise questions in the minds of his ad-

---

33. Naturally, my assumption that the Seventh Letter is essentially a veiled communication to Hipparinus could be wrong. What I would defend more strongly than this supposition is my identification of the issues that the epistle tacitly discusses.

dressees. Why does Plato discuss his youthful wish to go into politics, and his abandonment of that desire in reaction to the evils of Athens, in an account of the manner of the origin of Dion's opinion? If, as Dion's household associates and companions are likely to imagine, he is recounting the rise of his doctrine of justice, and if he insists on telling the story of how he came by that theory and later transmitted it to Dion, should he not credit Socrates with being the source of his view? Then why does he call Socrates his "man-friend" and "companion" rather than his teacher? Why does he not talk about the logical arguments that Socrates made to him? Why, instead, does he tell the irrelevant tales of his reactions to the "unholy" ways in which Socrates, the most just and pious man then living, was treated by the Thirty Tyrants and the democrats? Why does he drop the apparently irrelevant remark that the execution of Socrates occurred by "some chance"? Why does he make his own participation in politics and the possibility of effective political action dependent upon having "men who are friends and trustworthy companions"? What does it mean for his correspondents that he has merely called them Dion's "associates" and "companions," adding that man-friends and trustworthy companions are hard to find in the poorly governed cities that are ubiquitous? Why does he say that the incurability of cities compels the conclusions that the right philosophy enables one to perceive all kinds of justice political and private, and that right philosopher rulers are needed to end evil? What are the right philosophy and the right philosopher? Are Dion's associates right philosophers? My surmise is that Plato probably expects most of these questions from those of his correspondents who are clever but not truly philosophic. He probably also hopes that a thoughtful Hipparinus, upon hearing his father's associates and companions raise these sorts of questions, will judge that several of them (but not all) are misconceived.

Hipparinus should notice first that the questions as initially formulated are premised on a correct inkling. Clearly, Plato discusses his early political experiences and his reactions to them because they are the paradigm for the rise of Dion's opinion. However, it should also be obvious to Hipparinus that Plato concentrates solely on these experiences and responses. The text has nothing to do with the genesis of a theory of justice that was created by Socrates, taught to Plato, and handed on to Dion. Next, Hipparinus should recognize that if Plato does not connect the mode of the origin of Dion's opinion with the invention and transmission of a doctrine of justice, the reason for this omission surely is that Dion's opinion did not arise that way.[34]

---

34. It is equally plain that the text goes no further into Plato's autobiography because his youthful desire for justice and his reaction to Athenian injustice are the only facts about his life that are relevant to the origin of Dion's opinion.

Having made this much progress, Hipparinus should ask how his father's comrades could have fallen into the error that I have woven into their questions. This might help him to see what Plato really is doing. In my reconstruction, the associates have perceived correctly that Plato opens his treatment of the origin of Dion's opinion with a recollection not simply of his youthful political experiences, but also of his early yearnings for justice and his disappointments over extremely grave injustices. Then, however, they have jumped to three closely related, but still analytically distinct, misunderstandings.

First, in proposing his youthful political experiences as the model for the rise of Dion's opinion, Plato wants Hipparinus to comprehend that he had an early desire for justice, and that he reacted justly to Athenian injustices. However, Dion's companions are probably stuffed with things heard incidentally from philosophy. Therefore, they will probably move from Plato's words to the inference that his justice consists in adherence to a propositional theory. Plato never says this, though. If Plato agrees with the Socrates of the *Republic,* as he well might do at this elementary level of analysis, his justice is an ordering of the city and the soul, not an embrace of an ethical creed that dictates actions.

Second, in relating his youthful craving for justice to the origin of Dion's opinion, Plato probably gives Dion's associates the idea that he means to say how he himself became just, that is, how he learned his doctrine of justice. However, Plato already wants justice at the beginning of his story. He does not tell how he came to do so. On the grounds of the reasoning above, one suspects that if Plato were to say how this happened, he would discuss how his soul and character were formed. Here, he would not report that he was convinced of a moral code by Socrates' preaching or logic, which would be the same as to confess that Socrates had stuffed him. Rather, he would probably attribute the ordering of his soul to a divinely fortuitous long habituation, a divinely bequeathed firm character, and a divinely inspired ability to opine the truth (see *Meno* 99c–100b). If asked about the actual role of Socrates in his education, he would probably say that when he was already pregnant with his longing for justice, Socrates helped to deliver him of his own just deeds and philosophic insights into justice. This is not to claim that Socrates offered Plato no moral and philosophic arguments. However, it is to suggest that Plato's education by Socrates depended upon Plato's already present disposition to resonate with Socrates' reasoning.

Third, seeing that Plato introduces his concern for justice into his account of the rise of Dion's view, and leaping from this observation to the conclusion that Plato is discussing the origin of an opinion about justice, the household associates and companions forget that what is really being considered is the genesis of Dion's intention and opinion that Syracuse should be free and governed by the best laws. Accordingly, they fail to notice that Plato is actually analyzing the indispensable steps between his juvenile political ambitions and the framing of Dion's policy, and they mistake what Plato says for totally irrelevant and senile wandering, which it certainly would be if what he intended was a history of ideas. In the real argument of Plato's text, the formulation of Dion's intention had to be preceded by three events: Plato's career had to begin as the perhaps somewhat inchoate yearning of a young soul for justice, and as the resistance of that soul to existing injustice. Next, Plato had to see that political action is impossible without men who are friends and trustworthy companions. Then he had to praise the right philosophy by declaring that it enables one to discern all forms of justice political and private, and that there will be no end of evil in human affairs until philosophy and power are joined.

Were a thoughtful Hipparinus to restate the questions that Plato wants asked at this juncture, he would begin by inquiring whether his father and he himself embarked upon their political careers with an innate longing for justice in their souls, coupled with spiritual revulsion against the injustices of the Syracusean regimes under which they lived. This would already suffice to open Hipparinus to the much deeper wonder that Plato wishes to instill in him, prepare him for new discoveries, and enhance the prospects that Plato will come to his aid.

Hipparinus should conceive his more profound wonder when he attends to the still untreated questions on the original list, and when he adds a new one to them. The first of the remaining queries is this: Why, of all things, does Plato choose to apply the term "man-friend" to Socrates? The new puzzle pertains to the argument just completed: Why were Plato's deductions about friends, the discernment of the types of justice, and the need for philosopher rulers the indispensable steps between his youthful desires and the framing of Dion's intention?

The phrases "man-friend" and "men who are friends and trustworthy companions" conjure up images of the *hetaireiai*,[35] that is, the friendship, comradeship, and political action clubs that Athenian men often formed. Plato implies that he, Socrates, and perhaps a few others were united in the fellowship of such an alliance. The outrages perpetrated against Socrates caused Plato to think that cities could not be governed well without *hetaireiai*. This deduction looks crass. It seems to be the hackneyed idea that a successful politician needs a power base or a party, a truism that is beneath Plato's dignity to utter. However, this is a vulgar exegesis that misunderstands the nature of the *hetaireiai* that Plato envisages.

Plato's actual argument appears to be this: The evils done to Socrates were products of the injustice that prevailed in Athens. The only remedy

35. Cf. Edelstein, *Plato's Seventh Letter,* 30–31.

for such rampant injustice is to cultivate as much goodness in a society as one can (see *Gorgias* 513e5–514a2). This involves finding the young people who are divinely inclined to justice and delivering them of the beautiful virtue, true opinion, and philosophy with which they are pregnant. Genuine, as distinguished from false, *hetaireiai* are the mechanisms for this, the only authentic political activity (see *Gorgias* 521d6–e2). The true friendship group is led by a real friend. Socrates is the only person whom Plato is willing to call his man-friend; he pointedly refrains from bestowing this title on Dion's associates. In genuine friendship, as opposed to the merely nominal friendships that most people contract, it is the work of the friend "to exhort young people to the good and the just and thus to bring them on every occasion to friendship and comradeship toward one another" (328d6–e1). Without the true friend, and without this leader's action upon the beautifully pregnant young that makes them into friends, justice is not likely to emanate from any group into the political order. Thus, effective politics is impossible without men who are friends and trustworthy companions.

Plato's discovery of this political truth was probably necessary to the rise of Dion's opinion because it drove Plato around the world in search of a virtuous youth and landed him in Syracuse, where he met Dion, struck up a true friendship with him, and delivered the lad of his just deeds and right intentions with the help of the god. One of the things that Dion seems to have understood is that politics must be conducted by means of genuine *hetaireiai*. Dion knew that he needed Plato to lead the young to goodness and friendship. Dion lured Plato to Syracuse with the promise that he could found a real friendship group there, arguing that Plato could convert not only Dionysius II, but also Dion's nephews (his sister's sons, the half brothers of Dionysius II) and all Dion's house, a claim that Plato doubted but was willing to test (328a1–b6). Dion's household associates and companions do not appear to have much chance of repeating Dion's successful wooing of Plato. They are unlikely to understand the nature of true *hetaireiai*. Plato has quietly given them their answer.

It is likely that Plato's praise of the "right philosophy" was the final requirement for the framing of Dion's intention for these reasons: It is one thing to have an innate, noble, ardent desire for justice. It is quite another thing to know what justice is essentially, and what it is practically in each of the millions of pragmatic cases that present themselves for judgments and policy decisions, especially when those situations have been tangled by the well-nigh incurable illnesses of cities. Perhaps someone will ask how a person could want something without knowing perfectly well what it is. The answer is that although such behavior is mysterious, it is found everywhere in human life, from the hungry infants who have no rational knowledge of food to the children and adults who crave love to the mystics who long for God. At any rate, Dion's youthful yearning for justice and his membership in the genuine friendship group could not have eventuated in his intention to seek freedom and the best laws if he had not had a way to ascertain what were the best laws, both generally and for Syracuse. Plato's praise of the right philosophy as the means to knowing all the forms of justice and his call for a philosopher ruler were necessary to Dion's solution of this problem.

Well, then, what is the right philosophy? This term troubles us because it sounds like an invitation to dogmatomachy. We hear it and immediately picture whole armies of fanatics rampaging through their lands, proclaiming their doctrines as true and slaughtering enemies who laud their contrary teachings as the sole verities. There is no denying that this has been the modern experience of people who claim to be right. However, our projection of this experience back onto Plato is anachronistic. Given the manner in which Plato has praised it, the right philosophy could not possibly be a compendium of true doctrines. It is something that exists prior to the knowledge of any verities. It is something that resides in the soul, *by virtue of which* one can *discern* all kinds of public and private justice, when the needs for such insight arise. Perhaps, to rid ourselves of the connotations of dogmatic war, we should call it not the right philosophy, but the right love of wisdom. We should think of it not as a body of true propositions, but as a love that enables us to render a Solomon's verdicts, or to decide on the best laws for a Syracuse in extremely difficult times. Although we cannot say much more about it yet, we can probably distinguish a right love of wisdom from a wrong one by the real commitments of the former to justice and of the latter to illicit advantage. The right philosopher resembles Socrates, the most just man. One doubts that Dion's associates had teachers with Socrates' qualities, or that they had his virtues themselves, although they almost certainly believed themselves wise.

We must still consider Plato's attribution of the fate of Socrates to chance. What does this mean, and why is it relevant to the discussion? This is as good a place as any to ponder the Platonic concept of fortune. In the *Laws*, the Athenian Stranger remarks to Kleinias: "I was about to say that no human being ever makes any laws, but that chances and coincidences of every kind, happening in all sorts of ways, do all the lawmaking for us." The chance events to which the Stranger points are wars, poverty, diseases, weather, and the like. The Stranger continues by observing: "But one can speak equally well about these same things in suchlike manner . . . that in all things god, and with god, chance and opportunity, steers all the human things. It is more gentle to admit that a third must accompany these, art *(technē)*" (709a1–c1).

From this, it appears that the Stranger cannot decide between two opposite ways of explaining the ultimate causes of human destinies. It is equally good to say that chance determines everything and that god, fortune, and *technē* pilot everything. However, it is not clear to what extent the Stranger conceives of the two accounts as opposites, or of "chance" and "god" as different origins of human acts and outcomes. We soon hear him declaring that if things have worked out happily by "some chance" (τινα τύχην, 710c8), this has been wrought by "the god" (τῷ θεῷ, 710d2), so that good fortune, at least, becomes synonymous with divine guidance. However, bad luck could owe to spirits, too. Thus, the Stranger might think the two explanations equally good because the relationships among what strikes us as randomness, a benevolent providence, and an avenging or malevolent demonic interference are mysterious. It would require a serious analysis of the *Laws* to learn more about what the Stranger means, and whether his comments here represent a provisional or final position.

Whatever such a study of the *Laws* might show, we discover Plato speaking in the Seventh Letter only in the second of the equally good ways, and also adhering to Socrates' pious formula in the *Republic*: "Then the good is not the cause of all things, but is the cause of the things that are well; of the bad things it is not the cause. . . . Thus the god, inasmuch as he is good, is not the cause of all things, but is responsible for few things and not the cause of many. . . . Of the good things no other must be said to be the cause but of the bad things it is necessary to seek another cause than the god" (379b15–c7). It would not be surprising if the Athenian Stranger's statements turned out to be rigorous efforts to obey this rule. In any case, the Plato of the Seventh Letter has attributed possession of even the smallest measures of right opinion, conversion to Dion's intention, philosophy, any future success in carrying out Dion's policy, and the much desired joining of philosophy with power—all good things—to divine agency. Soon, he will confess that his unwitting participation in the preparation of Dion for his eventual overthrow of the tyranny of Dionysius II—another good thing—took place "possibly by chance" (ἴσως . . . κατὰ τύχην, 326e1), though it "seems likely" (ἔοικεν, 326e1) that "one of the ruling powers" (τινὶ τῶν κρειττόνων ἀρχήν, 326e2) was contriving it. He ascribes Socrates' execution, the failure of Dionysius II to respond to his instruction, and the defeat of Dion—all evil things—to "some chance" (325b5–6), a daimon who works through lawlessness, godlessness, and ignorance (336b4–6), and "some chance stronger than human beings" (337d8). Philosophy serves as the human art in this reflection. Thus, the deeper, less obvious meaning of Plato's attribution of Socrates' execution to "some chance" is that Plato wants this impious action to be assigned to the correct category of ultimate causality in order to avoid scandalous blasphemy. His solicitude to keep remote efficient causes straight is relevant to the origin of Dion's intention because Plato already wishes to begin warning Hipparinus that although he must become like the most just man to realize his father's plans, this step will not be sufficient to ensure his victory. The just face almost insuperable odds in the struggle against the ultimate causes of evil, be they symbolized as absurd randomness or malevolent demonic will.

Plato's narrative can now be resumed. Plato had reached his conclusions about the need for friends and philosopher-kings before going to Italy. Upon arriving there, he was distressed by the hedonism of the populace. No one could become wise or temperate or generally virtuous by living like that. No city could remain stable under laws of any kind if its citizens did nothing but spend, drink, feast, and indulge in sexual intercourse. In such cities, there would be endless transitions from tyranny to oligarchy to democracy, and their rulers would be unable to hear any talk of just government with equal laws. With these convictions, Plato continued on to Syracuse. Chance, or more likely a ruling power, was contriving the events that would follow. The higher power will cause similar incidents unless the addressees heed the counsel that Plato "now" (νῦν, 326e4) offers for the second time. Plato plainly regards Dion's household associates as thugs and is warning them that they will suffer the same fate as the deposed tyrant unless they change their ways.

This is Plato's first explicit mention of advice, and his correspondents, along with modern exegetes, must wonder when he dispensed the counsel for the first time. Readers must also wonder where the renewed advice is, for Plato seemingly does not offer it "now," but proceeds with his story of the rise of Dion's view. R. G. Bury says that the first occasion on which the advice was given was that of Plato's meeting with Dion at Olympia (see 350b6 ff).[36] However, the apparent failure of the second dispensing to materialize "now" suggests that both are hidden in our text. I think that the first dispensing stretches from the introduction to here and that it consists in the implicit argument that no one can share in Dion's opinion without having enjoyed a divinely bequeathed right habituation, noble nature, and capacity to believe the truth, and without having acquiesced in Plato's discoveries about genuine *hetaireiai* and philosophy—advice from which only Hipparinus might be able to profit. I suppose that the second dispensing extends from here to 334c3 in the section on counsel, and that it consists in the encouragement of Hipparinus to imitate another aspect of the rise of his father's intention. So, we must return to Plato's tale again.

Plato indicates that he will explain what he means by saying that his arrival in Sicily was the source of everything (good) that followed. In Syracuse, Plato associated with Dion, instructing him with words (or arguments, διὰ λόγων, 327a3) in what was best for mankind and urging him to realize it in action. Thus, he was unwittingly preparing the overthrow of the tyranny, for Dion was good at learning (εὐμαθής, 327a6) and responded

36. Bury, *Plato IX: Timaeus, Critias, Cleitophon, Menexenus, Epistles*, 326e4–5 n. 2.

to Plato's teaching more keenly than any other youth Plato had met. Dion vowed to live differently from the majority, honoring virtue more than pleasure. He was scorned for this decision until the death of Dionysius I, but hoped not to remain alone in his intention, which he had acquired through right words (or arguments, ὑπὸ τῶν ὀρθῶν λόγων, 327c1). After the demise of Dionysius I, he thought that, perhaps with the gods' help (ἂν ξυλλαμβανόντων θεῶν, 327c4), Dionysius II could be converted, thus bringing great happiness to the land. So, Dion persuaded Dionysius to summon Plato to Syracuse. Dion also begged Plato to come. He pointed out that Socrates' required stroke of divine good fortune had occurred. He spoke of the magnitude of the empire of Syracuse, and of his own power in that realm. He vouched for the desire of the younger Dionysius for philosophy and education and offered his own nephews as additional members of a new friendship group. He reasoned, in effect, that the time to try the experiment of the philosopher-king was now or never (327d7–328c2). Plato had his doubts about the young people, but judged Dion's nature stable. He eventually persuaded himself that he should not pass up what could have been a real opportunity to join philosophy with power, because he did not desire to seem to himself to be "word alone" (λόγος μόνον, 328c6). He also did not wish to be accused of cowardice and false friendship, for Dion was in danger, or of abandoning philosophy.[37] Therefore, he acceded to Dion's request, clearing himself of guilt before Zeus Xenios and from reproach on the part of philosophy.

Here, it is appropriate to interrupt Plato's narrative again, to ask why this history is rehearsed when counsel has been promised. Our already suggested reply is that the history *is* the advice, or at least the first part of it. Assuming that Hipparinus has passed all of the tests mentioned so far, that is, that he has received the divine favors of an innate yearning for justice, a strong character, and an ability to believe the truth, he is still not ripe for Plato's political help. Now he needs to be good at learning, and to be inducted into a friendship group headed by Plato. Apparently, he should volunteer to study in Athens, where he can enjoy Plato's oral instruction and learn from right arguments.

One is curious as to the nature of Plato's verbal teaching and "right arguments." Is my analysis now fatally contradicted, insofar as Plato has admitted to having educated Dion with doctrines? By no means. If we want a model of the instruction that Plato gave to Dion, we are surely obliged to examine Socrates' teaching of Glaucon in the *Republic*. There, Socrates does not hand Glaucon a list of syllogisms and dogmas to memorize. Rather, he guides him through all kinds of inadequate demonstrations and refuta-

---

37. On Dion's danger, see the eminently sensible discussion of von Fritz, *Platon in Sizilien,* 66–69.

tions, noble lies, myths, digressions, allegories, vague allusions, hints, and, perhaps, one or two vague stabs at a dialectical science that goes as far as human reason can push it. One infers that Socrates presents Glaucon with "right arguments" not in the sense of epistemologically certain proofs but in the sense of types of persuasion that maintain only a certain standard of rigor and that mainly are right for Glaucon. If Plato did the same for Dion, and if he now proposes to repeat the process with Hipparinus, he needs to get to know Hipparinus personally and tailor his teaching to the particular soul. This would explain why he does not simply jot the right arguments down, put them in the mail to Hipparinus, and publish them for everybody else.

Plato's report of his agonizing over Dion's plea can be interpreted as an apologetic digression. However, it also appears to be a logical next point of the counsel that Plato is giving to Hipparinus. At this juncture, it should occur to Hipparinus to pose a question: Suppose that he agrees to visit Athens, submit to the right arguments, and live virtuously. To what political benefits would this lead? By combining the stories of his education of Dion and his decision to return to Syracuse, Plato indicates the gravity of this topic and also gives his answer.

With regard to the importance of the subject, Hipparinus should grasp that although Plato's association with the young Dion owed much to the good fortune that the gods had created a Dion, it also resulted from Plato's art, and from a massive expenditure of Plato's resources. Itinerant philosophers do not meet young brothers-in-law of all-powerful tyrants by accident. Plato must have been traveling in Italy and Sicily not only to chat with his friend Archytas, but also for the express purpose of looking for someone like Dion, that is, a promising youth who was close to the throne of a tyranny and a possible successor to that throne. Why should Plato have been doing that? Because he had decided that there could be no end of evil unless philosophy and power were joined, because he wanted a chance to act by effecting such a union, and because he had probably already reached the Athenian Stranger's conclusion about that for which a lawgiver would wish: "Give me a tyrannized city . . . the tyrant being by nature young, able to remember, a good learner, courageous, and magnificent" (Laws 709e6–8). The question of the payoff that Hipparinus could expect from study at the Academy is of paramount importance for Plato because it involves nothing less than his last possible opportunity to educate a philosopher-king. One step in the origin of Dion's opinion certainly was that Dion, persuaded by Plato's urging to realize what was best for mankind in action, promised to try to become a philosopher-king himself, or to be the means to putting another in place. Plato is telling Hipparinus that he must commit himself to this goal, too. Then Plato will help with a countercoup. An unspoken implication is that the project almost certainly will require Hipparinus to let himself and Syracuse be ruled by a regent while he is being led up to philosophy, but his eventual power will be the better secured for the wait. As Dion understood, the ultimate benefit will be the establishment of the happy and true life without massacres (327d4–6).

To continue now with the tale, when Plato arrived in Syracuse, Dionysius II was ill-disposed toward Dion, whom he suspected of plotting against the tyranny. Soon Dion was exiled. His friends, including Plato, feared for their lives. However, Dionysius liked having Plato around for the sake of appearances and forced him to stay. The tyrant wanted Plato to praise him more highly than Dion, and he hoped to supplant Dion as Plato's friend. He could not be gratified because he avoided the requisite means to this end: hearing Plato's arguments. Finally, Plato went away. This concludes the second section of the letter.

Here, it appears that Plato has digressed again. The topic of the story seems to have shifted from the manner of the origin of Dion's opinion to the nature of Plato's relationship with Dionysius II. However, this excursus provides a final piece of advice for Hipparinus relative to the rise of Dion's view. If Hipparinus, like the tyrant, and unlike Dion, declines to hear Plato's arguments, he cannot be Plato's friend.

"Counsel"

Plato asserts that he will explain later, for the benefit of those who ask, why he visited Dionysius II a second time, and how this was most probable and just (ὡς εἰκότα τε καὶ δίκαια, 330c4). First, though, he must give the addressees advice, which he envisages himself as doing over seven Stephanus pages, not just the one that R. G. Bury credits to him. Plato states that he is deferring the topic of his return to the tyrant's court and dispensing the counsel now to avoid making the secondary primary. Bury takes this to mean that giving advice to Dion's "friends" is the ostensible purpose of the epistle.[38] Plato does not say this, though. He only forces readers to wonder in what sense the new counsel is primary, in what sense the explanation of the later voyage is secondary, and why he gives notice of the secondary material here rather than in its proper later place. One suspects that the rationalization of the return is mentioned here but then postponed because it ranks first in the order of importance but only second in the order of exposition. One also hopes to learn why Plato goes into the advice and the second visit to Dionysius II at all.

It seems that this section of the epistle has a preface followed by three subsections. The preface treats the practice of giving counsel. The first sub-

38. Bury, *Plato IX*, 330c9 n. 1.

section presents the same advice to the addressees as Plato and Dion offered to Dionysius II. The middle subsection surprisingly jumps to the tragic end of Dion's history. The third subsection offers what Plato calls the third repetition of the same teaching.

Plato opens the preface by asking whether a doctor whose patient is living in an unhealthful manner should try to change the man's life, counseling him only if he agrees to reform. A manly doctor, Plato says, should advise only the patient who will heed him, and abandon one who will not. In the same fashion, a person possessing reason will give advice to a well-ordered city that requests it, but not to a disordered city that warns the adviser not to disturb the regime on pain of death, or that wishes only to learn how to gratify its illicit desires.

Having said this, Plato immediately reexamines advising and changes his argument subtly but profoundly. He himself would counsel someone who requested it if the person were living well and would obey, but he would not assist or compel anyone, not even his own son, who was living badly and who would not listen. He would compel a slave, but not a father or a mother. This is the attitude that the sensible man should have toward his city. If the city is ill-governed, he should speak, but not if this will prove useless or cause his death. He should also refrain from revolutionary violence against his city and content himself with prayer whenever it is impossible to establish the best without banishing and slaughtering men. Plainly, these are not quite the same rules laid down just above. There, Plato did not ask whether a doctor should force cures upon his son, a slave, or his parents; he did not jump from the example of medicine to the dangerous subject of revolution; and he explicitly forbade speaking to disordered cities, especially when the adviser is warned to be silent or die. Now he demands the advising of bad cities except when this is useless or mortally dangerous. He also silently encourages revolution under certain conditions.

As usual, Plato has proved puzzling. One wonders why he discusses who should and should not be advised when he has already proclaimed his intention to counsel the addressees. Also, one should like to know why Plato speaks twice about advising individuals and cities, contradicting himself by recommending both quietism and its contraries.

It appears that these perplexities must be explained as follows: Plato has *not* decided to counsel all of his correspondents. Dion's household associates and companions will read the advice that Plato ostensibly gives them, but they will surely disregard it. Hence, Plato is actually indicating that he is putting these ruffians off with a merely cursory reply and otherwise not speaking to them at all (see 331b3–4). The person to whom he really offers further tacit guidance is the only one who might obey. Once again, an astute Hipparinus should look for the greater purpose that Plato conceals under the lesser.

This does not explain why Plato repeats the parallels between advising individuals and cities, changing his position before our eyes. To fathom this, one must imagine that by now, Hipparinus should be asking another question: Suppose that he agrees to come to Athens and hear philosophic arguments. Suppose that he even consents to invest thirty years of study in his preparation for philosopher-kingship, allowing Speusippus to act as his regent during that period. Does Plato not understand that he has immediate problems that are not solved by that advice? He has Callippus on his hands. He is also dealing with relatives whose intentions do not differ much from those of Callippus and who might do something terrible at any moment. He needs to act today, not thirty years hence. What does Plato say about that? In reply, Plato offers Hipparinus object lessons regarding policies that an expeditionary force financed by the Academy could be charged to carry out during the next months, if Hipparinus is willing.

The first policy to which Hipparinus must consent involves the tricky question of what to do about the relatives. Should Hipparinus and the expeditionary force remonstrate with them in an effort to temper their tyrannical appetites? Indeed, the goal of such advising being change, should Hipparinus and the Academy simply force the relatives to reform? Plato initially analyzes this problem from the standpoint of *technē*, that is, art. The lesson in his indirect analogy between medicine and ethical guidance, which is based less on biology than on knowledge of souls, is that moral betterment requires the voluntary cooperation of the person who needs it. It is technically impossible either to persuade or to compel someone to become virtuous if that individual does not wish it. To be sure, one could force a slave to improve, probably because all that is wanted of a barbarian is obedience to orders. This does not make for real goodness, though. Plato then indicates that this calculation is not affected by considerations of piety. Although piety would seem to require radical efforts to save one's own children and parents from immorality, it remains true that no persuasion or compulsion could overcome the technical impossibility of the task if the loved ones lacked the will to change. It would also be impious to hector one's parents, or to violate their freedom. Hipparinus must write his ignoble relatives off.

The second policy to which Hipparinus must agree concerns the problem of what to do about the Syracuse that is now ruled by Callippus. If people cannot be convinced or forced to reform ethically when they lack the desire to do so, could the physician of souls hope to improve an entire city? Plato informs Hipparinus that the answer to this question varies when the analyst changes perspectives. From the vantage point of a *technē* that looks at the polity as a whole, one reaches the same conclusion about cities that one drew about persons: no persuasion or compulsion will correct a polity that loves its corruption. The counselor should remain silent, especially when the city or its rulers would be provoked to kill him if he protests. However, from the standpoint of a piety that longs to save its city from evil, and that concentrates on parts rather than the whole, some action might be both possible and necessary. Pleading with the city could inspire the divinely favored few who long for justice. This is probably why the adviser should speak when he can do so without being slain (perhaps as Plato himself does). Further, although violence against the polity would be unholy when one would have to kill and exile men in order to establish the best, it might be pious to change the leadership forcibly, by attacking barbarian palace guards (who do not have the status of men), and, as Plato later says in qualifying his first statement, by banishing and executing the smallest feasible number of people (351c5–6). This could bring just rulers to power, thus altering the character of the city's authoritative decisions. Piety might well demand such an effort.

Perhaps it will be alleged that these last speculations err, because Plato has prohibited violent revolution simply. This objection betrays careless reading. What Plato's text actually forbids is using violence "whenever" the best cannot be achieved without flooding the world with citizen exiles and corpses. Thus, Plato quietly encourages just uprisings with the fewest possible absolutely necessary and justifiable ostracisms and killings.[39] He does not disapprove of Dion's liberation of Syracuse in principle and would have supported it in practice had it respected the demands of piety (333b2–3, 335e3–336a3, 350b6–351c5). What Hipparinus is being told is that if he opts for an alliance with the Academy, and if he is victorious, he must combine his attempts to enact the best laws with a policy of conciliation that repudiates the practices of Dionysius I, who styled himself a champion of the demos and banished and slaughtered the Syracusean nobles, and that equally abjures the wishes of the aristocrats who crave revenge. This was one of the elements of Dion's intention, and Plato will not support Hipparinus if he does not subscribe to it.

In the first subsection, Plato's advice to the addressees is the same as he and Dion gave to Dionysius II: A ruler should order his life so as to win self-mastery and trustworthy friends and companions. Dionysius I had failed to do this. Therefore, even though he had recovered a great many Sicilian cities from the barbarians, he had never been able to govern them as Darius and the Athenians had ruled their conquests, by leaving dependable friends in charge. Darius, who exemplified the character of the good law-giver and king, created a stable empire that has endured to Plato's day. The Athenians held their possessions for seventy years. Dionysius I managed

---

39. It is reported that Dion acquiesced in the murder of Heracleides. If Plato knew about this, he probably disapproved of it, given his own efforts to save Heracleides from the perfidy of Dionysius II (348e5–349c5). As will be seen later, he also objects to any plan that refuses ultimate reconciliation with Dionysius II.

all Sicily as a single polis, but was defective in virtue, had no friends to help him govern, and barely remained personally secure.

Brian Caven, the apologist for Dionysius I, objects that the tyrant never achieved the total unification of Sicily. This is true, but it does not take Plato's meaning, which is that Dionysius tried to rule all of his conquests directly from his seat in Syracuse rather than leaving subordinates in charge of loosely affiliated and largely autonomous areas. Caven also complains that Plato's accounts of the imperial methods of Darius and the Athenians unfairly conceal the tyrannies exercised by those rulers and the troubles that they had.[40] Here, Caven misses another point, that Plato was attempting to persuade Dionysius II and Dion's associates to become virtuous by offering them examples of conquerors whom they would admire. In this type of education, which appeals to one passion in order to moderate others, it is not necessary that the role models should have escaped all difficulties, or that they should have been virtuous in every respect, propositions that Plato certainly did not believe true of Darius and the Athenians, and that he would not have advanced in a history. All that is required for Plato's present purpose is that an honest man should be able to praise the models in the same spirit that Saint Augustine commends the Romans, of whom he says that they subordinated many appetites to their love of glory (itself a disordered passion), with the result that they had many virtues. Plato's silence about the problems and vices of his models is thus a bit of noble lying. It should also be observed that Dionysius I failed to hold his conquests precisely for the reasons that Plato gives. He escaped being murdered by those nearest to him only narrowly. He lost important battles because his vainglorious brother almost invariably disobeyed orders, so that he had to flee for his life to his fortress more than once.

Caven's further protests that the deeds of the elder Dionysius were typical of his time, or required by reasons of state, hardly excuse those acts. As Callicles saw, Socrates intended precisely to turn the ethical practices of the known world upside down (*Gorgias* 481b10–c4). Thus, Caven's defense of Dionysius I against Plato's criticisms would be more formidable if it dealt competently with Plato's philosophic and moral arguments.

Plato now repeats the counsel offered to Dionysius II, that he should have acquired virtuous friends and that he, being surprisingly deficient, should have become virtuous himself. Plato adds that this was said to Dionysius II in veiled terms, for openness would not have been safe. (This aside is another signal to Hipparinus.) Virtue was lauded as the road to empire: it would enable the tyrant to repeople the cities of Sicily, bind them together in league against the Carthaginians, defeat the barbarians, multiply his father's holdings, and save himself and all under his hegemony.

---

40. Caven, *Dionysius I*, 179–80.

This advice introduces a grave difficulty. The problem is not factual error. For example, it is not that Darius and the Athenians had no virtues. Following the Athenian Stranger (*Laws* 694e6–695d6), we may assume that Darius had the merits of a tough Persian shepherd, being able to live outdoors, keep watch without sleep, and control himself in ways that the Socrates of the *Republic* demands of his doglike soldiers. Similarly, we may suppose that the Athenians to whom Plato refers were the forefathers whose principles Athens had ceased to heed, thus making friends hard to find (325d1–4). Darius and these Athenians did have lower virtues that won them loyal allies and enduring power. The real trouble that Plato allows into his counsel is that Darius and the Athenian fathers were not by the furthest stretch of anybody's imagination philosophic—a defect in Darius about which the Athenian Stranger is fairly blunt (*Laws* 695d6–e2), and a failing in the Athenians frequently lamented by Socrates. Thus, the Plato who is trying to persuade Dionysius II and Hipparinus to prepare for kingship by listening to his arguments is showing these students examples of men who became strong rulers without ever having heard a whisper of philosophy. Worse, these paragons stand in sharp contrast to Dion, the one potential king who did listen to Plato, and whose reward is that he now lies dead at the hands of assassins. Why is Plato undermining his own cause?

Clearly, one reason Plato goes down this path is that he wants to moderate the behavior of Dionysius II, and of Dion's associates, by persuading them that virtue is the best means to gratifying their lusts for power. However, Plato knows that Dion's cohort will not be moderated, because their passions are already too excited, and because it is too late for them to begin to desire and acquire virtue, or to understand what genuine friends are. Therefore, I think that Plato has a more important purpose. He realizes that he has made a suggestion at which Hipparinus will finally balk. He anticipates that this new question will have occurred to Hipparinus: His father became virtuous and heard Plato's arguments. He agreed to liberate Syracuse with the smallest possible number of exiles and executions, and to institute a regime that conciliated hostile parties. Look what this got him. Now he is dead, having been rejected by the democrats upon whom he would have exacted revenge if he had known what was good for him, and having been murdered by those self-proclaimed enthusiasts for ethics who had promised to help him. All the successful politicians of whom Hipparinus knows have been, like his grandfather, vicious. He is beginning to think that a man who tries to be good all the time is bound to come to grief among the many who are not good, and that a prince should learn how not to be good to advance his own interests.[41] Why should he listen to Plato?

---

41. Cf. von Fritz, *Platon in Sizilien*, 116 ff.

It is this challenge that compels Plato to extol virtue as a means to a longer-lasting political power than the base arts of a Dionysius I or a Callippus can afford. Plato's implicit argument that the lower-order virtues of Darius and the Athenians yielded superior power-political results, and that this should deter Hipparinus from imitating the fox and the lion, is quite plausible. Nonetheless, it is not enough. Hipparinus should ask: Then why not be content to imitate Darius and the Athenians? Why try to do better than these conquerors by renouncing tyranny and by renewing the folly of the unrealistic quest for philosophic rule that killed his father?

These anticipated misgivings of Hipparinus force Plato to face a problem that has been lurking in the background of his epistle all along, namely, that attempts to yoke philosophy to historically existing power make virtually impossible demands on human beings as we know them. Plato will have to explain his failure to transform Dionysius and Dion into philosopher-kings by conceding that the conditions for the success of his experiment never existed. At the same time, he must convince Hipparinus that some approximation of them could exist or the lad will never take up his father's cause. Moving to the middle subsection of his counsel, Plato analyzes the difficulties by placing new object lessons in the careful reader's field of vision.

Disconcertingly to the inattentive, Plato returns here to the story of his first visit to the court of Dionysius II. This plainly is another occasion on which his tale *is* his advice. The young tyrant was deaf to the blandishments of Plato and Dion because slanderers had his ear and he feared plots. Specifically, the slanderers said that Plato and Dion meant to usurp the tyranny, placing Dion on the throne while Dionysius was distracted by his education. (This undoubtedly is precisely what Plato and Dion intended, except that they would have elevated Dionysius to the philosopher-kingship when he was ready for it.) So, Dion was exiled. When he returned to liberate Syracuse, the demos of that city twice listened to the slanderers just as Dionysius had done, believing that Dion had come not to free them, but to make himself tyrant. Playing upon these democratic fears, Callippus had Dion murdered. Those who now order Plato to involve himself in a countercoup against Callippus should hear, as it were, the real substance of these tragic events. As Dion's ally, Plato went to Syracuse to promote friendship, not war. He lost his battle against the slanderers. Still, as a captive of Dionysius, he refused the tyrant's enticements to betray Dion. For his part, Dion attached himself to two brothers while returning to Syracuse at the head of his small army. The friendship of these evil brothers was "not based on philosophy" (οὐκ ἐκ φιλοσοφίας, 333e1–2), but based on hospitality and epoptic association in the mysteries. These men murdered Dion, and Plato will not deny their shame. However, he will object to the charge that Athens was shamed by their deed, for it was also an

Athenian who became Dion's friend through community in free education
(διὰ δὲ ἐλευθέρας παιδείας κοινωνίαν, 334b5–6).[42] It is only the friendship
of this sort of community that should inspire the man of reason (τὸν νοῦν,
334b6) to give his trust. This, Plato adds, has been said as counsel to Dion's
"friends and relatives" (φίλων καὶ ξυγγενῶν, 334c3–4). It will become clear
in a moment that Plato is now speaking to a wholly different group from
that to whom the epistle is formally addressed, although the associates and
companions fancy themselves Dion's best friends and finest relatives and
Plato does not openly disabuse them of their conceit.

This advice translates into the following answer to the objections of Hipparinus: It is true that his father became virtuous. It is true that he heard
the philosophic arguments, and that he agreed to free Syracuse with the
smallest possible number of exiles and executions, instituting a regime that
conciliated hostile parties. This, however, did not cause his defeat. Rather, it
was the situation that destroyed him. Dionysius II turned out to be unripe
for philosophy and too insecure to ignore bad advice. Further—and this
was not the least of the obstacles—his father did not hear Plato's arguments
in a way that allowed him to become a man of reason. This caused him to
make a fundamental and fatal mistake. He befriended Callippus on a basis
other than that of community in free education. It was this error, not his
correct intention, that brought his assassin into the picture. Further, when
one proposes to establish a new order of conciliation of previously hostile
parties, it is necessary to persuade those who are about to lose the upper
hand that they have held so long, so oppressively, and so advantageously,
that the revolution will benefit them. The demos of Syracuse were wholly
unreceptive to right intentions. Dion not only failed to convince them that
they stood to gain by the loss of their champion tyrant, and by his own
rule, which would have been hard under the best of circumstances, but
also foreshortened the time that he needed to accomplish this task by injecting into the situation a man who could and did fan the flames of democratic paranoia. If Dion had become a man of reason, and if, accordingly,
he had obeyed Plato's counsel about liberating Syracuse according to the
rules of piety, he would have arrived on the scene with true, rather than
false, friends, and these trustworthy men would have at least spoken to
the people more soothingly. This would not have guaranteed the success
of the revolution, but it would have improved the chances for a happier

42. I do not have sufficient space here to respond fully to Edelstein's objection that
"free education" (or "liberal education") is not a Platonic term. I would say only that
in *Republic* 576a, 577d–e, Socrates envisages a genuine freedom that consists in self-
mastery, and that in *Laws* 720d, the Athenian speaks of a free medical doctor who inves-
tigates according to nature. Understood as aim and method, these criteria adequately
define liberal education, making it entirely likely that the real Plato would have used
the term.

ending. Dion's real friends and relatives, who will qualify as such on the basis of their association with Dion in free education rather than kinship of soul (affiliation in the mysteries) or body (334b7), will take the point, acknowledge their hero's shortcomings, and resolve to try to realize his right intention as the man of reason would do.

Here, commentators frequently assert that Plato is merely trying to blame Dion for his own blunders. I reply that although Plato might have erred in acceding to Dion's repeated requests, a possibility that will be discussed below, it was still Dion's mistake in befriending Callippus that led to his murder. Also, this question is boring in comparison with the terrible problems to which Plato has now admitted. It cannot have escaped Plato's attention that in explaining how the prerequisites for the success of his plans for Dionysius and Dion were absent, he has cast extreme doubt on the feasibility of the project of educating a philosopher-king by making an already powerful man philosophical.[43] He has alluded to three potentially insurmountable difficulties.

To elucidate the first, let us recall that for which the Athenian Stranger's lawgiver wishes: "Give me a tyrannized city . . . the tyrant being by nature young, able to remember, a good learner, courageous, and magnificent" (Laws 710e6–8). Let us compare the object of that prayer with Dionysius II. Syracuse was a tyrannized city. Dionysius II was young, and, as Plato grants, he was naturally gifted with the ability to learn (338d6–7). So far, so good, but those are the easy parts. Was the young, bright tyrant courageous and magnificent? On the contrary, Plato finds that he was afflicted with an amazing love of honor (338d7), that he lacked self-mastery (331d7–9), and that he was astonishingly deficient in harmony with regard to virtue (332d3–6). Further, Plato remarks that tyrannies entirely ruin both their slave and their despotic classes, the latter developing "petty and illiberal souls" (σμικρὰ δὲ καὶ ἀνελεύθερα ψυχῶν, 334d2) who know no goodness or justice divine or human. The Athenian Stranger also indicates that even in the reigns of benevolent tyrants such as Cyrus and Darius, the heirs to the thrones turn out badly because the fathers have no idea how to teach their sons rightly (Laws 694c–696a; see Plato's comment on the failure of Dionysius I to educate his son, 332c7–d1). It is astounding that Plato ever entertained Dion's suggestion that Dionysius II could be educated to philosopher-kingship, or that he ever thought that this dandy might not listen to Dion's slanderers, for the Plato who consults his own prudence never expects a tyrant's son to be the answer to the Athenian Stranger's prayer. It is doubtful that a real-world tyrannical environment would ever be conducive to the growth of a potential philosopher-king.

43. Cf. von Fritz, Platon in Sizilien, 15–16.

Nevertheless, suppose that against all odds, a Plato is fortunate enough to find a Dion. Here we have a youth who responds to Plato's teaching more keenly than any other Plato has met, who consequently becomes a model of virtue, and who nonetheless never becomes a "man of reason." It seems that even when the god almost grants the Athenian's prayer, providing an intelligent, good, young prince who is close to the throne of a tyranny, Plato finds it impossible to make this potential king into the right kind of raw material for his project. Indeed, he discovers that he cannot control his charge, keeping him on the path of virtue at the most critical moment (350d5–e2). What is the right stuff, and why is Plato unable to fashion it out of a nature as noble as Dion's? Noting that Plato has spoken of the origin of Dion's *opinion*, but never of the rise of Dion's *wisdom* or *reason*, we may assume that Dion never became "really philosophic, being familiar with and worthy of the matter by divine agency" (ὄντως ἦ φιλόσοφος οἰκεῖός τε καὶ ἄξιος τοῦ πράγματος θεῖος ὤν, 340c2–3). Why not? Perhaps because the god did not choose to make Dion philosophic. Or perhaps because an ambitious Dion did not spend the greater part of his life studying the subjects that are preliminary to philosophy, and then studying dialectic, coming finally to the state of synopsis, as outlined by Socrates in the *Republic*, book 7. Dion could not have done this, for he was too busy forging a career as a powerful minister and brother- and son-in-law to Dionysius I. Being a politician and becoming a philosopher apparently are quite incompatible for all or most human beings. If we suppose that Dion could have remedied his philosophic inadequacies by leaving Syracuse as a youth to study with Plato for thirty years, we can rejoice in this retrospective plan for the salvation of his soul, but we must also realize that the result would have been an emigrant philosopher who was completely forgotten at home, and who would never have been invited to play a political role in Syracuse after the death of the first Dionysius. There does not seem to have been any way for a Plato to transform a Dion into a philosopher-king in waiting.

Even if this difficulty had been obviated somehow, it would have still been dreadfully hard for a disciplined King Dion to legislate justice. Consider all the countries in history the rulers of which have maintained their power by enriching either the oligarchic or the democratic faction at the expense of the other. In which of these nations could one have hoped to find the favored group delighted to see its tyrant change course, rescinding its illicit advantages? In which of them could one have convinced the oppressed faction not to pursue revenge? Once again, it is astonishing that the author of the *Republic*, book 8, and of the remarks on counsel just above, could have imagined that the democrats of Syracuse might have embraced Dion's reforms and turned deaf ears to his slanderers. There appears to be no prospect that the subjects of a real tyranny could readily be transformed into the citizens of a just city.

So, it seems that Plato's experiment foundered on practical impossibilities. Hipparinus will hardly be reassured by Plato's excuses. Rather, he will worry that there could never be a situation in which an effort to realize his father's intention would not get him killed. However, he should think some more. Plato was not exactly oblivious to the alleged impossibilities before he sailed to help Dion. He still decided to go. Did he perceive some hope that the problems could be solved? If so, did he see truly, or was he hallucinating?

One possibility that Plato could have discerned is indicated by his frequent statements that Dion's intention must be realized with the aid of a divine dispensation. The barriers to a Platonic revolution are certainly so enormous that we can now understand why Plato would be serious about this necessity. Did Plato perceive divine fortune working in his favor? If he did, Hipparinus will not feel any great confidence in Plato's divination, or in his gods, for the event did not bear the prophecy out. This reminds us, though, that it was Dion who reported to Plato that the long-awaited divine dispensation had come. Well, then, did Plato have adequate reason to believe Dion? Or did he have solid human grounds for supposing that his project might succeed? As we cast back over Plato's account of his decision to go to Dion's assistance, we remember that the one supposedly known fact that weighed most heavily in his calculations was that Dion's character was measured. Plato evidently credited Dion's reports, and thought that all of the impossibilities could be changed to possibilities, because he assumed that he could rely on the harmony of Dion's soul. Here, we must admit that Plato was probably guilty of "extremely poor judgment."[44] However, this was an error of fact. On the level of principle, Plato could still make this argument to Hipparinus: All things are possible to the god. If the divine blessing had really been operating, reversing the usual odds against justice, Plato and Dion could have achieved their aims with relative ease. In human terms, they could have avoided the recent disaster had Dion been a fully measured character, indeed, a man of reason. Then he would have known better how to handle Dionysius II during his formative years, and Plato might not have had to be surprised to find how deficient the tyrant actually was upon arriving in Syracuse. Dion would also have known better how to introduce reforms without unduly alarming the demos. Moreover, the divine favor might be working now, if Hipparinus is reading and grasping Plato's letter. If so, Plato will not repeat his earlier mistake. Plato will help him to ascend higher toward philosophy than Dion did. Hipparinus will become the man of reason and pursue Dion's aims more intelligently.

Hipparinus might listen to this, but he will surely have two questions: (1) His father, Dion, knew Plato's arguments without having had to study

44. Ibid., 17.

a lot of tedious subjects, and he was virtuous, too. How and why was he not a man of reason? What on earth is a man of reason if his father was not one? How can he become one? (2) Specifically, how could Dion's errors have been avoided? Also, perhaps more to the point, what would a man of reason do now to oust Callippus, to replace him with a measured ruler, and to turn the political impossibilities of such a revolution into possibilities? Plato owes Hipparinus a profound reply to the former query. However, he will postpone this until he has treated the latter.

Plato begins the last subsection of his counsel enigmatically, saying that he must add something as he repeats the same advice for the third time "to you [plural] the third" (τρίτοις ὑμῖν, 334c5–6). Who are "the third"? A little further below, Plato indicates that the first was Dion and the second Dionysius (334d5–6). "The third" undoubtedly are Hipparinus, the third and last candidate for education to philosopher-kingship, and any other persons unknown to Plato who qualify as Dion's real friends and relatives (see 336c2).

In the first dispensation of the advice, Plato told the discerning reader that to share in Dion's intention, he must have been a lifelong imitator of Dion, having been good by virtue of a god's dispensation in granting him the right habituation, a strong character, and the ability to believe the truth; having joined the right kind of friendship group; and having acknowledged that there is a connection between yoking philosophy to power and curing the evil of cities. In the second, he reiterated that to agree with Dion's intention, one must imitate Dion, being willing to hear Plato's arguments, heed Plato's counsel, and conduct a just revolution piously, that is, without exiling and killing whole classes of the city (and also learning from Dion's mistakes). In the third, he will assert again that true followers of Dion must imitate him, and discuss a third way in which they must do that.

The final subsection of the counsel seems confused because Plato continues to employ the method of adducing object lessons as the premises from which he will draw conclusions. The initial step in his new argument appears to be a repetition of his demand for the renunciation of tyranny that is justified by an addlepated mixture of philosophic and religious claims, and buttressed by a petulant expression of bitterness. Plato declares that cities should be enslaved not to despots, but to laws, for those enslaved to despots ruin both the oppressed and the oppressor classes for generations, producing petty, illiberal souls who know no goodness or justice, divine or human. Then he reports that he tried to convince Dion and Dionysius II of this, and exhorts his readers to be persuaded for the sake of Zeus Third Savior. Then he cites the examples of Dion, who was convinced and died nobly, and Dionysius II, who was not persuaded and is now living no noble life as an exile from his palace. For suffering in the pursuit of the noblest is noble. No one is immortal, and no man would be happy if he were immortal, as the many believe, because goods and evils attach not to the soulless, but to soul whether or not it is united to body. We ought to believe the ancient, holy argument that the soul is immortal and that it is punished for being wicked, so that it is a lesser evil to suffer than to perform injustice. Whoever is poor of soul will scorn this teaching as he lives like a beast, plundering and gorging himself with food, drink, and the pleasures that are misnamed for Aphrodite, but he will pay in both this life and the next. Plato mentions that he tried to persuade Dion of all this, but says nothing of having taught it to Dionysius II. He continues by asserting that he is now justifiably angry with the assassins and with Dionysius II, because the assassins have destroyed the man who meant to practice justice, and Dionysius II refused to do justice when he had the power, thus injuring Plato and all mankind.

This seemingly softheaded reasoning is saved from legitimate intellectual condemnation by the fact that it is not really an argument, but a tough political marching order coupled with advice about allies and enemies. Here is the marching order: The first premise of Plato's advice to Hipparinus, and the absolute prerequisite for his agreement to help him, is that he must imitate his father by renouncing tyranny, because this sort of regime has harmful effects on all human beings. (I believe that Plato is serious about this because the truth of his warning about the consequences of practicing tyranny is proved by all historical experience.) Here is the counsel: Hipparinus should consider the inventory of arguments that Plato offered to Dion and Dionysius II. Both men were cautioned about the effects of tyranny. This reasoning was accepted by Dion, but not by the tyrant. Dion alone was given the well-known Socratic demonstrations about the nobility of suffering for the noble, the immortality of the soul, happiness, the relative merits of suffering and doing injustice, and the Socratic indication at the end of the *Republic* that independent of our ability or inability to know the literal truth of the ancient myths about rewards and punishments in the next life, it is good for us to believe the myths. One should note for future reference the essentially mythological character of the arguments presented to Dion. For present purposes, Hipparinus should observe the ways of life of those who reject, have not heard, or mock these teachings and myths. Thus can he know his allies and enemies among those who refuse to disclose their plans about tyranny. Also, it is true that Plato refused to lift a hand against Dionysius during Dion's campaign against him. Plato was morally obliged not to harm him, but the tyrant has also forfeited any right to Plato's help. He can be left out of account or bargained with as the present situation warrants. Finally, Plato is prepared for war against Dion's assassins.

Plato's next step in the last dispensation of his counsel appears to be a continuation of his complaint about the injuries done to him by Dionysius II and the assassins. Plato laments that the tyrant refused to practice justice when he had supreme power throughout his realm. If philosophy and power had been united in the same person there, this would have radiated throughout the world, leading Greeks and barbarians to the true opinion that happiness lies in subjection to justice and wisdom, whether cities or individuals have these virtues themselves or are governed by holy rulers. The tyrant's destruction of this prospect by refusing to strive for the goal is the injury that he has done to Plato and all mankind. As for the assassins, they have brought about the same result as Dionysius II. If Dion had gained possession of the kingdom, he would have liberated Syracuse, ordered the citizens by suitable laws of the best kind, and colonized Sicily after driving out the barbarians. If this had been done by a man who was just, courageous, sanely self-controlled, and philosophic, most human beings would have formed the same opinion of virtue that would have prevailed throughout the world had Dionysius II been converted. However, some daimon or sinful being fighting by means of lawlessness, godlessness, and *amathia* (ἀμαθίας, 336b6), that is, the ultimate spiritual ignorance that is the source of all evils for men, has wrecked everything a second time.

This apparent expression of frustrated and not altogether clearheaded wrath also has a straightforward message: The second premise of Plato's advice to Hipparinus is that he must imitate his father by committing himself to the aim of instituting philosophic rule. As with the renunciation of tyranny, Plato will not compromise on this point. If refused, Plato will not give aid. If Hipparinus agrees, they will follow Dion's program: first to win control of the kingdom, thus freeing Syracuse from despotism, then to legislate the best laws, and then to expel the Carthaginians and incorporate all Sicily into the realm. If Hipparinus frets about the practicality of this goal and plan, he should inquire into the ultimate cause of the two previous failures. In both cases, it was the work of the daimon who hitherto has always triumphed in human life, chiefly by cursing mankind with *amathia*. Plato insists, just as he caused Socrates to maintain in the *Republic* (473c2–4, 473c11–e2), that it is possible to bring the just city into existence by means of the neither small nor easy change of inaugurating philosophic rule. If a divine fate would only permit us to defeat the *amathia* just once, so that we could get a just, courageous, sanely self-controlled, and philosophic king, the rest of Syracuse and, indeed, the entire world would be brought around through general admiration of our happiness. If these expectations seem too sanguine, Hipparinus should consider that he does yet know what it means to overcome the *amathia*. That is the precise heart of our task. Perhaps Hipparinus will be skeptical about Plato's amazing claim that a philosophic ruler, once in power, would attract the nations to his felicitous mode of life. Plato's enthusiasm seems equivalent to that of an Isaiah who expects to see the mountain of the temple of Yahweh towering above all the other mountains, with peoples streaming to it seeking to learn God's ways (Isa. 2:1–3), or to that of a Christian looking forward to the New Jerusalem. One wonders uneasily whether Plato has lost his balance. Nonetheless, let us grant that Plato might be right. Or let us suppose that he is merely indulging in a hyperbolic description of a much improved human condition, and let us turn to the immediate pragmatic difficulty. An increasingly impatient Hipparinus has still not been told how a philosophic ruler could come to power in Syracuse at all.

Being fully aware of this, Plato draws his conclusions. He counsels Dion's "friends" to imitate Dion in his patriotism and sanely self-controlled life, and to try to carry out his plans under better auspices. He openly urges the real friends to dump any of their associates who cannot live virtuously and to call for the assistance of all Greeks who excel in virtue and hate the sin of killing hosts. He intimates that even the weakest intelligence must understand that there can be no end to the miseries of Syracuse until its warring factions cease and desist from their mutual assaults and revenges. He calls upon the winners of the coming civic strife (that is, Dion's friends) to master themselves, to enact laws that satisfy both the vanquished and the victors, and to compel the defeated to obey the laws by instilling fear and reverence—fear inasmuch as they will show themselves willing to use their superior power to enforce the law, and reverence inasmuch as they themselves will first and foremost subject themselves to the law. The winners should also imitate Dion by accepting the decision that he and Plato reached: to resort to the "second-best" course of action. They should call upon fifty excellent old men of ample property and good descent, and have them frame and obey equal laws that give no advantage either to the conquerors or to the conquered. This policy, which resembles that of the *Laws*, must still be realized with the aid of a divine dispensation and fortune. It is second best because it dispenses with direct philosophic rule for tactical purposes.

This language is so direct that it needs no interpretation. Hipparinus might wonder whether the idea of laws that satisfy both victors and vanquished in a long civic conflict is not utopian, and whether Plato's assembly of fifty gentlemen would not be, or seem to the demos to be, an oligarchic restoration. However, a policy of intimidation combined with moderation just might work if the propertied men, under a reasonable king's influence, actually moved toward true justice incrementally. This certainly would be a rare occurrence in human affairs.

"MY RETURN . . ." OR "THE LATER JOURNEY . . ."

Plato now offers to tell, to whomever wishes to hear, the story of his later journey by sea and how it most probably and harmoniously occurred.

Previously, he had promised that he would relate the story of this journey, and how it was most probable and just, to anyone who asked. Plato does not indicate why anybody should care about this new tale. He simply looks like a crank who has forgotten to reply to his correspondents' request for aid because he wants to answer criticism of his meddling.

Resuming his story where he left off, Plato reports that he escaped from Syracuse when he persuaded Dionysius II to release him because there was war in Sicily. He and Dion were supposed to be invited back after the war. When peace was made, Plato kept receiving calls from Dionysius to return without Dion, exhortations from Dion to consent, and reports that the tyrant was again amazingly desirous of philosophy. Meanwhile, Dionysius had been conversing with Archytas, and with various intellectuals who were "stuffed with some things heard incidentally from philosophy." Dionysius had let all these people believe that he had been instructed by Plato. He did not want his lie exposed, so he wished to bring Plato back and hear the arguments that he had formerly spurned. Therefore, Dionysius sent Plato a long letter promising to arrange Dion's affairs as Plato dictated, if he would come, and threatening harm to Dion if he refused. Archytas also greatly needed Plato's cooperation. Plato yielded, "blindfolding" himself with the reasoning that it was possible that the tyrant had come to love the best life and that he ought not to let Dion and Archytas down. He returned to Syracuse fearfully, and intent upon discovering how things really stood with Dionysius, namely, whether the tyrant was actually "inflamed by philosophy, as it were by fire" (340b1–2). There is a method of testing in such affairs that is suitable for tyrants, especially for the ones who are stuffed with things heard incidentally, as Plato perceived Dionysius to be immediately upon arriving in Sicily. This test is especially appropriate for those who are luxurious and incapable of enduring labor and stops them from blaming the teacher if they fail to learn philosophy. Plato lectures the tyrant on how much difficult study philosophy requires. Whoever is "really philosophic, being familiar with and worthy of the matter by divine agency," will not become discouraged, but will opt for an orderly life and work until he achieves the goal of his studies, perhaps eventually progressing without a teacher. While remaining in his present occupation, he will cleave above all to philosophy and the mode of life conducive to learning. Those who are "not philosophic, but superficially tinged by opinions" (ὄντως μὲν μὴ φιλόσοφοι, δόξαις δ' ἐπικεχροσμένοι, 340d5–6), like sunburned men, will be daunted, or assert that they are already learned.[45] Dionysius replied that he was already sufficiently accomplished. Therefore, Plato spoke to the tyrant philosophically only once. This criticism of Dionysius is tempered

45. My translation here coincides with the Loeb version simply because I cannot think of a better way to render the phrase.

by Plato's declaration of gratitude that the tyrant at least met the requirements of reverence by preventing Plato's murder.

At this point, Ludwig Edelstein objects vigorously that the real Plato
could not have devised this trial, for the following reasons: The "Plato"
of the epistle does not prescribe for Dionysius the same challenges and the
same curriculum of study, work, and philosophic leisure that the *Republic* variously specifies for promising youths in actual societies and for the
guardians of the just city. No Platonic dialogue ever expresses the fear that
a failed student will blame the instructor. The letter's test is inappropriate,
for it merely attempts to measure the stamina of the neophyte, without
probing his philosophic ability. The story of the test slanders Dionysius,
who is reported by most ancient writers to have been intelligent, excited
about philosophy, deeply immersed in geometry at least for a time, and
constantly surrounded by thinkers whom he invited to his court. In light
of these facts, which made it impossible for anyone to question the tyrant's
"intellectual endowment," the only course open to the forger was to de-
fame Dionysius on moral grounds.[46] Although these objections are obtuse,
they are worth considering because they frame the very issue that Plato
intends to raise with his discussion of the test: What is philosophy? Plato's
answer to this question starts with one implicit remark and two explicit
comments on what philosophy is *not*.

As even Edelstein grasps, Dionysius was the real tyrant of a real great
power, not some hypothetical talented boy in Athens, and not a guardian
of Socrates' city in speech realized on earth. When Plato asserts that he
has devised a trial *especially* suited to luxurious tyrants, one cannot expect
to find him directing a self-indulgent, paranoid, middle-aged dictator to
pass the same tests and follow the same schedules that Socrates requires
of capable youths in his hometown and fictitious guardians in his just city.
Similarly, it is easy to see why Plato's dialogues mention no anxiety about
failed students blaming their teachers and why the Seventh Letter does
express this fear. In the dialogues, there are no tyrants demanding to be
certified as great philosophers and possibly poised to murder instructors
who thwart them by refusing to give them lessons. The danger that Plato
faced in the real Syracuse surely explains not only why he was worried,
but also why he gave Dionysius one lecture on philosophy even though
he had determined that the tyrant was not qualified. We may infer that the
first thing that philosophy is *not* is an "-ism" with principles and programs
cobbled together from diverse theoretical contexts and mechanically applicable to human life without regard for practical situations.

With regard to the issue of whether the test is appropriate, we are obliged
to remember that in the *Republic*, Socrates devotes a lengthy discussion

46. Edelstein, *Plato's Seventh Letter*, 71–76.

to the problem of the corruption of natively philosophic natures (490c8–496a10). A youth who begins with the ethical virtues, facility at learning, good memory, beauty, wealth, and physical strength can, with bad rearing, turn all his virtues into their opposites. He then adopts the great beast's opinions of the noble and the base, good and evil, and the just and unjust. He becomes full of all sorts of intellectual pretensions, but the truth is that intelligence (νοῦς, 494d5) is not in him. He believes that he philosophizes, but, being unworthy of education, he utters only "sophisms" (496a8). We must also recall that Socrates lists moral prerequisites for admission to the pursuit of philosophy: keenness at study, unflinching courage in the face of difficult studies, and love of the labor of learning (535a3–c3). Thus, if Socrates spoke for Plato, as Edelstein thinks, the test is not only completely in character for the real Plato, but perfectly appropriate as a measure of the ethical requirements for philosophizing as well. There could be no such thing as a cowardly, intemperate, unjust, lazy person who enjoyed an actualized (as opposed to a nascent) philosophic ability, or who could be said to possess wisdom and reason. Philosophy is *not* something that can coexist in the same soul with vice, and philosophic ability is *not* synonymous with "intellectual endowment." What can exist is a vicious person who is good at churning out clever sophisms that are mistaken for philosophy by those who have no clue as to what philosophy is. This is why Plato broods that he will probably have to put up with people thinking that Dionysius (whose defects he knows well from both prior acquaintance and the test) exhibited "intelligence" (νοῦν, 339a5), a prophecy that came true in the authors whom Edelstein cites against the epistle and in Edelstein himself. We may be grateful that Hans-Georg Gadamer, unlike Edelstein, insightfully recognizes the need for a close study of the Seventh Letter that manages to discriminate between dialectic and sophistry.[47]

As we contemplate the resplendent court of Dionysius II, we see the tyrant seated in his great hall, occasionally with a philosopher such as Archytas, and always with a good many self-proclaimed intellectuals who enjoy his favor. These pretentious men drop names, pursue temporary enthusiasms for geometry and other subjects, recite arguments, try each other with syllogisms, and hotly debate "philosophies." They will seem wonderfully erudite to their historians. This does not recommend the historians. In Plato's view, these men are "stuffed with some things heard incidentally from philosophy" and "superficially tinged by opinions." They are not really philosophic, because philosophy is *not* a set of opinions and arguments that are poured into the mind like phrases into a parrot, so that the words are not grounded in a habituation of the soul to the order of being, in a stable character, and in a god-given ability to believe truth. Here, it is also

47. Gadamer, "Dialektik und Sophistik."

permissible to add that philosophy is *not* opinion that fails to rise to the opposite of *amathia*.

Given adequate understanding of Plato's positions on what philosophy is *not*, it would seem rash to accuse Plato of slandering Dionysius before learning what he thinks philosophy *is*. We must look into this. However, prior questions have been put off too long, and must now be addressed. Why is Plato concerned to have his reader agree that his second journey to the court of the tyrant was "most probable" and "just," or "harmonious"? Having announced the topic of the later journey, why does Plato launch into a discussion of whether Dionysius was genuinely desirous of philosophy?

I think that Plato wishes merely to look like a crackpot who is eager to establish that he has not misbehaved. His language effectively creates this disguise. However, many phrases could have achieved this end. Why does Plato twice use the term "most probable," with "just" and "harmonious"? The superlative suggests the existence of a standard of comparison, that is, a measure of the probable. What is that standard? It appears that Plato is asking the reader to consider how a philosopher would have been likely to act in his place. This, in turn, compels the reader to ask what a philosopher is, and this is the same question that is presented with the discussion of the real intentions of Dionysius. It seems, then, that the entire opening of this section of the epistle uses the lesser purpose of apologizing for an unsuccessful policy to cover the greater purpose of pointing to the question: What is philosophy? Why should Plato do that, though?

To solve this puzzle is to explain why Plato's so-called philosophic digression is not a digression at all, but the next logical step—nay, the fitting conclusion—demanded by both his drama and his argument. Dramatically, Plato must complete his clandestine offer of help to, and teaching of, Hipparinus. He still owes Hipparinus an account of the nature of the man of reason, and of what must be done to make good Dion's failure to become a man of reason. Theoretically, a comprehensive investigation of the problems of educating a potential king or an actual tyrant to philosophy, and of getting him into power or keeping him there, which is what the Seventh Letter has now been shown to be, requires an inquiry into the nature of philosophy.

Having finished his story of the test, Plato denies that he instructed Dionysius fully on that occasion. He then mentions that he has been informed that Dionysius eventually wrote a treatise about what he had heard, changing the teaching and claiming it as his own. However, Plato can vouch for this: It is impossible that Dionysius or other writers could know that about which he is serious (περί ὧν ἐγὼ σπουδάζω, 341c1–2), either as hearers of his, or as hearers of others, or by themselves. They could not grasp anything of the matter (περί τοῦ πράγματος, 341c3–4),

For there is no writing of mine about these things (περί αὐτῶν), nor will there ever be. For it is in no way a spoken thing like other lessons (ῥητὸν γὰρ οὐδαμῶς ἐστιν ὡς ἄλλα μαθήματα, 341c5–6), but, as a result of repeated being with (συνουσίας, 341c6) and living with (συζῆν, 341c7) the matter itself, it is brought to birth in the soul suddenly, as light that is given off by a leaping flame (οἷον ἀπὸ πυρὸς πηδήσαντος ἐξαφθὲν φῶς, 341c7–d1), and it maintains itself thereafter.

Plato is sure that the best statement of these things in writing or in speech would be his own. If he had thought that they should be transmitted to the many, what nobler action could he have done in his life than writing what is of great benefit to human beings and bringing "nature" (τὴν φύσιν, 341d7) to light for all? However, this would not be good for human beings, "except for some few who are able to learn by themselves with a little guidance." What would happen to the great majority is that "it would fill some with a contempt that is not right and that is in no way harmonious, and others with lofty and empty hopes, as if they had learned some mysteries" (341e3–342a1).

This fiery instruction to Hipparinus on false and real philosophy allows us to begin to answer a question raised early in the previous chapter: Is that about which Plato is serious not a spoken thing simply, or is it a spoken thing, but not in the way that other lessons are spoken things? It is clear beyond any doubt that Dionysius has never heard from Plato, and could not have heard from any other teacher, or read in any writing, that about which Plato is serious. Why not? To see this, imagine that that about which Plato is serious were a spoken thing in a unique manner. Suppose further that Plato had told someone about it, let us say Speusippus and Archytas, even if he had never written it for the general public. Dionysius knew Speusippus and Archytas personally. How, then, on these premises, could Plato be so sure that it is impossible for that about which he is serious to have been communicated to the tyrant? The only logical reply appears to be that Plato trusted Speusippus and Archytas to keep quiet. Nonetheless, there are indications in the epistle that Speusippus (350d) and even Archytas (339d) were prone to bad judgment. We must think again. Actually, Plato could be certain that no one has informed Dionysius only if he himself has told nobody, which must be the case. This inference is supported by Plato's remark that the best *oral* or written statement of his teaching *would* be his own (341d2–3), which implies that Plato has neither spoken nor written about that which he is serious. This reasoning is not yet decisive, but more will be adduced below. For now, we may proclaim a probable conclusion: Plato's serious things are "in no way a spoken thing like other lessons" in the sense that they are ineffable simply and not in the sense that they cannot be spoken in ways that other lessons are spoken. To place the latter construction on the phrase is to tear it out of context.

Perhaps it will be objected that this exegesis misses Plato's hints that he communicates with the few but not with the many, together with his hints at his refusals to express serious insights in writings or talks aimed at the many, which mean that he can articulate serious things when he wishes and that he does incorporate them into his speeches to the few. It is true that Plato addresses his arguments to the few and not to the many. However, the rest of the objection is a farrago of distortions and non sequiturs. The passage under discussion says not that Plato sometimes refrains from expressing serious propositional truth, but that he avoids it simply. Therefore, it does not assert or hint that the arguments that Plato addresses to the few contain serious propositional truth, or that he withholds it from the many, or that he can pronounce it whenever he wants. The passage also explains what would occur if Plato did try to publish his serious thoughts to the world. This would benefit only those who can learn by themselves with a little guidance—which seems to me to mean that the potential philosophers would still have to learn by themselves, because serious truth cannot be captured in words no matter how well crafted—and the incompetent would be harmed by being impelled into unwarranted feelings of scorn for philosophy or a ridiculous mumbo jumbo.

Why, though, should Plato's serious knowledge be ineffable, and why should attempts to teach it by speaking or writing fail to educate the intelligent and hurt the many? The answers to these questions depend upon what philosophy *is*. Plato tells us this by resorting to allegory or simile, just as Socrates does in the sun, line, and cave images of the *Republic*. Philosophy is a constant proximity to its matter that has rewarded Plato with flashes of illumination that resemble lightning. The reality thus brought to light is called "nature." *Amathia* is overcome only when one has experienced such enlightenment. Plato cannot give the competent verbal instruction because words differ essentially from the flashes of illumination. By implication, Plato can only counsel the intelligent on how to position themselves in order to receive the flashes, or lead them in the same exercises that were the occasions of his illuminations. This inference tallies with Socrates' statement that education consists not in putting vision into blind eyes, but, rather, in "the turning around" (τῆς περιαγωγῆς, *Republic* 518d3–4) of the soul, so that it might see for itself. If Plato tried to set the wordless flashes to words, the many who do not live in abiding nearness to the matter, and who therefore are unlikely to receive the illuminations, would find no referents for the words. This would inspire unjust contempt in some and make others ecstatic about speech that, to them, was unintelligible.

Now objections arise from opposite directions. Still striving to debunk the letter, Ludwig Edelstein declares it both fishy and inconsistent that "it is at this time and on this occasion that Plato tells what he has so far refrained from putting down in his published works."[48] In other words, it is suspicious that the epistle, unlike the dialogues, talks about flashes of light, or "non-discursive experience," and self-contradictory that it violates its own strictures against discussing such serious things. These charges are groundless. The allegories of the sun and the cave in the *Republic* abound in illumination images that are both epistemological equivalents and exact prototypes of that of the leaping flame.[49] Plato's resort to the analogy of the flashes in connection with his proclamation of his silence about serious things corresponds exactly to Socrates' promise to describe the offspring of the good in lieu of defining the good (*Republic* 506e3). The highest myth of the *Phaedrus* also alludes to silent viewing of the hyperuranian beings. It is precisely by using such similes that Plato refers to noetic experiences of serious realities without trying to analyze them.

Hans-Georg Gadamer, on the other hand, wants to place a completely different construction on the leaping-flame image. He believes that Plato trades only in propositional truths, that he has an esoteric oral teaching that was delivered in the lost lecture on the one and the indeterminate two, and that bits and pieces of this verbal doctrine show up both in the Seventh Letter and in the dialogues. Presumably, Gadamer's argument begins with the observation that Plato's flash of light illuminates "nature." Gadamer claims that this serious matter receives an expanded name when Plato mentions the treatise written by Dionysius "on the highest and first [things] of nature" (περὶ φύσεως ἄκρων καὶ πρώτων, 344d4–5). The language of *Statesman* 285d ff shows that the phrase "highest and first" is typical of Plato and that it refers to bodiless things. To write about the highest and first bodiless things of nature is to discuss serious reality with words. Further, at *Laws* 892c, the Athenian Stranger "calls the soul the essence of physis," so that Plato not only speaks about nature, but identifies its essence as well. All this implies that the simile of the flash of light cannot concern ineffable truth, and that it must refer to something else, such as the self-evident necessity that an insight must be able to maintain itself against all objections.[50]

Gadamer's argument cannot pass muster. First of all, it is probable that the name "the highest and first things of nature" was invented by Dionysius, not Plato, and that Plato greatly disapproves of it. It is also clear from

48. Edelstein, *Plato's Seventh Letter*, 108.

49. Plato's use of the identical images was called to my attention by Planinc, *Plato's Political Philosophy*, 85 ff.

50. Gadamer, "Dialektik und Sophistik," 111; "Dialectic and Sophism," 118; "Platos ungeschriebene Dialektik," 134, 143; "Plato's Unwritten Dialectic," 130, 142. "Dialektik und Sophistik," 95; "Dialectic and Sophism," 98.

the context in which Plato mentions this name that he thinks that nothing that anybody has written on such a topic could be sound. Plato does not even use the phrase "highest and first" at *Statesman* 286a5–6; he calls bodiless things "the most beautiful and greatest." Second, at the place cited in the *Laws,* the Athenian Stranger depicts nature as the ground from which all the things that come into being emerge. This is to speak not about nature, but about all of the things that come into being, just as Socrates declines to speak about the good in the *Republic,* but declares that the being and intelligibility of all known things come from it (509b6–10). Further, the Athenian Stranger does not call soul the essence of physis. What he actually says at 892c4–5 is that it is soul that preeminently comes into being by nature. Plato always talks about the highest things that come from nature, but never about nature, which is ineffable.

If it has not already done so, the so-called philosophic digression now begins (342a1).[51] Far from conceiving of this new discussion as irrelevant or digressive, Plato himself suggests that it might make that about which he has been writing clearer. Explaining why he has not tried to bring nature to light for everyone, he says that there is a true argument that confronts anyone who would write about these things, one that he has made frequently in the past and must now repeat again. Perhaps most of Plato's previous statements of the reasoning have been given in lectures. In his written works, a recognizable facsimile of it is found only in the *Laws* at 895d, where the analysis varies a little from that offered in the letter, perhaps because it is somewhat condensed.

What Plato is now doing is making a second approach to the summit of philosophy, or repeating what he has said in the simile of the lightning. Here is the argument: Three things are necessary to knowledge of each of the beings. The knowledge is fourth. Fifth is the being itself, which is knowable and true. First is the name (ὄνομα), second the definition (λόγος), third the image (ἔιδωλον), and fourth the knowledge (ἐπιστήμη). The circle provides an example. There is the name "circle." There is the definition that is composed of names and verbs. There is the image that we fashion and that can decay, and that is not the circle itself. There is knowledge and intelligence and true opinion (ἐπιστήμη καὶ νοῦς ἀληθής τε δόξα) about the circle, which must be assumed to form a whole that exists not in sounds or bodily forms but in souls, which makes it plain that nothing in this unit is itself the circle. Of these constituents of the fourth, intelligence (νοῦς) approaches the fifth most nearly. Going beyond circles, Plato remarks that this analysis holds true of the straight and the spherical, colors, the good,

---

51. Gadamer counts the "digression" as beginning here, that is, around 342a. See "Dialektik und Sophistik," 92; and "Dialectic and Sophism," 96.

the beautiful, the just, all bodies natural and artificial, all living beings, and all ethical actions or passions in souls. He does not declare that it applies to nature. One is compelled to wonder why, and one is forced to conclude that for the moment, Plato is talking about a science restricted to all the beings that come into existence from nature.

Next, Plato asserts that whoever fails to grasp the four will never acquire something new that he now introduces, "perfect knowledge" (τελέως ἐπιστήμης, 342e1–2) of the fifth. Here, Plato has distinguished two kinds of knowledge of the fifth, one of which is the fourth in the series "name, definition, image, and knowledge," and the other of which transcends the fourth, reaching the telos of efforts to know the fifth. The two sorts of knowledge must be different because the "knowledge" that is fourth is a prerequisite of the one that attains to the telos. The knowledge that is fourth cannot be a prerequisite of itself. Perhaps the perfect knowledge is a kind of union with the fifth, which itself is "knowable and true." Plato goes on to say that the four strive no less to express the quality (τὸ ποῖόν) of each (being) than to express the essence or being (τὸ ὄν) of each (being), this owing to the weakness of words (διὰ τῶν λόγων ἀσθενές, 342e2–343a1). So, it seems that the knowledge that is fourth in the series is a grasp of quality that has aimed at but fallen short of essence because words are inadequate. Thus, Plato concludes that no one who has reason will ever dare to put down (τιθέναι) the things known (τὰ νενοημένα, 343a1–3), especially not in unchangeable writing.

Plato says that the last statement needs explanation. Images such as circles are full of what is opposite to the fifth. Names can be changed at whim. Definitions are strings of names and, hence, suffer the same lack of firmness. The inaccuracy of each of the four is an endless topic. Now, the soul seeks to know not the quality but the essence or being. When the four offer the soul what it does not want, the disparity between the inaccurate four and the fifth makes statements easy of refutation and fills nearly everybody with perplexity and uncertainty. Worse, it is only words that can be used in oral and written accounts of beings, and the resulting gap between the four and the fifth allows any boor to make other people look ridiculous when they attempt to argue from the four to the fifth.

We may pause here to complete the argument that Plato's statement that serious things are "in no way a spoken thing like other lessons" means that they are ineffable simply and not that they are speakable in a unique way. As Kenneth Sayre remarks in his careful essay on the epistle, "The advice of passage 343a1–3 quoted above . . . is that no intelligent person would risk putting what he understands into language—into language (logos) of any sort—although written language is cited as particularly unreliable." To this, I would add that Plato has now declared explicitly that neither the

spoken nor the written word is adequate to put the soul in touch with the
serious things that it wants.[52]

Plato now repeats that the study of the four is necessary to knowledge
of the fifth, presumably meaning to the perfect knowledge of the fifth. One
must pass back and forth, up and down, among the four. Plato says nothing
about the manner in which one must pass back and forth, up and down,
among the four. He declares only that this passing fosters knowledge, "the
good-natured to the good-natured" (εὖ πεφυκότος εὖ πεφυκότι, 343e2–3),
with difficulty. When the individual is bad, though, as is the case with the
many either by nature or by corruption, not even Lynceus could make such
people see. Neither capacity to learn nor memory can help people to know
if they lack affinity with the matter. Without an affinity to the just and the
beautiful, even though there may be good learning and memory, there will
never be understanding of virtue and vice. Further, the truth about these
things must be learned in conjunction with the truth about the whole of
existence (τῆς ὅλης οὐσίας, 344b2). One must examine each being, pondering names, definitions, visions, and sense perceptions, proving them with
kindly proofs, inquiries, and answers that are void of envy. It is through
all this that the light of wisdom and reason about each being shines forth.
This is why the serious man (ἀνὴρ σπουδαῖος, 344c1) avoids writing about
the serious beings (τῶν ὄντων σπουδαίων, 344c2), lest he cast them as prey
to the envy and perplexity of human beings. So, whenever one sees written compositions, such as the laws of a legislator, these are not the serious
man's serious works. Rather, such works reside in the fairest region that
a person possesses. If written works are a man's serious ones, then it is
not the gods, but mortals who have ruined his senses. If Dionysius had
revered serious beings as Plato does, he would have never dared to write
about them, thus exposing them to unseemly and degrading treatment.

Although Plato's second ascent to the summit is difficult to follow, it appears to admit of this interpretation: Whoever seeks knowledge of each of
the beings is searching for two realities. The first is the essence of the thing
itself. One can use name, definition, and image to arrive at a science of this
essence, whether the thing itself is a quality, a substance, an action or passion of the soul, or even justice, the beautiful, and so on. However, one does
not arrive at what is sought, because the essence is mysteriously bound up
with nature. Perhaps this is why our minds are confined to knowledge of
the forms, or "looks," of things, or why we see only shadows on the wall

---

52. Sayre, "Plato's Dialogues in Light of the *Seventh Letter*," 95. Rosen denies that the
Seventh Letter implies that Plato's teaching "cannot be stated at all" (*Plato's "Symposium*," xliii). Sayre's analysis refutes him. Neither is Rosen right to charge that discerning ineffability in Plato is advocacy for a subjective passion of the Christian individual
(lv).

of the cave. The second reality sought is the ground of all things, nature. Name, definition, and image can provide no science or opinion of this. Nothing can be said about it. The name "nature" does not function like other names, pointing to things. It serves as a symbol of the unspeakable ground of all things.

It is necessary to operate in the medium of the four while seeking the fifth, the thing itself, or its essence. Gadamer has seen that to think in and through the four is to employ the dialectic in all its variants, such as division, combining opposites, and the like.[53] Now, in the simile of the lightning, that which was illuminated by the flashes was nature. In this "clarification" of the analogy, the perfect knowledge of the thing itself should also arise when nature is brought to light, for the essence of the thing must be grounded in nature. How are the essence and nature discovered in the ascent, though? Is it not by means of passing up and down among the four, that is, by means of the dialectic? Is it not necessary, then, to admit that this account contradicts the simile of the lightning by replacing something inexplicable and possibly supernatural, the flash, with a human method, indeed, a method that could be employed by evil men?

This inference is incorrect. The four cannot produce perfect knowledge of the fifth, owing to the weakness of words. It cannot be emphasized too much that manipulating the four in any manner whatsoever, or using the dialectic in all its forms, all of which rely upon words, does *not* cause the light of wisdom to shine. If there is to be union with the fifth, it must be wordless, and the soul of the seeker must have an affinity to the sought. This is why things known cannot be set down in speech or writing, or grasped by those who lack virtue. Every attempt to do so is confusing and opens the door to sophistry, a permanent potential in human discourse about the serious, an inclination to bandy words that have not and never could have reached to the perfect knowledge of the fifth.

Then why bother with passing up and down among the four? Dialectic has two uses. First, it leads to the knowledge that is fourth in the series. That is, it produces Plato's entire spoken and written analysis of soul, forms, the one and the indeterminate two, bodies, virtue, politics, and so on. This corpus of science is not so much false as incomplete. The dialectic does not lead to the telos of striving for knowledge. This is why the science is not serious. Thus, although dialectical technique is important throughout the four, philosophy is ultimately not a matter of finding and using right techniques.[54] The second and more important use of the dialectic is that it

---

53. Gadamer, "Dialektik und Sophistik," 114; "Dialectic and Sophism," 122.

54. Gadamer, despite his insight into Plato's refusal to equate philosophy with technique, tends to view dialectic and its results as the most important things about Platonic philosophy, missing the subordination of dialectic to illumination. He enables himself

prepares the soul for receiving the light of wisdom. Plato's language suggests that what is happening as one passes up and down among the four is a kind of habituation to being good-natured, or a sort of preparation of the soul's fairest region, so that the light can enter and shine in it, "good-natured to good-natured." This is why Plato brings the other prerequisites of philosophy back into the argument here. The crucial thing about philosophic inquiries is not that they are conducted by individuals who learn well and have good memories, like Dionysius, but that they are carried out by people who have divine, moral, and intellectual affinities for the subject, or by good characters whose hearts and minds have been purified, so that they can receive the light. Just as the first arguments that Plato gave Dion were useful because they produced moral conversion, the dialectic is useful because it refines intellectual affinity for philosophy's highest subject matter. Thus, Plato's first approach to the summit is really clarified and expanded by the second.

The debt to Hipparinus has been paid. Plato has told Hipparinus that his father was not a man of reason and did not escape *amathia* because he heard only Plato's mythological ethical arguments, but did not progress to the dialectic, and did not experience the flash of light. Hipparinus now knows everything that is expected of him if he wants to win Plato's friendship and support. Perhaps Plato should expect the youth to be incapable of grasping the teaching. That will not matter. If Hipparinus is philosophic, he will ask.

Returning from the "digression," Plato resumes his attack on Dionysius, and recites the history of his efforts to restrain the tyrant and Dion from evil. Here, Plato retreats behind his disguise while confirming Hipparinus in the distinctions among the tyrannical, true believing, and philosophic types. We have already extracted the theoretical essence of this discussion.

PLATO AS MYSTIC PHILOSOPHER

Ludwig Edelstein makes one last objection to the Seventh Letter that is worth pondering. He argues that for the author of the epistle, philosophy is "an affection of the soul comparable to the ancient mystic experience," and that the real Plato could not have agreed with that.[55] In this attack, Edelstein

---

to place dialectic at the pinnacle of Platonic philosophy only by taking the following steps. First, he tears the "digression" out of its context in the letter as a whole, thus freeing himself to neglect Plato's comments about the divine origin of philosophy and the necessary relationship of philosophy to virtue. Second, he ignores the fact that the "digression" is introduced as a clarification of the lightning simile. Third, he refuses to accept the plain meanings of Plato's statements that there are *no* writings of his on that about which he is serious.

55. Edelstein, *Plato's Seventh Letter,* 107; cf. the reply by T. M. Robinson in his "Review of *Plato's Seventh Letter,*" by Edelstein.

ill-advisedly invokes the aid of Immanuel Kant. He notes that in 1796, Kant found it expedient to criticize a newly arisen aristocratic tone in philosophy. Apparently, Kant had encountered people who were excited about secrets that could not be expressed or generally shared in speech, such secrets falling in the domain of *philosophus per inspirationem*. Kant charges that these individuals want to shirk the real labor of philosophy, namely, the dissolution and rebuilding of all concepts by the discursive understanding. He compares these "aristocrats" to the shiftless, lazy Mongol hordes who scorned industrious city dwellers, and he tells his diligent readers that the slackers espouse a "pretended philosophy" in which one does not need to work, but needs only to "listen to and enjoy the oracle" in oneself in order to possess all wisdom.[56]

Having vented his great displeasure with thinkers who want the rewards of philosophy without the necessary effort, Kant maintains that the paradigmatic offender is Plato. In his attempts to explain the existence of a priori notions that make synthetic statements possible, Plato postulates perceptions that have their sources not in human understanding, but in the primordial ground *(Urgrund)* of all things, the divine understanding. Plato needs to establish that these perceptions are more than subjective feeling. His effort involves a "mystical tact," a "jumping over *(salto mortale)* from concepts to the unthinkable that attains to no concept," a "mystical illumination," and, hence, a fall into *Schwärmerei* (that is, the enthusiasm of visionary charlatans) that is "the death of all philosophy." Hence, Plato is "the father of all *Schwärmerei* in philosophy."[57] Unfortunately for Edelstein, this severe polemic holds that the Plato of the dialogues is a mystic. However, Edelstein overlooks this difficulty because he is delighted by Kant's denunciation of the Seventh Letter as a forgery.

Kant does think that there is a second "Plato" who is worse than the first. When this pseudo-Plato advocates proceeding from the four to the fifth, he wants to reach "the object itself and its true being," an aspiration that is anathema to Kant, with his distinction between the phenomenon and the unknowable thing-in-itself. Criticizing the letter writer's lightning simile, Kant rhetorically asks: "Who does not see here the mystagogue who rants *(schwärmt)* not simply for himself, but who simultaneously is a clubbist insofar as he speaks to his adepts, as opposed to the people?"[58]

In weighing Kant's extraordinarily aggressive assault on the "two" Platos, I shall begin by adverting to some of Stanley Rosen's remarks. Rosen observes that Kant considers himself "the voice of reason," that Kant

56. Kant, "Von einem neuerdings erhobenen vornehmen Ton in der Philosophie," 377–79.
57. Ibid., 379–86.
58. Ibid., 388.

also believes that "reason is entitled to secure its authority by ad hominem argumentation when that authority cannot be scientifically or objectively enforced," and that "this is quite Socratic or Platonic."[59] I agree that ad hominem reasoning is Socratic or Platonic, in the sense that Socrates and Plato tailor their arguments to particular souls, striving to move each soul toward truth from its starting point along a spectrum of virtue and vice, or along a parallel spectrum defined by openness and opacity to the divine ground of truth, and reluctantly concluding that many souls will never attain to truth because they are too deeply mired in evil. However, there is another kind of ad hominem argumentation, one that tries to falsify proposed truths by vilifying those who suggest them, without regard for the actual characters of the persons thus condemned, the real relationships of those characters to truth, and the truth itself. This ad hominem reasoning is not Socratic or Platonic, but it is the kind of unworthy polemic that Kant directs against the Platos. What Kant attempts to do is to turn a nation of hardworking burghers against Plato and the author of the Seventh Letter by casting them as philosophic equivalents of inherently parasitical, presumptuous, yellow-skinned marauders, that is, good-for-nothing Asiatic types who want everything that makes life worth living without having to work for it, and also as nondemocrats. It would be fair to give Kant a dose of his own medicine. One could view with alarm the example of a supposedly liberal, enlightened "voice of reason" who tries to destroy the two Platos by appealing to the same petty-bourgeois, racist, populist prejudice that found expression on the gates of Auschwitz. However, the matter cannot be left at that. Although this response to Kant is not unjust, it is important to notice some of the philosophic questions that he raises.

The first such question is whether the real labor of philosophy is the dissolution and rebuilding of all concepts by the discursive understanding. Neither of the "two" Platos would concur in this description of the task. The chief concern of the author of the Seventh Letter is to educate a king who will know justice and introduce it into human society on the broadest possible scale. This is also one of the main cares of the Plato of the dialogues, or at least one of his chief exoteric preoccupations. The difference between the two interpretations of philosophy is profound. The barely concealed point of Kant's enterprise is to demonstrate that the rational mind originates, controls, and validates all of its own thoughts, or that the mind is its own place. The ostensible thrust of the Platos is to discover the right way of life for a man who exists in an order of being that is determined by a higher reality. Either of the Platos would be stunned to learn that his lifework had been to explain the possibility of a priori concepts that permit synthetic propositions, an activity that would be one of the steps

---

59. Rosen, *Hermeneutics as Politics*, 38.

in the dissolution and rebuilding of all concepts by the discursive understanding.

The second issue involves the identity of the faculty that is the seat or receptacle of the highest human knowledge. For the purpose of this analysis, it is permissible to say that Kant thinks that it is the discursive understanding. The author of the Seventh Letter holds that it is a person's fairest region (344c7–8), which is also the soul's smallest possible space (344e1–2). By a generous interpretation, one could equate Kant's discursive understanding with Plato's capacity for perusing name, definition, image, and knowledge, and the reasoning of Kant's discursive understanding with Plato's dialectic. Kant can follow Plato no higher, though. He refuses to acknowledge the reality of the fairest region. In arbitrating between the two, we would err if we demanded that the existence of the fairest region be proved by discursive understanding. This tiny space would become known to itself only after having experienced itself. The *Republic* seems to suggest that this expectation is Socratic.

The third question is this: What can the highest noetic faculty of man actually know? Kant's discursive understanding has extreme difficulty validating synthetic propositions and abandons hope of penetrating to the *Ding-an-sich*. His reason knows only what it controls or defines. The epistle's science at the fourth level aspires to more than this, but it admittedly falls short of grasping the Kantian *Ding-an-sich*. In proceeding to the perfect knowledge of the fifth, the author of the Seventh Letter alludes to a direct experience of illumination of nature, the ground of being. With this enlightenment comes comprehension of the *Ding-an-sich* and insight into all forms of justice public and private. The limits on Kant's discursive reason are thereby transcended, provided, of course, that a person really does enjoy such an experience. I think that Edelstein and Kant err in holding that in this regard, the writer of the letter goes further than the Plato of the dialogues. The epistle's claims do not seem to me to differ greatly from those of the *Republic* 508d–509b, 511a–e, and 515c–516c. Again, doctrinal evidence fails to prove that there necessarily are two Platos.

To be sure, Edelstein and Kant are right about one thing. If reporting experience of illumination of the ground of being is mystical, then the one Plato who seems to be talking is, indeed, a mystic philosopher. We now must consider the charge that this Plato is a *Schwärmer* and a mystagogue. It will be difficult to evaluate this ad hominem complaint because one is not quite sure what the essential attributes of a *Schwärmer* and a mystagogue are. I take the accusation to mean that Plato resembles religious people who become intoxicated by mixtures of their own desires, emotions, and imaginings; who try to lead others into their drunkenness; and who pretend to certain knowledge that they do not and could not possess. Is this a fair characterization of Plato's work?

In answer, I would say that Plato strikes me as austerely sober. Even his most playful dialogues are meticulous in the smallest detail and ever ready to repudiate their conclusions and begin anew. The Plato of the epistle stresses the need for a lifetime of hard work, during which insights are won only with difficulty. His possibly intoxicated view of the wonderful things that would occur if a philosopher-kingship were instituted is balanced by doubt that a just regime will ever see the light of day. Mystagoguery is entirely absent; Plato's silence in the Seventh Letter is opposed to and scornful of such proselytizing. Far from laying claim to certainty, Plato's Socrates always warns that he knows nothing, and definitely nothing that the god knows. He especially does this both before and after the allegories of the sun, the line, and the cave (*Republic* 506c2–3, 517b6–7). If his disclaimers are sincere, his mysticism is clearly not gnostic, or at least is less gnostic than Kant's assurance that he can dissolve and rebuild all human concepts by means of the discursive understanding. So, the accusation of *Schwärmerei* hinges upon this last question: Is the type of insight that Plato describes in the Seventh Letter possible?

Those of us who have not experienced illumination of the natural ground of being, or who have access to it without being aware that we do, can respond to this query in either of two ways, namely, with closed or open minds. Closed minds have no a priori grounds for denying the possibility of the flashes of light; they can only refuse to believe in the leaping flames because they see no evidence of them. Open minds will resist making blind leaps of affirmation. However, they will be ready to participate in an experiment, that of submitting to Platonic education, acquiring the virtues, striving for synopsis by going up and down the four, and waiting to see what happens. Is there then a good reason for the closed minds to become open, and to invest time and effort in the experiment? One could suggest that virtue is its own reward. One could also make the following calculation: Perhaps surprisingly for those who have not read him carefully, the author of the epistle agrees with Kant and modern positivists that logical science cannot transcend the fact-value distinction. This result should not be unexpected. Logical science is limited to the investigation of visible and mathematical things, whereas justice is thought to be a reality higher than those things. Justice could be found only by some means other than logical science. Hence, it might be worthwhile to determine whether Plato's reports are true. Of course, this reasoning will seem uncongenial to all those who, like Kant, insist upon making the mind its own place or, to say the same thing, to all those who aspire to be gods.

Meanwhile, it seems that our study of the Seventh Letter clearly supports the following conclusion: Plato is silent about serious knowledge for the reasons given by Friedrich Schleiermacher, Søren Kierkegaard, Eric Voegelin, and Paul Friedländer, not for the reasons such as those advanced by Friedrich Nietzsche, Leo Strauss, and Stanley Rosen.[60] That is, understanding of nature, and of all the forms of justice public and private, is mystical and ineffable. The very attempt to speak it distorts it. Those who have it cannot even say it to themselves, except with metaphors, for it does not consist in compendia of true propositions. Possessing it is more like being illuminated, or, to change the metaphor, more like having an internal gyroscope or an instrument of attunement to a homing beacon, than like owning an encyclopedia or a reference manual. Plato avoids setting the truth to words because he fears that such a perversion of its nature will cause the many to misconstrue it, thereby plunging themselves more deeply into a folly and injustice that will be bad not so much for him as for *them*. He is not, and in the nature of the case could not be, worried that revealing propositional truth will prompt the many to harm him, or that it will destroy some divine control over the many, or over being itself, that no philosopher has ever had.

It might be objected that this analysis ignores contradictions in the Seventh Letter that hint at esoteric doctrines contrary to what is adduced here. For example, Plato is vague about the relationship of chance and providence and treats it differently in different places. Further, his discussion of the leaping flames is "replaced" by his treatment of the five. I reply that the problem of chance and providence is not carried to a perfectly clear resolution because its mystery cannot be penetrated completely by human reason; even the serious people of faith do not pretend to be able to sort it out. The lightning metaphor is augmented, not replaced, by the account of the five. Generally, as shown above, the different treatments of subjects are complementary, not contradictory. Perhaps more examples of "contradictions" in the epistle can be adduced. There is not enough space here to anticipate every such objection. Suffice it to say that it would be possible but not reasonable to contrive these difficulties forever.

This concludes a long preparation for our study of eros and wisdom in the dialogues of Plato. What have we gained? I believe that we now have a much better understanding of what we can expect from a Platonic writing. Plato and his dramatic character Socrates try to move us toward knowledge of the serious things in two ways in the dialogues. First, they help us to comprehend the high realities, such as eros, by dragging us back and forth, and up and down, among these four: name, definition, image, and knowledge. Sometimes they employ myths in aid of this end; at other times they use the tools of dialectical logic. They lead us to sciences that grasp qualities of the serious things and related matters, such as the moral

---

60. To the extent that Schleiermacher views Plato as a mystic philosopher, it is incorrect to identify him as a modern. Cf. Rosen, *Plato's "Symposium,"* liv.

implications of what has been discovered. The propositions of these sciences are universally true and widely applicable, as far as they go. However, the sciences are incomplete. They do not yield what every soul wants, insights into the essences of the high realities and knowledge of the ground of those essences, nature. Still, the sciences are worth learning because they are true as far as they go—which is not to say simply true, a standard beyond the reach of propositional speech that fails to penetrate to essences and nature. Again, they are worth learning because mastering them—with all their historically and factually untrue myths; their names, definitions, and images that are never quite precise; their provisional hypotheses that are almost always refuted and transcended; and their "knowledge" that finally withstands every methodological test without yet being adequate— purifies souls for reception of the perfect knowledge that is promised to the good-natured. There are enough of these partially true and cathartic sciences to justify all of Plato's writing, even though, from the ultimate standpoint, going back and forth and up and down among the four does not suffice. Second, Plato and Socrates attempt to use their myths and sciences to maneuver our purified souls into position to receive the light of the leaping flames. Our task is to allow ourselves to be moved in these ways.

4

SYMPOSIUM: TITANIC EROS

We have seen that Socrates claims to have a science of eros. With regard to this subject of knowledge, he ranks himself as wondrously clever beyond any human being of the past or present. In Plato's dialogues, he gives us a series of definitions of eros. First he calls it desire and then yearning. He says that it is not a god, but a daimon, but then he indicates that it is a god or something divine. He leaves the definition hanging in ambiguity, never quite bringing himself to provide us with a precise, noncontradictory formula. Perhaps, on the testimony of the Seventh Letter, we may assume that he refrains from defining eros more exactly because it is one of the serious things and Plato maintains that words fail to capture the essences of the serious things. Socrates and Plato's other characters also attribute a great variety of objects to eros. It desires what everybody supposes, sexual intercourse. However, it is also desire for food, drink, job skills, fishing, moderate and just practices, wealth, ignoble gain, unlimited acquisition, and, indeed, all good things. It is desire for immortality in every way. At its noblest or most beautiful heights, in "right pederasty," it begins as longing for union with a beloved and then ascends to yearnings for virtuous souls, moderation, justice, beautiful laws, learning and the sciences, wisdom, and an ultimate vision of eternal beauty. At its lowest depths, it is desire for the things that tyrants want. Socrates thinks it important to have a science of eros because it is love that leads us to our felicity or misery, because eros is therefore the thing that teachers must know to help students fulfill their natures, and because eros is a powerful determinant of political behavior, such that a *technē* or science of eros is indispensable to anyone who aspires to political wisdom. These are the reasons we should know Socrates' erotic science. We may now begin our attempt to acquire it.

The Seventh Letter has taught us that learning the Socratic science of eros is not simply a matter of opening Platonic handbooks and extracting helpful true propositions from them. To be sure, we can find true Socratic sayings about eros. However, these doctrines are true in ways that are ultimately inadequate. They are nothing but verbal approximations of a serious reality, intended to propel us toward illuminations that constitute a more perfect knowledge. It is not clear that we know how to read Plato in a manner that yields these results. The only method of exegesis that I can recommend at the moment is to pay attention to everything in a Platonic dialogue, beginning with what is plain to the eye and hoping that we will be led from there to whatever lies beyond.

It seems to me that the most obvious thing about the first of Plato's erotic works, the *Symposium*, is that the dialogue is a dramatic poem, a play filled with interactions among the characters and with speeches that contain myths, arguments, and reminiscences. I think that in order to help Plato educate us as he wishes, we must take the *Symposium* as we find it. We must study it as a drama, examining its characters, actions, myths, arguments, and memories, and heeding the complex ways in which its author weaves these strands of his artistic creation together.

When we consider a play, we inquire first into its subject and plot. We ask: What is it about? What happens? When we pose these questions about the *Symposium*, we immediately get two sets of conflicting answers from different sorts of groups that are presently the sources of our orthodoxies.

One of the clashing groups is a mere aggregate. It consists of most of the scholars who have treated the *Symposium*. These authors share a basic assumption about the nature of the dialogue but little else. I can recount their common opinion but not their diverse arguments, which constitute a literature too vast to summarize. What these commentators agree upon is that the *Symposium* is a comedy about eros. In the drama, Socrates and his friends, a coterie of brilliant, well-educated, highly accomplished, and witty men, many or all of whom are gay in our anachronistic modern parlance, celebrate eros by staging camp performances, clowning around, showing off their erudition, and saying beautiful things about love. The product is a collection of Platonic perspectives on eros. Some proponents of this opinion believe that the Platonic viewpoints are meant more to entertain than to instruct. Accordingly, they declare it churlish to subject the dialogue to close philosophic scrutiny or to fuss about the logic or rectitude of its doctrines. Other members of the group think that some or all of the Platonic perspectives (especially those of Aristophanes and Diotima) are intended to add up to the whole philosophic truth about eros. Therefore, they analyze the dialogue by praising or blaming its various myths, propositions, and arguments as true or false, logical or fallacious, moral or immoral, inspiring or appalling, and so on.

The other group consists of Stanley Rosen, Allan Bloom, and probably other students of Leo Strauss. Although Rosen agrees that the *Symposium* presents itself as a play about eros, he interprets "Platonism" generally and this dialogue particularly as esoteric metaphysics. In his book on the *Symposium*, and in other essays that return to the dialogue, he employs Strauss's methods of reading in a sustained effort to prove that each character in the work contributes something to a coded ontological teaching on the question *quid sit deus?* Bloom's interests are ethical rather than metaphysical, but he uses the same methods in aid of the same result.[1] I cannot endorse either orthodoxy. In reply to the common opinion of the first group, I suggest the following points.

First, it is true that the *Symposium* is a comedy about eros. However, careful reading will show that the dialogue is simultaneously a tragedy about eros. When Plato has Socrates state near the end of the play that whoever knows how to make tragedy also knows how to make comedy (223d5–6), he is probably hinting at the dual nature of his work. The common opinion is invalid to the extent that it overlooks this. It is easy to laugh with Plato in the play—although one cannot be sure that one is quick enough to get all of Plato's jokes—but we need to do more than laugh. We must strive to see humor and heartbreak at the same time, perhaps even to discern humor in heartbreak and heartbreak in humor, so that we end up weeping and laughing simultaneously. It will not be easy to keep these elements of our task in balance. We could get dizzy and fall as we try to follow Plato across his tragicomical high wire. However, it helps to know the task.

Second, I understand that Socrates is on gracious and friendly terms with the other characters in the *Symposium*. However, I doubt that Socrates and the others are "friends" in any simple sense. We are obliged to recall that we met Phaedrus, Eryximachus, Pausanias, and Agathon in the *Protagoras*. Phaedrus and Eryximachus were pupils of the sophist Hippias. Pausanias and Agathon were students of the sophist Prodicus. Sometime after the dramatic date of the *Protagoras*, 432 B.C., Pausanias and Agathon abandoned Prodicus and went over to the sophist Gorgias—probably in 427 B.C., when Gorgias made his first visit to Athens. It is highly likely that men who have been educated by sophists have become sophists themselves. Indeed, after Agathon gives his speech in the *Symposium*, Socrates declares that it reminds him of Gorgias (198c1–2). Socrates at the least is worried about the health of the souls of sophists. We remember that before rehearsing his discussion with the great sophist in the *Protagoras*, Socrates tells his companion who attended the meeting, " 'And next I observed,' as Homer says" (315b9). He thus indicates that he descended spiritually into Hades when he entered Callias's home and that he is calling the roll of the

---

1. Rosen, *Metaphysics in Ordinary Language*, 52; Rosen, *Plato's "Symposium"*; Bloom, *Love and Friendship*. In my opinion, Rosen and Bloom, especially Rosen, thus succumb to Hegel's temptation to force Plato into one or more particular fields. This, together with Rosen's belief that there is such a thing as "Platonism," appears to me to be indicative of a fundamental misunderstanding of the nature of Platonic philosophy.

psychically dead. I believe that if Phaedrus, Eryximachus, Pausanias, and Agathon were spiritually dead in 432, their souls are probably still dead in 416, the year of the banquet in our drama. Further, we should recollect that the *Gorgias* opens with the words "war and battle" (447a1). The *Gorgias* competes with the *Protagoras* for the distinction of being the dialogue in which Socrates is the most nasty toward his interlocutors. Socrates has been at war with Gorgias and has probably been at war with Gorgias's students, too.[2] So, it makes sense that, as reported in our introduction, Socrates induces Aristodemus to go with him to the party by alluding to Homer, saying, "When two go together, one precedes another in devising what we shall say" (174d2–3), thus indicating that Agathon and his usual associates are an enemy army. His views of Aristophanes and Alcibiades surely must be equally complicated. After all, in his *Apology,* Socrates blames Aristophanes for having invented charges (in the *Clouds,* in 423) that have led to his trial and mortal danger (18d1–2, 19c2). As we shall see, he also hates Alcibiades' crimes. Thus, we must assume that Socrates is ambivalent toward all of his companions at the party. He must regard them both as friends and as enemies, or at least both as friends and as problems. The common opinion is defective to the extent that it misses this. We must improve upon it by inquiring how Socrates could see his fellows in such paradoxical lights.

Third, it is right to report that in the *Symposium,* Socrates and his friends-enemies celebrate eros by staging camp performances, clowning, displaying their erudition, and saying beautiful things about love. However, because the dialogue is both a comedy and a tragedy about eros, we cannot become so taken with the camp nature of the speeches that we focus on their styles totally to the exclusion of their contents, or delight in their playfulness without observing that most have profoundly disturbing undertones. Again, because the drama is a comedy-tragedy about eros, we cannot expect the speakers merely to exalt love. They also exemplify a kind of havoc that eros is wreaking in human affairs. Given that there are healthy and diseased forms of love, or good and evil erotes, the better eros is celebrated, whereas the worse is exposed as the source of the tragic troubles. Further, although the characters in the *Symposium* do say beautiful things about love, Socrates also happens to think that some of the statements are beautiful in extremely frightening ways (198c2). Beauty, or different forms of it, can have both elevating and destructive effects. The common opinion errs insofar as it fails to keep the paradoxes of simultaneous levity and gravity, celebration and censure, healthy and sick loves, and elevating and frightening beauties in view. It also ignores the Seventh Letter on the topic of science.

---

2. Cf. Voegelin, *Order and History,* 3:24.

In response to Rosen and Bloom, I shall say only a few general things here and take up particular issues later in my analysis. It is true that there is a great deal of metaphysics in the *Symposium*. However, this does not mean that the work is about metaphysics. It is also the case that the *Symposium* is filled with oddities that look like esoteric signals, but this does not imply that its characters are ironic tools of Plato's self-deification. The passages on ontology tend to be cynical sophistical jokes. Ultimately, the *Symposium* refrains from specifying the essences of the highest realities, offering its metaphysical insights not as scientific truths but as means to open souls to illuminations. The dialogue's contradictions, repetitions, silences, and the like have the same function. It is arbitrary to drive them all toward the *quid sit deus?* question. I could try to show this exhaustively, but refuting all of the esoteric moves of Rosen and Bloom would necessitate a tedious and endless polemic, for the possibilities of viewing Plato's words as ironic masks of self-deification are infinite. Disproving such interpretations is like hacking off the heads of a hydra. I hope to spare myself and the reader the tribulations of a perpetual polemic by mentioning only the most important arguments of Strauss and his students.

If I reject the prevailing orthodoxies, what do I say the subject and plot of the *Symposium* are? I can reply with a brief preview of what I think I have seen in the dialogue. I shall begin with what I have suggested already. I perceive the *Symposium* as a comedy-tragedy about eros. It is a comedy because its characters do and say inherently funny things. It is also a comedy because love is playful. The life of love is one of incessant games and laughter. Again, it is a comedy because human beings cannot capture serious things in words. As Socrates leads the others up to the loveliest vision, they all view mere images of beauty in playful myths and arguments. Finally, it is a comedy because lovers and philosophers must be the funniest playthings of gods who have sent eros to call them to their destinies. The dialogue is a tragedy because there are both healthy and sick forms of eros, or good and bad erotes. The happiness toward which the healthy or good eros leads us is marred or destroyed by the iniquity into which the diseased or bad eros can plunge us. Loves that are initially healthy, good, and beautiful can degenerate into sick, evil, and ugly tyrannical desires. This can occur both in individuals and in societies. In the *Symposium,* it takes place, or is on the verge of happening, both in the souls of most of the characters and in Athens as a whole. Thus, whereas the Seventh Letter implicitly depicts a struggle between the Socratic and tyrannical erotes in the real lives of Plato and Syracuse, the *Symposium* explicitly studies this sort of conflict in a play. Further, I suspect that the *Symposium* dramatizes a war between the Socratic and tyrannical loves that actually occurred in Athens in the years before its fall, a fight that unfortunately culminated in the victory of the evil eros and the consequent devastation of the city. In the medium of his play, Plato makes the war's erotes, antagonists, and events as true to life as possible.[3] He does so because he sees a philosophic need to analyze the forms that the tyrannical eros assumed in Athens, forms that we could classify as different types of "wrong pederasty," and also to contrast them with the "right pederasty" that would have saved the city.[4]

The fact that the *Symposium* dramatizes a war that really occurred between the good, Socratic eros and the evil, tyrannical eros explains why Socrates paradoxically views the other characters in the dialogue as both friends and enemies. Socrates cherishes these comrades for a number of reasons and worries about them on other grounds.

One of Socrates' less important reasons for treasuring his companions might be that he, perhaps like Plato, is a gay or bisexual man who finds himself in the company of physical beauties such as Phaedrus, Agathon, and Alcibiades, who are also gay or bisexual men. After all, Socrates discloses in the *Charmides* (155d) that he once was aroused to fiery passion when he happened to glance beneath a boy's garment.[5] Socrates might be sexually attracted to Phaedrus and Agathon. He is surely smitten with Alcibiades' beauty. However, as I do not tire of warning, this observation is anachronistic and ultimately unimportant to the argument, for Socratic love quickly ascends from bodies to souls, which are of decisive importance.

It is clear that Socrates loves his comrades for their souls. He, Agathon, Aristophanes, and Alcibiades are among the most talented Athenians of their day in real life. As a boy, Agathon had a "noble and good nature" in addition to being physically beautiful (*Protagoras* 315d8–e1). In the time of our play, he has become one of the most renowned tragedians in Athens. Then there is Aristophanes. Who could not love Aristophanes, who makes us laugh until our sides split? In the *Alcibiades I,* we see that Socrates loves the lad Alcibiades for his greatness of soul (103a–105e). In real life, when our banquet occurs, Alcibiades is on his way to becoming the political

---

3. This is something like the same sense that Shakespeare makes King Henry V and the battle of Agincourt as true to life as possible in *Henry V.* It is not that what appears in the play is exactly what happened in historical fact. Rather, the essence of what happened in historical fact is distilled into a concentrate that is presented in the dramatic characters.

4. The Jewish and Christian proposition that there should have been no pederasty at all would have been foreign to ancient thought. Plato approves of "right pederasty" while raising some questions about the role of sexual intercourse in this pederasty. Trapped in our time as we are, one cannot avoid speaking occasionally to intrinsically anachronistic issues.

5. One of my anonymous referees argues that Socrates is joking. I appreciate his point. Allan Bloom thinks that Socrates is serious. Either could be right. It does not matter, for Socrates and Plato seem able to discern the movements of love in persons of all orientations, whatever their own may be.

leader of Athens. For all we know, Phaedrus, Pausanias, and Eryximachus belong to the intellectual elite, too, although they shine rather less brilliantly than their fellows in Plato's dramas. Phaedrus possesses "something divine with regard to speeches," having elicited more speeches than anyone but Simmias (*Phaedrus* 242a7). Eryximachus and Pausanias have ample medical and rhetorical abilities. In short, Socrates loves and befriends all these men for their native beauty, goodness, talent, and greatness. He plays with them as lovers do. To some extent, they reply in kind, thus giving rise to many of the comic elements in our drama.

On the other hand, Socrates' comrades also resist him because they are erotically ill. Worse, their disease is ruining Athens. Unhappily, it is possible for the best and the brightest whom we love to go bad and corrupt everything around them. As Socrates argues in the *Republic*, the best natures turn out worst when they are reared improperly. Indeed, the best souls become exceptionally bad when they are taught wrongly. They become capable of the greatest crimes, for mediocrities never achieve anything great, whether good or evil. A philosophic nature badly nurtured spawns the greatest injustices (491b–492a). In other words, it becomes tyrannical. This is what is happening to Socrates' friends in the *Symposium*, with the horrifying result that the entire city of Athens is being perverted and pushed onto the path to disaster. This is why Socrates' friends are also his foes. Socrates must wage war on them. He must certainly be heartbroken. However, closing the circle of our paradoxes, he fights by loving these enemies. He practices right pederasty on them to recall them from their evil and to save his city.

The war between the Socratic right pederasty and the tyrannical wrong pederasty that rages in the *Symposium* is fought in three campaigns. These operations give the dialogue the peculiar tripartite, down-up-down structure that I mentioned in the introduction.

In the first campaign, the sophists and Aristophanes resist or attack Socrates by presenting their views of eros. The less able, noble, and inspiring thinkers lead off and are followed by those who are more able, inspiring, and noble. Therefore, the first campaign is paradoxically a simultaneous ascent and descent. It is an ascent with regard to the intellectual excellence and beauty of the speeches. It is a descent in light of the Socratic principle just cited, that the greatest injustices occur when the best souls go wrong. The less capable speeches are also the least worrisome; the intellectually and artistically superior orations of Aristophanes and Agathon are also the most dangerous to the health or right order of souls and societies. Accordingly, on the whole, this movement is a descent. The battlefield of this campaign is the culture of Athens. Whether or not the sophists and Aristophanes recognize and intend it, the erotic illness that they suffer and

communicate prepares the city culturally for the political and military adventures into which Alcibiades later leads it.

In the second campaign, Socrates lovingly counterattacks the sophists
and Aristophanes, struggling to pull them back from the brink of the abyss.
Speaking through Diotima, Socrates ascends to the vision of eternal beauty.

In the third operation, Alcibiades arrives at the banquet at the head of
a rabble. In his speech, he paradoxically loves and attacks Socrates, thus
creating a perverse mirror image of his former teacher's campaign. However, he has not heard Socrates' oration and never listens to him anymore.
His speech is a descent; he is tumbling straight toward the personal and
political disasters that he precipitates in his real life. Apparently, he cannot be recalled. By the end of the play, the sophists and Aristophanes have
laughed at Alcibiades' speech. Aristophanes and Agathon are still drinking
with Socrates and yielding to his persuasion until they doze off. Their behavior indicates, perhaps, that they can be kept from the abyss themselves
but that they are insufficiently vigilant against the political élan that they
have both fostered and scorned. Meanwhile, Alcibiades and his mob have
gone to their suicidal follies. In this chapter, I shall cover the first sophistical
campaign of the war.

It might be objected that Socrates' comrades in the *Symposium* look more
like pleasant fellows saying charming things at a party than budding tyrants at war. This is quite true if the question is what the speakers look
like. Plato wants them true to life. In reality, tyrants neither understand
nor present themselves as evil. They do not behave like the caricatures of
villains whom we encounter in novels, movies, and cartoons. Rather, they
think themselves just and justified, play and laugh like other people, and
are seductively attractive and hard to see through.[6] They are incarnate examples of frightening beauty. Plato wants us to recognize tyrants both as
they seem and as they really are.

It might also be objected that in blaming the fall of Athens on the likes
of Phaedrus, Eryximachus, Pausanias, Agathon, Aristophanes, and Alcibiades, I am taxing gays unfairly with a great responsibility for tyrannical
misadventures. Once again, this concern is rather anachronistic; Greeks did
not think in such terms. However, I answer that, as I observed in the previous chapter, sexual orientation has nothing to do with tyranny. Tyrannical
eros can arise with equal facility in the souls of heterosexuals, bisexuals,

---

6. For example, "Hopkins was elated by his intimate conversation with Stalin. He
found the Russian leader intelligent, courteous, and direct. . . . In four hours of conversation, Hopkins saw no signs of the cruel and ruthless temperament that lay behind Stalin's mask of politeness. Like so many other Americans who met Stalin during
the war, Hopkins came away impressed" (Doris Kearns Goodwin, *No Ordinary Time:
Franklin and Eleanor Roosevelt, the Home Front in World War II*, 257.)

and homosexuals. If Plato were to write a dialogue on the collapse of the French Revolution into Jacobinism and the tyranny of Napoléon, or a drama on the Russian Revolution and Stalin's dictatorship, the characters (as far as I know) all would be erotically sick heterosexuals. In the *Symposium*, the speakers are homosexual and bisexual because, by historical chance, gays were the best and brightest men of classical Athens and the comedy-tragedy of the polis played itself out in their souls. It was gay partisans of wrong pederasty who ruined the city, but it was also a possibly gay or bisexual philosopher, at any rate a philosopher of right pederasty, who would have saved it, had he been heeded. With this, we may turn to the reading of our play.

THE DRAMATIC SETTING

The *Symposium* contains a prologue in which the chief speaker, Apollodorus, consents to recount the speeches on eros given at a banquet attended by Agathon, Socrates, Alcibiades, and others. In the body of the dialogue, Apollodorus recites conversations that he heard not in person, but from Aristodemus of Cydathenaeum, also known as Aristodemus the Short.[7]

Scholars generally suppose that the dramatic date of this prologue must be 401 or 400 B.C. because Apollodorus, who is known to have been a late companion of Socrates, says that he has been following the master almost three years (172c3–6). Disagreeing with the majority, Leo Strauss dates the episode to 407 because that is the year of Alcibiades' return to Athens. Contradicting both of these views, Martha Nussbaum first argues that the conversation must be dated earlier than 401, for Glaucon thinks that the banquet occurred recently (172c2–3) and Alcibiades was murdered in 404. She then sets the time a few days before the assassination of Alcibiades.[8] I side with Nussbaum. Her argument against the majority is decisive. I think that she is also right against Strauss for the following reasons: Apollodorus says to Glaucon that Agathon has not resided at Athens for "many years" (172c6). Agathon is thought to have left Athens for Macedonia in 408. This date for Agathon's departure is speculative. Agathon could have actually

---

7. On the name "Short," see Xenophon, *Memorabilia* 1.4.2. Apollodorus also calls him "short" (*Symposium* 173b2).

8. Strauss, *On Plato's "Symposium,"* 24; Nussbaum, *Fragility of Goodness*, 168–71. The word that describes Glaucon's sense of when the banquet occurred is νεωςτὶ, which means "recently," but also has a flavor of "just now." Nussbaum's idea is that Glaucon thinks of Alcibiades as still living, and that nobody could have been unaware of Alcibiades' death for long.

left anytime after 411.[9] From 408 to 407 is not "many years." From 410, say, to 407 is still not "many." However, from 410 to 404 might be enough to be "many." Further, as I shall show below, the behavior of the companions of Apollodorus is more suggestive of 404 than of 407. Strauss chooses his time without looking closely enough at Agathon's date of departure and the comrades of Apollodorus. Let us date the prologue to 404.

Nussbaum also sets this dramatic scene beautifully. Athens has lost at Aegospotami. Lysander is menacing the city. Athens is gripped by faction. The oligarchic government of Theramenes is near collapse. The Thirty Tyrants are about to execute him at the behest of Critias. In this situation, a rumor circulates in Athens to the effect that Alcibiades has returned to the city and gone to a party with Socrates, where people gave speeches about eros. It seems credible to the Athenians that Alcibiades has been drawn back to the city by his passion for Socrates, apparently with Agathon in tow, and that he intends to lead a last-ditch effort to rescue Athens for Socrates' sake. However, the wealthy now think that the maintenance of an oligarchy approved by Sparta is the city's only hope to avoid destruction. They are dismayed by the news about Alcibiades and are trying to gather intelligence about the threat that he poses. The many are delighted by the word of Alcibiades' return because they are oblivious to his flirtations with oligarchs and regard him as the city's democratic savior. The widespread, groundless belief in the rumor explains the sudden upsurge of interest in the story of the banquet.[10]

Nussbaum's scenario accounts for incidents in the prologue that would be bewildering in any other setting. It is a seldom-noticed fact that whereas the table of dramatis personae at the head of the *Symposium* mentions only Apollodorus and a single comrade, Apollodorus addresses his audience with second person–plural verbs and pronouns. He is lecturing not one person, but a group with one spokesman. The character of this odd assembly is revealed when Apollodorus refers disparagingly to the vacuous prattle "of your wealthy and money-grubbing associates" (173c5–6). It seems most unlikely that a body of plutocrats would suddenly set out in quest of intellectual sustenance at any time, and highly likely that they would be acting as an investigative commission—in 404. Apollodorus is also impolite to this group in other ways, accusing them of doing nothing when they think that they are doing a lot and implying that they have no interest in philosophy. He reports that he was equally harsh with Glaucon two days earlier, when Glaucon asked about the banquet. He criticized Glaucon

9. See Pauly and Wissowa, *Real-Encyclopädie*, s.v. "Agathon."

10. Nussbaum, *Fragility of Goodness*, 168–71. It is ironic that Alcibiades should have been the darling of the masses, given that he tried to return to Athens at the head of a Persian-backed oligarchy, but this apparently did not affect his popularity.

for running around randomly, believing that he did things, and of thinking that philosophy was not his business. Ordinarily, it would be hard to grasp how Apollodorus could accuse people of not caring for philosophy at all when they have just requested recitations of philosophic speeches. However, in the circumstances of the drama, the crazy Apollodorus has an excellent reason for his incivility. He justly suspects that Glaucon and the oligarchical delegation are animated not by a real love of wisdom but by desires to spy upon and crush their political opponents.[11] The rich men may not even know that they are investigating theoretical discourses, imagining instead that the rumored speeches celebrated the resuscitation of an old political *hetaireia* and discussed plans for a coup.

Clearly, there is a difficulty with this reading. If Glaucon and the commission fear a new sedition, and have no interest in philosophy, why do they still listen to Apollodorus after they have heard that the alarming banquet took place twelve years earlier, when Agathon won a prize for his first tragedy (173a5–7)? One could reply that in view of the tense situation, their continued curiosity is plausible. They might doubt that Apollodorus is telling them the truth about the date and hope to use what he says to convict him of treachery after other witnesses contradict him. If they believe him, they might still like to gather evidence of a long-standing democratic conspiracy or religious outrage. However, the question also appears to have an answer that is a piece of this larger, more important problem: Why does Plato set the *Symposium* in such an intricate dramatic structure? Specifically, why does he date the prologue to the height of the real Alcibiades fever of 405–404, when the Athenians are grasping at straws to prevent Sparta from delivering the mortal blow to their empire?[12] Why does he juxtapose this moment of Athens's death struggle and the theoretical discussion of eros held on the earlier occasion of Agathon's triumph? Why does he mention the man named Phoenix? Why does he give his brother Glaucon a cameo part (172b2–3)? Why does he cause Glaucon to hurry to anticipate the enterprise of the investigative commission? Why does he have Glaucon and the delegation approach Apollodorus rather than Socrates himself? Why does he cause the banquet speeches to be related by an Apollodorus who heard them not from Socrates, but secondhand (173a9–b2), who checked only a few of the details of his informant's account with Socrates (173b4–6), and who cannot recall everything that Aristodemus

11. Cf. ibid., 170, on Glaucon's possible link to oligarchy. Nussbaum calls the companion a "friend" of Apollodorus. She does not see that he is probably acting as the spokesman of a hostile investigative commission. Cf. Rosen, *Plato's "Symposium,"* 12–13, on the legal character of Glaucon's language, this being an excellent point.

12. We know that there actually was such a fever. In the *Frogs,* which was staged in 405, and produced again in 404 with no change in the relevant line, Aristophanes has Dionysus remark that Athens is "in travail" about Alcibiades (1423).

told him (178a1–3)? Why does he make Aristodemus forget things (178a1–3) and too drowsy to hear the speeches to their end (223b9–c5)? Why does he exclude Socrates from the dramatic present of the play, thus letting Socratic wisdom inform it only at the third remove, in the rote learning of less than fully philosophic disciples (see *Phaedo* 117d) and, hence, as a shadowy image of itself?

I think that Plato's scheme of dramatic symbols quietly suggests this argument: The fall of Athens was tied to the earlier war between the good and bad erotes. When Athens was in its last agony, those who desperately wished to rescue the polis by giving it over to Critias or Alcibiades were twelve years too late and hoping in false saviors. The battle to save Athens was already lost on the occasion of Agathon's debut, when Agathon, Alcibiades, and Socrates were vying to determine the direction of its eros and the citizens gave their hearts to Agathon and Alcibiades. By loving these men, the city rendered Syracuse and Aegospotami inevitable, provoking the unjust, harmful reaction of Critias. Perhaps Athens could still have been saved had the most excellent young men of its next generation allowed Socrates to guide their eros. Glaucon's encounter with Socrates, dramatized in the *Republic,* was critical. Glaucon's eros was victory-loving and tyrannical. Socrates tried to cure it, but Glaucon proved unteachable. He spurned Socrates and joined the scramble for power, trying to outdo Critias. Ultimately, Glaucon became irrelevant and Critias won the day. Consequently, Socrates and his wisdom were absent from the public realm during the crisis of 404, except insofar as oligarchs culled thirdhand reports of private conversations for evidence of sedition.[13] However, even this was hopeful. The resurrection of an Athenian phoenix, whether that of the city itself or that of its better philosophic part, still had to begin with the Socratic wisdom that was present only in the faintest traces.[14] If anything was to be saved, one had to work from these shadows back to the substance that cast them.

To this end, Plato found it useful to write plays that fictitiously reversed history. It is well known that the *Republic* is a dramatic correction of the trial of Socrates. The dialogue addresses the democrats who refused to listen to Socrates and mythically forces them to hear him turn the tables, when he convicts the Athenian demos of depraving the young as he builds the just

13. American liberals will think of this behavior of the oligarchs as an early instance of "McCarthyism."

14. The Phoenix reference might also be an allusion to *Iliad* 9.168. Achilles has an elderly friend, a father figure, of this name. This man, who is dear to Zeus, leads the delegation that tries to persuade Achilles to come back to the war. Failing, he decides to remain by Achilles' side. Our Phoenix does not return from Socrates with a helpful report of his philosophy, and might be staying by Socrates' side. Thus, Plato might be casting the spurned Socrates in the role of Achilles in the events of 404, at least insofar as he now stays out of the war.

city in speech. Similarly, the *Symposium* imaginatively revises the events of 404. The play addresses historical oligarchs who shunned philosophy and who would have been bored by old, abstract ideas that did not confirm current charges of treason. It fictitiously constrains them to embark upon the examined life. Now they must consider essentially accurate images of the issues that Athens faced and the choices that the city had when it took the wrong side in the war of the erotes.

This is not all that needs to be said about the dramatic setting of the *Symposium*. Soon it becomes clear that the play is a mythical exercise in anamnesis, or recollection.[15] Apollodorus recalls what Aristodemus related. Aristodemus remembers what he heard in person. Socrates harks back to what he learned from Diotima. Most of the speakers recall mythical beginnings of gods and men. Alcibiades reminisces about his experiences of Socrates. At some points in the play, the reader is contemplating memories of memories of memories of memories, which are myths of myths of myths of myths. Eventually, it will be necessary to wonder why Plato creates this complicated anamnestic and mythical structure. For the moment, however, it will suffice to note that the prologue of Apollodorus contains a recollected prologue of Aristodemus, such that the *Symposium* has a dramatic setting within a dramatic setting. We are obliged to reflect on the significance of the earlier scene.

Here, we must inquire first into the occasion of the banquet. If Plato views Agathon's victorious debut as the beginning of the end of Athens, as I believe he does, he and his fellow citizens must have seen something genuinely explosive in it, for ill or good. We should like to know what that was. Unfortunately, history does not tell us much about Agathon. We have only a few lines of his tragedies, which classicists say are in the style of Gorgias. We hear from Aristotle (*Poetics* 1451b20–26, 1456a25–30) that he was an innovator: In his *Antheus,* he invented all his characters instead of taking them from legend. Also, he let choruses entertain audiences with songs rather than instruct them with various kinds of commentaries. Others inform us that he introduced the chromatic scale into his melodies. He is also caricatured in Aristophanes' *Thesmophoriazusae* as a passive homosexual and an effeminate transvestite, this perhaps being a bit of camp ribbing from a man who himself might have been far from what we call "straight." We know nothing more.

On the basis of this information, one can see that Agathon's debut would have caused a cultural, and, hence, to some extent, a religious stir. However, to us who daily weather new displays of artistic daring, many of which wander considerably far afield from contemporary religious and moral orthodoxies, Agathon's avant-garde exploits hardly seem enough to

15. Rosen deserves credit for this point (*Plato's "Symposium,"* 2).

justify accusing him of having ruined an empire. If Plato thought that the sky had fallen because of a playwright's tinkering with the cult of tragedy, we would have to say that he was a mindlessly rigid religious conservative. This is wrong, though. Aristotle, who was hardly more "liberal" than Plato, enjoyed Agathon's changes in the cult form.[16] Further, Plato, the author of the Socratic critique of the poets in the *Republic,* was not religiously hidebound. His philosophy was the most profound religious innovation in the history of Athens. One infers that Plato must have been upset by a terrible mistake in Agathon's art and its baneful political effect rather than by his cultural nonconformity as such. The error would have been something new that distorted the city's judgment, leading to fatal adventures.

Although we shall never ascertain the details, we would be well advised to expect Plato himself to alert his readers to the nature of his indictment of Agathon. I believe that he gives some particulars in the offhand remarks that he causes Socrates to direct to the triumphant poet. In one place, Socrates expresses anxiety that Agathon's upcoming speech will be a hard act to follow. Agathon retorts that Socrates is trying to drug and unnerve him by making him think that the audience has high expectations. Socrates rejects the idea that Agathon could get stage fright, recalling how he so recently looked a vast audience straight in the face, exhibiting manliness, magnanimity (or haughtiness, the Greek having both meanings), and fearlessness, confidently intending to display his own words (194b1–5). This exchange seems to consist merely in an urbane compliment, a disclaimer, and another accolade, but it really contains the mildest of several Socratic criticisms of Agathon. Plato's Socrates never voluntarily addresses the many en masse because he knows how to persuade only one man at a time (*Gorgias* 474a5–b1). He undoubtedly supposes that wisdom can never be instilled in the many qua many, that any speech to the multitude is risky because it necessarily leaves them foolishly ignorant, that public orations and performances should not be given at all without cautious concern for their consequences, and, thus, that Agathon erred in addressing his audience with less thought for the common good than for ingenious self-display.

A more serious charge is leveled against Agathon in Socrates' initial statements about his activities. At the beginning of the remembered prologue, Aristodemus meets Socrates and asks him where he is going. Socrates replies that he is on his way to dinner at Agathon's. He adds that

---

16. Whether this means that Aristotle also approved of their substance is an issue that would have to be explored through serious analysis. In the context of *Poetics* 1451b and 1456a, Aristotle is discussing what gives pleasure. This is not necessarily the same as what is good. It would be most unlike Aristotle to let capacity to produce pleasure be a decisive measure of the good. On the other hand, Aristotle would not have taken pleasure in the forms if they were intrinsically evil.

he skipped Agathon's celebration yesterday because he feared the crowd (174a7), but he accepted the invitation for today. This is surprising because we are used to a Socrates who goes to his death unflinchingly, who is not alarmed when the Athenian army is routed and his fellow soldiers are being slaughtered on all sides (220e9 ff), and who is otherwise quite hard to scare. Thus, we wonder why Socrates should have been nervous about yesterday's gathering. We begin to think that Socrates objects to crowds on principle. However, this cannot explain his fear, for we know that he saw Agathon's play with thirty thousand other Hellenes (194c4–5). He is not afraid of crowds in general, and he does not mind being jostled. It is specifically yesterday's throng that unsettled him. Why? Someone might argue that Socrates is concerned about riffraff who regularly work themselves into violent frenzies after Dionysian festivals (see *Protagoras* 327d). However, this hypothesis is inconsistent with evidence that Socrates is not more timid than his fellows and that the only injury that worries him is being induced to become a worse man (*Republic* 335c6–7). Indeed, such evidence suggests that the multitude could have frightened Socrates only because he was wary of its impact on his soul. He probably dreaded being infected with a newly rampant mob passion, on the premise that it is impossible to resist the clamor of the many without a divine dispensation (*Republic* 492a–493a). If so, his remark accuses Agathon of having taught the multitude a singular and virulent injustice.

This deduction is supported by an odd turn in Socrates' later exchange with Agathon. When Socrates scoffs at the notion that a man who braved a huge assembly could be flustered by an audience of "a few people like us," Agathon answers that a person of intelligence is more frightened by a few men of wisdom than by many fools. Socrates replies that he and the rest of the banquet guests were members of the theater audience and might not count as wise men in Agathon's eyes. Therefore, he asks Agathon to suppose himself with other men who really were wise. He suggests that Agathon would be "ashamed" to do something "shameful" before such individuals and solicits confirmation of this assumption. Agathon agrees. Then Socrates puts a leading question: "But you would not be ashamed before the many if you thought that you were doing something shameful?" (194c5–10). Thus, without any grounds in the previous discussion that are tenable, let alone compelling, Socrates suddenly tries to lead Agathon into a dialectical reflection on the shameful and all but flatly accuses him of having done something in his tragedy that he knew to be shameful, without being appropriately ashamed that he and the many were worsened. Phaedrus hastily terminates this line of inquiry, perhaps to prevent the hitherto charmingly civilized conflict from becoming openly savage.

What might Agathon's heinous act have been? Socrates' reproach reminds us again of his critique of the poets in the *Republic,* in which he censures theological stories that corrupt the young. Perhaps Agathon created such myths, for Aristotle quotes him as saying: "God is deprived of this only, to undo what has been done" (*Nicomachean Ethics* 1139b10–11). The deities of Socrates are denied more, such as gluttony, drunkenness, rape, telling true lies, and generally doing evil.[17] Socrates might be dismayed that Agathon lets some of the rowdy gods be unjust on stage. However, if Agathon does this, his offense is neither new nor unorthodox. It has been the stock-in-trade of poets since Homer. Hence, Agathon's repetition of it could not be regarded as a turning point. Plato must have seen something more in Agathon's work that, compounded with Homeric opinions of the gods, wrought catastrophe. He still needs to indicate what it was. I think that he will do this by having Agathon commit his misdeed again in the drama. Agathon remains silent when Socrates gives him a chance to deny that he takes his guests for fools. He will not be ashamed to duplicate his transgression before their eyes.

Agathon appears to repeat his outrage by halves. He inaugurates his feast by instructing his slave boys to pretend that they are the hosts, to serve whatever dishes they please, and to earn applause. In an aside, he says that he never has done this before (175b). This curious episode, which requires more attentive analysis than it usually receives, illustrates the political form of Agathon's shamelessness. Socrates remarks in the *Republic* that slaves are among the inhabitants of the *kallipolis* who are obliged to mind their own business (433d2). Socrates also declares that the ultimate in licentious democratic freedom is reached when slaves are as free as their owners (563b4–7). Agathon has incited his servants, who do not know which entrees are right for ordinary meals, let alone for a Dionysian banquet, to do the work of masters, and has made the measure of their success the diners' pleasure.[18] Plato's Agathon has plainly begun a radical project of fostering license. Extrapolating from his banquet to the tragic stage, we may infer that Agathon was one of the poets about whom the Athenian Stranger complained, namely, one who "bred in the many an illegality with regard to

17. Aristotle holds that Agathon was right to say what he did about revision of the past being the only thing denied to the gods. Perhaps he thinks that gods are capable of doing evil if they choose, even though evil is not what they would choose. This opinion is problematic. I side with Socrates.

18. Aristodemus reports that the company poured a libation and hymned the god as required by customary law (176a3). The god is Dionysus. If certain foods prepared in specific ways are mandated for a Dionysian festival, slave boys would not know this unless given instructions that Agathon deliberately withholds. The measure of the cooks' success should be compliance with the religious law and, otherwise, the health of the diners. It is a symptom of modernity that we should be surprised at philosophic objections to making the measure of culinary success the diners' pleasure. Plato's portrait of Agathon as one who demands that cookery give pleasure associates Agathon with Gorgias, whose rhetoric and sophistry, like cookery, are branches of the art of flattery (*Gorgias* 463a–c).

music, and made them so bold as to think themselves competent judges."
These poets "were ignorant about what is just and legitimate for the Muse"
and made the criterion of good music the spectators' pleasure. When they
spread "the opinion that everyone is wise in all things," and when the
many adopted their pleasure standard, they gave rise to "a knavish theatocracy" characterized by "knavish shamelessness" and an "exceedingly
audacious freedom." This led straight to manifestations and imitations of
"the ancient Titanic nature" (*Laws* 700d–701c). It is important that the theatocracy (rule by the audience) cultivated by the poets generated what we
may call "Titanism." The Stranger seems to believe that the worst political
disorders are directly connected with rebellion against the Olympian gods.
Agathon should grasp the shamefulness of fostering theatocracy, if not for
this reason, then because he regards the many as fools. Therefore, I think
that there is also an intellectual half of Agathon's political recklessness. We
must look for it later in his speech.

When Aristodemus meets Socrates, he finds that the master is fresh from
the bath and shod. This is unusual for Socrates. It means that he is going to
the banquet willingly. This is surprising, too. Here we have a Socrates who,
sixteen years earlier, had to be dragged to meet Protagoras with extreme
reluctance, who indicates by his quotations of Homer (174d2–3) that he is
conscious of being en route to the camp of the enemy, and who thinks of
Agathon as an irresponsible poet and an ally of Gorgias who is driving
Athens into the abyss. Why should Socrates have wished to avoid one relatively decent sophist while voluntarily celebrating with another who has
set the city on the road to ruin? Further, why should he expose his student Aristodemus to sophistry when he wished to insulate Hippocrates?
If Socrates' antipathies are known widely, we have to consider yet another
perplexity: Why should Agathon have invited Socrates to the banquet?

Socrates' motives are complex. Socrates undoubtedly remembers the
Agathon whom he met sixteen years ago at the house of Callias as a young
lad whose nature, he thought, was "noble and good" (*Protagoras* 315d9–10).
Further, starting with Socrates' comment that he has beautified himself for
the sake of his beautiful host (174a8–9), and continuing into his seriously
playful pass at Agathon after Alcibiades' exposé (222c–223a), it is evident
throughout the play that Socrates, in his idiosyncratic way, is erotically attracted to Agathon's native beauty and goodness. Socrates loves Agathon.
He never felt a similar attraction to the stuffy, pompous Protagoras, to
whom beauty could be attributed only ironically (*Protagoras* 309c–d).[19] At
the same time, Socrates knows that it is the noblest natures that can fall the
furthest and be turned to the greatest crimes (*Republic* 491e1–6). This must

19. The "beauty" of Protagoras lay in his supposedly superior wisdom, and the dialogue raises serious doubts as to whether he really was wise.

be the case with Agathon. It follows that Socrates wants to save Agathon. If he succeeds, he might also be able to get Agathon to undo the evil spell that he is casting on the demos now. Socrates cannot influence the many, but this might be in Agathon's power because the people love him. Perhaps pulling Aristodemus into this situation will be good for him, too. Aristodemus is a voluble atheist.[20] Socrates might see an opportunity to teach him the difference between superstition and a philosophic reverence for divine reality. So, Socrates accepts the invitation and brings his student along.

As for Agathon, it appears that there is a sense in which he reciprocates Socrates' love. A sexual spark is there, for Agathon tells Socrates that he wants to touch him in order that he might share a wise insight that Socrates must have had (175c9). Agathon has sexual contact in mind. He is also responsive to Socrates' later pass at him. Probably with comically overstated gestures and a tantalizing laugh at Alcibiades, he spurns Alcibiades and repairs to Socrates' side (222d–223a). Given that he speculates that Socrates must have enjoyed a wise insight, he also has some inkling of Socrates' greatness. However, I think that Agathon's love for Socrates is flawed. There are beloveds who want to control their lovers. Such beloveds are self-centered. Perhaps their sense of their worth depends on their ability to make lovers jump at their beck and call. Whatever the reason for their power libidos, they are displeased when the lovers fail to do their bidding. Socrates has already demonstrated that Agathon does not control him by refusing to attend the playwright's victory celebration. Agathon probably experiences this as a public humiliation. Now, when Socrates approaches Agathon's house, he remains standing outside, refusing to come in for dinner and flouting Agathon's repeated orders to enter. The playwright must think that this causes him to lose face, too. He seems to vent his wrath with a touch of obvious mockery in his speculation that Socrates has had a wise insight and with his attempt to touch Socrates, which, considering the relative ages and statuses of the two men, is an uncommonly aggressive dominance gesture. Socrates evades the touch by suggesting that wisdom cannot be transmitted that way, thus demonstrating a third time that Agathon is not his master. Agathon responds by declaring that he will soon take Socrates to law about their wisdom, with Dionysus as judge (175e7–10). This is a jocular but also serious threat. Agathon really intends to sue Socrates, in play, but in a kind of Dionysian moot court.[21]

Agathon's apparent desire to dominate Socrates and the fact that he already knows that he will be taking Socrates to court about their wisdom

---

20. Cf. Xenophon, *Memorabilia* 1.4.2–19.

21. This exegesis is consistent with both the comic and the tragic aspects of the drama. Many of Shakespeare's comedies are battles of wits between angry lovers. The laughter can turn to horror if one of the lovers' pranks leads to scenes that look like the end of *Hamlet.*

prompt me to go out on a limb with a guess about the plot. My essential argument, that the *Symposium* is a play about the struggle between the Socratic and the tyrannical eros, does not turn on this musing. However, I think that my hunch is correct and that it makes for a good story, so I shall advance it. I believe that Agathon invites Socrates to his party because he realizes that his recent conquest of Athens is unfinished and he has a carefully laid plan to complete it. Every Athenian but one, Socrates, has hailed him. He intends to subdue this man who has not yielded to him. So, Agathon has decided that he will sue Socrates in Dionysus's court long before Eryximachus proposes a night of tributes to the god Eros. Dionysus is Agathon's patron as the god of tragedians. Agathon expects to win because the judge is prejudiced. The witnesses are suborned, too. Agathon has prearranged the evening's agenda with Pausanias, Eryximachus, and Phaedrus, knowing that the Socrates who proclaims himself an expert on the things of eros could not decline to speak about eros in a quasi-legal, rhetorical contest (177d6–8). He is convinced that he can humiliate Socrates by beating him at his own game, and relishes the prospect. For good measure, he has also stacked the assembly against Socrates by inviting not only his allies but also Aristophanes, who has already attacked Socrates in the *Clouds*. Socrates eagerly accepts the challenge. He takes particular pains to prevent Aristophanes from scuttling the competition by pointing out that as a devotee of Dionysus and Aphrodite, Aristophanes could not object to praising Eros.[22] He also encourages Agathon's overconfidence, complaining repeatedly that he has not been given a fair chance in the trial by being forced to speak last (177e2–5, 194a1–4, 198a1–7). Again, my conjecture that Agathon has premeditated his campaign (but not, of course, the surprises that he has in store, more of which later) is not necessary to the philosophic results that I envisage. However, I shall read it into the rest of the play, hoping it worthy of Plato's dramatic skill.

Socrates is rarely or never caught unawares. He foresees that his eros for Agathon will be met with his host's animosity. He prepares for battle by doing four things, all of which are hybristic in one way or another, and all of which deviate from his usual practice.[23]

First, he orders Aristodemus to come with him to Agathon's for dinner, even though Aristodemus has not been invited. Everybody would recognize this as a display of shockingly bad manners.[24] Socrates rationalizes his

22. Addressing the audience in his own name in the *Clouds* (519), Aristophanes claims to have been nurtured by Dionysus.

23. The Greek "hybris," also transliterated and pronounced as "hubris," combines the English ideas of proud arrogance, wanton insolence, and aggressive violence.

24. However, there seems to have been a tradition of gate-crashing at symposiums. Uninvited persons who appeared had to be admitted and allowed to function as something like an official opposition, if they so wished. In the play, this accounts for Aga-

boorishness. He claims that he and Aristodemus may corrupt a proverb so that it asserts: "The good go unbidden to the tables of the Good" (174b4–5; the capitalized "Good" is Agathon's name in a pun).[25] This means that Aristodemus, being good, may dine at Agathon's unbidden. The excuse is both dubious and short-lived. Socrates immediately censures Homer for having perpetrated a hybristic distortion of the proverb by having the "soft spearman Menelaus" (174c1) go unasked to the feast of the good Agamemnon. The implicit comparison between Menelaus and Aristodemus demotes Aristodemus to a rank below that of the good, thereby depriving him of his alleged right to dine with Agathon. However, then Socrates seems to promote Aristodemus again by invoking *Iliad* 10.224, where Diomedes wants someone to accompany him to spy on the Trojans, because "when two go together, one precedes another in devising what we shall say" (174d2–3).[26] Aristodemus is now an Odysseus upon whom Socrates will rely for assistance in calculating how to outwit the enemy. However, then Socrates demotes Aristodemus again, by letting him go ahead while he stops dead in his tracks, lost in thought. When Aristodemus suffers the embarrassment of arriving at Agathon's house alone, he finds that his "Odysseus" function is not to give sage advice, but to serve as a socially expendable pawn who buys Socrates time to meditate on what he will say. Thus, Socrates is hybristic toward both Agathon and Aristodemus. Although we are appalled by his behavior, we cannot suppress our guffaws. The erotic comic rogue Socrates has begun to defend himself against his pugnacious beloved Agathon by gulling a short, soft spearman to act as his shield. Plato is subtly injecting the bawdy comedy of Aristophanes into his tragedy.

Second, Socrates stands outside Agathon's house thinking until the dinner is half over. This is another piece of effrontery that gets under Agathon's skin. That Socrates should stop someplace to meditate is not extraordinary.

---

thon's civility to Aristodemus and Alcibiades, for his attempts to co-opt them, and for his meek submission to Alcibiades' alteration of the rules of his proceedings. Cf. Pauly and Wissowa, *Real-Encyclopädie*, s.v. "symposium."

25. Apparently, nobody knows what the original proverb said or how Homer is supposed to have corrupted it. B. Jowett inserts into his translation of the *Symposium* the following sentence that does not appear in the Greek: "To the feasts of inferior men the good unbidden go." R. G. Bury appends a footnote to his translation, guessing that the corruption of the proverb might consist in the substitution of a dative for a genitive plural in the pun on Agathon's name, so that the original would have been something like "The good go uninvited to the feasts of those who are good."

26. In this account of the exchange between Socrates and Aristodemus, my own insights are mixed with some of Rosen's in *Plato's "Symposium,"* 23–24. I move to a conclusion that differs from Rosen's. Incidentally, Socrates misquotes or misuses Homer here. In *Iliad* 220–30, Diomedes asks for a partner who will help him discern useful actions, not useful words.

However, he is said to offend a host by doing this only once. It is also unusual that Socrates breaks off his reflections after what, for him, is no long time (175c3–4). The hybris of his tardiness is exceeded by the insolence of his judgment that he does not need a normally lengthy preparation for the coming battle.

Third, when Socrates finally condescends to appear, Agathon offers him a seat next to his. As suggested above, Agathon wants to touch Socrates so that he can share in the insight that Socrates won outside. Socrates permits nothing of the sort to happen. He comments that it would be well if wisdom could be transmitted from the more to the less gifted by touching. Then he would gladly sit next to Agathon and draw out Agathon's abundant wisdom, which the other day shone so brightly in the eyes of thirty thousand Hellenes, far excelling his own, which is as disputable as a dream. This language sounds gracious, but it is actually mocking. It rejects Agathon's reasoning, thus raising questions about his wisdom. It implies that Socrates scorns a wisdom that exists only in the eyes of the many. It subtly informs Agathon that if anybody mounts anybody to demonstrate superiority, Socrates will be on top. These points are not lost on Agathon. He answers: "You are hybristic, Socrates" (175e7), and then declares that he and Socrates will go to law about their wisdom.

Fourth, Socrates readily agrees to the program of oratory. Ordinarily, he cuts sophists off when they try to make long speeches, insisting on dialectical give and take.[27] This time he not only consents but arrogantly decrees that nobody could vote against the proposal as well.

Why is Socrates so hybristic, and why does he happily support the plan for a rhetorical contest? In aid of deifying philosophers, Stanley Rosen suggests that Socrates' behavior has to do with a necessary "philosophical hybris," that is, with the philosopher's "hybristic nature."[28] I greatly doubt this. Philosophy as such is not hybristic. If it is true, as Aristotle maintains, that "all men by nature desire to know" (*Metaphysics* 980a21), there is no hybris in aspiring to rise to the highest insights available to mankind. Neither is there any hybris in examining opinion to test its adequacy or in showing others that their beliefs are incoherent. Neither is it hybristic to react angrily to sophistical demagoguery. The philosopher is hybristic only when he tries to be a god or when he displays aggressive insolence. Socrates does not strive for godhood. I can think of a long list of men toward whom Socrates does not display haughty insolence, namely, all of the characters in all of the Platonic dialogues except those at the symposium and a few other sophists. In the present case, I should think that Socrates is doing what he always does: considering how to achieve his ends and tailoring his means

---

27. Cf. the *Protagoras* and the *Gorgias*.
28. Cf. Rosen, *Plato's "Symposium,"* 21.

to the character of the individual with whom he is dealing. Socrates wants simultaneously to ward off Agathon's attacks and to press his amorous suit on the beauty, a tricky task. Agathon is hostile and contemptuous but also docile. To succeed, Socrates needs to shock, disconcert, and perhaps even hurt Agathon, in order to shatter his hard exterior shell. Then he can shape Agathon's soft core. As for the speechifying, Socratic education always begins where the student is. Socrates must permit his pupil to declare himself, which Agathon chooses to do by dividing the labor of displaying the sophistical forms of eros among his allies and himself. This allows Socrates to grant Agathon's positions provisionally and then to lead him from those to better but still inadequate opinions that he finds acceptable, until he is finally compelled to leap to the truth itself. This accounts for Socrates' acquiescence in the program. It also explains why the sophists applaud Socrates' speech, although somewhat less exuberantly than they had cheered Agathon's (212c4–5). The sophists like some of the things they hear from Socrates but also feel distressed insofar as they are being pulled higher than they want to be.

When Agathon and his guests have eaten, poured their libation, and hymned the god, Pausanias pleads to be dispensed from hard drinking because he has a hangover. The company eventually decides by a formal resolution that there will be no constraint on anyone to drink (176e5). We should be curious as to why this action was deemed necessary. Why should the men have feared that they might be forced to drink? Why did they undertake to vote against such compulsion? Someone might answer that the Greek symposium was the predecessor of the Roman *convivium,* of which we know that the *magister bibendi* had the right to require participants to consume intoxicating amounts of wine on pain of being expelled or paying silly penalties. However, the Platonic *sympotai* (fellow drinkers) are not voting against a drinking game. Aristodemus says that the libation and hymn were mandated by customary law (176a3). The contemplated drinking is almost certainly required by law as well. In this instance, Agathon is celebrating his triumph in the Lenaea, a Dionysian festival. He has already had his *epinikios* (173a6), a ritual, orgiastic, public victory feast. A private extension of that ceremony would not qualify for exemption from Athenian law. The difficulty probably confronting Pausanias is that the meal is dedicated to Dionysus and the *sympotai* have a religious duty to get drunk again.[29] I think that with the prior connivance of Agathon and the other sophists, Pausanias is suggesting a grave impiety to facilitate the group's assault on Socrates and offering the flimsy excuse that he satisfied his obligation yesterday. The vote will aim to nullify the law.

---

29. Cf. Pauly and Wissowa, *Real-Encyclopädie,* s.v. "symposion" and "Lenaia," especially the descriptions of the orgiastic character of the Lenaea.

Aristophanes promptly supports Pausanias's request because he has a severe hangover, too. Plato thus signals that the Aristophanes who accused Socrates of impiety in the *Clouds* was also less than pious when it suited him. Eryximachus then comments that the others have spoken beautifully and inquires whether Agathon feels prepared for heavy drinking. The host begs off. Eryximachus replies that the weak drinkers would be lucky to find the capable ones exhausted. He then slides gracefully from this sigh of relief into an explicit denial of Socrates' right to vote on the matter. Socrates will be technically innocent of the impiety because he is excluded from citizenship in the sophistical city and obliged to comply with its law while he visits it. Next, Eryximachus compounds his own sin by denouncing drunkenness as a health hazard, thus asserting the superiority of modern science to the traditional religious norms. He pauses to let Phaedrus exhort everyone to do what is healthful, secures the consent of all who have the franchise to dispense with compulsory drinking, and then wins universal approval of his motion that the company dismiss the flute girl and gratify Phaedrus's desire for encomiums on the god Eros. By Athenian law, this plan is plainly unorthodox, too. If Eros is a god, he is not an Olympian, and he is certainly not a divinity worshiped in the city's cult. Socrates will also escape guilt for this heresy by letting Diotima conduct an argument that Eros is not a god. On the other hand, the sophists are foolishly ignorant of the danger in which they have placed themselves. It is not safe for humans to exalt and invoke Dionysus while denying him his due. When Greek gods are invoked and entreated, they come, doing their wills rather than those of their supplicants. Dionysus will come. He will punish the sophists' offenses and still exact his prescribed homage. If Eros is a supernatural being, whether god or demigod, he will fly to the banquet, too, and will work for divine rather than human purposes. It is also the case that if anyone talks indiscreetly about the proceedings, the *sympotai* will be subject to punishment by the city of Athens on charges of impiety and sedition. Even at a distance of twelve years, the oligarchs will perk up their ears upon hearing the rash Apollodorus repeat the prologue of the imprudent Aristodemus.

Eryximachus's remarks about drinking and subsequent events in the play reveal that the sacrilegiously sober revelers have diverse capacities for holding alcohol. The weakest drinkers are Aristodemus, Phaedrus, and Eryximachus. Pausanias is somewhat stronger. Aristophanes and Agathon are extremely formidable drinkers, Agathon being slightly better. The stoutest of all is Socrates, who can drain off a half-gallon wine cooler without batting an eye (213e12–214a1) and guzzle all night without feeling the slightest effect, although he often imbibes unwillingly (220a, 223d). In this regard, it should also be noted that Socrates almost always goes barefoot. He is immune to hunger (175c, 219e–220a), freezing cold, all other rigors of war (219e–220b), and sleep deprivation (220c–d, 223d). When he wants, he is able to resist the sexual attractions of beauties (216d–e, 217a–219d). The enticements of money and power mean nothing to him. Socrates clearly lacks or can discipline his eros for things that overpower many of his fellows. It is necessary to ask why Plato makes his characters call attention to these facts. Do the data have something to do with eros? For example, is there a correlation between a man's capacity to hold alcohol and the excellence of his eros, the better drinker being the better lover? Or do immunity to inebriation and the capacity to withstand the strongest erotic attractions imply that one is too coldhearted to be a good lover?[30]

We should not hasten to attempt to solve these problems, for we still lack criteria for judging. To illustrate, if we were to maintain that an inability to become inebriated implies an incapacity to be seized by sexual eros, or by an eros yet more noble, someone might retort that a miraculous invulnerability to the effects of alcohol, traumas, privations, and pleasurable enticements could occur only by virtue of a complete possession by the highest, most divine eros. If we were to argue that resistance to wine signifies a rejection of the self-abandonment that is indispensable to eros, someone might counter that if eros requires such abandonment, the ability to outdrink an army suggests absolute freedom from the self that is physically and mentally subject to ethanol. We cannot decide between these claims because we still have to find out what means what in the domain of eros. Hence, it would be wise to postpone these questions to a later chapter. For the present, we may finish our survey of the *Symposium*'s dramatic setting by sketching in the rest of its story.

Agathon, I think, has arranged his party seating in an effort to ensure that the *sympotai* will speak in a specific order. He intends that Phaedrus, the weak drinker and disciple of Hippias, should lead off. Phaedrus should be followed by Pausanias, the strong drinker and Prodicus-Gorgias student. Aristophanes should come in the middle. Then Eryximachus, the weak drinker and disciple of Hippias, should speak and be followed by Agathon, the mighty drinker and Prodicus-Gorgias student. Socrates, the best drinker, should come last. Agathon knows the views of the men whom he has pitted against Socrates. Also, he probably supposes that Pausanias is

---

30. The questions are fair because Plato puts the remarks about drinking ability and resistance to erotic attractions in his text. Rosen addresses them but ends, I think, with a fundamental contradiction in his argument. He asks whether the order of drinking capacities corresponds to "the order of erotic excellence" (*Plato's "Symposium,"* 30 ff). He seems to answer in the affirmative, for he interprets the rhetorical progression from Phaedrus through Agathon as an "erotic ascent." However, he also charges that Socrates' inability to get drunk and his failure to respond to Alcibiades' seduction make him "erotically defective" (xiii, xvii, xviii, xx, 5, 232, 251, 277, 279, 286, 311, 317). Indeed, he interprets the entire dialogue as Plato's comment on Socrates' erotic defects. I think that this is simply wrong.

intellectually superior to Phaedrus and that he himself is intellectually superior to Eryximachus. Relying on what the characters say later, I assume, then, that Agathon has concocted the following strategy for the prosecution of Socrates in the Dionysian court.

Phaedrus will present the sophistical wisdom of an *erōmenos* (beloved) whose ideas of eros are grounded on the science of Hippias, which consists partially in a metaphysics that asserts the ontological primacy of Earth. Pausanias will answer with the insights of an *erastēs* (lover) whose views of eros are founded upon the sciences of Prodicus and Gorgias and, thus, upon a metaphysics that presumes the ontological primacy of Uranus (Sky).[31] Ethically, both speakers will advocate a utilitarian egoism.

This will upset Aristophanes, who loathes sly talk, atheistic science, and selfish ethics because he fears that such things will ruin his city.[32] He will try to protect Athens's customary law, Olympian theology, and communitarian morals against Phaedrus and Pausanias. Hence, Aristophanes will have to be handled like a warhorse that is held tightly in the ranks in order that his force may be directed against the enemy and not against his own troops. If he can be controlled, he will be helpful to the sophists because he has been, and will continue to be, the scourge of a Socratic philosophy that he thinks devious, rationalistic, atheistic, and antisocial.

Agathon believes that his charger can be managed. Aristophanes' views on religion and politics have implicit sophistical premises. If the comic speaks after Phaedrus and Pausanias, condemning their egoism, Eryximachus and Agathon can demonstrate that his axioms lead to a sophistical communitarian view. Then his strictures will fall on Socrates alone.

Accordingly, after Aristophanes has spoken, Eryximachus will present the sophistical wisdom of an *erastēs* who adheres to the science of Hippias, assuming the ontological primacy of Earth, and who is also an Asclepiad advocate of the medical welfare of both individuals and polities. Agathon will reply with the ultimate sophistical sagacity of an *erōmenos* who is both a metaphysical follower of Gorgias, upholding the ontological primacy of Uranus, and a self-styled savior of individuals, cities, and mankind. This will fasten Aristophanes firmly in the ranks of the sophistical army while completing the attack on Socrates.

---

31. In Greek pederasty, the *erōmenos* was the boy or young man (probably ranging in age anywhere from twelve to twenty) who was the object of the affections of an older mature lover. He is generally thought to have been on the receiving end of homoerotic sexual intercourse. If the couple stayed together for life, he continued to be an *erōmenos* for life, even when older. The *erastēs*, on the other hand, was the mature man who loved the boy or young man. He is generally thought to have been on the giving end of homoerotic sexual intercourse.

32. "The novel comedy of Aristophanes defends the ancient polity" (Leo Strauss, *Socrates and Aristophanes*, 89).

The total effect will be three ascents to amended accounts of eros in which the defects of intellectually inferior arguments are surmounted while their strengths are both retained in and complemented by intellectually superior views. This is not to maintain that the speakers are expected to furnish a coherent system of the sophistical truth about love. Consistency and truth are concepts that are foreign to sophistry. Agathon will not recognize them as measures of rational or erotic virtue. He merely wants his program to cover every possible first premise relevant to eros, so that Socrates will be hemmed in by sophistical arguments no matter where he turns. It will be fun to watch Socrates flail.

The campaign does not go as Agathon intends. To say nothing of later developments, Aristophanes chances to get the hiccups and cannot speak in his turn. He and Eryximachus trade positions, thus ruining the symmetry of Agathon's design and setting the spooked warhorse loose in the ranks where it can trample everybody. Aristodemus speculates that Aristophanes' ailment comes from an excess "or some other cause" (185c5–7). In Plato, unknown causes are often supernatural intervention. The other cause is probably Eros, who is rearranging the schedule to his own liking. Eventually, Socrates escapes the trap that has been laid for him. He practices right pederasty on his *sympotai* in an effort to reclaim them, not without some positive effect. Then, however, Alcibiades surprises Agathon again by barging into the party.

We now may turn to the philosophic substance of Agathon's campaign, which consists in the orations of Phaedrus, Pausanias, Eryximachus, Aristophanes, and Agathon. I think that we shall be meditating on five examples of erotic tyranny. In keeping with what has been said about tyrants above, this will require us to recognize both the apparent beauty with which the tyrants cloak themselves and the savagery that lies just beneath their lovely surfaces.

PHAEDRUS

Speaking his first dramatic lines in the play, Phaedrus proclaims his absolute obedience to his *erastēs*, Eryximachus, in medical affairs.[33] Phaedrus is a valetudinarian who has had the sagacity to take a physician as a boyfriend. Now he is always ruled by the *technē* that leads to bodily health (176d5–7). His deference to the medical art somehow extends from the

---

33. This section begins by following the argument of Rosen, *Plato's "Symposium,"* chap. 2, fairly closely, but it does not do so for long. Rosen adheres to the text, so everybody would have to say much the same things as he at the basic levels. However, once I have shared his premises, I move rapidly to divergent conclusions.

realm of physical well-being into the affairs of love, for he allows his lover to deliver his public plea for suitable praises of Eros. Perhaps he thinks that erotic love most fundamentally is a matter of health. Whatever the reason, it is Eryximachus who relates that Phaedrus often grumbles that no poet has ever composed an ode to the great and ancient god Eros. Neither have "the useful sophists" written an encomium on Eros that rivals Prodicus's tribute to Herakles, which lauds the fabulous hero for preferring virtue to vice. This lacuna in the literature must be filled, for even trivial things such as salt have been celebrated extensively for their utility. These complaints make Phaedrus the "father" of all the talk that occurs during the banquet (177d5).

When we set out to praise some person or thing, we necessarily include an explanation of why the subject is praiseworthy. Phaedrus's words, as quoted by Eryximachus, have already indicated his standard. So far, Phaedrus has applauded certain sophists and salt, both because they are "useful." These statements embody the same spirit as his valetudinarianism. We infer that Phaedrus is a utilitarian who totes everything up on a balance sheet of personal profit and loss, an ancient "rational-choice theorist," as it were. He demands that poets and sophists rank Eros with other gods—nay, above them, for he ends by calling Eros "the most ancient, most honored, most powerful of gods" (180b6–7)—because love is useful.

The opinion that eros is useful seems crass. It might prompt us to judge that Phaedrus is not a terribly erotic man, for lovers are not supposed to be calculating. However, this reaction reflects an understanding of eros as selfless or abandoned sexual love. Those who want eros to be selfless might have the noble sort in mind; we hear of inspiring examples of ardent, self-less sexual love. However, it would be naive to forget that gross egoism and sexual eros frequently go together. The human race has had countless sexual exploiters of many kinds: for example, seducers such as Don Juan, others who have taken sexual pleasure from partners while giving nothing in return, others who have used their sexual attractions to obtain benefits that they have wanted from suitors, and rapists. Many such exploiters have been calculating. Those who want eros to be intoxicated forget that the sexual exploiters have been sober. Further, we must remind ourselves again that there can be eros for many things. Phaedrus, for example, clearly enjoys two kinds of sexual pleasures. If he did not like passivity, he could not have held on to his *erastēs*, Eryximachus. On the other hand, he is not inspired by the speech of Lysias in the *Phaedrus*, which aims to seduce a gullible boy, merely because he is a connoisseur of rhetorical flourishes. It seems quite likely that he is homoerotically "versatile" and enjoys the occasional fling with a younger lad, a pleasure that he would not scruple to obtain by clever speech from a youth whom he does not love. Beyond this, Phaedrus also relishes oratory with an intensity that borders on sexual lust, such that it is correct to refer to him as a "father" of speeches. To coin a phrase, he is a rhetorical satyr. He is also fanatically desirous of health. He seems to have an even more powerful eros, to which we shall come in a moment, that craves what he thinks is most useful and therefore his highest good. Phaedrus is obviously extremely erotic.

So, Plato has presented an intriguing erotic specimen for our edification. He is inviting us to examine some forms of eros that we do not usually perceive as eros, especially rhetorical satyriasis and the eros for whatever Phaedrus might regard as the summum bonum. He is also prodding us to ask what could possibly drive a man who is a crass, egoistic, "rational actor," a sexual *erōmenos* who also has an eye for younger boys, a rhetorical satyr, a health fanatic, and a utilitarian all at the same time. I think that the key to understanding what makes Phaedrus tick will be learning why he calls Eros a great god and the most honored, most powerful god, or, what is to say the same thing, discovering what he values as the highest good and why he presumes that eros is the means to it.

We shall have to allow Phaedrus to work up to his explanations of these matters. He opens his discourse with a cosmogony and a theogony based on a remark of the poet Hesiod: "Eros is a great god, wonderful among men and gods in many ways, not least according to his genesis. The god's honor is of the oldest. The proof of this is that parents of Eros neither exist nor are in any manner mentioned by private men or poets, but Hesiod says that first Chaos came to be, and next broad-breasted Earth, always stable seat of all, and Eros" (178a7–b7).[34] We gather that Phaedrus thinks Eros great for his genesis, his coming to be without generation on the seat of Earth. However, Phaedrus seems even more impressed by the fact that Eros is marveled at by gods and men and that the god's honor (as well as the god himself) is of the oldest. It is significant that Phaedrus emphasizes that Eros is the most honored god both at the beginning and at the end of his speech. This makes us wonder whether Phaedrus would call Eros great for the sake of his genesis without generation on the seat of Earth if no gods or human beings cared to celebrate him for this distinction. The answer seems to be no. Honor is revealed as Phaedrus's highest good.

Phaedrus's argument needs closer inspection. We should notice that Phaedrus does not prove his points by means of syllogisms. He affects to base his reasoning on Greek Scripture, so to speak, Hesiod's poems

---

34. The "private men" to whom Phaedrus refers are prose writers. The poets are public men. Rosen considers inserting additional lines in the text, lines that appear in the manuscripts but are rejected by contemporary editors (*Plato's "Symposium,"* 46–47). I do not have the expertise to judge this dispute among the classicists.

belonging to the Greek sacred canon. Phaedrus uses Hesiod selectively, though, suppressing passages on the immortal gods, thus disguising his heterodoxy.[35] He does not really accept the poets as authorities or their works as revealed truth. He is making a rhetorical joke in mock support of his ontology. Where, then, does he get his ideas? I think that he is symbolizing his own experience or perception of existence in his speech.[36]

What does Phaedrus see? The principal object in his field of vision is "broad-breasted Earth, always stable seat of all." Phaedrus lets this phrase from Hesiod's myth establish the secular claim, advanced by Hippias, that Earth is the ground of being. Phaedrus experiences Earth as the substance of nearly all things and the essential foundation of any reality not made of itself. He also espouses Hesiod's statements that Earth had a genesis from Chaos and that Chaos had a genesis, too. Earth, whether disorganized or organized, and a genesis that orders and disorders particles of Earth are the only eternal realities. Phaedrus accordingly suppresses references to immortal gods in his quotations from Hesiod. He adopts the physics of Hippias, which subtly demythologizes poetic, religious truths by recasting them as primitive or esoteric empirical observations.[37]

The next feature in Phaedrus's ontological landscape is Eros. In Hesiod, Eros arises on the seat of Earth by virtue of the same genesis that crystallizes Earth. Rendering this mythical portrait in secular language that might have suited Hippias, we could take it that Earth has an epiphenomenal aspect. We are not told what this epiphenomenon, Eros, is. However, we can talk about one form in which it displays itself and mark what it does. Phaedrus refrains from quashing Hesiod's view of Eros as a living god. Thus, his epiphenomenal dimension of Earth manifests itself most fully as an invisible principle of conscious appetite and intellect. What it does is to strive. Phaedrus experiences the unseen aspect of his matter straining to preserve the order of that matter against the power of the disordering genesis. The Athenian Stranger feels this, too, if his talk about eros for food and drink is any indication. Phaedrus also notices the epiphenomenon acting as a principle of generation, endeavoring to resist the extinction of man through sexual reproduction and to beget speeches for a reason not yet designated. Taking a new step in his exposition, he also says that the invisible aspect is "responsible for the greatest goods for us" because it creates in us "that which is necessary through all life to guide people who intend to live beau-

35. I owe this insight to Rosen, *Plato's "Symposium,"* 47–48.

36. It might be objected that Phaedrus is merely summarizing the conclusions of syllogisms that he learned from Hippias. However, such syllogisms are nowhere reported, and one wonders how there could be a logically airtight argument to the effect that Earth is the seat of all, and that Eros arose on the foundation of Earth without generation.

37. These insights are largely Rosen's.

tifully," namely, "shame with regard to the shameful" and "love of honor (φιλοτιμίαν) with regard to the beautiful" (178c2–3, 178c7, 178d1–2).[38]

We now are given to understand that Phaedrus defines eros as an epiphenomenal force of Earth that pulls its matter not only away from the fate that awaits it, but also toward a telos of honor with regard to the beautiful. Although eros appears to have three or four functions, it is one, and its work is one, in the sense that the preservation of existing conscious entities and the generation of new ones are the prerequisites for Earth's success in achieving the high telos of honor with regard to the beautiful, and presumably also in the sense that the generation of speeches is a way of ascending from the biologically secured ground to the supreme goal. We must observe that with this, Phaedrus has also told us plainly what his summum bonum is, not sexual pleasure, not health, not even the beautiful life, but "honor with respect to beauty." We do not know from whence this declaration came; it is certainly not a deduction from the cosmogony or theogony of Hesiod, or from the science of Hippias. However, we can see now that it has been present from the beginning of Phaedrus's hymn to Eros, where he declares that Eros is the most honored god. Eros enjoys the summum bonum to the fullest. Human beings can savor it, too. It seems possible that men could even surpass the most powerful god in this enjoyment by coming to be honored more than he, thus becoming more divine than he.

This account of eros begins to clarify Phaedrus's choices. His nebulous epiphenomenon of Earth exerts its pulls on each piece of matter that it instantiates as consciously appetitive and rational, seemingly aiming at the utility of individuals. Therefore, Phaedrus thinks that the very nature of reality requires and justifies his principled egoism. Each operation of the mysterious force strives first to ensure the foundation of the success of its own matter, that is, its existence. Thus, in Phaedrus's considered opinion, eros is actually one of the things of health and everybody who has any brains at all should be a health fanatic who is ruled by the medical *technē*. (Phaedrus would certainly applaud the millions of modern Americans who create the economic demand for the random health features that now fill television news programming. Television has democratized access to Eryximachus.) Hence, Phaedrus's crass selfishness and valetudinarianism now appear as symbols of a wish to become the most successful specimen of conscious Earth by being the most perfectly erotic. However, this raises a question about Phaedrus. If he intends to be so consummately erotic, why does he not participate in all the functions of eros? Why does he

38. The Greek φιλοτιμίαν is usually translated as "ambition," but this rendering does not capture the literal meaning that is important here. The word "ambition" does not convey the fact that Phaedrus loves not beauty, but the honor that he might obtain in relation to the beautiful.

not generate new human beings by lying with a woman, copulating with only men and lads instead?[39] His answer must run like this: Eros is not obliged to perform each part of its generative work in every portion of the Earth from which it arises. It can and does secure the existential basis for its activity in many while achieving its ultimate triumphs in a few, for honor would not be honor if everyone had it. The *erastēs-erōmenos* relationship to which some individuals are attracted is necessary for completing the climb to the telos. It is also superior to heterosexual intercourse, for two reasons.

First, it is more apt than birth to a noble family, privilege, wealth, or anything else to create (ἐμποιεῖν, 178c7) the shame with regard to the shameful and love of honor with regard to the beautiful that make a piece of conscious matter strive for honor. Pederastic union excels everything in generating libido for the highest end (178c2–d2).

Second, it locks the partners into a mode of life that does more than any other to keep the drive for honor at a fever pitch. Explaining why he cannot name "a greater good from his earliest youth than a useful lover and a boyfriend to the lover" (178c3–5),[40] Phaedrus argues at length that the *erastēs-erōmenos* bond deters shameful acts because the lovers are embarrassed to perform them in each other's presence, and also that the lovers are φιλοτιμούμενοι πρὸς ἀλλήλους (178e6–179a1), literally "loving honor toward one another," meaning, as I think the Loeb translator W. R. M. Lamb has seen best, that they are yoked in a "mutual rivalry for honor." Far from eliminating principled egoism from human affairs, erotic attachment is a relationship in which the lovers use one another in the universal competition for high status. In homosexual union, the lovers are especially "useful" to each other as goads. They intensify the striving to avoid shame and win honor because each hates to be outdone by the other.

If all this is true, we still do not see how Phaedrus's rhetorical satyriasis helps him attain to the end of honor. Phaedrus would reply that our trouble stems from our ignorance of how honor works. He gives several examples of people who have won praise. The people in these illustrations managed to become visible to men or gods and to be judged honorable by them. To be seen and applauded, they had to do things that seemed spectacular and potentially useful to the others. So, for Phaedrus, honor is in the eye of the beholder. His illustrations involve what men and gods consider to be extraordinary acts of courage. Here, it does not matter that the acts should

39. The answer might be that he does. We know that the historical Phaedrus, like many Greeks of his ilk, eventually married. This question and the subsequent analysis pertain only to the thinking of the character Phaedrus in his capacity as a representative of the wrong pederasty. It does not pertain to gays as such.

40. This ungrammatical but literal translation, which is absolutely necessary for an adequate understanding of Phaedrus's thought, closely follows Rosen's *Plato's "Symposium,"* 51.

really be intrepid. It suffices, or means everything, that eros should make the people who do these deeds "like" valiant ones, even if they are "bad in this matter" (179a7–8). It is appearance that counts, not being.[41] This is surely why Phaedrus speaks of "love of honor with regard to beauty" rather than love of beauty or beauty itself. There are appearances of beauty that some people prize more highly than the likeness of courage. We learn from the dialogue that bears his name that Phaedrus himself praises a speech and its author because the former has something in it that "made it elegant" (κεκόμψευται, 227c7) and because the latter is a "most clever (δεινότατος) speaker" (228a1). Phaedrus wants what he admires. He fathers speeches in order to command attention as a splendid producer of rhetoric and to be honored as a most elegant and clever wit. Insofar as he succeeds, and his activity does elicit expressions of amazement from no less a person than Socrates, his begetting gets him an Earth-based status that has a genesis but is not generated, for judgments that feats are phenomenal and elegantly clever must be, at some point, sui generis. They simply arise and hover over Phaedrus and his audience as his attained reality. Hence, Phaedrus imagines that his rhetorical satyriasis enables him to achieve a genesis analogous to that of Eros himself, such that he exists more beautifully or divinely than he could as a mere lump of conscious Earth. Eros is great, the most honored god, the most powerful god, and useful because he drives men to do the things that raise them to his own divine status.

At this juncture, it is appropriate to observe that Phaedrus is a thinker who attempts to imitate the ancient Titanic nature. His elevation of Eros to the rank of the most powerful god, which directly implies an attack on the kingship of Zeus, his removal of the Olympians from the Greek pantheon, and his intention to ride the wings of Eros to the pleasure of divine status himself are nothing if not a Titanic storming of the gates of heaven. To the extent that he can make himself heard, Phaedrus spreads Titanism in Greek culture.

One could argue that Phaedrus's eros is self-defeating. A brief glance at a few objections to his argument and his probable reactions to them will be illuminating.

First, Stanley Rosen maintains that Phaedrus entangles himself in the snares of G. W. F. Hegel's master-slave dialectic. He cites plausible evidence. Phaedrus's grammatically contorted statement that he cannot name "a greater good from his earliest youth than a useful lover and a boyfriend to the lover" betrays that his first impulse is to take his *erastēs* for everything he can get and that he is late to consider how this revelation will affect Eryximachus. In Phaedrus's examples of the blessings of love, eros

---

41. Up to this point in the present paragraph, I have followed Rosen, *Plato's "Symposium,"* 50–53. Hereafter, I diverge from him.

prompts the lovers to risk or sacrifice their lives for the beloveds in two of three cases. The beloveds selfishly accept this as their due and never dream that they should make the supreme sacrifice for their lovers. They get to live and enjoy the honor that accrues to them for not having been cowardly in war, or for having been such great beauties that lovers would die for them, whereas the lovers perish, hoping at best to receive posthumous homage. True, the lovers might be raised from the dead like the woman Alcestis, thus living to embrace their beloveds and to bask in the praise of men and gods, but this is most unlikely. The third case, that of Achilles and Patroclus, is unusual because the *erōmenos* feels agape for his *erastēs* and dies to avenge him. The gods reward him not with mere resurrection, as with the lover Alcestis, but with life on the Blessed Isles, because the beloved acts freely, whereas the lovers' sacrifices are necessitated by divine possession, that is, lust. Phaedrus just cannot resist broadcasting his conviction that the *erastēs* is a means to the honor of the *erōmenos*. He proposes to enslave his lover. Rosen objects: "Since utility is inseparable from visibility, the benefit to the beloved rests upon the presence of selflessness in the lover. Phaedrus cannot avoid offering a more serious praise of the lover than he intends." So, the master's dependence upon the slave and the slave's achievement of a greater nobility than the master's elevate the slave above the master, as in Hegel's myth.[42]

Phaedrus might reply that no one can be perfectly independent and that life's winners are those who squeeze more benefits out of universal interdependence than the losers. Also, he would certainly deny that anybody should be expected to be selfless because, on principle, he disbelieves in the existence of selflessness. He would maintain that self-sacrifice, where it is seen at all, is explained correctly only as the running of the risks that a lover, or occasionally a beloved, must run, or as the payment of the price that a love slave must pay, to get what he or she can in the struggle for honor. Further, he would declare that in a universe founded on Earth, and consisting entirely of individuated bits of matter and their epiphenomena, there is no ontological basis for selflessness.

There still seem to be two problems with Phaedrus's erotic self-genesis. One is that it is hard to imagine that a human "love" bond could be sustained on the basis of absolute egoism. Why would the subjugated lover not resent being openly disrespected and exploited, be further disgusted by the public reduction of his relationship with the *erōmenos* to a business deal that does not differ from prostitution, and leave in a huff? The other is that if everyone were a Phaedrus, a necessarily resulting war of all against all would destroy the city upon which the life of love depends.

42. Ibid., 51, 53–59.

Our ancient rational-choice theorist would probably meet the first criticism by saying that all erotic relationships *are* founded upon sheer egoism and that every liaison *is* a business deal. In the associations that survive, the partners are satisfied with their bargains. In the ones that break up, the ex-lovers bolt because they think that they should have gotten better deals.

There is no need to speculate about an answer to the second objection. Phaedrus gives it in advance, spinning out a compact little political theory in the process. He maintains that if there were a city or an army composed of lovers and their sweethearts, "there could not be better inhabitants thereof" (178e2–5), and the city-army would "be victorious over the world" (179a1–2). Thus, far from providing an impossible foundation for a polis, selfishness correctly understood would be the basis for the only genuinely excellent city. The individual citizens of this polis would be competitors for honor who were contented with the profit-to-loss ratios afforded by their erotic partnerships. As couples, they would seek to outdo other pairs in the race for applause. Thus, society would actually be a universal war of all against all. However, the conflict would be converted into cooperation, and the couples would be happy with the places they found in the social pecking order, because their political gains would exceed their social costs. As a whole, the city would strive for the same telos as each of its parts: honor. It would win glory by crushing other peoples and distribute it to all its soldiers, compensating the couples who had lost the fight for domestic prestige with imperial majesty. Under this arrangement, the entire polis could live beautifully. Apparently, Phaedrus has taken Pericles' Funeral Oration to heart, letting Pericles' boasts about honor represent the telos of politics.[43]

Phaedrus's political theory strikes the ancient ear, and also the modern one, as beautiful. Upon reading that an army of lovers would be "victorious over the world," one thinks: "Yes, yes! My love for my beloved and my beloved's love for me could conquer all!" This reflects the experience of all true lovers that their love could burst all bounds thanks to its selflessness. The thought is inspiring. One cannot help but feel the beauty of Phaedrus's words.

However, there is a problem with this beauty. It is false. In the first place, the beauty that true lovers project into Phaedrus's idea is not really there. As shown above, Phaedrus is not talking about their experience. He is discussing an arrangement wherein love is a business deal in which egoistic partners make mutual use of each other. It is fated in this relationship that one partner (the *erōmenos*, as Phaedrus would have it) gets the better bargain, in effect enslaving the other in order to profit more than he. Both partners, and all human beings, are engaged in a ubiquitous battle for

---

43. See Thucydides, *The Peloponnesian War,* 148.

honor. Accordingly, for Phaedrus, being "victorious over the world" cannot mean "triumphing over all the vicissitudes of human existence through
selflessness," a felicitous construction that many of Plato's readers might be
inclined to place upon the words. Rather, for Phaedrus, the general struggle for honor implies that armies must march out to wars of aggression in
which soldiers can win accolades for courage. Being "victorious over the
world" means murdering innocents in campaigns of imperial conquest.
Seen in this light, Phaedrus's words are only horribly beautiful. It seems
to me that true love transcends egoism, that love's real unity is infinitely
more than a business bargain, that my beloved and I are not rivals, that our
telos, whatever it may be, is nobler than honor, and that crushing nations
for the sake of glory is monstrous.

Before praising Phaedrus's political theory for its beauty, one should also
note that it omits all considerations of justice. Phaedrus denies the reality
of justice, effectively claiming that in a universe consisting solely of Earth
and its epiphenomena, justice has no ontological ground. To him, love of
honor, courage, and cleverness are the whole of virtue.[44] Therefore, he is
not squeamish about winning glory by strewing the world with corpses.
We begin to see how the sophistical eros drove Athens to fatal mistakes.
Phaedrus's speech is a rationalization of tyranny. Its Titanism and sham
beauty seductively enthuse the thoughtless for tyrannical political adventures. Plato wants us to understand this.

PAUSANIAS

To be able to tolerate an *erōmenos* such as Phaedrus, Eryximachus must be
blinded by his excessive libido for physical beauty or satisfied with some
obscure quid pro quo. Pausanias, who is burdened with no such handicap
or business sense, dislikes Phaedrus. His first words deflate the insufferable
erōmenos. One of the purposes of his speech will be to put Phaedrus in his
place, which is somewhere below the *erastēs*. Pausanias cannot do this if he
argues from Phaedrus's premises. Thus, he begins by moving to new theoretical ground. Phaedrus opened his oration with a quotation from Hesiod

44. This is the rationale for the cavalier attitude toward justice that Phaedrus presents
in *Phaedrus* 260a. On the sufficiency of honor, courage, and cleverness, Phaedrus, speaking in his own name and unprompted by the Socratic dialectic, mentions and embraces
only these virtues (the first two in the *Symposium* and the third in the *Phaedrus*), while
praising Eros (in the *Symposium*) as the provider of "all" virtue (180b7). Phaedrus really
sees no metaphysical basis for courage and cleverness; he counts them as virtues simply because they seem excellent to beholders. He might say that love of honor has an
ontological ground in eros. However, this is dubious. What is the metaphysical status
of an epiphenomenon?

that could be construed simultaneously as theogony, cosmogony, and ontology. Although Pausanias appears to start with theogony only, it will be seen that his statements speak volumes about cosmogony and ontology and revise Phaedrus's assumptions.

Pausanias introduces his argument with a crushing dismissal of Phaedrus's project: "Not beautifully does it seem to me, O Phaedrus, that the speech proceeds to us" (180c4–5). Proud Phaedrus aspires to nothing but honor with regard to beautiful speech, and Pausanias instantly denies him that with one cruel blow. The enterprise is not developing beautifully because, as Pausanias says patronizingly, the idea of an encomium on Eros is "simple" (180c5). It would be right to proceed in Phaedrus's fashion if there were only one Eros. However, "we all know that there is no Aphrodite without an Eros" (180d3–4). If there were a single Aphrodite, there would be one Eros, but there are two Aphrodites, so there must be two Erotes.

This reasoning seems illogical. If "there is no Aphrodite without an Eros," it would be logically acceptable for an infinite number of Aphrodites to share one Eros and there would not have to be multiple Erotes. However, Pausanias's use of the preposition ἀπὸ to describe the relationship of an Eros to an Aphrodite (181c8) indicates that the meaning of his postulate is that "[e]very Aphrodite gives birth to an Eros." Pausanias thus identifies an older Aphrodite who had no mother, having sprung from Uranus. He observes that "we" name her Uranian Aphrodite. He recognizes a younger goddess who is the child of Zeus and Dione. "We" call her Pandemic Aphrodite. It follows that there is a Uranian Eros and a Pandemic Eros (180c4–e3).

It will require a bit of effort to grasp what Pausanias accomplishes with this argument. Like Phaedrus, Pausanias starts with "Greek Scripture." However, the tradition contains more than one creation myth. Indeed, there are more genealogies of Hellenic gods than anybody could systematize in an orthodox creed. Phaedrus cites the story that has the goddess Earth emanate from Chaos along with an Eros whom she underpins. Pausanias refers to two other tales. In one, there is a process of genesis without generation in which Chaos gives rise to Earth, Earth to Uranus (Sky, a different element from Earth, one less solid), and Uranus to Aphrodite, who issues from Uranus's severed genitals and a foamy sea. Uranus becomes the ungenerated scion of Earth in this legend, leaving Eros to be born of the Uranian Aphrodite in a manner about which we are not informed. Eros may or may not have a father. In the other story, there is a shorter process of genesis without generation, with Chaos casting up Earth and Earth Uranus. Uranus then fathers the Titans upon Earth. The Titanic brother and sister Cronus and Rhea mate to produce the Olympians. Zeus eventually begets Aphrodite upon Dione, and one god or another fathers Eros upon Aphrodite. Pausanias obtains his two Aphrodites by assuming arbitrarily that the tales follow different chains of genesis and generation to distinct goddesses, justifying his move in Prodicus's manner by appealing to linguistic convention. He ignores the possibility that there might be different accounts of the same goddess. Next he resorts to the sophism that Phaedrus used. He suppresses portions of the myths that he finds inconvenient, leaving only premises that yield the conclusions that he wants. He sweeps Chaos and Earth under the rug, rhetorically depriving the female principle Earth of her role as the ground of all reality, and designating the male principle Uranus as the progenitor of presently existing gods and human beings. He thus affirms a theogony-cosmogony that proclaims the ontological primacy of Uranus. The primacy of Uranus permits Pausanias to insist upon the reality of soul as an airy matter; no longer will soul have the lesser status of an epiphenomenon. Thus, later, Pausanias can assert that the Uranian Eros, male principles, and soul are metaphysically superior to the Pandemic Eros, female principles, and body.

Pausanias next suggests that the company should investigate a crucial question: Which Eros deserves to be praised (180e3–4, 181a4–6)? He frames the problem of the relative worth of the two Erotes in ethical terms. He maintains that no act is intrinsically beautiful (noble) or shameful. Rather, a deed is beautiful if it is done nobly and shameful if done shamefully. This fact applies to love. Eros inspires noble and shameful modes of loving. One Eros stimulates the beautiful loving. The other encourages the shameful loving. The former is praiseworthy and the latter blameworthy (180e5–181a6).

We must notice a difficulty. If Pausanias rejects the concept of intrinsically noble and shameful acts, why do we not have something like a moral nihilism in which no deed is either praiseworthy or blameworthy? If Pausanias denies being a nihilist, he could refute the charge (1) if his theogony-ontology provided credible premises that demonstrated the impossibility of intrinsically noble and base acts while simultaneously providing universal criteria for deciding what is done nobly and what shamefully, or (2) if, like Aristotle, he posited a natural right for which variable prudential judgments strive. However, we have seen that Pausanias arrives at his Uranian ontology by interpreting linguistic convention arbitrarily and by suppressing the parts of myths that thwart his aims. He has no metaphysical basis for moral conclusions that anyone could take seriously. In fact, he himself does not appear to suppose that he has such a foundation, for he has not grounded his ethical analysis on his ontology. Neither has he given any other reason to believe in acts that are morally neutral by nature but noble or shameful in the doing. One begins to wonder why he has veered from his metaphysics to his ethics at all and why he expects anyone to concur in his moral judgments of the Erotes.

Perhaps we could solve this problem by hypothesizing that Pausanias is laughing as he playfully displays sophistical virtuosity, cobbling together a hilarious new ontology out of the old traditional myths and slipping in an unspoken, undefended assumption that metaphysical superiority entails ethical excellence. All good thinkers have something impish about them; they love to caper with intellectual outrages. We could picture Pausanias's comrades chuckling with him appreciatively, for they are educated and clever enough to catch the tricks that he has played. They also know that Pausanias's theoretical cynicism mimics that of Phaedrus, who must have drawn laughs, too. I agree that all are giggling. Nevertheless, we should not underrate Pausanias. His comedy is mixed with a sober purpose. He really wants to establish the moral superiority of the Uranian Eros and the loving that this deity inspires. He does not appeal to his ontology in this endeavor because he does not believe that such reasoning will be effective. In fact, his horseplay with metaphysics and his failure to cite it while setting forth his moral doctrines reveal that he sees a disjunction between nature and virtue. He intends to teach the ethical superiority of the Uranian Eros and his style of loving not as a conclusion drawn from his ontology but as a separate pillar of his larger argument. He emphasizes this by returning later in his speech to an explanation of how actions that are not inherently noble or shameful can become so in the doing.

In revisiting the issue, Pausanias states that from the beginning, he asserted that erotic activity is intrinsically neither beautiful nor shameful but noble if done nobly and shameful if done shamefully. Now he adds that to do it shamefully is to gratify a base man basely and to do it beautifully is to gratify a noble man nobly. A base man is a pandemic *erastēs* who craves the body rather than the soul, thus loving what is unstable rather than stable and consequently behaving unstably himself, forsaking the beloved (183d–e). Just prior to advancing this thesis, Pausanias has raised doubts about an absolute prohibition on abandoning the *erōmenos* (183b–c). Stability is not the measure of virtue. Therefore, Pausanias's ethics comes down to this: a sexual act is beautiful if it is done by a lover of soul to a lover of soul and shameful if done by a lover of body to a lover of body. That is all. However, the metaphysical superiority of the Uranian Eros to the Pandemic Eros, and of soul to body, has been proved comically. In the absence of serious ontological grounds for morality, the idea that the Uranian Eros is ethically superior to the Pandemic one becomes mere snobbery. Whichever party condescends to the other more hurtfully wins. The trick is to seize the (probably illusory) moral high ground by means of skillful rhetoric.[45]

Pausanias displays this snobbery in his initial appraisal of the Erotes. He says that the Pandemic Eros is truly pandemic, that is, characteristic of all the demos, or completely vulgar. It does its work randomly in men

---

45. Pausanias thus prefigures Kant, Kojève, and Strauss as understood by Rosen.

who are φαῦλοι, that is, common, low ranking, and thoughtless. These men love women as well as boys, bodies more than souls, and beloveds who are utterly brainless because they care more about physical intercourse than noble loving. They do good or evil indiscriminately, for their Eros proceeds from the younger goddess who participates in both the male and the female. The better Uranian Eros has no share in the female, but in the male only (181a7–c3). One must note here that Pausanias has now plunged into misogyny; he holds that evil is from the female. Also, it now seems that Pausanias's logic has derailed again. The Uranian Aphrodite has no mother, but she mothers her Eros, who therefore participates in the female.[46] However, if we are prepared to dispense Pausanias from the rules of logic, we can rescue his argument by reading it as an ontological proposition. If Uranus is wholly other than Earth despite the fact that he came from her womb, if the Uranian Aphrodite consists of the same airy substance as Uranus, so that she is an entirely "male" principle in the form of a woman, and if the Uranian Eros is airy, too, then this Eros takes no part in the female, but in the male only. This Uranian Eros is also the elder and without hybris (which might imply that Pausanias is mousy).[47] His character inclines him to the male. He has agape for the nature that is more robust and that has a greater share of *nous* (reason or mind) than the female, who seemingly tends to stupidity in Pausanias's misogynous opinion.[48] Those driven by this Eros love young men who are getting their first beards and who have begun to acquire *nous*. They pledge to stay with the lads as long as they live instead of abandoning them when their beauty fades (181c–d).

Here, Pausanias stops praising the Uranian Eros. Evidently, his position is simply that this Eros excels the Pandemic one because his male lineage and essence produce virtue, because he attracts men to the Uranian, male, metaphysically and ethically superior substance of souls, because he inclines men only to intelligent males; because he has no trace of the female descent and essence that cause evil; because he causes men to value soul loving more than body loving, or to place relatively more emphasis on caring for souls than on gratifying themselves on the metaphysically inferior, female matter of their beloveds' bodies (although only relatively, for they are obviously aroused by robust youths); because he disposes them to avoid women; and because he makes them faithful lovers. Having estab-

46. The illogic of this jump is so stark that some translators of the *Symposium* interpolate words into the text that are not there, causing Pausanias to speak of the Uranian Aphrodite as the one who partakes only of the male because she has no mother. This does not quite save the logic, though. How does a female partake only of the male?

47. I cannot think of any rationalization that would save the argument "older, therefore not hybristic," if that is what Pausanias means.

48. Agape is a kind of love. The distinctions among agape, eros, and *philia* would be worth a monograph by a classicist of superior ability and erudition.

lished this, Pausanias apparently forgets that he is supposed to be giving an encomium on Eros. Instead, he argues that the Athenian *nomoi* that regulate pederasty should be changed or interpreted in manners that favor the type of noble loving that he has described. He wants to shield his sexual tastes against legal action and social hostility. He might have an urgent historical motive for this. He is speaking only eight to ten years after Kleon moved legally and politically against the catamites, an attack that was obviously directed against *erastai* as well.[49] Virulent bigotry against gays of the sort now beginning to be decried in the West might have been as prevalent in parts of classical Athens as it still is in parts of modern America. Pausanias also has other motives that reveal themselves as he goes along.

Pausanias's first legal argument aims to remedy what he takes to be a bad situation. It happens that pandemic lovers seduce underage boys and then dump them. Pausanias furiously demands that the practice be outlawed. Good men voluntarily refrain from this atrocity. The new *nomoi* will keep the pandemic seducers away from the boys, just as it forbids them to love free women (181d–182a). I agree with his laws insofar as vulnerable children need protection. Whatever our moral opinions of various sexual activities may be, we all want them to wait for the age of real consent. Pausanias does not give this reason, though. His stated purpose is not to protect children, but to save a "noble," aging pederast like himself from investing his resources in boys before it is known whether they will turn out badly or well with respect to vice and virtue of body and soul (181d7– e3). Apparently, his noble pederasty requires that the lover should realize a decent return on his venture capital (that is, on his outlay of time, intellectual effort, emotion, self-abasement in the usual courting rituals, and money). Clearly, these rules hamstring Pausanias's competitors for good prospects, for pandemic lovers like to strike early. As he advocates his first laws, Pausanias is certainly not indifferent to this result. However, this is not his primary motive. He is sincere in his concern that the noble *erastai* should be protected against the risk of investing in boys before it can be ascertained how they will turn out. He wants the lover's reward to consist in the beloved's guaranteed maturation as a beauty and in his guaranteed receptivity to the lover's efforts to educate him as a paragon of intellectual and moral excellence. We should ask why.

I think that Pausanias's answer involves an issue that I discussed briefly in the previous chapter, education. Pausanias eventually takes up the question of whether it is good for the youth to gratify his *erastēs*. He argues that the coming together of *erōmenos* and *erastēs* is an exchange. The beloved obliges the lover. In return, the *erastēs* makes the *erōmenos* "wise" (σοφόν) and "good," this "able man" giving of his wisdom (φρόνησιν) and all other

---

49. See Aristophanes, *Knights* 875–80.

virtues, and the "needy one" (δεόμενος) being educated (184c–e). Pausanias makes his project sound beautiful, although it prostitutes the youth. He might believe that his rationale is true—not a guess about him that one should hazard often. However, we should contrast his claims with Socrates' views of education in other dialogues. In the *Theaetetus* (149a–151c), Socrates argues that his function is that of the midwife. He has no wisdom and he teaches nothing. However, by means of his art, all whom the god may have permitted (ἂν ὁ θεὸς παρείκῃ, 150d4) have found themselves pregnant with beautiful things and have brought them forth, the successful delivery being due to the god and himself (ὁ θεός τε καὶ ἐγὼ αἴτιος, 150d8–e1). Once again, in the *Republic* (518b–d), Socrates maintains: "Education is not what the boasts of certain people say it is. They say that they put knowledge into the soul that does not know, as if they were putting vision into blind eyes. . . . But the present argument . . . indicates that this power [is] in the soul of each." In the *Meno*, it will be recalled, Socrates argues that the slave boy somehow already knew the geometric theorem (82b–85b).

The differences between Pausanias's and Socrates' accounts of education should be clear. Pausanias claims that he has wisdom and that he imparts it to the "needy" one, together with all the other virtues. Socrates says that he has no wisdom and merely helps others to discover what the god has given them. Pausanias takes the credit for the lad's education; Socrates gives primary credit to the god. We can now articulate what has been bothering us all along about Pausanias's noble pedagogical enterprise: It is too patronizing. The noble *erastēs* clearly loves the *erōmenos* not at all for his own sake, only secondarily as a means to sexual pleasure, and chiefly for his value as raw material that will be incorporated in a creation or work of art about which the lover can boast.

With this, Pausanias has made it plain that it is the lover who uses the beloved for his egoistic ends and not vice versa, as Phaedrus had imagined. It is the *erastēs*, not the *erōmenos*, who achieves nobility. Originally, of course, there is no objective measure of human virtue. In this vacuum, the lover who molds the *nous* of his beloved creates the *erōmenos* in his own image. Harking back for a moment to G. W. F. Hegel's myth of the lord and the bondsman, we may conclude that the *erastēs* whom Phaedrus treats as a slave transforms himself into a new kind of master with a vengeance, changing the *erōmenos* who fancied himself the master into the product in which the *erastēs* finds himself mirrored. Accordingly, the *erōmenos* is humbled by being forced into a position partially comparable to that of Eliza Doolittle in a production that could be titled "My Fair Laddie." That is, he is compelled to submit to the *erastēs* not only physically, in sexual union, but also psychically, as to the divinity to whom he owes his intellectual being and life. Of course, the sexual submission of the beloved does not ennoble the lover greatly because every coarse vulgarian can manage it. The noetic subjugation of the *erōmenos* is more beautiful to Pausanias because the erotic sophist alone can "engender high thoughts" (φρονήματα . . . ἐγγίγνεσθαι, 182c2) that fashion young minds. Pausanias can contemplate his godliness in his creation of another *nous*, thus usurping the prerogatives and functions of the deity in Socrates' account of education. His project has more than a little of the intention to imitate the ancient Titanic nature in it. In his way, Pausanias is another Titanic tyrant.

Pausanias calls for additional laws. All these *nomoi* seem to aim not only at guarding gays against unjust prejudice, a purpose with which we may sympathize, but also at securing his own advantage in the competition for fair lads, a design that maneuvers his fellow citizens into complicity in his depredations. We may go through them quickly.

First, the laws will adopt Pausanias's moral relativism. Justice will be whatever the *nomoi* declare it to be. The statutes in this system of legal positivism will say that in love affairs, the nobly done is noble and the ignobly done is ignoble (182a). This will alter existing Athenian customs considerably, elevating Pausanias's style of loving to a position of legal favor.

Second, the *nomoi* will be complicated rather than simple. They will not state flatly that it is honorable to gratify one's lover. Neither will they merely outlaw pederasty. They will leave it to lovers to attempt to persuade youths by skillful speech (182a–d). This obviously rigs the game in favor of the sophistical rhetorician, who can outtalk the pandemic blockheads.

Third, the laws will say that success in the pursuit of an *erōmenos* is honorable and failure disgraceful. Hence, the statutes will allow all the types of self-abasement in which lovers must engage to entice their youths, even supplications, vows, sleeping on doorsteps, and the slavery to which beloveds such as Phaedrus subject them, provided only that the lovers win in the end (182d–183a). This will shield lovers from the contempt that they frequently suffer in Athens. Even more, it will endorse the snobbery of the winners such as Pausanias himself.

Fourth, the vulgar claim that a vow inspired by aphrodisia is no vow. On this, the gods, all lovers, and Athenian law will agree (183b–c). This bow to Pandemic Eros releases the pederast from any legal obligation to keep promises to the *erōmenos*. The sophistical lover may forsake his youth after all. This proves irrefutably that Pausanias regards the beloved as an object to be manipulated and that his morality serves his ego rather than some universal good.

Fifth, fathers try to prevent pederasts from getting at their sons. Boys shame schoolmates who gratify lovers. The *nomoi* will interpret this not as a social condemnation of pederasty, but as a social test of the mettle of lovers that aims to discover who will love nobly and who basely. Athenian custom regards not surrender to a lover but quick capitulation as a disgrace

(183d–184b). This exegesis of the social practice aims, again, not only at protecting gays from prejudice but at establishing Pausanias's style of gay loving in a position of legal preferment as well.

Sixth, the laws specify that beloveds may yield to lovers not for money, not for political or social advancement, and not out of cowardice or weariness, but strictly for the sake of virtue (184b–c). What Pausanias does in this argument is to seduce the city into acknowledging his superiority, his divinely creative act, and the beloved's inferiority in the *nomoi*. As he presents his case, it seems that no one could reasonably oppose it, for who wants to interfere with the cultivation of virtue? However, we have seen what Pausanias means by education to virtue and what kind of commitment he actually has to ethics. His speech is really a demonstration of breathtaking sophistical skill.

Finally, the statutes will decree that it is not dishonorable for an *erōmenos* to be deceived in his judgment that an *erastēs* will make him virtuous (185a–b). This shields the lover from the lawsuit that the beloved will want to file when he discovers that he has been tricked, or when he begins to doubt that he has received value for value. Thus, by a wonderful sleight of hand, Pausanias arranges for the putatively noble pederast to get his gratification risk- and cost-free. The *erastēs* ends with no enforceable responsibilities at all.

Pausanias ends this treatise on law by returning to his praise of the Uranian Eros. He has not forgotten his assigned task after all, but has digressed only to plead his case. Now, he argues that the Uranian Eros is precious to private and political life because it compels lovers and beloveds alike to attend to their virtue (185b–c). Thus, he has presented his audience with a short political theory. He has also engaged in one last act of one-upmanship against the previous speaker, Phaedrus, for he is maintaining that the proper end of political order is not honor, but virtue. Here, again, his sophistical talents are evident. It is clear that for Pausanias, to be honored *is* the essence of virtue. This does not differ greatly from what Phaedrus has said. However, Pausanias has succeeded in making Phaedrus appear selfish and himself noble while actually doing nothing more than claiming his predecessor's desired spoils for himself.

Like Phaedrus's love, Pausanias's "noble eros" might be thought logically suspect. Some of the objections to which Pausanias is exposed are essentially the same as those that Phaedrus faced, and they would probably receive similar answers. Pausanias tries to make himself into a master god by enslaving his beloved. However, it is difficult to see a master god in a man who depends for his being as a master god upon the testimony of a sexually desired slave. One also doubts, again, that a love bond could coexist with absolute egoism. Why would Pausanias's *erōmenos* not react to the revelation that he is loved only as a sex object and as great raw material for his lover's godhood by storming out of the relationship and exacting a terrible revenge? Pausanias might answer with Phaedrus that godhood for men is an affair of relative advantage rather than unmediated self-creation. He might also reply that a beloved who is taught virtue will agree that he has been compensated justly for his services. A more honest answer might be that the entire arrangement depends upon what the *erōmenos* can be induced to believe by clever speech and that the *erastēs* is not nearly so interested in a genuinely intelligent youth as he pretends to be. Also, Pausanias would certainly repeat Phaedrus's denial of the existence of the "real love" that his critics find lacking in his position. Although a Uranian ontology ranks soul higher than body, it does not conceive of soul as an immaterial reality that could be called beyond its inherently egoistic drives by attunement to a nobler transcendence, or by anything else whatsoever. Pausanias undoubtedly interprets his inward self as airy matter that seeks its own instinctive gratifications and that will dissipate when his body dies. Hence, he would see no sense in the self-sacrificing love of an Aristotelian *spoudaios*.

In the speech of Pausanias must also answer the objection that his egoism and snobbery are incompatible with political life. It appears again that pure selfishness would produce a war of all against all rather than a harmonious society. It seems further that a relativism that legislates the tastes of self-styled patrician lovers would necessarily lead to a perpetual flux of oppressive tyrannies as various groups seized power and enacted their preferences into law. I believe that Pausanias would concede the first criticism. His entire argument, with its relentless attacks on pandemic lovers, demonstrates that he conceives of social life as a struggle for domination. However, he denies that this strife must end in tyranny. Like Phaedrus, he replies to such misgivings with his political theory. He claims that his Eros resists tyranny by engendering wise thoughts and fostering friendships, as exemplified by the case of Aristogiton and Harmodius (182c1–7). This answer is a lie or an error. The envisaged assassination of Hippias was not directed against his tyranny as such; it was conceived as a method of removing a feared and powerful competitor for a beloved's sexual favors. Hippias would not have been threatened had he not been such a persistent lecher.[50] Pausanias is spreading the usual propaganda of tyrants, who always claim to be the opposite of what they are and who always manage to persuade the simple that they are not what they are.

In the speech of Phaedrus, Plato showed us an egoist who wanted his personal tyranny over his lover to be reinforced by the tyranny of his polity over foreign peoples. In Pausanias's oration, Plato has put another egoist on display, a predator who wants to extend his personal tyranny over his

---

50. Cf. Thucydides, *The Peloponnesian War*, 6.53–61.

beloved into a political one by co-opting the law as a guarantor of his success in achieving his selfish aims. In the climate in which we live, it will be appropriate to remind ourselves once again that although Phaedrus and Pausanias are gay men, Plato does not mean to smear gay orientation. I myself do not mean to imply that gay love is always egoistic and tyrannical. Plato's drama about diseased eros could have characters of any sexual orientation in other historical contexts. His subject here is not pederasty, but "wrong pederasty," which Phaedrus and Pausanias clearly represent. His concern is to illustrate the subtle ways in which the Titanic, tyrannical, sophistical loves found in Athens misunderstood, misrepresented, and insinuated themselves into the city's culture and politics. We have learned that two sorts of egoistic erotes thought themselves beautiful. They also portrayed themselves as beautiful in ways that probably attracted many besides Phaedrus and Pausanias. Thus, these erotes shaped tyrannical characters in the souls of many beloveds and lovers. They bewitched these people so that delirious souls thought it obvious that the polity existed to gratify their libidos for power on grand scales. The consequence was a perversion of Athenian expectations of foreign policy and law. Eventually, the erotes disposed these souls, with their unreasonable demands on the city, to respond to the appeals of a rising tyrant. The ultimate result was shipwreck. This process can occur in any society. Plato wants us to recognize and defeat it.

Eryximachus

When "Pausanias pauses," Aristophanes gasps that he needs Eryximachus either to stop his hiccups or to speak in his place until he can do it himself. Eryximachus replies that he will do both. He prescribes some remedies and gives his speech. His oration is superior to its forerunners in cosmological, theological, and scientific imagination and scope, although I must say that it is no more logical than they. It also exceeds its predecessors in Titanic ambition.

An adequate treatment of Eryximachus should initially advert to the dramatic context. Pausanias has just ridiculed Phaedrus as a simpleton who does not know the difference between a Uranian eros for soul and *nous* and a Pandemic eros for bodies. Eryximachus must defend Phaedrus against this attack to avoid succumbing to it himself. At the same time, he is obliged to attend to the sophists' common agenda. To amplify upon my dramatic argument, Agathon and his coconspirators wanted Aristophanes to speak after Phaedrus and Pausanias and before Eryximachus and Agathon. Aristophanes is dedicated to the preservation of the city, which he believes must be achieved by means of the strict enforcement of its customary laws and by exact adherence to the worship of the Olympian gods.

Aristophanes is no fool. He will grasp that the egoism of Phaedrus and Pausanias threatens Athens by fostering the war of everyone against everyone. He will not be convinced by facile claims that the selfish strife of would-be despots is changed into cooperative security by the pursuits of "honor, nobility, and virtue," especially not when these words are given relativistic definitions that favor legal positivism. He will also perceive that Phaedrus and Pausanias subvert the city's *nomoi* with their calls for social approval of their predatory eroticism and by preaching the adoration of Earth, Uranus, and Eros rather than the Olympians. He will equate these two sophists with the Socrates who corrupts the young by urging disrespect for ancient authority and disbelief in the city's gods.

However, as will be seen, Aristophanes implicitly reasons from sophistical premises. Had he spoken in his assigned place, delivering his complaints, Eryximachus and Agathon would have been able to snare him. They would have lectured eloquently on how the poet's assumptions about human nature resemble those of Phaedrus, on how these premises demand an art that harmonizes the relationships of men and gods, on their own knowledge of this *technē*, on the *erastēs-erōmenos* union as the noblest fruit of their science, and on devotion to Eros as an indispensable element of their technique that completes the established religion rather than undermining it. In brief, they would have hailed Aristophanes as a poetic, communitarian sophist. Under the rules of the symposium, Aristophanes would have had no opportunity to rebut them gracefully, so the full force of his fury would have been left to fall on Socrates alone, as Agathon intended.

Nonetheless, the best laid schemes o' mice and men gang aft a-gley when Eros decides to work his own will. Eros has come to the banquet and has taken Aristophanes and Eryximachus in hand. He has subjected Aristophanes to a comical malady that probably stems from a sort of erotic gluttony (thus affording Plato some revenge on the poet for his portrait of Socrates in the *Clouds*) and he has made Eryximachus foolhardy enough to think that he can depart from the plan.

Thanks to the intervention of Eros, Eryximachus is now forced to improvise. True, he cannot come up with an entirely new speech on the spot; he will stick to his outline as much as possible. However, to be sure of snaring Aristophanes, Eryximachus had to analyze the poet's words. Now he must invoke Aristophanes' principles before they have been declared, and he must parry his blows without knowing where they will fall. Worse, he has left Aristophanes free to reply, thus making his task extremely perilous. I think that this is why Eryximachus is nervously solicitous of the poet and why he bullies him when he shows signs of rejecting the proffered *technē*. Eryximachus would have been wiser to suggest waiting for

Aristophanes to recover from his indisposition, but his judgment has been clouded by Eros.

Having let Eros and recklessness get him into this fix, Eryximachus will have to solve a complex problem with his opening statement. His introduction must do four things at once: begin to defend Phaedrus and himself against Pausanias's critique; avoid vexing Pausanias again in front of Aristophanes; placate Aristophanes further by proving that a sophistical *technē* can reconcile antagonists, together with their conflicting theories; and lay the foundation for his synthesis of the religions of the Olympians and Eros. To accomplish all this, Eryximachus pretends to start with a partially conciliatory and partially critical remark about Pausanias. He avers that Pausanias "seems" to have begun his speech beautifully but not to have finished it becomingly, thus necessitating an effort to supply a more suitable conclusion. He promises to furnish the new ending. He also declares that he will give his *technē* the greatest reverence by speaking first from the vantage point of medicine. As a physician, he allows that Pausanias "seems" to have descried "a double Eros" beautifully. However, he also hints that Pausanias missed something. He says that he seems to himself to have observed "from medicine, our *technē*," that there is not only Eros of human souls toward beauties but also Eros of other things toward one another found in the bodies of all animals, in all growths in the earth, and in all beings; that the god's rule over human and divine affairs is universal; and that "the nature of bodies possesses the double Eros," for bodily health and sickness are unlike, "and the unlike desires and loves unlikes" (185e6–186b7).

Two questions now arise. First, how are we to read Eryximachus? Is his speech pure poetic tomfoolery meant to be comically entertaining? Or is it a serious lecture on principles of ancient medicine? Or is it a work of rhetorical deception? I assume that we have to take Eryximachus at his word when he says that he will speak from the standpoint of his *technē*. He purports to proceed by appealing soberly to medicine. Thus, we shall have to hold him to the standards of his century's science, or at least to rigorous rules of formal logic. However, we might come full circle in doing this, for Eryximachus's medical theories are so logically incoherent that they are funny. This might be both a camp joke and rhetorical trickery. The speech may be partially serious, partially comic, and wholly deceptive all at once.

Second, what does the principle "unlike desires and loves unlikes" mean? It must be clarified if we wish to understand Eryximachus. With its double negative, it could be read as an intricate version of the maxim "opposites attract"—for example, "Men and women are unlike, or opposites, so they are attracted to and love one another." However, I think that Eryximachus has something different in mind, namely, that opposites love things that are opposites of each other, not opposites of the lovers, and also that the opposites love things that are opposites of their opposites. Symbol-ically, his idea can be expressed with this formula: "A is unlike B. A loves C. B loves D. C is unlike B and D." This is why his homoeroticism does not violate his basic principle. When we think this through, we shall see that Eryximachus is right when he implies later that under his ambiguous axiom, opposites do not attract, but repel.

Eryximachus's solution of his strategic dilemma is skillful, but it is not philosophically or theologically honest. The most clever part of Eryxima-chus's speech has been his stress on "seeming." The verb "seem" is the first word out of his mouth. The verb is also repeated at each critical junc-ture. Eryximachus causes Pausanias to "seem" to have descried a double Eros beautifully. He professes to "seem to himself to have observed" the important facts—a queer expression. It can be shown that these invoca-tions of seeming strive to generate appearances, disguise aggression, and hide Eryximachus's real opinions. They appear to respect Pausanias. They appear to defend Phaedrus with soft, conciliatory language, words that suggest that the three sophists disagree merely because their subject is am-biguous and that they can quickly come to rational accord. They appear to establish the foundation for peaceful amity that will please Aristophanes. They affect piety by allowing medicine to acknowledge a divine rule over nature and, hence, apparently, the suzerainty of Zeus. Meanwhile, they create a hazy medium in which Eryximachus can surreptitiously humil-iate Pausanias by overpowering him with appearances, and they subvert Olympian piety by expressing a covert Asclepiad will to power over nature and the gods.

The manner in which Eryximachus "reconciles" the views of Phaedrus and Pausanias is extremely good evidence for the argument that his pur-pose is primarily rhetorical deception. Eryximachus's opening move, which consists in the statements that Pausanias seems to have begun beau-tifully but ended unbecomingly, and that Pausanias appears to have distin-guished a double Eros beautifully, looks like a proposal for rational com-promise. It says, in effect: "I will grant your partial insight into the truth; I ask you to acknowledge mine." The look, however, is deceiving. Pausanias does not *seem* to have identified a double Eros, beautifully or otherwise. He *really* asserted that there are two Erotes, which was to envisage something different from a single Eros with a double character. With this deliberate twisting of words, Eryximachus creates the appearance that Pausanias said something other than what he said. In doing so, he cleverly retracts his ostensible concession of partial validity to Pausanias's argument.

Further, given the other orators' metaphysics, the *sympotai* will wish to know what the double god's ontological ground is. When there were two Erotes, one was earthy and the other airy. Now that we are down to one Eros again, a deity with a split personality, most of the *sympotai* will suppose that the god must be either earthy or airy. When Eryximachus, speaking as a professional, finds his Eros in the bodies of all animals, in plants, and in all beings; when he affirms that "the nature of bodies possesses the double Eros"; and when, like Phaedrus, he mentions "soul" just once, in a "not only" phrase, and otherwise talks exclusively of bodies, he implies that all things are primarily body and that we must see the god as essentially earthy. He does not deny the existence of soul or Uranian Eros (that is, a Uranian aspect of the double Eros), but he leaves a cloudy, linguistic impression that soul and the double Eros are identical and that they are an epiphenomenon of Earth. Now Pausanias is the simpleton: he inanely committed the fallacy of concluding from opposite effects to opposite ontological causes, or to the duality of being, in the face of an empirical science that knows only bodies.[51] Phaedrus has been avenged. Clearly, Eryximachus's idea of reconciliation is to smile while stabbing or manipulating his foe secretly, so that no one, especially not the victim, realizes what has happened. By extrapolation, his concept of political harmony and a lovers' union is probably one of systems in which masters slyly govern slaves by selling them their servitude as freedom.[52] Phaedrus, who thinks that he competes successfully with his *erastēs* for honor, should beware.

The logic that Eryximachus uses to demonstrate his metaphysics also betrays that his purpose is essentially rhetorical. Eryximachus offers the company an implicit syllogism: "The double Eros is possessed by whatever exhibits the principle 'unlike loves unlikes.' The nature of bodies manifests this principle, for bodies display health and disease, which are affinities for unlike things. Ergo, the double Eros is found in the nature of bodies." Here, Eryximachus's major premise has been asserted gratuitously, with no basis beyond a vague claim that "studies show." It is also dubious. The proposition that "unlike loves unlikes" is no more evidently a general principle than its hackneyed contrary, "opposites attract." His minor premise means that bodies are dualistic organisms that simultaneously love healthy and sickly things (186b7–8). For example, hearts have healthy loves of rhythmic beating and sick loves of arrhythmia. This has a ring of plausibility, but the reasoning is specious, for organisms cannot really be said to love that

51. Although it might be true that opposite causes have opposite effects, it is not necessarily true that opposite effects have opposite causes.

52. Cf. Arlene W. Saxenhouse, "The Net of Hephaestus: Aristophanes' Speech in Plato's *Symposium*," 19. She says, "Eryximachus, who envisioned nature as inherently harmonious, ignored political life. Indeed, he made politics irrelevant. Politics as the resolution of conflict, as the choice of actions, as the protection of the city can be ignored for the doctor's art assures us that order exists by nature." I disagree. As we shall see, Eryximachus is far from believing that order exists by nature. Nor does he ignore political life. He subsumes it under his remarks on human affairs in 187c–e, in which he is still bragging that he specializes in resolving conflicts. More on this later.

which destroys them; rather, they resist it. The minor reduces to a deliberate obfuscation. There is an even greater difficulty. Let us start again with Eryximachus's major: "The double Eros is possessed by that which exhibits the principle 'unlike loves unlikes.' " When we proceed to the minor and the conclusion, we instantaneously perceive that the logic can take another path: "But the nature of *souls* manifests this tendency, for souls are the seats of minds, and minds display health and disease, which are affinities for unlike things. Thus, the nature of souls possesses the double Eros." Eryximachus should see this alternative, if not additional possibilities to which Socrates might point. However, he is silent about the problem, proving either that he is stupid or, more likely, that he loves victory in disputation more than truth.

One more note on Eryximachus's rhetorical intention is necessary. His obeisance to medicine and his claim to have observed all bodies, plants, and beings are calculated to give the impression that he is a reverent naturalist. After all, the doctors must heed Apollo, who surely taught them to study the natures of things because the medical *technē* is governed by a natural telos, health. Eryximachus apparently complies with this rule by citing the nature of bodies and explaining how it informs his *technē*. With a great ostensible piety toward nature, he establishes the law allegedly discerned in bodies: "unlike loves unlikes." Then he illustrates his art with an analogy. He maintains that he agrees with Pausanias that it is noble to gratify good people but shameful to gratify the licentious. He adds that by the same token, it is noble to gratify the good and healthy parts of bodies but shameful not to disappoint the bad and sickly.[53] The physician's *technē* produces the right gratifications and disappointments. Medicine is a knowledge of the "erotics of bodies" (that is, the things of eros that pertain to bodies) with respect to filling up and emptying. The greatest doctor distinguishes the noble eros from the base. He implants the one and eliminates the other, his choice depending upon which "should" be present. When he does this, "he will be a good demiurge" (186d4–5).

This outwardly naturalistic speech inspires admiration for Eryximachus's cunning, for it really supports a radical Asclepiad technicism that, far from being naturalistic or Apollinian, intends to dominate nature and the gods. Three considerations support this judgment.

First, as argued above, the rule "unlike loves unlikes" is not really based on observation of any universal natural behavior. Eryximachus imposes it on nature willfully. This becomes especially clear when the alleged principle is extended from bodies to human sexuality. Then, "unlike loves

---

53. The fact that there are bad, sickly parts of bodies that should be frustrated already refutes Saxenhouse's assertion that Eryximachus believes the world is orderly by nature. If he did think that, there would be no need for physicians.

unlikes" means that male homosexuality is a natural orientation, lesbianism is the opposite variety of natural sexuality, and heterosexual love is unnatural, or does not even exist.[54] It also means that by nature, "good" males
love "good" males, "bad" males love "bad" males, "good" and "bad"
females love "good" and "bad" females, respectively, and, to repeat, heterosexual love is unnatural for "good" and "bad" alike, for opposite sexes
repel each other. Eryximachus simply ignores the inherent attraction of
great numbers of men and women to one another, which is the natural
basis of human reproduction. Like Phaedrus and Pausanias, he conceals or
glosses over what is inconvenient.

Second, Eryximachus's reasoning slyly destroys nature's function as a
measure. In the classical conception, nature wants certain configurations
of organic matter. Living beings are healthy when nature achieves its aims
and sick when it falls short, so disease exists only in the mode of deficiency, even when it has efficient causes. When the double Eros belongs
to the "nature" of bodies as their principle, though, nature desires certain arrangements of organic matter and their defects simultaneously. The
bodies naturally pull in opposite directions. Hence, nature cannot tell us
which arrangements are healthy and which diseased. When we use these
words, they are conventional and depend upon our preferences.[55] (This
claim seems manifestly untrue. However, the thoughtless will think it true
because it superficially resembles the correct observation that organisms
naturally strive for self-preservation but are also naturally subject to destruction and decay.) However, neither conventions nor predilections bind
those who are determined to challenge received opinion. Eryximachus
thinks that he can decide for himself which loves of bodies are necessary in
each case. Inasmuch as he tacitly equates the terms "healthy" and "good,"
and "diseased" and "bad" (186c2–4), nature is also incapable of telling us
what is good and bad. In every human body, there is something that lusts
for other individuals conventionally denominated "good" and something
else that desires other persons conventionally called "bad," but this does
not show that the other people are good and bad by nature because human
nature wants both sorts. When Eryximachus agrees with Pausanias that it
is noble to gratify good men but not the licentious, he purposely omits the

54. Logically, the proposition "unlike loves unlikes" does not necessarily entail that
"like loves likes." A and B, being unlike, could love C and D, respectively, C being
unlike B and D, but also unlike A. However, if A and B constitute the entire universe,
as is the case with male and female, then "unlike loves unlikes" can mean only that
males love other males, and females love other females, or that "like loves likes." Thus,
male homosexuality and lesbianism are the only natural possibilities.

55. For example, you might like a clear mind, and I might prefer one addled by drugs.
The nature seen by Eryximachus wants both simultaneously, so it cannot be said to
inform us which alternatives are right.

qualification that the good are the ones who care about souls and have greater shares of *nous*. He offers nothing in its place because he recognizes no natural criterion of goodness. He can define not only the necessary outcomes of medical cases but also good and evil as he pleases.

Third, Eryximachus's declaration that the greatest physician can induce both the noble and the base Eros to appear and disappear is a staggering claim. Our surprise is not occasioned by the affirmation that the best doctor can work to make the sick healthy, which he might do, for example, by thwarting the eros in the heart that loves arrhythmia and gratifying the eros in the heart that desires life-sustaining rhythm. Neither is our surprise caused by the implicit suggestion that the most skillful healer of the sick also knows well how to kill the healthy by reversing his healing procedure. What floors us is something that goes far beyond the normal aspirations of medicine or crime by asserting that the greatest doctor can control what is or is not there by nature, so that, for example, the eros in the heart that loves arrhythmia can be eliminated and the eros that desires rhythm can be engendered. This best physician can refashion nature itself according to his own conception of what is "necessary." This is why Eryximachus states that the doctor will be a "good demiurge," leaving only the slow to wonder whether he means a "workman" or a "maker of the world."[56]

When we think long enough about everything that this could imply, we realize that Eryximachus has slipped a veiled hint into his argument, that the greatest physician is supreme because he will be able to rediscover the secret of Asclepius. This hero violated the Olympian order by raising someone from the dead—a crime for which Zeus killed him with a thunderbolt.[57] In his desire to emulate Asclepius, Eryximachus renews his forebear's assault on the gods. He concocts his own brand of Titanism, one that will be attractive to valetudinarians such as Phaedrus. He also hopes it will have a broader appeal in Athenian culture, that is, the many will put a conquest of nature and Zeus on the agenda of the polis, so that political support of physicians who seek to defeat death will wax. (The fantasy of an eventual triumph over death does become a durable strain in Western culture.) Eryximachus also believes that he can catch Aristophanes with this bait. Aristophanes endorses Olympian religiosity because its rites are supposed to bend divine wills. However, if Eros governs all human and divine things, and if the greatest doctor can compel the contrary elements of Eros to be and not be as he sees fit, even in gods, priests influence the gods

56. "Demiurge" literally means "a worker for the people." It would be interesting to trace the evolution of the term into a reference to a being who makes the world out of chaotic materials that he is given or finds at hand.

57. Zeus is the governor of the natural order. He has decreed that death is the lot of human beings. When Asclepius raises someone from the dead, he violates the order of Zeus, thus committing a crime. Piety toward the Olympian gods would accept death.

less than Asclepiad art does. Eryximachus is hinting to Aristophanes that the greatest physician can control the gods much more reliably than priests by transforming their natures, so that their wills are not free to accept or reject supplications.[58] This is grandly Titanic.

Eryximachus has purchased his *technē*, his fraudulent rapprochement with Pausanias, and his dominance of nature and the gods at a great logical price. If unlike loves unlikes, and if the double Eros is in all beings, causing their dissimilar parts to love dissimilars, it would appear that the cosmos should explode at once. Although "unlike loves unlikes" does not necessarily entail a subjective hatred of opposites, it does imply that the double Eros would naturally tear all bodies to pieces, forcing opposites to be objective foes. Eryximachus therefore assumes that "the greatest opposites are the bitterest enemies" (186d5–6), thus, incidentally, proving that his principle does not mean that opposites attract. Of course, his statement flies in the face of the fact that everything does not disintegrate at once. It also continues to ignore the mutual attraction of men and women, which secures the reproduction of the human race, making men and women the greatest enemies instead. It disregards the persistence of society, which consists not only of men and women, but of heterosexuals and homosexuals, young and old, rich and poor, as well as every other kind of opposites that one could imagine. Eryximachus must account for these realities in a way that simultaneously saves his universal principle and negates it. He must assume both his double Eros with its divisive tendencies and a cosmic force that unnaturally offsets it by harmonizing opposites, together with a human art that achieves the same end. This contradiction renders his reasoning fundamentally incoherent. However, he presses onward. Whether he does so humorously, seriously but incompetently, deceptively, or all of these at once is left to us to judge.

Leaving the larger problem of the cosmos aside for a moment, Eryximachus claims that the greatest physician will be able to change the bitterest enemies in the body into friends and mutual lovers (186d5–6). Eryximachus does not say how his doctor can transform the love of unlike for unlikes into the mutual love of opposites. Either he has no idea or he is refusing to disclose his most important guild secrets. Maybe he has other fish to fry. He is still making his play for Aristophanes. Gesturing toward both Agathon and Aristophanes, he declares that "these the poets" say that "our forefather Asclepius" composed "our *technē*" by knowing how to create eros and accord between opposites (186e1–3). He thus tries to co-opt

---

58. Accordingly, I also disagree with Saxenhouse's claim that Pausanias and Eryximachus "looked toward the Olympians" for their models of order ("Net of Hephaestus," 20). I regard it as sufficiently proved that to worship Uranus and Eros in the manner of Pausanias and Eryximachus is not to adore the Olympians, but to rise in rebellion against them. It should also go without saying that Uranus and Eros are not Olympians.

Agathon and Aristophanes as allies in the technical project of rendering human bodies viable by compelling their natures to become, or do, the opposite of what they are, or do. However, it is his great misfortune that he has forfeited his ability to force a muzzled Aristophanes to sit still for this account of his principles. The poet might contradict him.

Still omitting to explain precisely how his *technē* achieves its harmonies, Eryximachus does affect to lift the veil a little, letting on that mankind's most valuable *technai* are governed through (διὰ) the god Eros (186e4–187a1). He contends that agriculture, gymnastics, and music must treat the erotics of their objects in order to make harmonies of opposites. For example, music must blend the originally hostile acute and grave, and fast and slow, into loving unities in order to create harmony and rhythm. Only an expert in erotics can accomplish this.

Here, one surmises that Eryximachus is attempting to win his argument by pointing to existing harmonies and rhythms and giving his techniques credit for them, whether or not the melodies were composed by "modifying the loves" of their elements. For example, rhythm is generated either by holding a steady beat or by alternating fast and slow (tempos and note values). We have no reason to believe that fast and slow were ever "enemies," such that they had to be brought to "love" each other. Indeed, fast and slow are not even opposites, except in semantics. The two terms are relative and can be predicated of the same tempo, depending upon one's perspective. I believe that Eryximachus digresses to attack Heraclitus (regarding his analysis of "the one that is at variance with itself") in order to divert attention from the fact that his art really has nothing to do with such mysterious unities (187a).

Be that as it may, Eryximachus lets his musical illustration stand for the other *technai.* He thus creates the rhetorical impression that his medical expertise rules over the useful arts. Not content with this, he suggests that his *technē* is applicable "to the human beings," not by any ordinary man, to be sure, but by "a good demiurge" who can use education to bring the people "into a better order" (187c–e).[59] Apparently, he can turn the bitterest enemies in society into friends and lovers, too. This obviously makes social and political order technical artifacts. From here, it is a short step to the conclusion that the Asclepiad doctor not only is able to arrange love matches, say, between lovers and initially hostile beloveds, but also is the greatest political technician. Eryximachus reminds us of the enthusiasts who suggested to Albert Einstein that, as the world's most brilliant scientist, he should be competent to solve the most complex political problems. Eryximachus is nominating himself for the position of technocrat-king, or, more likely,

---

59. This is the explicit announcement of Eryximachus's political theory that Saxenhouse and many others miss. It is short but it is there.

technocrat-tyrant. Nevertheless, he lacks the wisdom of Einstein, who responded that physics is easier than politics.

Despite his theoretical inconsistencies, Eryximachus supposes that he has a good start on establishing Asclepiad science as the ruling method of the most useful *technai*, and he feels sufficiently secure to anticipate an objection. The difficulty is that although the technique of harmonizing opposites easily (but not rightly) can be touted as the secret of music, it does not appear to have much to do with cultivating crops (one remembers the Lysenko affair) or conditioning athletes or curing fevers.

Eryximachus handles this problem with a paradoxical—and not entirely coherent—explanation: It is simple to see the erotics of immaterial realities because the double Eros is not present in them. As the principle of corporeal natures, the double Eros exists only in bodies and there he is hard to discern. Thus, for example, the application of rhythm and harmony to human affairs in education is a tricky business that requires a good demiurge. Here, "the same logos" (somehow) recurs: One must gratify and preserve orderly men and bring the disorderly to the Uranian Eros of the Uranian Muse. (This is an inconsistent concession to Pausanias. Although committed to the metaphysical primacy of Earth, Eryximachus wants to assert his will to power over being [Earth] through the instrumentality of soul or mind [Uranus, Sky, Air].) However, the Pandemic Eros that belongs to the Many-Hymned One must be used carefully. Then its pleasure can be harvested without engendering license, just as cookery must be employed beautifully to get pleasure without disease. Hence, in music and medicine and everything else human and divine, one must watch for both kinds of Eros, for both are there.

In response to this argument, one can say only that Eryximachus is a master of the non sequitur. He tells his audience that they would stop doubting his ability to harmonize opposites if they had his expertise. He induces them to accept this petitio principii by promising them sexual and culinary pleasure, thus confessing that hedonism is the fundamental premise of all his calculations and that his distinction between the noble and the base Eros is meaningless. He finishes by hinting that it is now demonstrated that one must be appreciative of both halves of the double Eros, gratifying the "orderly" one without hesitation and indulging the other more carefully, so as to enjoy pleasure without suffering harm. This contradicts both of his previous doctrines, namely, the one that prescribed thwarting the licentious Eros and the one that prescribed changing opposites into lovers—unless reconciling opposites now means holding them in an uneasy union by satisfying each in turn. (I note in passing that the two parts of the double Eros have just lost cosmological and theological status. They now belong to Muses, not Aphrodites. I view this as a reflection of the fact that Eryximachus's eros values technical mastery more highly than the sex that he also enjoys. The "Many-Hymned One" is the Muse Polyhymnia. Eryximachus thinks that she inspires the successful techniques of the vulgar, who therefore praise her lavishly.) It may be that in the history of the world, a lot of irrationalities have been swallowed along with the promise of a good meal and a great night in the sack.

Whoever has been persuaded by this virtuoso performance might still inquire why the cosmos does not explode. Eryximachus illustrates his answer with the example of the seasons. He allows "the orderly Eros" (188a2–3) to cause fruitful, healthy seasons by harmonizing heat, cold, moist, and dry. He blames terrible, destructive seasons on "the hybristic Eros" (188a7). The orderly Eros is presumably the noble Eros, who up to now has been the principle of half of the opposites in the cosmos that needed to be harmonized. This Eros has amazingly altered his behavior. For example, he should be loving heat and fleeing cold (or vice versa), but now he is combining them. More strangely, he has effected his transformation into a reconciler of opposites, even though he has not begun to love or come into harmony with his own hybristic opposite. Indeed, he has abandoned control of the earth to his opponent for half of each year, permitting the hybristic Eros to threaten mankind with pestilence, frosts, and the like. Apparently, the world does not end because he periodically reclaims the earth from his foe, causing its cycles. (This new scientific account of the alternation of the seasons replaces the Persephone myth. It is surely significant that Eryximachus has done away with Hades and the queen of the dead.) We see that if Eryximachus has not fallen into self-contradiction, he is at least up to his neck in equivocation, making the order-loving Eros a blender of order and disorder. Instead of accounting for the earth's survival plausibly, he has lost himself in the double negatives of his postulate to the point of unintelligibility. Nonetheless, he sounds good. He and his friends might be laughing in happy enjoyment of the way that his sophistries make the average Athenian's head spin.

For Eryximachus, an especially wonderful consequence of the fact that the two halves of the double Eros determine the functions of the cosmos is that these operations can now be understood by an Asclepiad scientist who applies his knowledge of erotics to astronomy. This is significant not in itself but because astronomy is the technical basis of divination. When we acquire an astronomical grasp of the erotics of the cosmos, we can use divination, the means of communion between gods and men, to effect the preservation and cure of Eros (188b–c). This said, Eryximachus promptly infers that the Asclepiad physician can heal human impiety, for impiety is a refusal to gratify, honor, and prefer the orderly Eros and a surrender to the other in all questions of duty to our parents and the gods. Divination supervises the health of these human loves, leading us to pious observance. Aristophanes will be pleased. However, Eryximachus has lodged this claim in order to disguise a gross impiety. We know this because diviners can use their skills not only to get advice about remedies for human beings from the gods but also to influence the gods. This is the chief purpose of the *technē*. However, if divination is our means of getting at gods, our means of communion with them, and if the best physician can cure the double Eros, which governs gods as well as men, Eryximachus has repeated his intimation that the Asclepiad doctor can rule the gods and even the universe. Eryximachus has reaffirmed his Titanism. His ambition to overthrow the Olympian order is greater than it initially seemed, aiming not only to overcome death but to subject the entire cosmos to technical manipulation by man, replacing Zeus as its king, as well. In this form, his Titanism appears to prefigure a recurring Western dream, one that has gone under the rubric "the relief of man's estate."

If Eryximachus had followed rather than preceded Aristophanes in the speaking order, he might have felt free to utter this impiety much more openly. Then again, it is possible that sophists always feel a need to blaspheme in guarded ways. Whatever the case, Eryximachus makes one last play for Aristophanes. He argues that Eros, as a whole, exercises a complete power and that indulging in Eros with a good purpose and temperately, both with ourselves and with gods (παρὰ θεοῖς, 188d7; notice that he thinks this is possible), brings us complete happiness. Then we are able to forge concord with one another and friendship with the gods who rule us (188d). For Aristophanes' sake, Eryximachus has thus shown that his theories are pious and mindful of the common good. In conclusion, he allows that he might have inadvertently omitted praises due to Eros. Therefore, he suggests to Aristophanes that it is his task to supply the overlooked details now that his hiccups have been cured.

Aristophanes replies that he stopped his hiccups by following Eryximachus's advice about inducing sneezing and that this causes him to wonder that the orderly principle of the body should desire such noises and irritations. Eryximachus is stung to the quick. He warns Aristophanes to watch what he does if he wants to speak in peace. Aristophanes laughs him off, whereupon Eryximachus shows that he is not joking by renewing his warning in a nasty, intimidating manner. Complaining that Aristophanes thinks that he can simply hurl his darts and escape, he orders the playwright to say no more than he can say freely, that is, to say nothing that has not been sanctioned, or at least no more than he can say without challenge. Perhaps, then, Eryximachus will let Aristophanes go, if it seems good to him (189a–c).

Why is Eryximachus so agitated? The answer is obvious: With his seemingly innocent joke about hiccups and sneezing, Aristophanes has trampled Eryximachus's argument. If unlike loves unlikes, the orderly principle of the body should be incompatible with sneezing, and hiccups should be intensified by Eryximachus's prescription. If unlikes must be brought to love their opposites, the orderly principle of the body should be taught to coexist with the cause of hiccups, or to blend with it, and the sneezing remedy would be superfluous. If the orderly and licentious principles of the body can be reconciled by being allowed to take turns ruling, the sneezing cure would violate their agreement. There is no version of Eryximachus's theory under which hiccups should be treatable by inducing sneezing. Thus, Aristophanes has angered Eryximachus by exposing him as a ridiculous thinker. Eryximachus is literally a sophist who cannot take a joke because the first ripple of laughter batters down his intellectual structures. Aristophanes has also shaken off the harness that the sophists have tried to throw over him and is wreaking havoc in their ranks.

Aristophanes continues to trample the sophists by starting his oration with an explicit rejection of the arguments of both Eryximachus (and, hence, Phaedrus) and Pausanias, on the grounds that people seem to him to have failed completely to sense the power of Eros (189c2–5). This implies that the sophists, exacerbating a tendency of all men to underestimate Eros, have been stupid to believe that they could master Eros with their arts—a truth illustrated in the drama by their theoretical failures, which occur because Eros has vanquished them. With this criticism, Aristophanes renders the first three speakers hors de combat, relieving Socrates of the burden of answering them. When Socrates relates Diotima's teaching on Eros, he can address himself chiefly to Aristophanes and Agathon.

With the speech of Eryximachus, Plato has treated us to the spectacle of a man who has been infected with a novel, virulent strain of the tyrannical eros. For Eryximachus, it is not the essential point that he should dominate his fellow men. He does not consciously aspire to such mastery for its own sake. Rather, his Titanism makes him want despotic power over the cosmos, a technical ability to govern both the universe and social relationships, for what he wants to decree as the good of all his fellow men. There is something generous, noble, even frighteningly beautiful about his ambition. However, his final exchange with Aristophanes demonstrates that when need arises, he will grasp for tyrannical power over his countrymen, too. It is necessary to his project that all people should cooperate with it by turning their efforts to his purposes. It is no less necessary that all should yield to his ministrations when he intervenes in their affairs in order to attain the goals that he deems proper (including, just to add a dose of realism, his own sexual pleasure). Titanic do-gooders like Eryximachus brook no opposition when someone challenges their ends or their means. Up to these moments, the relievers of man's estate present fair countenances. When crossed, they become obnoxious, deny free speech, and think about clapping us in reeducation camps.

It is possible that by now, my treatment of Phaedrus, Pausanias, and

Eryximachus has provoked a rebellion. The *Symposium* is supposed to be a comic celebration of love. Every sophisticated reader of Plato believes, with Allan Bloom, that the dialogue's characters "speak openly about Eros, both taking it seriously and laughing about it." The speakers "are clearly having fun, without any opposition between edifying talk and enjoying oneself." Moreover, the men "represent what is most characteristic and appealing in the Athenian society that has been celebrated for so long." For these reasons, the *Symposium* has been "an inspiration for lovers throughout the ages."[60] On the contrary, my analysis, with its repeated crash landings in different sorts of tyranny, is becoming tragic. "Where," the anguished reader might cry, "are the comedy, the fun, the inspirations for lovers?" Because I already fear a loss of necessary balance between Plato's comedy and tragedy, I sympathize with this complaint. However, I judge it misguided because it misconceives both the eros and the comedy in the dialogue, in four ways.

First, clearly, we can take Phaedrus, Pausanias, and Eryximachus as representatives of what is "most appealing" in Athenian society and call their speeches inspirations for lovers throughout the ages only before having read what they have to say. It is extremely instructive to observe what happens as soon as thinkers of caliber do look closely at the three orations. Having actually examined Phaedrus's speech more carefully, Bloom begins his essay on it by reporting that "Phaedrus is not a very appealing character. . . . He seems to be in the love business, someone who gets a lot of attention from older men—and likes it—but who himself is essentially unerotic." Rosen agrees that Phaedrus "is not, despite his own beauty, a very erotic man." "Pausanias," Bloom continues, "turns out to be a rather timid fellow." As for Pausanias's "noble love," Bloom asserts: "To put it shamelessly, but as Pausanias really intends it, the boy is a prostitute." He decides that Pausanias's speech, "like Phaedrus', is not really a praise of Eros." Rosen also contends that Pausanias is a "coward" who turns his lad into a prostitute. Moving to Eryximachus, Bloom remarks: "Eryximachus, it turns out, is an utterly unerotic man. And this apparently is the natural accompaniment of the fact that he is a specialist." Further, Eryximachus's specialty is "imperialistic." His oration is also filled with "confused banalities." His science "does not do justice to the real experience of Eros." Rosen declares that Eryximachus is devoted to "selfishness." He denounces the Asclepiad physician as a "hedonist" for whom, "[m]orally, love is on the same level as eating." He concludes that the doctor's scientific interpretation of Eros not only is logically incoherent, but also "must lead to the suppression, not merely of the divine, but of the characteristically human

---

60. Bloom, *Love and Friendship*, 431, 435.

as well."[61] I permit myself to ask: Where are the "most appealing elements of Athenian society," the comic eroticism, and the eternal inspirations for lovers now? When the scholars who say such things actually read the *Symposium*, they promptly revise their own theses.

Second, the accusation that I am losing sight of the dialogue's comedy might arise from dislike of the fact that I am emphasizing the play's nature as a comic tragedy and bringing the tragic element into focus. People do not want eros to have a tragic aspect, but it can have one. Bloom, Rosen, and others err when they call Phaedrus, Pausanias, and Eryximachus unerotic because they have venal aims. These men are extremely erotic—for honor, for divine roles in creating other souls, and for a technical mastery of being, respectively. They are also rather voracious sexually. The errors of Bloom, Rosen, and others betray that they conceive of eros only as sexual appetite. This blinds them to the fact that the *Symposium* is a drama about the war between the Socratic eros (right pederasty) and a tyrannical eros (wrong pederasty) that is not the less erotic because its Titanic desires are more powerful than its extremely strong sexual lusts.

Third, anyone who thinks that I have missed the comedy in the first three talks seems to me to misunderstand the nature of their humor. It is true that the characters are laughing and enjoying themselves as they praise their erotes. We may not forget, though, that we have been listening to three sophists assiduously praising their own ideals of love. Sophists are hunters of youths (*Sophist* 223b). They love the young in the same way that hunters love deer, or, as Thrasymachus says, as shepherds love sheep. This suggests an analogy. Suppose fishermen swapping their favorite funny fish stories. We overhear them. Amused, we laugh heartily. Assume also, however, that people who love fish as living creatures are passing by, eavesdropping. Our humor is surely their horror. Our three sophists, the hunters of young men, are showing off their techniques for trapping prey. They laugh as they display rhetoric that is humorously potent but more conducive to tyrannical oppression of the young than to the common good. Their humor is a horror to Socrates, who loves the young not as hunters love animals, but for their own sakes. Thus, we have comedy that, in itself, is tragic.

Fourth, Plato's own comedy is somewhat like Shakespeare's in *A Midsummer Night's Dream*. Plato portrays the bantering sophists in his drama in a way that caricatures them, the comic flash of perception that stirs our mirth being not only that the orators say droll things but also that "Lord, what fools these mortals be." Also, Plato the comic playwright is even more like Aristophanes than Shakespeare. What evokes our laughter in the

61. Ibid., 453; Rosen, *Plato's "Symposium,"* 35; Bloom, *Love and Friendship,* 459, 466; Rosen, *Plato's "Symposium,"* 62, 87; Bloom, *Love and Friendship,* 470, 471, 472, 475; Rosen, *Plato's "Symposium,"* 93, 103, 115, 116, 119.

Clouds is essentially not the slapstick but a Socrates whose pretensions are ridiculous as compared with what is possible and important in the order of being, as that order is understood by Aristophanes. In making his characters as true to life as he can, Plato proves them ludicrous in light of the order of being as he understands it, simultaneously writing comedy and tragedy. Phaedrus, a prostitute and would-be imperialistic murderer who thinks that he is glorious in his speeches; Pausanias, a lecherous old legal eagle who imagines himself a creator of virtue in his *erōmenos* and in Athenian society at large; and Eryximachus, a mortal who aspires to sit at the controls of the cosmos, are much more laughable than the Socrates who floats above the sun while pondering the heavenly things and the farts of fleas. They are funny but tragically harmful cuckoos. So, I do not admit that I have lost my balance on Plato's tragicomical high wire. At least not yet.

Excursus on Socrates and Aristophanes

Aristophanes causes us special difficulties. Everybody loves him. So do I. This gives rise to issues that I must oversimplify by compressing their treatment into something less than a book. Our problems are caused by the fact that love of Aristophanes creates demands for—and often produces— two lines of sympathetic exegesis of his speech in the *Symposium.*

First, in his *Apology,* Socrates informs his jury that he has two sets of accusers who have said "nothing true" (18b2). The group relevant to our concerns has been libeling him since the jurors were credulous children. Socrates recites informal and formal versions of their charges. The informal indictment reads that "there is a certain Socrates, a wise man, a *phrontistēs* [that is, either a profound thinker, if the term is intended literally, or a "wise guy" in the pejorative sense] on the things high in the air, who has inquired into all things under the earth, and who makes the weaker speech the stronger" (18b6–c1). The accusers who say this are the dangerous ones, for "those hearing think that those who look into these things do not believe in gods" (18c2–3). The formal charge says: "Socrates does injustice and meddles by investigating the things under the earth and in the heavens, and by making the weaker speech the stronger, and by teaching others these things" (19b4–c1). Socrates regretfully confesses that he cannot name his long-standing accusers, except that one is a certain comic poet, Aristophanes (18d1–2, 19c2). Mary Renault draws the implication of this complaint sharply. Referring indirectly to Aristophanes' ridicule of Socrates in the *Clouds,* she has one of her dramatic narrators declare: "Mockery like this is a crucifixion, meant not just to hurt but to kill. Even in comedy it can finish a man; a few score know him, the whole city knows the lie."

Inasmuch as Socrates suffered judicial murder, "Aristophanes' hands are far from clean."[62]

Generally, lovers of Aristophanes reject this accusation. Their instinctive reaction is to think that Aristophanes must not have intended to portray Socrates as a bad man or to do him any real harm. Hence, they infer that there must be some misunderstanding here, one that a more sophisticated reading of the texts would clear up. Some argue that the *Clouds* was all in fun. Others contend that Aristophanes had just cause to censure Socrates and was attempting to help either him or his precious city, or both, by couching constructive criticism as humor.

Defending his beloved Aristophanes in the latter way, Leo Strauss offers the public a provocative book, *Socrates and Aristophanes.* Noting that an ostensible enemy might be fair, Strauss contends that Aristophanes "justly" depicts Socrates as "the first and foremost sophist," as seen by Athenians of the good old Marathon era. Observing that the *Symposium* closes with a conversation in which "Aristophanes agreed to a view propounded by Socrates," Strauss also claims that in the only Platonic presentation of the poet, Aristophanes is not Socrates' enemy at all, but "appears to be very close to Socrates." The *Clouds* is a comedy that strives to teach the imprudently outspoken Socrates caution. Following Strauss, Allan Bloom declares that the *Clouds* can be read "not as an act of petty enmity but as a kind of warning to Socrates as well as a thoughtful criticism of what was then his teaching. They disagree about some very fundamental things . . . but they agree about the important questions." Plato therefore makes the poet's speech in the *Symposium* central and "a tribute to Aristophanes' genius."[63] These arguments by Strauss and Bloom presuppose that both Aristophanes and Socrates are atheists, promoters of their own divinity, devotees of natural science, and aristocrats who uphold the right of better men to exploit worse men. Their notion that Aristophanes is giving Socrates a warning assumes that the poet is merely showing the philosopher what can happen to him if he is not more discreet about his beliefs and commitments.

Martha Nussbaum also sees Aristophanes as a just critic. Her Aristophanes represents traditional Athenian ethics. He blames Socrates for ignoring the necessity of habituation in moral education, for undercutting customary ethical norms with destructive critiques without offering

---

62. Renault, *The Mask of Apollo,* 195, 79.

63. Strauss, *Socrates and Aristophanes,* 8, 5; Bloom, *Love and Friendship,* 478. For some time prior to the quoted passages, Strauss has been summarizing Nietzsche's opinions. There is some doubt as to whether he means to assert what I quote here in his own name or in Nietzsche's name. Having read the relevant passages many times, I have decided that by this point in his discussion, Strauss has reverted to speaking in his own name, not Nietzsche's.

positive alternatives, and for neglecting to clarify the difference between his pompous disdain for Athenian values and outright "immoralism." Surveying these counts of the poet's indictment of Socrates, she judges that "there is a decent case to be made for convicting Plato's Socrates on all three." Plato's Socrates insists that ethics is a matter for experts. He demands that others show him their logically verifiable accounts of virtue. When they cannot comply, he demolishes their reasoning, leaving them without moral guidance. Aristophanes is not the only great thinker who levels these charges against Socrates. Nussbaum maintains that Plato himself endorses them in the *Republic*.[64]

The "all in fun" defense, the "just criticism" reasoning of Strauss and Bloom that again alerts us to esotericism, and the competing "just criticism" suggestions by Nussbaum save the day for Aristophanes' lovers. Now they can enjoy either a harmless spoof or just caricatures of Socrates in the *Clouds*, applaud the poet's amicable warning to the philosopher, and read Plato with an eye toward analyzing the continued agreement of Aristophanes and Socrates in their atheism, pursuit of godhood, scientism, and sophistry. Alternatively, they can commend Aristophanes' suggested reforms of Socratic morality and interpret Plato as a philosopher who uses Aristophanes as a model for improving Socrates. The general delight with these kinds of reconciliations of the two men exerts pressure on all subsequent commentators to explain the *Symposium* as a dramatization of the essential agreement of Aristophanes and Socrates (or the Platonically reformed Socrates) about the humor, ontology, and ethics of eros.

Second, among the lovers of Aristophanes, it is common to argue with Allan Bloom that "Plato makes Aristophanes the expositor of the truest and most satisfying account of Eros that we find in the *Symposium*."[65] The poet's myth of Eros in the dialogue is thought beautiful, so much so that nearly everyone demands and expects agreement with Bloom's proposition. It is rare to see such happiness and harmony among scholars.

The bliss is problematic. The "Aristophanes as jocular critic" and "Aristophanes as master of love" lines seem to me to misconstrue the *Symposium* and Plato's other dialogues. Thus, I do not want to be required to treat the *Symposium* as a proof that Aristophanes is just a wag or a friendly critic of Socrates, or that the two gleefully agree on their atheism, self-deification, scientism, and rhetorical manipulation of the Athenians, or that Plato presents a Socrates whose early "immoralism" has justly been corrected by Aristophanes. Nor do I want my interpretation of Aristophanes' speech to be denied a fair hearing by the existing prejudice in favor of the

---

64. Nussbaum, "Aristophanes and Socrates on Learning Practical Wisdom," 43–97, esp. 81, 85.
65. Bloom, *Love and Friendship*, 478.

comedian's myth of Eros. I perceive a need to prepare the ground for a more open-minded reception of my own view by departing briefly from the text of the *Symposium*. Thus, I shall offer a short excursus on the relationships between Socrates and Aristophanes in real history and in drama.

The excursus will focus on my first difference with the poet's lovers. It will ask whether Aristophanes intended the *Clouds* merely as good fun and friendly advice to Socrates or as a "crucifixion" of the philosopher; give some preliminary indications of my reasons for disagreeing with Strauss, Bloom, and Nussbaum; inquire whether the *Clouds* tells the truth about Socrates either in Strauss's or in Nussbaum's sense; show that Aristophanes and Socrates were not philosophically close; and speculate on Aristophanes' grounds for quarreling with Socrates about the most important things. Readers not interested in these issues may skip ahead to my next section, which will expound my differences with Aristophanes' lovers over the truth of his account of Eros.

So, I turn to the question of what Aristophanes means to achieve with his lampoon of Socrates. In the *Clouds*, produced at the City Dionysia in 423, Aristophanes portrays Socrates as a man who studies the things aloft (171–73) and as a teacher whose students investigate the things under the earth (188). He also depicts Socrates as an educator who shows men how to make the weaker speech defeat the stronger, although it advocates the more unjust things, so that the men can win both just and unjust causes by speaking (112–15, 98–99, 1105–6, 1148–53). He lets Socrates teach Pheidippides, a young man, the cunning speech that will procure his father's acquittal in lawsuits, no matter how unfairly (1148–53); that will turn the youth into a crafty perpetrator of injustice who has a reputation for justice (1173–74); and that will inspire him to beat his father, justify the act (1331–32), and consider beating his mother (1443–46). Finally, he causes Socrates to assert that "[g]ods are not currency to us" (247–48) and "Zeus is not" (367); to urge Strepsiades to confess only Chaos, the Clouds, and the Tongue as gods (424); to substitute an ethereal Vortex for Zeus (379); and to swear by the Air (627). In his grand finale, Aristophanes has Strepsiades upbraid Socrates for causing him to abandon the gods, ask Hermes what to do about the miscreant, hear Hermes' answering command to burn down Socrates' "thinkery," respond by setting fire to the building, and demand to know of the fleeing Socrates what was the idea of his hybris in advocating renunciation of the gods and study of the moon. Then Aristophanes brings Hermes himself on stage. Hermes shouts orders to chase Socrates and hit him with darts (lethal weapons like arrows) for wronging the gods 1476–end).

It is conceivable that Aristophanes means all this as a hilarious satire of a friend or as a fair critique in slapstick that teaches by drawing laughs. Although the parody does obviously include all of the elements that ultimately find their ways into the indictment of Socrates, one could speculate that it never occurs to Aristophanes that producing the *Clouds* will plunge Socrates into mortal danger, for Athens might be a genuinely cosmopolitan society in which no one seriously persecutes religious nonconformists or sophists who teach the young how to win lawsuits with clever rhetoric. After all, I. F. Stone is right to observe that the Athenians refrained from lynching Socrates in 423, that they probably left the theater laughing, and that nothing more happened for twenty-four years.[66] The twenty-four-year gap could also serve as a decent foundation for the benign-warning theory.

On the other hand, it is equally conceivable that Aristophanes intends to get Socrates murdered, despite the fact that it takes twenty-four years for the *Clouds* to achieve this effect. Stone goes too far when he suggests that few Athenians were ever really disturbed by religious nonconformity. Thucydides relates that Alcibiades faced the death penalty for defacing the Herms and profaning the mysteries, not seriously at first but imminently after the early defeat at Syracuse. Denying the existence of Zeus, replacing him with the elements, and corrupting the young could have also been irritants that the Athenians normally tolerated but were ready to punish ex post facto if their passions and fears became excited. K. J. Dover observes that it was not unusual for the Athenians to prosecute and kill people for injuring the polis; they did believe that gods would harm the city for the religious offenses of its citizens.[67] Given this, and given that the deeds and commands of Strepsiades and Hermes in the *Clouds* literally aim at roasting and spearing Socrates, there seems to be at least an even chance that Aristophanes wants Socrates executed and is disappointed that a foolish Athenian public makes him wait so long for the fulfillment of his wish.

Further, if Aristophanes' designs are benevolent—for example, if he thinks it necessary to warn Socrates against openness in certain speeches and actions because it might lead to the death penalty—I find it inexplicable that Aristophanes would give his "warnings" against openness so openly, before some thirty thousand people. If I have a "friend" who publicly bruits charges that I am an atheist, a heretic, and a sophist who corrupts the young, this in aid of persuading me to be more discreet about my atheism, heresy, and ruinous sophistry because they can get me killed, my "friend" has given me an amazingly indiscreet and totally irresponsible warning that can easily become a self-fulfilling prophecy.[68] Given the propensities of the Athenians to become homicidal when they were enraged or frightened, the same objection can be brought against the friendly-

---

66. Stone, *The Trial of Socrates*, 200–201.

67. Ibid., 199 ff; Thucydides, *The Peloponnesian War*, 6.27–29, 60–61; Dover, *Aristophanic Comedy*, 119. Stone's appeals to Athenian statutes pay insufficient attention to the possibility of the ex post facto legislation cited by Thucydides and Dover.

68. This point is so obvious that it seems unimaginable that Strauss and his students actually believe what they say about the "warning."

spoof defense. I conclude that Aristophanes is hostile to Socrates, or, at the absolute least, that he is much too blasé about the peril that he is creating for Socrates. Thus, I agree with Dover: the *Clouds* is simply "not good-natured fun which Socrates' friends could enjoy as much as anyone else." To be sure, some scholars contend that we have proof to the contrary. There is a story in Aelian that Socrates attended the play. Upon overhearing some visitors inquire who this Socrates was, he silently stood up to let them see him. People infer that Socrates was being a good sport and playing along with the joke. However, Aelian specifically observes that Socrates stood silently throughout the play in order to express his contempt for it.[69] This is as far as we can press this issue.

Before asking whether Aristophanes tells specific truths about Socrates, it will be well to consider general objections to Leo Strauss and Martha Nussbaum. There are dramatic reasons that it is wrong to argue that, according to Plato himself, Aristophanes justly labeled Socrates a prime sophist or immoralist, and also wrong to say that, according to Plato, Aristophanes agreed with Socrates. In the *Apology,* Plato causes Socrates to remark that his accusers have said "nothing true" (18b2). This necessarily implies that Aristophanes has said "nothing true." One could reply that we should expect a man on trial for his life to deny all charges and that Plato therefore makes Socrates speak naturally, although not credibly. This answer is wholly inconsistent with the rest of the dialogue, in which Socrates goads the jury into condemning him to death. Plato definitely does not represent Socrates as a man who would lie to save his life. Rather, he apparently means to convey the judgment that Aristophanes' charges are certainly false. Socrates also notes that no witnesses have testified that he has corrupted any youths (33c–34b). If these points are not convincing, I should permit Plato to speak in his own name. In the Seventh Letter, Plato declares that the accusations against Socrates were "most unholy" and that Socrates of all men least deserved them (325b6–c1). He also calls Socrates "the most just" man (324e2). These statements are absolutely incompatible with the argument that Plato regards the young or the old Socrates as guilty of atheism, impiety, sophistical injustice, or an "immoralism" that destroys all ethical guidance. Of course, we could now speculate that Plato himself is lying, either with esoteric intentions or to whitewash his beloved friend. Very well. Having made this move, though, we have surrendered any right to quote Plato as a witness against Socrates.

With respect to the claim that Plato has Aristophanes agreeing with Socrates, I think that the closing scene of the *Symposium* has a meaning contrary

---

69. Dover, *Aristophanic Comedy,* 119; Aelian, *Historical Miscellany* 2.13. Aelian is not a highly reliable source. He gets too many things wrong to be taken seriously. Nonetheless, his tale is the opposite of evidence that Socrates enjoyed the spoof.

to the one that Strauss gives it. Aristodemus does not say that Aristophanes "agreed" with Socrates, but that Socrates was "forcing" (προσαναγκάζειν, 223d2) Aristophanes and Agathon to agreement with reasoning that they had great difficulty following, until eventually they fell asleep. This envisages a slide from an initial discord to hope and then to frustration with a result rendered inconclusive by a lack of physical and cerebral capacity in the auditors. There is an immense difference between Strauss's "agreement" and the actual outcome of the conversation, a distinction great enough to generate radically different understandings of the dialogue.

The next question on our agenda is whether Strauss is right to argue that Aristophanes "justly" accuses Socrates of being the prime sophist in the eyes of the Marathon fighters. This notion presupposes that Socrates starts his career as a natural scientist and moves from there to atheism and duplicity. Thus, to evaluate it, we would first have to ascertain whether Socrates really studied things aloft and under the earth. We have no independent means of finding this out. We know only that our third observer of Socrates, Xenophon, disputes the poet's report. In his *Memorabilia* 1.1.11–13, Xenophon maintains that Socrates never spoke of "the nature of the all" or "the cosmos of the sophists." This supports neither Strauss's favorable view of Aristophanes nor his often repeated, but possibly exoteric, definition of philosophy as inquiry into the whole.

Strauss might mean, though, that Plato esoterically affirms Aristophanes' veracity. We are forced back upon Plato. Does Socrates' student secretly intimate that his great master actually investigated and lectured on things aloft and under the earth? Our only evidence about this is found in Socrates' account of his youthful enthusiasms in the *Phaedo*. Socrates informs Cebes that he was amazingly desirous of the sort of wisdom called "learning by inquiry into nature" (περι φύσεως ἱστορίαν, 96a8). He was eager to discover the causes of the generation, decay, and existence of all things (96a9–10), so he explored "the happenings of heaven and earth" (τὰ περὶ τὸν οὐρανὸν καὶ τὴν γῆν πάθη, 96b9–c1). He quickly decided that he was totally unfit for this sort of study and gave it up. This confession would already suffice to convict Socrates of a decadent, depraved sophistry in the eyes of the Marathon fighters, whose simple devotion to the gods, the city, and courage would render them incapable of understanding why anyone would wish to delve into nature. Hence, we are now obliged to wonder whether Plato signals in the *Phaedo*, more openly than esoterically, that Socrates lies in the *Apology* when he asserts that his accusers have said "nothing true." The Platonic Socrates clearly did study the *pathē* of the heavenly bodies and earth, that is, what befalls or happens to them, or their regular motions.

I believe that greater care with the texts will prove that they are not contradictory and that Socrates does not perjure himself at his trial. We must note exactly that in the informal rendition of the earlier accusations, Socrates is called "a wise man, a *phrontistēs* on the things high in the air, who has inquired into all things under the earth," and that the formal version asserts that "Socrates does injustice and meddles, by investigating the things under the earth and in the heavens." Our consideration of these indictments must focus on two things: the result of Socrates' youthful work and the precise nature of what the young Socrates studied.

With respect to the outcome of Socrates' inquiries, let us assume first that the charges are meant literally, such that Socrates is actually believed to be a wise man, a profound thinker about the heavenly things, and a man who has explored everything under the earth. In Plato's *Apology,* Socrates does not say that he has never studied nature. Rather, he denies that he is wise. He insists that his wisdom consists in nothing but his having become cognizant that in truth he "is worthless with regard to wisdom" (23b2–4). In effect, he also protests that he is not a *phrontistēs* on the things above, and that he has certainly not probed all things under the earth, for he holds that he "knows nothing, either much or little," about such things (19c4–5). If he is ignorant of them, he can say fairly that he does not share in these things (19c9). In the *Phaedo,* Socrates tells at length how his inquiries into the things of heaven and earth came to naught, so that he knew nothing of the causes of things (96a–97b). Accordingly, when he acknowledges having looked into the things of heaven and earth, he simultaneously refuses to admit to being what the informal version of the perennial indictment calls him. If we now suppose the opposite case, that the earlier accusations are anti-intellectual sarcasm, mocking Socrates as a "wise guy" who presumes that he walks on air above mere mortals and the sun, as in the *Clouds,* Socrates rejects them as "drivel" (*Apology* 19c4). This contempt is fair. So far, then, Socrates' remarks in the *Phaedo* do not prove that Aristophanes accurately depicted Socrates as a prime sophist.

It will be objected that this defense of Socrates is sophistical. The real concern of those who indicted him, it will be said, was that he investigated things aloft and under the earth, not that he was wise about them, and we cannot credit a refutation of the accusations that covertly changes the subject. I do not concede the premise of the objection. The early charges against Socrates imply that it is illicit either to possess or to seek knowledge of the things aloft and under the earth. It was just as needful for Socrates honestly to deny having a dangerous science as it was for the people accused of witchcraft at Salem to proclaim their ignorance of black magic. However, let us grant, for the sake of argument, that there is merit in the objection, because Socrates still seems guilty of *attempting* to know the things above and below the earth. Now we must turn to the question of the precise nature of the young Socrates' research.

With regard to this controverted issue, there are rather large differences between "the things under the earth and in the heavens," on the one hand, and "the happenings *(pathē)* of heaven and earth," as they affect the generation and decay of all things, on the other. This is to notice, in the first place, that it is one thing to ask what the heavenly bodies and the earth essentially are, which Socrates does not admit to having done in the *Phaedo*, and quite another to observe their motions and the natural effects of those *pathē*. The Marathon soldiers might not grasp this exact distinction. However, its relevance becomes clear when it is realized that Socrates is really being charged with doubting that the heavenly things and earth in themselves are divine and declaring that they are fire or rocks, positions that Socrates takes great pains to disown in the *Apology*, attributing those "absurd" (ἄτοπα) ideas to Anaxagoras (26d1–e4).[70] We should also note that Socrates goes out of his way in the *Phaedo* to denounce the opinion that the earth is held in place by a vortex, or by air (99b6–8). Socrates transforms neither astral divinities nor Zeus and his powers into inert matter and its functions. In the second place, to examine the *pathē* of earth and their effects on generation and decay is different from looking into "the things under the earth," a phrase that connotes the practice of witchcraft or alchemy. The heros of Marathon would not appreciate this nicety, either. If they did understand it, they might object that Socrates should have also refrained from investigating the motions of earth for fear of vexing the responsible ruling gods. However, their stated accusations mean that Socrates is guilty of witchcraft and dedivinizing the universe. Thus, Socrates does not commit perjury when he testifies that his accusers have said "nothing true." The *Phaedo* does not constitute prima facie evidence that Plato quietly confirms Aristophanes' picture of Socrates as "the first and foremost sophist" in the eyes of the Marathon fighters.

If Strauss means that Aristophanes intended a Nietzschean critique of Socrates, one mounted in the name of the Marathon fighters, and that such criticism is meritorious, I would answer further that: (1) Friedrich Nietzsche's *Birth of Tragedy* probably reveals more about the state of his own soul than about the Greek tragedians, a point that was argued by serious classicists in Nietzsche's own time; (2) although it might be plausible to attribute Nietzschean motives to Aristophanes, thus explaining his motives neatly, it would beg a host of philosophic questions to assert gratuitously that this justifies his attack on Socrates; and (3) it is implausible to put Nietzschean opinions in the minds and hearts of the Marathon soldiers,

---

70. In Plato's *Apology* 18c2–3, Socrates himself indicates that this is what the charges mean. Cf. *Republic* 508a4 and Xenophon, *Memorabilia* 4.7.2–7. Of course, Anaxagoras was right to deny that the heavenly things are gods. Socrates might even know this. However, Socrates might still object to Anaxagoras's denial that divine reality somehow moves and pervades the astral bodies, the point being that these bodies manifest the god. In this secondary sense, the heavenly things can be divine without being gods, just as human beings can be divine without being gods.

as if these hardy warriors were the tragic Dionysian types imagined in *The Birth of Tragedy.*

Perhaps we could defend Aristophanes by suggesting that he makes an honest mistake about Socrates' interests. If Aristophanes was born between 460 and 450, and if Socrates was treating the *pathē* of heaven and earth publicly, say, as late as 435, a precocious Aristophanes who was between fifteen and twenty-five could have heard him, failed to master the technical distinctions that I have just drawn, and formed his judgments. One would like to believe this. Nonetheless, even here there is something wrong with the timing. The *Protagoras* and the *Alcibiades I*, both set in 432, depict a Socrates who has long since turned from natural science to the human things. Aristophanes does not produce the *Clouds* until 423, when Socrates is forty-six. If Socrates is still discussing the *pathē* of heaven and earth in 423, this is no "quick" turn from a youthful false start.[71] Plato and Xenophon would have to be lying in portraying Socrates as having turned or having "never" spoken of such things. Perhaps they are. This still implies that we cannot use them to demonstrate that Aristophanes gives an accurate view of what Socrates "then was teaching." Having no reason to doubt Plato, I wonder why Aristophanes fails to disclose that the target of his mockery long ago gave up natural science as a dead end. K. J. Dover appears to be right in speculating that "Aristophanes decided to treat Socrates as the paradigm of the sophist and attached to him any attribute of the whole genus that lent itself to ridicule."[72] Therefore, Aristophanes was either woefully ignorant of the real Socrates or mendacious. Considering what ultimately happened, his falsifications were not justified for the sake of laughs.

Well, then, is it fair to charge that Socrates is an atheist or a heretic? There is no logical necessity in the claim that exploring the *pathē* of heaven and earth entails atheism. Xenophon emphatically denies that Socrates was an atheist. His proof is that Socrates always conducted the requisite sacrifices and practiced piety (*Memorabilia* 1.1.2, 4–9, 19–20). Socrates declares in Plato's *Apology* (35d6–8) that he acknowledges (νομίζω) the gods more than his accusers do.[73] In his debate with Meletus, he also asserts that everyone knows that he has been talking about his daimon for years and that everyone recognizes *daimonia* as gods.

Allan Bloom objects that anyone who thinks through Socrates' argument about the daimon will see that it fails to demonstrate that he believes in

---

71. I think that the same objection could be raised to the speculation that Socrates was still speculating on the physical "happenings" as late as 435, when he would have been thirty-five, but I will not press the point.

72. Dover, *Aristophanic Comedy*, 118.

73. This profession of belief is not contradicted by *Phaedrus* 229c–d, as will be shown in a subsequent chapter.

gods.[74] Strauss and his students also do this with Xenophon's apologies. They view the logic as an esoteric sign that Plato and Xenophon regard all proofs that Socrates acknowledges gods as exoteric claptrap. They also note that the public performance of religious duties proves nothing about interior piety. They are right that the arguments really prove nothing about faith or interior piety, but they err in moving to their esoteric conclusions. Logically, it is impossible in principle to demonstrate that one affirms the gods or that one is not an atheist. Socrates could never provide any evidence of his faith in gods that Strauss and others could not reduce to logical hash and, thence, to esoteric signals. Further, it is anachronistic to demand an interior piety of Socrates, for the ancient definition of piety focused entirely on external acts. Thus, it seems to me that rather than scoffing at Socrates' evidence of his belief, we could infer that he is forced by his accusers to offer some token of his faith and his piety and that he resorts to evidence that makes sense in his day.

Bloom is on more solid ground when he objects that Socrates never declares in the *Apology* that he recognizes the deities of the city.[75] Socrates' remark that he believes in gods more than his accusers do leaves a lot of room for heretical attachments to non-Athenian gods, especially to the astral divinities who seem to be acknowledged in the *Apology* and the *Laws*. The remark also admits of openness to a transcendent divine reality, one that Socrates thinks the Greek gods symbolize inadequately, the point being that the Hellenic myths envisage some divine verities but are still not true enough. So, we must grant that as religious reformers, both Socrates and Plato are heretics from the Athenian point of view, although their concession of partial truth to the Greek myths might save them from Aristophanes' accusations in their own opinion. Whatever the case, it is illegitimate to conclude from "hints" in Xenophon and Plato that Socrates was an atheist.

There is more to consider. Socrates relates in the *Phaedo* (97b–99d) that when he gave up his natural *pathē*, he was attracted to a promising teaching of Anaxagoras, that *nous* orders and causes all things. This *nous* had "daimonic force" (99c2–3), and it arranged all things with the aim of achieving the best.[76] Socrates was disappointed that Anaxagoras did not redeem his pledge to refer to *nous* when he assigned causes to the ordering of all things. He was also quite dissatisfied when others paid no heed to the good

74. Bloom, *Love and Friendship*, 538.
75. Bloom, *Closing American Mind*, 276.
76. Cf. the Eleatic Stranger on "all-perfect being" (*Sophist* 248e–249a). The *nous* that pervades or moves all things by directing them to their goods with daimonic power replaces heavenly bodies that are literally gods without dedivinizing the universe. It makes the whole divine in a higher sense. Xenophon's further testimony to this effect will be cited below. This story thus provides further evidence that Socrates did not perjure himself at his trial.

(*agathon*, 99c5) that must hold together and contain all things. Speaking on the day of his execution, he says that he would gladly become the student of anyone who could offer him a discourse on a cause of this kind. However, he found no such teacher and could not learn what he wished by himself, so he undertook his "second sailing in search of the cause" (99c9–d1), giving up the direct study of "beings" (99d5) in favor of the examination of "speeches" (99e5), which is an indirect exploration of the beings that still allows one to get at their truths (99e5–6). In describing this change of methodology, Socrates does not say that he abandoned his quest for a cause in which *nous*, the teleological aim of the best, and the *agathon* were associated. Rather, he seems to report that he changed the manner in which he sought "the cause" (99d1). His second sailing led to the discovery of causality qua participation, in which, for example, a beautiful thing is beautiful because it participates (μετέχει, 100c5) in "the beautiful itself." In the dialogues in which Socrates is characterized as a mature thinker, *nous* and the *agathon* play prominent roles. Although I cannot demonstrate the point here, I think that teleology is also preserved in the conception of participation as a cause. If so, Xenophon's Socrates agrees with Plato's by arguing that creation gives evidence of intelligent design by a wisdom *(phronesis)*, or even by an omniscient god, that dwells in the all (*Memorabilia* 1.4.4–7, 11–18). Socrates' cosmos is pervaded by a divine reality.[77] Again, it is impossible to prove that this means that Socrates believes in gods. However, all we need to infer here is that the available evidence does not support Aristophanes' charges.

Next we must examine Aristophanes' accusation that Socrates promotes injustice with sophistry, that is, that he teaches the young to serve evil by letting the weaker speech defeat the stronger. In the *Sophist,* Theodorus presents the Eleatic Stranger as "very much a philosophic man" (216a4). The Stranger takes the entire dialogue to arrive at a perfectly precise definition of sophistry (268c8–d4). His work affirms Aristophanes' portrait of the sophist as a wordmonger who makes the weaker speech defeat the stronger and improves it philosophically by giving it ontological foundations. Socrates does not object. He does act consistently with this negative view of sophistical rhetoric when he refutes or criticizes characters such as Gorgias, Polus, Callicles, Protagoras, Lysias, and Thrasymachus in other dialogues.[78] Thus, it seems that Plato's Socrates is inclined to behave like Xenophon's Socrates, who never taught or practiced the "art of words" (*Memorabilia* 1.2.31). Strauss admits the force of what I am saying when

77. Seth Benardete says that the second sailing is "designed to replace teleology" (*Socrates' Second Sailing: On Plato's "Republic,"* 4). I do not see textual support for this claim.

78. Planinc also shows brilliantly how the allegory of the cave in the *Republic* is a thoroughgoing rejection of sophistry (*Plato's Political Philosophy,* chap. 3).

he remarks that Aristophanes appears to make Socrates "a sophist in the Socratic sense of the term." To this, we must add that there is no evidence anywhere that Socrates ever deliberately "attacked" justice. In both Plato and Xenophon, Socrates always commends it. In the Seventh Letter, Plato calls Socrates "the most just" man (324e1). So does Phaedo (118a17). We may not project a Nietzschean nihilism onto Socrates anachronistically and gratuitously. In sum, Strauss's claim that Aristophanes tells the truth about Socrates seems baseless, except insofar as the superstitions and biases of the Marathon generation caused misunderstandings.

Martha Nussbaum's opinion, on the other hand, seems to have a basis in the texts and to have some truth in it. For reasons that will become clear below, I believe that she is right to argue that Aristophanes is an anxious representative of traditional Athenian morality. She also hits the target squarely when she says that the Platonic Socrates thinks that "the ordinary morality is in deep trouble and in need of 'salvation' " and that he spends a lot of time undermining the attachments that his interlocutors have to it, particularly in the *Protagoras*.[79] However, I do not agree that this is a fault in Socrates. An ethical tradition that encourages an entire nation to enslave its allies, follow Pericles in his policy of imperialistic expansion, elevate Kleon to a position of supreme power and authority, and produce men who reason the way the Athenian generals did on Melos prior to the genocide is not obviously worthy to continue forming the young. It might well need to be revolutionized utterly. In the *Gorgias*, Callicles realizes that this is what Socrates is trying to achieve. He declares that if we accept Socratic teaching, the world has been turned upside down and people everywhere are doing the opposite of what they should do (481b10–c4).

I also doubt greatly that Nussbaum is right to charge that Socrates neglects to replace the tradition that he blasts with something better. True, he does fail to supply an alternative in the *Protagoras* and some other dialogues. However, in the *Alcibiades I,* which is set before the *Protagoras,* Socrates not only shows Alcibiades that he could not have learned justice from popular education but also proposes joint meditations that will aim to make Alcibiades a just king. In this, he does not repudiate the traditional virtues; rather, he affirms them, in a way. He urges more nobly conceived versions of wisdom, justice, and temperance on Alcibiades, but not of courage, of which the lad already has enough. This is not "immoralism." Socrates does not speak to Alcibiades of habituation but that is because he is dealing with Alcibiades, not hypothetical children in a hypothetical polis. A spoiled young man who has been reared like Alcibiades can no longer be bettered by tutors or elders who habituate him by mixing mildness with severity.

79. Nussbaum, "Aristophanes and Socrates," 84–85.

Also, when we want Socrates to replace the Athenian tradition that he attacks with something better, we cannot expect him to teach morality on every occasion by articulating a full-blown theory of *paideia* containing all of the ideas in the *Republic*. We must be a little more sensitive to dramatic situations than that, letting Socrates try to reform Alcibiades as the circumstances demand. The same reasoning applies to the dialogues in which Socrates seems to negate tradition without offering any alternative. In the *Protagoras*, what is at issue is the great sophist's claim that young men can get an adequate education in virtue from the many and then come to him for instruction on how to become the most able in action and speech in their cities—a recipe for disasters of the sort that Athens is about to suffer. In the situation, it suffices for Socrates to prevent Hippocrates and Alcibiades from joining Protagoras's circle by proving that the sophist cannot do what he promises. The dramatic context does not permit the subsequent transformation of the home of Callias into a Socratic school in which everyone hears the ethical substance of the *Republic*, especially inasmuch as the angry Protagoras and Callias would not have stood for it. Finally, the fact remains that in the *Republic*, Socrates does begin to offer something like what Nussbaum seeks—although surely not a propositional science of the good. Nussbaum's idea that the early "immoralist" Socrates is not the Socrates of the *Republic*, who is a masked, moral Plato, is untenable.[80] Not only does it overlook the continuity between the Socrates of the *Alcibiades I* and the Socrates of the *Republic*, but it ignores the Seventh Letter on the topic of doctrines as well. To repeat, Plato's dialogues are not compendiums of propositional truths about the serious things, such as the nature of soul and the grounds of virtue. Doctrinal differences among the dialogues are not necessarily "developments of Plato's ideas," as Nussbaum infers with many others. Thus, it is still not clear that Aristophanes told the truth about the Platonic Socrates. Of course, we cannot learn whether Aristophanes told the truth about the historical Socrates. On that unknown Socrates, all must be silent.

There is still a great deal of value in Nussbaum's analysis. To show that Aristophanes does not tell the truth about Socratic "immoralism" is not to prove that Aristophanes does not believe that he is telling the truth about it. To repeat, I think it right to say that Aristophanes is a representative of the customary ethical education and that Socrates opposes it. If I had to guess how Aristophanes became a critic of Socrates, I would speculate that the poet probably had one or more encounters with the philosopher between 445 and 423, heard him submitting the old education to revolutionary critique (when Socrates was conversing either with simple artisans or with poets), and became too agitated to allow Socrates to move from the first

---

80. Ibid., 87.

step of his program (clearing away the rubble of the old education) to the second (supplying a new basis for courage, moderation, justice, and wisdom). Going away angry, Aristophanes would have been convinced that Socrates was an immoralist. From here, he could have taken an exceedingly short step to the conclusions that he had to fight the immoralist, that everything is fair in love and war, and that it therefore would serve Socrates right to tag him with all the features of the stereotypical sophist. The public would not have been in a position to separate the half truths from the outright misrepresentations. If thirty thousand saw the *Clouds*, Aristophanes would have reached more people in a day than Socrates could have inspired personally in individual conversations over a span of thirty years.[81]

My next tasks are to prove that Aristophanes and Socrates are not philosophically close and to identify the grounds of Aristophanes' quarrel with Socrates. This work will require an attempt to ascertain the poet's opinions by reading his plays. I recognize that such a venture will be perilous; characters in dramas are never simply identical with their creators. However, I maintain that it is possible to detect some constant themes in Aristophanes, themes that might well embody his views. What could be even more important is that the themes might represent opinions that Aristophanes effectively transmits to the demos, even if he is not committed to them himself.

One of these motifs is the idea that, with the exception of Prodicus (*Clouds* 360–61), all intellectuals are alike in principle and equally deserving of what is due to enemies. This is not something that Socrates thinks. Aristophanes appears to express this prejudice repeatedly in the ways that he portrays the characteristics of his successful protagonists and the opposite qualities of his ill-fated buffoons. His victorious characters tend to be simple, unlearned, and rustic men and women who directly intuit the essences of problems; say what has gone wrong with a few uncomplicated words; devise comically crude, impossible solutions; and persevere in funny campaigns to put things right against all kinds of reasonable warnings and divine and human obstacles. The single exception to this pattern might be the sophisticated Euripides in the *Thesmophoriazusae*, but even Euripides is wholly reliant upon his lowbrow in-law for his triumph.[82] The bunglers who falter or become absurd (for example, Socrates, Strepsiades, Philokleon) have been ruined by the new erudition.

Here we instantly see an example of the risk that we run by identifying Aristophanes' opinions with the views of his characters. It may be that the poet paints these pictures simply because they are funny and it is his job to

81. Therefore, I disagree with Nussbaum when she says that a false portrait of Socrates would have been widely repudiated (ibid., 86). The false picture was actually repudiated, not "widely," but by the small group that Socrates had won for philosophy.
82. In the *Frogs*, the god Dionysus succeeds in his aims. This Dionysus is also something of a hedonistic simpleton.

get laughs. He may also be satirizing the Athenian demos in the guises of both his heros and his buffoons, lampooning them for their simpleminded affinity for crazy schemes and reproaching both them and the few for having let themselves be corrupted by abstruse thought. However, it would be a mistake to expect the demos to grasp either point. They would miss the poet's sheer zaniness or the subtlety of his critique, take him to be advocating anti-intellectualism, and embrace this affirmation of their biases. For them, it would be true that all thinkers always spewed the same degeneracy, despite the most fundamental doctrinal differences, because all endangered mankind merely by thinking and uttering complex reasoned statements. Inescapably, they would also get the impression that the playwright is sympathetic to his heros. He apparently expects good of plain, rough-and-ready, thoughtless types and evil of all who are taught to think too much. He seems to be a proto-Rousseauian, celebrating only those who immediately hear the voice of a rudimentary nature and abhorring all who listen to a corrupt reason or a decadent tradition.[83] Without being able to prove the point decisively, I shall assume that this is Aristophanes' position, or at least the position that he unintentionally teaches the Athenian masses.

How could a simpleminded hearkening to an elemental nature be so beneficial and rationality so ruinous, though? Aristophanes' stance appears to depend on his ideas of the good life for human beings and of the necessary means to this felicity. Aristophanes' plays seem to show that unlike Socrates, he is a hedonist.[84] His heros, together with virtually all of his secondary characters, envisage the good life as one of pleasant feasting, drinking, and copulating with people of both sexes (his free men enjoying undisputed rights to intercourse with their wives, boys, male and female chattel, prostitutes, and consorts, and his free women being voraciously lusty and adulterous). They desire constant prosperity and innumerable honors. On the darker side, they take pleasure in cruelty that they practice upon enemies, slaves, barbarians, and others whom it is acceptable to oppress. True, the poet might intend to satirize this hedonism, but his aim would be lost on the masses, who will agree that he has captured the essence of the good life.

The obvious sine qua non for attaining to this happy life is that one should strive for it. People will pursue it wholeheartedly if they respond to their basic natural urges. A man who thinks too much, like Socrates, will become deaf to his nature and, hence, obtuse to his proper good. He will

---

83. Cf. the argument that the Weaker Speech makes to Pheidippides in the *Clouds* 1075–80, urging him to give free play to his nature by seeking pleasure, and, implicitly, to heed nature if he wants to know whether it is the Weaker or the Stronger Speech who tells the truth.

84. Cf. Nussbaum, "Aristophanes and Socrates," 94.

also imagine that he is something higher than he is, a man like any other with ordinary natural drives, while achieving nothing worthwhile. This will make him a legitimate target of Aristophanes' ridicule, which, among other things, aims to debunk boasters. This is why Aristophanes lampoons Socrates as a snobbish ascetic who starves, goes without a cloak and shoes, and is filthy, flea-bitten, and (most likely to inflame the contempt and animosity of a red-blooded Athenian) anerotic. Socrates is also a socially dangerous misanthrope, insofar as he induces others to aspire to his rationality and forget what is good for them. His thinking can potentially choke the happy life for everyone at its roots. This is why Aristophanes must deride Socratic philosophy as a ludicrous, useless pedantry; persuade Athens that Socrates is a menace to the city; and conclude the *Clouds* by inciting people to the salutary act of burning down Socrates' "thinkery." Given that Socratic reason represents the greatest threat to human welfare, Aristophanes can bill his antirational exposé of Socrates as his wisest comedy (*Clouds* 522) without intending irony. If this is not the comedian's argument, it will be hard for the many to understand why not.

Aristophanes' ordinary men naturally grasp that the good life is hedonistic and behave accordingly. Another crucial requirement for achieving the good life is that pleasure seekers should recognize the practical facts of existence and exercise a prudent regard for them. The first pragmatic fact seems to be that reality fundamentally lacks the highest conceivable justice, a divine or natural right. At least, no one in the *Clouds* contradicts the pronouncement of the Weaker Speech that there is no goddess Dikē (Justice, 901), nobody reverses the victory of the Weaker Speech over the Stronger Speech, and some heroic characters in Aristophanes' other comedies adopt the view of the Weaker Speech. Apparently, the missing Dikē would give all human beings their due, the pleasant life that nature makes them desire. Dikē being absent, what prevails by default is the empirical truth that might makes right, which allows the strong to take what they want. This is certainly not Socrates' sense of the reality of justice. If it is not Aristophanes' view either, the many would still mistake his satirical meaning and rejoice that somebody has finally endorsed their conviction.

Aristophanes might suppose that there is no Dikē and that might makes right because, as his funny Socrates teaches, the mythological gods do not exist, the cosmos is ruled by chaos and impersonal elements, and human affairs are governed by the tongue. Leo Strauss suggests plausible exoteric and esoteric grounds for inferring that Aristophanes holds this.[85] However, there is a serious ring to the proof for the existence of gods that Aristophanes' Nicias gives in the *Knights* (34), that is, that the gods hate him. It is not necessarily esotericism, and it might be plain sincerity, to posit a funda-

---

85. Strauss, *Socrates and Aristophanes*, 143.

mental reality principle (call it a god or whatever else we will) that harshly crushes human beings. Of course, it could be zaniness that makes Aristophanes put this proof into Nicias's mouth, but a people that has suffered long years of war could easily be persuaded to take the demonstration seriously, even while laughing.

Aristophanes' other plays also seem to envisage hordes of gods who are not good, but malevolent. In the *Clouds,* the Weaker Speech assumes that Zeus exists, that Zeus unjustly dethroned and bound his father (905), and that Zeus harms men for pleasure (for example, see 1077–81). The Weaker Speech thus declares Zeus's approval of the fact that might makes right and his enmity to humans. In the *Peace,* Trygaeus discovers that Zeus is striving viciously to destroy the Greeks by means of the Peloponnesian War. In the *Birds,* the human characters and the chorus of birds portray gods as usurpers who use their ill-gotten power to extract pleasurable burned offerings from enslaved men and who would betray each other for a square meal. The gods act these parts. In the *Plutos,* Xremylos discovers that Zeus has maliciously blinded the god Wealth in order to prevent him from conferring himself on just, wise, and orderly men. Zeus does this because he is jealous of mankind. He is especially hostile to usefully good men (87–92). The thoughtless heros in these plays—for example, Trygaeus, Pisthetairos, and Xremylos—are believers who make war on Zeus, or on all the gods. Thus, it is possible to see Aristophanes as a predecessor of Ivan Karamazov, that is, as one who acknowledges that there are gods, regards them as the supreme criminals who are responsible for all the evils that befall the human race, and hates them with a Titanic passion. In this view, the poet's verity that there are malignant deities who are inimical to mankind and his truth that there is no Dikē are two sides of the same coin and stand together as the primary practical fact of life that average men naturally know.[86] Again, if Aristophanes himself does not believe this, the Athenian many could mistakenly derive it from his plays and espouse it themselves, thinking that they had learned it from the poet.

Aristophanes' perception of malevolent gods leads him to a paradoxical rebellious piety. On the one hand, Aristophanes joins Prometheus in hating all gods (with the possible exceptions of Dionysus, Aphrodite, and Eros), blasphemes constantly, and exults in fantasies of rebellion against Zeus and the order over which this wicked tyrant presides. He goes so far as to celebrate a fictitious man, Pisthetairos, who supplants Zeus as the highest god. He would approve the overthrow of Zeus, if anyone could arrange it, or

---

86. This interpretation of Aristophanes' belief in gods is perfectly compatible with his great cynicism about oracles. Human beings could easily err about signs of the gods' wills while still being sure that there are misanthropic gods out there. To arrive at the latter opinion, the people would have to experience their lives only as unmitigated oppression.

any lesser effort to relieve man's estate that could prevail against divine powers. On the other hand, he evidently despairs of the possibility of a successful effort to get rid of the gods. Therefore, in the *Clouds,* he causes Strepsiades to suffer for accepting a rationalistic scheme of frontal attack on the gods, and he recruits Hermes to direct the punishment of the master schemer, Socrates. This teaches that the oppressed slaves of hostile deities had better endure their miseries, couch their blasphemies as jokes that the gods will ignore as long as they receive their tributes, keep sacrificial smoke wafting heavenward to avoid being smitten by divine power, and conduct their metaphysical rebellions as small, oblique attacks that succeed as spiritual passive resistance, not as outright violent overthrows of the despots.[87] So, human beings are born to misery, and Aristophanes' comedy is tragic. His piety is a sullen and pragmatic obeisance that actively mollifies hostile, stronger powers while jokingly defying them and eluding their governance in the interstices of being, where they do not bother to intrude. Even if his humor is sheer wittiness without any serious intent, Aristophanes' perhaps merely zany disrespect for the gods can be understood by the many as incitement to a real disrespect that combines rebellion with a tactical piety.

Meanwhile, alleged atheists such as Socrates harm Athens not because their frontal assaults on the gods are evil, but because they are unsafe. Also, if Aristophanes knows anything at all about the Socrates of Plato and Xenophon, he is aware that this perhaps more actual Socrates believes in good gods. This man's refusals to attribute evil to the deities and his reasoning that envisages the possibility in principle, or even the slightest practical chance, of a reform of the world's injustice presupposes the nonexistence of Aristophanes' real gods, that is, the ontological pillars of the present evil order that rustic men recognize naturally. This kind of utopianism is unsafe, too, because its naive practitioners are headed for disaster. Whichever Socrates is the real one, Aristophanes, or those who misconstrue his humor as I, perhaps, have done, would know that Socrates had to be destroyed by any means, honest or dishonest.

The next basic fact of life that hedonists must observe is that injustice is sewn into the nature of man. Aristophanes makes this clear in the *Clouds* by forcing the Stronger Speech to appeal lamely to Athenian tradition while letting the Weaker Speech appeal more persuasively to nature (1075) in their wooing of Pheidippides. The injustice of human nature displays itself especially in the absence of any authoritative or legitimate principle of moderation in the soul (1060–80). Thus, characters such as Dikaiopolis,

---

87. It is especially ironic that Hermes, the divine prince of thieves, wants to punish Socrates for teaching injustice. However, when might makes right, gods are concerned about injustices to themselves without insisting on justice as a universal principle. This is Hermes' point (1508–9).

Trygaeus, Pisthetairos, and Xremylos celebrate their victories with licentious feasting, drinking, and sexual orgies. They also revive cruelties that they themselves had denounced (for example, in an act verging on cannibalism, Pisthetairos, who has become a man-bird, roasts and eats birds who have rebelled against his new regime). They perpetuate practices that, even in Athenian times, must have been repugnant to decent people (for example, Dikaiopolis purchases two starving Megarian girls from their desperate father for future sexual use, to the tune of puns on obscene Greek words for "pudenda" and "pigs").[88] Pisthetairos delights a wanton son by legalizing the injustice that Socrates was blamed for teaching, that is, by approving of the bird custom of father beating. Pisthetairos also allows his unbridled lust for power to expand into his own despotism over the birds, men, and the gods, and Aristophanes invents no character who can think of a sound objection to him. Clearly, the achievement of boundless pleasure and unlimited tyrannical power is the natural telos of every human being, which is not what Socrates thinks. However, this causes problems for all who cannot hold sway like Pisthetairos. The difficulty is that human nature is self-destructive. If we all gave free reign to our natures, there would be ubiquitous injustice and incessant warfare. No one could pursue pleasure and power successfully for long. The human condition again proves to be tragic.

This trouble has the paradoxical implication that nature can approach its ends only by conventional means. Naturally unjust men must devise a conventional justice and abide by its dictates to attain to any part of their natural telos of the full enjoyment of unlimited pleasure and power.[89] Although the Weaker Speech easily vanquishes the Stronger and nature trumps convention, Aristophanes will insist on prudential validity of the Stronger Speech. Thus, he will urge the Athenians to return to their original mores. Though glorifying hedonism, he will advise moderation. Though coveting the delights of tyranny, he will condemn demagogues and the flatteries that persuade the demos to accept tyranny, or at least tyrants other than himself. Of course, this seems utterly self-contradictory. The bonds of justice and moderation curtail pleasure, inconsistently with the aim of infinite enjoyment. Justice forbids cruelty but cruelty is fun. Obedience to self-imposed law is not the ecstasy of absolute power.

The obvious solution of this dilemma that naturally occurs to ordinary

88. The father disguises the girls as pigs, and tries to trick Dikaiopolis into buying them for sacrificial use in the mysteries. When this fails, the father suggests that the girls can be offered to Aphrodite and skewered on the "spit" of a phallus, whereupon Dikaiopolis agrees to the deal.

89. The fact that justice is unnatural makes any effort to create an artificial right Promethean and, hence, Titanic. The invention of justice is, so to speak, an attempt to improve man's lot against the will of the gods.

human beings is that they should try to have it both ways. These men spontaneously form associations that aim to ensure justice and temperately shared pleasure for all in their internal relations and that unjustly and immoderately kill, enslave, and rob outsiders to generate pleasure, these alliances being called cities. Aristophanes condones this. He puts Everyman's solution into the mouth of Bdelykleon, who thinks it outrageous that crooks such as Kleon should enrich themselves with the tribute paid by Athens's one thousand vassal cities but believes it just that twenty thousand Athenians should live sumptuously by dividing up the profits of imperial tyranny (*Wasps* 698–712). He also counsels this solution in the example of Dikaiopolis, whose name means "just city."[90] The hedonistic Dikaiopolis is a just city unto himself in that he arranges pleasures only for himself and (to a lesser extent) his family, refuses to share his goods with anyone who did not support his policies from the beginning, and heartlessly exploits weaker cities whenever he can.[91] In light of these examples, the unnatural justice that hedonists naturally create must be defined as "helping friends and harming enemies," "help" being that which produces common pleasures and "friends" being the associated brigands, that is, citizens. If Aristophanes knew that Socrates rejected this view of justice, as in the *Republic*, he would gather that the rationalistic sophist was "attacking" justice and defeating it by making the weaker case the stronger, that is, by confusing simpletons with his questions about it.

To make his justice work, Aristophanes needs to reconcile some clear contradictions. For example, Demos (the personification of the people in the *Knights*) is naturally the greatest hedonist (1121–30), but he must let himself be pared down to the good fighting trim of the Marathon soldiers if he wants to keep his empire and his freedom (1321–61). All of the naturally warlike men in the *Acharnians*, *Peace*, and *Wasps*, who have built an empire by fierce deeds, must stop resisting peace between Athens and a clearly invincible Sparta to enjoy the fruits of their victories and to escape being beggared by endless warfare. The poet who can make Pisthetairos describe the

90. Dikaiopolis may be the character in Aristophanes' plays who most perfectly embodies the poet himself. At one point in the *Acharnians* (500 ff), he speaks in the person of Aristophanes.

91. Cf. Strauss, *Socrates and Aristophanes*, 76–77. I disagree with Strauss's opinion that Dikaiopolis, strictly speaking, is minding his own business, or refraining from meddling in the affairs of other cities. The people who visit his market stand for cities, just as Dikaiopolis himself does. Thus, he injures Megara by exploiting its weakness in bargaining. He stirs up trouble in Thebes by exporting an informer, or a troublemaker, to that city. Also, I am not sure that Dikaiopolis has the positive ethical impact on the Acharnians that Strauss envisages. The line in the play that Strauss cites to prove that the Acharnians have been made better by Dikaiopolis (650) refers to no such event. Rather, the chorus leader is putting praises of Aristophanes into various mouths, all saying that the poet has made the Athenians better.

greatest bliss as a situation in which he is surprisingly invited to fondle a fair boy (*Birds* 137–42)[92] and make the Sausage Seller say that Kleon moved against catamites only for fear of their potential popularity as rival orators (*Knights* 875–80) must let the Stronger Speech warn that rampant public pederastic flirting breeds unmanly soldiers. He must also let the Stronger Speech admit to the Weaker that nearly everybody is a "wide-anus" and desert to the catamites while deriding Agathon as an effete drag queen and denying being a buggered "wide-anus" himself. Hedonism generally, pederastic eros particularly, and ferocious militarism are the marks of excellence, but only up to limits beyond which they become self-destructive. In every case, Aristophanes must require his rustic men to toe a paradoxical line along which unlimited pleasure and imperialism remain finite and prudent without reducing hedonistic delights.

If there is such a line, one wonders how Aristophanes proposes to pull off the miracle of inducing his simple men to obey. (In the *Knights,* he causes this wonder to occur off stage mysteriously, under the tutelage of the Sausage Seller, during a choral speech, 1264 ff.) I believe that his reply is that his comedies reeducate the demos to prudence without recourse to a corrupt logical reason. In the *Acharnians,* Aristophanes has the chorus praise him as the poet who makes the Athenians better (650) and who leads them to felicity (656) by speaking justice to them (645) and giving them the best teaching (658). Here lies Aristophanes' claim to superiority over Socrates and the "other" sophists. Unlike sophists, the poet does not need to manipulate human beings by making the weaker speech the stronger; he can get people to act well simply by dramatizing the truth. Unlike them (or unlike the alchemists among them, such as Eryximachus), he does not have to pretend that he has a magical power to change nature; he needs only to find a poetic way to let nature take its true course, as far as the tragic position of the human race will permit, with the aid of conventional rites and mores.

Such, then, is the Aristophanes to whom Plato assigns a role in the *Symposium.* He is an enemy of Socrates who bears false witness against him. He tries to destroy Socrates because he hates sophists and attacks Kleon because it hurts to suffer tyranny. He loathes sophists and demagogues because the former, with their rationalism and sly rhetoric, and the latter, with their flattery, confuse and corrupt ordinary rustics, with the result that these worthies cannot hear the voice of nature that guides them truly when they heed it. He is a principled hedonist. He is a Titanic rebel. He hates the

92. Various editions differ on whether this speech is given by Euelpides or Pisthetairos. This might be a matter of indifference, for both characters seem to speak for the poet in the *Birds,* one for each side of the somewhat self-contradictory truth that he maintains, that is, one for the value of comfort seeking and one for the value of Promethean aggression.

gods for having created an intrinsically unjust world and for afflicting human beings, who naturally seek pleasure, with a tragic incapacity to satisfy all their desires without destroying themselves. He would gladly dethrone the gods to punish them for causing human suffering. However, he has a keen eye for power relationships and perceives that men are no match for gods. Accordingly, he grudgingly insists upon a public piety that placates gods with sacrifices, so that the deities will not become even more obstreperous and wreck human life entirely. He also thinks that in keeping with the injustice of the universe as a whole, human nature is inherently unjust. He believes that his rustics must find a way to gratify their natural lusts for injustice and immoderate pleasure without suffering the natural consequences of such striving. He hears nature telling him that the means to this end is the city, an artificial association that guarantees justice and produces pleasure for members while unjustly exploiting nonmembers. That is, he thinks that nature calls for a conventional justice under which citizens help friends and harm enemies. This requires his rural stalwarts to strike balances between a totally immoderate hedonism and an absolutely strict adherence to the wholesome way of life of the Marathon heros. He blames sophists and demagogues for depriving the demos of the virtues necessary to this life and writes his comedies to reeducate the people to the only justice that will ensure happiness while preventing the annihilation of Athens.[93] Although he envisages himself as an enemy of the sophists, damning them for their rationalism and slick rhetoric, he fails to realize that although he rejects their logos, he endorses their purposes, for the sophists (such as Phaedrus, Pausanias, and Eryximachus) are also Titanic hedonists. For the last time, I add this caveat: If this is not the real Aristophanes, it is still the one that the many will see, so he might as well be the true one for practical purposes.

ARISTOPHANES

I return to the text of the *Symposium*. In keeping with my assumption that Plato tries to make the dialogue's characters as true to life as possible, I believe that he intends the speech of Aristophanes to reflect the poet's actual views, or at least his impact on Athenian culture.

It appears to me that Plato repays Aristophanes for having misrepresented Socrates by sketching the poet fairly in the *Symposium*. Clearly, when Plato makes Aristophanes lament that he is too debilitated from yesterday's inebriation to drink today, and when Plato pictures him as gorging

---

93. Annihilation is the logical outcome of the war of all against all. Aristophanes also had good reason to fear genocide by the Spartans, in retaliation for Athenian atrocities.

himself to the point of an indigestion that leaves him mute, he gently sat-
irizes the hedonism of the creator of Dikaiopolis. When Plato causes Aristophanes to assert that he will speak "in a different manner" (ἄλλη, 189c2)
from his predecessors, he depicts not merely his dramatic character's intention to offer different praises of Eros but also the real poet's resolve
to substitute his openly mythical teaching of the edicts of nature for the
sophists' degenerately clever lies and pseudoscience. When Plato makes
Aristophanes dependent upon Eryximachus for his capacity to talk, he is
being consistent with the now self-evident fact that Aristophanes' poetry is
subordinate to the doctor's medical expertise, or to sophistical technicism,
for three reasons. First, a person who behaved like Dikaiopolis at a banquet
would really need medical care to be able to speak. Second, a purely hedonistic life would reduce individuals and cities to animality by destroying all
speech not symbolic of pleasure and pain. To hope to lively solely for pleasure while writing poetry, and to aspire to teach cities to be both hedonistic
and just, is to seek ends that can be realized only by *technai* that purport
to harmonize unlikes, insofar as they seem to convert libidinous, mindless
bestiality into moral and rational humanity. Third, no matter how different
his poetry might be from sophistical rhetoric, Aristophanes must finally say
what the sophists say, that men should win their paradise of pleasure by
devising a *technē* that somehow defeats the gods. I anticipate that in the
poetic myth that the fictitious Aristophanes tells in the dialogue, Plato will
have him paint a portrait of Eros that reflects this sophistical ambition of
the real poet.

   Having stated that he will speak differently from Eryximachus and Pausanias because mankind has failed to sense the power of Eros, Plato's Aristophanes does not proceed directly to explain the misapprehended power.
Instead, he argues that if people did realize the power of Eros, they would
dedicate temples, altars, and sacrifices to him on a grand scale because he
is the god who is most friendly to human beings. This call for a new cult
of Eros could expose Aristophanes to suspicion of heresy. If the poet is not
exactly advising adoration of a hitherto unknown god, he is advocating
a novel worship of a previously neglected deity who is not an Olympian.
Aristophanes' remark that Eros is the most philanthropic god also hints
that the gods tend toward misanthropy, thus suggesting the desirability of
waging war on them, or at least the necessity of devising defenses against
them. In this, the Aristophanes of the dialogue tallies with the historical
one. If this fictitious Aristophanes wants to stay out of trouble, and if he is
to continue to correspond to the real poet, he will need to reconcile his position with Athenian customary law soon. Evidently, he is confident that
he can avoid prosecution, for he urges the *sympotai* to teach his account
of Eros "to all." This distinguishes him from the three previous speakers.
Phaedrus and Pausanias were proponents of rhetorical arts that secured

the victories of their personal interests over the competing ambitions of the many; these sophists were not eager to teach the many anything helpful. Eryximachus belonged to a secret society, the Asclepiad order, that could reveal its scientific principles and aims but not the procedures of its *technē;* his fee for sharing this limited portion of his wisdom with others, and for giving them medical treatment, was that they should acknowledge his exclusive, personal apotheosis. The Platonic Aristophanes, like the historical one, differs by having democratic tendencies.

Aristophanes introduces the subject of the power of Eros by saying that the god cares for mankind, healing the sicknesses the cure of which would constitute the greatest happiness of the species. This implies that the nature of man is inherently diseased, or that the natural state of mankind is one that we today would call alienation. The real Aristophanes, with his concerns about the intrinsic inability of human beings to achieve the happiness for which they naturally yearn, held the same opinion. This raises the extremely important question of what the diseases and the cure are. Before replying, the Platonic Aristophanes must answer a prior question: How can we distinguish health from illness? Like the Weaker Speech in the *Clouds,* he takes certain drives of human nature as the measures of what ought to be. His recognition of natural things as teleological measures and his immediate, prelogical grasp of the decrees of nature distance him from Phaedrus, Pausanias, and Eryximachus. Though paying lip service to cosmic nature as a teleological norm, these sophists either were heedless of nature or intended to dominate or transform it to obtain their pleasures. They distorted traditional cosmologies, and, hence, views of nature, to acquire premises for their pseudoscientific arts.[94]

Aristophanes analyzes mankind's native ailments or alienation with a myth of his own invention: Our nature is not what it once was. Originally, human beings came in three sexes: the double male, the double female, and the androgyne. They resembled Siamese twins joined back to back, but only a little, for they were "round" (στρογγύλον) and had two faces at the head of one cylindrical neck. We are overcome by laughter: these earlier people were built like cartoon caricatures of scrotums with four arms and legs and erect penises for heads.

It is necessary to dwell for a moment on this shocking and outrageously funny image. Virtually none of Plato's readers since antiquity have understood his joke. Scholars have had ponderous debates on whether Aristoph-

94. It is true that in the *Birds* 467 ff, Pisthetairos persuades the birds to support his rebellion against Zeus by using Aesop to twist the theogony of Hesiod, making birds senior to the gods. In intention, substance, and form, Pisthetairos's argument greatly resembles those of Phaedrus, Pausanias, and Eryximachus. Thus, the poet who takes his cues from the Muse and nature can lapse into propagandistic, sophistical speech inside his myths.

anes' people were στρογγύλον (round) as in "disklike" or "spherical."[95] For moderns, this dispute would be settled in favor of "spherical" by the poet's remark that the earlier humans inherited their forms from the sun, earth, and moon (190b3–5). However, we are not certain as to how Plato or Aristophanes conceived the shapes of these bodies. At any rate, the debates are obtuse to the humor. We must recall that we are dealing with Aristophanes, who is famous for his ribald language and dirty jokes. Given that the word στρογγύλον connotes the hemispherical curvature of the hulls of ships;[96] given Aristophanes' statements that seem to make his creatures all fronts and sides, thus pouchlike; and given that the creatures had heads on cylindrical necks, with only "half necks" remaining to us now, it is quite clear that their entire form was neither disklike nor spherical (perfect circles and spheres do not have appendages), but "round" in a sense more in keeping with both Aristophanes' penchant for risque humor and the contours of other hull-shaped objects that appear as packages of two in one with heads on cylindrical necks.[97] It might be objected that this exegesis makes the creatures' heads too small in comparison with their bodies. This might be true: the point is moot for want of information. However, I think that the incorrect proportions, if they are in the picture, are intended by Plato as an ironic comment on, and an accurate reflection of, the relationships between the body and the mind in Aristophanes' view of human nature.

The appearances of the original human beings will soon be seen to be representative of their hybris. Plato, foreseeing the satyr play that will be presented by Alcibiades later in the dialogue, makes Aristophanes portray the early people as beings whose outsides reflected their hybristic insides and, hence, unlike Socrates, whose outsides and insides were different.[98]

To continue, with their two pairs of arms and legs, the creatures could walk in either direction or tumble rapidly like acrobats. They had amazing strength. The double male was descended from the sun, the double female from the earth, and the androgyne from the moon. (Perhaps they resulted from the mating of these astral divinities with Chaos, Uranus, or Zeus. Aristophanes does not see fit to tell us everything about the genesis of these heirs to godhood.) These three types generated young not by means of sexual intercourse, which did not exist yet, but upon the ground, like grasshoppers or cicadas. Given their forms, strength, ancestry, and virtual

95. For example, Rosen calls the people "circle-men" (*Plato's "Symposium,"* 138). Saxenhouse makes them spherical ("Net of Hephaestus," 21).

96. Cf. J. S. Morrison, "Four Notes on Plato's *Symposium*," 48.

97. Pat Edwards, a fine reader of Aristophanes at McMaster University, has alerted me to the fact that Aristophanes himself uses στρογγύλος in the *Clouds* (676) in an evident sexual pun. I think that this tends to confirm my reading.

98. I am grateful to Zdravko Planinc for pointing out this connection, in response to his reading of my earlier drafts.

self-sufficiency in reproduction, these beings were disposed to think that they were entitled to divine status.[99] Aristophanes reports that they had "great thoughts" (φρονήματα μεγάλα, 190b6) and thus conspired to attack the gods by mounting heaven, like Ephialtes and Otus in Homer.[100] So, the earlier people suffered from their first dissatisfied unhappiness not by virtue of an injury to their natures but by dint of the place of their natures in the hierarchy of being. Their "illness" was anger over the fact that they were inferior to the gods in rank. When Aristophanes classifies their attitudes as "great thoughts," he applauds their alienation and metaphysical rebelliousness and indicates that the true remedy of their malady would be the gratification of their *libido dominandi*.

With this, the dramatic Aristophanes reveals a secret passion of his historical model. The playwright made a show of hating the gods because they were unjust. Plato replies that Aristophanes thinks the gods unjust because he hates them, regarding their very existence as an unfair slight to any lower being who aspires to their sovereign rank. The fictitious poet also involves himself in the same political dilemma as the historical one: By identifying human nature with the will to power and by approving its gratification, he makes it doubtful that there could have been peace, order, and universal pleasure among the previous human beings had they defeated the Olympians, and equally dubious that we can achieve these goods today. Aristophanes also entangles himself in metaphysical difficulties. He has portrayed the Titanic élan as chronologically prior to the existence of Eros, thus making it impossible for Eros to have cured human alienation in the earlier age. This raises a question: If the cause of Titanic élan is human nature qua will to power, if the gratification of our lust for power is the remedy for our malaise, and if Eros is offered as the nostrum that will heal us now, will not our nature simply attempt to press Eros into service as an ally in new assaults upon the gods, and will not these attacks necessarily be futile, such that Eros could not really cure us? Or will the help of Eros render our new offensives successful?

It seems highly unlikely that the Platonic Aristophanes believes that present men could destroy the gods. This improbability might be hard to discern at first. The poet continues his myth by saying that Zeus and the other Olympians were perplexed when they were besieged. They perceived that they could not slaughter the upstarts without annihilating the donors of their honors and sacrifices. Dispensing with these services was quite out of the question, as in the *Birds*. This could mean that men always

99. Cf. the perceptive discussions of Saxenhouse, "Net of Hephaestus," 21–22; and Rosen, *Plato's "Symposium,"* 138–39.

100. It is instructive to read the story of these Aloeids in the *Iliad* 5.385–90 and *Odyssey* 305–20, but it is not necessary to recite it here.

have some power over the gods because the gods have an essential need to be succored by men. However, it would suffice to postulate that the gods could have given up their pleasures but hated to do so. Thus, we cannot suppose that the power of Aristophanes' gods over the round beings was incomplete or necessarily diminished by an ineluctable dependence. Zeus could have killed them had he wished, but he preferred to spare them to ensure the gods a more delightful immortality.[101] When he selected his course of action, he did what he liked with them, without the slightest resistance. The human beings of the present time merely serve the gods as their ancestors did and are much weaker than their forerunners (190c), so they have no essential power over the gods. Even with the assistance of Eros, they are still totally at the mercy of Zeus (190d4–6). I conclude that Aristophanes judges their prospects in another war against the gods nil and their condition tragic.[102] The question of how he supposes Eros to be a remedy for our most fundamental ailment remains open.

Aristophanes' comic references to the gods' addiction to human worship and to their befuddlement in the face of the attack of the round men reflect the historical poet's fondness for blasphemy. So does his story of Zeus's solution of the problem of the uprising. Zeus cuts the hybristic rebels in half, vertically, compelling them to go on two legs rather than four. He then orders Apollo to twist their faces into line with their gaping insides and to close them up with new fronts by stretching and tying their skins at the formerly nonexistent navel, with wrinkles at the stomach and navel to remind them of what they had suffered. Zeus, the king of the gods and the creator of the order of the universe, and Apollo, usually hailed as the god who restores human nature to health by teaching physicians their art, are thus blasphemed as the sources of an order of being destructive of the original Titanic nature of man and inimical to the health and happiness of people now. Henceforth, the divided human halves must live with outraged feelings. Further, none of them will have quite enough stretched skin left to be comfortable in their own tightly wrapped bodies; their very physical existence will be painful to them. Aristophanes' symbolism thus amounts to a total rejection of the present order of human existence and its rulers.

The new human beings are more valuable to the gods than the old ones, for now there are twice as many of them from whom to extract sacrifices. They are also less troublesome to the gods because they are weaker. Zeus threatens to slice them again, thus compelling them to hop around on one

101. Cf. Rosen, *Plato's "Symposium,"* 142–43. Rosen, following Strauss, has Aristophanes make the very existence of the gods dependent on human worship. I do not think that this follows from a close reading of the text.

102. Therefore, Seth Benardete's description of the present situation is just right: "Within the constraint of the laws of the city smolders a defiance of the gods that is too weak to succeed" (*On Plato's "Symposium,"* 55).

leg, if they do not "keep quiet."[103] In taking these measures, Zeus invokes no principle of justice. One wonders by what right he subjugates and punishes his underlings. The obvious answer is that he does it because he can. His might makes right. The dramatic Aristophanes thus reproduces his prototype's universe without Dikē, a cosmos in which the only possible justice for gods and men is a conventional agreement to help friends and harm enemies, which is exactly what Zeus does.

With Zeus's punitive surgery on mankind's ancestors, we arrive at the second illness, or alienation, that is inherent in human nature. This time the sickness consists in two wounds to the nature, one inflicted by Zeus and one by Apollo. The harm that Zeus does to the nature is the more fundamental. Zeus afflicts the new human beings with an essential lack of wholeness that they experience as a constant torment. Apollo's violence to the nature might be the more galling. The people still suffer from the first illness, the Titanic élan. However, the shame of their inability to gratify their hybris is written in their bodies, doubling the pain of their hated inferiority by adding injury to insult, as it were, compounding their humiliation by making their material damage both a physical agony and a sign of the warning to "keep quiet," that is, to refrain from new mutinies and from serious advocacy of the round men's "great thoughts."

In Aristophanes' theology, Zeus is not omniscient. He can err. His suppression of the rebellion goes completely awry. The freshly crafted humans pine for their other halves. Zeus has accidentally created Eros, whom the poet defines by saying, "The desire and pursuit of the whole is named Eros" (192e10–193a1).[104] (In context, Aristophanes' definition of Eros as "desire of the whole" clearly does not refer to any longing for the Cosmos or the All; Eros is a longing for the original wholeness of the earlier human beings.) Zeus has erred because the now erotic people hug their other halves when they find them and perish in those embraces; they cannot live without their primal wholeness. Thus, by nature, Eros is friendly to neither men nor gods, and he is a remedy for no disease. In his debut, he simultaneously destroys the new human beings and deprives the gods of their pleasures. We wondered how Eros could be a cure for mankind's first alienation. Now we see that, originally, he was a fatal reaction to the second, like a high fever in the plague.

When Zeus surveys what he has wrought, he takes pity, certainly more

---

103. One could judge this an empty threat because the cutting would destroy genitalia. I do not think the threat empty. It will soon be seen that Zeus has a capacity to rearrange human reproduction as he likes. After another cut, he could think of something new again, probably making reproduction a cooperative venture of four quarter-people rather than of two half-people (quarter and half as compared with our original natures).

104. Cf. Saxenhouse, "Net of Hephaestus," 25.

on himself and his fellow deities than on the people. He rushes his creatures back to his surgery, moves their genitals from their initial positions around to their new fronts, and changes their reproductive functions, inventing sexual intercourse. Now the man begets upon the woman, and when two men unite they are satiated and relieved, so that they can pay attention to work and the rest of life. Therefore, Aristophanes deduces that the eros of human beings for each other has been ingrained in us for a long time and that it brings together the original nature, striving to make one of two and to heal human nature. We observe that the character of Eros has not changed. He is still desire for and pursuit of the whole. He continues to act as he did from the moment of his creation. What is new here is that Zeus, rectifying his mistake, has harnessed Eros for his own purposes by altering the constitution of man again, so that the natural action of Eros has become less deadly for the sundered halves than it was previously.

Aristophanes' depiction of the results of Zeus's remedial operation on the human beings quietly differentiates the benefits of the three new kinds of sexuality. Of course, in one way, the male-female, male-male, and female-female sexual acts have identical effects: the separated halves are joined briefly in processes that try to heal their second illness by fusing them— but the striving does not achieve its aim. Aristophanes does not say that the coitus actually makes two lovers one, even for a moment. Perhaps we should assume that it temporarily alleviates their pain by affording them a pleasurable illusion of wholeness. The illusion, however, is fleeting, the yearning resumes, and delusive wholeness looks more like another of the tortures inflicted on human beings by Zeus than a genuine cure of our ailments. The poet does envisage a truly positive result of the androgyne union, the reproduction of human beings, and two different benefits of the male-male liaison: satiation and an attendant ability to focus on work and the other business of life. However, he does not say that one type of sexuality shares the blessings of another. This means that only the androgyne union ends in procreation, which is obviously true, that only male-male intercourse produces satiation and a capacity to manage important affairs, and that there are no benefits of female-female sexuality at all (191c).

These distinctions make it impossible for us to go on ignoring issues that have needed attention for some time. Here I shall focus on only one set of such problems, reserving others for later. When Aristophanes painted the earlier people as male genitalia with erections, our laughter drowned out a legitimate question: Should not the double women have been shaped like pudenda, and the androgynes like a combination of male and female organs? Perhaps it was permissible to neglect this difficulty because all of the round creatures could have been formed externally by an internal hybris best symbolized by the aroused male members. Nonetheless, we cannot escape the next question so easily: How could the double females have done their "begetting and bringing forth" (ἐγέννων καὶ ἔτικτον, 191b7–8) upon the Earth, itself a female principle? Did they spray seed upon the ground? If so, would we not have to deny that they were female in any sense intelligible to us and conclude that Aristophanes views present-day femininity as a degradation of a once completely masculine human nature, a debasement that resulted from a divine mistake? Or did the double females lay eggs in the borrowed womb of Earth, there to wait for fertilization by a male, thus showing that as the only previous human sex that could not generate offspring autonomously, they were inferior? Perhaps this query could be dismissed as an excessively literal nitpicking of a poetic image. However, now that Aristophanes has slighted women again by failing to ascribe value to lesbian intercourse, the question acquires an undeniable theoretical relevance. It forces us to suspect Aristophanes of misogyny and to face that phenomenon in the sophists' and poet's speeches squarely.[105]

Here is the argument: The *erōmenos* Phaedrus is the only orator who has extolled a woman (Alcestis) so far in our dialogue.[106] The *erastēs* Pausanias was virulently antifeminine. The *erastēs* Eryximachus envisaged opposites as mortal enemies, thus silently declaring his view of women. Aristophanes, another *erastēs*, now delivers himself of antifeminine views, too. I infer that *erastai* in the *Symposium* hate women as much as they detest the Olympian gods. We should observe that their antagonism to the gods and their antifeminism increase in intensity as their inherent greatness of soul increases. Aristophanes, a superb poet, is the first speaker in the drama who openly embraces the Titanism that the Athenian Stranger attributes to the poets who are ignorant of what is just and lawful for the Muse. Simultaneously, he is the first to suggest that women are relatively useless and unproductive aberrations of the male nature, a slander that outstrips even Pausanias's description of them as naturally mindless. We need to ask why Titanism and misogyny are related in this increasingly passionate fashion.

Actually, we now have two or three unsolved problems on the table. Aristophanes has promised to explain the power of Eros by showing how the god treats the diseases the cure of which would be the greatest felicity of the human race. He appears to be making an extremely poor job of it. He has identified mankind's primary ailment as a Titanic élan and its remedy as the gratification of our will to power, but he has not shown how Eros can

---

105. This is as good a place as any to mention that the speculations of Bury about the reproductive practices of the round beings, to the effect that Plato intends to ridicule the physiological doctrines of Hippocrates, lack apparent foundation in Plato's text. They fail to explain how such a seemingly random attack on Hippocrates was demanded by the economy of Plato's developing argument. See Bury's comment in Plato, *The Symposium of Plato*, xxxi–xxxiii. Aristophanes' intentions are spiritual, not biological.

106. This does not make Phaedrus a feminist. He praised her for doing a manly thing.

help us defeat the gods. He has diagnosed mankind's secondary sickness as an essential lack of wholeness compounded by a configuration of our bodies that constantly reminds us of our primary shame. The cure for this would appear to be the achievement of genuine wholeness and, again, the satisfaction of our *libido dominandi,* so that we would not suffer the shame of which our bodies presently remind us. However, Aristophanes' Eros appears to offer little more than brief moments of an illusory wholeness that torture us by permitting the immediate resumption of our longing. This Eros seems to be less a philanthropic remedy than a cruel, misanthropic exacerbation of our diseases, for he denies us a merciful release from our misery in premature deaths and the quick annihilation of our misbegotten race. Evidently oblivious to these lapses, Aristophanes has blended his hatred of the gods with antifeminism, thus worsening mankind's fractured condition by stirring up the war of the sexes. Why has he taken these positions?

In my opinion, these puzzles have a single solution, the key to which lies in the power of Eros. Aristophanes has really been explaining the power of Eros all along, in a completely open yet stealthy way. In a limited but crucial sense, Eros is superior to Zeus because he is the one reality that Zeus cannot purge from human existence. It is quite true that Eros was created by Zeus; that Eros cannot prevent Zeus from using love for the advantage of the gods; that Eros cannot keep Zeus from ruling, mangling, or exterminating human beings just as he pleases; and that Eros cannot help men overthrow Zeus. However, as long as the king of gods wants people around for his pleasure, he must accept the unchangeable fact that Eros will have them in his grip and that Eros will act as desire for and pursuit of their whole. It is precisely this narrowly circumscribed but decisive superiority to Zeus that makes Eros divine, even though he is not necessarily immortal, his life depending upon Zeus's desire to preserve human beings.

Now, to speak euphemistically, the power of Eros is a finger in Zeus's eye that advances Aristophanes' causes. The human beings can actually press Eros into service as their ally in a new kind of conquest of the gods. By embracing Eros, giving themselves over body and soul to Eros, and defining themselves as devotees of Eros, they can partake of the power of Eros, at least vicariously. They can flaunt the truth that no matter what Zeus does to them, he cannot force them to stop being erotic unless he is willing to destroy them in the process. Thus, in a limited manner, they too are superior to Zeus and triumph over him even in their subjugation to him. Their Titanic élan is gratified, and their first sickness is cured by Eros after all. Their eroticism also thwarts Zeus by adopting an egocentric telos. The people yearn for wholeness, but they insist upon satisfying that desire by receiving themselves back into themselves. This is to say that Aristophanes' myth of the round men is a precursor of the symbol articulated by Friedrich Nietzsche in Zarathustra's "Night Song": "But I live in my own light; I drink back into me the flames that break out of me."[107] Men refuse to accept a completeness that Zeus or nature might have wanted them to enjoy in their proper ontological places. Zeus cannot force them to renounce a self-sufficient wholeness, so they defeat Zeus and satisfy their Titanic élan again. This victory compensates them for their inability to acquire the wholeness that they want. As long as they can be defiant Titans, they are prepared to settle for the temporary pleasures and ersatz unity of intercourse instead of real fulfillment. They resemble Prometheus chained to the rock, ready to let his liver be eaten by day for the sake of his opposition to Zeus.

Finally, Aristophanes' heartfelt misogyny also appears to serve as a kind of symbolic weapon against the gods. In the eyes of the first round men, and in the view of the poet who epitomizes the previous human beings as male genitalia, the phallus represents man's demand to give himself his own happiness actively. Pudenda and femininity symbolize passivity in the quest for completeness, that is, receptivity to elements of wholeness that come from without. (I do not mean that female organs and femininity symbolize passivity in reality. Rather, this is a convention adopted by the metaphysical revolutionary Aristophanes in Plato's play, probably because female organs receive male organs and seed. The poet's word does not make it so.)

Aristophanes proceeds next to an ostensible explanation of the ontological origins of heterosexuality and homosexuality in Zeus's punitive division of the round beings and in the subsequent rise of Eros. Heterosexuals, with their adulterers and adulteresses, are descendants of the androgynes. Homosexuals are descendants of the double males and females. The poet makes this point not for its own sake, but to create an opening for his immediately following speech on the superiority of male homosexuality to heterosexuality and lesbianism. His ideas on this probably have little to do with male homosexuality, heterosexuality, and lesbianism in themselves. Aristophanes is advancing his Titanic agenda, in which he has simply co-opted male homosexuality and, more specifically, pederasty as his symbols of auto-salvation without having asked any gay men who are not Titanic whether they consent. He has done this in the spirit of the Sausage Seller's behavior in the *Knights;* he declares the male-male couple superior because he thinks that they have the hybris required for his erotic rebellion.

Aristophanes begins his speech on the superiority of male-male sexuality by building on a suggestion noted above, that heterosexuals, unlike gay

107. Nietzsche, *Also sprach Zarathustra,* in *NW,* 6.1.132.16–17; *Thus Spoke Zarathustra,* in *The Portable Nietzsche,* 218.

men, are insatiable. It is time to observe that this idea is dubious. We discover that Aristophanes maintains it because he wants to tax heterosexuals with a unique disposition to adultery gratuitously, casting doubt on their ethics, as if there were no infidelity among other groups. Next, after acknowledging the existence of lesbians again, he moves to defend boys, but not girls, who gratify lovers against the charge that they are shameful. As distinct from the adulterers, adulteresses, lesbians, and promiscuous girls, whom Aristophanes implicitly holds up as the genuinely disgraceful ones, these boys who gratify lovers are the best and bravest, the most manly, for they cleave to their kind. A great proof of this is that upon maturing, these boys alone prove to be men (ἄνδρες, 192a7) in politics and become pederasts themselves. Aristophanes does not mean here that only homosexual boys become politicians, but, rather, that the only politicians worthy of the title of ἄνδρες, men (for example, the Sausage Seller in the *Knights*), have pleased male lovers and have then become pederasts themselves. Thus, in a single stroke, Aristophanes has shifted public opprobrium from the pederasts to the heterosexuals, justified the Sausage Seller's censure of Kleon's attack on catamites, and claimed eternal glory for the pederasts, proving his previous problematic claim that only male homosexuals can manage important affairs.

Like the preceding speakers in the drama, Aristophanes has also suggested a miniature political theory. If pederasts are the only real men in public affairs, the telos of political order must be identical with that of the original humans whom the pederasts most resemble in their hybris. That is, the telos must be the Titanic defeat of the gods, which can now be achieved only by embracing Eros. Right political order must be the Zeus-like rule of the pederast who has usurped Zeus, such as Pisthetairos. By requesting that his speech be taught to "all," the poet seeks to recruit the entire human race for his cause. He is democratic because he wants his metaphysical rebellion to be universal. He probably embraces the traditional virtues of the Marathon era not because he loves moderation and justice, but because he wants to make the old order's martial temperament the foundation on which his radically new order can rest. Only thus can he reconcile the conservative and the revolutionary strains of his thought.

One additional observation is appropriate here. With his portrait of the previous men as aroused male genitalia, his use of the phallus as the sign of man's Titanic triumph over the gods, and his call for the transformation of political order into the organization of society for the achievement of this conquest, Aristophanes has given a sneak preview of the meaning of the defilement of the Herms. At least, his myth makes sense of an event in Athenian history never before understood as anything but absurd. In the language of Pisthetairos, the revolt of the Titanic males intends to "forbid the gods to go back and forth through your space with hard-ons" (*Birds* 556–57), so that the Titanic pederasts might do this instead.[108] The sailing of the armada against Syracuse marks the political triumph of this revolution. The sacrilegious dismembering of the Herms is the deed that symbolically celebrates the realization of its aim, perhaps consciously so in Alcibiades' mind. Hence, Plato is indicating through Aristophanes that when sophistical eros grows into the Titanic "wrong pederasty" of the poets, striving to involve the city and even all mankind in an assault upon the gods, the attendant hybris makes it impossible for the many to hold to the calculating hedonism of Dikaiopolis. Mass ardor for fatal errors like the Sicilian adventure becomes inevitable.

Pushing his discourse on pederasty further, Aristophanes asserts that the beloved boys who become mature pederasts have no natural intention to acquire wives and children and do so only under the compulsion of customary law. They really yearn to find their other halves (which would seem to be impossible for the descendants of the original halves, a difficulty that indicates that Aristophanes is more interested in the spiritual symbolism of his myth than its scientific cogency). When they do encounter their other halves, they cling to them joyously, refusing ever to leave their sides. The mates cleave to each other throughout life, even though they cannot imagine what they want from one another. Aristophanes tells the pairs that they are ignorant of their goals. Then he graciously clears up their confusion by declaring that it is not the aphrodisiac coitus that they crave (a fact that might surprise at least some of them), but something else that their souls only faintly divine. What is that? Aristophanes answers with a hypothetical myth. If Hephaestus should come to them as they lie together, asking what they desire, and if he should be forced to dissolve their perplexity by asking again if they wish to be fused into a single whole, the two having become one both in this life and in the next, not one of them would refuse the offer. All would realize that this was exactly what they had wanted all along. They would beg for that union (thus demonstrating that in Aristophanes' eyes, sexual intercourse by itself never achieves it).

It is at this juncture that Allan Bloom and nearly everybody else becomes lyrical about the superior truth and beauty of Aristophanes' account of Eros. I wish to divide my response to Bloom's claim into two parts.

First, Bloom states that Aristophanes' speech is the first in the *Symposium* that "gives an erotic account of Eros." Aristophanes, declares Bloom, "describes embraces and orgasms." The embraces and orgasms "are what Eros is about and are splendid as ends in themselves."[109] I disagree. Aristophanes' oration is not the first erotic speech in the dialogue. Bloom has simply

---

108. I follow Alan Sommerstein's lead in opting for a crudely vulgar translation here.
109. Bloom, *Love and Friendship*, 478.

missed the fact that there is eros for different objects. Accordingly, he has reduced eros to sexual desire, dismissing everything in the dialogue up to here as essentially irrelevant and also ignoring Diotima's warning that eros is defined too narrowly when its meaning is restricted to sexual longing (205b–c). It follows that Eros is not "about" embraces and orgasms. It is about much more that Bloom has failed to discern. I am also doubtful about Bloom's designation of embraces and orgasms as "ends in themselves." They do afford us a beauty and felicity nearly unsurpassed. However, the idea that they are ends in themselves, which claims to capture the spirit of Aristophanes, distorts the poet's teaching summarized just above. Aristophanes says that it is *not* the aphrodisiac coitus that is the point, but something that the souls of the lovers divine only faintly, thus necessitating the telling of the myth of Hephaestus about the longing for eternal oneness. In other words, for Aristophanes it is metaphysical rebellion that is the point, not orgasms. Further, it seems to me that in a man's union with his wife, for example, embraces and orgasms are clearly not the point. For him, she is the point. The beauty of her being and intense desire for her happiness are the point. Even more beyond this might be the point. Saying that orgasms are "ends in themselves" appears to betray hedonistic blindness to the true ends and to reinforce earlier concerns about Bloom's choices of words.

Second, Bloom asserts: "To say, 'I feel so powerfully attracted and believe I want to hold on forever because this is my lost other half,' gives word to what we actually feel and seems to be sufficient."[110] Aristophanes does actually have a nebulous sense of a sublime truth and beauty here. It is true that every human being feels an essential emptiness, a fundamental something missing. It is also true, for example, that a man's wife fills up so much of that void that he believes that his eternity would be diminished if he could not share it with her. Still, it seems to me that Aristophanes and Bloom sully this exceptional truth and beauty. Why should the lover construe the beloved as his or her own "lost other half"? Taken literally, this is a species of narcissism; it requires an attempt to charm a beloved by gushing: "I love you because you remind me of me." The beloved is precisely not the self of the lover but an *other* who, thanks to the beauty and mystery of his or her own being, fills the essential void in the self of the lover. Aristophanes' love, which overlays the beloved's self with his own, is a monstrous tyranny. Further, why should we understand our experience of a fundamental something missing as a proof that being is dysfunctional?[111]

110. Ibid.
111. With allowances for my shift from mythical to metaphysical language, Bloom recognizes that this is exactly the issue. Explaining why the round men rebelled against the gods, Bloom argues that they were rising against "tyrants who give *nomoi*, before which these free-spirited circular men refused to bow. They apparently wanted only to

Why not read it as a natural consequence of our ontological place, as a condition of being human that is certainly difficult but also indicative of the path that we should be following and, hence, manageable without whining? Again, why should we construe the filling of this emptiness by love as a triumph over an evil reality rather than as our natural fulfillment in a benevolent order of being? The mere telling of Aristophanes' myth does not make his alienated interpretations of being true. His grievances only seem true to those who are seduced by his association of his metaphysical rebellion with the truth that we want union with our beloveds forever. The practice of permitting a great truth to tinge falsehoods with the aura of truth is a trick that does credit to any sophist.

Aristophanes closes with several urgent injunctions to religious piety. He reminds us that we formerly were whole and one and that now the god has separated us for our injustice, as the Lacedaemonians dispersed the Arcadians. This switch from the story of the Zeus who cut up mythical round men to the historical example of the Spartans who shattered Mantinea in the year 385 serves the rhetorical purpose of evoking fear of a credible threat. The fictitious Aristophanes does not want his audience to think that gods can harm them only in fairy tales; if vexed, the gods can still visit Athens with destruction at the hands of a Sparta that is always strong and hostile. (The reason for Plato's anachronism is obscure. It might have to do with the fact that Diotima is a Mantinean. It is also possible that there is no anachronism because Aristophanes is referring to another event that occurred in 418.[112] Either way, Aristophanes' purpose would be the same.) Those who seek personal and political unity in Titanic rebellion must therefore manage divine-human relations adroitly. Shifting back to Zeus's threat to split us again if we do not keep quiet, Aristophanes declares that we ought to exhort everyone to a pious observance of the gods in order to escape injury and win happiness under the hegemony of Eros (note: not under the hegemony of Zeus). No one should oppose Eros, and incurring the hatred of the gods is to oppose him (a point that is true not because Eros loves the gods but because inciting the gods to destroy us would result, ipso facto, in the destruction of Eros). If we make friends with him, we shall find our sweethearts, as few presently do. Indeed, all men and women should become happy through Eros, finding their sweethearts or other lovers to their liking,[113] thus returning to their first natures.

---

revolve in freedom like their parents" (*Love and Friendship*, 479). I think that Bloom is naive or disingenuous not to add that the round men would have probably behaved like Pisthetairos after their victory.

112. Cf. Morrison, "Four Notes," 44–46.

113. This qualification indicates that Aristophanes is not serious about finding our original "other halves." Any pleasing lover or beloved will do in the campaign against Zeus.

If we minister to the gods piously, Eros will restore our original nature and lead us to a blessed happiness.

Aristophanes' teaching here is clear. As long as we do not irritate the gods so much that they decide to exterminate us, and Eros with us, and as long as we please the gods enough to make them want to preserve us, and Eros with us, we can continue to gouge Zeus in the eye by flaunting the divinity of Eros, thus winning heavenly bliss for the entire human race in our rebellious existence. We risk losing everything, though, if we deprive the gods of their sacrifices. Therefore, like the real Aristophanes, the Platonic one advocates a pragmatic adherence to the Olympian religion. (It should be observed here that this Aristophanes nowhere recommends friendship with any god other than Eros.) This is the poet's reconciliation of the adoration of Eros with the worship of Zeus, a propaganda feat that turns all mankind from sincere piety to an ironically reverent metaphysical rebellion.[114]

In his peroration, Aristophanes says that he will repeat his request to Eryximachus not to mock his speech comically.[115] The doctor answers that he will comply because he enjoyed the talk. Eryximachus believes that he has luckily gotten away with his tactical blunder, for Aristophanes not only has held to the sophists' Titanic line but has also presented it much more beautifully than his predecessors. Eryximachus forgets that Aristophanes has rejected the first two speakers' cavalier neglect of nature's aims, as well as the Asclepiad project of changing or controlling nature. He has envisaged nature as a teleological measure instead. Eryximachus also forgets that Aristophanes has invalidated the first three speeches, so that Socrates is by no means beset from every side.

I think it sufficiently proved that Plato depicts an Aristophanes who deliberately and openly injects Titanism into Athenian culture, thus preparing Athens for what the poet would consider the right sort of tyranny. In personal relationships, this despotism would consider its beloveds as the selves of the lovers—definitely a tyrannical "wrong pederasty." In politics, it would mobilize all society behind the projects of metaphysical rebellion and, quite probably, an intelligent imperial domination of the ancient world that would be approved by characters such as Dikaiopolis, Bdelykleon, and the Sausage Seller. Aristophanes' support of religious piety

---

114. Again, Saxenhouse's analysis of these issues is excellent ("Net of Hephaestus," 30–31).

115. Rosen thinks that Aristophanes lies about having made this request earlier (see *Plato's "Symposium,"* 164). I disagree. The final such plea occurs at 193d7–8. An earlier one occurs at 193b6–7, and, in essence, an even earlier one at 189b4–7. One might wonder why a comic poet should object to comic ridicule of his comedy. This is no great puzzle. As seen above, the real Aristophanes was profoundly serious about the truth of his teaching. That had to be exempted from mockery.

is calculated to bolster this tyranny, for it subordinates such faith as the Athenians have to the purpose of maintaining the cultural hegemony of the despotic eros. Socrates will be obliged to answer Aristophanes in some detail. It will be difficult for him to counter the influence of the comic poet, whose attraction is all the more seductive for its portions of great real beauty and its lyricism.

AGATHON

Having been exhorted by Phaedrus to stop answering Socrates' questions about shame, Agathon begins his oration by saying that he wants to speak first about how it is necessary for him to speak, and then to speak. He immediately charges that his *sympotai* have failed to give an encomium on Eros, choosing instead to felicitate mankind on the goods that the god causes for them. He explains: "What sort (ὁποῖος) he himself is who is giving these things, no one has said. There is one right method of all praises of all things: to go through in speech what sort (οἷος) of cause there is of those things that the speech happens to concern. Thus, it is just for us to praise Eros first for what sort (οἷός) he is, and next the gifts" (194e7–195a5).

Standard English versions of the *Symposium* mistranslate this text, causing Agathon to remark that none of the previous speakers has said what the "nature" of Eros is. Even Stanley Rosen, whose translation has inspired mine, says that "Agathon's statement of method is a demand that we consider the nature of the god."[116] This seems wrong, or at least in need of extremely careful qualification, for three reasons. First, Agathon almost totally avoids the word "nature" (φύσις). He replaces the concept of "nature" with the idea of "sort." Second, it is surely too soon for Agathon to have forgotten, as we ourselves should not forget, that Aristophanes has defined Eros as "the desire and pursuit of the whole" (192e10–193a1). Aristophanes has stated *what* Eros *is*, thus telling us what the god's nature is, as most people use the concept "nature." Further, Phaedrus, Pausanias, and Eryximachus have implied that Eros is an epiphenomenon of earth, or that he is sky, thus alluding indirectly to his nature. If Agathon recalls this, he must be criticizing his *sympotai* not for having neglected the nature of Eros, but precisely for having concerned themselves with the deity's "nature" rather than his "sort." Third, Agathon consistently shows what his replacement of "nature" with "sort" means by refusing to speak of substance, concentrating instead on traits. That is, he eschews definitions of Eros that employ nouns to clarify what the god is, favoring accounts that use adjectives and verbs to describe his phenomenal qualities, typical habits, and behavior.

116. Rosen, *Plato's "Symposium,"* 171.

He wants to get rid of essences and focus on attributes. Only after he has achieved this does he remark that Eros was "born" (πέφυκεν, 195b3) to hate old age, saying not what Eros is, but what he detests, by nature, thus referring to nature (φύσις) indirectly only once, not as essence, but as an inherent antipathy. Thus, we may assert that Agathon demands consideration of the "nature" of Eros only in a sense, only after the concept has been redefined as a synonym of "sort," so that it means not essence, but traits.[117]

With this clarified, we are obliged to ask why Agathon finds it "necessary" to speak as he ordains. Clearly, his judgment has nothing to do with the propriety of using a philosophic method, as distinguished from the impropriety of failing to utilize one, as prejudices inherited from the Enlightenment would cause us to suppose. Rather, it has to do with the propriety of rejecting one method (inquiring into natures, or into natures qua essences) in favor of another (investigating sorts, or natures qua sorts). What is the "necessity" of such a change?

In this matter, it is relevant that Agathon has promised to take Socrates to court about their wisdom, and also that Agathon will have no compunction about committing a shameful act in his speech. It is likely that Agathon's shift from essences to sorts is the opening gambit in his lawsuit. Socrates is known for his "what is" queries, which lead to studies of essences.[118] Agathon objects that true wisdom asks "what sort" questions, investigating traits. In turn, this procedural ploy probably strikes Plato as Agathon's first intellectual step in his subversion of the Athenian demos. So, to repeat and expand our question, why does Agathon assert that the wise necessarily speak of sorts, and why should Plato judge this a radical outrage?

I think that to deal with these issues properly, we must recall that all of the previous speakers in the *Symposium* have had Titanic libidos. Accordingly, all four have attempted to deify themselves in one way or another.[119] Phaedrus was eager to attain to a genesis without generation analogous to that enjoyed by the oldest god, Eros. Pausanias intended to usurp the divine role of forming souls by generating beautiful thoughts in them. Eryximachus ventured to portray himself as the governor of the erotics of gods, men, and the cosmos. Aristophanes sought godhood in an erotic defiance of Zeus through which people bestowed their salvations upon themselves. These schemes all fail in the same way to achieve the perfect deification of human beings: in none of them does a man go beyond the rebellious appropriation of a divine function to himself, arriving at pure iden-

---

117. Cf. Bloom, *Love and Friendship*, 490.

118. Perhaps Agathon will remember having heard the discussion in the *Protagoras*, in which Socrates says near the end that his object has been to learn what virtue "is in itself" (360e8). Cf. Rosen on "what is" as "Socrates' favorite question" (*Plato's "Symposium,"* 204).

119. Cf. Rosen, *Plato's "Symposium,"* 50, 65, 145, 169.

tity with a godly essence. We shall see that Agathon is Titanic, too, longing for the most perfect possible self-deification.[120] However, the wish to achieve divinity on the level of essence would raise the daunting problem of how a human being could become divine, that is, the question of how any man could become something that by nature he is not. The "necessity" of Agathon's method probably roots in the insight that this problem would evaporate if essential natures were demolished, leaving only traits as the foundations of divinity. If so, Agathon thinks that he is wiser than Socrates because he assumes that everyone who aspires to nobility wishes to become a god and that exhibiting certain traits will succeed where striving for new essences fails. Plato's judgment that Agathon's method is ignoble and politically ruinous would then be related to its objective of self-deification.

Having established his methodology, Agathon delivers his oration. I wish to skip over his presentation to its end for a moment. Agathon concludes by saying: "There, Phaedrus, is my speech that I shall offer to the god, mixing play and seriousness in a measured manner, as I am able" (197e6–8). With this, we are advised that Agathon's talk is partly jocular and partly serious. However, we are now at a bit of a loss. About which parts is Agathon talking? And which part is jocular and which serious?

Although no one may judge without having studied the speech, we may be permitted a preliminary speculation that follows the lead of Socrates, where he says (198b) that the bulk of Agathon's speech was not so marvelous but that the beauty of its words, especially toward the end, was breathtaking. This indicates, I think, that the parts that Agathon has in mind are not the discussion of this topic as opposed to the analysis of that one, and not a sequentially earlier part as opposed to a sequentially later one, but, rather, the intellectual substance that might be aimed at understanding as opposed to the rhetorical form that might be calculated to produce emotional effects. Further, I believe that Agathon is jocular about the former and extremely serious about the latter. When one pays attention to Agathon's rational substance even with the firmest of resolutions to read sympathetically, one still sees that it is riddled with obvious sophisms, logical fallacies, contradictions, begged questions, gratuitous assertions, and other analytic inadequacies. Socrates is right; it is not remarkable. I imagine that Agathon knows well that his reasoning is frivolous, for he intends it mainly as an entertaining spoof of philosophy. When we come to the beauty of Agathon's words, though, we find ourselves agreeing with him despite our rational qualms, so moving is the beauty. Socrates delivers himself of a pun (198b–c) that suggests that the beauty of the poet's words paralyzes

---

120. Cf. "Agathon . . . makes the strongest claim in the dialogue: identification of himself with the ruling god" (ibid., 163) and "Agathon is the only man to achieve genuine immortality, and he is a god" (191).

thought, much as a glimpse of the Gorgon Medusa turns people to stone. I hypothesize that Agathon is serious about producing this effect, in aid of winning universal acknowledgment of his divinity.

Agathon turns his Gorgon's rhetoric on his guests with the words: "Thus I say that of all the gods who are happy, Eros, if it be customarily lawful (θέμις) and blameless to say so, is the happiest of them, being most beautiful and best" (195a5–7). Agathon has boldly uttered a shocking, dangerous statement at the beginning of his speech. In context, his assertion seems risky for two reasons. First, it is anything but conventionally lawful to maintain that Eros is the happiest, most beautiful, and best god. Agathon could be accused of impiety for advancing this novel evaluation.[121] Evidently, he does not fear this outcome because he is confident that the beauty of his comic sophisms will cast a hypnotic spell on his auditors, one that will cause them to believe docilely that it is customarily lawful to proclaim Eros the most excellent god. Second, Zeus or Apollo or Aphrodite might have something to say about who is the happiest, most beautiful, and best deity, and the Olympians might not absolve Agathon of blame for an insult. Agathon seems unconcerned. Does the poet think that he can mesmerize the gods, too, or does his courage have another basis? Whatever his reason, Agathon has clearly made light of Aristophanes' allegedly grave peril.

As suggested above, Agathon's assertion that Eros is the happiest, most beautiful, and best deity is not epistemologically serious. However, the proposition appears well founded to the thoughtless because Agathon casts it in the form of a syllogism and pledges to demonstrate his minor (195a7–8). In effect, he says: "The happiest god is the one who is most beautiful and best. As I shall prove, Eros is the most beautiful and best. Therefore, Eros is the happiest god." If inferior intellects can be dazzled by good rhetoric in the course of the demonstration of the minor, they will think that Agathon's inference is customarily lawful because it is true. To foster the impression that he is demonstrating the minor, Agathon initially adduces poetic reasons for saying that Eros is the most beautiful god. Next he offers the same sort of reasons for affirming that Eros is the best. We shall follow each argument.

Agathon maintains that Eros is the most beautiful god because he is the youngest, soft, fluid, elegant (or graceful), and colorful of skin, like the flowers among which he dwells. It is easy to see, logically, that no one is compelled to confess that a god who is the youngest, soft, fluid, elegant, and flowery of hue is the fairest, let alone that Eros himself has such qualities. We can imagine that other deities with other traits might be more comely yet, and that Eros might have totally different qualities. Agathon's

---

121. I pass over the interesting hint that there are gods who are unhappy. There is not time for everything.

statements are gratuitous. However, Agathon is not counting on logic to sway his audience. Instead, his images create an aura that powerfully stimulates our emotions to assent joyfully, crying, "Yes, most beautiful."[122]

Granted that Agathon is reckoning on the emotional effect of his word images to carry his argument, we might still ask why he settles upon the constellation of adjectives "youngest, soft, fluid, elegant (or graceful), and well-complected, like flowers," rather than some other, perhaps more moving, set of traits to create his aura. The answer is provided by Aristodemus in his description of the reception given Agathon's speech. Aristodemus, who is swept off his feet by Agathon, reports that the poet's oration was applauded raucously because "the youth" had spoken in a manner "suitable to himself and the god" (198a1–3). He means that Agathon's adjectives were predicable of both Agathon and Eros. In his analysis of Eros as beautiful, the poet has projected his own qualities onto the god. He will do this again in his analysis of Eros as best. He is cultivating his serious aim, emotionally contriving the qualitative assimilation of his being to that of the god. He is also promoting his lawsuit against Socrates, denying divinity to a man whom he regards as ugly, old, hard, stiff, ungraceful, and sallow.

Agathon returns to arguing more comically than seriously as he moves to his account of the constituents of the adjective "most beautiful." He starts by addressing Phaedrus, telling him congenially that Eros is "the youngest of the gods." He states that Eros himself supplies a great proof of this, namely, that he flees from old age, which clearly is swift, for it comes nigh to us more quickly than is needful. Eros naturally hates old age and will not get near it; he is always with the young, and is such, for the proverb says well that like draws nigh to (or weds) like. (By endorsing this motto, and otherwise remaining silent about women, Agathon denies females a role in his felicity, thus implicitly approving the misogyny of his comrades.) So, Agathon says, he agrees with Phaedrus in much else,[123] but he denies that Eros is older than Kronos and Iaretus and reaffirms that Eros is the youngest of the gods and always young.

122. An example of this nearly irresistible emotional power of Agathon's rhetoric is found in Leonard Bernstein, *Serenade after Plato's "Symposium": For Solo Violin, Strings, Harp, and Percussion,* corrected ed. (1956; reprint, n.p.: Jaini Publications, Boosey and Hawkes, 1988). Composing movements that reflect the dialogue's speakers, Bernstein makes Agathon's movement, an adagio, the most melodious, serene, and beautiful of all. There is a good argument to be made for the view that Bernstein should have made Socrates' movement the most beautiful. Instead, he creates a Socrates-Alcibiades movement that is the most playful and riotous, which is not far off the mark but still deficient in the necessary beauty.

123. In what else? Agathon does not tell, but I think that the agreement lies in several areas: the ungenerated character of Eros (Agathon totally ignores the question of the parentage of Eros); the superiority of speech, at least poetic speech, to sexual reproduction; the supremacy of the narcissistic *erōmenos* to the *erastēs*; and the great desirability of fame.

We can laugh uproariously at the sophisms that Agathon adduces to establish that Eros is eternally the youngest god, which include the equation of an aversion to aging with youth, a smug and deceitful hint that sexual love is only for the young, a Prodicus-inspired appeal to the Homeric adage that like loves like (the popular form of Eryximachus's maxim that unlike loves unlike), and the substitution of frequent repetition for rigorous logic. We can also laugh at Agathon's gross self-contradictions, the chief of which are that he voluntarily maintains a sexual relationship with the aging Pausanias, parties happily with older men, and makes a god who is the being of love a natural hater. However, we must recognize Agathon's rhetorical skill when we observe that the poet, who at thirty to thirty-four is still "young," but no spring chicken, no boy in bloom, has persuaded Aristodemus and nearly all the other guests to think of him as "the youth," as if the image of perpetual youth were right both for himself and for the god. Suddenly, the comical has become quite serious again; Agathon's implicit appropriation of immortality bespeaks his apotheosis as Eros.

This result forces the tension between Agathon's comedy and seriousness out into the open. We are obliged to inquire how Agathon's rhetorical *technē* prompts most of his guests to overlook his sophisms and contradictions and accept his conclusions, or how he gets these people to take his comedy seriously. True, we have already said that the beauty of his words carries his argument against his logic, but how far can we push a disjunction between beauty and logic? How illogical can a speech become before someone ceases to think it beautiful? Specifically, when Agathon adduces nothing but a facile trick to rid himself of the problem of essences, nothing but images that manipulate emotions to prove that Eros is beautiful, nothing but clever fallacies to demonstrate that Eros is young, and, especially, nothing but intimations to establish the identity of his qualities with those of the god, how does he move Aristodemus and the others to accept his lyrical jesting as beautiful truth, agreeing that he has spoken in a manner appropriate to himself and the god? Just what is it in his words that strikes others as beautiful in the face of the mounting illogic? Is it merely the images or more?

Someone might suggest that Agathon succeeds through superior sophistry. I doubt it. It is inconceivable that a group of the best sophists in Athens would miss his jokes or be duped by the deceptions that they themselves practice so well. Likewise, it is out of the question that Socrates should think these artifices as dangerous to himself as Medusa. Socrates was not born yesterday. Agathon's tricks are merely tools for hoodwinking the foolish many.

A more helpful suggestion could be Socrates' accusation in the *Gorgias* (463b1, 6) that sophistry is a branch of flattery. Agathon's oratory clearly attempts to flatter the pederastic *erastai* and Socrates into forgetting not only his sophisms about the youth of Eros but also his offensive pronouncement that Eros habitually flees from older men such as themselves. The suddenly beneficent Agathon has offered his elders hope that old age comes to them more quickly than is *needful*. This suggests that through Eros-Agathon's grace, the *erastai* and other guests can postpone (or escape) the aging process that has been proclaimed unnecessary. Indeed, it hints that by stooping to party with these graying lovers, the ageless god-man has confirmed their own status as eternally young. Actually, there is some beautiful truth in what Agathon is saying: Surely, somehow, love keeps our souls eternally young. Agathon probably lets this truth tincture his quite different suggestion that old age can be put off, making it seem possible to elderly men that youth of soul can delay decay of the body. The resulting goodwill could render the ideas that Eros is the youngest god, and that he is somehow incarnate in the ever youthful Agathon, quite beautiful indeed. However, it is unlikely that the *sympotai* would easily fall for this. Presumably, adroit flatterers know when they are being flattered.

Further, it is one thing to persuade desperate oldsters that they look young and have several years left and another to convince them that anybody could be divinely immortal, no matter how much this idea might appeal to their aesthetic sensibilities. Agathon appears to have overstepped himself by reminding his guests and us of a fundamental difficulty in his project. Everybody agrees that to be a god is to be eternal (and more besides). Everybody can see that time moves at the same rate for all men, aging them with inexorable necessity, so that it is ridiculous to apply the term "eternally young" (ἀεὶ νέον, 195c1) equally to gods and human beings, as Agathon implicitly endeavors to do in his own case.[124] When we experience movements of "eternal youth" in our souls thanks to love, this does not mean that we, like gods, will always be. Agathon's humor unintentionally demonstrates that he and his art are human, not divine, at least to the rational understanding.

Despite these apparently insuperable obstacles, Agathon delivers explicit proclamations of his victory over necessity, insisting that the kingship of Eros has replaced the rule of the goddess Necessity. Rejecting the cosmologies cited by Phaedrus, Pausanias, and Eryximachus, he argues that it was Necessity who caused all the internecine violence and castrations among the gods that Hesiod and Parmenides relate, if there is any truth in their accounts. Now, with the coming of the reign of Eros, all that is in the past, and friendship and peace prevail among the gods (195c). The immediate consequence for our present discussion is that the Olympian order of being arranged by Zeus, which was driven by Necessity and featured the

124. Another problem for Agathon is that if all gods are immortal, they must all be eternally young.

inevitability of human aging, has been overturned by the Titanic assault of Eros-Agathon. Although all of these assertions are gratuitous, Agathon is appealing to some beauty that enables his *sympotai* to assent to his aesthetic gravity about his proposition that he and his lovers can be eternally youthful. Aristodemus and the sophists, who have not succumbed to crude logical swindles and flattery, are swayed. Socrates, who is surely immune to hoaxes and delusions, considers Agathon's rhetoric challenging. It is also striking that in the *Thesmophoriazusae*, which dates to 411, when Agathon is thirty-five or older, Aristophanes makes Euripides' in-law call Agathon "young sir" (νεανίσχ', 134) and "child" (παῖ, 141). Agathon's "youthfulness" must have been widely recognized. It becomes ever more important to put our finger on the beauty of Agathon's rhetoric that compels the agreement of everyone but Socrates to impossibilities and that also worries Socrates.

It seems to me that the effective beauty of Agathon's speech lies not in his sophistry, not in the seduction of his flattery, and not in any power to make men believe impossibilities, but in the attitude that the oration exhibits, or the volition that it symbolizes. The discourse flaunts a sheer audacity that thrills its auditors, making them experience a kind of beauty. More specifically, the oration represents something in Agathon's soul that generates the audacity. Aristophanes, who appears to have been more familiar with Agathon than with Socrates, helps us fathom that spiritual reality. In the *Thesmophoriazusae*, he lets the in-law ask Agathon why he dresses like women. One could speculate that Agathon's behavior is just comical camp. I think that it is camp and much more. In his answers (148–52, 154–56, 167), Agathon explains not only his cross-dressing, but the whole of his poetic activity as well. He replies that he wears what corresponds to his intention (γνώμη), which depends on the subjects of his plays. His poetic creation (the Greek for which, ποιεῖν, translates literally into English as "to make") requires him to use mimesis, or imitation, to acquire the habits (τρόπους) of those whose dramas he makes, when he lacks what they have. By necessity, he makes in ways that reflect his nature. Accordingly, whenever he has the intention to do so, Agathon can become what he is not by imitating it because it is in his self-creative nature to become it. By extension, he becomes eternally young through mimesis of the eternal and becomes immortal insofar as he acquires the habits of immortality. Therefore, Agathon does not expect to be eternally young in the sense that he will exist forever. Rather, he expects to spend all his mortal days infused with the might, and exercising the prerogatives, of eternal youth, and he promises to confer these powers on his lovers. His soul is filled and imbues others with a triumphal Titanic will. This is what his auditors experience as beautiful, so that they are moved by his sophisms. The glow of this beauty will carry the *sympotai* over many a rough spot. This prompts us to ask whether Agathon and his lovers have not fallen prey to refined, rather than primitive, forms of self-delusion and flattery.

A Greek who sympathized with Agathon might object that we should inquire instead whether he is not right. To an extent, Agathon's self-interpretation in the *Thesmophoriazusae* resembles that of the earliest worshipers of the cosmological gods, who win sacred being and resist profane life by imitating the sacred.[125] Hellenic believers would see little difficulty in the proposition that Agathon can share in the life of Eros through mimesis. Still, they would be missing Agathon's point. Sophists and moderns would support Agathon for reasons that were truer to his thought. Agathon imitates according to his own intention. By the necessity of his will, he produces in ways that reflect his nature. His mimesis is not a participation in a reality above him but in icons engendered by and characteristic of his creativity. Through his cross-dressing and his other imitations, he bestows divinity on himself. This, again, is what strikes both sophists and moderns as beautiful.

That Plato agrees with the historical Aristophanes' views of Agathon's intent is proved by two observations. One is that Plato's focus on Agathon's insistence on traits is equivalent to Aristophanes' attention to his proclivity for miming habits. The other is that Plato makes Agathon state that Eros is a good poet (196e4), in the broadest sense of a "maker" of all things. Eros generates all life. He is responsible for musical making and the demiurgic making of all *technai* (196e–197a). He is the sort who generates what he naturally conceives. If Agathon is Eros, Plato's Agathon is thus the same as Aristophanes' Agathon. However, Agathon is Eros. He says that Eros needs a Homer to sing his softness (195c7–d1). The soft Agathon is that Homer. His self-made traits mimetically participate in those of the deity who "creates" him, whom he also poetically creates on the model of the traits that he generates. As Agathon intends, we lose track of the difference between the divine and the human poets. His making blends into that of the creator of all things. The implication for Agathon's lawsuit against Socrates is that poetry, not philosophy, is the means to self-deification.

In his treatment of Eros as soft and therefore beautiful, Agathon gives an exhibition of the divine power of the human poet. He remakes the goddess Ate by tearing some lines from Homer (*Iliad* 9.91–96) out of context. In a speech that blames gods for the evil that men do, Agamemnon excuses his affront to Achilles by pleading that Ate, the eldest daughter of Zeus, caused it. She walks with delicate feet on the heads of men, stirring up their evil to hurt them. This Ate is hard. The daintiness of her feet enhances her harshness, for it prevents her victims from feeling her noxious presence. When the droll Agathon gets through with her, Ate is

---

125. Cf. Mircea Eliade, *The Sacred and the Profane: The Nature of Religion.*

soft because she has delicate feet and retains none of her odious qualities (195d). Eros-Agathon can soften the gods over whom he rules.[126] Indeed, he can mold gods however he likes because he holds that they are products of poetry. Thus, Aristophanes' piety and Eryximachus's medical expertise are rendered unnecessary by poetry. This is why Agathon fears no retribution from the Olympians for judging Eros more beautiful than they.

Continuing with his jocular logic, Agathon declares that he will prove the softness of Eros in the same way that Homer demonstrates the delicacy of Ate. Eros, he says, resembles Ate in that he refuses to walk upon the earth. However, Eros also avoids stepping on heads, which are not soft. He walks and dwells in the softest of all things, the characters and souls of gods and human beings. He does not abide in all souls. When he comes upon one with a hard character, he leaves. When he finds one that is soft, he colonizes it. Because he always grasps the softest of the soft with his feet and his whole self, he is necessarily most soft (195e2–196a1). This clowning prepares the ground for a decisive offensive against Socratic wisdom. Agathon associates hardness with the head and, hence, implicitly, with reason. In contrast, he connects softness with characters and souls. A more modern romantic writer would say that he makes softness a quality of the heart. Agathon then proclaims the inferiority of the head and reason to characters and souls, or the heart, on the grounds that the former cannot be permeated by Eros, whereas the latter are receptive to him. Socrates cannot be called wise if he closes himself to happiness. He commits that error by letting reason control his soul, thus fatally hardening his heart. Agathon has also replied to Socrates' doubt that wisdom is imparted by touching. Wisdom expresses itself in erotic generation, and Eros spreads himself by touching, with his feet, which undoubtedly are now a euphemism for another part of the anatomy.

Agathon's discourse on Eros as fluid, elegant, and flowery of hue is noteworthy chiefly for its comment that Eros and unshapeliness are always at war (196a6–7). It is necessary to ask why there should be war when Eros, the divine champion of friendship and peace among the gods (195c), is sovereign. Also, how Eros could win the war if he is soft? Agathon indicates that Eros is warlike for natural reasons. When he asserts that Eros pacified the Olympians, he does not thereby make his god a prince of peace on earth. Rather, he lets Eros despise anyone whose qualities are opposite his own. As mentioned above, it is surprising that a god who is the being of love naturally hates, but we understand this when we perceive that Agathon is projecting his habits onto the god. It is Agathon who abhors old age, reason, and ugliness. Similarly, we comprehend why there is war during the reign of the god of peace when we realize that it is Agathon

---

126. I owe this insight to Rosen, *Plato's "Symposium,"* 179.

who wants to vanquish everything he hates, as it is found, for example, in a gnarled, aging philosopher. The irenic mood on Olympus protects Agathon from the gods' wrath but not distasteful men from the poet's ire. All this enhances Plato's portrait of Agathon's Titanism. Agathon intends to revise the order of being so that it is a realm of freedom rather than necessity, an existence in which he is not compelled to lack for eternal life, walk upon a hard earth, be subject to the abrasiveness of rational thinkers, or be forced to gaze upon ugliness. When his enjoyment of this new world of beauty is marred by the existence of hated irritants, Agathon is provoked to bellicose rage, and his sympathizers with him. This is an interesting emotional effect of speech-induced beautiful emotion.

As for the measures that the soft-hard Eros-Agathon adopts to win his battles, the most important is presented as the epitome of delicate nonaggression. The deity softly slips away from those who repel him, thus devastating them (195e–196b). The poet's actions give the lie to his words, though. It was Agathon who sought Socrates and invited him to the symposium, in order to master him. True, Eros-Agathon withholds love from the men he hates, but this clearly happens simultaneously with efforts to subjugate them that are advertised as innocent flight, for propaganda purposes. Further, if I withheld my love from someone who displeased me, and otherwise lived and let live, the event would be an isolated one that involved only me and the other. However, if I were the divine embodiment of love, it would seem that I could not prevent someone I hated from enjoying me unless I made sure that he had no lovers at all, so that he was entirely desolate. I would have to mobilize his entire community against him. He would have to become loathsome to all, and all would have to show him how loveless he was. As suggested by Socrates, Eros-Agathon has a powerful effect on the many. Perhaps he would make a crowd exert moral and physical pressure on a philosopher to stop being so hard and ugly if he turned up at the poet's *epinikios*. Agathon might even believe that this strategy has worked, for the unsightly Socrates has made a pathetic attempt to prettify himself for the banquet. Apparently, if the beautiful, young softie needs ugly, hard threats or brawling done to secure a victory, he can let his foe be softened up by fear of, or the fists of, his followers.

When Agathon asserts that Eros is the "best" god, he means that the deity is superior in virtue (196b5). He ascribes to Eros the traditional virtues of justice (or, more precisely, lack of injustice), moderation (or sane self-control, σωφροσύνη), courage, and wisdom. His discussion of the manner in which Eros manifests these excellences is facetious. For Agathon, the most critical point under the heading of the peerless virtue of his god is that "Eros neither does injustice to a god nor receives injustice from a god, neither does he injustice to a human being nor receive it from a human being. Neither does he suffer violence nor violently cause suffering, for

violence neither touches him nor governs his actions. For all serve Eros
in all things willingly, and where the willing agree with the willing, the
saying 'the laws are king of the city' is just" (196b6–c3). This speech is a
jest because, as weighed against his earlier arguments, every statement in
it is contentious. One is even rather far-fetched. The insinuations that it is
not unjust to despise people for being elderly, rational, and ugly, and not
unjust to deprive them of love, are, to say the least, highly debatable. They
could be true only if there were no justice, such that cruelty would not be
unjust, or if old age, rationality, and homeliness had no legitimate claims to
anything as their due, so that nothing done to them could be unjust. Also, it
might be that a god, Eros, suffers no violence at the hands of gods or human
beings. Then how is it not violent to deprive someone of love, thus denying
him or her the one thing most needful for human fulfillment? Further, there
are no grounds for the idea that violence could not touch Eros-Agathon and
his armies. When Lysander appears, he will not be impressed by the fact
that Athens is full of lovers. Further, it would be dishonest to contend that
rape victims serve Eros willingly, or that the deceived prey of men such
as Pausanias really are willing partners in their relationships. The proverb
that the *nomoi* are king of the city when the willing agree with the willing,
a principle of legal positivism quoted from the sophist Alcidamas, also ignores the possibility that the willing could agree with the willing to enact
unjust laws—unless, once again, justice is not natural but, rather, a mere
convention.

The flimsiness of Agathon's argument about justice prompts us to ask
why something so weak should be rated as "the most important" (μέγιστον,
196b6) item in his analysis of the god's virtues. I think that the reasoning
derives its prominence from its function as a political theory: Agathon is
teaching his adherents the presuppositions of his erotic polity. The axiom
that Eros does no injustice is really the propaganda version of a claim that
no act of Eros may be challenged. Agathon has recurred to a theme that has
appeared in one guise or another in all of the previous speeches: for Eros
and his followers, everything is permitted. The idea that everyone willingly
serves Eros in all things is also propaganda, intended to make palatable the
legal fiction that all the acts of Eros rest on a foundation of perfect unanim-
ity, perhaps because those opposed can be induced to agree by guile or fear.
Those slated for bondage "want" to be love slaves when they have freely
submitted, so it cannot be said that they are being forced.[127] This is a beautiful notion in the eyes of those who are doing the forcing. Meanwhile, in a

---

127. This is the most plausible explanation of Agathon's refusal to inquire into the
practices of Pausanias, which would amount to statutory rape in the United States. The
same principle is argued by Thomas Hobbes in the seventeenth century: All consent is
voluntary, no matter how obtained.

cosmos naturally devoid of justice, like Aristophanes' universe that has no goddess Dikē, this universal consent serves to legitimate a new justice of which man is the creator, so that the sophism "where the willing agree with the willing, the saying 'the laws are king of the city' is just," becomes the basic principle of the polis. Like his associates, Agathon either wittingly or unwittingly works in the sphere of culture to condition Athenians to accept tyranny.

To demonstrate that Eros is moderate, Agathon states that everyone defines the virtue as control of pleasures and desires, that no pleasure is stronger than Eros, that all pleasures are therefore under the control of Eros, and, accordingly, that Eros must be moderate. To prove that Eros is courageous, Agathon reasons that Eros for Aphrodite caught Ares, that Eros must be stronger than Ares, and that to subdue the otherwise bravest god implies superior courage. Agathon's version of the Ares-Aphrodite-Hephaestus story substitutes Eros for Hephaestus; it argues that poetry is a soft, spiritual *technē* superior to the hard, mechanical bodily regimens of Eryximachus and Aristophanes. Agathon's zany fallacies must have evoked great outbursts of mirth among the sophists. They are an exhibition of the cavalier attitude that a student of Gorgias would bring to discussions of virtue.

Coming at last to wisdom, Agathon declares that he must do his best to omit nothing about the topic. His concern is motivated by the fact that this is the subject over which he has filed his lawsuit against Socrates, with Dionysus waiting in the wings to judge. Speaking as a poet, he says that, first, he wants to honor his own *technē* as Eryximachus did his (196d6–e1). A little later, he remarks that the god is a wise poet (196e1), that poetry (making) is Eros's own wisdom (197a2), and that Eros is responsible for the demiurgic creation of the *technai* (197a3). Unlike Socrates in many contexts, and unlike Aristotle in his classic discussion of the noetic virtues in book 6 of *Nicomachean Ethics* (especially 1139b15–20), Agathon uses the concepts wisdom (σοφία) and *technē* (τέχνη) as synonyms. Indeed, he collapses wisdom into the poet's *technē*. Why? It appears to me that Agathon has ontological, epistemological, and Titanic reasons. If essences have been abolished; if wisdom in the Socratic, Platonic, and Aristotelian sense can be defined provisionally (and somewhat incorrectly) as noetic attunement to the natural structure of being; and if Agathon sees the function of mind as determining how to remake the order of being in the image of his own creative will, there is no place in reality for the type of wisdom advocated by Socrates, Plato, and Aristotle. There is room only for a wisdom qua *technē* that renovates being by generating qualities and habits.

Honoring his *technē* after the fashion of Eryximachus, Agathon contends that Eros is a poetic maker so wise that he makes others poetic makers, for everyone becomes a poet, even if he were unmusical before, if Eros touches him (196d6–e6). Agathon is repeating his insistence that wisdom is transmitted by touching. This is consistent with his basic premises. The only knowledge that a reality without essences could support would be a knack of imparting form to a flux of qualities and randomly regular actions that had no stable metaphysical basis. The fluctuating nonessence receiving the form in its traits could simultaneously be said to have been given its form, the will to have that form, and the knowledge of how to have that form by the creative and teaching touch of the maker of the form.

Meanwhile, we must notice the broader implications of Agathon's teaching. Eros is a wise poetic maker who makes others like himself by touching them. Everyone becomes a poet, even if he were unmusical before, if Eros touches him. Who has not been touched by Eros, though? The wise god Eros makes all biologically mature human beings wise poets at once. Eros-Agathon goes further, however, intimating that all these newly musical people are divine. His touch makes all whom he touches into gods at once. If in order to win the prize for best play at the Lenaea, Agathon broadcasts his doctrine from the tragic stage in a manner that everyone can understand, and Plato seems to accuse Agathon of this flattery, the result is as follows: The thirty thousand are taught that they are gods who are wise about all poetic making, to whom everything is permitted, whose collective will creates justice, who may subdue all who offend them, who are served "willingly" by all whom they overcome, and who cannot be touched by force. This is heady stuff for fools. Agathon's shameless pandering certainly has the capacity to generate the theatocracy about which the Athenian Stranger later complains. Theatocracy is the soil in which tyranny grows. The political and intellectual halves of Agathon's ignoble deed converge: Agathon transmits the virus of Titanism to the many. Perhaps this is one of the most important reasons that in the year 416, the demos veer out of rational control and lurch down the path to excessively brazen freedom, Syracuse, and Aegospotami. This surely explains why Agathon's crowd frightens Socrates.

This is not all. It was mentioned above that Agathon credits Eros with the generation of all living beings, all musical making, and the demiurgic production of all the *technai*. In the case of the *technai*, the person who has the god for a teacher becomes famous. It is not only human beings whom Eros renders famous. Eros and Desire taught Apollo archery, medicine, and divination. Eros tutored the Muses in music, Hephaestus in the blacksmith's art, Athena in weaving, and Zeus in the governance of gods and human beings. Agathon proves this claim by implying that *technai* were created for the love of beauty (197a–b), a dubious notion. He is relying on passionate language to carry his arguments again. Of the several important things about Agathon that these remarks reveal, we shall notice this: If Eros is authoritative in all the useful arts, and if Agathon enjoys the power of Eros and imparts it to the thirty thousand, too, Agathon gets to be the god of all gods. It is not proved, though, that Eros rules all the arts useful to human life. This is why he slyly posits a link between *technē* and fame. Agathon claims that he is a god and wiser than Socrates because he can stimulate the many to applaud him, whereas Socrates is the butt of popular jokes.

Having finished his analysis of what sort Eros is, Agathon proceeds to praise the god's gifts. In the first tribute, he portrays Eros as a prince of peace after all, arguing that the god makes "peace among human beings" (197c5). Or does he? A few lines later, he also calls Eros the best παραστάτης (197e1–2), that is, the best comrade in arms who fights on one's flank. Can this contradiction be reconciled? Perhaps. Though maintaining that Eros taught the gods their arts for love of beauty, Agathon repeats that his deity has "nothing to do with ugliness" (197b5). Just before asserting that Eros is the best comrade in arms, he indicates that the god is "careful of the good, careless of the bad" (197d7–8). One gets the impression that Eros is the god of peace among men in the sense that he is a "savior" (a σωτήρ, as Agathon states, 197e1) who will fight on behalf of the beautiful to expel ugliness and evil from the earth, so that the beautiful will *eventually* not need to wage war, have anything to do with ugliness, or have any care for the bad. When Agathon praises Eros as a god of peace, the peace that he has in mind is the peace that conquerors enjoy. It anticipates the Pax Romana.

Agathon's remaining praises of Eros's gifts are a bouquet of lovely flowers that does not enlarge upon his theory greatly. Therefore, our scrutiny of his speech may be concluded with these observations: Agathon says that it is Eros who brings people together in gatherings such as the present one (197d2–3). This is another identification of himself with the god. Agathon ends with the exhortation that Eros is he whom "all men should follow, singing beautifully, participating in songs of praise, enchanting the mind of all gods and human beings" (197e3–5). This, however, is the siren song of the would-be tyrant who beguiles his fellow citizens with visions of divine happiness.

As subsequent events demonstrate, Agathon's lawsuit presents the judge with at least one true proposition: the poet can win more votes and louder acclamation than Socrates. This, however, is not the same as the judgment of Dionysus, which we must await. In the meantime, we can profit from a look at Socrates' evaluation of the speech. Immediately after the round of applause for Agathon, Socrates glances at Eryximachus and asks whether he was not right to fear that the poet would speak wonderfully. Elaborating, he exclaims: "But who would not have been scared out of his wits at hearing the beauty of the words and phrases toward the end?" (198b4–5). Socrates has given Agathon a compliment with a barb. He is suggesting that certain kinds of beauty can be frightening.

Socrates gives Agathon another compliment, an accolade less likely to be suspected as a double entendre than the previous one: "Dear Agathon, it seemed to me that you introduced your speech beautifully in saying that it was necessary first to display what sort (ὁποῖος) Eros is, and then his works. I thoroughly admire those words at the beginning" (199c3–6). Socrates surprises us as much with this remark as he does Agathon. He admits, nay, proclaims, that there is something fundamentally right about Agathon's shift from essences to traits. Further, the first five of Socrates' own direct references to what can loosely be called Eros's "nature" are allusions to traits. Socrates soon accepts the task of asking "who and what sort (ποῖός) Eros is" (201e1). He makes Diotima tell him that Eros is a "great daimon" (δαίμων μέγας, 202d13), and this looks like a definition of Eros in substantial terms, but then a "great daimon" is itself depicted as "something between mortal and immortal," so that the name is really a definition of Eros that delineates quality and ontological rank. He causes Diotima to announce that the "nature" (φύσις) of Eros is to be between wise and ignorant (204b7, 5), and this again defines Eros with respect to quality. Then he has Diotima maintain that Eros is "of such character" (τοιοῦτος, 204d2) as she has stated. It begins to look as if Socrates has been converted to the study of natures qua sorts. Nevertheless, the philosopher then suddenly reverts to his former custom and gives a generic, substantial definition of Eros as "all desire of good things and of being happy" (205d1–2), which accepts Aristophanes' account of Eros as desire, but corrects his notion of the object of the desire. We must ask what all this means.

It might be suggested that the inexactness of Socrates' language implies that Plato never cared to make an issue of the difference between essences and traits. I would reply that a Plato who took pains to make Socrates invoke the distinction in other settings (for example, in his discussion with Polus, *Gorgias* 462c–d, and at the end of his conversation with Thrasymachus, *Republic* 354a–b), is highly unlikely to have disregarded it in the *Symposium*. Socrates' behavior in praising Agathon must intend to convey the judgment that in the case of Eros, it is proper to speak almost entirely in terms of traits, without overlooking essence altogether. Why?

To dissolve our perplexity, we must jump ahead a little in the story. In the *Phaedrus*, Socrates reports Stesichorus as stating that we human beings have never seen or appropriately grasped a god with our intellect (*nous*) and that we cannot give an account of the immortal in any logos (246c6–d1). Even to declare what sort (οἷον) immortal soul is would be utterly and wholly a divine matter (246a4). In this perspective, at least, there is no serious sense in which we could maintain that the all-important question that is coeval with philosophy is *quid sit deus?* In the *Phaedrus*, Eros has divine status. Hence, the only medium in which Eros can be treated is myth. At the present juncture in the *Symposium*, Socrates lets Diotima demote Eros to the rank of "great daimon," which is "something between mortal and immortal." It follows that insofar as Eros tends to the immortal, there can still be no logos of him. There can be no account of what he is simply and no description of his qualities or acts. However, to the degree that he tends to the mortal, there can be a logos of him. There can be a partial substantive definition of Eros because there is something about his nature that shows up in the mortal soul as desire of the good. This desire cannot be elucidated further because everything about it other than its manifestation in the human soul tends to the immortal. Something in Agathon's restriction of his speech to his god's traits is a response to the real being of Eros. It corrects the hybristic pretense of his allies (other than Aristophanes) to know more about the essence of Eros than is humanly possible. This is why Agathon merits some praise.

Well, then, where does Agathon's speech break down? In effect, Socrates answers: "In nearly everything." After complimenting the beauty of the peroration, Socrates asserts that "the rest," which includes the introduction, was "not equally wonderful" (198b4). If Socrates likes Agathon's introduction so much, why does he not deem it wonderful? Socrates' reference to Eros's essence in his general discussion of the daimon's qualities and acts indicates the reason. Even when it is impossible to know what a being is, we remain obliged to acknowledge that it is what it is and that this distinguishes it from other beings that are not what it is. To share a being's traits is not to become it. Therefore, although Agathon's decision to examine Eros's traits rather than his essence agrees with sound epistemology, it is unsound when it aims at Agathon's identification with the eternal reality, or his self-deification. What is great in Agathon's stress on Eros's qualities and what is noble in his silence about his god's essence are polluted by the hallucinatory character of his project.

In Socrates' opinion, the body of Agathon's speech has even less to recommend it than the peroration and introduction. After a devastating dialectical assault on Agathon, Socrates gets the poet to admit that he knew nothing of what he was talking about (201b11–12). Eros is not beautiful. He does not possess beautiful things. He lacks good things, including wisdom. Socrates thrice repeats that Agathon and the others have said nothing true about Eros (198d–199b, 201c). Thus, insofar as Agathon's soul is erotic, Socrates does not grant that it is either defensible or persuasive to contend that the nature of the poet's psyche is divine creativity. In fact, Socrates could not concur in this view if soul is immortal and if there can be no logos of the immortal. We have come around again to the conclusion that Agathon's wisdom of Eros is a self-delusion, a lie in the psyche.

We come now to the heart of frightening beauty. Delusions can be beautiful, but they remain illusory. Beautiful delusions paralyze our power to live in the reality that we inhabit. Probably, one cannot reason with people who suffer from such delusions. They might well be beyond rational help (although one can still try to heal their spirits by loving them). At the rational level, the most one can do is offer them a diagnosis of their condition. Socrates seems to do this for Agathon. He tells Eryximachus that Agathon's discourse so reminded him of Gorgias that he discovered himself ἀτεχνῶς (absolutely, or exactly) in the situation related by Homer. He was afraid that near the end, Agathon would show him "the Gorgias head," thus turning him to speechless stone (198c1–5). This puns on the plight of the hero in *Odyssey* 11.632. Having just spoken with the image (εἴδωλον) of Herakles in Hades, Odysseus suddenly finds himself besieged by the myriad tribes of the dead wailing frightfully. He is overcome with fear that Persephone will set the Gorgon's head on him, so he flees immediately.

Why is Socrates' state like that of Odysseus? Here are the parallels: (1) In Hades, the souls of the dead lack *nous,* and exist only as shadows of their living selves (*Odyssey* 10.494–95). By identifying himself with Odysseus, Socrates hints that his *sympotai* are lifeless souls who have lost their *nous* and exist as mere shades of their real selves. The entire *Symposium* is a conversation of Odysseus-Socrates with the dead in Hades. (Plato uses Homer to the same effect about the same people in *Protagoras* 315b9–c3, c8–e1). To desire salvation through illusion is to win living death in insubstantiality.[128] (2) In Hades, the myriads of the dead want to ameliorate their condition, thus upsetting the ordained relationships of heaven, earth, and hell. The departure of Herakles, the mortal hero who gave Atlas a rest from holding heaven above earth, triggers their uprising and terrible outcry. In Athens, the many living dead want betterment. Agathon's rhetorical removal of Herakles, that is, his negation of the task of keeping heaven above earth, metaphysically, produces their appalling metaphysical rebellion and much howling. In both cases, the result of Herakles' elimination is mass Titanism, and this scares the real living men who have *nous.* (3) In the legend, Atlas joins the Titans' revolt. For this, he is condemned to prop heaven above earth for all eternity. After Herakles deserts him, he is shown the Gorgon's head and turned into Mount Atlas. This ensures his eternal compliance with Zeus's command that he always uphold the Olympian structure of reality. In Hades, Odysseus fears that his voluntary presence will aid the Titanism of the dead myriads; that Persephone, the dread queen of Hades, will blame him for their insurgency; and that she will restore order to her realm by subjecting him to the same fate as Atlas. In Agathon's hellish party, Socrates fears that his potential acquiescence in the host's seductively beautiful temptation will further the Titanism of the demos and that he will be shown the "Gorgias head" by an Agathon who wants to be Eros

---

128. This warning is not precisely an accommodation of philosophy to sophistical poetry.

but ends as Persephone, for the illusory triumph of Agathon's revolution is simultaneously its own punishment that maintains the ineluctable order of being, freezing the rebels in postures that involuntarily support man's metaphysical firmament.

The comparison between the situations of Odysseus and Socrates may be extended into a brief digression that points to coming chapters. What about the person of Socrates himself? Is Socrates really an Odysseus? Stanley Rosen thinks not. He objects: "Odysseus has somewhere to go, namely, to his wife and home in Ithaca. . . . There is a homelessness about philosophy, a detachment from the city which is essentially alien to the wily Odysseus." Accordingly, the homesick Odysseus flees, whereas Socrates stays at the party.[129] I believe that a consideration of the *Phaedrus* suggests the opposite conclusion. Odysseus is forced to wander the earth because he has sinned against Poseidon. In the myth of Stesichorus, souls are compelled to sojourn on earth because, in their previous existence, they have been filled with forgetfulness and evil, lost their wings, and fallen into the world of matter. Odysseus recalls his lost home with longing. In the *Phaedrus*, Socrates' soul has a home, too—not the house in which Socrates dwells with Xanthippe, for the philosopher's wife is a fellow exile, but the realm from which it fell, and in which it beheld sublimely beautiful visions that nourished it. The philosophic soul enjoys remembrance, or anamnesis, of that former abode and yearns for it. Socrates' assumption of the role of Odysseus quietly suggests the anamnesis theme that must be taken into account in any final reckoning with the *Symposium*. Further, Odysseus travels to Hades in search of the prophecy that will guide him home. Socrates solicits Diotima's prophecies at the symposium for the same reason. Odysseus hastily leaves Hades. Socrates stays at the banquet, but quickly repudiates his agreement to play the sophists' game of lies and illusions in favor of the pursuit of truth (198c–199b). He thus extricates himself from their hell with all deliberate speed.[130]

EROS AND TITANIC TYRANNY

Plato has used the discourses of Phaedrus, Pausanias, Eryximachus, Aristophanes, and Agathon to show us living portraits of the tyrannical eros. He has not told us what this eros is, except to indicate that on its mortal side, it is desire. Probably, he can go no further toward defining its essence

---

129. Rosen, *Plato's "Symposium,"* 204–5.
130. Cf. Planinc, *Plato's Political Philosophy.* In his conclusion, Planinc instructively argues that Socrates' identification with Odysseus is at the mythological heart of the Platonic corpus.

because the greater part of its being lies in the immortal. However, he has clarified an important question. At the beginning of this chapter, I used the phrase "the things that tyrants want" without giving that concept any content. What are the things that tyrants want?

Plato's living portraits indicate that tyrants have the same biological erotes as ordinary men. They want food, drink, comfort, and sexual gratification. However, they have erotic desires for much more. Each in his own way, they all crave sexual slaves, mass adulation, power over as many of their fellows as they can subdue, victory in Titanic assaults on divine reality (which may be conceived as existent or nonexistent), and their own godhood. They try to convert Eros, who may have his own ends (or eros, which may have its own ends) into a means of achieving their aims. This makes it inevitable that their erotic relationships with their beloveds, who are expected to adore them, will be sick. As will be seen, they inevitably pervert what Socrates takes to be the true ends of pederasty. It is bad enough that every time this occurs, human misery increases. It is disastrous that in Athens, representatives of this wrong pederasty are gaining credit with the masses, preparing them not only to accept some future tyranny, but also to yearn for one enthusiastically because they cannot resist its seeming beauty.

5

SYMPOSIUM: PROPHETIC EROS

The drama of the *Symposium* consists in Socrates' efforts to save his beloved Agathon from the evil that he has devised. Agathon was once a noble and good-natured youth, but now he is in no mood to be rescued. He and his friends have embarked on a project of Titanic self-deification. Their enterprise is driven by the tyrannical eros and takes diverse forms of what I have called "wrong pederasty." Through cultural appeals to the demos, Agathon and his allies have drawn the many into their metaphysical rebellion, their tyrannical loves, and their tastes for perverse sorts of pederasty. The result seems to be that they have transformed Athens into a theatocracy, unwittingly unleashing political passions that endanger the city. Socrates hopes to redeem Agathon by leading him toward a nobler eros and a right pederasty. If Socrates can win Agathon, he might be able to save Athens, too, for Agathon has the ear of the many.

I believe that Agathon has invited Socrates to his party in order to sue him in the court of Dionysus in the matter of their wisdom. He wants to dominate and humiliate Socrates, the only Athenian who has not acknowledged his cultural hegemony. Even if he has not planned the evening's program in advance as an attack on Socrates, it remains true that the sophistical, tyrannical eros and the Socratic eros meet in combat in the *Symposium.* Socrates has a hard assignment. He must simultaneously court and repel his beloved in a tricky situation of love requited by war. He will try to do this by lavishing right pederasty on Agathon. This will involve educating the poet.

In most people, there are deleterious connections between passion and reason. It is also possible, or probable, that the most sublime truths are ineffable. Therefore, Socrates' loving rehabilitation of Agathon cannot simply be a matter of proclaiming propositional verities to him, with the advice that he write them down in his copybook and memorize them as a creed. Before he can start, Socrates must fight to get a hearing. He can do this only by cracking Agathon's proud bellicosity and inordinate self-confidence. He needs to turn the tables on Agathon, giving him a dose of humiliation to make him acutely aware of his lack of wisdom. This discipline will begin where the student is. Socrates must permit his beloved to declare himself, which Agathon does by dividing the labor of praising sophistical erotes among his allies and himself. Then Socrates must detach Agathon from all these loves with subtle honesty. He must acknowledge whatever is true in them. He must also disentangle truth from falsehood. Therefore, he must grant sophistical errors for the sake of argument and expose them gradually. In these ways, he must guide Agathon up through improved but still deficient postures, repeating the process until Agathon is forced to leap to the truth itself (perhaps, as the Seventh Letter has it, jumping from the four to the fifth). It will be so much the better if this pedagogy also engages Aristophanes and the other *sympotai,* but Agathon is the primary target.

Given that Socrates will educate Agathon in the manner just described, we must expect him to teach as he does in the *Republic.* That is, we must anticipate that, occasionally, he will invent myths and voice falsehoods or partial truths provisionally, with a view toward revising them later. This causes certain readers to fall into hermeneutic difficulties quite unnecessarily. People observe that Socrates' positions in the *Symposium* on immortality, anamnesis, forms, the good, and beauty vary from those in other dialogues.[1] Then, some who expect philosophy to be the consistent elaboration of doctrines are baffled. Others who choose to portray Plato as an esotericist or a fool pounce on the discrepancies triumphantly. None heed the warning that Plato's serious insights are neither written nor spoken. None consider the dramatic point that if Socrates concedes Agathon's ideas in order to refine them, he cannot speak here as he does elsewhere. Our present task is not to worry about doctrines, but to let Socrates lead us to the truth gradually, too.

Socrates reports that he learned his erotic wisdom from Diotima, a Mantinean woman. Although it will necessitate looking ahead in the story, it will be convenient to consider first who Diotima is and what function she has in the dialogue.

Diotima as a Character

Every commentator on the *Symposium* has something to say about Diotima's identity and role. Some regard Diotima as fictitious and treat her as one of Plato's mouthpieces, along with Socrates, the Athenian and Eleatic

1. For example, Harry Neumann, "Diotima's Concept of Love." Sometimes the differences are not as great as the scholars think.

Strangers, and Timaeus. Others maintain that she is a genuine historical figure whose ideas Plato has either adopted or garbled. One scholar argues that she is real because her teaching is "inconsistent with Platonic philosophy" and because if she were mythical, she would be "the only fictional character in all of the Platonic dialogues." This author is confident that Diotima is the heiress of a high Minoan-Mycenaean civilization in which women held prominent positions, presided at religious ceremonies, and worshiped a goddess. After Mycenae declined, the descendants of these priestesses preserved the religion of a central female divinity and resisted that of a supreme warrior father god. Thus, in historical context, Diotima must be seen as "part of a religious order that had maintained its authority" from the Minoan period, an order like those of the Pythia at Delphi and the female votaries at Eleusis. This would make it likely that she was Socrates' authoritative teacher. By co-opting her, and by turning her "loving conversation" into the "Socratic *elenchus*," Plato succeeds in becoming "not the authoritative founder of Western thought" but "a rebellious student who manages to transform Diotima's complex teaching on personal identity, immortality, and love into the sterile simplicities of logical form."[2]

The hypothesis that Diotima, together with Socrates, the two Strangers, and Timaeus, is one of Plato's mouthpieces once again ignores the warning of the Seventh Letter that Plato's serious thought is not found in his writings. With regard to Plato's conception of the highest truths, no character in his dialogues could play the envisaged role. The opinion that Diotima is a historical figure could be right. However, we cannot demonstrate this by pointing to the deviations of Diotima's statements in the *Symposium* from "Platonic philosophy," for there is no such thing as a propositional Platonic philosophy. Neither can we show it by arguing that there are no fictitious characters in Plato's works. An Athenian Stranger who visits Crete and climbs to the cave of Zeus with Kleinias and Megillus is certainly fictitious, even if he is based on Socrates or Plato, and the Cretan and Spartan are also imaginary. To cite closer, perhaps more telling, cases, the companion to whom Apollodorus narrates the symposium speeches is transparently fictitious, and there is no historical record of the Phoenix to whom Apollodorus refers.[3] Further, Diotima could hardly be the priestess of a female divinity whose Minoan cult has staunchly resisted father gods. Diotima's name means "Honor to Zeus," "Honor of Zeus," "Honored by Zeus," "Zeus Honor," or even "Zeus Honored," depending on which case

2. Andrea Nye, "The Hidden Host: Irigaray and Diotima at Plato's Symposium," 46, 53, 57, 45.

3. Nye's argument simply ignores the Seventh Letter and the latter part of the *Phaedrus*. Even if there were such a thing as Platonism, it would not follow that Diotima was real because she disagreed with it. Leo Strauss says that Phoenix is "a figure in Xenophon's *Symposium*" (*On Plato's "Symposium,"* 19). I cannot find him there.

of the word Ζεύς and which use of the root τιμ are intended. These would be rather odd names for a militant feminist sibyl.[4] Further, if we cheerfully and lovingly concede a point that the mists of history have obscured, that anonymous women deserve more credit than Plato for having founded Western civilization, it also remains unhappily true that we have no idea what a real Diotima said as she taught the feminine wisdom, if that differed from what Plato causes her to say in the *Symposium.* It would be a highly arbitrary and illegitimate procedure to attempt to distill Diotima's "actual" views out of their Platonic "distortions," much as Thomas Jefferson tried to extract a "genuine" historical Jesus from the Gospels.[5] If we stick to the available evidence, we can affirm only that Diotima is a possibly real individual whom Plato makes a character in his drama, and we must deal with her teaching as it appears in the text.

We can expand upon this modest conclusion by turning from Diotima's identity to her function in the *Symposium.* Here, it is necessary to make a distinction. Everyone knows that most of Plato's characters are real people whom he takes into his books. However, everyone should also know that the speeches that Plato assigns to his characters are fictitious. True, the orations probably represent Plato's perceptions of the actual opinions of the historical figures,[6] as argued above in the case of Aristophanes. Still, the words in the dialogues were not actually uttered as they stand; they are Plato's poetic creations, invented to suit his dramatic purposes. Hence, Stanley Rosen is right to declare that "the energy that has been expended in the effort to determine the historical existence of Diotima might have been better invested in reflection upon her dramatic significance."[7]

To grasp Diotima's dramatic import, we must first think a little more about her name. Socrates is confronted with metaphysical rebels who aim to overthrow the reign of Zeus and replace it with the rule of an Eros who is a mask of their despotic will. By choosing a person whose name combines "Zeus" and "Honor" as his teacher of erotic wisdom, Socrates indicates that it is only within the framework of piety, that is, of a humble acceptance of the given order of being, that the human race can profitably heed

---

4. Not only is it unclear whether "Diotima" intends the genitive, dative, or accusative forms of the word "Zeus," and unclear whether the root for the word "honor" is meant to be extended into various of its noun and verb forms, but the ambiguity might be intended to convey *all* of the possible meanings together. Thus, no feminist priestess would tolerate such a name. Nye has additional problems in this regard. The Pythia is a servant of Apollo. The women of Eleusis are servants of Demeter, the sister, incestuous lover, and subject of King Zeus.

5. This is the difficulty that I have not only with Nye, but also with Luce Irigaray, "Sorcerer Love: A Reading of Plato's *Symposium,* Diotima's Speech."

6. Not always, though. The myth attributed to Stesichorus in the *Phaedrus* is undoubtedly wholly above and beyond anything that the real poet invented.

7. Rosen, Plato's *"Symposium,"* lix.

its erotic inclinations. The name Diotima is a single word that symbolizes and advocates the opposite of everything for which Agathon and his allies stand. It is like a burr under the sophists' saddle. Whenever Socrates pronounces the name, he abrasively shows his *sympotai* which path they must renounce and which they must take to avoid disaster and be happy. If Diotima is a real person in Socrates' past, Plato is lucky that he can adapt her name to his purpose. If there is no historical Diotima, as I suspect, Plato would want to make Socrates invent her to achieve the desired effect.

Next, it is significant that Socrates calls Diotima a Mantinean (that is, a citizen of the city of Mantinea). The word "Mantinean" (Μαντινικῆς) closely resembles the word "prophetic" (μαντική). Thus, by saying that Diotima is Mantinean, Socrates almost suggests that she is a prophetess.[8] A few pages prior to that, Socrates asks Eryximachus: "Does it seem to you that I did not speak prophetically?" (198a4–6). With this, Socrates almost suggests that he himself is a prophet. Shortly after calling Diotima a Mantinean, Socrates declares that she obtained a ten-year postponement of the plague by advising the Athenians to offer sacrifices (201d3–5). It is hard to know what to make of Socrates' undemonstrated and entirely undemonstrable report, except that it comes as close as possible to saying that Diotima is a prophetess without actually saying so and indicates that Socrates has prophetic knowledge. Later, Socrates observes that it would require prophecy or divination (μαντείας, 206b9) to grasp one of Diotima's remarks. This virtually calls her a prophetess. We are prompted to inquire why Socrates should so guardedly work up to asserting that he and Diotima have prophetic powers.

I think that these cautious intimations are directly related to Socrates' pedagogical task and that the key to understanding them lies in the *Phaedrus*. I have argued that Socrates needs to educate Agathon by letting him declare his opinions, by acknowledging whatever is true in them, by granting provisionally whatever is false in them, and by baring the defects gradually, so that Agathon arrives piecemeal at new opinions that are improved but still inadequate, whereupon the process will be repeated indefinitely, lifting Agathon ever closer to the truth. As an equivalent to that, I could have maintained that Socrates must aim at progressive reforms of his student's soul. In the *Phaedrus* (248c9–e2), Socrates-Stesichorus ranks human souls according to merit. The hierarchy is as follows, in descending order: (1) a philosopher or a lover of beauty, or a musical and erotic individual; (2) a lawful king or warlike ruler; (3) a statesman, household manager, or financier; (4) a lover of gymnastic labor or a doctor for the body; (5) a prophet or celebrant of mysteries; (6) a poet or other mimetic artist; (7) a craftsman

---

8. Bloom points out that, in this grammatical form, the word Μαντινικῆς is identical with the word for the science of divination (*Love and Friendship*, 501).

or farmer; (8) a sophist or demagogue; and (9) a tyrant. Prophets rank just above poets. To improve Agathon's soul now would be to raise it from the poetic level to the next highest, the prophetic. Socrates and Diotima must therefore teach Agathon first by accepting and then by elevating his poetic opinions so that they rise up to the level of prophetic insight. They themselves must appear as poetic prophets whose teaching points to prophetic truths (compare Socrates' reason for speaking as a poet in the *Phaedrus,* 257a5–6). I say "*appear* as poetic prophets." If Diotima is an alter ego of Socrates, as I believe she is, she is certainly a philosopher who couches philosophic truths in prophetic terms or, alternatively, who takes the truest prophetic insights up into philosophy. For now, however, it is pedagogically useful for her to soft-pedal this fact, making philosophic arguments in prophetic forms that might attract Agathon and elevate his soul.

Socrates' pedagogical strategy requires him to set every opinion that Agathon loves for its poetic chutzpah in flight toward prophecy. Therefore, in his own name and in his Diotima persona, Socrates will review all these ideas systematically. From time to time, he will take up a pronouncement of Agathon's, or an assertion of one of the poet's allies, embracing each and then amending it, priming it for takeoff, as it were. When Socrates-Diotima is finished, she will have given all of the previous orators pointed replies with references to specific items in their arguments—a fact that guarantees that Diotima's speech is fictitious, for it would be too marvelous a coincidence that Plato should find in Socrates' library an old address by Diotima that prophetically foresees what five men will say years in the future and that answers them in detail. The need for Diotima's survey explains moves in her speech that puzzle and annoy many readers, probably because they have paid too little attention to the other speeches. For example, when Luce Irigaray complains that Socrates attributes incompatible positions to Diotima, one a monument to eternally free love and one slavishly teleological,[9] she misses the facts that Diotima is actually examining the previous arguments dialectically and that her jumps are not erratic initiatives, but methodical responses. It is not that Plato-Socrates is spoiling Diotima's insights. Rather, Socrates-Diotima is digging up sophistry's erotic fault lines.

Last but not least, it is dramatically significant that Diotima is a woman. The sophists' Titanism and misogyny have become increasingly virulent in tandem, the former entailing the latter. Agathon and his partners view the phallus as the symbol of their despotic will and wrongly perceive pederasty as the symbol of active human auto-salvation. They interpret the vagina as the token of a fulfillment that is base because it is endured passively. Except for the praise that Phaedrus accorded Alcestis, they have

---

9. Irigaray, "Sorcerer Love," 32. Incidentally, I do not agree with Irigaray's interpretations of the passages in question, but that is not relevant to my present point.

scorned everything feminine as mindless and subhuman. Socrates compels them to contemplate a woman's wisdom. He incessantly repeats that Diotima is wise, continuing to nettle them. Diotima's superior wisdom will teach them that in the affairs of the psyche, they must practice "feminine" receptivity to win their proper felicity. The receptivity is "feminine" in this sense: Biologically, women conceive new life by receiving seed. Spiritually, human beings cannot initiate the new life of their salvation, as the sophists desire, but must receive its quickening germs from without. It is ironic that Plato is savaged by feminists for his use of Diotima when his intention is that she should represent the spiritual analogue of biological feminine receptivity as the way to human perfection.[10]

Socrates and Agathon

Resuming now the action of the play where we left off, Socrates has been praising the introduction and peroration of Agathon's speech, but expressing great fear that he will not be able to compete against the beauty of the poet's words and that he will be turned to stone by the Gorgias head. He slides from these comments into a long repudiation of his obligation to participate in Phaedrus's round of encomiums on Eros. He laments that he was a fool to agree to Eryximachus's proposal and to call himself clever in erotic affairs, for he was ignorant of the manner in which encomiums should be made. He had imagined that one was supposed to tell the truth about the object of praise, picking out its most beautiful features and arranging them in the most comely manner. He had presumed that he would speak well, for he had supposed that he knew the truth. However, now it seems that beautiful praise is expected to ascribe all of the greatest and most beautiful things to the object, whether it has them or not, that is, whether the attributions are false or not. In other words, it seems that the *sympotai* were supposed to give apparent, rather than real, eulogies of Eros. The sophists relate every kind of "moving logoi" to Eros, applying them to his character and work to make him appear most beautiful and best. They convince individuals who are ignorant of Eros, but certainly not those who know him. Abrogating his contract because he was ignorant of its requirements, Socrates paraphrases an infamous saying of the protagonist in Euripides' play *Hippolytus*, pleading, "The tongue promised, but not the mind (or heart, φρὴν)" (199a5–6).[11] With that, he bids farewell to his obligation,

10. In other words, Diotima stands for the tale of Penia that she will tell. Cf. the analysis of Nussbaum, *Fragility of Goodness*, 177.

11. Cf. Euripides, *Hippolytus* 612. Socrates does not quote the line exactly, changing "swore" to "promised."

firmly declaring that he cannot be a eulogist in the sophists' sense. However, he offers to give Phaedrus a substitute for his unpaid rhetorical debt. Rather than rival the sophists' talks, thus making himself their laughing-stock, he would be happy to tell the truth about Eros. Phaedrus and the others give him permission to speak as he likes (198c–199b).

One can suppose that Socrates' disavowal of his obligation strikes the sophists as a sign of cowardice and weakness. One can also assume that his invocation of Hippolytus's devious rationalization for breaking an oath evokes their contempt. Athenians condemned Euripides for having put these words into Hippolytus's mouth, and Aristophanes will mock Euripides in the *Frogs* (1471) by making Dionysus quote them as his excuse for leaving Euripides in Hades. The sophists surely suspect that Socrates is ripe for the kill and judge that the sneaky coward deserves it. Moreover, they are unfazed by his accusation that they have lied and his pledge to tell the truth, for they do not believe in truth. This is why they readily agree to give Socrates latitude. Of course, Socrates knows what and what not to fear. He is far from beaten and has tricked his *sympotai,* drawing them onto terrain on which he can fight more easily.

Socrates' reaction to Agathon's speech requires us to confront a philosophic issue that we have been skirting for some time. Socrates' remark that Agathon's praises were beautiful and his denial that they were true oblige us to ask how there could be a beauty that is false, or how there could be a disjunction between beauty and truth. Later, Socrates induces Agathon to confess that he did not know what he was talking about, and Socrates consoles him with the reply that he nevertheless spoke beautifully (201b11–c1). This makes it seem that for Socrates, there is also a chasm between beauty and knowledge. However, could beauty really be inimical to or separable from truth and knowledge? Does this jibe with what Socrates says elsewhere?

In my opinion, we should not overreact to this unsettling puzzle, rushing to announce the discovery of gross metaphysical confusion in the *Symposium* and Plato's other dialogues. We should notice that so far, Socrates has said nothing about the relationships among beauty, truth, knowledge, and philosophy as they are in themselves, essentially. He has only reported how these relationships look when they are reflected in sophistical "moving logoi" (198e5). If beauty, truth, the highest human knowledge, and philosophy in themselves are always linked, as they might be, they can be disjoined in speech. Words that are comely because they usually refer to beautiful realities can be detached from those realities and falsely applied to things that are not beautiful. This is one of the manners in which logoi "move." When this happens, the words carry the beauty of their associations with the beautiful realities with them and attract human beings both to themselves and to the ugly things that they artificially beautify. It is the ability of moving logoi to deceive us about the degrees to which hideous things participate in beauty that is dangerous to philosophy. It is Agathon's capacity to take words with beautiful connotations and move them to ugly things that allows him to give speeches that are beautiful, false, and ignorant all at once. Agathon's power to conjure up apparent beauty by transferring the logoi frightens Socrates, so he flees from the Hades of spiritually petrifying lies.[12]

Socrates' comments on Agathon's speech also raise some ethical questions. It appears that Socrates was prepared to give what he took to be a real encomium, a speech that chose the most beautiful facts about Eros and arranged them in their fairest guise, meanwhile remaining silent about ugly facts. Thus, he was willing to deliver praises that disclosed part of the truth while passing over or even concealing another portion of it. Is Socrates in a position to accuse the sophists of lying when he was ready to be so dishonest himself? I think that this objection is too fastidious about eulogies. We all know that when we mean to speak well of someone, it is polite to refrain from mentioning the person's shortcomings, too. No one is duped. No one is exposed to the lie in the soul about fundamental realities. It is interesting to observe in this respect that when Socrates discovers the sophists' intentions to mislead people about Eros, he changes his original plan to give a real encomium. Diotima's speech reveals both beautiful and ugly truths about Eros (or approximations of truths that Agathon can reach). What, then, about Socrates' repudiation of his obligation? Is it not unethical to break promises? And what about his deception of his *sympotai* in order to secure his competitive advantage? Is that just? These are easy problems. We learn in the opening pages of the *Republic* that justice does not demand keeping promises when evil will result. We are also taught in that dialogue that some lies are noble, especially those that further education and the attainment of just aims in war.

Having obtained permission to proceed as he likes, Socrates immediately asks Phaedrus to condone what he had formerly forbidden, the dialectical questioning of Agathon. When he wins this right, too, he is elated, for he knows how to persuade one person, and Agathon is the beloved whom he hopes to convince. He will speak chiefly to Agathon and start by breaking his hard character. The leitmotif of the questioning has already been sounded. When Socrates remarked that the moving logoi persuade only the ignorant that Eros is beautiful and best, he was referring explicitly to

12. Rosen remarks: "It is by no means self-evident, as many readers of Plato have concluded, that beauty, truth, and goodness simply coincide at the highest stage of his teaching" (Plato's "Symposium," 224). I agree. Neither is it self-evident that they do not coincide, though. For now the question should be left open, and we should be prepared to distinguish the cases obtaining in different ontological realms if that is what Plato eventually does.

Agathon's thesis, indicating that it was nonsense that could impress no serious person. Now Socrates will vindicate that assessment, swiftly and brutally forcing Agathon to contradict himself.

Socrates approaches Agathon with an innocuous-looking question: Is the character of Eros such that he is eros for something or not? Digressing momentarily, Socrates says that he should not be understood as asking whether Eros is eros for a mother or father, which would be laughable.[13] What Socrates wishes to be told is whether Eros is the same kind of thing as a father, mother, brother, or sister. One could not be a parent or sibling without being a parent or sibling of somebody. Can Eros not be Eros without being eros for something?

We should ponder the ontological implications of this question. The words "father," "mother," "brother," and "sister" do not distinguish substantial beings; rather, they refer to relations of these beings. For example, the diverse substantial beings man, bull, stallion, and gander can all be called fathers, provided that they have sired offspring. When someone says "father," it is not clear who or what is a father until the speaker specifies the being that is contemplated. If Agathon answers that the term "Eros" functions like the words "father," "mother," and so on, he will mean that the term points less to a substantial being than to a relationship; it will not reveal, but hide, if not abolish, the being that is related. Then, Agathon can still avoid speaking of Eros as an essence; he will have to say only what sort of relation Eros is.

Socrates knows that Agathon will decide that Eros is eros for something. Previously, Agathon suggested that Ares was caught by "Eros for Aphrodite" (196d2), thus making Eros a relation as well as a congeries of qualities, and his speech prescinded from essences. Agathon now gives the expected reply. However, Socrates is not required to agree with him. He may perceive the possibility that Eros is a self-subsisting being (or an emanation of such a being) with an eternal essence that human words cannot apprehend. The presence of this being or its emanation in souls could be the ground of all experiences of desire. Such a presence might be perceived by many as nothing but a libidinous relatedness of their own to objects of desire. This would cause Agathon to gather that Eros must be eros for something. If Socrates induces Agathon to reason on the basis of this premise, what we get is not a Socratic dogma, but an example of Socrates

---

13. In a dubious excursus, Rosen argues that "those who wish to be gods, or *causa sui*, must come to terms with, or laugh at," fear of incest (*Plato's "Symposium*," 215). This implies that Socrates calls the question of incest laughable because he hopes to be a god. I disagree. I have shown above that one infers that Socrates hopes to be a god only by construing selected texts contentiously. I think that Socrates calls the suggestion of eros for parents laughable because it is out of the question philosophically, even if it is consistent with the sophists' principles. Cf. Bloom, *Love and Friendship,* 498.

provisionally granting Agathon's position to him in order to lead him to an impasse and, subsequently, to higher insight. The later leap is suggested when Diotima exhorts Socrates to rise above his eros for individual things to loving meditation on the whole "open sea" (πέλαγος, 210d4) of beauty.[14]

Socrates next asks whether Eros desires that for which he is eros. Without reflecting, Agathon answers yes. The alacrity of his reply is dictated by the facts that he regards Eros as a relation and needs to stipulate what type of relation Eros is. Given his experience of Eros, he hastily assumes that Eros is the relation of desire for the desired. However, now Eros is a congeries of qualities, a relation, and the act that generates the relation. Logoi are moving again. Once more, Socrates need not agree. In his eternal essence, Eros could be a substantial being who is neither quality nor relation nor act. Socrates is still setting Agathon up for a fall.

Now Socrates inquires whether Eros possesses that which he loves and wants before he loves and wants it. Agathon finally tumbles to the fact that trouble is coming and balks. He answers that Eros *probably* does not have what he desires prior to desiring it. Socrates refuses to tolerate this evasion. He insists that Agathon say whether Eros *necessarily* lacks the object of his desire, adding that this looks necessary to him. It seems to me that Agathon's premises force him to agree. Substantial beings can possess objects that they want. Qualities, relations, and the acts that establish them cannot do this. For example, if I want a child, I can have one, but beauty, fatherhood, erotic desiring, and begetting cannot have one. An Eros who is not a substantial being but a floating congeries of qualities, a relation, and an act can never possess what he desires. Suddenly, it is Agathon who seems ready for the coup de grâce. However, Socrates does not dispatch Agathon by resorting to the logic just outlined, although he has pointed to it clearly. Probably because Agathon is attached to what we now call deconstructionism, and also because Agathon would assail a logic of categories as contemptible quibbling, Socrates extends his inquiry further, hoping to bring about Agathon's surrender by other methods. Curiously, Socrates' final steps make for appalling reasoning.

Socrates' further explication of the position maintains that living beings cannot desire and have what they desire simultaneously. This seems counterintuitive. For example, I think that I love my wife, want her companionship, and delight in it at the same moment. However, Socrates denies this. He argues that beings never desire and have what they want at the same time, on the grounds that possession prevents or terminates desire. Rich,

---

14. Planinc, *Plato's Political Philosophy*, chap. 3, establishes the point that Socrates does not necessarily endorse the premises that he suggests to his interlocutors, because the assumptions are not really his, but are implicit in the positions of the interlocutors.

strong, healthy, and tall people could not aspire to be rich, strong, healthy, and tall because they have these goods already. If they say that they want what they already have, we must take them to mean that they want what they do not have yet, the future enjoyment of the objects of their desire (200a–c). So, rejoicing in the companionship of my wife right now, I cannot want it too, but must be said to long to possess it in time to come.

In response, I admit that some desires temporarily subside when they are gratified. If I am hungry and eat to satiation, I am not hungry anymore. I cannot be both full and hungry. However, it also seems to me that my love for my wife and my desire for her companionship initially impel me to her and then persist and hold me fast to her even as I enjoy my life with her. If I stopped loving her, I could not cherish her company when I had it. Similarly, if my love for my wealth, strength, health, and present height suddenly died, possessing them would become intolerable. Clearly, if all these desires subsided when they were satisfied, then, just as I push food away when I am full, I would certainly cast off my wife, renounce my riches, stop exercising, live unhealthfully, and cut off my legs, thus becoming solitary, poor, nasty, weak, sick, and short. Socrates is dead wrong: My abiding desire for that which gladdens my heart is what makes me cleave to it even as I possess it.[15] However, Agathon does not raise this objection. Why not?

Probably, there are multiple reasons. Agathon's refusal to attribute essence to Eros requires him to deny it to human beings, too. It would be hard for him to explain how people could possess anything. If this difficulty does not trouble the poet, he must also consider the implications of his belief that Eros is always young. If the life of Eros is an infinite succession of beginnings that keeps him ageless—a possibility similar to one that Diotima will suggest to Socrates not long hence (203e, 207d–208b)—every instance of desire and satisfaction would have to be temporally separate. We must also take Agathon's experience of eros into account. As a selfish *erōmenos*, Agathon does not feel eros for his suitors but lets them want him. He observes that their sexual urges visibly wane upon gratification. He also values Pausanias and other suitors chiefly for his effects on them,

---

15. Perhaps it would be helpful to suggest that desire usually resembles the phenomenon of secondary magnetism. Remove the primary magnet and the metals that it has magnetized fall apart. Cf. *Ion* 533d–e. By analogy, remove the "Heraclea stone" Eros and the lovers would fall apart. My thanks to Zdravko Planinc for reminding me of the *Ion* passages. Nussbaum mentions that Socrates' claims "about the logic of wanting and possessing" are "controversial" (*Fragility of Goodness*, 177). She deserves credit for noticing that there is a problem. Many commentators on Plato, especially those who stress his irony, swallow this particular piece of irony hook, line, and sinker, taking it for a dogma.

for the effects testify to his godhood. It may be that his craving for every particular affirmation of his divinity perishes in the having because false testimonials gratify egos only momentarily while still leaving real voids in human hearts. Thus, it seems likely that Agathon readily accepts Socrates' fallacies because they represent his own opinion. Again, it is doubtful that Socrates subscribes to what he postulates.

Socrates is now ready to finish Agathon off. He asks the poet whether he remembers having argued that the gods did their acts for love of beauty. Agathon admits this, whereupon Socrates answers that he spoke fittingly and adds that Eros must be eros only for beauty, not ugliness (201a). We already know that Socrates is granting another of Agathon's assumptions, and not announcing a doctrine in which he himself believes, for he soon makes Diotima deny that Eros is defined properly as eros for beauty (205c–206e). Socrates next supplies a premise to which Agathon previously agreed, that Eros loves what he lacks. The conclusion seems to follow irresistibly: Eros cannot be beautiful (201b). However, the reasoning is equivocal. Starting with the proposition that Eros must desire a beauty that he lacks, namely, an external beauty such as a lover might find in a beloved, Socrates infers that Eros cannot possess a beauty of his own, as if a man who desired a beautiful beloved could not be good-looking himself.

One wonders how Socrates could propose, or how Agathon could accept, this inanity. Martha Nussbaum, who does a fine job of formalizing the logic and exposing the fallacy, suggests that the argument can be saved by assuming that beauty is one and uniform, so that you lack all beauty if you lack any.[16] This is helpful, but I doubt that Socrates is serious. In the *Phaedrus*, Eros is divine (242e2). The divine is beauty (246d8–e1), so Eros is beautiful. Socrates defines eros as desire in his first speech (237d2). He allows this teaching to stand in his second speech, although he makes eros yearning rather than desire (251c7). The desire or yearning of eros is for the beauty of the beloved (251c–252b). Thus, within the matrix of the equivocations in the *Symposium*, the Socrates of the *Phaedrus* contradicts the propositions that beings cannot want what they have and that the beautiful cannot desire beauty, proving that the Socrates of the *Symposium* is playing sophistical logical games.[17] Agathon falls for these tricks, confessing that

---

16. Nussbaum, *Fragility of Goodness*, 177–79. I would put it differently. Socrates' actual opinion seems to be that we all lack real beauty. However, it is too early in the argument to expect Agathon to have any inkling of this truth, and just now Socrates is relying on the poet's own logic to obtain his agreement to conclusions.

17. One could argue that the fact that Socrates only pretends to refute Agathon's thesis means that he secretly adheres to it. However, this would miss the points that Socrates is not interested in doctrines for their own sakes and that it serves Socrates' pedagogical purpose to let Agathon's position destroy itself on its own basis. If leaving Agathon's fallacies in the argument helps to persuade him that he is not wise, thus

he spoke in complete ignorance of his topic. Why? I think that Socrates has trapped him in his own perspectives again. In Agathon's experience of eros, none of his many suitors have his beauty: eros is invariably an affair in which lovers desire what they lack. The poet fails to see through the fallacy because it appeals to his narcissism. It is vanity that causes Agathon's humiliation.

His battle being won, Socrates mops up with one last syllogism. Agathon thinks that good things are beautiful. If Eros is not beautiful, he cannot be good, either. Nothing is left of Agathon's argument. Agathon laments that he cannot contradict Socrates, who replies that it is easy to contradict Socrates, but not truth. This is funny. Agathon could have contradicted Socrates easily with the truth. He has fallen victim not to truth, but to his own sophisms.

DIOTIMA

Socrates now introduces his mentor Diotima, proclaims her wise in erotics and many other matters, and says that he learned erotics from her. He promises to relate her teaching to the group. He declares that he will transmit it in the question-answer form that Diotima used. He also commits himself to Agathon's procedure (201d8–e2). First he will analyze what "sort" of thing Eros is and next describe the works of Eros. Apparently, he will not analyze Eros as a substantial being but as qualities or a relation or an act. This furthers the policy of granting Agathon's assumptions. The question of method being settled, Socrates reports that he once shared Agathon's beliefs about Eros and that Diotima refuted him just as he has now refuted Agathon. This autobiographical story might be set in the time when the young Socrates was seeking the causes of the generation, decay, and existence of all things in the *pathē* of heaven and earth. This would hint at a necessary connection between the limitations of a physics of cosmic phenomena, whether that of the young Socrates or that of the sophists, and the habit of considering Eros in an ignorant, Titanic manner. However, Socrates' meeting with Diotima could have also occurred after his turn to the human things. Plato does not really indicate when it happened. Whatever the case, we wish to learn what Diotima has to say about erotics.

Diotima's primary task is to cure Agathon of Titanism. Socrates has already begun the treatment with his mock refutation of the argument that Eros is beautiful and good. The fake rebuttal challenges Agathon's wisdom,

---

achieving the only intended result of the exercise, this would be both eminently fair and practical. Thus, the therapy administered to Agathon implies nothing at all about esoteric Socratic teachings.

the characteristic of his godhood for which he is most eager to be lionized. Now, Socrates causes Diotima to launch a frontal assault on Agathon's appropriation of divine status by consigning his alter ego, Eros, to an "in-between" (μεταξὺ) mode of reality.[18]

Inside the Diotima story, Socrates reacts to the refutation of his and Agathon's opinion that Eros is beautiful and good by presuming that the god's only alternative is to be ugly and evil. Socrates draws this conclusion because he realizes that it is the only one that Agathon's Titanic narcissism will allow him to imagine; again, he is stating and granting Agathon's view provisionally so that he can deal with the problems underlying the opinion. Speech about the "in-between" is the required therapy, so Diotima asks Socrates whether "not wise" is the same as "ignorant," or whether there is not something "between" wisdom or knowledge or prudence, on the one hand, and ignorance on the other, that is, right opinion. Trusting that Agathon will accept common sense, Socrates recognizes this mean. Implicitly arguing by analogy, Diotima then commands Socrates not to compel whatever is not beautiful and good to be ugly and evil. As he listens to the tale, Agathon is supposed to infer that Eros possesses qualities between the beautiful and the ugly and between good and evil. However, Diotima's analogy does not show that there is something between beautiful and ugly, or between good and evil. It only suggests the possibility of such middling qualities. Socrates fails to notice this and rushes ahead to his next question. One wonders momentarily whether he and Diotima should be criticized as careless thinkers.[19]

The previous course of the conversation points to a better explanation of the omission: Diotima and Socrates can safely shirk their logical obligation because they know that Agathon will not catch the oversight. Agathon's original proposition was that of all the gods who are happy, Eros is the happiest because he is the most beautiful and best (most virtuous). Because Agathon has gone to great lengths to identify himself with Eros, this statement symbolizes his will to be the supreme deity himself. The implied agreement of Diotima and Socrates that the qualities of Eros lie between beauty and ugliness and good and evil negates the god's primacy. Instead of being the happiest god because he is the most beautiful and best, Eros must now be a less happy god of mediocre qualities, or maybe no god at all, depending on whether Agathon thinks that superior felicity, beauty,

---

18. Voegelin was the first to notice the theoretical significance of this "in-between" mode of reality, or *metaxy* (a word that has mystified many of Voegelin's less enthusiastic readers, but one that is merely the Greek preposition "between" elevated into a symbol or an index for an experienced mode or dimension of being). See *Anamnesis*, 266–67, 278; *Anamnesis*, 129 ff.

19. Bloom thinks that Socrates has fallen into a profound confusion (*Love and Friendship*, 503).

and virtue are indispensable attributes of divinity. This demotion of Eros denies Agathon's divine supremacy. Diotima and Socrates have purposely stung Agathon, simultaneously focusing his attention on his pain and diverting it from their logical transgressions. Thus, when Socrates hurries to ask Diotima: "What about the universal agreement that Eros is a great god?" (202b6–7), he gives voice to Agathon's immediate concern and great personal anguish.

Diotima mercilessly laughs at the worried claim that everybody believes that Eros is a great god. She sets out to prove that Socrates (that is, Agathon himself) does not believe that Eros is a god at all. She asks whether Socrates would say that not all gods are happy and beautiful.[20] Socrates replies: "Not I, by Zeus!" This might go beyond Agathon's position, but the poet would at least contend that a *great* god must be happy and beautiful, so Socrates is still answering more or less faithfully for his beloved. However, now Diotima reminds Socrates (that is, Agathon) that he equated happiness with the possession of good and beautiful things, and, further, that he confessed that Eros desires and, therefore, lacks them. Eros cannot be a god.[21] Of course, the implication is that Agathon cannot be a god either, not even a deity of minor rank. What, then, asks Socrates on behalf of the reeling Agathon, is Eros? A mortal? Diotima responds by extending her earlier postulate of the existence of "in-between" qualities into an affirmation of the reality of "in-between" ontological states. Eros is something "between" the mortal and the immortal. Socrates inquires what that is. "A great daimon," answers Diotima, "for the whole of the daimonic is between the divine and the mortal" (202d13–e1). It would appear that, here, Diotima departs from Agathon's basic premise, for she applies a noun to Eros, thus implying that he has an essence and that he is a substantial being.[22] However, as argued in the previous chapter, Diotima does not tell Socrates what a daimon is. She uses the term not to disclose the content or structure of an essence or a substantial being, but as an index of Eros's metaphysical status. A daimon ranks below a god, having a middling place in reality.

20. Here, Rosen tries to make esoteric hay out of "Diotima's striking failure to mention wisdom or truth as a possession necessary for happiness" (*Plato's "Symposium,"* 228). However, the failure is not so striking. Socrates-Diotima has just demolished Agathon's wisdom, so he-she can be expected to play that down for a moment. Although Eros has also been shown to lack beauty and goodness, Agathon still thinks that he himself is happy and beautiful, so he might hold out hope that he qualifies for divine supremacy on these grounds.

21. Because Diotima's dedivinization of Eros relies on the fallacies analyzed above, such that we have here no real proof that Eros is not a god, Socrates can contend that Eros is a god in the *Phaedrus* without contradicting what he says in the *Symposium.* This implies that the diverse accounts of Eros in the two dialogues do not necessarily have to be interpreted as esoteric signals.

22. This seems to be the opinion of Bloom, *Love and Friendship,* 503.

Incidentally, we are not informed how Diotima knows of this in-between dimension of being.

Socrates next asks what "power" the whole of the daimonic has. Some commentators have thought this a strange question. However, the query makes perfect sense when we recall that Socrates is still speaking for Agathon. The poet's dreams have just been dashed to pieces. Now he fears that he has nothing. "Having what power" is his question. It means: "How can a daimon with mediocre qualities and a middling rank be 'great'? What capacity would I have to promote myself if I were an Eros like that?"

Diotima replies that the daimonic has the power to interpret and convey human things to the gods and divine things to human beings. Through the daimonic, petitions and sacrifices go up to the gods and ordinances and recompense for sacrifices go down to the human beings. Placed in the middle of divine and human, the daimonic is filled with both and binds together the whole to itself. Through it are conveyed all prophecy and the *technē* of priests regarding sacrifices and initiation into mysteries and all divination and sorcery. "God does not mingle with the human, but through it [the daimonic] all dealing and converse between gods and men occurs whether waking or sleeping" (203a1–2). Whoever is wise about this is a "daimonic man" (δαιμόνιος ἀνήρ, *daimonios anēr*, 203a5). To be wise in other things, such as the *technai* and crafts, is to be a *banausos* (a vulgar, illiberal tradesman—thus, a person of contemptible social status). There are many diverse *daimones*, and Eros is one of them.[23]

To appreciate Diotima's answer, we must exercise our historical imaginations. Assume that a survey researcher asked all of the ancient Greek prophets and prophetesses what power they had. To me, it seems certain that every last one would claim the power to interpret and convey human things to the gods and divine things to human beings. All would maintain that pleas and sacrifices go up to the gods and that ordinances and payment for sacrifices go down to the human beings through them. (This is exactly what transpired when Diotima arranged for the ten-year postponement of the plague.) All would assert that their class has a monopoly on prophecy, priestcraft, divination, and sorcery. All would swear that there is no mixing of gods and human beings except through the mediation of qualified specialists, namely, themselves, the prophets and prophetesses. All would declare that prophetic wisdom alone is worthwhile and that all other wisdom is merely vulgar. Thus, just as Eryximachus praised his *technē* and

---

23. These lines in the *Symposium* inspired Saint Augustine to break with Plato over the issue of whether daimonic intermediaries between God and man are necessary (*City of God*, 8.18). Augustine evidently was not terribly sensitive to the uses of myth. However, with a major adjustment of ontological rank, the image of an intermediary who is filled up with both the divine and the mortal reappears in his own thought.

made Eros a physician, and just as Agathon extolled his art and made Eros a poet, so Diotima has celebrated her *technē* and made Eros a prophet.

We must also notice something curious. Diotima has implicitly described herself as a *daimonios anēr*. Hence, she has presented herself not only as a woman who has risen further than Agathon toward the same rank as Eros but, more remarkably, as a daimonic male.[24] This means that Diotima is a spiritual androgyne. She has a "male" aspect of her soul that generates an activism appropriate to human beings in the pursuit of their felicity (we are all responsible for pursuing our perfection and happiness actively) and a "female" element of her psyche that sustains her receptivity to salvation from the external source of our felicity. Her androgyny mirrors that of her alter ego, Socrates, who is both himself and Diotima.

Diotima's praise of prophecy would not startle Aristophanes, Agathon, or their fellows, or strike an average Athenian as unusual. It would all look like familiar religiosity. If some, such as the sophists, were skeptical of the prophets' claims, many Greeks would believe them.[25] Certainly, the rhetoricians Phaedrus and Pausanias, the doctor Eryximachus, and the poets Aristophanes and Agathon would be irritated by Diotima's insulting dismissal of their *technai* as vulgar. However, given their common exertions to deify themselves, they would notice no exceptional hybris in her self-portrait as a *daimonios anēr*. If anything, they would be disdainful of her self-restraint in claiming something less than divinity, or even something less than the middling status of the daimon, for a *daimonios anēr* seems to be slightly below a daimon, even if above an ordinary man. Indeed, in the context, it is not hybris that Diotima is advocating, but piety. She is teaching that, god not mingling with human, the noblest rank to which mortals can aspire is that of the *daimonios anēr*. The sophists should be happy with it if they can get it, renouncing their quest to be gods. To persuade the sophists of their need for the recommended humility, Diotima will have to dispel their skepticism about prophecy and continue working to dissolve their hybris. Ironically, to convince students of philosophy of their need for the suggested humility, Diotima might have to dispel their

---

24. This might not have been as shocking to a Greek as it is to us. Many Greeks would have assumed that Diotima was making herself not literally a male, but a woman who deserved the status of an *anēr*. The Pythia, for example, undoubtedly had social status equal to or greater than that of a male citizen-warrior. Further, the ancient mind was open to the possibility of transmigration of essences or characteristic traits, such that maleness could be the fundamental core of a female and so on. We have already seen this in Pausanias's view of the Uranian Aphrodite as male.

25. Thus, I fear that I cannot agree with Voegelin, *Anamnesis*, 266–67, 278, 129 ff, when he argues that the *daimonios anēr* is a new type who emerges in the field of history with the advent of philosophy. Much that Voegelin says about this character is important and true, but the type seems to have already been on the scene with prophecy, before philosophy.

skepticism about prophecy and strive to dissolve their hybris, too. The students of philosophy will probably be disappointed that Diotima has foisted something as questionable as prophecy on Socrates and Agathon. However, prophecy, whatever its shortcomings, possesses a degree of truth that would-be philosophers must discern before they can rise to their highest goal.[26] For the Socrates and the Agathon who are being taught by Diotima, attaining to this truth is their next necessary step.

If we wonder what the prophetic truth is, we may consider the likelihood that, insofar as it can be spoken, a portion of it has already been revealed to us, namely, that there is such a thing as a *daimonios anēr*, a man who has some daimonic qualities. Inasmuch as the whole of the daimonic is in the in-between, this man's soul must behold the close but unmixed meeting of the divine and the mortal. Thus, he knows the in-between because he is aware of his own condition, by virtue of experiencing it. This explains why Diotima's question-answer session with Socrates has veered from the logical examination of propositions into the symbolization of a mystery.

This means that if Diotima wishes to bring Agathon to see the truth of prophecy, she will not be able to do it with empirical or logical demonstrations. Rather, she must continue trying to cure Agathon's Titanism in order to open him to daimonic experience. Therefore, Socrates raises no objections to Diotima's accounts of the powers of prophecy and the wisdom of the *daimonios anēr* but hastens to ask another question about Eros that apparently changes the subject: "Who are his father and mother?" He moves to this topic because all the sophists have used theogony as a means to self-deification. Phaedrus appealed to the myth of an Eros who enjoyed genesis without generation. He hoped to appropriate divine reality mimetically by arranging for his own genesis without generation. Pausanias changed the story of the birth of Eros, making the god the scion of a purely Uranian line. This permitted Pausanias to strive for mimetic self-deification through the formation of souls. Eryximachus implicitly accepted Phaedrus's theogony because it made for gods and a cosmos entirely composed of Earth, such that the Asclepiad physician could rule them with the medical *technē*, thus becoming a god of gods. Aristophanes had Eros being generated entirely out of human raw material through the mistake of Zeus and achieving divinity for mortal lovers when the Olympian king could not get rid of him. Agathon was completely silent about traditional mythical theogonies because he invented his own, in which he had generated himself as Eros through his mimetic poetry. With the putative grounds of his god-

---

26. In the myth of Stesichorus in the *Phaedrus*, every human soul, even that of the tyrant, has seen some truth in the upper world before falling to earth. Prophets might not remember the truth that they saw, but philosophers must know the prophets' portion of truth in order to be philosophers.

hood being progressively destroyed, Agathon might still be hoping that his theogony will save his erotic divinity and, hence, his enterprise.

Diotima answers Socrates with another myth of the birth of Eros: When Aphrodite was born, the gods, including Poros (a Way, Contrivance, or Resource), son of Mētis (Craft, Skill, or Cunning), were feasting. When they had dined, Penia (Poverty) came begging at the door. Poros became drunk with nectar, for as yet there was no wine. He went out to sleep in the garden of Zeus. Penia, because she was without resource, contrived to lie with Poros and conceived Eros. Because Eros was begotten on Aphrodite's birthday, he serves and waits on her. Furthermore, Eros by nature is an *erastēs* (φύσει ἐραστὴς) of the beautiful, Aphrodite being beautiful. As the son of Poros and Penia, Eros is subject to this fate: He is always poor and extremely lacking in the softness and beauty that the many suppose him to have. Indeed, he is hard, dried up, shoeless, and homeless. He sleeps uncovered on the ground, in doorways, and in roads. Having his mother's nature (φύσιν), he always dwells with need. Owing to his father, he plots against the beautiful and the good. He is brave, bold, intense, a clever hunter, always weaving artifices, desirous and resourceful of prudence, philosophizing throughout his whole life, a clever sorcerer, a poisoner, and a sophist. By birth (πέφυκεν) he is neither immortal nor mortal, but on the same day he will bloom and live, prospering, and then will die, only to be resurrected by his father's nature (φύσιν), his resources always flowing out, so that he is never either resourceless or wealthy. He is in the middle of wisdom and ignorance, for gods do not philosophize or desire to become wise, being wise already. Neither the wise nor the ignorant philosophize or desire to become wise. The ignorant are self-satisfied, do not realize that they suffer their defect, and accordingly desire no remedy (203a–204a). Diotima's myth has at least the following lines of poetic-prophetic significance.

(1) The myth is great poetry. The poets Agathon and Aristophanes and their sophist allies who have mined poetic stories for their self-deifying theogonies will feel attracted to Diotima, or less menaced by her, because her poem is delightfully beautiful and charming and because she works in a plastic medium that they believe to be totally subject to the poet's will.

(2) As a poetic prophetess, Diotima will not insist on the literal truth of her tale. She means it as a mythical symbolization of divine-human realities. At the same time, she will not admit that it stands merely for her subjective desires. She intends to draw Agathon away from willfulness and toward truth. She speaks not as she wills, but as she must.

(3) With Socrates' *sympotai* waiting eagerly to see which of their theogonies has snared him, thus compelling him to affirm the assumptions of one of their schemes of self-deification, Diotima snatches him from their grasp by spinning a yarn about the birth of Eros that is not a theogony at all,

Eros being a demigod. Further, she signals that once the mythical reality of theogony has been posited, prophecy must remain silent about the manner in which theogony operates because knowledge of the process is not given in the in-between. We cannot say that gods come to be by means of a divine aphrodisia or erotic intercourse, for the gods are already there before the births of Aphrodite and Eros. We do not hear that Aphrodite was generated by copulation, either, only that Eros was. Neither may we accept esoteric intimations that the tale agrees with Agathon about the generation of gods by poets. As we shall see in a moment, the story is set in a time before there are human beings. Indeed, we would do well to analyze the myth as an anthropogeny, for Eros will soon appear to be the principle of the human soul. Here, we might speculate that the generation of Eros and his human instantiations does have something aphrodisiacal about it, for Aphrodite is present at the conception of Eros, and Poros lies with Penia. However, this generation is not erotic. A nonexistent Eros could not drive his own generation.

(4) Diotima answers Phaedrus, Pausanias, and Eryximachus. Through her silence, she declares Chaos, Gaia, and Uranus irrelevant to knowledge of Eros; rejects the cosmologies and theogonies based on the pseudosciences of Hippias and Prodicus; and informs the first three speakers that their theogonies merit no comment. She also advises Eryximachus that Eros is a natural unity of opposites that exists without internal warfare thanks to a divine resource and, hence, without the intervention of a quasi-magical Asclepiad medicine.

(5) Diotima pays special attention to Aristophanes. Her invention of Poros and Mētis by hypostatizing nouns (Resource and Craft) recalls Aristophanes' practice of creating gods in the same manner (Wealth and Peace). Her remark that the gods were feasting and, in at least one case, becoming intoxicated by nectar reminds us of Aristophanes' opinion of the habits of the gods. However, it does not constitute a Socratic statement about flaws of the Olympians. Nectar is not alcohol. It makes gods immortal, and we must inquire what it means to become intoxicated by that. Also, Socrates insists vehemently in the *Republic* (389d–391e) that neither gods nor demigods should be seen as intemperate in drink, sex, and eating. By adopting but changing Aristophanes' technique and teaching, Diotima begins to answer him. What is she saying, though? I think that we can ascertain this with a little comparative mythology.

First, in Aristophanes' story, all the Olympians are present. Zeus and Apollo are featured. They are forced to use all their wit (or, let us say, all their craft, skill, or cunning) to hit upon a means (or, let us maintain, a way, contrivance, or resource) for putting down a rebellion. In Diotima's tale, all the Olympians are there again, but not in leading roles. The inferior deity Mētis (divine Craft, Skill, or Cunning) is mentioned prominently, but he plays no part in the drama. The non-Olympian Poros (a divine Way, Contrivance, or Resource) becomes nearly comatose by imbibing the essence of that which makes him a god. In this state, he performs the only divine act that directly affects the outcome of the fable, thus effortlessly improving the situation of a mendicant.

Second, in Aristophanes' talk, there are round creatures who represent the human Ur-nature. They have the shapes of cartoon caricatures of male sex organs. They proudly storm the gates of heaven and are punished for their uprising. In Diotima's story, we meet Penia, begging at the door of Zeus's palace. Who and what is she? The mythical datum that the mating of Poros and Penia spawns a cross between god and mortal implies that Penia is the primordial human nature. This nature is feminine, poor, and humble. In Aristotelian terms, it is a potency with only one characteristic act, a needy begging. However, its very lack of resources drives it into a "masculine" activism in the inventive pursuit of salvation through impregnation by the god, to which its "femininity" is receptive. It is rewarded for its efforts.

Third, in Aristophanes' poem, Eros results from Zeus's deliberate splitting of the primordial humans, and he is the accidental deification of a human drive. In Diotima's myth, Eros is the product of a minor god's unintentional coupling with the primordial human potency. Eros is neither entirely divine nor completely mortal.

This should suffice to clarify the thrust of Diotima's reply to the comic poet: It is not true that in the mythical Ur-time, the Olympians could have been hard-pressed to stamp out an insurrection by a first human nature that was full of its own hybris. It is even less true that the existence of Eros demonstrates the incompetence of divine skill and, consequently, that it deifies men. Rather, the Olympians were scarcely aware, or wholly unaware, of a primordial humanity that had to beg for divine charity because it was absolute poverty. The existence of Eros is the result of a godly act in which divine craft and consciousness were not even needed, that is, the reflexive, generative outflow of divine capacity into the near emptiness that mankind originally was. Eros is not human godhood but something daimonic in our soul between god and mortal. Human nature perfects itself not by perverting pederasty into auto-salvation but by means of a "masculine" activism that cleverly seeks a "feminine" reception of seed from the god. Human individuals perfect themselves not by making pederasty a self-deifying adoration of an Eros who resists Zeus but through acceptance of the daimonic life that is nascent within them, thanks to the gift of divine Poros. They can approach this act of "feminine" receptivity only by making decent progress in a "masculine" quest for help with their condition. Thus, in both its universal and individual modes of existence, the role of human nature in its salvation is androgynous.

(6) By singing of a god, Poros, who fertilizes the original human nature, Penia, Diotima holds that the seed of Divine Resource inseminates the womb of resourceful resourcelessness, or potency, in every instance of the nature. Eros becomes a simultaneously divine and mortal "fetus" that matures in each human body-soul womb until it is born into man's erotic actions, which are both material and spiritual manifestations or incarnations of the daimon's powerful presence. Hence, Diotima's tale replies to Agathon as well as Aristophanes. Agathon is right to believe that Eros is the presence of something divine in a human being. However, it is not true that this supernatural something is a self-deifying and, thus, divine, human poetic *technē*. Rather, it is a seed of Divine Resource that is twice removed from Divine Practical Wisdom. Thus, it is not true that the divine something is caused by the self-creative will of the mortal. Rather, it flows from the god into the individual human nature that needs support. Finally, it is not true that only a physically beautiful *erōmenos* who happens to be a popular poet carries the divine seed. This blessing belongs to every person. A mortal's erotic excellence evidently depends on how the daimonic fetus fares in his or her body-soul womb.

(7) Diotima's fiction thus totally repudiates Titanism, denying not only that Agathon can be a god, but that he is able to revise the order of being that is known to the *daimonios anēr* through the prophetic soul's experience of itself. However, Diotima also qualifies that denial with a new vision of the "in-between," the spiritual reality that Eric Voegelin calls the *metaxy* (transliterating the Greek word for "between," μεταξὺ). Diotima argues that god and man do not mix. She is serious about that. However, the *metaxy* is the principle of the human soul, the whole of the *daimonios anēr*'s conscious experience of the core of his or her being. In this reality, "god" and "man" are both unmingled and mingled poles in a natural continuum. They cannot be either simply identified or simply hypostatized as two separate entities. "God" is still not "man," and "man" is still not "god," but the two blend into one another, in a manner analogous to that in which the characteristics of human fathers and mothers blend indistinguishably into their children, making it impossible to tell where "god" leaves off and "man" begins. It seems that two things are true simultaneously: Man is not and cannot be god, as Titanic souls would have it. However, divine and human realities pervade each other. In this sense, every human being is divine in principle. We all need to become aware of that to lead divine lives.[27]

---

27. Again, see Voegelin, *Anamnesis*, 266–67, 278; *Anamnesis*, 129 ff, and virtually all of Voegelin's mature works after *Anamnesis*. For a decent secondary account of Voegelin's understanding of the *metaxy* in the context of the *Symposium*, see M. W. Sinnett, "Eric Voegelin and the Essence of the Problem: The Question of Divine-Human Attunement in Plato's *Symposium*," 410–39. Generally appreciating Sinnett's summary, I dis-

(8) Diotima tersely supplies some symbolic information about the conditions necessary for the proper development of Eros in the human body-soul womb. The mythical details that Eros was conceived on Aphrodite's birthday, that Poros was drunk with nectar, that wine did not exist yet, that Dionysus therefore had no decisive role in the generation of Eros, and that Eros attends Aphrodite prove the following: The begetting and nurture of Eros are functions of the presence of Aphrodite, the imbibing of nectar (the mysterious drink that immortalizes and intoxicates gods), and service to the goddess. They have no necessary relationship to the presence of Dionysus, wine, alcohol-induced inebriation, and service to Dionysus. This means that Eros flourishes in the context of a divine madness inspired by beauty and superabundant immortalizing substance, not in that of an alcoholic fog. Aristophanes and Agathon are hard-drinking servants of Dionysus. Eros will not mature properly in their body-soul wombs.

(9) We can now think a little about erotic excellence. This virtue is clearly a product of intoxication by nectar. It is not the eminence in wine drinking that wards off drunkenness for an unusually long time while still ultimately yielding to the power of the grape. It does not need Dionysian orgies. We now see how Socrates could be subject to erotic mania, represent the pinnacle of erotic excellence, be the best drinker of wine insofar as he can hold out against Bacchic drunkenness forever, yet be indifferent to alcohol. A philosopher who is seized most completely by erotic madness has been touched more potently by Aphrodite and has drunk more nectar than his fellows. The goddess and the immortalizing drink of the gods are too powerful to allow Dionysus and wine to have their usual effects. The lovers who fail to attain to erotic excellence have known too little of Aphrodite and have drunk too little nectar. Their capacities for holding alcohol correspond, but only roughly, to their shares in the more divine madness that the Dionysian variety poorly mimics.

(10) This concludes the initial ascent from poetry to prophecy in Diotima's teaching of Agathon. However, the tragedian might not be ready to surrender yet. He might think that although he cannot be a god, he can still behave like one, in the sense that he has the power to do whatever he pleases (see *Republic* 359b–360c). After all, Agathon is riding high on the wave of his current popularity. If he cannot compete with Socratic wisdom in metaphysical eristic, he might still believe that he enjoys a superior political wisdom, that is, a greater tactical guile.[28] Thus, having pulled

---

agree with his argument that Voegelin's philosophy has no place for Christian grace. Voegelin's theory of the *metaxy* is the Platonic equivalent of the symbol of grace. Cf. Meister Eckehart, *Deutsche Predigten und Traktate*, predigt 57, *Dum Medium Silentium*, 415–24; and *Sermons and Treatises*, vol. 1, sermon 1.

28. When Socrates defeated Agathon by "demonstrating" that Eros could not be beautiful or most virtuous if his characteristic act was desire, it was inevitable that

Agathon through an ontological-ethical ascent from poetry to prophecy, Diotima must drag him through another utilitarian-ethical ascent. This accounts for the next turn of her story.

(11) Again defining "nature" (φύσις) as Agathon does, Diotima analyzes the nature of Eros as a set of qualities and typical acts. As mentioned above, she says that Eros by nature is an *erastēs* of the beautiful. (Calling Love a lover by nature repairs Agathon's earlier absurdity, in which Love was a hater by nature.) Then she gives Eros the traits related previously. It is said frequently that Diotima thereby identifies Eros with Socrates, an erotic, poor, hard, ugly, shriveled, normally shoeless, courageous, bold, intense, clever, and prudent philosopher who plays sophistical tricks and drugs minds to win the beautiful and the good. It is true that her Eros is like Socrates in these ways. However, we hear nothing of a homeless Socrates sleeping in fields or doorways. We know from the *Phaedrus* that Socrates would be ashamed to be a lover who, like the "nonlover" in that work, or like Pausanias, plots to exploit the beautiful and the good. We know from the *Republic* that his gods eschew vicious sorcery and harmful acts. In light of the *Phaedrus,* the *Sophist,* and the *Republic* (especially 496a), we know that there is no such thing as a "philosophic sophist." Hence, I suggest a revision of the usual thesis.

I think that Diotima intends to identify Eros with the Socrates who has been Odysseus in Hades in this dialogue. This Eros-Socrates-Odysseus is provisionally endowed with both the inspiring and the unsavory attributes of Homer's hero.[29] Socrates-Odysseus is homeless as represented in the *Phaedrus,* as a broken-winged soul sunk from its eternal abode. If the sense in which Eros plots against his prey is left vague, Eros-Socrates-Odysseus can seem as crafty as Homer's Odysseus, especially if we define the "wisdom" that Odysseus displays as tactical shrewdness, as Socrates' *sympotai* do. Thus, Eros could be a philosopher and a sophist under a sophist's definition of a philosopher. Next, equating Eros with the Homeric Odysseus lets him become a composite character who absorbs not only the Socrates who craftily charms and drugs people, but also the selfish Phaedrus, the cunning Pausanias who pursues his quarry by sleeping in doorways, the Eryximachus who aspires to be a life-restoring sorcerer and who could be an able poisoner, the Aristophanes who thinks that he can outwit gods, and the rhetorically slippery Agathon who uses word-magic to deify himself. This flatters the sophists, conceding their wisdom and granting their ethical

---

Agathon would try to regain the upper hand in his lawsuit by redefining wisdom, thus shifting the grounds of his argument like Thrasymachus in the *Republic.* Therefore, although wisdom was omitted in an earlier list of qualities necessary to happiness, Diotima will bring it back in the guise of the prudence of Eros. This prudence will be one of the qualities indispensable to Eros's pursuit of happiness.

29. Again, this analysis is indebted to Planinc, *Plato's Political Philosophy.*

assumptions provisionally, giving Diotima an excuse to show where they really lead.

(12) Diotima needs to establish two things before she can subvert Agathon's belief that he is wise enough to be a divine, politically savvy Odysseus. The first refers back to the poet's assertion that Eros is eternally young. Diotima now finds it convenient to raise the question of how this could be so in a reality that is wholly immersed in time, as the sophists suppose. She answers that Eros enjoys an infinite succession of new beginnings that keep him youthful. Being neither immortal nor mortal, he exists and prospers with his resources always flowing out, dies, rises from the dead, and repeats the cycle. Socrates-Agathon accepts this explanation of Eros's youth because it is the only one compatible with Agathon's cosmology and because it matches the poet's experience of sexual eros. (For those who do not get the joke, Diotima is depicting the life of Eros as an allegory on what happens to the phallus as it becomes aroused; "prospers" in intercourse; ejaculates, its resources always flowing out; collapses in a kind of death; and then is restored to its capacity to become aroused again—this being a witticism for Agathon's benefit.) Diotima will bank this result for future use.

(13) We must recall the agreement that to want beauty and virtue is to lack them. Eros cannot be supremely wise. Diotima reminds Agathon that the daimon's virtues are middling. Thus, Eros stands between wisdom and ignorance. This having been reiterated, Diotima baits Agathon by declaring that gods, being wise, do not philosophize.[30] Neither do ignorant men. Only men who are neither wise nor ignorant philosophize. However, this means that no man who philosophizes in any manner, be he Odysseus, Socrates, or Agathon, can pretend to be wise. Diotima has filed Socrates' reply to Agathon's lawsuit.

On behalf of Agathon, Socrates now rises to Diotima's bait. There are certainly many unproved assertions in Diotima's myth of the birth of Eros that Socrates could challenge, if he were so disposed. However, Socrates knows that Agathon will be preoccupied with Diotima's insult to his wisdom. Therefore, Socrates ignores all of the possibly debatable remarks in Diotima's tale and inquires: "Who, then, Diotima, are the ones who philosophize, if they are neither the wise nor the ignorant?" (204a8–9). She exclaims that by now it would be clear to a child that these persons are the

---

30. Gods do not philosophize because they *are* what philosophy seeks. Diotima's reasoning depends on the assumption that beings cannot have what they desire, that is, Agathon's position. Thus, her remarks about gods and wisdom are too sophistical and frivolous to be the basis of a serious theology. The fact that Diotima intends the ethical improvement of Agathon rather than an ontological tract suggests the same conclusion. Accordingly, I think that Rosen errs by trying to deduce a serious theology from her comments (*Plato's "Symposium,"* 236–38).

ones who stand between the two sides of wisdom and ignorance and that Eros is among them. Thus, she undermines Agathon's conviction of his superior political wisdom by intimidating him, aggressively setting Eros, all who philosophize, and Agathon insofar as he philosophizes in middling places. Having cracked Agathon's hard shell, she is displaying some hybris to take advantage of his inner softness.

Psychological aggression cannot be expected to keep a sophist down for long. Diotima therefore escalates her campaign against Agathon's pretensions to tactical genius by preparing her next rational initiatives, which will eventually lead back to the subject of Eros's perpetual youth. She begins by anticipating a possible protest by Agathon that his cleverness is already knowledge, and, hence, not identical with the philosophy of mediocre men. She appeals to a maxim that Agathon readily concedes because it is one of his famous boasts: Wisdom pertains to the most beautiful things. (Diotima might also assume this because Socrates himself teaches it, apart from his strategic need to reason from Agathon's premises; see *Republic* 476b–d, 508e–509a, 517b–c.) Then, she argues that if *philia* for wisdom is *philia* for the greatest beauty (that is, if *philia*, like eros, is defined as a kind of desire for the greatest beauty), and if Eros is eros (or desire) for the beautiful (which, as agreed, cannot be possessed if it is desired), it follows that Eros is not wise and must be a philosopher. By extension, the human devotees of Eros cannot be already wise about the beautiful, either. This argument, replete with sophistries and hidden premises about the identity of *philia* with eros as it is, gives one pause, but it catches Agathon. Diotima adds that when Socrates (that is, Agathon) said that Eros is all-beautiful, he was viewing Eros as the *erōmenos*.[31] It is the beloved who is beautiful, soft, perfect, and blessed. However, Eros is the *erastēs*. The vain poet will imagine that Diotima is giving him a choice: he can abandon Eros and erotic lovers to the in-between or forfeit the role of a godly beloved in which he gets to be perfect and, thus, still as wise as he thinks. If Agathon takes the godly part, Diotima will have destroyed his identification with Eros. Agathon will cling to his godhood, so his proxy renounces the view that Eros has transcended philosophy, saying: "Well, then, Stranger. You speak beautifully. But, Eros being such, of what use is he to human beings?" (204c7–8).

Diotima informs Socrates that this is the next item on her agenda. Of course, Socrates poses the question because it again reflects Agathon's misgivings about an Eros who must be a mediocre daimon. It is the next order of business because it provides an opening for Diotima to drive the discussion toward the heart of Agathon's self-image as a clever Odysseus, namely, his notion that he has a superior knowledge of human ends and

31. This is true, for Agathon equated himself with Eros.

means. Diotima moves to this task by inquiring: "What does he who loves beauties love?" (204d5–6). (More accurately, "For what does he who has eros for beauties have eros?" meaning: "What does the lover of beauties want?") Socrates selfishly replies: "That they may become his."[32] This seems unproblematic. However, now Diotima startles Socrates (that is, Agathon) with another query: "When the beauties are his, what will be his?" (204d7–9). She means: "What is the use of making the beauties his?"[33] Socrates, still playing Agathon, surprises us by confessing that he is baffled. Diotima therefore changes the object of the question, inquiring: "What does he who loves good things (ἀγαθῶν) love?" Socrates selfishly answers: "That they may become his." Diotima restates her follow-up question: "When the good things are his, what will be his?" Socrates-Agathon replies that he can do better with this problem: he who gets good things "will be happy" (204d10–e7). Diotima concurs and adds that the answer is ultimate.

Socrates' replies are strange. We remember well that Agathon's original thesis was that Eros is the happiest god, inasmuch as he is the most beautiful and the best. The poet was sure that possessing beauty and the traditional virtues, in the sense of being beautiful and virtuous oneself, made one happy. It might be thought to follow that obtaining possession of beauties and good things, in the sense of making others who are beautiful and virtuous one's own, namely, by seducing them and by getting all the other good things into one's grasp too, should result in happiness as well. At least, it might be supposed that if getting good things causes bliss, it should follow that procuring beauties has the same effect. If Socrates is speaking for Agathon, why, then, is he stumped when asked about the utility of having beauties, but quick to reply that getting the good things makes one happy?

This difficulty might tempt us to believe that Socrates has stopped talking for Agathon and that he is quietly teaching that getting beauties and good things produces different results because the beautiful is fundamentally different from the good. However, we must mistrust this conclusion. At *Phaedrus* 246d8–e1, where Socrates is speaking much more philosophically than he does to Agathon, he declares that the divine is beauty, wisdom, goodness, and the like. Assuming the logical principle that if A = B, and B = C, then A = C, in the *Phaedrus* beauty and goodness are somehow the same in divine reality, even if not on the level of moving logoi, on

---

32. Nye's effort to make the Greek say something else, that "the beautiful should come into being for us," simply does not work ("Hidden Host," 47–48). The Greek contains a dative of possession.

33. We know that the question concerns utility rather than metaphysics because we have just been told that utility is the subject now under discussion.

which Agathon, Socrates, and Diotima are now operating.[34] Socrates is not teaching Agathon anything seriously here. Therefore, it seems that Socrates answers Diotima as he does because he is still representing Agathon and because something in the present argument would cause the poet to doubt that possessing beauties leads to happiness. What would that be?

This is not a hard question. If, as Agathon assumes, it is having beauty in the sense of *being* especially beautiful that causes felicity, and if, as Diotima has now "proved," Eros and other lovers neither are singularly lovely nor become so by seducing beauties, sexual love does not seem to offer any essential link between sleeping with beauties and being happy. Socrates cannot say what the lovers will have when they seduce the beauties because Agathon cannot imagine how his rather plain lovers could become happy by copulating with him, a beauty.[35] In other words, Agathon's problem is clearly not that the beautiful and the good are different, but that possessing beauties differs essentially from the good of being beautiful oneself. This is another reason that Socrates-Agathon has taken to suspecting that Eros is useless to humans.[36] To be sure, it is undeniable that the lovers hanker to seduce the beauties and that they expect to become happy by doing so. However, it now appears that their bliss would have to come from something above and beyond the possession of the beauties. Socrates-Agathon declines to argue that sexual pleasure is the additional felicitous element, probably because he knows that it is gone as soon as one enjoys it, so that the lovers could not expect a permanent delight from it. This would tally with Agathon's experience of the dilemma of his lovers, who start lusting for his body again fairly soon after they have had him. Thus, Diotima has persuaded Agathon that some unknown ingredient must be coupled with the secondary possession of the beauty of beauties in order to extract happiness from the secondary possession—a logical need that arises on the basis of Agathon's narcissistic attitude to eros, not from some personal quirk of Socrates.

With this, Diotima has forced Agathon to admit that neither Eros and his ilk nor he himself are as divinely wise as Odysseus about the ends and

34. Thus, for the moment, we need not be terrified by Bloom's citation of John Locke's argument that it would be ridiculous to declare "a good bowel movement" beautiful (*Love and Friendship*, 499).

35. It might occur to someone to argue that beauty and the good cannot be identical precisely because beauty cannot be transferred from a beloved to a lover, whereas a virtue such as wisdom can be transferred from one person to another. Agathon certainly believes this. He has not given up his notion that wisdom can be transferred by physical touching. However, Socrates argues in the *Republic* (518b–e) that people cannot bestow wisdom on others, as if they were putting sight into blind eyes. The argument fails.

36. We have come a long way from the sophists' paeans to Eros as the source of mankind's greatest blessings. I am grateful to Rodrigo F. Sánchez for the conversations in which this solution was thrashed out and tested for possible oversights.

means of erotic men. Agathon's ethical premises have again led to the result that he does not know what he thinks he knows.[37] However, Agathon still holds that wisdom can be transmitted by touching and that the concept of "good things" embraces more than the virtues. Thus, Agathon does not think that the good is subject to the same problems as beauty, and Socrates-Agathon can say immediately that having good things yields happiness, the ultimate end. This suggests to Agathon that for a "lover of beauty" to become happy, he must really love a good thing other than beauty and acquire it with his possession of beauties. Accordingly, when Diotima shifts the definition of eros from "desire for beauty" to "desire for good things," her jump will strike Agathon as logically well prepared and not as incomprehensible, as it has appeared to insufficiently thoughtful readers.

Diotima effects this correction promptly. She begins by broadening the conversation, seizing the chance that she has just contrived to clarify the general telos of Eros. She asks her student whether the love (that is, desire) of happiness is common to all human beings. Socrates admits that it is common to all. Diotima thereupon asks whether all men love. Socrates does not know what to say, for Agathon has been accustomed to thinking of lovers as people who crave sexual intercourse, and it is clear that not all human beings do so, if only because we have the examples of children and the exhausted elderly. However, it is plain that everyone "loves" happiness.[38] Agathon will be uncertain as to how to escape this logical quandary.

Diotima tells Socrates-Agathon that he need not be confused. We have restricted the term "eros" unduly. We narrow the word in the same way that we limit the term "poetry." As Agathon has already intimated in his own speech, everything that passes from nonbeing into being is the product of poetry (*poiēsis*, making). Nevertheless, we give the word "poet" only to the makers of music and meter, excluding the makers of all other things, thus confining the name "poetry" to a part of the whole activity of making. Socrates unhesitatingly agrees, just as Agathon would. Diotima asserts that it is the same with eros. Generally, eros is "the desire of all good things and of being happy" (205d1–3). So, those who are erotic in moneymaking, love of gymnastics, and philosophy are not called lovers, but those who are serious about Eros in one of his forms (the sexual) are said

37. Anyone who thinks that this is not the point of the passages under consideration has forgotten that the *Symposium* is a lawsuit about the wisdom of Socrates and Agathon. Attention to Plato's dramatic context remains necessary.

38. If we accept the proposition that one cannot have what one loves, the gods who are happy could not love happiness, and people who love happiness could not be happy. Cf. the parallel discussion of Rosen, *Plato's "Symposium,"* 236 ff. However, as argued above, this premise is Agathon's position, granted by Diotima for dialectical purposes. Thus, it remains too shaky a foundation for Rosen's continuing effort to infer a serious theology of Diotima from these passages.

to be lovers, receiving the name that all should have.[39] This implies that eros is a force that impels us to all the goods that make us happy, especially material wealth, bodily health, the goods associated with possessing beauties, and the good of philosophy, wisdom. Diotima has now made eros substantial and has equated *philia* with eros openly. Socrates agrees rather dubiously, for Agathon is now in unfamiliar territory. Diotima reacts by criticizing Aristophanes. There is a saying, she declares, that all who seek their other halves are lovers. However, eros is neither for the half nor for the whole, unless a half or whole chances to be good, for human beings expeditiously amputate their own body parts if they are harmful rather than good. Aristophanes got the telos of Eros wrong: people love their good, not their wholeness.[40] The attack on Aristophanes apparently persuades Socrates-Agathon completely, for he swears an oath by Zeus to emphasize his agreement with the result. Maybe Agathon is repelled by the idea that he might be the other half of the horrible old Pausanias.

At this point, I must interrupt the narrative for a short excursus on Diotima's concept of the good, the necessity for which will become evident in a moment. When Diotima states that Eros is the desire of all good things, she does not give a definition of "good," although she does hint at the identities of the most important good things. Despite the omission, can we tell what her notion of good is? I think that we can make some headway with this problem by adverting to her story of the birth of Eros. Our results will be mythical, but that will be consistent with Diotima's entire presentation, so it will do.

In posing our question, what we want to know precisely is what "good" for human beings is. In Diotima's myth, the original human nature, Penia, is virtually nothing, or, if not nothing, then a hypostatized potency. Penia desires divine resources that will bring her into being, or to a greater fullness of being. We may suppose that the good of this Ur-nature is the same as what it seeks. When Poros inseminates Penia, the beings who instantiate

39. This use of poetry as an example does not provide grounds for an ontology or a theology. For example, it does not restrict making to human beings, thus demonstrating Plato's atheism. If gods pass from nonbeing into being, as all ancient myths envisage, they are surely products of poetry, but the poet could be a reality even higher than the gods. Once again, Rosen tries here to infer an ontology from remarks that are not intended to be metaphysical (ibid., 236–43).

40. Rosen concludes that Diotima denies that the whole is good and, again, that the good and the beautiful cannot be identical on Diotima's account (ibid., 244–45). His deductions are elementary mistakes. The whole to which Diotima refers is not necessarily or even probably the cosmos, but the whole original human being in the myth of Aristophanes. The error is compounded by the facts that Rosen defines "the whole" as a mathematical sum of all beings and that he includes bad things, or badness and ugliness themselves, among the beings, thus making Diotima teach that human beings love only the part, not the whole. The fact that nothing in Diotima's speech justifies this is another illustration of why it is dangerous to treat her remarks as secret ontology.

the resulting nature have the fetus Eros as their principle of desire. What will their good be? Presumably, it will be half the good of Eros's mother and half the good of Eros's father. As an heir of Penia, the erotic person will continue to be a resourcelessness who wants divine resources that bring him or her into being, or to a greater fullness of being. These constituents of being or a fuller being will be the individual's good. They will include everything that keeps the person from the void and also all the things that fill his or her residual emptiness. Obviously, among them will be material wealth and bodily health, which ancient myths interpret as divine gifts. Also among them will be whatever it is about having beauties and about philosophy that protects the person from the void, or that fills his or her emptiness. As the heirs of Poros, who eagerly drank immortalizing nectar, and thus could not avoid fertilizing Penia, the erotic persons will love eternal life and will be unable to avoid transferring some portion of their shares in divine resources to still empty potency. Immortality and the reflexive discharge of divine generative capacity will be added to a human being's goods.[41] Diotima will have to treat these matters as she teaches Socrates how Eros is useful, or how he helps us achieve our ends, although she will not take them up in the same order as I have done. As she instructs Socrates, her oration will pass over from the explication of the "sort" and nature of Eros to a description of his works.

Having established the general telos of Eros, Diotima is now in a better position to do her analysis of the utility of having beauties. She asks whether human beings love (desire) the good to be theirs. Socrates answers yes, for Agathon's egoism has not diminished at all during the previous discussion. Diotima then inquires whether they want the good to be their own always or eternally (ἀεί), and Socrates vehemently agrees that she speaks "most truly" (206a12–13). It is important to notice Socrates' eager response to the "always," for it reflects Agathon's yearning for perpetual youth, a passion so robust, and so single-mindedly pursued, that Stanley Rosen believes that Agathon is "the only man to achieve genuine immortality."[42] Even here, where Diotima wants to lead Agathon toward her own insights, her argument begins with Agathon's premises, and not with her arbitrary whims. We might go so far as to say that we are now proceeding from the real center of Agathon's concerns. Therefore, we may also speculate that we are on the threshold of the final destruction and elevation of Agathon's opinions, at which Diotima has been aiming throughout her speech.

41. This is another answer to Eryximachus: Human beings are unities of opposites by nature.
42. Ibid., 191. Rosen appears to have an interesting idea of "genuine immortality." Agathon looks as dead as they come to the Socrates who classes him with the living dead in Hades.

Diotima continues this line of investigation by asking what the method (τρόπον), acts, and work (ἔργον) of those who want to make the good eternally their own are. It has already been made clear that Socrates-Agathon was ignorant of both the ends and the means of Eros, so Socrates is perplexed again and pleads that he came to Diotima to learn these things.[43] The prophetess rejoins that their work is "begetting on beauty (τόκος ἐν καλῷ) by means of both the body and the soul" (206b7–8). Socrates is mystified. He complains that it would require prophecy to comprehend Diotima's statement and that he does not understand. This signals that Agathon is about to be led up to prophecy again. As we follow, we must mark carefully the male and female sex roles connoted by the terms for generation that Diotima uses. It will be difficult to sort these functions out because many of Diotima's words can have both male and female senses—an ambiguity that Plato likes, for we have learned that his Socrates has a mystical view of the relationships between male and female in spiritual androgyny. So, what are we supposed to gather from Diotima's description of the work of lovers of the good?

Diotima explains that all people "are pregnant (κυοῦσι) in both body and soul" (206c1). In this declaration, Diotima uses a form of the verb κυέω, which J. S. Morrison says can refer to either the male or the female generative act.[44] She has already used κυέω at 203c1, to report what Penia did as a result of having lain with Poros. Thus, I take it that "are pregnant" is the correct translation of κυοῦσι here and that Plato at least temporarily means κυέω to stand for what women do in generation, namely, to "conceive." Now we wonder what Diotima means by stating that all people "are pregnant in body and soul" and how she learned this amazing fact.

It is here that one realizes the necessity of relating Diotima's concept of the good, and, hence, her idea of our means of obtaining it, to her myth of the birth of Eros. The answer to our question is not that Diotima proposes to instruct us in the science of physiology and that she is relying on some laughable ancient medical theory of human reproduction. Rather, her statement means that when Poros lay with Penia, inseminating human nature, he planted the seed of Divine Resource in every human body-soul womb. All men and women are "pregnant in body and soul" with the daimon Eros, and, thus, with his neediness and his godly resources, in a

43. Again, we do not need to believe literally that a Socrates who was ignorant of erotics went to a real Diotima to learn them. Socrates' reply hardly proves that he suffered from an erotic defect.

44. Morrison, essay on KYEIN, in "Four Notes." H. G. Liddell and R. Scott restrict the term to the female. Morrison takes issue with them, arguing that Diotima usually employs the verb in the male sense (52). I am not in a position to challenge Morrison's authority, but it seems to me that Diotima's use of the verb originally is female and gradually becomes androgynous.

mythical-mystical-ontological sense, not physiologically. Diotima knows this because she is a *daimonios anēr.*[45]

How does this clarify Diotima's bewildering remark that the work of those who desire always to have the good is "begetting on beauty (τόκος ἐν καλῷ) by means of both the body and the soul"? The words seem meaningless. Begetting "by means of the body" is intelligible, but how does one beget "by means of both the body and the soul"? Before tackling this issue, we must deal with another semantic problem. The noun τόκος and the related verb τίκτειν can refer to either the female or the male role in reproduction, depending on the context. The terms can be translated properly either as "bringing forth" or as "begetting." The phrase τόκος ἐν καλῷ can therefore mean "bringing forth (or giving birth) in beauty," as some experts have it.[46] However, in Diotima's first use of τόκος, in a context in which the work of an *erastēs* is in question, the word logically entails the male generative act, "begetting."[47] Therefore, we are compelled to ask how a pregnant *erastēs* can beget. Again, our answer must refer to Diotima's tale. Because the *erastēs* is pregnant with Poros's seed, he will surely reach a stage at which he cannot avoid conveying his divine assets into empty potency. Insofar as he is simultaneously a body and soul pregnant with Eros, he will be moved to transmit both his bodily and his spiritual divine resources. His act of communicating bodily and spiritual resources will be an integral whole employing bodily and spiritual means at once. Diotima sums up by saying that "upon reaching a certain age, our nature (ἡμῶν ἡ φύσις) desires to beget (τίκτειν)" (206c3–4). Once again, Diotima means this in a mythical-mystical-ontological sense, although these words can also be flattened into a physiological truth when read out of context.

The fact that Diotima says that "our nature" desires to beget implies that both women and men beget on beauty by means of body and soul. To make sure that we do not miss this, Diotima bludgeons us with a mystical linguistic usage. Pointing to human reproduction, she tells Socrates that "the συνουσία [literally, the being together, thus, the sexual intercourse, the union] of a man and a woman is a τόκος" (206c5–6), that is, a τόκος for both sexes. It seems too that Diotima is begetting on Socrates spiritually by teaching him. So, all people are pregnant, and all are driven to

45. Cf. Morrison's disquisition on Plato and ancient medicine (ibid., 54–55), which I think is misplaced. One also regrets Rosen's use of the term "Physiology" in his relevant section heading (*Plato's "Symposium,"* 245).

46. For example, see Alexander Nehamas and Paul Woodruff, *Symposium,* in Plato, *Complete Works* 206b7–8.

47. The woman in a male-female pair would not be called an *erastēs.* Thus, Phaedrus does not refer to Alcestis as an *erastēs,* although, so to speak, she might be the one who wore the pants in her marriage. Socrates would not be discussing female-female pairs in his present company, so, here, he would not be extending the term *erastēs* to a member of this pair, either.

beget on beauty by means of the body and the soul, all this on a mythical-mystical-ontological plane. It follows that all are metaphysically androgynous in their pursuit of the good. This is the reason Plato makes Diotima so steadfastly ambiguous in her use of terms for generation. He wants her to speak accurately in androgynous double entendres. Thus, I have rendered her statement that "the συνουσία of a man and a woman is a τόκος" as if "τόκος" meant a "begetting" for both the man and the woman, but Diotima would be glad if we understood her to say that it is a "bringing forth" for both. Indeed, she would be happy if we took her to mean that the sexual union is both a bringing forth and a begetting for both the man and the woman, for both are giving birth to that with which they are pregnant by the god, and both are begetting by passing their inherited resources into empty potency. Giving birth and begetting are the same. Let us call the androgynous act "engendering."

As enlightening as these instructions are, they leave Socrates-Agathon with a problem pertaining to the relationship of the good to beauty. Let it be granted that beauty is a good for someone such as Agathon because being beautiful makes him happy. Also, let it be admitted that Agathon's beauty is not the good of a lover who does not share it. Thus, let it be allowed that the eros of an *erastēs* lacking in beauty is eros for all good things and happiness, and that this *erastēs* must obtain a good other than beauty in connection with the possession of a beauty in order to be happy. Why, then, should Diotima say that it is the work of an *erastēs* to seek his or her good by "engendering on beauty"? It would appear that the lover could concentrate on his or her good, seduce those who offer it, and do without beauty in the *erōmenos* altogether. To defend her analysis of the work of an *erastēs*, Diotima must explain why the lover of the good is constrained to beget–bring forth, or engender, on beauty.

Diotima responds. Speaking of our nature, she insists, "To beget (τίκτειν) on the ugly (or shameful; αἰσχρῷ) it cannot do, but only on the beautiful" (206c4–5). So, although the beloved's beauty is not the good of the lover, the lover must engender on beauty to secure his or her good because doing otherwise is impossible. Why? Diotima says: "It is a divine affair (θεῖον τὸ πρᾶγμα), conception (κύησις) and generation (γέννησις), being something immortal in the mortal animal. These things cannot occur in the inharmonious. The ugly is inharmonious with all the divine, but the beautiful is harmonious. Therefore Beauty is Moira [the goddess Fate] and Eileithuia [the goddess of parturition] to birth" (205c6–d2).[48]

Diotima's explanation is obviously not an empirical observation or a

48. I believe that in this passage, Diotima changes from τίκτειν to γέννησις because the former has a great deal of the feminine in it and Diotima wants us to know that she includes the masculine in the divine affair.

logical deduction from premises evident to everyone. Its reference to Moira tells us that it is a proclamation of a divine edict, a decree of inexorable Fate, that has been passed down to us through the medium of a *daimonios anēr*. As a revelation of this type, Diotima's declaration is consonant with her genealogy of Eros and consists entirely in repetitions of points in her tale or inferences drawn from it. Diotima has taught that Poros fertilized Penia and that Eros attends and freely serves Aphrodite and loves beauty because he was conceived during the birthday celebration of the goddess. Mythically, this already suffices to demonstrate that (1) human generation is a divine act in a mortal animal, being a deed of Poros that we can reenact because we are pregnant with his resources;[49] (2) our conception and generation are a single androgynous affair that only seems twofold to us (observe that in Diotima's usage, κύησις and γέννησις have become one θεῖον τὸ πρᾶγμα); (3) beauty and the beautiful are harmonious with divine reality, whereas ugliness and the ugly are inharmonious with it; and (4) Eros will not freely serve ugliness or the ugly. In the logic of the myth, it follows that divine-human conception and generation can take place only in the presence and service of the beauty that is personified by Aphrodite. Only Beauty-Aphrodite can be the Moira-Eileithuia who rules the fertilization and opening of the human body-soul womb as inexorable destiny.

It might be objected that we know of many cases in which lovers have united with the ugly or the plain. In two such incidents, Xanthippe has allowed the homely Socrates to father children upon her, and Diotima is spending a lot of time on this same Socrates. It will also be seen that Alcibiades, once Socrates' *erōmenos*, has become his *erastēs*. Therefore, it seems that erotic individuals can engender on the ugly, and not only on the beautiful.

This apparently mighty objection does not necessarily refute Diotima's proclamation. It merely raises a hitherto overlooked question: What is beauty, or, better, what sort of beauty does Diotima envisage when she argues that we can engender only on the beautiful? It may be that lovers engender on beauty even when we judge otherwise. We need another digression, this one on Socratic concepts of beauty. Three are relevant to our difficulty, as follows.

First, in the *Phaedrus,* Socrates-Stesichorus maintains that "the divine is beauty" (246d8–e1). In the *Symposium*, we are informed that all gods are beautiful, particularly Aphrodite (202c6–7, 203c4). Diotima probably

---

49. If we are reenacting the deed of Poros, does this demonstrate that we know how divine generation works after all, because Poros must have copulated if we copulate? The answer is no. The stories of coitus are mythical and are not the point. What we do not understand is how divine resource is passed into empty potency. Inasmuch as we do this without the least comprehension of how we do it, skill, competence, and cunning have no role in our act, just as Mētis had nothing to do with what Poros did in the myth.

thinks that the essence of divine reality involves beauty and that Aphrodite personifies divine Beauty in the same way that Poros personifies divine Resource.[50] Meanwhile, Agathon and Socrates have agreed that Eros cannot be beautiful because he desires beauty (201a–b). The fact that this doctrine was reached via a sophism does not imply that the daimon is perfectly fair; it means that the speakers do not know that he lacks beauty, but only believe it. Diotima probably does know that Eros cannot be perfectly beautiful by virtue of experiencing the in-between as a conscious *daimonios anēr*. Diotima also makes erotic people philosophers and lovers of beauty (204b2–3). By her sophistical logic, this means that human beings cannot be perfectly beautiful, either. Again, her fallacies are probably vindicated by her prophetic insights, namely, by the revelation that god does not mingle with mortal (203a1–2). If the divine is essentially beauty, people cannot possess perfect beauty. Thus, although we have not heard what perfect beauty is yet, we may assume that it belongs to the nature of divinity, such that it could not be predicated of a less than divine being.

So, when Diotima says that the work of lovers of the good is τόκος ἐν καλῷ, she may have divine beauty in mind. If so, we would have to render τόκος ἐν καλῷ not as "begetting on beauty," but as "engendering in the presence of beauty."[51] I think that, ultimately, this is the most correct translation of the phrase, for it would be most consistent with the mythical facts that Aphrodite's presence was needed for the generation of Eros, that Poros begot not on Aphrodite but on Penia (a lady of dubious, and not divine, beauty), and that Eros by nature is an *erastēs* of beauty who serves and waits on Aphrodite. Accordingly, when Diotima asked Socrates-Agathon, "For what does he who has eros for beauties have eros?" Socrates should have said: "You are asking what it means that Eros is an *erastēs* of Beauty-Aphrodite, or what an *erastēs* of beauty desires. The truth is that the lover yearns to serve Beauty-Aphrodite, not that the lover desires to make the beauty his." Thus, the thesis that our nature can engender only ἐν τῷ καλῷ would mean that our birth giving–begetting occurs only when Divine Beauty moves potential lovers, giving them an irresistible invitation to serve her voluntarily.[52] Then, the details that Socrates is ugly and that

50. One is reminded of Saint Augustine's explanation of the possibility of the mystery of the Trinity. Socrates-Stesichorus-Diotima would respond that Augustine has too few persons in God, perhaps infinitely too few.

51. Nehamas and Woodruff suggest "in the presence of" as a possible translation of ἐν, but then, unfortunately, do not render it this way (Plato, *Complete Works* 489 n. 41).

52. When Diotima remarks that Eros is a servant of Aphrodite, she uses the word θεράπων (203c2), which means that he serves her freely rather than as a slave. This is why I have been insisting on the freedom of the daimon's service throughout the analysis. I leave it to others to solve the mystery of how an irresistible invitation is consistent with freedom.

others nevertheless couple with him would not contradict the statement that erotic people can engender only "in the presence of beauty."

Second, although Diotima probably thinks that, strictly speaking, people cannot be beautiful because beauty is divine, she appears to conceive of beauty in a looser sense when she says that it is the *erōmenos* who is "beautiful and soft and perfect and blessed" (204c4–5). Or does she? It might be Beauty-Aphrodite who is desired as the soft, perfect, blessed, beautiful ruler. However, let us suppose that Diotima has a second idea of beauty, a concept of a less than divine beauty that can be predicated of a human *erōmenos*. Taking beauty in this sense, could it still be true that the work of lovers is to engender in the presence of beauty when some want union with the ugly Socrates? Here, it will be helpful to notice that at the end of the *Phaedrus,* Socrates prays to Pan that he might "become beautiful within" (καλῷ γενέσθαι τἄνδοθεν, 279b8–9). In our present dialogue, Diotima mentions beautiful souls (209b6), indicating the location of inner beauty. Perhaps Socrates already possesses some of the inner beauty for which he prays. What would this inner beauty be? Diotima might explain it thus: Given that, by definition, the inner beauty could not be a divine beauty in a person's nature that essentially deifies him or her, and given that divine beauty is the most truly real beauty, the inner beauty might still be related to the divine beauty, existing as a kind of pervasion by it. In the close but unmixed meeting of the divine and the mortal in the in-between, the soul of the *daimonios anēr* might behold the divine beauty, freely serve that beauty, and become derivatively beautiful by virtue of being filled with the vision and doing the service.[53] Diotima speaks of just such a vision of beauty later (210e–212a). If Socrates reflects it, Alcibiades would be closer to the truth than he realizes when he relates how he once looked inside Socrates and saw images (that is, statues that celebrate the gods, ἀγάλματα) there that were "divine, golden, all-beautiful, and wondrous" (216e5–217a2). Thus, the human inner beauty of Socrates would be an image of divine beauty in his soul. Then, the fact that lovers unite with him would not belie the assertion that lovers can engender only in the presence of beauty.

Third, Socrates seems to speak of beauty in an even looser sense when he refers to Agathon as beautiful (174a9). Agathon certainly does not possess the divine beauty of Aphrodite, and he has closed himself to the inner beauty of Socrates by wishing to be beautiful autonomously rather than as a vessel for images of divine Beauty. Hence, Socrates must mean here that the poet is a physical beauty. Diotima also speaks of bodily beauty (209b4–5). On this level, could it still be true that lovers can engender only in the

---

53. One thinks of the "old doctor" in Alexander Solzhenitsyn: "The meaning of existence was to preserve unspoiled, undisturbed and undistorted the image of eternity with which each person is born. Like a silver moon in a calm, still pond" (*Cancer Ward,* 432).

presence of beauty, or do lovers who unite with the ugly Socrates refute the axiom? We could answer that the perceived physical beauty of an ugly beloved depends on the taste, hormones, and degree of intoxication of the lover, so that the lover would always mate with an imagined beauty. However, such relativism would render Diotima's law meaningless. Besides, I think that even with regard to physical beauty, she would insist that her dictum is objectively valid. So far, our analysis of Diotima's ideas of beauty has been rather hard on the human race, denying people a real beauty properly their own. However, Diotima's myth is not so relentlessly stingy. We must recall that as a god, Poros is beautiful and that every human being is pregnant with Poros's seed in body and soul. Hence, there must be something in the nature of every person's body and soul that is, if not divinely beautiful, then at least humanly fair in a way that is reminiscent of the god's beauty. Perhaps not every potential lover will see this inherited beauty in every potential beloved. However, one potential lover might catch a certain smile, a certain look, or a certain air in the potential beloved that reveals the potential beloved's natural share of divine beauty. Then the potential lover will see real human beauty and become a captivated lover. Diotima's proclamation will be verified because no human being is unrelievedly ugly by nature.

This concludes our digressions, which we have pursued in order to grasp an especially subtle section of Diotima's argument. Now we must return to the main line of her reasoning, lest we lose our way. We need to recall that Socrates refuted the central thesis of Agathon's speech by showing that Eros could not be beautiful and good. Then Diotima frustrated Agathon repeatedly. She proved that Eros is not a god. She characterized Eros as a daimon of middling qualities. She described Eros's power as that of an intermediary who binds gods and men together and who represents them to one another without mixing them. She portrayed prophecy and the *technē* of the *daimonios anēr* as superior to poetry and the vulgar *technē* of the poet. She endowed Eros with a genealogy that interprets the Olympian order of being as inviolable; makes Eros a willing servant of Aphrodite; and leaves humans beings ontologically inferior to gods, poor, and dependent upon an infusion of divine resources for their existence, or at least their happiness. She raised Agathon's hopes by letting Eros be as sly as Odysseus. However, she demonstrated that for all his wit, Eros is a philosopher who cannot be wise. The consequence was that Agathon's claims to wisdom were severely challenged. Certainly, Agathon could not be Eros and a wise god, too. Socrates-Agathon therefore gave up Agathon's identification with Eros, but inquired: Of what use to human beings is Eros—that is, of what use is a mediocre Eros who does not deify his followers?

We are presently studying Diotima's reply about the utility of the daimonic, mediocre Eros. To discuss utility intelligently, one must ascertain what ends are being pursued and then what means are conducive to the ends. Agathon was ignorant of the purposes of an Eros who desires to make beauties his. Diotima suggested that the telos of Eros is all good things, and, finally, happiness, adding Agathon's proviso that lovers want to make the good things theirs eternally. In the penultimate step of this analysis, Diotima is teaching Agathon that the means adopted by those who desire to make good things theirs forever is an androgynous begetting and giving birth in the presence of beauty. Thereafter, Diotima will be obliged to finish her explanation of the utility of Eros by becoming more specific about the good(s) that Eros seeks. What unknown thing(s) must lovers win when they beget–give birth in the presence of beauty in order to be happy? Must they acquire all the good things, a few, or one in particular? The prophetess will wrap up the argument that I have been summarizing here and then answer the still open question.

Diotima's synopsis of the conclusions reached thus far focuses on the goods of the part of human nature that owes to Poros. The prophetess delivers her account with an explosion of androgynous double entendres. She tells Socrates how "the pregnant" (τὸ κυοῦν) repairs to the beautiful and overflows with "begetting and generation" (τίκτει τε καὶ γεννᾷ). When it encounters the ugly, it withdraws into itself and goes without generation (οὐ γεννᾷ).[54] Then it withholds that which has been conceived (τὸ κύημα), carrying it heavily and painfully. However, a great excitement about the beautiful befalls those who are pregnant (τῷ κυοῦντι) and, hence, σπαργῶντι (a wonderfully ambiguous concept that simultaneously means "full to bursting" when applied to females and "swollen with passion" when applied to males, as in the portrait of the condition of the *erastēs* at *Phaedrus* 256a2). This exhilaration is caused by the fact that the possessor of beauty can relieve the pregnant–full-to-bursting–phallically swollen individual of great birth pangs (206d3–e1). Diotima means that the divine resources with which people are pregnant must be transmitted into empty potencies that they actualize; they must out, or the persons pregnant with them feel like exploding.[55] Beauty-Aphrodite triggers their release by

54. Rosen makes this line the basis of a dualistic Platonic ontology in which the beautiful and the ugly exist and are eternally at war (*Plato's "Symposium,"* 247–48). The evidence is too flimsy to support this judgment. To uphold it, one would have to scour the Platonic corpus for commentary on "the being of the ugly." Rosen does not prove that "the ugly" of which Diotima speaks has positive being. It could exist only in the mode of defect.

55. The standard translations of this passage—for example, those of Lamb, Jowett, Joyce, and Nehamas and Woodruff—are wildly disparate, indicating serious confusion in the ranks of professional classicists. Morrison tries to argue, vainly, that τὸ κύημα refers to a withheld male seed, and that the σπαργῶντι are only the passionate male lovers ("Four Notes," 52). However, others give the lines an exclusively feminine cast, just as vainly. The problems of these observers would be solved if they paid attention

showing herself to the σπαργῶντι in the bodies and souls of beauties. She does so as the beautiful goddess who calls into being ever new beauties that her birth continually demands, namely, beautiful new children and perhaps equally beautiful representations of the beautiful truth of being over which she rules, that is, beautiful inquiries, conversations, and speeches. She does not relieve the lovers by serving as the beloved who is possessed. For eros is not (eros) for the beautiful, as Agathon supposed (and as Pausanias thought before him, as he imagined himself creating souls by introducing grand thoughts into unformed minds). Rather, eros is (eros) for generating and engendering in the presence of beauty (τῆς γεννήεως καὶ τοῦ τόκου ἐν τῷ καλῷ, 206e5), and in the service of beauty.

Socrates-Agathon reluctantly answers: "So be it (εἶεν)" (206e6). He has turned mulish because Agathon's wisdom has been refuted again and because Agathon has probably foreseen a new defeat coming. We must picture the Agathon who is listening to Socrates' monologue beginning to sweat like the soon-to-be-vanquished Thrasymachus in the *Republic*. Diotima will not let Socrates-Agathon escape by introducing the doubt implied by his "So be it." She attacks, crying: "Certainly it is!" Then she asks: "Why for generating (τῆς γεννήεως)?" She replies: "Because genesis (γέννησις) is everlasting being and immortality to the mortal. From what has been agreed, it is necessary to desire immortality with the good, if indeed eros is for the good to be one's own always. This reasoning makes it necessary for eros to be [eros] for immortality" (206e7–207a4). The coup de grâce has been delivered.

Why should it trouble Agathon to be told that the utility of Eros is that lovers achieve the mortal equivalents of divine generation and immortality by begetting–giving birth in the presence of beauty, especially when a name for godly poetic creativity and perpetual youth are his heart's greatest desires? The answer clearly is that Diotima has struck a devastating blow at his pride. When Agathon said what "sort" Eros was, he himself was the omniscient creator, especially the creator of himself, and he achieved a genuinely divine immortality by doing the acts and acquiring the habits of gods. Diotima has taken his godly wisdom, his auto-creation, and his divine perpetual youth; refashioned and downgraded them in her myth; and returned them as a third-generation inheritance of divine wisdom, a secondhand participation in divine resources in which lovers and poets exercise the dispensed generative powers of a god, and an ersatz immortality that Agathon hates because his only share of eternity is the ability to

---

to the meaning of Diotima's myth and the philosophic issues that arise from it. They need to see that Diotima is trying to symbolize an experience vaguely similar to, but more complex than, that of the prophet Jeremiah. She is attempting to do this by using an ambiguous language of spiritual androgyny.

transmit assets with which the god has fertilized him. In short, Agathon is distressed because Diotima has forced his proxy to confess that he does not enjoy fully divine generation and immortality, but *only* their mortal equivalents. If Agathon thinks the genuinely divine acts and traits the only true or gratifying ones, then Diotima is far from agreeing that Agathon is "the only man to achieve genuine immortality," and she warns him that no mortal ever acquires it.

Diotima dwells on this point in order to show Agathon some of its ramifications. She asks Socrates what "the cause of this eros and desire" is. This provocative question intends to establish not the origins of the daimon Eros, which have not been under discussion, but what it is that causes the mortal craving for engendering. Here, it is not clear what Diotima means by "cause" (αἴτιον). Is she referring to Aristotle's "efficient cause" or "final cause"? In either case, it would seem that the cause of the mortal desire has already been disclosed: beauty is the efficient cause, and immortality is the final cause. However, just when it seems that Diotima is repeating herself merely for emphasis, she takes a new tack. She inquires whether Socrates knows what drives animals to reproduce and rear their young. Humans, she indicates, might be thought to do this on the basis of calculation (ἐκ λογισμοῦ), but what about animals?

Her question is both fair and ironic. It was Eryximachus who, rightly in Diotima's opinion, saw Eros as a force working throughout nature. An explanation of the workings of Eros that covers people must account for animals, too. It is not evident that Agathon's erotic desire for poetic self-deification could be attributed to animals. Neither is it plain that human beings have so much control over Eros that they could indulge their erotic impulses simply on the basis of calculation, as Agathon's speech envisaged. Like animals, human beings really are totally in the grip of Eros, whether they recognize this or not.[56] Thus, Diotima's request to be told what she has already announced has the aims of emphasizing that immortality is the final cause of engendering, observing that the immortality to be expected is closer to that of animals than that of gods, and exposing absurdities in Agathon's talk. Accordingly, Socrates-Agathon might be more than a little truculent when he replies that he does not know what the cause of erotic conduct in animals is. Diotima seizes her chance to intimidate him again, wondering aloud how he hopes to become clever at erotics if he cannot answer such questions.

With Agathon back on his heels, Diotima continues to batter him. She presents a new perspective on the idea of a wholly temporal immortality that is achieved through an infinite series of new beginnings. Justly appealing to her earlier agreements with Socrates, she argues that the mortal

---

56. If Moira is involved, as Diotima says, there is no choice at all.

nature always tries to become immortal, according to its ability. It can do this in only one manner, by generation, through which it leaves behind young in place of the old. Each of the living things is said to live and be itself from childhood to old age. However, even though it is called the same, it never possesses the same things. It is always becoming new. Its body varies constantly. Further, the ways, habits, opinions, desires, pleasures, pains, and fears of the soul never remain the same; some come to be and others are lost. (Notice that Diotima has surreptitiously stopped talking about animals and is discussing human beings again; as far as we know, animals do not have opinions.) The person's knowledge is always changing, too. Small particles of it die through forgetting. When we try to get them back, we replace them with new ones that are different, even though they look like the old ones. Everything mortal is preserved this way, not by keeping it completely the same, like the divine, but by replacing the old and the lost with the new. This is how the mortal participates in the immortal, both in the body and in all other ways. It cannot do so in any other manner (207c–208b).

This argument checkmates Agathon, we might say, by pinning him between a pair of major pieces that his assumptions have permitted Diotima to mobilize. We must distinguish between the act of engendering and the product of engendering. Diotima has offered the first major piece, the act of engendering, to Agathon as something divine in the mortal animal, that is, as a divine act that a mortal can reenact because it is pregnant with the seed of divine resource. A human being therefore participates in immortality in the act of engendering insofar as he or she repeats the deed of the immortal Poros and shares in the life of the quasi-immortal Eros, who, according to Agathon's cosmology, is eternally young only insofar as he always dies and rises again in an infinite succession of new beginnings.

When Agathon contemptuously turns his back on the immortality of Diotima's act of engendering because, as a loan from the gods, it is not the work of his own poetry, and also because the immortality of this Eros is only daimonic and not divine, Diotima confronts him with the other major piece, the product of engendering and its immortality. The product of engendering that Diotima shows him is, once again, the only such product that his cosmology allows. In his cosmology, there is nothing but genesis and two varieties of matter, earth and air. A time-bound genesis and matter can be nothing but the river of Heraclitus. As in the existence of the daimon Eros, there is still an infinite series of new beginnings, but the entirely material world does not even permit new beginnings of the same. Much to Agathon's horror, it only admits of new beginnings of the different. The only immortality available to Agathon in this domain is entirely animalistic, being the eternity of the species, and the only enduring continuation of his person for which Agathon can hope is an illusory identity in non-identity that persists over time. It is in vain that the pathetic Agathon tries to forge and symbolize his eternal youth by dabbing makeup on his wrinkling face, draping young women's clothing on his middle-aged body, and writing his self-deifying poems. All his efforts are carried away by Heraclitus's river. Reacting to this tragicomical predicament, Socrates-Agathon "wonders" and cries out: "Well, O most wise Diotima, can this truly be so?" (208b8–9). This protest is both Agathon's cry of despair and his expression of sheer unwillingness to believe that he and his sophistical friends have been wasting their time so fruitlessly.[57]

In a brief aside, we may inquire whether Diotima's bleak portrait of the immortality of the mortal represents Plato's "real" opinion of human immortality. The many commentaries on "Plato's doctrine of immortality" that come to hand are certainly right to observe that the picture painted by Diotima contradicts others found in the *Phaedo, Republic,* and so on. Thus, do we find here in the *Symposium* proof that Plato does not believe in the stories of immortality that he concocts in other works? I doubt that we can answer confidently. In the *Symposium,* Diotima leads Agathon to the conclusions that his premises demand. We do not know what she would say to other people with other presuppositions. Further, we cannot be certain that Diotima intends her comments about the animalistic, lesser immortality of the mortal to refer to the part of human nature that owes to Poros, which she still might regard as deathless. Her remarks might relate only to mankind's heritage from Penia. Nor can we know that Socrates does not have strategic reasons for teaching immortality to interlocutors such as Cebes, Simmias, and Glaucon. Plato never discloses his opinion. We would be well advised to stop attempting to ferret a Platonic doctrine of immortality out of the dialogues.

In reporting Diotima's reply to his question as to whether her reasoning could be true, Socrates adds a personal observation. He states that Diotima speaks "like the perfect sophists" (ὥσπερ οἱ τέλεοι σοφισταί, 208c1) in answering. Diotima says that to know that she is not being absurd, all Socrates has to do is notice the love of honor (φιλοτιμίαν) in human beings, who are greatly disposed to love winning names, and who try to "lay up immortal fame for all time." Why does Socrates indicate that this argument is sophistical?

In our investigation of this question, our first task is to permit Socrates

---

57. Rosen's account of this response differs substantially from mine. He says of Socrates: "It is not difficult to see what puzzles him. . . . The denial of continuity excludes numerical identity and stable mathematical properties. . . . Diotima excludes the possibility of a reconciliation between Pythagorean mathematics and pre-Socratic process physics" (*Plato's "Symposium,"* 256). This is a surprising, and perhaps not quite so obvious, inference, for it has no foundation in the text. It is also unclear why numerical identity and mathematical properties would require the continuity of material beings.

to say what he says. Standard translations of the *Symposium* go to impressive lengths to keep Socrates from accusing Diotima of sophistry.[58] Plato could not have meant that his own mouthpiece played sophistical tricks! However, Diotima does not teach Platonic dogma. As I have contended all along, she administers therapy to Agathon by reasoning from his premises. Among the assumptions that she grants to Agathon is that it is fair to argue the way he and his friends do, not just for them, but also for her. To cure Agathon of Titanism, Diotima must finish grinding his claim to perpetual youth to unpalatable dust. In aid of this cause, Diotima commits one of the most egregious sophisms in the history of philosophy. Plato causes Socrates to call attention to it for fear that seekers of doctrines will miss it.

What is the fallacy? We could guess that it consists in equivocation: If we wanted to prove that human beings engender merely to achieve the lesser immortality of the mortal, it would be illegitimate to do this by citing a universal human desire for fame—the eternity of the species and the replacement of the old and extinct by the young or new are not exactly the same sorts of lower immortality as a long-lived name and endless glory. However, we ought not to press this point. If I console myself with the idea that my children will represent me after I am gone, or if I congratulate myself on exceptional triumphs that will continue to elicit praise after I die, I desire in either case to replace my old and soon-to-be-lost self with a new symbol of my being that survives me, either for a short while or indefinitely. Diotima is right on that score. She knows that Agathon will agree.

Diotima's actual offense is manipulating passions to secure the victory of a lie. There is no *universal* human longing for immortal fame. There are many people who want nothing to do with glory and the wearisome labor necessary to win that fool's gold, the most prominent being the soon-to-be-reincarnated Odysseus who chose the quiet life of a private man when he met Lachesis at the *axis mundi* (*Republic* 620c–d).[59] However, Diotima perceives that she is dealing with men who do crave eternal fame and that people who are ruled by their appetites tend to project them onto everyone. She rekindles the *libido gloriae* in Socrates' *sympotai*, thus easily inducing them to affirm her thesis. Among those whom she dexterously steers in this manner are Phaedrus, who openly covets glory and calls love of honor a virtue; Pausanias, who wants new Athenian laws to declare his pederasty honorable; Eryximachus, who hopes to be revered as a physician who can govern the cosmos; Aristophanes, who flies into rages when the judges of comedies do not give him first prizes; and Agathon himself,

58. For example, Lamb (Loeb edition): "like our perfect professors." Jowett: "She answered with all the authority of an accomplished sophist." Joyce (Hamilton-Cairns anthology): "with an air of authority that was almost professorial."

59. See also *Republic* 347b1–3, where Socrates tells Glaucon that the love of honor is said to be a reproach.

who demonstrates his wisdom by citing his popularity. To reinforce this subtle manipulation, Diotima invokes the examples already provided by Phaedrus, those of the self-sacrificing Alcestis and Achilles, and adds that of Codrus, the Athenian king who gave his life to save his city. She argues that none of these heros would have died for their beloveds if they had not expected to win a deathless memory for virtue.

Diotima-Socrates must know that this reasoning is venal, but she also realizes that it will set her auditors' heads to nodding, and that is her purpose. Socrates-Agathon succumbs to the sophism and lets Diotima proceed without interruption for the rest of her speech. The reduction of Agathon's vaunted divine eternal life to the lower immortality of the mortal animal is complete. With his argument lying in ruins, what remains is to elevate his opinions.

Diotima will continue to argue from Agathon's premises as long as she can. This will make it difficult for her to improve his opinions much. However, it is pedagogically wise to start here. She does what she can, giving ethical instruction specifically directed at her Titanic, glory-loving audience.

Diotima opens by contending that men who are pregnant in body repair to women, opining that they will acquire immortality through their children. Her purpose in saying this is to validate eros for heterosexual intercourse as a worthy longing for immortality in the eyes of the *sympotai.* She attends to this matter because her auditors are misogynists. (She does not mean a principled critique of gays as misogynists, which would be untrue, but she thinks that the "wrong pederasts" to whom she is speaking need this reminder.)

Next, alluding to homoerotic sexual intercourse only in passing, the prophetess takes up "pregnancy of soul." She says that there are people who "are pregnant in their souls even more than in their bodies," people who "conceive and beget (κυῆσαι καὶ τεκεῖν)" what befits souls. Who are these pregnant individuals? Diotima is probably referring especially to gifted gays such as the *sympotai,* giving them new terms with which to think of themselves. What do they conceive and beget? "Prudence [*phronesis*] and the rest of virtue. All the poets are generators of these things, as are those craftsmen [demiurges] called inventive [Eryximachus imagined himself an inventive demiurge]. And by far the greatest and most beautiful part of prudence is the ordering of the things of cities and households, which is named moderation and justice" (209a3–8).

Diotima omitted moderation and justice from her first list of Eros's virtues. We now see that she did not intend to exclude them from the nature of Eros. When she narrated the myth of the birth of Eros, she had to give the daimon a prudence identical with the supposed predatory instincts and cunning of Homer's Odysseus because Agathon esteemed that kind of rapacious slyness. She could not ascribe a prudence of genuine moderation and justice to Eros because Agathon, in the most flippant part of his oration, had made satirical mockeries of all the cardinal virtues except his wisdom, conceived as poetic *technē*, and because the poet would have rejected a truly temperate and just Eros as inconsistent with the hedonistic savagery that he and his friends intended. (For present purposes, we may define true moderation and justice as the opposites of the licentious exploitation admired by Agathon in his jokes, or, as Socrates once informed Alcibiades, as the opposites of absolute license and despotic power [*Alcibiades I* 134c–d, 135b]).[60] Diotima could not counsel genuine moderation and justice until Agathon's smugness about his wisdom as the one needful virtue had been dispelled. Now that condition has been satisfied, so Diotima is free to talk about other virtues and to change her account of their role in Eros's "nature" as easily as she altered her definition of the daimon's telos. In the logic of her myth, moderation and justice clearly do belong to the "nature" of Eros. If human souls are "pregnant" with moderation and justice, that must be the result of the insemination of Penia by Poros. The locus of these virtues must be the nascent Eros.

Having given Eros a prudence that includes a serious moderation and justice, Diotima offers the company new political and pedagogical ideals. She wants the sophists to adopt these models in place of the miniature political and educational theories that mark their rebellious aspirations now. Her account of politics is that its telos is an ordering of cities and households in moderation and justice—not the world conquest of Phaedrus, not the lovers' hegemony of Pausanias, not the medical domination of nature craved by Eryximachus, not the metaphysical rebellion of Aristophanes, and not the organized worship of the poetic god-man that Agathon hopes to set up, with himself as the object of adoration. Her argument about the means to the moderate and just society, one that will have to be amended or qualified soon, is that the poets and creative demiurges must and do strive to educate moderate and just citizens. Poets ought not to attempt to educate admirers who obediently shower them with gifts, reflect their divine creative power, and support imperialistic, self-deifying schemes, as the *sympotai* do.

The role of Eros in bringing about the moderate and just society is that he (it) inspires poets and inventive craftsmen to educate citizens to the requisite virtues. This evidently takes place in the contexts of both individual and mass relationships. When a person who has been divinely pregnant

---

60. Of course, this still begs the question of what real justice and moderation are. Diotima and Plato themselves beg the question in the *Symposium* because it is impossible to treat every problem in adequate depth at once. Plato must assume the possibility of a knowable answer for now and save the actual inquiries for other dialogues. In the meantime, he avoids giving a dogmatic definition.

(ἐγκύμων) in his soul from youth with moderation and justice comes of age and experiences the desire to beget and generate (τίκτειν τε καὶ γεννᾶν), he seeks the beauty in whose presence he may generate (γεννήςειεν), for he can never do this in the presence of the ugly. Being pregnant (κυῶν), the individual embraces beautiful rather than ugly bodies. If a beautiful body should happen to have a beautiful, well-born, good-natured soul, he greatly welcomes this mixture and straightaway addresses the beauty with resourceful speeches about virtue and the qualities and pursuits that behoove a good man, thus undertaking his education. By being with the beauty, the lover begets and generates what he has borne from of old (ἃ πάλαι ἐκύει τίκτει καὶ γεννᾷ, 209a–c), the aforementioned virtues. Both men nurture the resulting "children" together. As in the Seventh Letter, they build a fuller community and a surer friendship than biological parents and children do because their offspring (the virtues) are fairer and "more immortal" than the biological sort. Everyone would prefer these kind of children to the human variety.

This ideal of the individual lover's education of the beloved is aimed at Pausanias and Agathon. Diotima reminds these worthies that spiritual begetting is androgynous. The Ur-nature of the *erastēs* has been fertilized by Poros. Thus, when the lover wants to beget, he really desires to bring forth that with which he is pregnant. So, the excellences that he yearns to engender are not creations of his own that prove his divinity; he has actually been pregnant with them from of old, when Poros inseminated Penia, and they are inherited divine resources that he is bringing to birth.

Further, the lover must see that he can give birth to that which has been conceived in him not simply by an act of his sovereign will, under an arrangement in which he may choose his beloved, but only in the presence of a beauty that controls him. When he does bring forth his inheritance from the god in the presence of beauty, seeking the betterment of his beloved, his offspring are carried not in his semen, but in his edifying speeches about goodness. Virtues do not jump from body to body via physical touching, as Agathon argued.[61] Rather, they are evoked in the beloved's soul by the words that proceed from the lover's soul. These speeches are not seeds with which the *erastēs* begets virtues in the sense that he pumps moderation and justice into his *erōmenos,* installing in the beloved's soul something that was not there before. Rather, the *erastēs* begets insofar as his good words trigger the labor of a beloved who himself is already pregnant with the virtues, for the beloved's soul is already beautiful, well born, and good-natured, and the two nurture the offspring together. Finally, Diotima has just become sexually austere. She has barely mentioned that the lover embraces

---

61. Diotima would probably add that vices do not jump from person to person through the semen either, as in Augustine's idea of original sin.

beautiful bodies and has harped on virtue a great deal. She might be trying to maneuver the *erastēs* into the disciplined state to which Glaucon is
eventually led in the *Republic* (403b). If not that, she still rejects the "wrong
pederasty" of Pausanias. Her lover does not force the *erōmenos* to prostitute
himself in return for an education. It is spiritual partnership in the virtues,
not Pausanias's sexually exploitative transmission of excellence to his re-
made fair laddie, that produces the permanent friendship that Pausanias
promised Agathon.

If Pausanias and his friends now wonder what incentive the lovers have
to educate the beloveds if sexual gratification is not the point, Diotima
replies by stimulating their libidos for immortal glory again, pointing to
the relationships that famous poets and lawgivers have had with whole
civilizations. She directs their gaze to the ethical offspring of Homer and
Hesiod, which have won deathless fame and even temples for their authors. Lycurgus and Solon have been equally successful with their laws. It
is far more glorious, Diotima intimates, to educate Hellas to moderation
and justice than to conquer nations and exploit beloveds.

This raises questions. Homer and Hesiod do not shine in the pages of
the *Republic* as teachers of moderation and justice; rather, they appear as
ignoble liars who corrupt the young. Why, then, does Diotima call them
glorious teachers of virtue here? Obviously, our answer must be that Diotima is attempting to use the fame of Homer and Hesiod as an inducement
to Socrates' fellows to do what those poets should have done and perhaps
really did, rather than what they seemed to do in the texts castigated in
the *Republic*. However, why does Diotima expect Homer, Hesiod, all poets,
and the inventive demiurges to be able to become ideal teachers of moderation and justice? Poets rank in the lower half of Stesichorus's hierarchy of
souls. The doctors do not rank much higher. They saw little truth in their
mythical former lives. They cannot begin to approach perfection in virtue
themselves or have any profound grasp of it.

The solution of our puzzle lies in the design of Socrates' first program of
education in the *Republic*. Socrates proposes to oversee the makers of stories (the poets), requiring them to tell tales that educate auxiliary guardians
properly. The auxiliaries are supposed to become philosophic and wise
in the same manner that dogs have these virtues—as well as courageous,
moderate, and just. This means that the poets are asked to teach wisdom
and the other virtues to the auxiliaries in the forms of true opinions and
habits that are instilled by rote drilling and strict discipline. Diotima probably envisages giving her poets the same assignment. Thus, she does not
believe that the poet-engendered virtues will be real virtues. Later, she
says that only the man who reaches the pinnacle of the ascent that she
is describing will be able "to beget not images (εἴδωλα) of virtue . . . but
virtue" (212a3–5). When Diotima tries to interest Socrates' poetic *sympotai*

in engendering moderate and just cities as a means to their eternal fame, she tactfully neglects to add that philosophers will have to govern these polities to compensate for the shortcomings of the poetic and technical teachings.

This concludes Diotima's effort to educate Socrates-Agathon by reasoning on the basis of Agathon's premises. Before examining the rest of her speech, I need to advert to a serious problem. I have been waiting for the right moment to bring this issue into the limelight, and it seems best to start thinking about it now. The problem is this: Important contemporary commentators accuse Socrates of having been "erotically deficient." This charge seems to have two meanings. I shall deal with one of them here and allow the other to arise in due course. The first sense of the accusation is that Socrates was sexually abnormal.[62] On the grounds of his behavior and speech so far—particularly his stuffy reaction to Agathon's suggested touch, his resistance to wine and drunkenness, and his alter ego Diotima's rush to skip reflection on homoerotic intercourse in order to discuss pregnancy of soul and virtue—and on the further grounds of his rejection of the sexual advances of Alcibiades and, we might as well add, his comments on intercourse in the *Phaedrus* (which will be discussed in subsequent chapters), it is said that Socrates lacked the Dionysian self-abandonment necessary to a healthy eroticism. Is this true? Is Socrates' whole argument nothing but the bile of a sexual crank?

Socrates' critics apparently presuppose that pederasty, homosexuality, and bisexuality should be considered normal for our analytic purposes. That is, they assume that a healthy, red-blooded Athenian man would have been expected to be eager for sexual intercourse with boys, other men, and women, and to engage in these acts often. I am willing to accept their premise, in the spirit of Plato's present lack of attention to this anachronistic concern. I know that some question its historical accuracy, but that is irrelevant in the context of our dialogue. Granting the premise, I may challenge the conclusions that the critics draw from it. So, let's have a look. Is Socrates erotically deficient?

I begin with a known biographical fact. Socrates married and produced children with Xanthippe. Diotima apparently approves of this, for she teaches that this is what those who are pregnant of body do. It would be difficult to portray this behavior as evidence of sexual abnormality. (For want of solid data, this is all that we can say about Socrates' relationships with his wife. Stories of his coldness to her are rumors based on his decision to send her home on the day of his execution.)

---

62. For this view, see Rosen, *Plato's "Symposium,"* xiii, xvii, xviii, xx, 5, 232, 251, 277, 279, 286, 311, 317. It is the primary thesis of Rosen's book that Plato wrote the *Symposium* as a critique of this flaw in Socrates. The other sense of the accusation is represented by Gregory Vlastos and Martha Nussbaum. I shall take it up presently.

On the homoerotic side of the ledger, we see in the *Charmides* (155d) that Socrates was aroused by the sight of a boy's genitals—unless this is a lie or a joke. We also gather from the *Symposium* that Socrates was attracted to Agathon. We also hear Diotima suggesting that the man who is pregnant of soul goes about seeking the beauty on whom he might beget and that he "embraces" (ἀσπάζεται) beautiful bodies (209b5). We read in the *Alcibiades I* that Socrates followed his beloved young Alcibiades around town with the other lovers in the lad's train. If we reserve the rejection of Alcibiades' advances and the *Phaedrus* passages for later discussion and base our initial judgment solely on these facts, we seem to be proving under our stipulated definitions of classical normality that Socrates was a sexually typical Athenian.

Well, then, it will be asked, what about his reaction to Agathon and his resistance to drink? These points are inconsequential. No one would accept sexual groping that was open to interpretation as a dominance gesture. The notion that erotic excellence requires drunken self-abandonment is insupportable. Eros serves Aphrodite, not Dionysus.

Well, what about Diotima's rush past homoerotic intercourse in order to get to virtue? This is where I must question the reasoning of Socrates' critics. Diotima seems to me to leave the *sympotai* undisturbed in their "embraces" of beautiful bodies. She does not have a change of heart, storm into bedrooms, and tear lovers apart. Again bracketing the disappointment of Alcibiades and the *Phaedrus* passages for later analysis, why is that not enough to save Socrates from the charge of erotic deficiency? Why should Diotima not pass over a few sexual scenes in order to reach pregnancy of soul and virtue? Do the critics maintain that eros necessarily culminates in the lovers' embraces? Do they therefore expect Diotima to celebrate orgasms at exuberant length as "ends in themselves"? Is Socrates erotically deficient because he does not make Diotima conclude her lecture in the style of American movies, with scenes of carnal love everywhere triumphant?

Socrates has been arguing that there is more to eros than genital sexuality, indeed, an entire realm of eros that pertains to souls more than to bodies. One is free to disagree with him, but it is thoughtless to adduce his opinion as evidence for judging him bizarre. I would add that there is a time and a place for everything. Sometimes, lusty celebrations of sexual love are exactly what a situation needs. For example, Carl Orff's *Carmina Burana* are great cultural treasures and wonderful tonics for people in the doldrums. However, Athens in the year 416 is not a society that needs performances of some ancient equivalent of *Carmina Burana*. Socrates is confronted not with repressed Puritans or Victorians who need to loosen up but with oversexed egoists who have driven their sexuality into tyranny and beyond, into a great Titanism of the spirit that threatens to destroy the city. In these circumstances, might it not be important for a sexually normal philosopher to pay more attention to eros of the soul than to eros of the body? Might Socrates not have sufficient reasons for drawing the attention of his *sympotai* away from their orgasms and toward reflection on the erotic diseases that are eating their souls? Such considerations begin to make it doubtful that Socrates is "erotically deficient" and doubtful that Plato wrote the *Symposium* to convict him of this fault.

The problem of Socrates' alleged sexual abnormality will have to be revisited in some later pages on Alcibiades and the *Phaedrus*. For now, I shall suppose that Socrates-Diotima is right to leave sexual embraces in the bedroom where we last saw them and right to ascend to a meditation on eros and souls. Even if the *Symposium* dramatically begins as a struggle over bodies, the dialogue ultimately is about an effort to cure a Titanic eros in souls.

Diotima has gone as far as she can in her endeavor to improve Agathon's opinions by reasoning from his premises. To advance his education further, she must set him on a higher path, with more suitable foundations. To give him a look at the better way, she commences an ascent of what she calls a "ladder" of beauty (211c). She gradually drops prophetic language in favor of philosophic speech as she rises, thus proving herself Socrates' alter ego or kindred spirit, for a prophetess could not know the things about philosophy that she knows unless she were a philosopher, too. She has always been a philosopher who spoke prophetically.

Still declaiming prophetically, and still addressing Agathon through Socrates, Diotima says: "Into these erotic matters, Socrates, perhaps even you might be initiated. But I do not know if you could approach the perfect revelations (or final revelations, τέλεα καὶ ἐποπτικά) for the sake of which these exist, if someone should follow them rightly. I shall speak, then, nor shall I abandon my eagerness. Try to follow me, if you can" (209e5–212b2). This compact statement has three important elements that need emphasis, as follows.

First, Diotima is not certain that "Socrates" has grasped the foregoing erotica. Why not? Probably, it is unclear that Agathon will understand that reasoning from his own premises leads to all these conclusions fatal to his claims, because this will contradict his strongest passions. It is even less certain that he will have sufficient intellectual integrity to yield to Diotima's therapy gracefully if he does understand, which he must do before he can make real progress.

Second, Diotima doubts that "Socrates" is ready to hear higher revelations. Why? Probably, the reason is that being led to the boundary of poetry and prophecy is one thing and ascending to higher levels, such as prophecy or even philosophy, is another. The problem is that there is a fundamental disparity between what Agathon needs in order to rise and what he has gained so far. "Perfect revelations" are coming. This implies that what Agathon has been shown up to now are "imperfect revelations." In the *Republic*, Socrates warns: "Nothing imperfect (ἀτελὲς) is a measure of anything" (504c2–3). After all this lovely talk, with all its (sophistical) refutations of Agathon's positions, and all its beautiful myths that are intended to be (and are) closer to the truth than Agathon's views, Diotima has still given Agathon no real knowledge of eros and no genuine openness to the presence of the healthy Eros in his soul.

What, then, has been the point of Diotima's speech so far? Diotima asserts that the imperfect revelations have been for the sake of the perfect revelations. This plainly means that Diotima has given Socrates-Agathon the imperfect revelations in order to purify his soul for the reception of the perfect ones. Her *technē* of eros, which is later taken over by Socrates, is not a science of eros, and not an art of injecting knowledge of eros into souls, but a *technē* of preparing souls for the flowering of the healthy Eros by removing toxins from them. However, the purging of the poisons does not guarantee that Agathon's psyche is still healthfully pregnant with the seeds of the higher revelations. A soul cleansed of blights might be barren because it has suffered a miscarriage through extreme trauma, or pregnant with a fetus deformed by the illnesses. Agathon's behavior has not inspired confidence that he still bears the healthy seeds. Thus, Diotima cannot know that her speech will trigger Agathon's fruitful labor. By the way, this means that the Socrates who professes to know (ἐπίστασθαι, 177d8) erotic matters does not contradict the Socrates of the *Apology* who says that he is "worth nothing with respect to wisdom" (23b2–4). One could know things about erotics—for example, how to eliminate impediments to the highest revelations—without knowing how to ensure the desired results, or what eros is in itself. We need not agree with Bloom that at least one of Socrates' two remarks is ironic.[63]

Third, Diotima fears that "Socrates" will not be able to follow her new arguments. Why? The difficulty here is not that Diotima will use abstruse reasoning intelligible only to the most subtle minds. Neither is it that she will traffic in ponderous language or jargon; she will speak ordinary words. Neither is it that she will lack patience to explain things to "Socrates" in as many different ways as he requires to comprehend them. Rather, everything will depend on Socrates'—that is to say, Agathon's—abilities. Diotima will say what she has to say, and the poet will be able to follow only if her oration activates seeds with which his soul is pregnant, initiating the process by which he brings forth what he has borne from of old. Thus, Diotima refers to epoptic, a concept borrowed from the mystery religions, to whet Agathon's curiosity and capture his attention. Agathon and his allies

63. Bloom, *Love and Friendship*, 431.

will imagine that they are about to be told a secret that may not be legally divulged to the uninitiated. They will be all ears. However, Diotima cannot tell them the secret even when she announces it. They must give birth to it by being what Friedrich Schleiermacher calls good "auditors of the inner."[64]

Lest we, in our innocence, should think ourselves better able than Agathon to follow Diotima, we should try to understand as clearly as possible what we are about to receive. We are not about to be given the several details of a propositional revelation. Indeed, the coming paragraphs of Diotima's speech do not look anything like metaphysical information. Rather, they look like instructions on what we must do to prepare ourselves for the higher revelation. In the end, we are told to expect a vision of beauty. We are taught what the beauty is not, but we still receive little or no data on what the beauty is. What we hear is the proclamation of a silent vision. Thus, we cannot excel Agathon by being more attentive than he. Again, we are not about to be given syllogisms that can be understood as grand metaphysical verities only by unusually astute logical minds. Diotima merely tells "Socrates" that he must do X to permit Y to occur. We cannot do better than Agathon by being superior logicians. Our only hope of succeeding where the poet will probably fail lies in letting Diotima guide us and in waiting to learn whether we see anything resembling what she says we are supposed to see.

Diotima's first piece of advice to the would-be initiate is: "It is necessary for one who proceeds rightly in this matter to begin when young by going to [or longing for, ἰέναι] the beautiful bodies" (210a4–6). Why does "Socrates" need to be told this? Given that the real Socrates is as red-blooded as any Athenian or American young man, I doubt that the counsel has much to do with his alleged erotic failings.[65] Also, the matter that "Socrates" must handle correctly is seeing revelations, not proving his manhood. What Socrates (that is, Agathon) really needs to be taught is that there is a necessary connection between seeing the perfect revelations and being attracted to the beautiful bodies, a point that is not immediately obvious to a Greek who wants to be initiated into the mysteries, on the one hand, or who craves beautiful bodies merely out of sexual ardor, on the other. The point is less clear to the typical American, who would never stop to think that intellectual life and sex are related. We need to learn that we cannot fracture our being into compartments, separating our reason and our sexual longings, soaring rationally to a great vision of beauty while ignoring our

---

64. Therefore, I cannot agree with Strauss's argument that the *Symposium* reveals what really happened when mysteries were profaned, that is, that it was Socrates, not Alcibiades, who disclosed the secrets (*On Plato's "Symposium,"* 23–24).

65. Cf. Rosen, *Plato's "Symposium,"* 265.

sexuality as if it were wholly irrelevant to the flight, or treating sexuality as if it were its own end. We are all subject to the order of Beauty-Aphrodite-Moira that Eros should initially awaken us to Beauty through the appeal of bodies to bodies. We must obey that fateful decree, even though we are not privy to its rationale. We meet the same situation in the *Phaedrus*, where the black horses in our souls behave as if they were incorrigible sexual maniacs but are nevertheless the naturally required initiators of the flights of lovers to their former home. All the aspects of our being are pulled by the same Eros.[66]

Continuing, Diotima tells the neophyte:

> First, if his guide leads him rightly, he must love one body and gen-
> erate beautiful words in it [or in its presence, ἐνταῦθα]. Next, he must
> observe that the beauty of any body is brother to that of any other body,
> so that if it is necessary for him to pursue beauty in form, it is great folly
> not to assume the beauty of all bodies to be one and the same. Having
> understood this, he must make himself a lover of all beautiful bodies,
> thereby diminishing his feeling for one, disdaining and counting it for
> naught. (210a4–b6)

A little later, having ascended to the level of souls and beyond, Diotima declares again that her initiate may not, like a lowly slave, love beauty in a single instance, whether in a boy or a man or a custom (210c6–d3).

It is speeches such as these that give rise to the other sense of the charge that Socrates is erotically deficient, namely, that Socrates is incapable of real love of particular human beings. Indeed, Diotima's ideas cause Gregory Vlastos to accuse not only Socrates but also Plato of being erotically flawed. It will help us to consider Vlastos's objections to Diotima, for his concerns provide an entree to the meaning of what she says. Vlastos argues that, in the *Symposium:*

> It is not said or implied or so much as hinted at that "birth in beauty"
> should be motivated by love of persons—that the ultimate purpose of
> the creative act should be to enrich the lives of persons who are them-
> selves worthy of love for their own sake. . . . We are to love the persons
> so far, and only insofar, as they are good and beautiful. . . . If our love
> for them is to be only for their virtue and beauty, the individual, in the
> uniqueness and integrity of his or her individuality, will never be the
> object of our love.[67]

---

66. This is not a pitch for the seduction of students by professors. To recognize the reality of attraction and its relevance to the life of the spirit is not to react to every instance
of attraction by proceeding to the joys of Aphrodite. There are other considerations.

67. Vlastos, *Platonic Studies,* 31.

We may open our reflection on Vlastos with a glance at Martha Nussbaum's appraisal of his charge. Although she has qualms about what "uniqueness" and "individuality" might be, Nussbaum asserts: "And yet, despite our questions, we feel that Vlastos must somehow be right." She means that it seems true that Socrates cannot love a person. However, she thinks that Plato himself can be saved from Vlastos's critique. She reasons that what Vlastos demands but does not get from Diotima, "a story of passion for a unique individual as eloquent as any in literature," is contained in Alcibiades' upcoming speech, such that Plato must realize that a passion for a unique individual is "fundamental to our experience of love."[68]

I would go further and defend not only Plato but also Diotima against Vlastos. With his hermeneutic that seeks dogmas in Plato, Vlastos unwittingly shows that Diotima disagrees with him about an ontological issue. Her opinion strikes me as much more tenable than his. The hermeneutic and metaphysical problems must be laid out step by step. To begin, I would endorse Nussbaum's view that Vlastos wrongly disregards Plato's drama. We have now seen enough of Plato's art to know that we cannot read him as Hegel does, distilling out doctrines and ignoring contexts. Even if we aspire merely to an understanding of Plato's argumentation that falls short of his serious insights, we must still take into account everything in his poems, including the dramas, the contexts, the reasoning, and the actions.[69]

Next, it appears necessary to append a logical point of order to Nussbaum's criticism: Diotima does not volunteer the theory of love that Vlastos demands because the topic of this section of her talk is the path to the perfect revelations, not our time's romantic ideal of a love relationship between individuals. What Diotima holds is that *if* it is necessary for the neophyte to pursue beauty in form, *then* he must suppose beauty to be one and the same in all bodies, become a lover of all beautiful bodies, find the same beauty in all souls, and become a lover of the one beauty in all souls, too. This is to maintain that *if* the initiate feels impelled to seek out the highest reality of beauty, and to attain to the loftiest vision of it, *then* he must adopt an ontological postulate, that the beauty to which he responds in each body or soul is one and the same in all. Then he must take the rational step of loving this beauty in all equally. Diotima says nothing about ceasing to love an individual particularly, with all one's heart. She insists only that her initiate should put the love in metaphysical perspective. This exercise should lessen the intensity of the initiate's feeling for the beloved in the sense that the lover stops attributing singularity to the merits of the

68. Nussbaum, *Fragility of Goodness,* 167, 166.

69. Many of Vlastos's complaints against Socrates are based on the *Lysis.* Vlastos's comments on this text are applied to Plato's other dialogues, thus wrongly disregarding context.

beloved and begins to see the beloved as one of many who are constituted as beauties by participation in a common beauty. The lover then realizes that the common beauty must be loved infinitely more than the individuals who share in it. This new love helps to elevate him or her to the perfect revelations of beauty.

Vlastos would probably object that this still amounts to a failure to love the individual in the uniqueness and integrity of his or her individuality, for now we must love the common beauty, not the unique individual for his or her own sake. This brings us to the fundamental ontological issue. The problem is already indicated by Nussbaum's inerrant sense that there is something questionable about Vlastos's ideas of uniqueness and individuality. Vlastos thinks it self-evident and undeniable that one should love the individual in the uniqueness and integrity of his or her individuality, and that this is to love the individual for his or her own sake. However, what is an individual? What is uniqueness? What is integrity of individuality? Is there such a thing as a "unique" individual in Vlastos's sense?

Perhaps a unique individual would be a self-contained entity endowed with no essential nature that could be replicated, a random, inimitable mixture of particles, motions, and traits. Perhaps integrity of individuality would be a wholeness that allowed this self-possessed entity to be itself by itself, owing its existence and structure to no one. Perhaps, therefore, Vlastos's unique, integral individual would be the godly self willed by Agathon, which would resemble the modern self on whose behalf Immanuel Kant especially insisted that it be treated as an "end in itself." Perhaps all this would imply that the ultimate purpose of the creative act should be to enrich the lives of persons who are themselves worthy of love for their own sake. However, none of this is necessarily so.

Diotima allowed Agathon to depict himself as a "sort" with no essence for pedagogical reasons. Her present invocation of a beauty that is common to all bodies and souls establishes that she never really subscribed to that picture. Her individuals are definitely not perfectly unique because they share a nature and, therefore, are destined to essentially the same kinds of beauty and virtue no matter how singularly and unrepeatably manifested in each. Again, they are not autonomously integral because they are descendants of Poros and Penia, that is, because they have a ground of their being that is common to all while allowing them to differ. They surely cannot be loved strictly "in the uniqueness and integrity of their individuality" for their "own" sakes because someone who intends to love them for who they are will love them for who they *really* are, beings who share in a common beauty and virtue even though they are uniquely instantiated. It will certainly not be the highest purpose of the creative act to enrich the lives of these lovers because they love essentially to serve Beauty-Aphrodite, not to make Beauty serve them. Of course, the act of love does enrich the lovers simply by virtue of being what it is, the fulfillment of the lovers' wish to belong to Beauty-Aphrodite, so we could state that this enrichment is *one* important aim of the act. However, it is not the *ultimate* end. So, who is right, Vlastos or Diotima? It seems to me that there is a common human nature and that it shares in a common beauty and goodness that flower differently in each individual, so that to love the common *is* to love the individual and to love the individual *is* to love the common. I think that the palm goes to Diotima: without the common, there is no individual.

Vlastos would dispute this. He would contend that "Plato" is wrong simply because a theory of love that discerns what love really is *should* regard individuals as ends-in-themselves who are unique and whole by themselves. In reply, I would speculate that Diotima foresaw the possibility of such protests when she wondered whether Socrates-Agathon could follow her. If there is a common human nature with a common beauty and virtue, and if the nature gives all people their special identities in the diverse ways that they participate in the common beauty and virtue, these truths might not be accessible to someone who cannot experience the common because he insists upon being an autonomous individual. The dispute between Plato and Vlastos is the same as the debate between Diotima and Socrates' *sympotai,* the same as the dispute between prophecy and sophistry. It could be resolved only if Vlastos agreed to open himself to the possibility of the experience that Diotima teaches him to seek and waited to see whether it came to him.

Whether Vlastos consented to attempt this experiment or not, he would still offer one last rebuttal. He would argue that holding "Plato's" theory of birth in beauty certainly means that one would "never" love an individual for his or her own sake, for "Plato" does not speak about this, and therefore must not know about it. Nussbaum would probably also continue to agree with Vlastos's critique of Diotima. However, his charges are wholly false. Clearly, under the concept of "individuality" held by Plato, Socrates, and Diotima, we may not and cannot love the common ground of beauty, virtue, and being while refraining from loving individuals for their own sakes. Just as obviously, Plato and Diotima both know this truth. This is where Nussbaum's insistence upon Plato's drama and context must be brought to bear, and not only by pointing to Alcibiades' speech in the *Symposium.* If, as I have assumed, Diotima functions as a mask of Socrates, we may demonstrate Socrates' ability to love a real individual by finding stories of "a passion for a unique individual as eloquent as any in literature" in other Socratic speeches.

We do not face a long or arduous search. In the *Alcibiades I,* Socrates abruptly speaks to Alcibiades after having followed him around silently for years. In his salute to Alcibiades, Socrates identifies himself as "the first of all your lovers" (πρῶτος ἐραστής σου, 103a1–2). In the ensuing conversation, Socrates explains that he has singled Alcibiades out for his special greatness of soul. Later, he beseeches Alcibiades to obey the command of the Delphic oracle, "know thyself" (124a8–b1). He convinces Alcibiades that he is not his body, but his soul. He argues that he who loves Alcibiades loves his soul, and tells Alcibiades that he alone has loved his soul (131c–d). With evident fervor in his voice, he says to Alcibiades: "I was the only lover of you" (131e10) and urges him to keep his soul beautiful. In the *Gorgias*, more than twenty years later, Socrates still declares that he loves Alcibiades (481d). These are not the pronouncements of a rationalistic cold fish who has "never" loved or could "never" love a unique person. They are the words of "a passion for a unique individual as eloquent as any in literature."[70]

However, perhaps I overreach myself. There might be even more eloquent words that meet this description, those of the brokenhearted lament for Dion that Diogenes Laertius attributes to Plato. I refer to the epitaph quoted fully above, the poem that ends with the line: "After making my heart rage with eros, O Dion!" Vlastos is plainly wrong to think that Plato, Socrates, or Diotima could "never" love a unique person. His ideological commitment to the autonomous individual blinds him to what is a matter of public record.

We return again to Diotima's ascent of the ladder of beauty for the benefit of Socrates-Agathon. Having required Socrates to become a lover of all beautiful bodies, Diotima orders him to regard the beauty of souls as more valuable (210b7) than that of bodies, so that the least bloom in the soul will suffice to elicit his love and care, causing him to beget the speeches that improve the young. Although Socrates is not enjoined to stop loving bodies, Diotima's words imply that he should be attracted to youths with minimally beautiful souls, even if their bodies are not especially beautiful. This is consistent with his earlier statement to Alcibiades that the true *erastēs* loves not his beloved's body, but his soul, and it explains how the Socrates whose physical beauty is substandard can enjoy lovers. Assuming that there might be a lot of young folk whose souls are slightly beautiful, Socrates will have a lot of loving to do—one wonders whether Diotima has not just ordered Socrates to teach all mankind. Further, Socrates will not be permitted to stop loving a beloved whose soul becomes less beautiful, at least not until the youth loses every scintilla of spiritual beauty, which might be a metaphysical impossibility. I think that this is why, Vlastos notwithstanding, Socrates still loved Alcibiades after breaking with him, just as Plato loved Dion despite his flaws.

---

70. Socrates threatens to leave Alcibiades if he fails to remain as beautiful of soul as he needs to be. However, he does not say that he will stop loving Alcibiades. This is an issue that I am reserving for later treatment.

Next, Diotima argues, preferring souls forces one to behold the beauty in customs and laws and to notice that all this beauty is akin to all, so that one will think the body's beauty a small thing.[71] Although the initiate still has no idea what beauty is, he must experience it as a single, uniform reality that draws a teacher to the soul of a promising student, a citizen to the beautifully moderate and just order of a city, and a sexual *erastēs* to the body of a beloved. He must also know beauty as a reality that pulls him more strongly to the soul of the promising student and to the beautifully moderate and just order of a city than to the body of a beloved. Although we scarcely understand the meaning of our words, beauty is starting to look like the metaphysical ground or essence of the perfection of all natures. Its attractiveness to prophetic-philosophic souls is apparently increasing to the extent that it permeates natures that resemble itself in substance and scope.

The erotic prophet-philosopher will now begin to seem sexually aberrant to ordinary folk and to poets such as Aristophanes because he or she will appear more thrilled by chances to engender well-ordered souls and polities than by opportunities for intercourse with beautiful bodies, much as the vulgar lover of bodies will become more aroused by opportunities to sleep with physical beauties than by invitations to bed the plain and the elderly. However, it is not the erotic prophet-philosopher who may be justly called defective, for his or her responses will be more in tune with the relationship of Eros to Beauty-Aphrodite than that of a man who never experiences the relative strengths of the erotic attractions to beautiful souls, cities, and bodies. Nor has Diotima suggested that her initiate necessarily becomes sexually repressed. Diotima's lover of beauty will have a robust natural eros for beautiful souls, cities, and bodies. The man who is impervious to Diotima's experience will know only the natural eros for bodies, and, as with mental illness, his deficiency will cause him to believe that it is the healthy philosopher who is sick. In this regard, it should be noted that Diotima's ladder establishes a hierarchy of loves, with eros for bodies ranking below eros for beautiful souls and laws. One can imagine that if the love of a body somehow became incompatible with the love of a soul or a city, the lover would have encountered an unwelcome but still compelling reason for abstaining from love of that body. By the same token, Diotima would require everyone to give up all carnal loves that threaten to mar the beauty of souls, customs, and laws.

Nearing the end of her preparation of the initiate, Diotima now tells him that he must ascend to the sciences (ἐπιστήμας), pondering their beauty.

---

71. The jump from souls to cities is perfectly logical. The neophyte has been commanded to love all beautiful souls. Ideally, the well-ordered city is the community of all beautiful souls.

Having beheld beauty on a great scale, he will become incapable of loving only one beauty. He will turn toward the open sea of beauty, and, looking at it, he will engender (τίκτῃ) many beautiful and magnificent speeches in unenvious philosophy. Diotima's insistence that the philosophy be devoid of envy presages the same stipulation in the Seventh Letter (344b), where Plato discusses the proofs of names, definitions, sights, and sense perceptions always associated with going up and down among the four. The "sciences" and "philosophy" to which Diotima refers are the incomplete knowledge and lower-level, dialectical philosophy to which Plato attains in moving up and down among the four. This is why Diotima promptly informs Socrates that, strengthened and augmented by his many beautiful and magnificent speeches about the sciences, he might perhaps descry a single science of a beauty of which she has yet to speak. The previous sciences do not produce the new one inevitably; they only prepare the soul for it. The new one approaches the perfect knowledge of the fifth, which is philosophy proper, in Plato's Seventh Letter. The beauty of the sciences that passing up and down among the four affords, in a process that evidently is still androgynous generation, and the relationship of the sciences of the four to that of the fifth, could be known only to a philosopher. Diotima has ascended from prophecy to philosophy. Now she will be harder, and perhaps impossible, for Agathon to understand, and this explains why she pauses one last time to urge Socrates (that is, Agathon) to give her his best attention.

Diotima notifies Socrates: "Whoever has been thus far educated in erotics, seeing the beautiful things in succession and rightly, now coming to the end of erotics will perceive suddenly (ἐξαίφνης) something wondrous and beautiful in its nature. And it is on account of this, Socrates, that there were all the previous labors" (210e2–6). Diotima's report that the initiate has the vision "suddenly" corresponds to the fact that the leaping flame illuminates the soul of the philosopher "suddenly" (ἐξαίφνης) in the Seventh Letter (341c7). I think that Diotima is describing the same experience that Plato recounts in that epistle. She does not say what the object of her vision is, probably because she cannot. This seems to mean that eros leads us to a wisdom that is silent because it is ineffable, not because it is secret.

It might be objected that Diotima has quite a lot to say about the object of a vision that is supposedly ineffable. She declares that it always is, neither coming to be nor passing away, neither waxing nor waning, neither beautiful in one part nor ugly in another, nor at one time and not another, nor in one respect and not another, nor in one place and not another, nor to some and not to others. It is not visible in a face or hands or in any other part of the human body. It is neither a logos nor a science, nor is it in anything, such as an animal, earth, heaven, or anything else. It is ever itself according to itself, with itself, one in form (μονοειδὲς).[72] Although all beautiful things participate in it, coming to be and passing away, it grows neither greater nor less and suffers nothing (210e6–211b5). Should we not judge that there are too many words in this speech for something allegedly wordless?

This complaint overlooks the widely recognized fact that Diotima's description of the object of the vision is entirely negative. We are told everything that the highest beauty is not. Even the language that seems obviously positive is negative: To assert that something is always "according to itself," "with itself," and "singular in form" is to say that it is not like anything in human experience. The phrases evoke no images in our minds because we have never seen anything that corresponds to them. The negative terminology is used by Diotima to indicate that the ultimate beauty is absolutely incomparable to everything in our ken. By "absolutely," I mean "absolutely." The highest beauty is so utterly different from everything we know that it must be said to have no spatiotemporal presence, for that which is exempt from every kind of change, that which is contained in no body, that which is identical with no logos or science, and that which "is not in earth, heaven, or anything else" is nowhere. Hence, it is in no time. It follows that the ultimate beauty does not share our mode of being and that if we attribute existence to it at all, we can do so only analogically. The beauty is beyond being.[73]

Diotima continues by informing Socrates that when a person ascends from these stages by means of "the right pederasty" (211b5–6) and begins to perceive beauty, he will "almost" be at the end. There is more to come. What? Perhaps Diotima indicates the necessity of rising above the vision of the ultimate beauty to the vision of the good. Diotima does not speak of this. She has already flown too high for sophistical poets.

We come to Diotima's peroration. Retracing the steps of her ascent up her ladder, the prophetess-philosopher tells Socrates that he must always climb until he knows what beauty is itself. A human being finds this life alone worthwhile, meditating on the beautiful itself (αὐτὸ τὸ καλόν, 211d3). The "Mantinean woman" maintains that such a life is far superior to that spent chasing gold, raiment, and beautiful boys and striplings, as "Socrates"

---

72. In other words, it seems to succeed in being what Vlastos might have wanted the unique human individual to be.

73. Rosen says that "there is nothing in this brief description of beauty in itself which renders it in a realm altogether separate from its appearances to man" (*Plato's "Symposium*," 271–72). It seems to me that he denies the plain meaning of Diotima's words. Nor does it make sense to claim that the separateness of beauty should be understood as that of "a unique form, visible not in something else, but by virtue of those instances which dwell within it." Diotima has just said precisely that the beautiful is "visible" (analogically, to the soul) apart from the appearances of beauty in everything in the universe. Beauty itself does not appear "in" these things, and, being entirely "according to itself" and "with itself," it does not depend upon them for its own proper visibility.

(now representing not only Agathon, but all the sophists) presently does. Diotima draws this contrast between the life of philosophic contemplation and the quest for gold, raiment, and sexually attractive lads not because she wants to establish another metaphysical point, but because her *sympotai* desire nothing less than the wealth, power, and erotic pleasure that Glaucon desired when he fantasized about the ring, and she hopes to save Athens by converting these popular figures. With her audience still in mind, she asks what would happen if one of them could see beauty itself, whole, pure, and unmixed with corporal and mortal things, and she inquires: "What if he could see divine beauty itself in its oneness of form?" (211e3–4). Diotima knows that her companions still want to be gods, and she is suggesting to them that real ecstasy lies not in self-deification, but in the enjoyment of the philosopher's vision of the divine beauty. Almost as an afterthought, she thus indicates that the beautiful itself (αὐτὸ τὸ καλόν) is divine.

Warming to her rhetorical task, and turning especially to Agathon and Aristophanes, Diotima now asks whether they think that a life spent seeing and being with beauty would be trivial. Would it not be true, rather, that a man living thus would generate not images of virtue, but true exemplars, inasmuch as he is beholding not images, but the truth? When he does this, he will be loved by the god, and, if any human being can do so, he will also acquire immortality (211e4–212a7). What Diotima is saying is that if Agathon wants to attain to the greatest happiness by means of being associated with the greatest beauty and virtue, he must give up his attempt to achieve supreme beauty and virtue in his own divine person. The real beauty itself can be seen and tied to oneself only by beholding the divine beauty in the manner that Diotima has described, with a faculty of the human soul suited for the purpose. Likewise, real virtue can be won only by embracing the gift of Poros that allows us to participate in the androgynous engendering of true speeches about wisdom, moderation, courage, and justice. Further, if Agathon wishes to be a delight to the gods, and if Aristophanes hopes to gain their benign neglect, if not their friendship, they must do so by acquiring the true virtues that result from contemplating beauty itself, not by engaging in Agathon's poetic self-construction, and not by practicing Aristophanes' combination of the spiteful flaunting of Eros with the sullen performance of required sacrifices. If the two poets want to be immortal, their only means to the end in this life is to allow their souls to be permeated with the vision of the ever abiding beauty.

Diotima falls silent. Socrates resumes speaking in his own name, telling Phaedrus and the others that he is persuaded of what she said and that he hopes to persuade everyone else to seek the help of Eros in the pursuit of the immortality just described. He exhorts all human beings to honor Eros in this manner and asks Phaedrus to accept this account of Eros in place of the promised eulogy. When Socrates finishes, everyone applauds except

Aristophanes, who begins to remark about something in Socrates' speech that referred to his own. The ovation for Socrates' talk is probably a polite tribute paid to a surprisingly worthy opponent under the rules of civilized competition. It does not match the thunderous applause that the audience gave to Agathon, whose cause the assembled sophists passionately loved. Generally, it is believed that Aristophanes was starting to reply to Diotima's argument that we love the good rather than our wholeness. This could be so, for Aristophanes has seen no proof that our good is other than our self-deifying wholeness. However, Aristophanes could also have been working up to an attack on Diotima's entire myth of Penia and Poros, which, far from agreeing with his own poem, contradicts it at every turn.

This is a good place to tie up a loose end. Earlier, we were puzzled as to why Socrates was so adamant about forcing Protagoras to abandon long speeches in favor of dialectical give-and-take but prepared to tolerate long speeches at Agathon's party. We know now that he did not cease to insist on dialectic in the *Symposium.* Having heard Agathon, he compelled him to submit to dialectical therapy first in his direct dialogue with him and then in the fictitious exchange between Diotima and the younger Socrates. He abandoned the dialectic only upon reaching the beginning of Diotima's ascent to the vision of beauty, a point at which Agathon had run out of premises that could be examined dialectically.

RIGHT PEDERASTY VERSUS THE TYRANNICAL EROS

Diotima's ascent to the highest rungs of the ladder of beauty has been breathtakingly lovely. One did not wish to interrupt it with poor words of one's own. However, we must now consolidate what we have learned from her speech by commenting on the revolutionary implications of her concept of "right pederasty." In doing so, we must remember that in the higher reaches of her teaching, Diotima is referring to an ineffable vision. It would be foolish to imagine that we have discovered how to do more than she in the way of transforming her highest insights into propositional doctrines. On the other hand, keeping the Seventh Letter in mind, we may permit ourselves a few imperfectly scientific statements about matters that admit of discussion at the level of "the four."

Diotima's symbol of "right pederasty" is revolutionary in two ways. First, as hinted in Chapter 3, it surprises certain members of Athenian society and challenges various modern religious and moral beliefs with the news that there is such a thing as right pederasty. We are obliged to entertain this hypothesis and to ask in what right pederasty might consist.

In response, we may not bowdlerize Plato's text by alleging that "right pederasty" has nothing to do with gay sexual orientation. As mentioned in

Chapter 3, I think that Plato and Socrates were probably gay. If I am wrong about this, they certainly had great insight into the souls and sensibilities of gay men, and they undeniably addressed themselves to gays in the *Symposium*. To repeat, one of the most insightful modern religious teachings on the question of homosexuality, namely, that of the Roman Catholic Church, advises us that "the homosexual condition" is not chosen.[74] This counsel is confirmed by the testimony of the gay individuals whom one knows. This means that nature wants or allows gay sensitivity and that gay people discover, rather than decide, that they are gay. Plato and Socrates were serious philosophers. As such, they investigated every aspect of the order of being, including a sexual disposition that might have been their given personal destiny and that was certainly the fate of many of their brilliant contemporaries. They had to ask whether there are right and wrong ways to be gay, just as heterosexuals should inquire whether there are right and wrong modes of their sexuality. Right pederasty is the right order of gay existence. It is also the right order of teachers of the young who do not happen to be gay.

Diotima's theory of right pederasty holds that gay sexual attraction, like all sexual attraction, is intrinsically beautiful. It is ravishing because it is a call of the divine-human eros that arises from the union of divine resource with human poverty. Diotima has not told us what eros is. That is an ineffable matter. However, we have been taught what eros does. We have learned that eros, whatever it might be, is a force that pulls our entire being and, hence, every element of our essence toward the natural telos of our entire being and the natural aims of its elements. Our bodies belong to our natures. Eros calls us to love beautiful bodies, that is, to desire to beget in the presence of corporal beauty, for the sake of our integral good. The way to our ultimate good passes through the love of beautiful bodies. An attempt to attain to our highest good without passing through the love of beautiful bodies would be unnatural, wrong, and doomed to failure because it would be out of keeping with the order of being.

It is rather unclear whether Platonic right pederasty progresses from gay sexual attraction to homoerotic intercourse. It was seen that Diotima leaves the lovers undisturbed in their bedrooms. However, as mentioned previously, some texts in the *Republic, Phaedrus,* and *Laws* appear to forbid homoerotic union. Other passages in the *Phaedrus* might allow or encourage it. It goes without saying that many gay persons would think urging to celibacy absurd. Indeed, it would seem right to wonder why an inherently beautiful attraction should not be consummated. I need to postpone an effort to clear up Plato's apparent ambiguity on this issue to my later analysis of the *Phaedrus*, a dialogue in which the question is addressed more directly.

74. *Catechism of the Catholic Church,* sec. 2358.

Whatever Plato's opinion, we need to move to some different considerations that Diotima suggests.

The fact that Diotima requires her neophyte to ascend the ladder of beauty implies that she does have two definite teachings about gay (as well as straight) sexual attraction. One is that whether or not the lover and his beloved consummate their love physically, they may not divorce their intrinsically noble love of bodies from the telos of their being, misconstruing carnal love as an end in itself, as in hedonism. Ultimately, eros is about souls, not bodies. To put this another way, sexual unions are prohibited if they prevent ascents of the ladder. The other is that lovers may not pervert their inherently good eros for bodies into an instrument of some artificial telos of their whole being, such as self-deification. As integral beings, they are required in right pederasty to proceed from their love of bodies to the love of souls, from there to the love of virtue and beautiful laws and customs, from there to love of the sciences, and finally to the contemplation of the divine beauty. In other words, the pull of eros on bodies must be accepted along with the attraction of eros on every other dimension of our being as we are drawn to the ultimate goods of our souls, which come to us from a divine reality. No rung on Diotima's ladder of beauty may be treated as an end in itself until we have ascended to the highest.

When Diotima calls gay men to right pederasty (and, implicitly, gay women, and also straight men and women, to their right loves), she intimates that gays are especially "pregnant of soul." Throughout history, gays have suffered for being gay. One cannot console them by patronizing them. However, Diotima might be suggesting that the gays who suffer for being what they are pay a price for gifts that qualify disproportionately high numbers of them to lead their fellows up the ladder of beauty.

The second way in which Diotima's notion of right pederasty is revolutionary is that it opposes the prevailing ethic of Athenian culture. I mean that it resists the tyrannical eros. In our time, we take condemnation of tyranny for granted. We see criticisms of tyranny such as those found in Plato's *Republic* and yawn, thinking that they are old hat. We thereby fail to appreciate how radically novel, or at least how extremely unpopular, Socrates' disapproval of tyranny was. Indeed, we miss Plato's explicit declarations that the tyranny that he is fighting is favored by the many. Plato bludgeons us with these statements. All of the initial pages of book 2 of the *Republic* are devoted to Glaucon's presentation of the *popular* view of tyranny as the best life and to Adeimantus's reply that even where the demos censures the tyrannical morality that interests Glaucon, it unwittingly betrays its love of the tyrant's pleasures in its denunciations of immorality. In the *Gorgias*, Polus is flabbergasted by Socrates' claim that he would not wish to be a tyrant. He assumes that Socrates must be misrepresenting his real desires. He gets Socrates to agree only that "almost everybody" would say that the tyrannical life is best (469c–472c). Callicles believes that Socrates is joking, too, and contends that if what Socrates says is true, the life of mortals has been turned upside down and everywhere we are doing the opposite of what we should do (481b–c). Here, in the *Symposium*, Socrates observes that the thirty thousand roared their approval of Agathon's play. In contradistinction to Leo Strauss, one feels compelled to infer that if Plato were really an esoteric writer who meant to conceal his ideas from the many, he would have had to disguise his opposition to despotism, not his approval of the way of Thrasymachus, which was in vogue.[75]

It is significant that, as she concludes her teaching of "Socrates," Diotima calls the eros that she commends the "right" pederasty (211b5–6). She employs this symbol as the capstone of her presentation, thus stressing the necessity of rightness in right pederasty. This, in turn, implies the possibility of "wrong pederasty." Given that Diotima has explicitly contradicted every orator who preceded her, it is clear that she intends her *sympotai* to understand that they all are partisans of various kinds of "wrong pederasty," even if she does not use the term.

Wrong pederasty can display itself in the personal relationships between lovers. When it does, it always involves exploiting partners for sexual pleasure and other selfish ends. Plato has shown us a Phaedrus who wants to use his *erastēs* as an instrument of his aggrandizement and glory, a Pausanias who proposes to make his *erōmenos* a prostitute who exchanges sexual favors for an education that testifies to the instructor's divine creativity, an Eryximachus who applies his *technē* to his beloved's eros in order to control his behavior, an Aristophanes who interprets his beloved as an extension of himself, and an Agathon who casts his lovers as ugly ciphers whose lusts for him demonstrate his supremely beautiful divinity. These erotes are all examples of a tyrannical wrong pederasty; they pervert eros into a tool for enslaving others in order to gratify selfish desires. In dramatic contrast, Plato has shown us a Socrates who does not see his beloved as a mere source of sexual pleasure; who asks nothing from the *erōmenos*, except for love; who educates his beloved generously, for the sake of the lad's perfection in virtue; who regards the education not as the transfer of his knowledge into the *erōmenos* but, rather, as the awakening of what is already in the fair beloved's psyche; who treats his already noble *erōmenos* as an equal partner in the nurturing of the spiritual products of their union, and who strives with might and main to rise with his beloved, hand in hand, to the vision of the eternal beauty. Right pederasty consists in this.

Wrong pederasty can also manifest itself in various political agendas.

---

75. Granted, the way of Thrasymachus entailed fleecing the many. This is no contradiction. It seems that virtually every ordinary Athenian would have loved to fleece all his fellows.

Plato has shown us a Phaedrus who dreams of world conquest, a Pausanias who wants to stack the laws against his sexual competitors, an Eryximachus who relishes the prospect of creating a society to his liking by means of technical-medical engineering, an Aristophanes who teaches the desirability of mobilizing entire societies in support of metaphysical rebellions, and an Agathon who hopes to organize Athens as a cult devoted to the worship of himself. These erotes are forms of the tyrannical eros, too. It is not for nothing that Socrates urges his *sympotai* to abandon their pursuit of gold, raiment, and sexually attractive lads, considered altogether as measures of the fulfilled life. Socrates is pleading with them to perceive the emptiness of tyranny, the form of government that parades its gold, dazzling vestments and sexual courtesans. By way of dramatic contrast, Plato has shown us a Socrates who is passionately dedicated to regulating cities in moderation and justice and who hopes to contribute to this end by educating beloveds to virtue. Right pederasty consists in this.

Wrong pederasty also appears as Titanism. Plato has shown us a Phaedrus, a Pausanias, an Eryximachus, an Aristophanes, and an Agathon who attempt to use eros as an instrument for dethroning Zeus and deifying themselves. This eros is tyrannical inasmuch as it embodies the master passion of tyrants, an overwhelming craving for power over the order of being. In dramatic contrast, Plato has shown us a Socrates who leads his beloved to a joint fulfillment in the *metaxy.* Right pederasty consists in this.

The Judgment of Dionysus

Before Aristophanes can state his objection, he is interrupted by the sounds of revelers and a flute girl outside the house. Agathon orders his slave boys to go see who is making the noise, and to admit τις τῶν ἐπιτηδείων (212d1), that is, anyone who is a friend in the sense that he is useful or necessary. A few moments later, the flute girl leads Alcibiades into the room. Alcibiades is being supported by members of his entourage because he is falling-down drunk. He is shouting loudly that he wants to be taken to Agathon. He is crowned with a wreath of thick ivy and violets. He is also wearing a great array of ταινίας *(tainias),* ribbon headbands that are customarily awarded to victors.

The entry of the flute girl signals that the program of encomiums on Eros has reached its climax and that Agathon's lawsuit against Socrates has ended with it. Authorities ranging from Pauly to Rosen and Nussbaum agree that Alcibiades is acting as the head of a Dionysian procession, that his intoxication and his wreath of ivy represent Dionysus, and that the violets in his crown symbolize Aphrodite. We have also learned from Mircea Eliade and many other sources that in all ancient religions, the high priest who conducts the rites of his god becomes the deity, without ceasing to be himself.[76] Thus, Dionysus has appeared, coming "suddenly" (212c6), that is, in the same manner as the light in the Seventh Letter and the vision of beauty in Diotima's oration. Like all gods, he will immediately exact his due from the mortals. Also, Agathon had declared that in his action against Socrates about their wisdom, Dionysus would be judge. We may assume that the god will reveal a verdict.

Moving first to claim what is owed to him, Dionysus-Alcibiades asks the men whether they will drink with him—an inquiry that, in the mouth of a god, is a command rather than a question. After some drunken judging that occasions laughter, he repeats the query. At that, Aristodemus reports, "all cheered him boisterously" (ἀναθορυβῆσαι, 213a3, which is to say that they greeted him with exactly the same applause that they had bestowed on Agathon, 198a2), "and Agathon also invited him." There could be no other human response to a god's wishes and directives. The *sympotai* must get drunk whether they like it or not. As host, Agathon must validate the new arrangement officially. He goes along reluctantly because another god is supplanting him and because he is losing control of the evening's agenda. After attending to the verdict, which will be discussed presently, Dionysus-Alcibiades appoints himself archon of the drinking bout and commands that the guzzling commence. He promptly drains off a half-gallon wine cooler, easily enough to stagger a horse. Then he enjoins Socrates to do the same, even though he knows that Socrates is immune to the grape (probably because the philosopher is under the protection of Aphrodite and nectar, as maintained above). Socrates instantly and silently complies, thus demonstrating his perfect piety. However, Eryximachus, the instigator of the original impiety, tries to resist. He informs Dionysus-Alcibiades that the company had agreed on a round of tributes to Eros and demands compliance with this arrangement (214a–c). Dionysus gives a mock promise to do whatever the gentleman physician prescribes. Then he does what he likes anyway, delivering a satyr play with a besotted praise of Socrates. When he concludes, the many come pouring through the doors and turn the party into a drunken rout. The god has his way. Except for Socrates, the party ends under the hegemony of Dionysus.

With regard to the lawsuit, it is not a good sign for Agathon that Dionysus has arrived with violets in his wreath. Deities who are the lords of their own persons do not display the symbols of other divinities in their crowns. Dionysus is apparently subordinate to Aphrodite, who will not look kindly upon human efforts to elevate Eros above her. Although Agathon may not see this initially, it also bodes ill for his hopes that Dionysus has come on yesterday's errand. Agathon won first prize at the Lenaea two days ago.

76. Eliade, *Sacred and Profane.*

The god should have appeared at the *epinikios* yesterday to present him with a *tainia*. However, the hard-drinking Dionysus is a comically irresponsible, flighty, and bumbling god (this when he is not acting in his other character as a ferocious, bloodthirsty horror), so he flippantly pleads that he could not make it yesterday and means to fulfill his intention today. He is also unaware of Socrates' presence. He has not even been paying attention to today's proceedings in his court.

Dionysus begins to transact yesterday's business by saying that he will take the *tainias* from his head and entwine them around the head "of the wisest and most beautiful." Agathon probably thinks that the god is both affirming the triumph of his tragedy and judging today's lawsuit in his favor. What happens next is misrepresented in the standard translations, which make Dionysus-Alcibiades transfer his wreath of ivy and violets to Agathon. This definitely does not occur: Dionysus does not yield up the symbol of his divinity to the mortal poet. The text explicitly states that Dionysus-Alcibiades gives Agathon *tainias* (212e7). Having received these tokens of an earlier victory, Agathon learns next that he has lost his lawsuit. Dionysus-Alcibiades soon discovers Socrates sitting beside him and exclaims, "Oh, Herakles," associating Socrates with the hero who held heaven above earth. This suffices to settle the case. The god soon requires Agathon to give back some of the *tainias,* so that he can also entwine Socrates' amazing head. He explains to the humiliated poet that Socrates "is victorious in speeches over all men, not once like you the other day, but always" (213e3–4). Dionysus allows Agathon to keep some *tainias* in recognition of his victory at the Lenaea, but he determines that Socrates has defeated the tragedian without having bothered to hear the arguments.

6

SYMPOSIUM: DIONYSIAN EROS

Let us return to the dramatic moment in the *Symposium* when Socrates has concluded his speech and everyone is applauding except Aristophanes, who is beginning to comment on something that Socrates has said about his myth of the first suggestively shaped humans. It would seem that Plato could justifiably end his play at this point, or take it in the direction of a fruitful dialectical exchange between Aristophanes and Socrates. After all, Agathon's lawsuit against Socrates has run its course. Although Agathon has won louder applause than Socrates from his sophistical friends in the company, he must realize in his heart that the philosopher has beaten him, for he was forced to admit that he was totally ignorant of the things of which he had spoken. Agathon does not need the judgment of Dionysus to be convinced that he has lost, for he has delivered the crushing verdict himself.

Socrates, for his part, must be satisfied with his evening's work. If my analysis has been correct, he had set out to stop or impede the rapid spread of several virulent strains of the sophistical tyrannical eros in Athenian culture, a disease that had been fanned into an epidemic by Agathon's effective manipulation of Athens's growing theatocracy. He has made some headway. He certainly could not and did not expect to convert Phaedrus, Pausanias, Eryximachus, and Agathon to right pederasty and philosophy with one speech. However, he has successfully taken the first step toward this goal, reducing Agathon and everyone else who applauded his oration to consciousness of their ignorance and to a grudging acknowledgment that they need to weigh his dialectical teaching. There is a real possibility that, given sufficient time, Socrates could win the sophists over completely and get them to use their influence to reverse the damage that they have done. It is an unexpected and extremely gratifying bonus that Socrates has apparently managed to draw Aristophanes into a serious debate. In my opinion (which might be biased because Agathon's plays are not extant, and because Plato's Agathon seems to be a rather silly fellow), Aristophanes is a greater thinker than Agathon. If Socrates could engage Aristophanes in the dialectic and attract him to philosophy, too, he could win his cultural war outright. Why, then, does the *Symposium* continue with the intervention of Alcibiades? Why did Plato write no more plays about the education of Agathon and no dialogue titled *Aristophanes*?

I believe that the answer to these questions is that Plato wished to remain dramatically true to Athenian history. Athens might well have been corrupted culturally by sophists and poets. However, the city was also led to its ultimate political degeneracy and to its fall by Alcibiades. Again, the historical Socrates might have been making tolerable progress with the sophists and poets in 416 B.C., the time of Agathon's victorious debut. If he was making such headway, his work was cut short by Alcibiades' disastrous political triumph soon thereafter. I think that the *Symposium* takes its turn toward Alcibiades to mark this development: The cultural war between Socratic right pederasty and Titanism, in which the right pederasty was gaining ground, was complicated by a political struggle between the right pederasty and Alcibiades' imperialistic strain of the tyrannical eros, which, in view of Plato's casting of Alcibiades in the drama, I shall call Dionysian eros. There are no more Platonic plays about the education of Agathon, and, much to our disappointment, there is no Platonic dialogue called *Aristophanes* because a budding rapprochement between Socrates (philosophy) and Agathon and Aristophanes (poetry) was rendered ambiguous and politically irrelevant by the loss of Alcibiades and the Athenian many to the Dionysian tyrannical eros.

This intuition suggests the need for a treatment of Alcibiades' satyr play and Socrates' response as the third campaign of the war between Socratic right pederasty and the tyrannical eros. I shall turn to this analysis in a moment. However, it would be a mistake to forget that there is also a dramatically (and, probably, historically) relevant relationship between Agathon and Alcibiades. Before studying the third campaign, we should consider two questions: Why did Agathon not invite Alcibiades to his banquet in the first place? Why did Alcibiades decide to come without having been invited?

We have good reasons to assume that Agathon deliberately avoided inviting Alcibiades to the symposium. When Alcibiades does appear, Agathon refrains from extending him even the elementary courtesy of the lie that he told Aristodemus: "I went round to invite you but did not find you home." Not only that, but his formal welcome to Alcibiades also seems to be belated and grudging (213a). Why? I think that Agathon's reluctance is explained partially by a poet's antipathy to politicians. Artists who create pure forms in the media of culture tend to disdain politicians who frequently create messes because their raw material is refractory real men.

However, Agathon also senses an adversary in Alcibiades. Agathon wants to be a god. It will be seen below that Alcibiades has the same ambition. The two would-be deities are competing for the same worshipers because they need adoration to confirm their divinity. The god who has succeeded in winning thirty thousand devotees by writing a tragedy in the realm of culture evidently does not wish to risk sharing his wealth with the god who is trying to win adherents by promising glorious victories in the domains of politics and imperialistic war.

Alcibiades, on the other hand, has been spending his time lately struggling to marshal voters behind various bellicose proposals in the Assembly. He has already started planning his Sicilian adventure, too. Although he cannot commit himself to the precise details of Agathon's ideology, he probably wants to associate with the tragedian for the same reason that U.S. presidents like to be photographed with celebrated entertainers and champion athletic teams: he can garner more Assembly votes, thus ensuring that he can be the god that he aspires to be, by hopping on every popular bandwagon that happens to come along. Thus, while Agathon attempts to hold Alcibiades at arm's length, Alcibiades tries desperately to embrace Agathon. This is a comical love match that has an explosive potential for the order of the polis, for the new cultural and political darlings of Athens are both spreading tyrannical erotes.

Alcibiades obviously does not expect to find Socrates at Agathon's home. He does not know specifically what has been said at the banquet. However, when he arrives and discovers Socrates sitting next to Agathon, he will naturally assume the worst. That is, he will infer that Socrates, who opposes his political and military ventures, has been scheming to turn Agathon against his Dionysian imperialism. If Socrates succeeds, Agathon's popular appeal will probably be thrown into the balance against Alcibiades' projects. This inspires Alcibiades to try to destroy Socrates' credit with Agathon. The effort will hurt Alcibiades, for he himself is torn between Socratic right pederasty and the tyrannical eros and, hence, between love and hatred for Socrates. The tyrannical eros masters him, and he lurches ahead. It is in this way that the third campaign of the war between right pederasty and the tyrannical eros begins.

As ever, I think that Plato attempts to make his characters true to life. Accordingly, I shall weave my analysis of the final scenes of the *Symposium* together with an excursus on the relationships between Alcibiades and Socrates in Platonic drama and in history.

Excursus on Alcibiades and Socrates

Alcibiades appears in the *Symposium* not only as the god Dionysus but also as himself. We must ask why Alcibiades has the dramatic features that

Plato attributes to him in the dialogue. That is, we need to know why Alcibiades is leading a Dionysian procession, why it is suitable for him to behave as a drunken Dionysus, why he is wearing not only a Dionysian wreath of ivy generously sprinkled with Aphrodite's violets but a great plethora of victory *tainias* as well, why he wants to award Agathon *tainias* as "the wisest and most beautiful," why he meant to reach the poet yesterday but failed (as distinct from Socrates, who could have reached him yesterday but deliberately refrained), why he is unaware of Socrates' whereabouts, and why Agathon's slaves might mistake him for one of Agathon's useful intimates (τις τῶν ἐπιτηδείων), even if not for a friend (φίλος).

To handle these questions, we must go back to the beginning of Alcibiades' love affair with Socrates in 432 B.C. and then trace the history of this match forward into the present of the symposium in 416 B.C. As reported previously, Socrates opens the *Alcibiades I* (which is set in 432) by calling himself Alcibiades' first *erastēs*. Alcibiades has had many other suitors. He has discouraged the others by expressing contempt for them. He has informed them that he needs no man because his superb assets of body and soul make him self-sufficient. Socrates observes that Alcibiades thinks himself foremost in beauty and stature, a scion of the noblest family in the greatest city of Hellas, better connected than anyone (especially because Pericles is his guardian), and rich. Although his suitors were μεγαλοφρόνων, that is, possessed of "great thoughts," like Aristophanes' first men, Alcibiades has overwhelmed them with his personal forcefulness. Socrates depicts Alcibiades as ὑπερπεφρόνηκας, meaning that he has surpassed the suitors by conceiving "hyperthoughts," as it were, ideas many magnitudes more hybristic than those of Aristophanes' round people. Socrates does not say whether Alcibiades has more laudable qualities of soul, for he is discussing the youth's self-image, and what has already been recounted has sufficed to make Alcibiades think himself superior. However, now the lad is coming of age, being not quite twenty (123d5–6). He is no longer attractive to vulgar pederasts. His suitors have forsaken him, perhaps hurting his pride, his disdain for them notwithstanding.

Socrates remarks that Alcibiades must be surprised to see that a man who has followed him around town for years without saying a word—owing to a certain daimonic opposition that can be discussed some other time— has not yet abandoned his suit or set aside his eros. Alcibiades' response is unfriendly. With considerable justification, he answers that, indeed, he does wonder why Socrates has been "bothering" him by dogging his steps. Socrates pledges to give an account of himself, but only on the condition that Alcibiades will stay to listen, for the youth frequently stalks away from people who are speaking to him. Alcibiades is so intrigued by Socrates' strangeness that he agrees to hear the philosopher out.

Socrates' next statement surely astonishes Alcibiades exceedingly. Socrates says that if he beheld Alcibiades content with his good looks, noble birth, high social position, riches, and hybris, he would have set his love aside long ago, or so he wants to believe. Unlike his fellow suitors, Socrates is not mastered by his desire for the beauty of Alcibiades' body, and he cares not at all for the youth's other supposedly enviable attributes. Before Alcibiades can begin to suspect Socrates of a clever lover's ploy, Socrates astounds him again by telling him his secret ambitions. Socrates observes that if some god were to ask Alcibiades whether he preferred to live with his present possessions or die if he could not acquire greater ones, Alcibiades would choose to die immediately. In fact, Alcibiades supposes that when he makes his debut in the Athenian Assembly a few days hence, he will show the people that he is more worthy of honor than Pericles or anyone else. After this, Alcibiades expects to attain to supreme power in the city, in Hellas, and in Europe, among both the Hellenes and the barbarians. However, this will not satiate his appetite. If the same god were to tell Alcibiades that he had to content himself with Europe and leave Asia alone, he would still elect to die. He wants all human beings to know his name and power, and he thinks that the only worthy men who ever lived were Cyrus and Xerxes. In short, Socrates maintains that Alcibiades hopes to become an Alexander the Great, seventy-six years before the birth of Alexander. (One wonders whether Alexander conceived his project when Aristotle showed him Plato's *Symposium*. That would be an ironic twist.) Socrates claims that he knows all this. He is not guessing. If this is true, Alcibiades has been infected with his Dionysian tyrannical eros from an early age. Judging from his self-image, Alcibiades also has latent ideas about his own godhood.[1]

Here, I must confess that if I discovered such "hyperthoughts" in a conceited, insolent princeling of the most powerful country on earth, I would lament that no one had smothered him in his crib. I would be sorely tempted to do mankind a favor by rectifying the oversight. Being more visionary than I, Socrates undoubtedly sees Alcibiades as a prospective "lawful and warlike king and ruler," that is, as a potential member of the second-highest tier of human beings in Stesichorus's hierarchy (*Phaedrus* 248d4–5). Socrates loves him for his sexual beauty and for his promise. Hence, he will try to win Alcibiades over. He suggests that his power over the affairs of Alcibiades is so great that he is indispensable to the realization of the youth's dreams. He also declares that, just as Alcibiades hopes to prove himself supremely worthy in the city and thus rise to power, so he himself aspires to achieve the greatest power over Alcibiades by proving that he alone can give Alcibiades the power that he craves, provided only

1. Unlike Stephen Forde, I am not moved to doubt that Alcibiades had this ambition. See "On the *Alcibiades I*," in Plato, *Roots*, 224. Alcibiades' confidence in his own self-sufficiency, attested by Socrates in 104a, is already an incipient belief in his own divinity.

that the god helps. This might not be to assert that he really intends to help Alcibiades conquer the world after the fashion of Cyrus and Xerxes. However, Alcibiades assumes that Socrates means this. He hints that he might deny Socrates' description of his plans, but he asks the philosopher to tell him more, thus betraying that the "hyperthoughts" are at least stirring at the back of his mind. He wants to learn a wisdom that will gratify his Dionysian eros.

Having caught Alcibiades' attention, Socrates subjects him to a dialectical examination. He asks Alcibiades on what subjects he proposes to counsel the Athenian Assembly. He notes that Alcibiades' prior education has been limited to writing, kithara playing, and wrestling—a shockingly insubstantial foundation of expertise for someone who proposes to subjugate and govern all mankind. The unwary Alcibiades replies that he will advise the Athenians on their own affairs. When pressed to specify which of these matters he means, Alcibiades proves that Socrates was right about his ambitions all along, answering that he will speak about peace and war, along with "other" civic affairs. Especially, he will say with whom Athens should make peace and war, when, and how. When Socrates inquires by what *technē* Alcibiades will know when it is better to make peace or war, the youth is stumped. Socrates asks him whether it is not shameful to be ignorant of this art, and he admits that it is. With this concession in hand, Socrates apparently changes the subject, inquiring whether Alcibiades intends to encourage the city to wage war on those who are acting justly or unjustly.

Alcibiades artlessly reveals more about his character every time he speaks. He answers that Socrates' question is difficult, for someone who decided to make war on those who were acting justly would never say so. He would be constrained by the facts that waging an unjust war is illegal and that it appears to be ignoble. However, Alcibiades agrees that he would necessarily have to speak about justice and injustice when giving war counsel. Whether he believes in the existence of justice or not, he is ready to wage wars usually called unjust in the service of his ambitions and to rationalize them with propaganda.

Socrates acts as if he has missed this implication. He asks Alcibiades whether it does not follow that "the more just" is the measure of better and worse in matters of war and peace, as if the youth had admitted the necessity of discussing the reality, rather than the appearances, of justice. Socrates is playing the blockhead ironically. Far from having mistaken Alcibiades' meaning, he has understood perfectly well and sees that he must use a rhetorical stratagem to force the would-be conqueror to think about justice more seriously. Alcibiades must be made to appreciate that he has no good idea of justice if he fancies that it can be violated and twisted with propaganda whenever it forbids his plans. So, Socrates has inquired whether "the more just" is not the measure of decisions about war and peace as a means of getting the problem of real justice on the table. Alcibiades senses that something is wrong with Socrates' logic, but he is uncertain of the philosopher's intention. Socrates could be setting a sly example of how to pretend to respect the reality of justice while actually stage-managing the appearances. He could also be attempting to trap Alcibiades by inducing him to argue that "the more just" is not the measure of options for war and peace, which would amount to a confession of illegal, ignoble aims to a stranger. Alcibiades opts to reply safely. Perhaps with doubt in his voice, he says that Socrates is "apparently" right (109c12), not "certainly" or "clearly," as some translators have it. If Socrates can get nothing more than this from his pupil, he will have wrought a "conversion" of Alcibiades to justice that everyone would have to recognize as counterfeit.

Socrates continues to insist upon his sophism. He suggests that Alcibiades has failed to notice his ignorance of justice, or, alternatively, that he himself has failed to notice Alcibiades taking lessons on justice and injustice despite having shadowed him everywhere, whenever he stepped out of his house. He asks Alcibiades who his teacher was, begging to be introduced to him so that he can learn from him, too. Alcibiades can check himself no longer. He exclaims, "You are joking, Socrates!" It is not only Socrates' demand to be told the name of the teacher that strikes Alcibiades as flippant, but also his dogged determination to take justice seriously as the measure of right and wrong in war and peace, and his affected inability to understand that Alcibiades means to dispense with justice when it becomes inconvenient. Alcibiades does not see how Socrates could be so crass as to be earnest about a real justice. Socrates shocks him by swearing on his Friendship for Alcibiades that he is serious (as if the friendship were a god). He again requests the name of Alcibiades' expert on justice. Alcibiades has been goaded to the point of frustration. In his pique, he inquires rhetorically whether he could not know the just and unjust without having had an instructor. However, he has now tacitly claimed to know justice. The focus has shifted from appearance to reality, and Socrates has him where he wants him.

Socrates readily grants that Alcibiades could have insights into the just and unjust if he had discovered them, that he might have discovered them if he had sought them, and that he might have sought them if he had thought that he did not know justice. Socrates leaves out of account the possibilities that Alcibiades could have had an innate understanding of justice and that he could have had a divine revelation. Alcibiades overlooks the omissions and accepts the premise that he could have acquired knowledge of justice only through a teacher or through his own investigations. Socrates rapidly proves that there was never a time when Alcibiades did not think that he knew justice. He recalls that as a boy, Alcibiades frequently accused his playmates of competing unjustly. Alcibiades replies with hot anger that the other boys were really playing unfairly—and that he knew this, too (110b–c). However, this only establishes Socrates' case. Socrates has demonstrated that Alcibiades never learned justice from a teacher and never inquired into it himself because he always thought he knew it. According to the logic of the argument, Alcibiades should admit that he is ignorant of justice. Whether he knows justice or not, we observe that although he is prepared to inflict injustice on others promiscuously, Alcibiades is unwilling to suffer it passively, even in the most trivial affairs.

It is a sign of Alcibiades' imperious spirit, and also a harbinger of things to come, that he refuses to yield when he is beaten. He shifts his grounds, asserting that he did learn justice, from the many, just as he learned to speak Greek from them. Socrates disposes of this claim easily by showing that the people could not teach anybody justice because they disagree about it, thus proving that they do not know it. The result, Socrates remarks, is that Alcibiades, by his own answers, has convicted himself of planning to speak to the Athenian Assembly about matters of which he is ignorant. Alcibiades will still not concede defeat. He shifts his grounds again, revealing what he has really thought all along: that the Hellenes have never been overly inquisitive about justice, that the point of political discourse is to identify the expedient rather than the just, that many have profited greatly from injustice, and that others have gained little from justice (113d). Socrates obviously has a terribly difficult project on his hands. He hopes to make a lawful and warlike king and ruler of a spoiled young aristocrat who is fully intent upon a life of unlawful and warlike world conquest and tyranny.

Socrates wastes no time attacking Alcibiades' new position. Observing that Alcibiades has investigated the expedient no more than he has studied the just, Socrates demands that the youth demonstrate that the expedient differs from the just. Alcibiades counters by calling him hybristic (114d7). Inasmuch as this is the first, but by no means the last, time that Alcibiades taxes Socrates with hybris, we ought to consider whether the charge is fair. To me, Socrates' intimation that Alcibiades should defend his opinion looks entirely courteous and reasonable. Alcibiades seems to apply the adjective "hybristic" to Socrates not because it fits, but because he resents being held to rational account for evils that he intends to commit, especially when it appears that sophisticates "know" that everyone who could perpetrate the crimes would do so immediately. Alcibiades thinks that gentlemen wink at injustice, and he regards Socrates as rude and aggressive for trying to embarrass him over such matters.

If this is the definition of "hybristic," Socrates willingly admits the charge (114d8). He then makes short work of Alcibiades' new argument. Relying on Alcibiades' earlier equation of the just with the "noble" (that is, the beautiful), he gets the youth to call the noble good and the good expedient. Thus, the just is the expedient. This refutation is facile. Alcibiades need not have admitted its first premise. Instead, he could have replied ironically with Thrasymachus that justice is the sign of a "noble" (in the sense of well-born) good nature, that is, the mark of an aristocratic simpleton (*Republic* 348c12). However, Alcibiades is young and inexperienced at eristic; he does not see this way out. Finding himself tied in knots, he swears by Zeus that he has been reduced to a strange condition by Socrates' questioning, such that he does not know what he is professing and varies his positions from one second to the next. From this moment forward, Alcibiades appears to be a changed lad. Now he stands in real awe of Socrates and is putty in the philosopher's hands. However, the result is not a genuine conversion to the ways of justice, for Socrates could not effect such a transformation so cheaply. Rather, it seems that Alcibiades has fallen under the spell of Socrates' rhetorical power. His enchantment probably consists in enthusiasm for Socrates' ability to make him say anything he pleases, a talent that could have marvelous political utility. He has come to admire Socrates for the wrong reason.

Socrates advises Alcibiades that his bewilderment has been occasioned by nothing more than his ignorance of matters that he thought he knew. He warns the youth that he is wedded to *amathia,* the illness that Plato blames in the Seventh Letter for all the evils of mankind. He admonishes his beloved that it is dangerous to go into politics without being educated, as the Athenians, evidently including Pericles, typically do. Socrates' scolding produces some comic relief: Alcibiades speculates that he can omit his own education if all his Athenian competitors are ignorant too, for his natural abilities excel theirs so much that he should be able to defeat them easily. (This adolescent notion is so precious that the historical Alcibiades must have actually expressed it to Socrates, Plato hearing of it later.) The alarmed Socrates responds that if Alcibiades intends noble actions that distinguish him in the city, he really needs to get a better idea of the identity of his opponents.

Alcibiades affirms that he does intend such actions, thus proving again that Socrates was right about his goals. He asks who his enemies are. Socrates answers that they are the kings of Persia and Sparta. Perhaps kicking himself for missing the obvious, Alcibiades agrees. Socrates proceeds to relate a highly fanciful story about the superb educations of the Persian and Spartan kings in prudence, justice, moderation, and courage—a tale that is completely at odds with the scornful account of Persian royal education given by the Athenian Stranger in the *Laws.* He also scares Alcibiades with reports that the wealth of those kings dwarfs his own, this with a view toward convincing him that if he wants to defeat his opponents, he must rely on superior virtue, not on his beauty, stature, birth, and relatively meager resources. Alcibiades finally asks what he must do to realize his desires

(124b). His question represents a grudging opening to education. Socrates must be dismayed that he has had to work so hard and artfully to move Alcibiades so little, and depressed by the danger of the game that he is playing. Although Alcibiades is now ready to submit to a bit of training in the cardinal virtues, and, hence, could be assumed to be on the path to philosophy, his commitment is to education for the sake of victory, not for the sake of the good. He could veer off the road to virtue at any moment, whenever he loses sight of the connection between ethical excellence and success. The probability that Alcibiades will reject Socratic education is extremely high, for character is formed early in life. It would be surprising if Socrates could rescue a lad who has been developing bad habits for fourteen years under the permissive eye of the most useless of Pericles' servants (122a–b).

Undoubtedly sighing, Socrates begins the training of Alcibiades from scratch. Trying to get a stronger grip on his student, he hints that it is only through his god and himself that Alcibiades can enjoy his epiphany. Alcibiades is quick to accuse Socrates of joking again. The philosopher's effort to introduce piety as the principle of his teaching and to keep Alcibiades from perverse influences has been premature. Alcibiades' education will have to continue to appeal to calculations of political advantage, for the would-be conqueror and deity will hear nothing of divine tutelage. It will be subject to abrupt changes of direction, for Alcibiades will listen to Socrates now only because he is suffering the probably temporary fear that he might be inferior to his chief adversaries. It may be with an eye to Alcibiades' vanity that Socrates has already suggested that his only hope for success lies in obedience to the Delphic command to "know thyself" (124a). Now Socrates repeatedly pleads with Alcibiades to cultivate himself. The youth likes this advice much better, so Socrates leads him through a study of himself, in search of the desired political wisdom.

The remainder of the *Alcibiades I* meanders because Alcibiades' first self-discovery is that he hopes to be "good," with "goodness" meaning ability to rule Athens (124e–125b), and he proves hard to lead toward a more adequate understanding of virtue. However, Alcibiades is eventually brought to proclaim the necessity of a political order in which all citizens attend to their own business. He agrees that this situation is "just," but is embarrassed to see that he does not know what the basis of the justice is (127d), a failing that raises questions about his "goodness," or his ability to rule the city.[2] Perhaps he must learn justice after all.

Leaving this problem in abeyance, Socrates uses Alcibiades' discovery of his ignorance as a lever to force him to reconsider his needs for a god's

---

2. It is telling that, in the context, this boils down to Alcibiades' inability to understand friendship.

favor and Socratic divination (127e), and also his need to look into himself more seriously. Now the question becomes who or what his self is. Socrates suggests enigmatically that this inquiry will eventually involve knowledge of "the same in itself" (αὐτὸ ταὐτό, 129b1, or "itself in itself," αὐτὸ τὸ αὐτὸ, 130d4), but he does not pursue this. Ultimately, he induces Alcibiades to proclaim that he is not his body but, rather, his soul (129e–130c), and to infer that he who would know himself must know his soul.[3] He points out that as the only lover of Alcibiades' soul, he is the only *erastēs* Alcibiades has ever had. He will not forsake him merely because his bodily beauty has faded. He will not leave unless Alcibiades is ruined by the flattery of the Athenian people. This is a threat not to stop loving Alcibiades, but to abandon him if he becomes hopelessly corrupt, a remedy that true love dispenses in the last resort. Socrates fears that Alcibiades will become a *"dēmerastēs"* ("*erastēs* of the people," δημεραστὴς, 132a2), a lover of popular flattery. This would deprave him, so the bond that Socrates offers is not unconditionally guaranteed. If it were, we should think ill of Socrates, who has no business letting a would-be tyrant believe that anything goes.

Having suggested that he who would know himself must know his soul, Socrates urges Alcibiades to examine the soul by looking in that region in which its virtue, wisdom, is found. This is the most divine part of the soul, the element that resembles god. Alcibiades is suitably moved, perhaps assenting because he regards his own wisdom as godlike. Socrates then recalls that he and Alcibiades had previously judged that self-knowledge is moderation (σωφροσύνη, sane self-control, 133c18). It is true that they had said this (131b4–5), although one is at a loss to know why, for Socrates seems to have slipped the equation past his student without proof. Perhaps Socrates bases the equation on a part of his story of the Persian kings that Alcibiades had swallowed even earlier (122a), that is, on the claim that the wisest Persian magus teaches the heir to the throne everything that pertains to being a king, and that the most temperate tutor teaches him not to fall under the power of any pleasure, so that he may be free and a king. If so, Alcibiades must reason that "I am a free king, wisdom is my knowledge of myself as such, and free kingship is rule of everything, including my pleasures." If he does think this, he has espoused temperance as a telos of the will to power. Socrates has played a neat but risky trick.

From here, it is a simple step to the inferences that virtue is more needful to cities than triremes, that a ruler must impart virtue to citizens, that the archon must be virtuous himself, and that to be a good ruler Alcibiades should seek justice and temperance rather than license. Alcibiades

---

3. The implication of Socrates' association of "itself in itself" with the problem of the self-knowledge of the soul is that the soul is not its own ground. A human being who is a soul that uses a body is not "the same itself," or "itself in itself."

probably affirms these teachings for the sake of mastery, too, not for the sake of the good. True, Socrates promptly persuades Alcibiades to abjure despotism, but one suspects that his vow owes more to his inability to resist Socratic logic than to a heartfelt conversion. Like Thrasymachus in the *Republic,* Alcibiades has been charmed like a snake. Socrates next urges him to assent to the proposition that he can escape his ignorance "if god wishes" (135d6). The now docile Alcibiades agrees. He vows to follow Socrates everywhere and to care for justice. He might even feel sincere, for now. However, Socrates still fears that Alcibiades will become a *dēmerastēs.* He knows superficial persuasion when he sees it (see *Republic* 412b ff).[4]

We next encounter Alcibiades in the *Protagoras.* Like the *Alcibiades I,* this dialogue is set in 432 b.c. It cannot be more than a few months since Socrates first spoke to Alcibiades. Socrates' affair with Alcibiades has become a gossip item. People are asking the philosopher how his pursuit of the young man is going. Simultaneously, they are twitting him for chasing a lad whose beard has grown out—inexplicable behavior to the vulgar, akin to waiting until a beautiful woman has become matronly before trying to seduce her. However, the most interesting thing about the opening scene of the *Protagoras* is that Alcibiades is not in it. He has not kept his promise to attend Socrates everywhere he goes. One suspects that his ardor for justice has evaporated as quickly as his determination to honor his pledge.

This suspicion is intensified by Alcibiades' initial appearance on stage. The young man enters the house of Callias in the company of Critias. This Critias, a relative of Plato, is one of the men denounced in the Seventh Letter. In 415 b.c., he was implicated in the desecration of the Herms, indicating that Alcibiades and he were known allies at the time. In 404 b.c., he became one of the Thirty Tyrants, the most murderous of the lot. Thus, far from cleaving to the Socrates who preaches against tyranny, Alcibiades has taken up with a companion who is likely to encourage his worst tendencies.

Alcibiades is silent in the *Protagoras* until Socrates starts to leave in a huff because the great sophist refuses to engage in dialectic. When Alcibiades speaks, he indicates that he is still in awe of Socrates, but his reason for valuing his lover still disappoints us. He does not revere Socrates as a teacher who is leading him to virtue. Rather, he asserts that he would be

---

4. Since the rise of higher criticism, *Alcibiades I* has been suspected of being inauthentic because of the shoddiness of its philosophic reasoning. I think that this quality of the dialogue is evidence of its Platonic authorship. The drama perfectly reveals what the historical Socrates could have expected to achieve with the historical young Alcibiades at a first meeting. It also points directly at the defects in Alcibiades' character that ultimately prevented Socrates from getting anywhere with him. As with so many critiques of Platonic dialogues, the "reasoning unworthy of Plato" argument ignores dramatic context and fails to consider that the purpose of *Alcibiades I* was not to demonstrate doctrines, but to give an appropriate analysis of the problem of Alcibiades.

amazed if Socrates gave place to any person in dialectical disputation, or in understanding the give-and-take of reasoning. He adds that if Protagoras would confess his inferiority to Socrates in this style of argument, Socrates would be satisfied (336b–c). In other words, he perceives Socrates as a master at winning dialectical brawls. He also assumes that Socrates craves victory in these altercations and fails to consider that what Socrates really desires is to make progress toward truth and virtue (see *Republic* 537e–539d). He wants Socrates and Protagoras to continue their debate because he likes to see a rousing fight and relishes the prospect of Socrates mauling the sophist. Critias, who has unfortunately come to know his Alcibiades well, confirms that he is ἀεὶ φιλόνικός (always victory loving, 336e1) and, hence, disposed to support Socrates in the quarrel. Critias probably applauds Alcibiades for being φιλόνικός, strengthening and fixing this trait in the lad's character. So, Socrates' early efforts to improve Alcibiades result only in temporary reforms, as do his later endeavors down to 416. Alcibiades always relapses. Thus, for example, he awards Socrates *tainias* in the *Symposium* because Socrates "is victorious in speeches over all men" (213e3–4). His esteem for his *erastēs* still flows from his love of victory.

Shortly after the events of the *Protagoras*, the Peloponnesian War broke out. We catch only a few glimpses of Alcibiades and Socrates from 432 to 422. We gather from Alcibiades' speech in the *Symposium* that they promptly went to war and fought together at Potidaea in 432, that Socrates saved Alcibiades' life when the latter was wounded at Potidaea or on some other battlefield, and that as a mounted knight Alcibiades covered Socrates during the retreat from Delium in 424. Although Alcibiades made his political debut soon after the *Protagoras*, he clearly spent most of the next ten years soldiering rather than politicking because the war gave him opportunities to distinguish himself that were too good to miss. He won a prize for valor in the battle in which he was wounded, partially with the connivance of Socrates, who exhorted the generals to give the award to his beloved rather than himself. Alcibiades deserves some credit. Courage was the one virtue to which he could lay some legitimate claim.

Our first reports of Alcibiades as a politician are recorded in the pages of Thucydides and Plutarch. Plutarch relates that when Alcibiades first addressed the Assembly (at the time, Alcibiades was still a "stripling"), he promptly humbled all the demagogues except Nicias and Phaeax, a competitor who was vanquished later. True to his victory-loving nature, Alcibiades envied the honors that the city bestowed upon Nicias. This demonstrates that Socrates' fears were well founded. By late 422, Alcibiades was plainly a *dēmerastēs*, a man who longed to be gratified by the praises of the demos and who was jealous of rivals for the favor of the people. When the Peace of Nicias, a fifty-year armistice, was concluded, Alcibiades opposed it because Nicias had the credit for it and because the cessation of combat denied him good opportunities for heroism and advancement. In 420, he contrived to sabotage the peace by hoodwinking a Spartan delegation into behavior that enraged the Athenian Assembly and by making Nicias look "soft" on Sparta.[5] These swindles were proof positive that Alcibiades preferred victory, power, and lies to justice, as he had revealed in the *Alcibiades I.* They were also foul crimes in which Alcibiades knowingly sacrificed thousands of lives for the sake of his *libido dominandi.* His tyrannical temper was really Dionysian, reflecting not only the god's drunken exuberance but also his character as a murderous horror.

Alcibiades got what he wanted from his villainy, for the Peace of Nicias was destroyed and he was appointed general. Next, in 419, he persuaded the Patrensians to side with Athens. Then he concluded an alliance with Argos, Mantinea, and Elea and incited them to confront Sparta, thus causing the battle of Mantinea in 418. Plutarch reports that nobody liked the way Alcibiades achieved this but that the effects of his scheming were great. The Peloponnesus was thoroughly agitated. Enormous armies were quickly raised up against the Spartans at Mantinea, at no risk to Athens, and with no advantage for the Spartans when they won. In 417, the neophyte general led a force to Argos and stabilized its democratic government, thus winning favor and power both for himself and for Athens.[6] In his campaign to become the king of the Hellenes, Alcibiades could now count five triumphs, although his rapidly growing party of enemies would not have been so generous in the reckoning.

Having advanced his cause this far, Alcibiades began to promote imperialistic passions among the Athenians, urging them to take seriously their military oath, wherein they pledged to consider as their own all of the earth that anyone could use. If we may jump ahead in our story a little, by looking past the dramatic date of the *Symposium,* we may note that the first practical step in Alcibiades' imperialistic agenda was to take Melos. Plutarch informs us that in the summer of 416, approximately six months after Agathon's banquet, Alcibiades was the moving force in the slaughter of all the grown men of Melos, having supported the Melian decree. Next, he took advantage of Athens's longstanding wish for territorial conquest in Sicily. Plutarch tells us that Alcibiades was the man who fanned the Athenians' desire into flame, persuading them not to try anymore to grab the island piecemeal, but to sail there with a massive force and conquer it entirely. Further, Alcibiades regarded Sicily as only a start, for he was also dreaming of Carthage, Libya, Italy, and Peloponnesus. In the city, the young men were transported by his hopes, and their elders joined in raising the expectations. Thus, from 417 to 415, Alcibiades was busy building

---

5. Plutarch, *Alcibiades* 13–14.
6. The history in this paragraph is gleaned from ibid., 15.

an imperialistic movement, one that did not blink at genocide or hesitate to risk the safety of Athens in the very manner against which Pericles had warned.[7]

Returning to the year 417, Plutarch also reports that it was around then that Alcibiades began to engage in extremely unusual behavior:

> But all this political meddling and speaking and prudential calculating and cleverness, on the other hand, was in turn [accompanied by] a great softness of life, with most hybristic drinking and loves, with effeminacy of dress—drawing long purples through the agora—and with overweening spending. . . . He had a shield made out of gold, not with a device of the fathers but an Eros armed with a thunderbolt. The people held in repute looked on all these things with hatred and disgust and feared his contemptuousness and lawlessness as something tyrannical and monstrous. (*Alcibiades* 16.1–2)

It is indispensable to an understanding of Alcibiades that the meaning of this behavior be interpreted correctly.[8] The "great softness of life" and the "most hybristic drinking and loves" (πότους καὶ ἔρωτας ὑβρίσματα) show that Alcibiades rejected the Socratic teaching that self-knowledge requires moderation; he apparently reached the conclusion that his will to power compelled him to flaunt a limitless self-indulgence. The effeminacy in dress is less easy to explain. It might have been mere camp, some harmless fun. However, in conjunction with the purple, it was more probably a public proclamation of the course that Alcibiades' eros was taking, that is, a symbol of the tyrannical eros, an ostentatious embrace of the "wrong pederasty." The purple robes are important. They are the crimson of the tapestries that Clytemnestra spreads before Agamemnon upon his return from the Trojan War in her attempt to induce him to sin. Agamemnon initially refuses to walk on the crimson cloths, protesting that this is for gods alone (see Aeschylus, *Agamemnon* 910, 922, 946).[9] By dragging his long purple (or crimson) robes through the agora, Alcibiades was parading his wealth, advertising his dreams of royalty, and proclaiming his divinity, or

7. Ibid., 15–17.

8. For example, in *Fragility of Goodness*, Nussbaum uses Plutarch's report of the Eros with thunderbolt as the epigraph of her Alcibiades chapter. She makes the Eros a sign of Alcibiades' nature as a warm, sensitive lover who cherishes the beloved for his or her unique self (193). Alcibiades' images do indicate the sort of being he claims to be. However, the image of Alcibiades as a "sensitive" lover is inconsistent with everything else known about his character, especially including the remark of Plutarch that his loves were ὑβρίσματα (most hybristic). Nussbaum's dreamy liberalism prompts her to lift the story of the shield out of its context in Plutarch's report in order to give it an anachronistic color.

9. This relationship was called to my attention by Patricia Marquardt, my colleague who teaches classics at Marquette University.

his challenge to the gods. It is in this context that we must view the golden shield with its sign of an Eros holding a thunderbolt. The shield was a token of Alcibiades' belief that he had achieved apotheosis. As a god who denied himself no delight, Alcibiades now personified an Eros most unlike Diotima's daimon. The thunderbolt signified that he had usurped Zeus. Alcibiades, like the sophists, saw himself as a successful Titan. The shield was a perfect symbol of the tyrannical eros. It is no wonder that Athenian notables condemned Alcibiades' conduct as tyrannical.[10] They understood what it meant.

It would not be too much to assume that by the time that Alcibiades started to exhibit this behavior, Socrates would have judged him wholly corrupt. Therefore, Socrates would certainly have made good on his threat to abandon Alcibiades in 416. He would have been eager to influence other popular figures who could dissuade the Athenian demos from the course of action counseled by Alcibiades. This would explain his decision to make a play for Agathon. However, this does not mean that Socrates stopped loving Alcibiades. In the *Gorgias,* which is set with studied vagueness at every, any, and no particular time from 427 to 405,[11] Socrates still refers to Alcibiades as his beloved (481d), one whom he tries periodically to educate. The result is always the same. Socrates complains that Alcibiades always changes his words (482a–b). The fickle beloved leans whichever way the last wind blew and remains a *dēmerastēs.*

The rest of Alcibiades' career is well known to all. Alcibiades persuaded the Athenians to undertake the Sicilian expedition. The night before the fleet sailed, the Herms were defiled. The next morning, Athens was in an uproar. Alcibiades was accused. One tends to suppose that he was guilty. The imminent departure of the armada represented his greatest victory in his campaign to become tyrant of the world. To celebrate, he would have gotten quite drunk, as was his wont. In his inebriated state, this Eros who had usurped Zeus would have thought of Pisthetairos's advice to the birds, that they should prohibit the gods from passing to-and-fro through their territories "with hard-ons." He would have judged that the dismembering of aroused gods was a fitting observance of his political and ontological triumph. He and his cronies would have therefore laughed and hacked away in an orgy of hybris typical of egoistic tyrants, who eventually always lose the self-control needed to avoid overreaching themselves. However,

10. If Nussbaum's interpretation of the shield were correct, it would be difficult to see why Alcibiades' contemporaries judged his behavior tyrannical and monstrous.

11. On Plato's deliberately ambiguous dating of the *Gorgias,* I am entirely persuaded by the argument of Seth Benardete, *The Rhetoric of Morality and Philosophy: Plato's "Gorgias" and "Phaedrus,"* 7. By the way, this dramatic setting means that Socrates was at war with Gorgias during the entire period of the latter's sporadic activity in Athens, a time encompassing most of the Peloponnesian War.

firm evidence was lacking. It was decided to have Alcibiades sail for Sicily. After he departed, in the midsummer of 415, other charges were brought against him, especially that he had profaned the Eleusinian mysteries by reenacting them in a drunken revel in which he himself played the role of the high priest and revealed the mysteries, a capital offense. Now it was decreed that Alcibiades should return from Sicily for trial. Realizing that his enemies had the upper hand, the man who would not lose at dice as a boy slipped away to Sparta. There, he betrayed Athens, doing incalculable military harm to his city.[12] In 411, he was obliged to flee Sparta. According to Plutarch, his flight was necessitated by the fact that he had seduced the wife of the Spartan king, Agis. He went to the court of the Persian satrap, Tissaphernes. Finding himself in danger there, too, he began to angle for a recall to Athens and won this by helping to defeat the Four Hundred. Critias was the man who got the motion of recall passed. Alcibiades then served Athens well. In 407, the demos gave him gold crowns and made him general. However, they deposed him when Antiochus, his deputy, lost the battle of Notium in 406. He withdrew to Thrace. Critias and Lysander had him assassinated in Phrygia in 404, just when Athens was rife with rumors that he would return yet again to save the city.

Plato's reasons for giving Alcibiades the dramatic traits that he has in the *Symposium* now seem clear, at least to me. Alcibiades is leading a Dionysian procession and wearing the ivy wreath of Dionysus because, as the usurper of Zeus, he has supplanted all the gods; because he therefore has a penchant for playing the roles of the high priests who become those gods, as he probably did in the case of the profanation of the Eleusinian mysteries; and, as mentioned above, because he has become a drunken and murderous terror. He has the violets in his ivy crown not because he reveres Aphrodite, but because they symbolize Athens. Once again, he is advertising his aspirations to kingship. He is drunk because he has become Dionysus and also because he likes to practice his principled immoderation. He has wrapped several *tainias* around his head because he is inordinately proud of his victories in his struggles to best Nicias, ruin the Peace of Nicias, forge alliances and incite wars against the Spartans in Peloponnesus, and stabilize Argos. He wants to give *tainias* to Agathon and calls the poet "the wisest and most beautiful" because he understands that he needs to court a popular man who teaches the many a version of the tyrannical eros akin to his own, aiding his world conquest. However, he could not reach Agathon yesterday because he was too busy working the crowd, hoping to win recruits and Assembly votes from the same mob whose overwhelming influence caused

12. Socrates' refusal to escape his unjust death sentence stands in sharp contrast to Alcibiades' treason. His decision to stay might have been precipitated, at least in part, by the behavior of his beloved.

Socrates to fear for his own soul and for that of his beloved. He does not know that Socrates is present at the symposium because he has long since ceased to attend the philosopher and Socrates has forsaken him.

It is telling that Alcibiades fails to see Socrates because he is holding *tainias* before his eyes (213a). He is blind to philosophy because he is φιλό-νικός (victory loving). Agathon's slaves probably view Alcibiades as his useful intimate because an alliance with an up-and-coming tyrant could be profitable to his career.[13] However, Agathon does not regard Alcibiades as a friend because the leaders of metaphysical rebellions all wish to be the highest god. Agathon and Alcibiades might be allies as long as it is expedient, but would-be gods have only present and potential enemies, never fast friends. Plato permits Alcibiades to deliver the last speech in his dialogue on eros because this proto-Alexander incarnates the last tyrannical eros that Socratic right pederasty must resist, the Dionysian eros. Alcibiades arrives only after Socrates has spoken because, after 417, Alcibiades never truly hears Socrates again.

ALCIBIADES

Near the beginning of his speech, which he has billed as a praise of Socrates, Alcibiades says to the philosopher: "I shall speak the truth. But see if you will permit it" (214e6). A little later, he tells the *sympotai* that they do not know Socrates, but that he will reveal him, for he once caught Socrates when he was serious and "opened" him,[14] spying divine images—statues of gods—inside (216c–217a). Every student of Plato would be happy to hear the truth about Socrates, particularly from an intimate who is in a position to know it. Is Alcibiades a reliable informant? Some scholars think that this question is settled by the following evidence: Before starting his presentation, Alcibiades exhorts Socrates to contradict him if he utters a single lie, if Socrates so chooses (214e–215a). Socrates never complains that one of Alcibiades' assertions is false. Hence, these commentators infer that Alcibiades, of all men, reveals Plato's insights into the crucial truth about Socrates. In the process, they maintain, Alcibiades gives Plato's critique of Socrates' alleged erotic deficiencies.[15] I hope that I may be allowed to ex-

13. A few years after Alcibiades fled to Sparta, Agathon bound himself to another autocratic patron, Archelaus of Macedon.

14. I assume that Alcibiades means this in an intellectual sense, that is, he gained access to the secrets in Socrates' mind. Given Alcibiades' later story of his attempted seduction of Socrates, I see nothing here that would justify a homoerotic reading.

15. Among the observers who take this position are some who issue dire warnings against equating Socrates' statements with Plato's opinions. They inconsistently permit Alcibiades to be Plato's spokesman. This procedure strikes me as simply arbitrary. We

press a few doubts about this analysis. A number of considerations militate against it, as follows.

First, shortly after Alcibiades gains admission to the banquet, he begins to transfer some of his *tainias* to Agathon, saying: "I shall entwine the head of the wisest and most beautiful, if I may speak the—thus. But do you laugh at me because I am drunk? Well, and even if you laugh, I know well that I speak truly" (212e7–213a1). However, the Delphic Oracle, whom Socrates could not disprove, informs us that no one is wiser than Socrates (*Apology* 21a). Agathon is not the wisest. Socrates' examination of Agathon has demonstrated this. When a man's first substantive words are false, whether as lies or as errors, we have good reason to distrust him when he promises to disclose a verity that he "knows well." We are entitled to suspect that his judgment might be flawed. Knowing Alcibiades' victory-loving character and Dionysian eros as we now do, we would also do well to suspect that propaganda is coming.

Second, Alcibiades reports that many of his experiences of Socrates, including his "opening" of his lover, date to the days before they went to Potidaea (219e). Thus, he allegedly "opened" Socrates in 432, when he had all the philosophic acumen that he exhibited in the *Alcibiades I* and the *Protagoras*. It seems that if the young Alcibiades saw something divine in his lover, which may well be, he was in no position to understand it. Indeed, the "divine" something that he thought he saw might well be Socrates' imagined godlike ability to rule men. Hence, his claim that he "opened" Socrates could be a vain boast. It would be simplistic and uncritical to accept it at face value.

Third, we have seen in the *Alcibiades I* that Socrates warned Alcibiades in 432 that he was wedded to *amathia*, the ignorance that destroys noble human endeavors. Alcibiades' *amathia* took the form of a naive belief that he knew what he was talking about when he was devoid of any conception of his topics. We must inquire whether Alcibiades cured himself of *amathia* between 432 and 416. If he did, it was certainly not in the *Alcibiades I*, when he took Socrates as an *erastēs* for despotic, victory-loving reasons that were philosophically foolish. It was not in the *Protagoras*, when he had already befriended Critias despite his solemn pledge to follow Socrates. Indeed, in the *Protagoras*, Alcibiades displayed another facet of his *amathia* when he stated that Socrates was invincible in dialectics, which seemed true, and that Socrates would be satisfied by a surrender, which was false. This proves that Alcibiades was attuned to outward facts or appearances but failed to discern the realities inside them. One could speculate that Alcibiades overcame his *amathia* sometime after the *Protagoras*. However, the

---

can make "Plato" say what we want when we gratuitously decide who his spokesmen are. The choice of Alcibiades is largely unsubstantiated by evidence.

similarity between his motives in sabotaging the Peace of Nicias and those of Callippus in the betrayal of Dion, the sheer stupidity of his violation of Pericles' warning in his agitation for the Sicilian expedition, and the almost inconceivable imbecility of his seduction of the wife of Agis when he was dependent upon the king's good grace for his very life should make us hesitate to credit this conjecture. It is far more likely that Alcibiades was never cured of *amathia.* Therefore, it seems probable that, in the *Symposium,* Alcibiades still tends to imagine that he knows what he is talking about when he is ignorant. We can put this another way. If we grant generously that Alcibiades sometimes sincerely means to tell the truth, we must suspect that he will relate not the truth simply, but the truth as he misconstrues it in his ignorance.

Fourth, Alcibiades testifies that he is torn between irresistible attraction to Socrates and the wish that Socrates were gone (215d–216c). I believe this. It will be said that an Alcibiades who loves Socrates so much could surely discover authentic truths about him. Let it be so for the sake of argument. In return, I expect it to be granted that an Alcibiades whose tyrannical eros wants Socrates dead could not refrain from casting these truths in false lights.

Last, those who assume that Alcibiades is a truth teller are right to observe that Socrates never denies any particular remark that Alcibiades makes about him. However, these writers try to erect too weighty a structure on this slight foundation. It should be noted that Socrates does not agree to obey Alcibiades' injunction to protest every time he believes that he is being maligned. Socrates could have sound, innocent reasons for holding his peace while Alcibiades is building his case. There seem to be two explanations for his long silence now. The first is that Alcibiades' points incorporate facts and appearances. They are examples of his propensity to focus on externals while missing inner realities. It is hard to object constantly to reports of apparent facts without being seen as suspiciously defensive. The second is that it is economical to refrain from repeated denials of details when the whole of a falsehood can be refuted in one fell swoop. When Alcibiades finishes, Socrates charges that his aim was to stir up antagonism between Agathon and himself (222c–d). Some hold that this denies nothing in Alcibiades' talk. They are logically right about external facts but philosophically wrong about inner meanings. When Socrates unmasks Alcibiades' vicious intention, he indicates that Alcibiades has mixed his empirical brew into a spiritual lie, that Socrates is bad for Agathon. In this way, Socrates denies the whole of Alcibiades' speech.

In view of these reflections, I cannot agree that there is a prima facie case for assuming that Alcibiades tells the essential truth, or any significant untainted truth, about Socrates. I think that if we keep Alcibiades true to his character in the *Alcibiades I,* the *Protagoras,* his biography as recorded by

Thucydides and Plutarch, and his first speeches and deeds in the *Symposium*, his words are likely to be those of a man who is torn between Socratic right pederasty and his Dionysian eros, and who is leaning heavily toward his tyrannical eros.

It will be objected that we should not read these other materials into the *Symposium*. I see no reasonable grounds for the objection. Why should Plato endow the *Symposium* with an Alcibiades who differs from the one in his other dialogues and in history, allowing the new Alcibiades to deliver infallible pronouncements about Socrates? To me, this idea bespeaks an illegitimate desire for a key to an absolute understanding of Socrates, or an arbitrary intention to construe the *Symposium* as a modern American romance between a dashing, noble beloved who is acutely sensitive to the souls of others and his wise lover. The longing for a key to an absolute grasp of Socrates is illicit because it violates Plato's warning that his serious teachings are not found in his writings. The romantic view of Alcibiades as a noble, sensitive beloved is silly because it superimposes wishful thinking on the portrait that Plato paints. Alcibiades is pictured not as a sensitive darling, but as a man who is anything but sensitive in his treatment of Agathon, in his approaches to Socrates, and in his claims that he has been outraged, which elicit laughter. He is depicted not as a youth who nobly returns his lover's affection, but as a man torn between attraction to his lover—an attraction that the text of the *Symposium* still attributes to his great admiration for eristic skill rather than to love of the good—and desire to see his lover dead because the lover makes him ashamed of the things that he says and does, which we know to be the things of the Dionysian eros.

Thus, what I look to see in Alcibiades' speech is a mixture of the real truths (perhaps lover's insights cast in false lights), partial truths about facts that misconceive inner realities, hasty opinions, errors, and propagandistic lies that have typified his assertions all along. His words will be expressions of a love that seems to be wrongly motivated, at least in part, and of a hostility that inspires acts of war on behalf of the Dionysian tyrannical eros. It will not be so easy to distinguish the truths from the bellicose lies. Nothing that Alcibiades says can be accepted as true simply because he has promised to adhere to the truth—as if every character in a play who gives this assurance should be believed.

When Alcibiades notices Socrates reclining at the same table as Agathon, he is shocked. He accuses Socrates of "ambushing" him. He demands to know Socrates' purpose. He asserts that Socrates has intrigued to sit with the most beautiful member of the group when he could have been paired with somebody such as Aristophanes, who is deliberately ridiculous. In keeping with the charm of Athenian society, he undoubtedly expresses all this in a humorous manner that lightly veils his chagrin. As argued above, he is incensed because he assumes that Socrates is there to turn Agathon against him.

Adopting the same jocular demeanor as Alcibiades, Socrates cowers behind Agathon in a mock terror that has an authentic aspect. He begs Agathon for protection, saying that ever since he became Alcibiades' *erastēs*, Alcibiades has jealously kept him from looking at or conversing with other beauties and that Alcibiades has groped at him incessantly. (These accusations are consistent with what we know of Alcibiades' victory-loving character. The charges also tally with the story that Alcibiades tells on himself later.) Interestingly, Socrates urges Agathon to reconcile him with Alcibiades. This probably implies that Socrates still loves Alcibiades and hopes against hope that something can be done to call him back from his evils. Socrates also begs Agathon to protect him if Alcibiades should resort to force. Given Alcibiades' hybristic nature, Socrates' fear of violence is not entirely groundless. It is ironically funny that Socrates appeals to the soft Agathon for hard protection.

Alcibiades spurns Socrates' offer of reconciliation, thus calling into question our contemporary ideas about who in our dialogue can and cannot love real individuals.[16] He threatens to take revenge "hereafter" for Socrates' ambush. "Hereafter" turns out to mean "forthwith." After Alcibiades has forced Socrates to quaff the wine cooler, in a vain effort to get his revenge by reducing Socrates to a humiliating drunkenness, Eryximachus insists that Alcibiades should abide by the rules of the symposium and praise Eros. Alcibiades replies that it is not fair to expect him to compete against sober speakers when he is drunk. Changing the subject, he adds that Eryximachus should not believe what Socrates just said. It is Socrates who keeps Alcibiades from praising any man or deity but Socrates, not vice versa, and it is Socrates who cannot keep his hands off Alcibiades. I believe this accusation, insofar as it concerns outward looks. Socrates has certainly been at pains to keep Alcibiades from praising people such as Critias and gods such as those cited by the Athenians at Melos. He has undoubtedly caressed Alcibiades while trying to reason with him. He has surely held himself and philosophy up as examples superior to those Alcibiades is emulating. However, these acts have been philosophically motivated. Alcibiades is twisting their import. Thus, Socrates exclaims, "Will you not speak well?" (Οὐκ εὐφημήσεις, 214d5). This idiom has the force of the command "Don't blaspheme!" Socrates is protesting the libel on philosophy and the impious suggestion that he elevates himself above gods.

---

16. Every sensible person knows that love matches involve real people who inevitably need forgiveness from time to time. Love cannot exist apart from a constant readiness to forgive.

Alcibiades reacts by swearing by Poseidon (a significant choice, for Poseidon has always disputed Athena's rulership of Athens, wanting it for himself), claiming that he cannot praise anyone but Socrates when Socrates is present. Thus, he induces Eryximachus to allow him to celebrate Socrates. He then construes this permission curiously, asking if he should really feel free to "take revenge" (τιμωρήσωμαι, 214e2). It is when Socrates protests again that Alcibiades pledges to be truthful. It is possible that truthful praise could simultaneously be vengeful. However, Alcibiades' self-conscious vengefulness does nothing to allay the fear that his speech will mix his usual truths, errors, and propagandistic lies in a way that serves his Dionysian eros, both unintentionally and intentionally spinning these ingredients into a false whole.

So, Socrates orders Alcibiades to tell the truth. Alcibiades exhorts Socrates to interrupt him if he tells falsehoods. Then he launches into the body of his oration. Much like Agathon and Socrates, he specifies his method at the outset. Whereas Agathon and Socrates described Eros in terms of "sorts," Alcibiades will reveal Socrates with icons, or images. He insists that he does this not for the purpose of ridicule but for the sake of truth.

Alcibiades begins his encomium by likening Socrates to the little Silenus statues sold in shops, the kind that have pipes or flutes in their hands and can be pulled apart vertically, revealing statues of gods inside. Further, he asserts that Socrates resembles the satyr Marsyas. When we envisage satyrs, we immediately think of rabid sexual lust. Hence, we wonder how these icons could be the truth about Socrates. However, the analogies are not offered chiefly as commentaries on Socrates' sexual habits. Alcibiades says that Socrates is like these satyrs in all respects, which he proceeds to enumerate, and he discusses Socrates' sexuality only near the end of this discourse. The images will be the truth about Socrates if he has the characteristics indicated. We also wonder whether equating Socrates with satyr statues and with a real satyr is praise or revenge. Perhaps the claim that there are effigies of gods in Socrates' breast and the suggestion that the supernatural powers of satyrs inhere in his soul are intended to sound like praise.[17] On the other hand, Alcibiades is thinking of dismembering statues. The satyr icon also demotes Socrates to a status in which he is half man and half beast. (Although Alcibiades is unaware of what he has done, he has just disputed Diotima's claim that Socrates, together with the rest

---

17. Perhaps the *sympotai* would share the opinion of Nietzsche, who maintains that "the satyr was the archetype of man, the embodiment of his highest and most intense emotions," as well as a *Schwärmer*, "one who proclaims wisdom from the very heart of nature, a symbol of the sexual omnipotence of nature" (*Die Geburt der Tragödie*, in *NW*, 3.1.58.8–12; also in *Basic Writings of Nietzsche*, 61). In Nietzsche's account, a *Schwärmer* is not so much a humbug, as in Kant's denunciation of Plato, as an ecstatic speaker of tongues who is maddened by the closest possible contact with the core of reality.

of mankind, is half human and half god.) This is probably meant to disgust Agathon. The Marsyas image also recalls a terrifying story. Marsyas challenged the god of the flute, Apollo, to a flute contest that he could not win. He was skinned alive for his brashness. By calling Socrates a Marsyas, Alcibiades could be warning Socrates that he faces a similar fate if he challenges the new god of politics to a political contest. Alcibiades also hates the flute as an instrument unfit for free men.[18] He might be revenging himself upon Socrates by calling him slavish. Given all these possibilities, we are not ready to say whether Alcibiades' words are laudatory, damning, or both at once.

The first satyric property that Alcibiades imputes to Socrates is a similarity of physical form. He doubts that even Socrates will deny this likeness. Of course, the comparison is not literally correct; Socrates does not have the lower body of a goat. However, let us assume that Alcibiades means that Socrates is as ugly as a satyr. Prescinding from the question of whether or not there is an objective physical beauty or ugliness, this critique of Socrates might be true in the eyes of many beholders. Socrates cannot be troubled to dispute it. We notice only that Alcibiades' truth can scarcely be construed as praise. Rather, it intends to focus attention on Socrates' worst feature, his looks. Alcibiades could know that Agathon loves beauty and hates ugliness without having heard his symposium speech. One infers that he is trying to alienate Agathon from Socrates. His opening gambit appears typical of his tendency to stress external appearances while overlooking or obscuring inner realities.

The next satyric characteristic that Alcibiades attributes to Socrates is hybris. He says: "You are hybristic, aren't you? If you disagree, I'll bring witnesses" (215b7–8). It is plain that whereas Alcibiades did not expect Socrates to object to being called ugly, he does anticipate that Socrates will deny being hybristic. Therefore, he tries to head Socrates off by threatening to produce witnesses. Alcibiades can undoubtedly find many Athenians who will back him up. Agathon even accused Socrates of hybris within moments of his arrival at the banquet. However, witnesses are worthless with respect to the truth unless we have ironclad guarantees that they are not lying or mistaken (see *Gorgias* 471e–472a). The witnesses whom Alcibiades means to produce are likely to be Socrates' enemies: would-be tyrants, sophists, and Athenian democrats who have been embarrassed by his refutations of their errors and lies, or by his objections to their injustices. Socrates' combative bluntness and honesty with these people will certainly seem hybristic to them. However, this does not prove that Socrates is hybristic in any of the senses found in H. G. Liddell and R. Scott: "violent," "wanton," "insolent," and inclined by one's "pride of strength

---

18. Plutarch, *Alcibiades* 2.4. Plutarch probably relies here on *Alcibiades I* 106e6–7.

or passion" to "outrage" others. Socrates could be disposed to fight tyrants and sophists and be hybristic to them without being violent, wanton, or insolent because he is proud. As Alcibiades contemplates Socrates, he probably fears that he will rise to make this obviously valid point. That is why he tries to silence him in advance. Quite apart from the question of whether the charge is true, we wonder how calling Socrates hybristic is supposed to be flattering.[19] Probably, it is meant as censure rather than praise. Alcibiades has known Socrates for a long time; he knows how Socrates treats sophists. He has not heard the speeches tonight, but he can guess that Socrates has been gruff. He believes that his accusation will play well with the crowd. He is trying to alienate Agathon from Socrates.

Alcibiades understands well that his description of Socrates as hybristic needs proof. He lays the groundwork for this demonstration by assigning a third feature of satyrs to the philosopher. He asks Socrates: "But aren't you a flautist (αὐλητής)?" (215b8). Answering his own question, he declares that Socrates is a more amazing piper than the satyrs. Marsyas could charm the human beings with his flute. Anyone who pipes his tunes can do the same, that is, bring about possession and reveal those who are ready for gods and mysteries (215c1–6). However, Socrates surpasses all flautists. He can "flute" without a flute, by speaking. Often, the best orators speak and nobody pays attention. (Apparently, even in ancient Athens, incessant speechifying and propaganda had the result that has become so well known in our time, mass apathy. On occasion, Alcibiades must have seen this happen.) However, whenever anyone hears a Socratic discourse, whether spoken by himself or another, "we are transported and possessed" (215d5–6).

Here, Alcibiades has told the truth. Socrates' speeches possess people. His sophistical opponents are reduced to silence by his dialectic, as if they were paralyzed by snake venom or drugs (see 218a). Others appear to become enchanted, falling into trances, following him and wishing to hear only his words. Although Alcibiades has observed this phenomenon rightly, it is not certain that he has understood it. I say this because he immediately moves to present it as something bad. I doubt that he could do this if he perceived it properly.

Alcibiades depicts Socrates' stunning, enchanting fluting as evil or undesirable when he describes its effects on his own person: When he hears Socrates speak, he becomes worse than the Corybants. His heart pounds and he weeps copiously. He has heard good orators such as Pericles, but none have made him suffer as Socrates has done. These other orators have not left his soul in turmoil, and they have not made him feel like a slave taken

19. Some scholars in our time would understand it as praise, of course. They celebrate the alleged hybris because they think it essential to Socrates' self-deification and theirs.

in war. However, Socrates has made him think his life not worth living (215d–e). This reaction is the opposite of that of the "crazy" Apollodorus, who thought that he had been doing nothing with his life until he filled it up with the speeches of Socrates. I agree with Apollodorus: Socratic philosophy is fulfilling, not stifling. Alcibiades has cast a false light on the truth about Socrates. Socrates does enchant, but the effects of this are liberating, not enslaving. True, Alcibiades does suffer. However, he suffers not from Socratic possession but from his resistance to it.

We should ask why Alcibiades misunderstands the effects of Socratic possession in this manner. He replies for himself. He asserts that, even now, if he listened to Socrates, he could not resist him. Then he would suffer in the same ways as before, for Socrates compels him to confess that whereas he needs to hear what Socrates has to say, he neglects himself in order to conduct Athenian affairs. So he stops up his ears as against the Sirens and runs away, lest he should sit next to Socrates until he grows old (216a4–8). Socrates brings him to a state that no one would expect to discover in him, shame. He claims to be aware that he should do what Socrates orders, but as soon as he is out of earshot he falls victim to his love of the honor of the many, which is to say that he does not really see that he should do what Socrates commands. Often, he could have wished Socrates dead. However, if this wish were granted, he would feel worse than he does now, so he does not know what to do (216b–c). I judge that these words are candid.

This certainly clarifies the problem. Alcibiades misunderstands the effects of Socratic piping because Socratic possession shames him for his Dionysian eros and for taking pleasure in his democratic popularity, which is a major part of his tyrannical eros. It may be asked why I assume that this means that Alcibiades misunderstands what he is describing. Why not suppose that he deliberately misrepresents it? Let us explore the latter alternative. If it obtained, we would have a Pauline or Augustinian affair in which Alcibiades grasped the truth perfectly but was torn between good and evil desires, succumbing to his evil will.

Every Christian might say that this is his trouble. However, Plato is not a Christian. When he speaks in his own name in the Seventh Letter, he attributes worldly evil not to the defective will of the Christians, but to *amathia*. Plato would find the Pauline and Augustinian stories of spiritual struggles between two wills, one that knowingly chooses good and another that knowingly opts for evil, preposterous. He would declare deliberate choices for what one knows to be evil impossible. Accordingly, in the drama of the *Symposium,* the situation must be that (1) Socrates can always compel Alcibiades to admit his shortcomings by subjecting him to dialectical logic, as in the *Alcibiades I;* (2) this process always has an emotional impact on Alcibiades, again as in the *Alcibiades I,* for dialectical reason is powerful; (3) Alcibiades still needs a vision of the good, or an experience of the illumination that comes to the soul like a leaping flame, because he needs to know perfectly, rather than merely accept a proof at the level of the four, that it would actually be good for him to sit by Socrates' side until he grows altogether old and that it is bad for him always to be a victory-loving *dēmerastēs;* and (4) this always leaves Alcibiades in the condition of which Adeimantus complains in the *Republic* (487b–c), namely, that rather than being completely convinced of the truth of Socrates' reasoning, he fears that he has been refuted for want of dialectical skill. This implies that it is true that an internal struggle is raging in Alcibiades' psyche. However, it is a battle between something in his reason that yields to dialectical persuasion and something more vital in his reason that is still shrouded in the darkness of *amathia.* Alcibiades is torn between the conclusions of a logical reason that are not yet the highest knowledge and the ignorance of a reason that still cannot see why victory, popularity, and tyranny are not true goods. This lack of full understanding explains why he always vacillates in his words and his choices.

Proud men do not like to be shamed. Alcibiades loves Socrates for the cogency of his logical dialectic because it enables him to make people say whatever he likes. Simultaneously, he thinks it unfair that Socrates uses this dialectical skill to shame him for acts that seem good rather than shameful. So, paradoxically, he loves and hates Socrates for the same qualities and cannot decide whether he should listen to him or have him killed. However, he admits that, lately, he has been fleeing from Socrates. This means that he is leaning toward the tyrannical eros. This implies, in turn, that his simultaneous praise of Socrates and revenge on Socrates is more revenge than praise. He is issuing a warning to Agathon: "Beware! What Socrates has managed to do to me, he wants to do to you. His hybristic piping will enslave you!" This is false, for Socrates leads his beloveds to liberty.

Alcibiades is not finished. He thinks of another way to develop the theme of Socrates' hybris. It is now that he assures the *sympotai* that they do not know Socrates, but that he will reveal him. Finally turning to homoeroticism, he attributes a fourth property of the satyrs to Socrates, a characteristic that resembles intellectual irony, and that might be labeled as "erotic irony." Socrates, he says, is always erotically involved with "the beauties." At the same time, he affects to be "entirely ignorant and to know nothing." This, Alcibiades affirms, is just like a Silenus. The amorousness and the ignorance are an outer shell that Socrates wears, like the surface of a Silenus. However, if you open Socrates, you find that he is full of moderation (σωφροσύνης). It does not matter to him if someone is a beauty; he hates (καταφρονεῖ) beauty. Similarly, he is contemptuous of wealth, honor, "and us." Consequently, he "spends his whole life being ironic toward and making sport of the human beings" (216d–e, especially e3–5).

These lines necessitate an inquiry that is becoming our regular exercise. It is clear that Alcibiades has accurately described some facts and appearances that pertain to Socrates. It is true that Socrates is always erotically involved with the beauties; he is doing nothing more nor less than obeying Diotima's command to rise from the love of one beautiful body to the love of all of them. It is also true that in doing so, he appears to be lacking in the sexual passions and emotions usually connected with such flirtations. Once again, he is following Diotima's injunctions, that he should ascend from the love of bodies to the love of souls, and from there ever higher on the ladder of beauty. It is true that you can tell from Socrates' visible acts that he is full of temperance. Socrates has also told him that he is relatively unimpressed by the beauty of bodies, as compared with the beauty of souls and higher eternal realities, and that he cares not at all for wealth and honor. Alcibiades is "revealing" the obvious; he did not have to open Socrates to learn this. However, we must now ask whether it follows from these observations that Socrates spends his whole life ironically making game of the human beings. Is it true that Socrates is "full of moderation" in Alcibiades' sense of the phrase? That is, does Socrates only pretend to be attracted to beauties? Is he, unlike satyrs, a sexless cold fish who, like the satyrs, feels only scorn for human beings? Does he hate physical beauty? Does he really only affect love and friendship for beauties, secretly mocking their naïveté and intellectual inferiority when they fall for his line, thus amusing himself at their expense? Does he hold his present company in contempt? Is he a sexual Silenus? Or has Alcibiades repeated his characteristic error of getting external facts right and inner meanings wrong?

To answer these questions, we must begin by allowing Alcibiades to offer his evidence. He attempts to persuade his *sympotai* that his accusations are true by telling a long, important story, one that brings the theme of his satyr play back into focus. He does not know, he says, whether anyone else has laid Socrates open when Socrates was being serious. However, he did it once and beheld *agalmata* (ἀγάλματα, statues created for the religious purpose of honoring and adoring gods) inside. So, Alcibiades reaffirms that Socrates is like Silenus figurines insofar as his outside differs totally from his inside.

Alcibiades continues by reporting that the statues that he saw in Socrates were "divine and golden and all-beautiful and wonderful," so that he had to do what Socrates ordered. He believed Socrates to be attracted to his youthful beauty. Therefore, he says, "I thought it was a gift of Hermes and wonderful good luck for me, by gratifying Socrates, to hear all that he knew. For I thought I was amazingly beautiful" (217a2–6). That is, Alcibiades decided to seduce Socrates, hoping in that way to induce Socrates to give him the "divine" things that he saw and wanted but had not been given yet.

Alcibiades next reviews the tactics that he used in his comical, protracted campaign to bed Socrates. First, he dismissed his attendant when he went to meet Socrates, hoping that the liaison would heat up in private. He

Eros, Wisdom, and Silence

laments that Socrates merely conversed with him in the usual way. This
is to say that he disdains dialogues that serious students of philosophy
would have given anything to hear, without so much as a word regarding
any memory that he might have had of their contents.[20] Then he persuaded
Socrates to wrestle with him. Nothing came of it. Then he asked Socrates to
dinner. Socrates was reluctant but went to Alcibiades' home twice. On the
second occasion, Alcibiades chatted him up for hours and then convinced
him to stay the night. Again, Alcibiades gives no report of the dialogue. His
whole concern is his attempted seduction of the hybristic sexual Silenus.

    Now Alcibiades assumes the aspect of an Athenian citizen in a law court
who is acting at once as victim, witness, and prosecutor. In Athens, hybris,
defined as the willful outrage of a fellow citizen, is a serious legal offense.
Alcibiades is suing Socrates, who is now facing the second lawsuit filed
against him this evening. Alcibiades addresses his fellows as men who
at once are victims, witnesses, and jurors. He casts Socrates in his standard role as the accused. As victim-witness-prosecutor, he appeals to the
victims-witnesses-jurors to convict the hybristic Socrates of outraging him,
on the grounds that his seduction was rebuffed.

    To prepare his jury, Alcibiades says that, so far, his story has been noble.
However, he would not proceed if wine and truthfulness were not urging
him on. It would be dishonest if he did not tell everything about Socrates'
"magnificent-arrogant deed" (ἔργον ὑπερήφανον, 217e5). Alcibiades is acting as if only wild horses could drag his next words out. He is really eager to
broadcast them. We are supposed to think: "Poor Alcibiades! How terrible
that he is forced to rehearse Socrates' arrogant treatment of him in public! Look at his tears of shame!" Alcibiades resorts to this rhetorical dodge
to deflect attention from the fact that he is claiming victim status under a
bizarre interpretation of the laws of outrage: He, Alcibiades, to whom such
things are not supposed to happen, felt disgraced when his sexual solici-
tation of Socrates was rebuffed. It follows that the "hybristic" Socrates has
violated him!

    Suddenly looking more wily than drunk, Alcibiades continues to work
his jury with a politician's psychological tricks. He recalls the case of a
man who suffered a snakebite. The man refused to describe his symptoms
to anyone who had not been bitten too, on the grounds that only fellow
victims could understand him. Alcibiades declares that he has been bitten by something more painful, and in the worst way, "in the heart or the
soul or whatever one must call it."[21] He has been hit, as if by a missile or

    20. Alcibiades stands in stark contrast to Aristodemus, who memorized every word
of the master's philosophic conversations with others.
    21. This deliberate ambiguity about the soul neatly sidesteps the sophists' quarrels
about the reality and alleged primacy of the soul, disputes about which Alcibiades may
have heard in other places and times, even though he has not heard them tonight.

lightning, and bitten by Socrates' philosophic discourses, which grip more fiercely than an adder and force a young, not incapable soul to do or say what it will. Embracing his audience with a gesture, Alcibiades says that he has only to look around to see a Phaedrus, an Agathon, an Eryximachus, a Pausanias, an Aristodemus, and an Aristophanes—he need not speak of Socrates—all of whom have known the madness and Bacchic frenzy of philosophy. "All of you," he insists, shall stand and confirm what follows (217e–218b). I have already observed that it is true that Socrates' discourses have the described effects and that Alcibiades has mistakenly cast them in a negative light. He repeats this move here, portraying the effects as painful. He hopes that his victims-witnesses-jurors will share his experience and cry with rage: "Yes! Philosophy is just like that! It is painful and degrading to be refuted, to be forced to contradict our own positions, to be capable youths and compelled to do Socrates' will!" Alcibiades wants these jurors to perceive Socrates as a Dracula who has gotten them under his hypnotic power, or as the witch of the charges that have been brought against him since Aristophanes produced the *Clouds*. He is working them into the frame of mind in which he wants them to hear his personal tale of woe.

Still preparing his jury, Alcibiades adopts another role, that of the priestly guardian of a mystery. He orders all present except the initiates to cover their ears. Then he narrates his story, without being scrupulous to ensure that only initiates can hear. (It is not hard for us to deduce what Plato thinks about the charge that Alcibiades profaned the Eleusinian mysteries.) However, Alcibiades does not care about that. He wants the jurors to feel privileged to enjoy his revelation of his Socratic mystery because this will make them more likely to support him.

At last, Alcibiades resumes his tale. He says that when the lights were down low and the slaves were gone, he told Socrates that he considered him the only worthy *erastēs* he had ever had. Therefore, he thought it irrational not to gratify him erotically, or with property of his own or his friends. He declared that nothing was more important to him than becoming the best, so he would feel more shame at not gratifying the friend who could help him than he would feel before the mindless many for gratifying the friend. Hearing this, Socrates put on a tremendously ironic air and replied: "My dear Alcibiades, I daresay that you are not vulgarly stupid (φαῦλος) if what you say about me chances to be true, and there is a certain power in me through which you could become better" (218d7–e2). Socrates continued by observing that Alcibiades must have seen an extraordinary beauty in him, far superior to Alcibiades' physical beauty. If so, Alcibiades was hoping for no mean profit in the mutual exchange of beauty for beauty, for he was trying to get true beauty for seeming beauty and attempting to pull off the old bargain of gold for bronze. Finally, Socrates warned

Alcibiades to be more wary, for the supposed helper could prove worthless to him (219a).

Alcibiades was not deterred by this answer. He imagined that Socrates had been hit by his "bolts." The new Eros-Zeus was so far gone in pride that he could not hear a definite "no." So, he slipped under the covers with Socrates and wrapped his arms around him, whereupon the two lay like stones for the rest of the night with absolutely nothing transpiring. When he had done all this, Alcibiades grumbles, Socrates "was superior to me" (or "prevailed over me," ἐμοῦ . . . περιεγένετό, 219c3). Furthermore, he was "contemptuous of," "scornfully laughed at," and was "hybristic toward my youthful manhood" (ὥρας, 219c4–5). Alcibiades addresses this testimony to the "gentlemen of the jury," explaining, "You are jurors in the matter of Socrates' magnificent arrogance (ὑπερηφανίας)" (219c5–6). He finishes with an oath by "gods and goddesses" that, as a result of his efforts, he had no more slept a night with Socrates than if he had been in bed with his father or brother.

All those who consider Socrates erotically deficient, whether they accuse him of gross "indifference to human things," sexlessness, or an inability to love, cite this anecdote as proof of their thesis. In their view, Alcibiades ought not to have been treated in this manner, with his heartfelt love having been heartlessly rejected.[22]

It appears to me that these scholars have been fooled by Alcibiades' rhetoric; they vote with his ideally gullible jury. If a crime against love has been committed here, it is Alcibiades, not Socrates, who is guilty of gross insensitivity. I propose a mental experiment. Suppose that you have devoted a great deal of time and effort to the cultivation of a beauty whom you love, to whom you may well wish to make love, and whom you hope to educate to virtue. Assume also that one day, the beauty invites you to an intimate dinner and seizes the moment to say: "You are privy to information that I want. I'll sleep with you in exchange for that information. In addition to that, I'll pay you any sum of money you ask, and my friends will contribute, too." I believe that you would realize that your beauty had just tried to reward your love by suggesting a commercial exchange: not love for love, but sex and riches for desired instruction. I think that you would be stunned that the beloved hoped to sell you sexual intercourse in return for what you would have given freely if you had judged it good to give. Being deeply hurt, you might even shout, "Whore!" and storm out of the house. It is certainly not a sign of Socrates' "coldness" that he replied

22. Rosen is not beguiled by Alcibiades as much as other scholars in the "erotic deficiency" camp and does not fall for this sob story. Still, he agrees that Alcibiades' tale is one of many pieces of evidence that Socrates "lacks the human Eros" and that he is possessed of an inner coldness.

to Alcibiades with ironic asperity. Alcibiades was as far as possible from the right pederasty.

We may now evaluate Alcibiades' sexual accusations against Socrates rapidly. Does his story prove that Socrates is a sexless cold fish who only pretends to be attracted to beauty, that Socrates hates beauty, and that Socrates is guilty of an erotic irony in which he teases beauties, induces them to offer sexual intercourse, and then laughs in their faces? Does it demonstrate that Socrates is a sexual Silenus whose outside differs from his inside?

I think that totally opposite conclusions are warranted. We must recall that Socrates was aroused by the sight of a boy's genitalia. He does not fake passion. By Alcibiades' own account of the failed seduction, Socrates also reacted to it by recognizing Alcibiades' great physical beauty. He did not "hate" Alcibiades' beauty, but commented that Alcibiades must have seen an even greater beauty in the man with whom he was trying to strike a deal. Here, Socrates said something that Alcibiades probably construed as hatred of his beauty, namely, that the inner beauty that Alcibiades saw was "real," whereas Alcibiades' physical beauty was only "seeming." However, to say this about the relative ontological ranks of spiritual beauty and physical beauty does not entail hatred of physical beauty.

Further, Alcibiades could hardly claim that Socrates had kept this opinion secret from him. We remember well that Socrates had already informed Alcibiades at their first meeting that he cared less for the beauty of bodies than for the beauty of souls and that Alcibiades needed to cultivate his soul. We also know from Diotima's teaching, even if Alcibiades has not heard it, that a Socrates who might have been happy to make love to Alcibiades if their spiritual affairs had been in order would refuse to do so if the sexual romance hindered either or both of the lovers from ascending the ladder of beauty. Far from being erotically deficient, Socrates' conduct presupposes that when a spiritual situation calls for sexual self-restraint, the exercise of that restraint is healthful rather than pathological. The decision for sexual restraint in such cases will appear inhuman and erotically deficient only to those who are obtuse to the fact that the things of the soul outrank the things of the body, and who are therefore incapable of imagining any reasons for putting off sexual gratification. I should think that Alcibiades' decision to repay love with a business deal certainly set off alarms in Socrates' soul, warnings that the ascent of the ladder of beauty could not proceed on these terms. Alcibiades should have known from Socrates' first conversation with him that the alarms would ring. On this topic, Socrates is not a Silenus. He is a philosopher whose outside is always the same as his inside. Socrates' spurning of Alcibiades was not an act of erotic irony, but a straightforward act of tough love.

However, enough of Socrates, at least for a few moments. If my arguments have been right, Plato intends Alcibiades' speech not as a study of

Socrates, but as a study of Alcibiades and the Dionysian tyrannical eros. Alcibiades claims to reveal Socrates, but, in attempting to do this, he unwittingly reveals himself. I infer from Alcibiades' words that when the Dionysian eros takes its sexual form, it craves sexual pleasure, yes, but it is essentially much more interested in perceived advantage. It does not respond to purely sexual sparks with purely sexual sparks, or to pure friendship with pure friendship, or to pure love with pure love, but always desires to turn sex, friendship, and love into means of control, that is, its personal control of the individual beauty, friend, or lover, and also its technical control of such tools of political power as can be generated from the association. Thus, the tyrannical eros perverts the noble eros. It will even betray love for political advantage. Socrates loves Alcibiades, and, let it be granted, Alcibiades loves Socrates in some inchoate manner. Alcibiades still cannot stop himself from betraying Socrates by misrepresenting the real issues in his failed seduction, if that is what it takes to win Agathon. Nor can Alcibiades refrain from waging war on his lover. His tale of the seduction has been not a praise of Socrates, but false witness in a lawsuit, an undisguised act of war in the service of the tyrannical eros. Alcibiades has given Agathon another warning that is mistaken and mendacious: "Beware! Socrates will romance you, but he really hates aristocratic beauties. He will deceive you, disappoint you sexually, and laugh in your face." This is not a profound psychological analysis of Socratic "erotic irony." Rather, it is a slander of a perceived political rival whom Alcibiades loves but must defeat for the sake of tyrannical expediency.

It will be objected here that this analysis sells Alcibiades short, for two reasons. First, Alcibiades claims that his tactics in the attempted seduction of Socrates aimed at virtue. After all, he did say that nothing was more important to him than that he should "become the best" (ὅτι βέλτιστον ἐμὲ γενέσθαι, 218d2) and that this was why he proposed to gratify his lover. Further, he did say that the *agalmata* that he had seen in Socrates were "divine and golden and all-beautiful and wonderful," so that he had to do what Socrates ordered (216e6–217a2). It has been established by Diotima-Socrates that there is something divine in Socrates (and, in fact, in all of us), so Alcibiades must have opened Socrates with some profound insight.

In answer to the first objection, I would remind the apologists for Alcibiades that the failed seduction of Socrates occurred in 432, before the two courting lovers left town to fight at Potidaea. We must ask what Alcibiades is likely to have meant in the year 432 when he said that he desired to "become the best." Given that Socrates does not appear to have made much progress with his *erōmenos* between the *Alcibiades I* and the *Protagoras* (or even between the *Alcibiades I* and the *Symposium*), it seems probable that on the night of his spectacular flop, Alcibiades defined "virtue" (a word that he does not even use in this context at *Symposium* 218d) in the same way that he did at his first meeting with Socrates. Then, he described it as that at which "good men" (οἱ ἄνδρες οἱ ἀγαθοί) aim, that is, as superiority in "the management of affairs" (οἱ πράττειν τὰ πράγματα, 124e4, 6). Thus, Socrates would have been persuaded that Alcibiades was offering to sell him sex in return for the keys to supreme political power. The lad was displaying not the desire for virtue that his apologists so facilely attribute to him, that is, virtue understood in the Socratic sense that embraces moderation, wisdom, and justice, but a desire for technical political skill. Socrates' reaction still seems proper to me.

With regard to the second objection, I think that it is time to inquire into the *agalmata* that Alcibiades says he saw. Did Alcibiades really see them? If so, what were they? I believe that Alcibiades did see something in Socrates. However, we must distinguish between what he probably did and certainly did not see. The evidence of the *Alcibiades I* and the *Protagoras* suggests that what Alcibiades probably did see was the Socratic dialectic and its results. The products of the dialectic are conclusions of the incomplete sciences to which one attains by passing up and down among the four. These conclusions are lovely because they are verbal images of eternal realities. It would be fair to say that they are "divine and golden and all-beautiful and wonderful" because they are the most excellent representations of the eternal realities that human speech can craft. Thanks to their logical rigor, they also have the power to force auditors to do what they say, as long as the auditors are willing to listen to logic. The beauty and power of these verbal facsimiles of the eternal realities would dazzle a talented man such as Alcibiades because beauty always attracts a soul that is noble in its original nature and because the power to compel people to do as one commands appeals to the Dionysian eros. This beauty and power explain Alcibiades' positive response to right pederasty, his love of Socrates, and his understanding of the dialectic as "divine." However, the conclusions of the dialectical science are not the perfect truth itself. They are only effigies of the living realities, sculpted to pay homage to those eternal verities. I believe that this is why Plato has Alcibiades call them *agalmata*. Being mere verbal images, they share the weaknesses of all words and can be made to appear ridiculous. Unless one has seen the realities of which the words are mere representations, one's convictions can succumb to attacks on the words.

Alcibiades does succumb to such assaults. He inclines toward Socrates when he hears Socrates but wavers toward Critias when he listens to Critias. Hence, I cannot imagine that Alcibiades has seen the realities themselves, or that he has experienced Diotima's vision of the eternal beauty. Furthermore, it is impossible for Alcibiades to have enjoyed Socrates' vision of eternal beauty precisely because he uses the term "*agalmata.*" Statues have heads, faces, torsos, arms, and legs. They are likenesses of composite wholes carved in dead stones. According to Diotima, "divine beauty itself" never presents itself in the guise of face or hands or any part of the body. It never exists in a substance other than itself. It "outshines gold." I suppose that if Alcibiades had seen Diotima's vision, he would have observed this about divine beauty. Then, he could not have called what he saw in Socrates' soul golden *agalmata*. Alcibiades was right when he insisted that Socrates' outside differed totally from his inside. Ironically, he did not appreciate why he was right. Socrates' outside was his ugly physical exterior and his humanly beautiful public arguments. His inside, which Alcibiades never discerned, was the presence of the living eternal beauty (Aphrodite) to the erotic daimon (Eros) in the core of his soul.

However, we are now compelled once again to say "enough of Socrates." Alcibiades' speech is a study of the Dionysian tyrannical eros. What more have we learned about it? I answer with an analogy. Plato had his Dion and his Dionysius II. Many decades earlier, Socrates had his Alcibiades, who was a Dion and a Dionysius rolled into one, overbalanced in the direction of the Dionysius. Plutarch says that Dionysius loved Plato "with a tyrannical love" (*Dion* 16.2). It seems to me that Alcibiades loved Socrates with a mixture of a small true love and a great tyrannical love. The essential characteristics of the Dionysian soul, as found in both Plato's Dionysius and Socrates' Alcibiades, are that the soul is sufficiently noble in its native nature to experience the divine beauty of the Socratic dialectic, surely capable of philosophy itself, and, nevertheless, resistant to philosophy and ignorant of the divine beauty because it has eros for power over all men. In Alcibiades' case, at least, there is also eros for power over gods and the order of being. These traits of the Dionysian tyrannical soul explain why Socrates says that when noble souls fall, they fall the furthest, to the horrifying depths of murderous tyrannical acts; why there is still much good that Socrates loves in a bad Alcibiades; why Alcibiades loves Socrates mostly for the wrong reasons; and why Alcibiades is torn.

For the time being, Alcibiades is finished with his figurine-satyr icon. He proceeds to other praises of Socrates. We should note that because Alcibiades is "always victory loving," he has conceived of Socrates' virtues in terms of competition. Socrates always defeats all men in speech. Socrates is hybristic, which is bad when directed against Alcibiades but good when it can be channeled into helping him to victory in glorious pursuits. Socrates forces others to do his will, not vice versa. Socrates is victorious in love relationships—a strange concept for lovers who might not have realized that they were supposed to be antagonists but certainly not a surprising idea for the likes of Phaedrus and Pausanias who conceive of the life of sexual love as predatory hunting. As he moves to different fields of endeavor, Alcibiades continues to celebrate Socrates as a superior competitor.

Socrates, Alcibiades announces, excels other men in the following ways: He can endure the hardships of combat more easily than others. For example, he can go without food longer than anybody. At the same time, he enjoys food more than everybody and can drink anyone under the table. He can walk in ice and snow barefoot when no one else dares to venture out, causing other soldiers to believe that he is contemptuous of them. He can do without sleep, as exemplified by the incident in which he began to weigh a problem at dawn and stood thinking about it until the following dawn, with the Ionian contingents of the army watching because no one had ever seen anything like it. He fights heroically, as illustrated by his saving of the life and armor of his wounded comrade. He spurns awards for courage, urging his superiors to give them to his beloved. Unlike others, he is fearless in the face of death, as demonstrated by the incident in which he vindicated Aristophanes' comments by proudly strutting off the field at Delium while the army was in a general panicky rout (219e–221c).

These observations of Socrates' public behavior are all drawn from military life. They are the sorts of compliments that a tough soldier such as Alcibiades would think to confer upon a comrade in arms. They testify to the truth that the philosophic soul can attain to astonishing control of the passions. They surely express sincere admiration. However, even in this praise, there seems to be a vengeful barb. Pericles remarked in his Funeral Oration that praise of other people is tolerable only up to the point at which one still believes that one could do some of the things being lauded. Beyond that point, people get jealous and incredulous.[23] Alcibiades has not been inattentive to his guardian. He might hope that his accolades for Socrates will have this "Periclean effect," driving the company toward the inference that the inhumanly stolid Socrates feels contempt for them, as the winter soldiers thought. Alcibiades is still attempting to convince his jurors to convict Socrates of hybris.

Encouraging more envy, Alcibiades says that Socrates has many other meritorious and wonderful qualities but that he will concentrate on the philosopher's uniqueness. Socrates is like nobody else in history or literature. Brasidas, the marvelously successful Spartan general, has his Achilles, and Pericles has his Nestor or Antenor, but Socrates has no human precursor. His only models are the Silenoi and satyrs. It might be true that Socrates had no forerunners, although Parmenides and Heraclitus could certainly lay tenable claims to that distinction. If Socrates was so different from other human beings, his singularity consisted in his awareness of the vision of beauty and its implications for human order. However, this is not what

---

23. Thucydides, *The Peloponnesian War,* 144.

Alcibiades has in mind. With his return to the figurine-satyr image, Alcibiades is reviving the notion that Socrates' external looks conceal *agalmata*.[24]

This brings Alcibiades to his last substantive point. Previously, he says, he neglected to mention something. Just as Socrates resembles satyrs, his speeches are like satyrs, too. On the outside, his speeches are ridiculous, like the hide of a hybristic satyr. When you open them by getting past all the talk of pack asses, cobblers, smiths, and such like, you find that they are the only speeches that have reason in them. They are most divine, they are filled with *agalmata* of virtue, and they are indispensable for anyone who cares to become a *kalos k'agathos*, which is to say, a nobleman who is good according to the standards of the Athenian aristocracy.

With the possible exception of the reference to hybris, this speech contains Alcibiades' most heartfelt praises of Socrates. Alcibiades sincerely believes that his lover's discourses are absurd outside and rational, divine, filled with statues of virtue, and useful to a *kalos k'agathos* inside. He is willing to bestow these compliments because he admires the rationality, divinity, and *agalmata* of virtue that he imagines will make him the greatest *kalos k'agathos* in the history of Athens, if only he can obtain them. Alcibiades' honesty in this regard forces us to rethink the question of whether he has penetrated Socratic irony. If he has done so, Alcibiades might be telling us important things about philosophic esotericism.

I believe that Alcibiades is right to argue that the outsides of Socrates' speeches conceal their insides. Diotima's speech has shown that the reason for this is that his words can never be adequate to the realities that they represent. Alcibiades does not know this. We have seen that he admires the rationality and divinity of Socrates' speeches because they have the power to force people to do what they will. Socrates would rejoice in this if it meant that he could compel people to be virtuous but not if it implied what Alcibiades thinks, that he could force Athenians to do his political bidding. I am also worried again that Alcibiades sees *agalmata* of virtue in Socrates' speeches. The really virtuous Socrates yearns to generate real virtue in his beloveds.[25] Hence, Socrates does not offer instruction on how to become a

24. Rosen argues that, from this section of Alcibiades' speech, "[W]e learn a deep truth about Socrates . . . from being told that the philosopher is not a hero, a general, a statesman, or a political orator. The lesson, in fact, is obvious: Socrates is not a political man" (*Plato's "Symposium,"* 318–19). I am sure that this is what Alcibiades thinks, because the would-be god-king of the universe certainly defines a political man as one who strives to be god-king of the universe. However, Socrates maintains in the *Gorgias* (521d) that he is the only person in Athens who practices "the true political art." I would sooner believe Socrates than Alcibiades or Rosen.

25. Rosen argues that with regard to the virtue in Socrates' soul, "the language of Alcibiades' 'iconography' is on this point in conformity with the teaching of Diotima." He purports to demonstrate this by citing *Symposium* 212a3–4, where he makes Diotima contend that he who sees beauty itself becomes immortal "by generating images of

kalos k'agathos. That was Protagoras's boast. Instead, he wants his beloveds to become good men. Thus, I am left with the conclusion that Alcibiades is quite close to the truth about Socrates' speeches but still misses the true reason that they are satyric. He remains true to his Dionysian tyrannical form, misconstruing exhortation to real virtues as models of means to power. If this is so, the satyric quality of Socrates' discourses has nothing to do with esoteric needs to conceal dire verities from unreliable men. Alcibiades probably suspects that it does, but he and his modern imitators seem to me to be simply wrong.

In this respect, it is significant that Alcibiades calls the outer hides of Socrates' orations (that is, all the discussion of pack asses and whatnot) hybristic. In saying this, Alcibiades drops a little more poison into his ostensible praise of Socrates. He suggests to the group that Socrates outrages them by speaking in a fashion that draws asinine veils over his marvelous rhetorical strategies for dominating other men. Socrates should share his tricks with worthy gentlemen such as themselves to help them become *kaloi k'agathoi* more readily. Alcibiades wants them all to have the same grudge against Socrates that Hippocrates had against Protagoras (310d).

Alcibiades arrives at his peroration. Addressing the "gentlemen" (who will remember that they are still "gentlemen of the jury"), he declares that these are his praises of Socrates and that he has mixed them with a bit of blame, especially in the matter of Socrates' hybris toward himself. However, Alcibiades says, he is not the only person whom Socrates has served after this fashion. Charmides, son of Glaucon; Euthydemus, son of Diocles; and many others have found Socrates' eros so perfidious that beloveds who believe themselves pursued discover that they have been transformed into lovers who do the pursuing. It is no accident that Alcibiades appeals here to a once promising beauty who became one of the Thirty Tyrants (Charmides, Plato's uncle) and to another once promising beauty who became the beloved of Critias and, therefore, to witnesses whose careers paralleled his own. Alcibiades reveals himself by the company whose grievances he recites. In conclusion, Alcibiades turns to Agathon, remarking solicitously: "I say this to you that . . . you may protect yourself by learning from our sufferings, and do not, like the fool in the proverb, learn from suffering" (222b4–8). On this note, he submits his case to the jury.

---

excellence in another's psyche (τίκτειν . . . εἴδωλα ἀρετῆς)" (*Plato's "Symposium,"* 319–20). Rosen's argument is that the ἀγάλματα of Alcibiades are identical with Diotima's εἴδωλα. I do not think that these two Greek words connote exactly the same things. However, that is not entirely relevant. What does matter profoundly is that Diotima says "τίκτειν οὐκ εἴδωλα ἀρετῆς," not "τίκτειν . . . εἴδωλα ἀρετῆς." Rosen replaces the "οὐκ" ("not") with an ellipsis, perverting her meaning into its direct opposite. The person who sees beauty transmits *not* mere εἴδωλα of virtue, but real virtue. Alcibiades is as far as possible from being in conformity with Diotima's teaching.

THE AFTERMATH

Aristodemus reports that when Alcibiades had spoken, there was some laughter at his freedom of speech, which betrayed that he was still erotically inclined toward Socrates. This indicates that Alcibiades had underestimated his jury. His cunning rhetorical techniques have worked like magic on the clods in the Assembly and other crowds, but he is now dealing with professionals who have seen and used his tricks many times themselves. It is in character for Alcibiades particularly and, perhaps, for imperial tyrants generally that sooner or later they underrate the people with whom they have to deal. Alcibiades manifested this tendency as a young man, in the *Alcibiades I*, when he was totally unaware of the might and prowess of the kings of Sparta and Persia. In real history, he displayed the trait in his planning of the Sicilian expedition and in his double-crossing of the Spartans and Persians. These mistakes led more or less directly to his assassination. It may be that Alcibiades and other tyrants sink so far into self-love and the love of victory, and become so accustomed to holding *tainias* before their eyes, that they blind themselves not only to philosophy but to their own vicious interests as well.

Be that as it may, Alcibiades' miscalculations in the present drama cost him his lawsuit. It is true that Alcibiades still has eros for Socrates. The *sympotai* see this and, hence, probably infer that Alcibiades has not been half so outraged as he claims. Although Alcibiades does not know it, they have been won over a little by Socrates themselves. They are already somewhat disposed to acquit Socrates. When Alcibiades reveals his passion for his lover-turned-beloved, thus evoking their laughter, he pushes them right to the brink of this decision.

Socrates astutely exploits this advantage. He quickly remarks that Alcibiades must be sober, for no drunk could have cloaked his intention so gracefully, appending it to the end of his speech as if it were a mere afterthought. He charges that Alcibiades' true purpose has been to provoke a quarrel between Agathon and himself. What Alcibiades actually wants is to keep Socrates as his sole lover and to be the sole lover of Agathon. However, now his satyric and Silenic drama has been exposed. Having said this, Socrates urges Agathon not to let Alcibiades divide them against each other.

Agathon promptly agrees that Socrates has hit upon the truth. I believe that Socrates has told the truth, too, and, hence, have let my analysis of Alcibiades' speech be guided by his remark. Whether right or wrong, Agathon's opinion represents the only vote that matters to Alcibiades' lawsuit. Agathon demonstrates this physically by moving to sit next to Socrates again. The frustrated Alcibiades swears by Zeus that "the mortal" makes him suffer. (He is speaking like a Homeric god, perhaps like Poseidon frustrated with Odysseus.) He asks that Agathon sit between himself and Socrates, but Socrates will not allow it. Socrates pretends that the revised rules of the symposium require him to praise the person on his right. He says that he cannot do this if Agathon sits on his left, for then Agathon would have to praise him and he is eager to praise Agathon. The company fails to notice that Eryximachus decreed no such rule. Socrates undoubtedly knows this. He is helping the truth along with a little adroit manipulation of Agathon, hoping to put a quick, victorious end to this third campaign in the war between the right pederasty and the tyrannical eros.

Agathon is delighted to hear that Socrates wants to praise him, so he laughingly moves to the spot that Socrates has specified. Socrates prevails: Alcibiades is denied his alliance. However, the victory is insufficient. Just when Agathon sits next to Socrates, the many tumble through the doors and transform the party into a drunken, chaotic rout. Phaedrus and Eryximachus are scandalized by the opening of the alcoholic floodgates and take their leave. Aristodemus falls asleep. When he awakes, Socrates, Aristophanes, and Agathon are drinking and talking, but all the others are either sleeping or gone. At dawn, Aristophanes and Agathon doze off, too. Socrates tucks them in and leaves to spend a normal day. He is followed by Aristodemus, but otherwise he is alone and Alcibiades is out there somewhere with the mob. Although he managed to avert an alliance between Agathon and Alcibiades, Socrates could not contract one between Aristophanes and himself, or between Agathon and himself, because these poets were too sleepy. He also failed to regain his hold on Alcibiades, so he cannot stop the young, aspiring tyrant from embarking upon the course that will prove fatal to Athens.

When Socrates, Aristophanes, and Agathon were speaking just before dawn, Socrates was trying to persuade the two poets that the same man could write both comedy and tragedy. This is what Plato has done in the *Symposium.* The two-front war that pitted Socratic right pederasty against the sophistical eros and the imperial tyrannical eros was a comedy because the right pederasty was delightfully roguish in its nature and in its play with the others, and because the sophistical and imperial tyrannical erotes were farcical in their natures and in their aspirations. The war was a tragedy, the tragedy of Athens, for two reasons. Although the right pederasty could begin to win over the sophistical tyrannical loves that infested the realm of culture, it could not keep them awake. Although it could be loved for the wrong reasons by the Dionysian imperial tyrannical eros, it could not prevent that eros from encouraging the many to unjust, stupid adventures. Tyrannical pederasty was not dissuaded from its course because, ultimately, it would not listen. The tragedy can be summed up in words that are nearly the first that Homer's Muse applies to Odysseus in the *Odyssey:* "Many the human beings . . . whose minds he came to know, and many the tribulations he suffered on the sea, in keeping with the desire to win his own life force (ψυχήν) and the return of his comrades. But he did not save his comrades, eager as he was, for they perished utterly through their own recklessness—childish fools" (1.1–5).[26]

The *Symposium* has been a series of memories of memories of memories of memories. Why? This question can be answered now that we have discovered the dialogue's aim. Plato wished to understand the disorders that brought his city down. That required analysis of the essential natures of those disorders, as they were reflected in the persons who perpetrated and bore them. That, in turn, necessitated anamnesis. However, disorder cannot be understood except against the background of the order of which it is a perversion. The disorders that destroyed Athens, the Titanic eros and the Dionysian eros, cannot be comprehended except in contrast to the right order that should have prevailed, a polity founded upon the true eros that leads to real virtue and the vision of beauty. The disorder that ruined the natural leaders of Athens, which I have called "wrong pederasty," cannot be understood except in light of the order that should have prevailed in those men, which Socrates calls "right pederasty." However, right order is not known easily. The philosopher must seek it in the reality that first suggests to him that such order is there to find, that is, in his soul. However, what is perceived in the soul is seen only dimly, cannot be spoken directly, and can be communicated only poetically. The philosopher must therefore invoke the Muse. However, Hesiod tells us that Zeus fathered the Muses upon Mnemosyne (*Theogony* 53 ff). This teaches the philosopher that the introspective search for the ineffable order that can be symbolized only poetically must honor the Great Mother. The quest must be anamnestic. We shall learn more about the reasons this is so from the dialogue to which we now turn, the *Phaedrus*.

26. The significance of these words dawned on me while I was reading Planinc, "Homeric Imagery," in *Politics, Philosophy, Writing*.

7

PHAEDRUS: DEMOCRATIC TYRANNICAL EROS

Plato's *Phaedrus* is at once sublimely beautiful and hard to understand. One important cause of the difficulty is the dialogue's structure. The *Phaedrus* has five parts, as follows.

First, the prologue. Socrates hails Phaedrus, who is heading for a walk outside the walls of Athens, concealing the written text of a speech by Lysias under his cloak and attempting to memorize the words. Phaedrus tells Socrates that the speech is somehow about eros. He does not quite fathom how it is about eros, for it portrays a beauty being seduced by a nonlover. Socrates joins Phaedrus and makes him read, rather than summarize, the speech. The two men walk along the Ilissus, looking for a place to recline while considering the text. As they stroll, Phaedrus raises certain mythological issues, which Socrates declines to discuss seriously because he is too busy trying to obey the Delphic injunction to know himself. Phaedrus leads the way to a spot with a plane tree and a willow, a place filled with figurines of nymphs and Achelous, father of the nymphs. Socrates praises the beauty of the grove. Phaedrus remarks that Socrates is behaving like a stranger who has never seen the countryside before. Socrates explains why he usually remains in the city. Then he confesses that Phaedrus can lead him all over Attica like a domestic animal by shaking leaves (of writing) before his eyes.

Second, the reading of Lysias's oration. Phaedrus gives voice to the speech of the nonlover as Socrates reclines. Phaedrus performs his task like an ecstatic Corybant.

Third, the first speech of Socrates. Phaedrus asks Socrates how he liked Lysias's oration. Socrates replies ironically. The irony is not lost on the disappointed Phaedrus, who demands to know who could give a better speech in the same vein. Socrates answers that he heard one somewhere and that he himself has a superior version in mind. Phaedrus is delighted and asks to hear it. Socrates turns coy, protesting that he was joking. Phaedrus compels him to deliver the new oration by swearing on the plane tree that he will never tell Socrates another speech if he does not comply. Socrates yields, saying that he will veil his head to avoid embarrassment as he speaks. Then he gives the speech, which depicts a lying lover who pretends not to be in love as he seduces a beauty, and which waxes eloquent on the evils of eros. Shortly before the middle of this talk, Socrates comments that he feels himself falling victim to "nympholepsy" and expresses the hope that he can avert the attack. He continues but then stops abruptly and unexpectedly. Phaedrus complains that Socrates has covered only half of the material that he had promised to improve. Socrates nevertheless refuses to go on. He repeats that he is under siege by nymphs and begins to depart across the stream.

Fourth, Socrates' palinode. Phaedrus implores Socrates to stay, pointing out that it is nearly noon and extremely hot and proposing that they talk things over while waiting for the weather to cool. Socrates answers that Phaedrus has something divine with regard to speeches in him, for he has inspired more talks than anyone but Simmias of Thebes. He also says that his daimon has prevented him from leaving without expiating an offense against the god. He is a mantic prophet, although not a good one, but he now sees that he must offer Eros a palinode for his impious attack on the god. He uncovers his head and speaks beautifully, ending with a prayer to Eros that asks for forgiveness and for Phaedrus's conversion to philosophy.

Last, a discussion of speaking and writing. Phaedrus declares that he joins the prayer, if what Socrates has requested is good for them. He says that Lysias will probably decline to compete with Socrates' palinode for fear that he could not produce anything as beautiful. Not only that, but a politician has daunted Lysias by calling him a "speechwriter." Socrates replies that this would not deter Lysias and suggests a joint analysis of good writing. Phaedrus agrees. Socrates then opines that the cicadas singing loudly overhead would laugh to see them dozing like sheep. However, if the cicadas were to see them conversing, unmoved by the charms of buzzing Siren voices, the cicadas might favor them with the gift that the gods have empowered cicadas to give to human beings. Phaedrus has no knowledge of this gift. Socrates explains and then undertakes a long dialectical discussion of rhetorical speaking and writing, a conversation that reviews current theories, digresses into an Egyptian myth, and ends with appeals to Lysias and Isocrates. Socrates then prays to Pan, Phaedrus adds an amen, and they take their leave.

The problem with this structure is that the two halves of the dialogue, namely, parts 1–4, which are about eros, and part 5, which analyzes rhetoric, do not clearly amount to an intelligible whole. The renowned Catholic philosopher Josef Pieper notes that the two halves "seem to have nothing whatsoever to do with each other." Representing the students of Leo

Strauss, Seth Benardete also remarks on the "nonevident unity of the dialogue" and states: "The speeches on Eros seem to be an unprivileged occasion for the conversation on the art of writing, to which any other topic would have given Socrates equal access." Benardete regards this as especially puzzling because in the *Phaedrus,* Socrates argues that a good writing should be articulated like a living being, with head, feet, and middle members arranged in appropriate relationships to one another and the whole (264c). Benardete expends great effort to avoid the inference that Plato "went out of his way to show himself incompetent." Greatly respected commentators also have trouble understanding the play's individual episodes. For example, Joseph Cropsey finds that he must grasp "at any straw" to explain the interlude of the cicadas.[1]

Nearly everybody who has ever written on the *Phaedrus* has offered an opinion on the problem of the thematic unity of the dialogue. Many have concluded that the play simply has no unity because Plato wrote it when he was either too young to know what he was doing or too old to still enjoy his once vaunted mental competence. Others assume that the drama has a unity that does not disclose itself immediately to the casual reader.[2] I think that this is true. The design of the *Phaedrus* is no more bewildering than that of any other Platonic work. Plato is up to his usual trick of concealing his argument from the inattentive. He wants us to extend ourselves to discover wherein the unity of the dialogue consists. Hence, this question must be answered, and the roles of the particular dramatic episodes must be clarified before we can claim to understand the play. Past efforts to solve the problems have been unpersuasive. I think that the recent scholarship of Zdravko Planinc gets closer to solutions than the previous studies have done.[3] I hope to make a modest contribution to his momentum, this with a view toward settling our original theoretical question: What belongs to Socrates' art of eros? The relationship of eros to rhetoric that unifies the *Phaedrus* is evidently one of the things that we must master. I shall begin my inquiry by examining the setting of the dialogue.

---

1. Pieper, *Begeisterung und göttlicher Wahnsinn: Über den platonischen Dialog "Phaidros,"* 15; cf. Pieper, *Enthusiasm and Divine Madness: On the Platonic Dialogue "Phaedrus,"* xiv. Benardete, *Rhetoric of Morality,* 103; Cropsey, *Political Philosophy and the Issues of Politics,* 248.

2. At the extreme reaches of this opinion, see the first sentences of Jacques Derrida, "Plato's Pharmacy," in *Dissemination,* 63. With other postmodernists, Derrida does not believe that a text ever discloses anything, whether about itself or anything else whatsoever. If this is so, I hope that I am not writing a text.

3. I have been privileged to read the manuscript of a forthcoming book by Planinc, *Plato through Homer.* I am grateful to him for allowing me to see his work in advance. Planinc has a good summary of previous attempts to solve the problem of the thematic unity of the *Phaedrus.* He, in turn, partially relies on a summary by G. J. de Vries, *A Commentary on the "Phaedrus" of Plato,* 22–24.

THE DRAMATIC SETTING

It seems to me that the dramatic setting of the *Phaedrus* reveals the unity of the work. This background consists in two kinds of features that Plato intertwines: historical and poetic allusions and episodes. Of these two types, the historical is the easier to elucidate. Plato's historical allusions can be expounded best by asking questions. The first crucial queries are these: What is the dramatic date of the play, and what is its relevance?

The earliest possible dramatic date of the *Phaedrus* is determined by the *Republic*. As I have argued in the Introduction, the *Phaedrus* mentions that Polemarchus has been turned to philosophy (257b). This conversion obviously takes place in the *Republic,* if not later. However, it is clear from the reference to Theages (469b–c) that the *Republic* is set sometime after 409. It is probable, as Planinc has concluded, that it occurs during the week of the Plynteria in 407, a bit before Alcibiades' return to Athens on the holy day. The Plynteria fell on 25 Thargelion, an Athenian month that, in 407, spanned late May to early June.[4] The *Phaedrus* (257b) also supposes Polemarchus still alive. Polemarchus was killed by the Thirty Tyrants in early 403. Further, Phaedrus and Socrates walk outside the walls of the city. Lysander besieged Athens in October 405 and razed the walls in March–April 404. Therefore, the *Phaedrus* must be set in the summer of 407, after the first week of June, or in the summer of 406 or 405.

We might be able to pin the date down more precisely. K. J. Dover observes that a recently discovered inscription shows that the historical Phaedrus was implicated in the mutilation of the Herms and the profanation of the Eleusinian mysteries. Another inscription testifies that an Eryximachus, who could be Phaedrus's historical lover, was also accused.[5] Evidently, both men joined forces with Alcibiades after leaving Agathon's banquet. Both fled when they were charged, and, along with Alcibiades, both were exiled and cursed in 415. With this in mind, we next surmise that the *Phaedrus* occurs years later on one of the hottest days of the summer. Phaedrus would not have been relaxing in Athens before Alcibiades' homecoming in 407, but he could have been doing so a month or two later in the midsummer heat. When Alcibiades sailed into the Piraeus in June, he was greeted with a general democratic euphoria. The stelae that exiled and cursed him were tossed into the sea. Adeimantus, son of Leukolophides, who had also been exiled for his part in the sacrileges, came home with Alcibiades on that glorious day.[6] If this Adeimantus could return so easily,

4. Perhaps 25 Thargelion, 407 B.C., was approximately June 7 on our calendar.
5. Dover, "The Date of Plato's Symposium," 7 n. 15; J. K. Davies, *Athenian Propertied Families, 600–300 B.C.,* 462. This Eryximachus was prosecuted for "staying in the city" in 404/403.
6. Donald Kagan, *The Fall of the Athenian Empire,* 288–89.

Phaedrus could have drifted back to Athens in Alcibiades' wake, too. I think that the possibility of this is illustrated by Socrates' tart comment that in democracies, people condemned to death or exile show up in the city every day and attract practically no attention (*Republic* 558a). It will be objected that there is a serious problem for this scenario. Dover does not believe that Phaedrus could have returned to Athens prior to the recall of the exiles in 404. Neither does Martha Nussbaum.[7] However, they leave Socrates' miffed observation out of account. The recall to which Dover refers probably favored unpopular oligarchs who were repatriated by Lysander. To me, it seems unlikely that Phaedrus would have returned at that time. As for other dates, Alcibiades became unpopular and went back into exile after his deputy Antiochus was defeated at Notium in 406. Phaedrus might not have wanted to show his face much during the summers of 406 and 405. I therefore think it likely that the *Phaedrus* is set in midsummer 407, at the height of the tremendous Alcibiades delirium attendant upon the end of the general's first exile. This would balance the drama nicely with the prologue of the *Symposium,* which is set at the height of the other great Alcibiades agitation, that of 404, which arose in erroneous anticipation of the end of the general's second exile.

If this dramatic date is correct, it would indicate that the *Phaedrus* has something to do with the democratic aspect of the fall of Athens. The *Symposium* focuses on oligarchs. The oligarchs were responsible for Athens's calamity because they failed to see that Socratic right pederasty was the only true salvation from the Titanic and Dionysian tyrannical erotes that had laid the city low and because their class had been the chief bearer of these diseases, having spawned the sophists, Alcibiades, and Critias. However, the demos who so loved Alcibiades were far from guiltless. I think that the *Phaedrus* will assess their susceptibility to the fatal illnesses and their role in Athens's demise. Someone might object that the 407 date could show equally well that the drama is also concerned with the oligarchical aspect of the tragedy. After all, Xenophon reports that both the people and the oligarchs turned out to welcome Alcibiades home on the Plynteria in 407.[8] True, but the demos were more enthusiastic about Alcibiades in 407 than the nobility were. Further, the dialogue's concern with the democratic features of the fall is demonstrated by the answers to our next questions about the dramatic setting: Why Phaedrus? Why not some other interlocutor from the *Symposium,* such as Alcibiades? Also, why Lysias in his present-absent role?

It is time to take a closer look at Phaedrus. Once again, I advert to my belief that Plato makes his characters as true to life as possible. We know a

---

7. Nussbaum, *Fragility of Goodness,* 212.
8. Xenophon, *Hellenika* 1.4.

few things about the real Phaedrus. As mentioned above, he fled Athens in 415 when he was accused of sacrilege. The record also shows that his property, which was confiscated, did not add up to much—household chattels, a rented house, some rented land. He was, in brief, a member of the upper level of the demos. His *erastēs*, Eryximachus, seems to have been a member of the propertied liturgical class and, hence, well-to-do. It is also interesting that sometime after 415, Phaedrus married a daughter of the richest Athenian of his generation, realizing a dowry of four thousand drachmas.[9] It is apparently no coincidence that the historical Phaedrus twice made financially profitable love matches, one with the daughter of the rich man and the other with his physician-lover, Eryximachus. This is in keeping with his speech in the *Symposium*, which is easily the most mercenary of the lot. In life and in the *Symposium*, the man is a valetudinarian and a social climber.

Phaedrus remains true to form in the dialogue that bears his name. His opening lines indicate that he is still a valetudinarian, one who wants good health without having to work unduly hard for it—he is taking his exercise outside the walls because his physician has advised him that the extramural roads are "less fatiguing" (227a–b). In the same vein, his ecstatic joy in the rhetoric of Lysias betrays that he still thinks of love in terms of balance sheets. As in the *Symposium*, he also fancies the idea of obtaining love's benefits without rewarding his partner with anything in the way of personal commitment. In sum, we can picture Phaedrus as one of Socrates' democratic "drones" whose pasture is the rich (*Republic* 564e), who live by sucking honey. I think that Plato intends Phaedrus's dramatic character as the quintessential example of this species. If so, he makes Phaedrus Socrates' interlocutor because he wants to study the democratic aspect of the fall of Athens.

Lysias was one of three sons of the *metic* Cephalus.[10] His brothers were Polemarchus and Euthydemus. All four appear in the *Republic*, Cephalus and Polemarchus in speaking roles and the other two silently. Cephalus was persuaded to relocate from Syracuse to Athens by Pericles, probably sometime after 463. He built up an armaments factory in the Piraeus, dealing chiefly in shields. When he died, his sons inherited the factory. Sometime after 443, the family moved to Thurii, the mostly Athenian colony on Sicily. Lysias, who was fifteen when he moved to Thurii, studied rhetoric under Tisias there. He returned to Athens, either with or without the possibly deceased Cephalus, and with the rest of the family, in 412, again residing in the Piraeus. He and Polemarchus ran the weapons factory. They

9. Davies, *Propertied Families*, 200–201, 462–63. Phaedrus made out quite handsomely with a dowry of this size.

10. *"Metic"* is a technical Athenian term meaning "resident alien without rights of citizenship."

became exceptionally wealthy. History does not tell us whether Lysias practiced rhetoric professionally on the side from 412 to 403. He certainly gave private displays during those years.

Lysias's life changed drastically with the advent of the Thirty Tyrants. As protégés of Pericles, he and his family were ardent democrats. Being both democratic and rich, they were natural prey for the Thirty when the Tyrants discovered that they needed money in early 403. Lysias and Polemarchus were arrested. Their houses and factory were looted. Most of their funds, inventory, and slaves were appropriated by various oligarchs. Lysias luckily escaped through an unlocked door of the house in which he was imprisoned and sailed to Megara, but the less fortunate Polemarchus was murdered. When the democrats ousted the Thirty, Lysias composed an impassioned speech for delivery by an Athenian citizen, "Against Subverting the Ancestral Constitution of Athens." In recognition of his loyal services to the democracy, he was granted Athenian citizenship himself, only to lose it again because there was a technical defect in his papers. He used his moment as an Athenian to prosecute Eratosthenes, the man who had arrested his brother. Thereafter, he made his living by writing speeches for plaintiffs and defendants in lawsuits. As a *metic*, he could not deliver the orations himself. Rather, he had his clients memorize the speeches and perform them at their trials. He also specialized in tailoring his orations to the personalities of his clients. He was extremely successful. Thus, in his way, he was quite influential in Athenian politics until his death around 380.

If we inquire why Plato has Lysias appear in the *Phaedrus* in his present-absent mode, that is, as the author of a speech that is recited by another person, I answer again that Plato makes his characters true to life. That is how Lysias always appeared, except on the occasion when he briefly held citizenship and prosecuted Eratosthenes in person. If Lysias remains in character in this manner in the drama, I should think that he stays in character in other ways, too. For example, the Platonic Lysias probably tailors his written speech to the personality of a specific client, namely, Phaedrus. Sometimes it is said that this oration could be "spoken by anyone to anyone."[11] That is manifestly untrue. The speech is a masterful display of what I have called the ancient equivalent of rational-choice theory. It could not be spoken by anyone who finds rational-choice theory intellectually or ethically unsatisfactory. However, it could be spoken by Phaedrus, who, as we have seen in the *Symposium*, was an eager partisan of this kind of thought. Further, the oration conjures up the image of inducing a rather gullible lad to exchange his sexual favors for his own present pleasure and future benefits (which may or may not materialize). We must see that this

11. For example, see Benardete, *Rhetoric of Morality*, 116.

topic is not merely accidental, as if a certain style of rhetoric could have been illustrated as well with any other theme. The subject is essential to the intended impact of the speech. The oration could not be given by a person who thinks that reducing beauties to prostitution is morally abhorrent, or who regards erotic love as more than a pleasurable bodily service that people may trade like a commodity. However, it could be spoken by Phaedrus who, as we have seen in the *Symposium*, conceives of eros in precisely those terms, and who identifies the substantive point of Lysias's speech as just the element that is really clever about it (227c). Again, the talk contemplates the achievement of gratification without any significant giving of oneself. It could not be spoken by someone who would be ashamed to be a drone, but it could be declaimed by Phaedrus, a shameless drone. Finally, as Socrates himself observes, the oration lacks any notion of generous love (243c–d). It could not be spoken by a nobleman who would be embarrassed to be heard talking like a low sailor, but it could be spoken by Phaedrus, whose outlook is decidedly vulgar.

The fact that Plato gives a zealous democrat such as Lysias a role in his drama shows once again that he intends the *Phaedrus* as an investigation of the democratic aspect of the Athenian tragedy. Plato's division of the people's labor between Lysias and Phaedrus also represents an interesting opinion that the philosopher has of democratic regimes. Lysias is a counterpart of the gray eminence who sometimes stands behind royal thrones: he is the prompter who stands at the bases of democratic platforms. Plato evidently believes that oligarchs who are verbally facile and who hire themselves out to the demos are necessary to the ability of democracies to get what they desire, the demos themselves being a wee bit short of imagination and rhetorical skill. Elevating this observation from the personalities of Lysias and Phaedrus to the level of symbolism, we may deduce that Lysias represents the most persuasive logos of democracy and Phaedrus its libido. I hasten to add that in this discussion, I am talking about the empirically existing democracy that Socrates and Plato knew in Athens, not about democracy generally, which is a vast topic that would require a more complex analysis.[12]

This brings us to our first conclusion about the thematic unity of the *Phaedrus*. Lysias and Phaedrus together represent a single eros. Their logos and libido are democratic yet intent upon the exploitation of innocent victims. It would be fair to say that their eros is the "democratic tyrannical eros" and that all those who possess it are carriers of the drone-desires that buzz around the great winged drone of the eventual tyrant, planting the sting

---

12. It will be recalled that the American authors of *The Federalist*, James Madison, Alexander Hamilton, and John Jay, declared the Athenian democracy a horror that, by itself, would have justified despair of the possibility of a successful democratic regime.

of longing in it (*Republic* 572d–573c). The *Phaedrus* is about Socrates' confrontation with the democratic tyrannical eros and, thus, continues the saga of his war against tyrannical erotes. Inasmuch as the logos of the democratic tyrannical eros expresses its libido and its libido informs its logos, the logos and the libido appear as a unified phenomenon. They cannot be treated separately. Hence, I must expand the statement that I just made. The *Phaedrus* is about Socrates' struggle with the democratic tyrannical eros that gratifies itself best with rational-choice rhetoric. The dialogue's unifying theme is eros-logos: the democratic tyrannical eros-rhetoric, its nature, its most effective appeals, and its necessary cure by means of Socratic right eros-logos.[13] As Plato analyzes diseased and healthy erotes-logoi, he can now let his emphasis fall on the forms that they employ to express themselves, that is, on the varieties of logoi, and then let his emphasis fall on the substances of the styles of logoi, that is, on the types of erotes, but the logoi and the erotes are always implicit in each other.[14]

I should add here that Socrates' war against the democratic tyrannical eros has the same pattern as that in the *Symposium*: down-up-down. There are three campaigns. In the first, a descent into evil, Lysias and Phaedrus (who speaks through the mouth of a charmed Socrates) mount a rhetorical offensive on behalf of the democratic tyrannical eros. In the second, an ascent to the highest reality, Socrates pits a philosophically prophetic and poetic eros-logos against the vile one. In the third, another fall into untruth, Phaedrus raises up an army of challengers to the philosophic poetic eros-logos that Socrates must defeat.

Let all this stand as a historical-philosophical hypothesis about the unified theme and structure of the *Phaedrus* until corroboration can be supplied. Meanwhile, it is still necessary to account for the dialogue's poetic features: Socrates' voluntary excursion outside the walls of Athens, which is unique to the *Phaedrus* (unless Socrates is the Athenian Stranger); Phaedrus's questions about a myth and Socrates' replies; the Ilissus; the grove with the plane and willow trees and the figurines of the nymphs and Achelous; the nympholepsy; Socrates' daimon; the cicadas; the Egyptian myth; Pan; and more that I do not have space to enumerate here. What is the function of these interludes and allusions, and why are they in the dialogue?

It was seen in the *Symposium* that the playwright Plato is exceedingly skilled in the art of embedding dramatic settings in dramatic settings. In the *Symposium*, Plato embedded the setting of Agathon's party in that of

13. Ronna Burger, *Plato's "Phaedrus": A Defense of a Philosophic Art of Writing*, 6, approaches this formulation with the statement that the theme of the dialogue is "erotic dialectics." However, I prefer to broaden "dialectics" to "logos" because Lysias's speeches are not dialectical. Neither are some of Socrates' own mythological speeches.

14. Thus, it is not true that any topic other than eros would have given Socrates equal access to the subject of rhetoric.

the approach of the oligarchical investigative commission to Apollodorus. He did this in order to suggest the causal relationship of a spiritual event, the triumph of Titanic and Dionysian tyrannical erotes in Athens, to a political one, the military destruction of Athens. For Socrates personally, the spiritual event, the victory of Titanic and Dionysian tyrannical erotes, had a negligible effect: he continued to go about his business. I believe that in the *Phaedrus*, Plato once again embeds a dramatic setting in a dramatic setting, and that he uses his poetic allusions in aid of this layering. This time the situation is reversed. A political cause, the birth of the tyrannical democracy on the occasion of Alcibiades' return from his first exile, and its growth to maturity after the toppling of the oligarchical tyrannies installed by Sparta, has a spiritual consequence, Socrates' philosophic preparation to embrace his telos. This spiritual outcome, in turn, produces a tremendous personal effect on Socrates: he becomes willing to accept his death, after which he no longer goes about his usual business, at least not in the ordinary, mortal human way. Plato's poetic allusions embed the dramatic site of Socrates' spiritual progress, along with an account of his development, in the context of the democratic movement that burgeoned in 407.

So, what is the spiritual dramatic setting of Socrates' philosophic preparation to accept his fate? It is at this juncture that we turn to Zdravko Planinc. In *Plato through Homer*, Planinc offers compelling analyses of both Homer's *Odyssey* and Plato's *Phaedrus*. He interprets the tale of Odysseus's journeys as an allegory on shamanistic spiritual travel along the *axis mundi* in the direction of the supreme divine reality, a voyage that never reaches its goal in this life. In the course of his wandering, Odysseus is transformed from a wily scoundrel into a more just man who is open to the formation of his soul in accord with divine order. I have noted previously that Planinc construes the Platonic Socrates as a new Odysseus. Socrates is the Odysseus who met Lachesis at the *axis mundi* and chose the life of an unheralded private man, that is, Socrates' life (*Republic* 620c–d). Planinc maintains that in Plato's dialogues, Socrates repeats Odysseus's travels and trials spiritually as he rises toward the highest reality. Plato causes Socrates to do this by refiguring tropes from Homer's poems, thus proving himself the poet's most capable, discerning reader and making Socrates relive Odysseus's adventures on philosophic planes.

More specifically with regard to the *Phaedrus*, Planinc shows that Plato freely refigures and rearranges numerous tropes from the *Odyssey*. Socrates' voluntary exodus from the city is Odysseus's departure from Ithaca (both of which symbolize the fall of Socrates' soul from its home in the divine region, as in the later story). Socrates' meeting with Phaedrus is Odysseus's encounter with Nausicaa in book 6 of the poem. Phaedrus is a comic Nausicaa: "The divine Nausicaa is present in the dialogue, but the man playing her part has none of her character and substance; he goes through the motions, walking through the role as her phantom."[15] Being a ludicrous "virgin" in the sense that he prefers oratory to sex, being ridiculously warlike in his boasting of world conquest that is backed up only by exercise on the least fatiguing roads, and being credited humorously with rulership of nymphs, Phaedrus also bears a comic likeness to Artemis.

Nausicaa more seriously resembles the goddess. Lysias's text, which excites Phaedrus because it promises him the love matches for which he would pray, is the dream that Nausicaa receives from Athena, which animates her because it promises the marriage for which she has prayed. The Ilissus, the stream that is the site of Socrates' encounter with the pseudo-divinity Phaedrus, is the river on the banks of which Odysseus has been cast up so that he can converse with the godly human Nausicaa. The place in which Phaedrus and Socrates recline subsumes a number of woodsy-watery Homeric locations: the meadow in which Odysseus first spies the princess and her maidens; the place in which Nausicaa has Odysseus bathe and dress; the grove in which Odysseus stops to pray on his way up to Scheria, the city of the Phaeacians; and the isle of Calypso. The plane tree is the omphalos symbol of the *axis mundi* that Homer repeats in numerous tree scenes. Phaedrus's queries about the tale of Oreithyia, her maiden playmates, and her rape by Boreas evoke Homer's sketch of Nausicaa, her maids, and her fear of rape by the monstrous-looking Odysseus. Socrates' two speeches divide the single plea that Odysseus makes to Nausicaa with a divided heart. His palinode corresponds to Odysseus's purification in the river after his blasphemy against the gods. The cicadas recall the episode of the Sirens. The excursus on division *(diairesis)* and collection *(synagōgē)* represents the tools that Calypso gave Odysseus so that he could leave her island. I venture to suggest that Socrates' survey of popular rhetoricians is Odysseus's enraged slaying of the suitors.

Planinc says much more, but this suffices to indicate the gist of his thesis: On the spiritual level, the unity of the *Phaedrus* is constituted by the unity of Homer's Odysseus legend. The setting of the dialogue is the *axis mundi,* and the action is Socrates' reenactment of Odysseus's travel along that passage to divine reality in his own soul. One might quibble with this or that construction that Planinc places on a Platonic use of a given Homeric trope. However, I believe that his argument is fundamentally sound and that it illuminates many things in the *Phaedrus* that have mystified generations of scholars. Accordingly, I shall blend my analysis with his as occasions warrant.

15. Planinc, *Plato through Homer,* page not yet determined.

THE PROLOGUE

Socrates opens the *Phaedrus* with a greeting: "O dear Phaedrus, where are you going, and from where do you come?" (Ὦ φίλε Φαῖδρε, ποῖ δὴ καὶ πόθεν, 227a1). The question has three meanings. Socrates wonders whither Phaedrus goes and whence he comes literally. Socrates also seems to be prodding Phaedrus to ponder the wisdom of continuing to head in his habitual revolutionary political direction and reminding him of his recent return from the debacle of the Herms. Finally, as I stated in the Introduction, Socrates conceives the question sub specie aeternitatis, hinting that Phaedrus should consider his spiritual destiny and origin. We know from the *Cleitophon* (407b1 ff) that Socrates makes a habit of asking, "Where are you carried, O human beings?" and chiding people for seeking wealth to the detriment of their characters.

Phaedrus catches only the trivial meaning of Socrates' salute. Even on this level, he is not exact. He changes and reverses the subjects broached by Socrates, reporting from *whom* he has come and where he is going and disclosing that his whence has determined his whither. He has come from Lysias. He is going for a stroll, for he has been sitting with Lysias for quite a while, perhaps since dawn. He will walk outside the walls, for the doctor Acumenus, whom he assumes to be Socrates' friend as well as his own, has advised him that the exterior roads are less fatiguing. Socrates replies that Phaedrus speaks beautifully and speculates that Lysias must have been in town. Phaedrus confirms this, reporting that Lysias has been at Epicrates' house, the one that formerly belonged to Morychus, near the Olympieum.

This exchange is heavily charged with political import. Phaedrus, who represents the libido of democracy, has been listening to Lysias, who stands for the ideal logos of democracy, for a long time. Symbolically, Phaedrus's activity is already being determined by his extended association with Lysias. Without Lysias's influence, Phaedrus might have gone about his usual valetudinarian business ineptly, but now Lysias has offered him the most effective rhetoric for realizing his aims.[16] (The rhetoric will be revealed presently.) Phaedrus, the pure democratic libido, is still trying to learn what Lysias taught him throughout the morning, the democratic logos best calculated to produce gratification. For his part, Lysias normally confines himself to the Piraeus, but today he was in the city. Symbolically, this implies

16. We may wonder whether Phaedrus is really pursuing his normal valetudinarian affairs. Why is he taking medical advice from Acumenus, the father of his *erastēs*, Eryximachus? Why not from Eryximachus himself? The most likely reason for this is that Eryximachus is away with the fleet. There is evidence that Eryximachus served as trierarch at Aegospotami (see Davies, *Propertied Families*, 463). During his exile, he probably caught on with the democratically inclined Athenian fleets that were plying the Aegean and the Hellespont. If Eryximachus is at war, it would make sense for Phaedrus to cadge free medical counsel from the next best source, his lover's father.

that Lysias's crude type of rational-choice reasoning has made its way from the fringes of Athenian political life to its core. Perhaps it has also reached the center of Athenian religious life: the Olympieum is the temple of Zeus. Phaedrus and Lysias have chosen alarming cronies. Epicrates is a dema-gogue who will eventually be executed for treason and bribery. Perhaps he is the spiritual heir of a theatocracy fostered by Morychus, a tragedian who cared more about culinary pleasures than tragic excellence.[17] Sym-bolically, the most compelling democratic logos and its characteristic li-bido have lodged in the minds and hearts of Athens's rabble, just when these elements of the demos have become excited about their political prospects.

Socrates asks what the conversation was. Before Phaedrus can reply, Soc-rates surmises that Lysias must have feasted the company with speeches. We need to reconstruct the events of the feast correctly. Lysias obviously came with written texts in hand. Given his character, he had designed them for particular persons. He did not appear at an evening's entertainment like one of our modern comedians, equipped with monologues intended to amuse anyone who happened to be present. Rather, he made a special trip up to town to attend an early morning political meeting, he knew who would be there (or, at least, what kinds of people would turn up), and he intended to put the right speeches into the right mouths. Symbolically, the most clever democratic logos went looking for an alliance with the quintessential democratic desire and found it. Lysias was delighted with his match, as evidenced by his devotion of the entire morning to Phaedrus. Phaedrus was just as enraptured by his new tutor, who seemed to have given him the key to paradise. Now he is trying to memorize his magical new lines, just as all the clients of Lysias will eventually do. Socrates has taken all this in with a glance.

Phaedrus offers to tell Socrates what was said if he will come along. Soc-rates exclaims: "What? Don't you think that I would consider it, with Pin-dar, a 'more important affair than business' to hear how you and Lysias passed your time?" (227b9–11). This reply is curious. If Socrates already knows essentially what transpired and what Phaedrus is doing, why does he want to waste his time on the drone, who already proved to be a rather unpromising student on the occasion of the *Symposium*, whose grave religious-political crimes and illegal presence in town do not inspire much hope, and whose present activities appear entirely discouraging? If Soc-rates is already familiar with Lysias's crassly rationalistic democratic ori-entation, as he must be if Lysias is being scorned by citizen politicians, why does he consent to hear Lysias's speech? Why does he consider this more important than his normal business (ἀσχολία, literally, "lack of leisure"), which we understand to be his striving to obey the oracle? If he does have

17. See Pauly and Wissowa, *Real-Encyclopädie*, s.v. "Epicrates" and "Morychus."

a good reason for learning the details of the oration, why is he prepared to get them from Phaedrus, or even from a text that Lysias has written? Why not go ask Lysias in person, so that he can urge Lysias to clear up ambiguities in the piece? Why does he agree to go outside the walls, especially considering that Phaedrus is so eager to celebrate the speech that he would probably be content to remain in the city if Socrates insisted?

It seems to me that Socrates consorts with Phaedrus for the same reasons that he once attended Agathon's banquet. The first words of the drama, "O dear Phaedrus," and Socrates' direct and implied declarations of affection for Phaedrus (for example, ἐγώ σε πάνυ μὲν φιλῶ, 228e1) indicate that Socrates loves Phaedrus, as a friend if not romantically. Although I have said much against Phaedrus's character, he has some strong points. At forty-three, he still attracts older men sexually. He does have something divine with regard to speeches in him. His soul was graced by every soul's native beauty. Like Agathon, he would be worth redeeming from his folly. Socrates probably wants to hear Lysias in order to save Phaedrus. (Odysseus hopes to get his comrades home because he cares for them [*Odyssey* 1.4–8].)[18] Then again, Socrates is worried about the direction that Athenian democracy is taking. If he can guide the libido of the demos into more healthful channels, he might still be able to save his city. This partially explains the quotation from Pindar, which, in its original version, presupposes that patriotic duty ranks higher than personal business. Such a political intent would account for Socrates' decision to remain with Phaedrus rather than seek Lysias. Better to mold the democratic libido directly than to try to reform all the sophisticated logoi that buzz around it. The aim of saving Athens also accounts for Socrates' extraordinary voluntary sojourn outside the walls. Socrates has left Athens on other occasions, as a soldier, whenever the city needed him to fight for her survival. Evidently, he goes on extramural excursions when the city's welfare requires it. If there is even a slim chance that Socrates can serve the city well by following Phaedrus outside, he seizes it. His exit thus implies the opposite of philosophic disdain for the city.[19]

18. Benardete argues that "Phaedrus and Socrates are two nonlovers" (*Rhetoric of Morality*, 110), and he describes the relationship between them as a struggle to extort gratification from one another (106–11). In this, he seems to construe the interaction between Socrates and Phaedrus as an early example of Hegel's dialectic of the lord and the bondsman. Benardete is probably right about Phaedrus but wrong about Socrates, the textual evidence uniformly contradicting the proposition that Socrates is a nonlover. Students of Strauss appear to assume as a matter of course that the lord-bondsman relationship is the paradigmatic situation, probably thanks to the influence of Kojève. However, that is not necessarily so.

19. Typically, students of Strauss cite Socrates' departure from the city in the *Phaedrus* as proof that philosophy ultimately cares only for itself, not for political order. The Pindar quote suggests the contrary.

To be sure, this reading leaves a question open. Is Socrates' special reason for lacking leisure, that is, his obligation to obey the oracle by getting to know himself, truly less important than his duty to make one last—and predictably futile—effort to help his friend and rescue his city? Is his soul really less important than the debased pastimes of Phaedrus and his failing polity? I do not think that we are forced to this disturbing conclusion. Happily for Socrates, his obligations to the oracle and himself, on the one hand, and to his comrade and city, on the other, converge. His quotation from Pindar is ironic in a way that our modern connoisseurs of irony generally fail to perceive, for his duty to know himself actually requires him to listen to Phaedrus's recitation of Lysias's speech. This is the reason that Socrates' daimon chooses not to mount a vigorous resistance to his decision to join Phaedrus's ecstatic exercise.[20]

To show why listening to Phaedrus read Lysias's oration is Socrates' personal business, I must return to Planinc's paradigm, extending it in directions that it suggests and drawing out some of its implications. Homer's Odysseus does not leave Ithaca, fight at Troy, and journey from middle earth to the poles of the cosmos because he wants to enjoy a pleasure cruise. He embarked upon his expedition because he had a legal obligation to the Achaean league and, to be more truthful, because he was an avaricious, treacherous, murderous pirate. He persists in his travels for the theological reason that various gods want to punish him. He also continues for a spiritual reason that he does not understand until nearly the end: that he had to wander the *axis mundi* to know himself, that is, to learn who he was and who he had to become.

As Odysseus's trip gradually turns from a historically real campaign of war and piracy into a symbolic but spiritually real journey along the *axis mundi*, Odysseus himself is changed from an epic historical hero into a mythical bearer of the shamanistic life of Homer's psyche. Odysseus's discovery that he has incurred divine wrath is the poet's dawning perception that something in his soul is out of harmony with the order of being. Odysseus's ignorance of the causes of his trouble is the poet's admission that he suffers a spiritual disease (one that we can analyze as a prefiguration of the Platonic *amathia*). The revelation that Odysseus hears from Teiresias in Hades—that he has endured shipwrecks, catastrophic struggles with Polyphemus and Circe, and the frightening voyage into Hades because of his uncurbed *thymos,* and that he must rein his *thymos* in as he suffers further trials before he can return home—is an oracle to the poet that

---

20. Cropsey, in *Political Philosophy,* thinks that the daimon spends much of its time in the dialogue asleep at the switch, failing to prevent Socratic choices that it should have forbidden (240). However, Plato has a somewhat more expansive view of the things allowed to Socrates, or even required of him, than Cropsey does.

he too must curb his *thymos* as he faces edifying ordeals in his shamanistic spirit life.

The tests of Odysseus are paradigmatic experiences of all the evils to which he has been prone, or, if I may have recourse to a convenient Christian concept, paradigmatic experiences of the temptations to which he has been subject. Odysseus must experience all of his vices or temptations again to the fullest, this time seeing them for what they are with absolute clarity, feeling the total force of their powerful pulls upon his *thymos*, yielding to them in act while no longer succumbing to them in desire, suffering their consequences in perfect consciousness of his guilt, knowing complete misery as his punishment, and emerging purified. Hence, for example, he must deal with the effect of lotus-eating, a euphoric forgetfulness of home, for he himself ate the lotus of gratifications that made him forget the true joys of his home. He must appear in the cave of Polyphemus as a marauding bandit who pays no heed to Zeus, the duties of guests and hosts, and the rights of suppliants, just as he often did at Troy, only to ascertain to his sheer horror that the Cyclops is a mirror image of himself who will repay him in kind. He must visit Circe's island, see his comrades transformed into swine with human minds who epitomize his own vice, swallow Circe's magic pig-making drug (or poison, or medicine, or charm: Greek φάρμακον, *pharmakon*, which carries all these meanings), enjoy a divine grant of immunity to the drug's effects, and embrace Circe (as a symbol of the piggish life) sexually while fearing that he might be hers forever. He must hear the Sirens singing to him of the evil glory of his own deeds while he is tied to the mast of his ship, thus being tempted again by his pride while learning who he really was. He must hear Calypso's enticing promise that he can become a human immortal on a par with the gods, live this pseudodivine life as her prisoner, and embrace her (as the symbol of her pledge) in erotic union, too, just as he has always done before, again in agonies of terror that he might never escape. While he does all this, he must preserve the memory of his true home in a manner that prevents him from sinking back into the raging passion *(thymos)* for vice that made him leave home in the first place. As Odysseus endures these challenges in the story, his poetic creator is experiencing them in his shamanistic spirit existence as he progresses toward his own purification. Thus, it transpires that for both Odysseus and Homer, the way down is the way up.

Norman Austin, an excellent commentator on Homer, maintains that Nausicaa fuses a number of characters in the *Odyssey* in herself.[21] Planinc accepts this principle and extends it. Following their lead, I infer that at any moment, Nausicaa can be Circe, Calypso, Penelope, or anyone Homer

21. Austin, *Archery at the Dark of the Moon: Poetic Problems in Homer's "Odyssey,"* 200–202.

wants. This brings us back to the plot of the drama of Socrates' encounter with Phaedrus. Socrates is the philosophic Odysseus who has fallen from his spiritual home. Plato is the philosophic Homer who chants his tale. Socrates-Odysseus needs purification, as does Plato-Homer, who has been discovering that his soul is prone to all the vices that drove the first Odysseus and the original Homer. For both Socrates and Plato, as for both Odysseus and Homer, the way down will be the way up. Socrates has had a terrible shipwreck insofar as he has sunk down from the divine region under the vault of heaven (as in the myth that he will eventually tell) into an earthly body. In the aftermath, he happens upon Phaedrus, who is the Nausicaa who subsumes several characters in herself. I suppose that, just now, Phaedrus is Nausicaa-Circe. Normally, Socrates' daimon would forbid him to associate with any kind of Circe. However, Socrates-Odysseus must face the ordeal in which he is threatened with being changed into a pig with a human mind, or perhaps I should say a human being with a pig's mentality, for Plato-Homer understands that he is subject to the human temptation to be such a creature. Therefore, Socrates-Odysseus is obliged to ingest the *pharmakon* that transforms men into swine. He understands that Phaedrus-Circe is purveying the *pharmakon* (230d6), namely, the contents of Lysias's oration. Homer says in the *Odyssey* that Circe is a "dread goddess of human speech" (10.136), meaning that she converses with humans, sweet-talking them into swallowing the deadly *pharmakon*. Hermes perceives that Odysseus is addicted to such cajolery and gives him special protection against the *pharmakon*. Socrates-Odysseus himself realizes that he is "sick with craving to hear arguments" (228b6–7) and that he will fall for the invitation to hear the poisonous oration, as, indeed, he must do in order to know himself and advance the self-knowledge of the poet Plato-Homer. The daimon will be Socrates' divine immunity to the *pharmakon*'s effects, so that he will not choose to be a pig again. So, the business of knowing himself requires Socrates to hear Lysias in an effort to save Phaedrus and Athens, and the daimon supports the enterprise.

When Socrates affirms that he would like to hear about the conversation at Epicrates' house, Phaedrus answers that Lysias's speech was right up Socrates' alley because, in a way that he does not quite grasp, it was an erotic thing (227c4–5). Lysias has represented an attempt on one of the beauties that is not made by an *erastēs*. It is just on this account that the oration is elegant, for Lysias asserts that it is better to gratify "the nonloving" rather than "the loving"—literally, if I may beg leave to coin new English, the "non-erosing" rather than the "erosing." Lysias's meaning is plain. He has composed a speech for an older man who wants to say to a boy or a stripling: "Look, I am not in love with you. I do not ask you to love me. I am the one with whom you should have it off." Phaedrus's confusion is easy to understand. He cannot quite make out how Lysias's oration is about eros if the speaker is not erosing. Phaedrus is not terribly bright. Clearly, the speaker is not erosing in the sense that he is not in love with the lad, but he is erosing in the sense that he has a sexual appetite for him. To the extent that the speaker lets the true part of his statement misrepresent the false part, thus deceiving Phaedrus and the presumably witless young sex object, he is a liar. At the beginning of his first speech, Socrates will point this out to the obtuse Phaedrus.

All this has implications for both Socrates' war against the democratic tyrannical eros and for Socrates-Odysseus's and Plato-Homer's needs to win self-knowledge. It is essential to the democratic-tyrannical eros that it separates the nobler feature of eros (being in love with the beloved) from its appetitive aspect (craving someone as an object of pleasure), consigning the former to nonexistence and letting the latter become the whole of eros while pretending that it is not what it is, naked appetite. This is necessary to the democratic-tyrannical eros because it is not in love but wants pleasure from victims whom it can exploit. The pretense is carried by a deceptive eros-logos. This can happen on the personal level, as in the relationship between a man and a youth, and also in politics, as in the relationship of a demagogue with his people, or of a tyrannical majority with its subjects. Spiritually, the psyche that falls from its home also embraces this mutilation of eros, forgetting the genuine felicity of the higher beauty because it is now devouring the lotus of mere appetitive satisfaction. Phaedrus-Circe, a dread goddess of human speech, has employed an eros-logos to disguise perpetual entrapment in this piggishness as elegance.

Upon hearing of Lysias's suggestion that the non-erosing rather than the erosing should be gratified, Socrates exclaims: "O nobly-born man!" (Ὦ γενναῖος, 227c9). Then he wishes, probably with a wistful sigh, that Lysias would write that sexual favors should be dispensed to the many who are poor, old, and otherwise disadvantaged like himself, for such words would be witty and "helpful to the demos" (δημωφελεῖς, 227d2).

This answer is extremely complex. On one plane, it is flattery, for democrats like to think that they are noble. Democracy never aspires to pull the high down, but always wishes to lift the lowly up. Socrates flatters Lysias's democratic tyrannical idea to get Phaedrus to tell him the speech. On another level, Socrates' response is comic irony. Lysias is not noble and not speaking nobly. He is a *metic*. He is demanding something for nothing (gratification in return for no commitment), a demand typical of the vulgar. Phaedrus is so taken with Lysias's thesis and so swayed by Socrates' flattery that he misses the irony. On another plane, Socrates is serious about calling Lysias noble. His exclamation hints at something that Phaedrus has not noticed. Lysias is rich. In this respect, he is a member of the upper class. His interests do not coincide entirely with those of the demos. There might be something less useful to the people than to the rich in his arguments, this being a permanent potential in the relationships between democrats and their moneybags spokesmen. There is also a spiritual sense in which Socrates' outcry is not ironic. In his Odysseus persona, the Socrates who lands in the realms of Circe, Calypso, and Nausicaa always finds himself in the situation of a have-not, for as long as he is prone to vice he has insufficient resources to resist it. He must always beg favors that goddesses would grant because a suppliant is needy, not because it would be rational for them to gratify him without being loved. He will always feel a need to flatter his potential helpers. Thus, he is in the most dire democratic situation. The soul that has forsaken the noble eros belongs to hoi polloi of spirits and will naturally incline to democratic sentiments.

Phaedrus responds to Socrates' request to hear the speech by turning coy. He suggests that he cannot recite from memory an oration that cost Lysias, the cleverest writer of the day, a great deal of time to compose, although he would rather have that talent than a heap of gold. Phaedrus prefers the ability to recite Lysias to fabulously great wealth because he assumes that the power to make people grant favors gratis is an infinite asset, whereas piles of gold, however large, are finite. Socrates counters: "O Phaedrus, if I do not know Phaedrus, I have forgotten myself!" He denies that either part of this conditional is true (228a5–6). Then he reveals what he has known all along: Phaedrus spent the morning getting Lysias to repeat his speech. Not happy with that, he borrowed Lysias's book, using it to memorize the oration. Upon meeting "the man sick with craving to hear arguments" (τῷ νοσοῦντι περὶ λόγων ἀκοήν, 228b6–7), he was pleased to find a fellow Corybant. However, when asked to speak, he played coy. So now, Socrates says, Phaedrus should do what he really wants to do and talk. All this time, Phaedrus has been hiding Lysias's text under his cloak. He is too dense to grasp that he has been discovered, so he proposes to lecture Socrates on the general sense of Lysias's speech without attempting a verbatim recitation. Socrates responds that Phaedrus may do this after he has revealed what he is holding in his left hand under his cloak, for he thinks that Phaedrus has the speech. Although he is fond of Phaedrus, he refuses to permit Phaedrus to practice on him if Lysias himself is present. Phaedrus owns up and agrees to read.

Socrates' comment that if he does not know Phaedrus he has forgotten himself gently broaches the necessity of self-knowledge. Like Socrates' dear Alcibiades, Phaedrus must learn to know himself to be saved. If being sick with craving to hear arguments is to be a Corybant, and if Phaedrus and Socrates are both Corybants, both are suffering an ailment that deprives them of self-knowledge by plunging them into an ecstasy of delight at hearing incessant talk, so that they fail to examine themselves sufficiently well. It is a joy in contemplating clever speech that procures delirious satisfaction of all the desires. This oblivion exacerbates, or is identical with, the essentially democratic lotus-eating euphoria (see *Republic* 560c5) that comes with massive enjoyment of appetitive gratifications. It is a madness that admits of degrees. It is possible for Socrates to be subject to this illness while denying that he has forgotten himself. Socrates-Odysseus has not forgotten himself in the sense that he preserves a blurry memory of life in his true home. This faint memory distinguishes him from Phaedrus, here considered as a shipmate, who has forgotten everything. The dim recollection, with the indispensable help of the god, will pull Socrates-Odysseus through his ordeals. However, Socrates is still sick and needs to acquire self-knowledge in the sense that he has forgotten too much. Thus, he indicates that his desire to hear Lysias's speech and Phaedrus's wish to speak it are symptoms of a disease that consists in a destructive variety of mad self-forgetting.

Socrates' ensuing demand upon Phaedrus, that he should show what he holds in his left hand under his cloak, alludes to Phaedrus's role as Circe-Calypso-Nausicaa. In the *Odyssey,* all three divine or nearly divine ladies intend to capture Odysseus. Circe first desires him as a pig and then as a paramour. The others want him as a mate or spouse. All three hide secret erotic agendas from Odysseus. Circe does not want him to know that she means to turn him into a pig. Calypso does not want him to discover that he cannot be an immortal deity. Nausicaa is keeping the dream of a husband that she received from Athena to herself. Hence, they all play coy. Their behavior is simultaneously intellectually misleading about Odysseus's true situation and sexually flirtatious. This represents the deceptive natures of the erotic attractions that the temptations of Odysseus exercise on Homer. At this moment in our Platonic poem, Phaedrus specifically is Circe. Phaedrus-Circe is yearning to possess Socrates-Odysseus as a pig, perhaps as a piggish bedfellow. She conceals the text of Lysias's speech in her left hand (meaning that she is being sinister) because she does not want her prey to know the true origin and power of the *pharmakon* that she will use to change him. She thus symbolizes the misleading nature of the erotic attractions that the temptations of Socrates exercise on Plato. The proposition that Phaedrus-Circe receives in reply, that he-she should reveal what he is holding under his cloak, is clearly homoerotic foreplay. It is fated that Socrates-Odysseus will lie with Phaedrus-Circe (as the symbol of the swinish life) in erotic union—at least in the intellectual shaman life of Plato-Homer. Socrates-Odysseus recognizes coquetry when he sees it. He is easily seduced. He commences the affair with a sexual innuendo that a low sailor would think comically subtle.

Phaedrus and Socrates have reached the countryside, and they turn to wade barefoot in the Ilissus, searching for a place to rest. Phaedrus comments that he is fortunate to be barefoot today, as Socrates always is, for it is easy and pleasant to wade in the stream at this time of year. Then Phaedrus spies a particularly tall plane tree. He informs Socrates that the tree marks a shady, grassy place in which they could sit or lie down. So much for exercise for the sake of physical fitness. The easiest pleasures are now the order of the day, and the seduction is on. The representative democrat is going about his ordinary affairs. However, he is unaware that he is steering Socrates toward the present locus of the *axis mundi,* along which all kinds of divine things might come into their lives unexpectedly.

Apparently out of the blue, Phaedrus then asks Socrates a question about a folk myth that concerns the Ilissus.[22] The abruptness of this inquiry might be taken for a literary flaw in Plato's construction of his dialogue. However, it is no coincidence that the query has popped into Phaedrus's mind at the very moment that he has pointed out the plane tree. A tree can talk when it serves as the *axis mundi,* for it has become the avenue of divine communication with human beings. A god communing through the tree has put Phaedrus's question in his head. The same god will influence Socrates' reply. Henceforth, the conversation between Phaedrus and Socrates will not be entirely under their control. It will be divinely inspired, or guided, or supervised, just as the exchanges between Circe, Calypso, and Nausicaa, on the one hand, and Odysseus on the other, are subject to the management of Hermes and Athena. We must attempt to learn what the god is trying to accomplish by directing the conversation. In other words, we must try to discover the divine principles that govern the poet-philosopher's shamanistic voyage along the *axis mundi* and his reactions to his spiritual trials.

Phaedrus's question is this: Is it not from someplace along the Ilissus that Boreas is said to have carried off Oreithyia? Phaedrus refers to the tale in which the daughter of Erechtheus, the king of Athens, is abducted by the North Wind. Socrates responds: "So it is said" (229b6). Phaedrus inquires if they have reached the spot now, for the waters are pure and it looks like a fitting place for girls to play. Socrates answers that the site is farther down, close to where an altar to Boreas stands. (The altar was erected by the city in thanksgiving for Boreas's aid in the victory over the Persian fleet.) Swearing by Zeus, Phaedrus asks Socrates whether he believes the myth. Socrates replies that if he disbelieved, as "the wise" (οἱ σοφοί) do, he would not be unusual. Then, "playing the sophist" (σοφιζόμενος, 229c6), he might argue that a blast of the north wind, later personified as Boreas, pushed Oreithyia off the rocks while she played with Pharmaceia (Enchantment, loosely translated), killing the princess and giving rise to the story. However, Socrates contends that such pretty interpretations are

---

22. Benardete refers to Phaedrus's question as a "casual remark" (*Rhetoric of Morality,* 111). It is hardly that. To believe otherwise is to violate Socrates' (and Strauss's) doctrine of logographic necessity. Even without that doctrine, the topic is too important to be casual.

the inventions of an overly clever, laborious, and unfortunate man, for this kind of analyst immediately incurs an obligation to explain the forms of Hippocentaurs, the Chimera, Gorgons, Pegasuses, and the like. If he sets out with "some boorish wisdom" (ἀγροίκῳ τινὶ σοφίᾳ, 229e3) to explain all such strange creatures, he will need a great deal of leisure. However, Socrates has no time for this enterprise, for he has not succeeded in knowing himself and it is ridiculous to investigate these things when he has not yet heeded the oracle.[23] Accordingly, obeying or being persuaded by the customary lawful opinion about such myths, he explores himself, attempting to discover whether he is a wild animal more complicated (literally, "multiply twisted") than Typhon or a tamer, simpler "animal who participates by nature in a divine, un-Typhonlike [that is, nonarrogant] fate" (ζῷον φείας τινὸς καὶ ἀτύφου μοίρας φύσει μετέχον) (230a5–6).

Insofar as the Boreas-Oreithyia tale maintains that the god kidnaped the maiden, it is a story about a rape. Planinc is right to argue that it evokes the Odysseus-Nausicaa encounter, in which Nausicaa fears that Odysseus will rape her. However, Plato refigures the trope in a way that packs several meanings into the image, corresponding to the multiple dramatic roles that Phaedrus is playing just now. In this refiguring, it is the feminine character too who is the prospective rapist, a circumstance that is consistent with what occurs in the *Odyssey*. In one sector of his soul, the feminine Phaedrus is Boreas. He is contemplating the use of the power of Lysias's words (contained in an object under his cloak) to dupe both Socrates and the hypothetical young man into giving him what they would otherwise be unwilling to yield up, their sexual favors. Considering that the objects of seduction must be presumed to be more than a little vapid, it would not be too much to assert that Phaedrus is savoring the idea of a rhetorical rape of the two of them.[24] In another layer of his soul, Phaedrus is Circe and is attempting to transform Socrates-Odysseus into a pig with her *pharmakon*, thus perpetrating another sort of rape. In yet another part of Phaedrus's soul, in which he is a comic Nausicaa, he-she is planning to use what she laughably believes to be truly wise words to invite Socrates-Odysseus to take her. In all these cases, the god in the tree has caused Phaedrus-Boreas-Circe-Nausicaa to betray all too obviously exactly what is on his-her mind, this with a view toward helping Socrates-Odysseus know his fatal penchant for succumbing to words that seductively promise pleasurable advantage. The god in

23. The fact that he does not know himself sufficiently is proof that there is a degree to which he suffers the illness of self-forgetting.

24. Benardete declares that the Boreas story "presented silent violence as the truth about love" (ibid., 123). Try as I might, I cannot follow his logic to this strange conclusion. I must ask when rape became love. Benardete should have argued that the story presented the truth about seeking sexual gratification when one is not in love, which is precisely the point of the attempt that Lysias's speech makes upon the beauty.

the tree wants the shamanistic voyage along the *axis mundi* to make it clear to Plato-Homer that what is at stake in yielding to his temptations is erotic violence to his person. The deity also inspires Socrates-Odysseus to give Phaedrus a warning that parallels the admonitions that Hermes gives to Circe and Calypso: temptresses who try to rape divinely protected heros by playing with *pharmaceia* are also self-ignorant in that they are trying to step out of their places in the order of being. They will be divinely thwarted.

The god in the tree also inspires Socrates-Odysseus to recognize the correct procedures for navigating the *axis mundi* in the depths of his soul. The revelation concerns the right use of myth. When Phaedrus raises the question of the Boreas fable, Socrates answers in a manner that leaves no doubt that the tale is not his and that he does not believe in its literal truth. However, he hints that there are right and wrong modes of unbelief. The wrong mode of unbelief is that of the "wise," namely, the sophists. These intellectuals, whom Socrates calls "the wise" ironically, are boors. Having only a churl's sense of reality and its divine-human continuum, they seize upon one reductionistic idea that squeezes being into the narrow confines of their vision, declaring what they cannot see unbelievable and then explaining the whole of reality as an effect of the only causes of which they are certain. In this instance, they discredit the traditional myths by treating all statements about divine reality as superstitious accounts of physical phenomena; then they conclude to their pet anthropological and ethical doctrines. The basic error here is that the stories are not intended as literal truths about supernatural entities. Missing the purpose of the myths, the sophistical boors jump straight to the nonreality of divine being, an inference that is not warranted by their mishandling of the stories. In view of the extraordinary bluntness of Socrates' language, one must entertain the gravest doubt that Plato means the Boreas discussion as an esoteric sign of approval of the rationalistic debunking of myths, which would make Plato a sophistical boor. That is a boorish idea.[25]

The right mode of unbelief "obeys" or "is persuaded by" the customary lawful opinion about the myths. This does not mean that the poet-philosopher "accommodates" his teaching to the law by pretending to believe in the literal truth of the tales, as modern interpreters of Plato as an esoteric atheist would have it. It has already been established that worrying about the literal truth of the stories is for bumpkins. The poet-philosopher obeys or is persuaded by the legally sanctioned myths by adhering to their real intention. In what sense, then, does he assent, and what is the true intention of the fables?

---

25. Accordingly, I cannot sympathize with Benardete's interpretation of the Boreas interlude (ibid., 111–15), which has Socrates embracing the sophists' position, making him into precisely the kind of boor that he proposes not to be.

The right mode of unbelief, which is actually a sort of persuasion by the myths, begins with the realization that inquiring into their literal truth is to ask the wrong question. In his second speech, Socrates makes it perfectly clear why asking about the literal truth of the stories is to put a flawed question. Speaking of the form, or idea (τῆς ἰδέας, 246a3), of the soul, Socrates says: "What sort of thing it is, is completely in every way a matter for a long, divine accounting" (246a4–5). With reference to god, Socrates says that we speak of the divine "without either having seen or adequately comprehended him in thought" (246c7–8). To inquire into the literal truth of the myths is to ask a bad question because it is beyond the power of the human mind to discover answers to such a query.

One must ask the right question. To ask the right question is to try to know oneself—a task that especially involves knowing one's ground. One's self is not surely an autonomous, self-grounded being. Socrates says that there are two alternatives: he is either a wild animal more "multiply twisted" than Typhon or a tamer, simpler "animal who participates by nature in a divine, un-Typhonlike fate." In his second speech, Socrates opts for the latter alternative: he is an "animal who participates by nature in a divine, un-Typhonlike fate." Thus, he needs to discuss soul and god rightly, which he cannot do literally. However, it is possible for us to say what soul "is like" (ἔοικεν, 246a5). Equally, it is possible for us to say what an unknown divine reality that we experience is like. This is the true function of myth: to describe with symbols or metaphors what we encounter as we travel along the *axis mundi* (which term itself is a metaphor) in our souls (which term is also a metaphor), trying to understand ourselves as tame, simple beings who *participate by nature* in a divine fate. Homer and Plato do just that as they sing their poems of Odysseus and Socrates. As Planinc observes, Socrates' second speech therefore unabashedly brings mythical creatures such as Hippocentaurs and Pegasuses back into the picture as images that try to capture the soul's experiences of higher reality. Human beings must be content with this kind of insight into the mysterious grounds of their existence. This, perhaps, is the most important principle that governs spiritual travel along the *axis mundi*.

Given that Socrates postulates the two alternatives, that he is either a wild animal more "multiply twisted" than Typhon or a tamer, simpler "animal who participates by nature in a divine, un-Typhonlike fate," it will be inquired why I maintain that he opts for the latter. To answer adequately, I must relate the story of Typhon. Hesiod (*Theogony* 819 ff) tells us that when the Titans had been defeated and imprisoned in Tartarus, Earth lay with Tartarus and conceived Typhon. Typhon had a hundred serpent heads. His eyes flashed fire. His mouths uttered every kind of sound. According to other poets, he was the largest monster ever born. From his thighs down, he was nothing but coiled snakes. His arms opened a hundred leagues in either direction, also being composed of snakes. We can understand why Socrates describes Typhon as "multiply twisted." This Typhon was brother to the Titans and had the same sorts of aspirations. He assaulted Olympus. Although it might be stretching a point beyond what our text supports, I suspect that Socrates sees in the enormous, many-voiced, multiply twisted Typhon a symbol of the tyrannically disposed demos who, like their sophistical and imperial tyrannical kin from the upper classes, wish to usurp Zeus. If Socrates does not take Typhon as an apt likeness of the tyrannical many, he surely regards him as an image of the potential that every human soul has for adopting an infinite variety of poses and urging an infinite number of grievances against the gods. Be that as it may, in the poems of Hesiod and Pindar, Zeus has to fight a hard war against Typhon, who, as Hesiod says, could have easily become the king of Olympus and the gods had Zeus not been watching. Zeus smites Typhon with his bolts and incarcerates him in Mount Aetna. Now, in Socrates' second speech, the souls who inhabit the divine region follow in the trains of gods (246e–247a). They do not display hybris against Zeus and the other Olympians. Rather, they could be said to be un-Typhonlike, that is, nonarrogant (ἀτύφου). Like Zeus, they appear as charioteers driving pairs of winged horses around in the ether, caring for everything that lacks soul, thus "participating in a divine fate." They do not end up buried under Mount Aetna, although some get trapped in matter.

When Phaedrus and Socrates reach the plane tree, Socrates exclaims: "By Hera, it is a beautiful resting place!" (230b2). Then he expands upon this observation, explaining that the plane tree is far spreading and lofty; the full, shady *agnus castus* (willow) is quite beautiful and fragrant; the spring is pretty and cool; the spot, as indicated by its statuary, seems sacred to nymphs and Achelous; the good ventilation of the grove is lovely and pleasant; the place is resounding with a shrill, summery cicada chorus; and the most exquisite thing of all is the grass that is just right for relaxing. This is another point at which those who like to read Plato as an esoteric atheist misconstrue the text. They observe enigmatically that of the seven items listed by Socrates, the only one not praised is that in the middle.[26] We are expected to understand that the central element of a list is being singled out for esoteric notice and that Plato is teaching the inferiority of religiosity (nymph statues) to real physical nature. I think that this interpretation tears the passage out of its plainly Homeric context. Odysseus encounters Nausicaa in a place that Homer explicitly describes as having beautiful streams and a grassy meadow (*Odyssey* 6.85–87, 120–25). He is terribly nervous

---

26. For example, see ibid., 114–15. It is telling that Benardete judges the word "sacred" not to be a term of praise. He stands in opposition to a long tradition of singers of "Sanctus."

about nymphs (6.123), understandably so, having only just escaped from Calypso, whom he also met in a paradise of natural beauty (5.55–70), and having suffered terribly at the hands of Circe as well. Socrates-Odysseus is now meeting Phaedrus-Nausicaa and discerning in him-her a vision of the ordeals to which Phaedrus-Circe and Phaedrus-Calypso soon will subject him. (Here, Plato is clearly rearranging Homer's poetic tropes to suit his dramatic purposes.) Socrates places the nymph statuary at the center of his list of features of the grove because the nymphs whom they evoke are present and soon will take over the action of the play. If he does not praise the figurines, the reason is that he is nervous about nymphs, only this time with prophetic foresight rather than hindsight, or perhaps even with anamnestic hindsight if he is Odysseus reincarnate. Soon he will be apoplectic about the nymphs as he feels himself in their clutches. In the shaman life of Plato-Homer, Socrates' perhaps ambivalent attitude toward the nymph statuary symbolizes the philosopher-poet's trepidation as he gives himself over to the torments of his trials.

When Socrates so effusively praises the grove and commends Phaedrus for being such an excellent guide, Phaedrus erupts. He calls Socrates an "amazing" and "most strange" man, declares that Socrates behaves like an artless foreigner being led around, and expresses doubt that Socrates ever leaves the city or even goes outside the walls. Socrates apologizes, pleading that he loves learning, that country places and trees are not willing to teach him anything, and that people in town are willing to teach him. However, Phaedrus has found the *pharmakon* to lure him out. Just as people lead hungry animals around by shaking branches or fruit before them, so Phaedrus can lead him all over Attica by dangling speeches in books before him.

Socrates' plea that he loves learning, that country locales and trees are not disposed to teach him, and that people in the city are willing to teach him explains clearly enough why he usually remains in town. His rationale is mistaken, for he does not realize yet that a tree (or a god in the tree) just taught him something. However, his error is pardonable, for we do not normally expect to receive instruction from trees. Still, his argument seems to be incoherent in light of some of his later remarks, to the effect that oral teaching is superior to written teaching, which has serious defects (276a–277a). His resolve to study a written speech seems inconsistent with this opinion.

I think that the apparent gap between the premise and the conclusion of the reasoning has a lot to do with the fact that Socrates cannot tell Phaedrus everything. Socrates' inability to be perfectly informative attaches to both of the roles that he is playing. This can be seen by considering the matter from two standpoints.

First, in his existential persona as himself, Socrates is walking outside the walls because he wants to save Phaedrus and Athens from the democratic tyrannical eros. It would be a tactical blunder for Socrates to be candid about this purpose before Phaedrus has become amenable to being saved. Therefore, Socrates omits any mention of it from his apology and explanation. As a lover of learning, he lets Phaedrus think that he expects the *pharmakon* to educate him. Having gained Phaedrus's confidence, he will rescue him by undermining Lysias's speech later. In his Odysseus persona, Socrates still recognizes his responsibilities to Phaedrus and Athens. However, he has regressed into a lower area of his soul that must be illuminated and examined so that he and his philosophic-poetic creator, Plato-Homer, can be purified. In this stratum of his consciousness, he is drawn to the same kinds of things that attract Phaedrus and the demos. It is not entirely clear to him that salvation is not identical with preserving the life of pleasure and piracy that Athens is still attempting to lead in 407. His sense of obligation to his friend and his city therefore resembles Odysseus's concept of his duty to the Achaean league when he left Ithaca, which was one part grudging willingness to abide by the provisions of a treaty and several parts lust for booty, as witness what he took away from Troy. Consequently, at the moment, Socrates-Odysseus is spiritually incapable of raising the problem of the democratic tyrannical eros with Phaedrus. His now dubious love of learning makes him eager to learn all about the *pharmakon* understood as a new weapon invented by the arms merchant.

Second, in his existential persona as himself, Socrates remains the same philosopher of erotic wisdom whom we followed through the *Symposium* up to the vision of beauty, the entry to his true home. He loves learning understood as the ascent to the vision. This Socrates cannot simply tell Phaedrus the ineffable truth. He must try to turn Phaedrus's psyche around so that Phaedrus sees for himself. This education must begin where Socrates finds Phaedrus, in thrall to Lysias's speech. Thus, it must start with a provisional acceptance of the oration. Only later can Socrates lead Phaedrus beyond it. Socrates must love this sort of education and, therefore, Phaedrus's variety of learning, too. This creates a nexus between Socrates' love of learning and his willingness to hear the *pharmakon*. In his Odysseus persona, in which he has relapsed into the lower level of his soul, Socrates suffers from *amathia*. Accordingly, he is inclined to annul or ignore the noble eros that loves the beauties and to seek mere appetitive gratification. He cannot tell Phaedrus that Lysias's speech is poison because he does not quite know this himself. He is offered the *pharmakon* in the guise of advice on the means of achieving his pleasure. He loves this learning, reaches for it, and falls from his true home with his Penelope, the vision of beauty. When he jokes that Phaedrus can lead him away from the city like a domestic animal, it is really no joking matter. The stratum of his soul that is sick with *amathia* is on the verge of ingesting Circe's potion. The domestic beast to which his joke refers is the pig. The lower portion of his soul is already starting to oink. Plato-Homer, who sees all this happening to his shaman spirit, is not laughing. Like Odysseus looking at his men, he is terrified. Luckily for Socrates-Odysseus, there is a willow next to the plane tree. As Planinc mentions, the willow is the symbol of Asclepius. Contrary to the intentions of Phaedrus-Circe, Socrates-Odysseus is taking the *pharmakon* in order to become healthy.

Lysias Spoken by Phaedrus

The speech written by Lysias for Phaedrus begins with the assertion that the addressee knows the speaker's affairs and has heard how he thinks it would be advantageous to arrange these things. Either someone else has informed the youth or the speaker has made a blunt proposal. The speaker notifies the addressee that he hopes to be spared the misfortune of not obtaining what he wants merely because he does not happen to be an *erastēs* of his. In the remainder of the speech, the speaker contends that the youth should gratify the non-erosing rather than the erosing.

With respect to form, Lysias's composition has a subtle structure. It looks disorganized and repetitive. Commentators assume that Lysias deliberately wrote the oration this way to give it "an effect of haphazardness and spontaneity."[27] In democracies, these qualities are taken as signs of honesty, the idea being that chaotic, spontaneous oratory could not be calculated.

In tone, the speech is businesslike. It breathes a professionalism that is impatient with sentimentality and irrelevant prattle. In democracies, this tone never fails to convince people that the speakers who adopt it know what they are talking about. Everyman knows how he approaches his own business or trade, the essentials of which he has grasped, and supposes that he can recognize the technical expert's attitude in others. Oftentimes, he is right.

With regard to substance, Lysias leaves many of his premises and conclusions unstated. The rhetorical effect is to imply that the unspoken matters are already too well known or too clear to everyone to need discussion. In democracies, appeals to public opinion are the most persuasive forms of reasoning. In addition, the speaker insinuates that smart, chic individuals already understand the premises and conclusions and that the addressee is smart and chic, so that these things need not be explained to him. If this hint contradicts the previous one, the logical trifle is overlooked in the glow of the flattery. The auditor is convinced. Lysias is a rhetorical force to be reckoned with.

27. G. R. F. Ferrari, *Listening to the Cicadas: A Study of Plato's "Phaedrus,"* 52–53.

It is not easy to summarize the argument of an oration that is deliberately scrambled, brusque, and reticent about its affirmations. One does so at the price of depriving the piece of its intended capacity to generate psychological pressure. With the warning that readers should examine the speech for themselves to experience this effect, I shall present a brief synopsis that supplies Lysias's unspoken premises and conclusions in brackets, as follows.

(1) [All eros reduces to desire (ἐπιθυμία, *epithymia,* 231a2). This is an overwhelming compulsion that unaccountably seizes human beings and later releases them again. Those who are subject to it have no control over their actions. When they do favors, their *epithymia* has forced their hands. Naturally, the addressee is interested primarily in these favors.] When the desire of the erosing abates, they repent the favors they have conferred. [The non-erosing are not subject to *epithymia.* The speaker is not dominated by passion for the addressee.] There is no time when the non-erosing repent their gifts, for they are benevolent "not by necessity" (231a4), but voluntarily, as dictated by their considered self-interest. [If the addressee gratifies the speaker, therefore, he may be sure of reaping and keeping great rewards.]

(2) [People resent compulsion (see 240c4–5). Therefore, the erosing are prone to miserly behavior.] The erosing keep ledgers that balance the expenses and gains of their erotic affairs. When they do their sums, they always conclude that their outlays for romance have been too high. [Logically, no one complains about his free choices.] The non-erosing, whose works are not governed by necessity, do not engage in miserly accounting. [We have seen that they act as their enlightened self-interest ordains.] They readily do what they think will be gratifying. [Hence, the addressee, whose sole concern is his own advantage, can expect bigger payoffs if he obliges the speaker.]

(3) The erosing claim to be friends who gratify beloveds by word and deed, even if this means incurring the hatred of others. [However, everyone knows that *epithymia* inevitably dies.] If the erosing are telling the truth, they will surely injure old beloveds to please new ones. [The non-erosing pay as they go. Once they have settled accounts, they have no further commerce with ex-providers. As sharp businessmen, they make sure that their sexual transactions entail no third-party complications. Therefore, they have no motives for damaging ex-providers to please new ones. The addressee, whose desire for benefits understandably includes an aversion to being wounded, may be certain that he runs no risks of this by gratifying the speaker.]

(4) It is unreasonable to involve oneself with the erosing, who suffer a misfortune so overwhelming that no experienced person would try to cure it. They themselves admit that they are "more sick than sanely self-controlled" (νοσεῖν μᾶλλον ἢ σωφρονεῖν, 231d2–3), that they think poorly,

and that they "are not able to rule themselves" (οὐ δύνασθαι αὐτῶν κρα-
τεῖν, 231d4). When they recover [as they invariably will], they will repudiate the decisions that they made when they were ill. [The non-erosing
are healthy, sane, clearheaded, self-ruled, and constant. If the addressee
gratifies the speaker, he can expect predictable behavior.]

(5) Those who eros for the addressee are few. [The speaker needs to establish his bona fides as a non-*erastēs* by delivering the occasional insult, which
merely compounds the original and fundamental affront, the declaration
that he himself is not an *erastēs* of the addressee. The youth should not
take this amiss. Everybody knows that businessmen haggle by disparaging
the commodity for which they are negotiating. The sharp trader wants his
counterpart to be a little desperate to make the deal.] Those who do not eros
for the addressee are many. Thus, the addressee has a statistically higher
probability of finding someone worthy of his friendship if he decides to
gratify the non-erosing rather than the erosing.

(6) Perhaps the addressee is worried about customary law and gossip.
[He must recall that the erosing are insane and cannot control themselves.]
He should know that the erosing will certainly disgrace him because they
cannot refrain from boasting of their conquests. However, the non-erosing,
"being rulers of themselves" (κρείττους αὐτῶν ὄντας, 232a4–5), are discreet. Further, the many notice lovers keeping company. They always gossip about this. However, they pay no attention to the non-erosing who
meet, for everyone must speak with somebody, either for the sake of friendship or for "some other pleasure."

(7) The addressee might be afraid that all friendships inevitably die.
[They do.] When the addressee envisages the breakup of his relationships,
he might worry that he will have lost something [that is, everything that
goes into giving oneself in sexual intercourse] that he regards as more valuable than the rewards that he will have received. The addressee should be
aware that in this regard, the erosing are more to be feared than the non-
erosing [who, to be tacitly honest, are also to be feared. The erosing, it will
be recalled, are insane and lack self-control.] Every little thing hurts the
feelings of the erosing. Therefore, they hinder their partners from associating with men of superior wealth, education, intellect, and so on. The result
is that the addressee will either lose good social connections or lose his
erastēs. [Either way, his profits will be down.] However, the non-erosing
who are gratified owing to their virtue [namely, their great rationality and
sane self-control] are never jealous. When their protégés find other associates who benefit them, they feel benefited, too.

(8) Many of the erosing desire the body. They leap headlong into affairs before getting to know the character, traits, and associates of their
beloveds. It is uncertain that when their desire ceases, they will still want
to be friends. The non-erosing [who are not blinded by lust and who can

accordingly make adequate assessments of personalities] who were friends before they engaged in the matters under discussion will not see their friendships lessened after they have been gratified. [The addressee may assume that the speaker and he are friends because the speaker is favoring him with these tips, which are not given to just anybody. The addressee is what our modern advertising deftly calls a "preferred customer."]

(9) The addressee will be improved more by gratifying the speaker than by gratifying the erosing. The erosing are ruled by fear of being hated and desire, which has a deleterious affect on judgment. Hence, they corrupt beloveds with flattery. [Now the speaker comes out from behind the screen of generalities that he has erected and openly presses his own suit.] "But if you are persuaded by me" (233b6), the speaker says, he will plan for future advantage rather than immediate pleasure, and he will not be overcome by eros but will be in control of himself. He will not stir up great animosity over trifles, he will anger slowly when offenses are great, he will forgive involuntary transgressions, and he will attempt to prevent intentional ones. This demonstrates that the friendship will last a long time. [However, not forever. Everyone knows that interests change over time.]

(10) The addressee might wonder how there can be friendship without eros. However, there is friendship with sons, fathers, mothers, and faithful friends without eros.

(11) If one must gratify those most in need, the speaker says derisively, perhaps it is also best to confer benefits not on the best but on those in greatest want. Such people will be the most grateful. On the same grounds, the addressee should invite not friends but beggars to feasts; soon these guests will be hanging around asking for favors all the time.

(12) Reversing course, the speaker muses that perhaps it would be better to gratify not the neediest, but those most capable of returning favors; and not the erosing, but those most worthy; and not those who will ravish the addressee and then dump him, but those who will keep giving him good things as he gets older; and not those who will boast of their conquest, but those who are discreet; and not those who will attend upon him only for a short time, but those who will be friends for life; and not those who will look for excuses to end the affair when the bloom of his youth is gone, but those who will display their virtue then.

(13) The friends of the erosing warn them that their affairs are bad for them. Nobody has ever warned the non-erosing that they deliberate badly about their affairs.

(14) The erosing and the non-erosing agree on one thing: The addressee should not be promiscuous, gratifying all of the non-erosing. No one values what is common.

(15) If the addressee has any questions, he should ask.

Lysias's argument is recognizable as a generality that we have seen dressed in countless fashionable guises from the sophists to highly acclaimed modern thinkers: Life is nothing but pleasure and pain. The point of human existence is to maximize pleasure and minimize pain. Therefore, everybody is on the make. You and I are too smart to pretend that this verity does not include us. Although everyone is on the make, people divide into two classes. Some pursue their interests rationally all of the time. However, there are others who become impassioned and sometimes pursue their interests irrationally. When the human beings who are always on the make want things from one another, the best deals are struck when all the parties calculate their interests rationally and choose accordingly. This is true of all matters ranging from war (see the Melian Dialogue in Thucydides' *History*) and politics to personal relationships. The application of this principle to the present case is as follows: Sexual affairs do not differ from other kinds of human business: their point is to maximize pleasure and minimize pain. Every single value in these affairs is an interest that a person may declare inviolable, compromise, or trade away like a commodity in his or her effort to increase the pleasure quotient of an entire ensemble of interests. The addressee should calculate his interests rationally. He will see that his sexual favors have a reasonable price and that he can get a good bargain by selling them to someone who is willing and able to advance all of his interests, so that he turns a tidy profit of pleasures on the whole. He will also appreciate that his rational, non-erosing suitor is a better business partner than an irrational *erastēs*. The addressee should make the rational choice.

I have already indicated that Plato views this argument as a *pharmakon* that makes pigs of the people who internalize it. That is my opinion, too. However, the argument contains a certain worldly wisdom. It is no easily refuted straw man. At this point in his dialogue, Plato does not make Socrates supply a refutation; he concentrates instead on the rhetorical form of Lysias's speech. I shall follow suit. Before doing that, however, I must call attention to a few things in the substance of the oration.

Previously, I mentioned that although it is true that Lysias's speaker is not erosing for the addressee in the sense that he is not in love with him, he is erosing for the youth in the sense that he has a sexual appetite for him. It could not be otherwise: who would offer copious gifts for sex with a beauty whom he or she did not desire? To the extent that the speaker maintains that he is not in the grip of *epithymia*, he is lying. This observation is not made in a spirit of moral outrage (although that would certainly be justified). It is a technical criticism. It would seem that the lie is so clumsy, and that it would be so incredible to the addressee, that it would destroy the intended rhetorical effect of the speech. The implausibility of the lie accounts for Phaedrus's suspicion that Lysias's oration is actually erotic, although it claims not to be. Lysias would have done better to declare that there are two kinds of *epithymia*, the irrational and the rational, and that he represents the rational. Socrates is aware of this substantive defect. That is one reason he opens his second speech by hinting at the crudity of the deception.

In view of the flimsiness of the oration's basic lie, the addressee might also notice that he has been given no real guarantees that he will receive any benefits or be held safe from any harm if he gratifies the speaker. The speech could be given successfully only to a dimwit. However, there might be a sufficient number of those on the scene to ensure that the speaker will thrive. One thinks of P. T. Barnum's favorite saying: "There is a sucker born every minute." This is a thought that would have delighted the Odysseus of the *Iliad*.

The speaker's sarcastic suggestion that the addressee should gratify those who are most needy looks at first as if Lysias intends to accommodate Socrates' wish that the speech be helpful to the demos. However, then Lysias has the speaker argue against democratic interests by conjuring the specter of hordes of beggars coming to the addressee's door if he does gratify the neediest. Then he causes his mouthpiece to support oligarchical interests by having him suggest that it would be better for the addressee to gratify someone who has the means to keep a paramour in classy style. Again, Plato seems convinced that the demos are manipulated by their aristocratic and wealthy spokesmen.

The speaker's concluding directive to the addressee that if he has questions, he should raise them, is meant not so much as an invitation as intimidation. What young beauty would want to convict himself of stupidity by revealing that he did not understand such rationality? The addressee is undoubtedly feeling pressure to answer that, no, he comprehends everything and agrees to gratify the speaker without further ado.

Lysias is absolutely consistent in one respect. His speaker never represents himself as erosing for the addressee. He intimates that the addressee may count on his friendship, but he even hedges on that, implying that the addressee should know that it cannot endure.

For the moment, this is enough on the substance of Lysias's composition. We may pick up the action of the drama. When Phaedrus finishes, he asks Socrates whether the speech was not supernatural (ὑπερφυῶς, 234c7) in every regard and especially in diction. This is comical. James H. Nichols has done a translation of the *Phaedrus* that strives to be as close to perfectly literal as his art can make it. I admire Nichols's competent realization of his intention. However, Lysias's speech in literal English is an utter horror with respect to diction. Although its tone is businesslike, its form is impossibly convoluted (one could say "multiply twisted," Typhonlike) and its high-sounding words are packed into vague dangling clauses that are hard to fathom. It is completely lacking in beauty. I suspect that its original would have read the same way to an educated speaker of Attic Greek. This would imply that Phaedrus probably enjoys its diction because it sounds a lot like himself, a half-educated dilettante. Lysias has given a display of his talent for tailoring speeches to the traits of his democratic clients.

When Odysseus ingests Circe's *pharmakon*, Circe smiles in the happy expectation that Odysseus will immediately drop to all fours and take to grunting. When Socrates-Odysseus swallows Lysias's *pharmakon*, the comic Phaedrus-Circe smiles in the happy expectation that Socrates-Odysseus will be instantly turned into a spiritual pig. However, when Odysseus has drunk to the last drop, he obeys Hermes by rushing upon Circe with his sword drawn. The stunned Circe shrinks back in terror and begins to parley. When Socrates-Odysseus has heard Lysias's speech to the last word, and when Phaedrus-Circe asks him whether it was not supernatural, Socrates-Odysseus attacks Phaedrus-Circe with irony, a figurative drawn sword. He answers that he found the speech "daimonic" and that he was overcome by it because he perceived that Phaedrus was brightened by it. Hence, thinking that Phaedrus knew more about the matters touched upon than he, he had joined Phaedrus, "the divine head" (234d6), in the revelry of the Bacchus, meaning that he had tagged along inanely with Phaedrus satirically conceived as the enthused (that is, divinely possessed) leader of a Dionysian procession. The irony stuns Phaedrus, who now demands to be told in the name of Zeus, the god of friendship, whether any other Hellene could speak better or at greater length than Lysias on the same matter.

In mock surprise, Socrates asks whether Phaedrus means that Lysias's speech should be praised for its comprehensive coverage of the needful rather than for its finely honed phrases. He, Socrates, did not notice that, for he had been paying attention to the rhetoric alone. This is an appropriate response for Socrates-Odysseus, who has not yet overcome the defects in his spirit that incline him favorably toward piggishness. His natural tendency at this point would be to consider the creator of the *pharmakon* as a fellow predator and to evaluate the technical merits of the potion as a weapon for overcoming prey.

As for the rhetoric, Socrates doubts that even Lysias could have been satisfied with the piece, which was redundant, as if the author could not think of many things to say about the subject. Phaedrus is incensed. He probably approves of Lysias's redundancy because the first principle of the art of propaganda is that incessant repetition persuades audiences of the truth of propositions more effectively than good arguments. More important, Phaedrus believes that it is the special merit of the speech that Lysias has said everything that anyone could possibly say on the topic.

Socrates dissents. Ancient wise men and women have spoken and written about these things. They will refute him if he agrees that Lysias has exhausted the subject. Phaedrus is all ears and asks: "Who has done better?

Where have you heard it?" Socrates feigns forgetfulness. Perhaps, he remarks, he heard something better from Sappho or the wise Anacreon (of whom Socrates seems to be thinking as poets whose wooing was much more subtle and capable than that of Lysias). However, he himself could give a speech that makes other points and is not worse. He is being evasive about its source because he does not want to disclose that the unwitting author of the new oration is Phaedrus himself (243e9–244a1). Like Circe, Phaedrus thinks that he can still extort some gratification from Socrates. Like Circe, he begins to parley.

PHAEDRUS SPOKEN BY SOCRATES

Phaedrus doubts that Socrates has forgotten his source. He responds by giving Socrates the same compliment that Socrates had given Lysias, except that he ironically renders it in the superlative, exclaiming: "O most nobly born man!" He implies that it is just like a nobleman, especially the noblest of all, to hold out on a democrat. However, he also thinks that Socrates, like all men, has his price. He assumes that although he is relatively poor now, he will be able to amass tons of gold if he can get Socrates to show him the more powerful *pharmakon,* far more than he could gain by using Lysias's rhetoric. Therefore, he can offer Socrates rewards beyond the wildest fantasies of the ordinary democrat. As compared with his anticipated new wealth, Socrates' price would be chicken feed, for Socrates seems too doltish to perceive the wonderful uses to which his rhetorical power could be put—if, indeed, he possesses it. So, Phaedrus says to Socrates, look, forget the source, I do not care about that. Just tell me the speech, confining yourself to the things that differ from what Lysias has said and speaking at the same length. If you do, I promise that I will erect life-size golden images in Delphi, one of myself and one of you. Athenian archons are compelled to swear that they will set up gold statues in Delphi if they break the law. Phaedrus knows that he has already violated the law and is doing so again by planning to build the images. He envisages for himself, and is offering to Socrates, golden idols that are usually dedicated to worship of the gods. Thus, he is tempting Socrates not only with the golden idol—the chicken feed—but also with a prospect of deification and immortality.

With this pledge, Phaedrus-Nausicaa-Circe becomes Phaedrus-Nausicaa-Circe-Calypso. According to Homer, Calypso, like Circe, is a "dread goddess of human speech" (*Odyssey* 12.449). She is dread because she uses human language to persuade Odysseus of the fatal delusion that he can become immortal by embracing her in erotic union. Even after allowing Odysseus to leave Ogygia if he wishes, she tempts him to stay by arguing

that she is more beautiful than Penelope, that he can escape a great deal of
suffering to which he is destined if he tries to return home, and, once again,
that he can be immortal if he keeps house with her (5.206–13). As Zdravko
Planinc has pointed out, the promise is false. Hermes proclaims the truth:
If Odysseus stays on Calypso's island, it will be his fate to die there far
from his friends and his home (10.110–15). Odysseus's real telos is to suffer
his trials and return to his true home. In the shaman odyssey of Homer's
soul, Calypso symbolizes the poet's temptation to employ word-magic in
the vain attempt to transform himself into an immortal god.

Phaedrus unwittingly relishes the idea of being Circe and Calypso simultaneously. He craves gratification of the base appetites. This disposes him
to be swinish and to make others pigs who will supply his lower wants.
He also longs to enjoy his satisfactions forever. This causes him to hope to
be divinely immortal and, thus, to receive worship from others. It is the
powerful connection between Phaedrus's yearning for base pleasures and
his craving for immortality that now moves the philosopher-poet Plato to
view the same argument twice in our dialogue, once from the standpoint
of the nymph who makes men pigs and once from the vantage point of
the nymph who sings beautifully of a deathless life. Phaedrus's wish to
be both Circe and Calypso, or to attain to eternal gratification of the base
passions and eternal adoration as a deity, at the expense of victims charmed
by words, is the essential aim of the democratic tyrannical eros. In his role
as Circe-Calypso, Phaedrus sings the song of this eros by "enchanting"
(καταφαρμακευθέντος, more literally, "sending down into the grave with
a *pharmakon*") Socrates' mouth so that he sings it to himself (242d11–e1),
thus tempting him to believe that he is the one who has an ability to extract gratification from others in a divinely immortal way. However, this
promise is no less false than the one that Calypso gave to Odysseus. A lot
of good it will do Socrates to have people burning incense before a dead,
golden image or memento of his body while that body molders in its grave
and his soul is lost.

We have gotten a little ahead of our story. These types of objections do not
occur to Socrates yet. As Socrates-Odysseus, he must face another ordeal.
He must embrace Phaedrus-Calypso erotically. Therefore, he is required
to experience attraction to his-her promise and to yield to her beautiful
song in act. In his lower soul, he must continue to desire the piggish pleasures and begin to covet the false immortality. Without losing the memory of his home and, therefore, without desiring the piggish delights and
the false immortality in a nobler part of his soul, he and his philosophic
shaman-poet Plato must both endanger their abilities to go home and suffer punishment for their vice, pining away like Odysseus shedding tears
on the shores of Ogygia. Therefore, Socrates haggles over the terms under which he will receive the gift of the golden image. He objects that his

speech could not be 100 percent different from that of Lysias. At least he must be permitted to claim that the non-erosing man is prudent, or wise, and the erosing man imprudent, or unwise. With regard to this particular, he demands to be praised for his superior rhetorical presentation, not the discovery. However, when he presents new ideas, he should be praised for both the presentation and the discovery. Phaedrus thinks that Socrates' objection is measured (that is, reasonable), so he makes a concession: Socrates may argue that the erosing man is "sicker" (236b1) than the non-erosing.

The bargain having been struck, Socrates gets cold feet and turns coy. Like Odysseus becoming unhappy as Calypso's captive, he is beginning to sense the enormity of his danger. He tells Phaedrus that he was only joking: he does not really have a speech superior to Lysias's production. Phaedrus compels Socrates to deliver his oration by swearing on the plane tree that unless Socrates speaks, he will never relate another speech to Socrates. Stricken, Socrates cries: "Oh woe! O blood-guilty one!" (ὦ μιαρέ, 236e4). He laments that Phaedrus has learned too well how to enslave a man who is sick with the love of discourse and yields.

Seth Benardete asserts that Socrates here "casually makes a plane tree into a god."[28] However, that is not quite what has happened. It is the will of Zeus that Socrates-Odysseus should undergo his ordeals. To enforce Zeus's sentence, the god in the tree has inspired his unwitting minion, Phaedrus-Calypso, to swear by the *axis mundi*. Socrates-Odysseus, who is only beginning to know himself, and who is therefore less attuned to the god in the tree than to his diseased desires, is equally inspired by the god to bow to an oath not on a "casually created god," but on the avenue of all divine communication with human beings in this world. The oath could be more solemn only if the person swearing it knew what he was doing.

Socrates has agreed to speak. However, he now says that he will veil his head as he speaks, so as not to be perplexed by the shame that looking at Phaedrus would cause. The veil has three functions. It symbolizes the divinely prescribed conditions of Socrates-Odysseus's ordeal, that he must yield to the temptations of Phaedrus-Calypso in act while not succumbing to them in desire, or, to put this differently, that he must crave the piggish pleasures and the false eternal life in a lower element of his soul while remaining mindful of his true home and ultimately ashamed of these wants in a nobler part of his psyche. As Planinc astutely notices, it also symbolizes with a sort of pun what is happening to Socrates-Odysseus right now.[29] The Greek term for "being veiled" that Plato chooses is ἐγκαλυψάμενος (237a4), in the pun, "en-Calypsoed," "engulfed by Calypso," as it were.

---

28. Benardete, *Rhetoric of Morality*, 119.
29. The rest of this paragraph follows Planinc, *Plato through Homer*.

Plato uses the same term for the veiling of Socrates' face after he has drunk the hemlock *pharmakon* and is dying (*Phaedo* 118a6). Spiritually, Socrates-Odysseus and the philosophic shaman-poet Plato are dying the death, being sent down into the grave by a *pharmakon*. Finally, the veil recalls the wrap that Ino gave to Odysseus on his raft, to shield him from Poseidon's wrath and bring him safely to Scheria. Zeus wants Socrates-Odysseus to survive and learn from his trial. This is why Socrates' daimon does not stop his first speech.[30]

The shrouded Socrates begins his oration by invoking the Muses, singing: "Come then, O Muses, whether you are called clear-voiced because of the form of your song or because of the musical tribe of the Ligurians. 'Take up with me' the story, being forced as I am to speak by this best of men, so that his comrade, who earlier seemed wise to him, now will seem yet wiser" (237a7–b1). Then he chants, in storybook fashion, that once upon a time there was a boy or, better, a stripling, a young man, who was exceptionally beautiful. This youth had many *erastai*. One of them was sly. He was erosing for the lad as much as anyone but had convinced him that he was not erosing for him. To persuade the youth that he should gratify the non-erosing (that is, the speaker, who is actually erosing) rather than the erosing, he gave the speech that will now be recounted.

This opening seemingly creates a great difficulty. On the one hand, the veiled Socrates invokes the Muses. On the other hand, he proceeds forthwith to the story of a lie and invents the lie in the story that the Muses supposedly sing through him. Not only that, but when he has finished speaking, he also charges that Phaedrus has been enchanting him to deliver the oration at the cost of his spiritual life (καταφαρμακευθέντος, sending him down into the grave with a *pharmakon*), and he asserts explicitly that his speech, like the accusations of Aristophanes that will lead to his physical death eight years hence, contained "nothing healthy or true" (μηδὲν ὑγιες . . . μηδὲ ἀληθὲς, 243e5–6). The problem is that this dramatic construction apparently makes the Muses responsible for poisoning Socrates and telling lies. There was a time when this would not have been shocking. Hesiod reports that the Muses' first words to him were: "Shepherds of the fields, creatures of evil disgrace, mere bellies, we know how to tell many lies that are similar to truths" (*Theogony* 26–28). However, it is just this sort of claim that motivates Socrates to denounce the poets. Muses are goddesses, daughters of Zeus. Socrates insists in the *Republic* that gods are the authors of no evil (379b–c) and tell no lies (382e). The Muses could not be responsible for poisoning Socrates and prevaricating. Plato, therefore, has caught himself in an arguably deliberate contradiction, the most sensible

---

30. Thus, the daimon is not "an easily detectible subterfuge," as Cropsey argues (*Political Philosophy*, 240).

resolution of which would be that the speech that Socrates is about to give is true, no matter that he exoterically declares it a lie.[31]

In my opinion, this difficulty is a fiction, an artifact of inexact exegesis. The Muses do not poison Socrates or tell lies. Nor do I contradict myself by trusting that the coming speech is completely false. We must observe the following points: Just for the record, it is Phaedrus, not Socrates, who invokes the Muses, for it is Phaedrus who speaks through Socrates' mouth. Phaedrus asks the Muses for proof that Lysias is even wiser than he originally believed. This would require Socrates either to deliver a speech that is formally inferior to Lysias's oration or to give a presentation that excels Lysias's exhibition in form but fails to outdo its rationality in the comprehensive coverage of needful arguments. The Muses do not grant Phaedrus's prayer. Socrates' hooded speech is superior to that of Lysias in both form and substance. Even worse for Phaedrus, and also for those who eagerly claim that Plato deliberately contradicts himself in a way that makes the coming oration true, the Muses slip something into their answer for which Phaedrus had not bargained, the preface that comes between the prayer and the speech proper. This preface announces to Phaedrus, Socrates, and the reader of the dialogue that the coming oration is a lie. When the Muses affirm that the upcoming speech is a lie and, in fact, it is a lie, then the Muses have told the truth. Presumably, they have done so in order to help Socrates-Odysseus overcome his addiction to the lie. Just as Odysseus had to swallow Circe's potion under a divine grant of immunity to its effects in order to become spiritually healthy, and just as Socrates-Odysseus had to listen to Lysias's *pharmakon* under the protection of his daimon as a means to his spiritual healing, so he must now undergo an even more powerful magic spell, another *pharmakon* that Phaedrus-Calypso charms him into casting on himself, in order to rid himself of his susceptibility to the evil magic. Socrates is once again protected by his daimon, who is not sleeping on guard duty. The operation is like a spiritual "vaccination" that causes death to renew life. It is true that the Muses administer poison. However, when a *pharmakon* is administered as a medicine that produces healing, the physicians who dispense it are doing good. Therefore, we should not let the entry of the Muses into the play deceive us into believing that Plato esoterically makes Socrates' first oration true.

Turning to his speech proper, Socrates addresses his hypothetical auditor with a respect that Lysias's speaker never showed to his addressee, using the vocative, "O boy" (237b7). This is already better calculated to win a favorable response than Lysias's gruff discourtesy. Socrates informs the youth that the ruling principle of wise deliberation is that one should know

31. For example, see Nussbaum, *Fragility of Goodness,* 202–3; Nussbaum follows earlier scholars in this, such as Hackforth.

what one is talking about. However, many people do not know that they are ignorant of the essences of things. This causes disagreement at the beginnings and ends of deliberations. The question at hand is whether the erosing or the non-erosing should be befriended. Hence, it is necessary to arrive at an adequate definition of eros, ascertaining what sort of thing it is and what its power is. Everyone sees that eros is a kind of desire *(epithymia)*. We also know that the non-erosing have desire (again, *epithymia*) for the beauties. Thus, it is openly declared that the distinction between the erosing and the non-erosing is not the presence or absence of *epithymia*. Ergo, it is necessary to discover the real difference. The gist of Socrates' argument will be that eros is irrational desire and that non-eros is rational desire. This means that Socrates quickly jettisons Lysias's absurd, self-defeating introductory lie, replacing it with a distinction that at least has a ring of plausibility. This, in turn, implies that Socrates' speech is more evil than Lysias's effort, for it makes Lysias's essential lie harder to detect. As in the first campaign in the *Symposium*, we are descending morally even as we ascend intellectually.

Socrates gets his distinction between irrational and rational desire by observing that in each person, there are two ruling and leading ideas, the desire of pleasures that is natural to us and an acquired (hence, unnatural) opinion that aims at "the best." Sometimes these principles agree, and sometimes they are in conflict. When opinion leads with reason to the best, its rule is called moderation—better translated as sane self-control (σωφροσύνη, *sophrosyne*). However, when desire without reason governs us, its sway is named hybris. Implicit in these assertions is the inference that all human beings are naturally drawn to pleasure by *epithymia* and that not all, but only those who unnaturally acquire reason, aim at what is best. The democratic impulses are being managed again so that they redound to the benefit of sophistical aristocrats. Socrates preserves Lysias's intent in this. Another point to notice is that Socrates neglects to define "the best" for which the reasonable are able to strive. He does not want to raise this question because his young man might get too curious about the assumption of his argument. This supposition is that the *only two* principles that govern human behavior are the natural desire for pleasure and an acquired reason. By logical extrapolation, this assumption means that reason, when present, must serve the desire for pleasure, for there is nothing else in man about which it could deliberate. "The best" is rationally maximized pleasure. Socrates walks softly here because he does not want his lad to ask whether there is more to life than a choice between stupid and enlightened hedonism.[32]

---

32. Thus, I think that Benardete obscures an important issue when he contends that Socrates' first speech is "wholly concerned with the good" (*Rhetoric of Morality*, 120).

Socrates now has good reason to be ashamed of his words. He has mis-appropriated the name of that noble virtue, *sophrosyne,* for one of its con-traries, rational hedonism. His lad has never learned that real *sophrosyne* recognizes higher goods and beauties. It perceives the pursuit of these greater goods and beauties to be its first priority. It also knows that hu-man beings are made to take pleasure in lesser goods and beauties, which, indeed, are goods and beauties, not intrinsic evils, and that this is its sec-ond priority. Its function is to prevent us from reversing our priorities. It directs us to pursue all goods, beauties, and pleasures in a way that pre-serves their proper hierarchy, so that we can attain to fulfillment in union with the higher and also possess the lower in ways that do not destroy our ability to reach the higher. (Thus, *sophrosyne* is not Puritanism.)[33] Soc-rates' shame is that he has just taught his youth that there are no nobler goods and beauties. He has perverted *sophrosyne* so that it aims not at our ordered enjoyment of both the (allegedly nonexistent) higher goods and the lower but, rather, at maximizing the pleasures of all the lower goods and beauties in manners that do not destroy our abilities to enjoy them all whenever we wish. For example, genuine *sophrosyne* would object to chronic drunkenness (but not to drinking) because it totally incapacitates us to fly up to Diotima's vision of beauty. The sophistical *sophrosyne* just preached by Socrates would discourage alcoholism because it spoils our ability to become wealthy, seduce beloveds who find drunks disgusting, savor fine foods, live longer lives, and the like. The stupid hedonism being denounced by the hooded Socrates would lack the sophistical *sophrosyne* and degenerate into chronic drunkenness. Rational, enlightened hedonism would be informed by the sophistical *sophrosyne* and enjoy all of the lower pleasures to the fullest always. Drunkenness would be acceptable up to the point at which it interferes with the other pleasures.

Having intimated this doctrine of *sophrosyne* to his ignorant lad, Socrates employs it to expand his definition of eros as hybris. He maintains that eros is the irrational hybris that stands to sex as gluttony stands to eating, drunkenness stands to drinking, and so on. Eros is desire without reason that masters the opinion that strives for what is right (the nature of the

---

The good, that is to say the ultimate good, in the *Republic* is definitely not pleasure, but a reality beyond being in dignity and power. Better to say that the oration is about a liar's conception of various goods.

33. Ferrari says that the anthropologies of Lysias and Socrates differ radically. The former is hedonistic, whereas the latter explicitly opposes pleasure as a whole to the notion of the good. Ferrari even says: "We have heard in Socrates' nonlover the voice of puritanism, by which I mean an automatic hostility towards pleasure as such, and an in-ability to integrate pleasure in an honest fashion with the pursuit of the good" (*Listening to the Cicadas,* 96, 99, 98). Ferrari fails to observe the exclusivity of the ruling principles to which Socrates appeals. He thus manages to make Socrates say the opposite of what he means in this context: pleasure *is* the good, but the wise pursue it intelligently.

right again being left to the youth to infer), leading toward the pleasure of the beauty of bodies and (according to a highly suspect etymology that Socrates here introduces) taking its name from a word for "force" because it tyrannically forces people toward the carnal pleasures. (Non-eros will later be defined as the opposite of eros. As we have seen, the non-erosing will be the opposites of the erosing not in the sense that they abjure the carnal pleasures, but in the sense that they are not forced toward them like stupid slaves, instead choosing them rationally and freely as their estimates of their goods dictate.) Eros is a brutish tyrant.

Having said this, Socrates appears to emerge temporarily from his trance. He asks his dear Phaedrus whether it seems that he has been afflicted with a divine pathos (θεῖον πάθος πεπονθέναι, tribulation or experience, 238c5–6). Phaedrus replies that he is speaking with an uncustomary good fluency. We are not surprised to learn that Phaedrus is normally not all that impressed by the speeches of Socrates but genuinely likes what he is hearing now. Socrates commands Phaedrus to listen silently, for the place appears to have a divine presence. Then he counsels Phaedrus not to wonder if he is soon in the throes of nympholepsy (νυμφόληπτος, seizure by nymphs, 238d1). He blames Phaedrus for his exposure to this danger, hopes that the attack may be averted, and piously sighs that it is in the hands of the god. We recall the nervous anticipation that Socrates had when he entered the grove, so that he neglected to extend manifest praise to the nymph statues. Now he is experiencing the death agony that the nymphs intend for him, for he is really already possessed by Circe and Calypso. Phaedrus is actually responsible, for he is Circe-Calypso and is charming Socrates so that he pronounces the speech. The onset of nympholepsy is truly in the hands of the god: Zeus wills this ordeal for Socrates-Odysseus. Plato inserts this interlude in his play because he wants to be sure that we understand the dramatic spiritual situation.

Socrates returns to his trance and his oration. He remarks: "So be it, O bravest one." It is not perfectly clear whether he is addressing himself (encouraging himself in his capacity as Odysseus to persevere in his trial) or addressing his lad (exhorting him to accept the rational consequences of their reasoning). Perhaps both. At any rate, he proceeds to draw conclusions from the premises that he has established. The topic is now the power and works of eros. He who is ruled by *epithymia* is a slave to pleasure and will try to make his *erōmenos* as pleasing to himself as possible. To the sick man, everything that does not oppose him is pleasant, but everything that is stronger or equal is hateful. Thus, the *erastēs* will not permit his darling to be stronger or equal but will strive to make him weaker and inferior. Accordingly, the *erastēs* will attempt to ensure that the *erōmenos* is unlearned, cowardly, dumb, and slow-witted. He will necessarily be jealous, too, and keep the *erōmenos* away from helpful associates, especially from the wise and divine philosophy. He will try to make his beloved's body soft, pale, lazy, and unfit for war. Further, he will strive to make his *erōmenos* dependent by impoverishing him and depriving him of his parents, relatives, and friends. He will not want the *erōmenos* to marry and have children (which bisexual Athenians such as Socrates usually did).

As if this were not enough, the *erastēs* is an unpleasant pest. People such as flatterers and courtesans at least have something pleasant about them, but not the *erastēs*. This scourge of a man cannot leave the *erōmenos* alone. He hounds him constantly, forcing his company on him. Necessity impels the *erastēs* always to desire to see, hear, and touch his darling. The *erōmenos* will inevitably get sick of his lover but will be unable to get rid of him. The ugly old face, the unmentionables of the aging body, the gushing excessive praises and intolerable reproaches, the slobbering drunkenness—what pleasure can the *erōmenos* take in all that? What, then, of the time when the *erastēs* has ceased from his desire? The hour has come for the nasty old coot to make good on his mighty oaths, but he cannot be found. He has recovered from his illness; he is now rational and moderate and hopes to renege on his promises. *Erastēs* and *erōmenos* change places. The latter becomes a pursuing debt collector and the former the pursued. By then, the *erōmenos* will have understood to his sorrow that he should have never gratified the *erastēs*, who is necessarily without *nous*, and that he ought to have gratified the non-erosing, who has *nous*. By yielding to the *erastēs*, he hands himself over to every kind of harm, especially including terrible harm to the nurture of his soul, for "as wolves love lambs, so do lovers befriend boys" (241d1).

We must pause to observe that Plato-Socrates has now finished an excellent portrait of the democratic tyrannical eros and its characteristic man. It is Phaedrus who has been talking. Speaking through Socrates, he has been pretending not to be erosing while he has really been erosing. Thus, in his denunciation of the *erastēs*, he has been pretending not to be describing himself while he has actually been describing himself. Now, in the mien of a corrupt archon, Phaedrus represents the depraved, tyrannical Athenian demos as a whole.[34] In his role as the democratic tyrannical man writ large, he experiences only the tyrannical eros in his soul. He accordingly equates his tyrannical eros with eros simply. In his persona as Circe-Calypso, he defines his tyrannical eros as a "natural" desire for pleasures that everyone must follow. It is a craving for eternal gratification of the lower appetites together with eternal adoration as a god.

I set "natural" in quotation marks because this tyrannical eros is actually a longing for pleasures most unnatural to a man. It is a passion for delights appropriate to a creature who is simultaneously a beast and a god and,

---

34. I owe this insight to Rosen, *Quarrel between Philosophy and Poetry*, 95.

hence, to a monster such as Typhon, but not for human beings who, according to Diotima, are naturally possessed of an eros that stands between gods and their prime natures. We become Typhon by joining the speeches of Lysias (Circe) and the veiled Socrates (Calypso) together. Phaedrus pretends to himself that as a "non-erosing" man, he is the master of his Typhonic *thymos* because he can maximize its pleasures rationally. However, this is not mastery, for he is still serving his desire for pleasure that he cannot resist. Far from being a master, he is only a slave who serves his master rationally. Under the lash of his inner tyrant, he strives to gratify his Typhonic cravings by tyrannizing over others. On the level of his personal relationships with his beloveds, he attempts to extract erotic pleasure from them, perhaps even love, without giving in return. He tries to secure this arrangement by means of rhetorical rape, in which he dupes his victims, sometimes with promises (as with Lysias), and always with sophistical arguments that yielding to him is the only rational thing to do. When he succeeds, he next reduces his darling to abject helplessness and dependence upon himself, so that the prey becomes totally incapable of resistance.[35] He will neither release the victim nor keep his promises unless he is forced by a god, just as Circe and Calypso were constrained by Hermes to let Odysseus leave. However, then he always goes back on his promises. On the level of Athens's relationships with allies, the tyrannical demos proceeds in exactly the same way. The alliances are founded on solemn guarantees and rational-choice arguments (this when the city has not raped polities forcibly, like Boreas). Soon Athens has sucked the physical and moral fiber from its victims and will neither let them secede from the alliance nor honor its pledges to grant them the greatest possible rational human freedom inside the union. The tyrant polis demands that its slaves minister to it constantly. The slaves grow weary but cannot escape.

It might be objected that it is contradictory for the tyrannical eros secretly describing itself to denounce itself as tyrannical. However, tyrants always attain to their positions of power by promising to deliver their victims from tyranny, pretending that they themselves are not what they are. It is absolutely in character for Phaedrus's democratic tyrannical eros to speak in this manner through his charmed Socrates. Further, a tyrannically inclined demos always screams bloody murder when a tyrant is tyrannizing over it. This demos intends to be free of masters so that it can become the master of others. This is the true telos of rational hedonism, Rawls with his fanciful veil of ignorance notwithstanding.

Socrates abruptly snaps out of his trance again and breaks off. He tells Phaedrus that his speech is finished. Phaedrus protests that the oration is

---

35. Cf. Benardete, *Rhetoric of Morality*, 124. On this point, Benardete is insightful.

only half finished; he is still owed an account of the case for gratifying the non-erosing. Socrates replies that if he continues, he will surely be possessed by the nymphs. He means forever. A half dose of the *pharmakon* is all that his soul can bear without expiring completely and hopelessly, so he must throw off the spell of Phaedrus-Calypso and escape. Therefore, if Phaedrus is interested, he may assume that the praises of the non-erosing are deduced by making all his qualities the opposites of those of the erosing. When pressed for an explanation of his default a while later, Socrates adds that both Lysias's speech and his own were *pharmakons,* that both were ridiculous, and that neither contained anything healthy or true. With this, he forfeits his golden idol.

After my summary of Lysias's oration, I stated that it was no mere straw man because it contained a certain worldly wisdom. Socrates' speech greatly improves upon Lysias's effort. It is better both formally and substantively. With respect to form, whereas Lysias's oration was disorganized and repetitive, Socrates' presentation is systematic, proceeding first to establish an agreement upon premises and then moving with inexorable logic from those assumptions to conclusions that compel the auditor's assent. In doing so, it never repeats anything until it reaches the peroration, in which the speaker is expected to provide a concise synopsis. With regard to substance, whereas Lysias's speech began with a lie so incredible that even a moron might dismiss it out of hand, Socrates' oration starts with the extremely plausible distinction between rational and irrational desire and uses it as a new, more solid foundation for all of the points that Lysias made, together with a few new ones. Accordingly, if Lysias's speech was no straw man, Socrates' amended version of it is positively formidable. This means that we have an obligation to make our own assessment of the truth of the two speeches.

The worldly wisdom of which the two orations may legitimately boast is encapsulated in the following propositions: There are no higher goods and beauties. Human life is nothing but physical and psychosomatic pleasure and pain. The point of our existence is to maximize the pleasure and minimize the pain. Reason is the handmaid of the passions. Everybody is on the make. In this situation, everybody ought to use reason to calculate his or her enlightened self-interest and conclude to choices that maximize the pleasure and minimize the pain. The rational self-control that can do this is the only *sophrosyne.* Erotic affairs, like all others, are subject to these rules. This worldly wisdom is formidable because it seems true to many that there are no higher goods and beauties. This granted, everything else follows. However, if there are higher goods and beauties, Socrates is right to say that the two speeches say nothing healthy or true. His task in the next section of the dialogue will be to convince Phaedrus, if he can, that there are higher goods and beauties. Being already persuaded of this myself, I also agree with Socrates that the two orations are lying *pharmakons* that lead us to our spiritual deaths.

This evaluation seems clearly correct to me but, apparently, not to others. By way of anticipating some important objections, I must take notice of a remarkable fact. In our time, many scholars appear absolutely zealous to dispute Socrates' judgment of the two speeches and thereby to bring Plato into secret or even open alignment with Lysias's position. Perhaps one should also say that their view has come to constitute a contemporary orthodoxy. Therefore, it is necessary to take a brief look at their opinions.

A number of commentators argue that the presence of the Muses and the failure of the daimon to interfere with Socrates' participation in the proceedings imply that Plato approves of Lysias's and Socrates' speeches. I have already disposed of that claim. Actually, the Muses and the daimon vindicate Socrates' judgment. We may move to different arguments.

Martha Nussbaum takes partial exception to Socrates' position, contending that Lysias's and the hooded Socrates' positions are not so much true as worthwhile, because they represent something that Plato once "seriously endorsed." We may assume that these opinions "merit the attention of an aspiring young person of . . . talent and beauty" for the following reasons: Plato never inveighs against straw men. The speeches are blamed "above all" for their naïveté. The Muses are present. It is a "real Platonic view" that eros is a madness and a disease. In the "middle dialogues," there are "ascetic arguments" that one must "not only attack the passions but also pretend that he himself is not a humanly erotic personality." For example, through Socrates, Plato has taught us in the *Republic* that one must rehearse arguments against eros as a countercharm against its spell. The recantation that is coming in the *Phaedrus* is therefore "a serious recantation of something that Plato has seriously endorsed." Further, there is value in the moral advice that Lysias and Socrates give to Phaedrus. Take an analogous case, that of a young woman in our culture entering a male-dominated profession. She would want to "live a full personal life" yet protect her "autonomy, her chance to live and work on reasonable and non-threatening terms" with her predominantly male colleagues. "If we imagine what a concerned feminist would say to such a young woman (or what she would say to herself) we will be on the way to understanding what is serious about Lysias." It is not surprising that a "young vulnerable person concerned with fame and autonomy" should find Lysias's proposal attractive: "We do not need to ask how most feminists would advise a female Phaedrus; and we know that, given a certain picture of the person in love, a picture that is true a good part of the time, they would be right." Lovers do love in the way that wolves love lambs. That is a good reason for the lambs to protect themselves as well as possible. The self-defense should be premised on the understanding that in no case should the person "go mad." When it comes to preserving sanity, we may judge that having sex in Lysias's spirit "might be, for some people, a very good way precisely of distancing oneself from its power and gaining intellectual control." It all depends on "the individual, the culture, the time of life."[36]

Stanley Rosen refers to Lysias's speaker as "that much and unjustly maligned character, the nonlover." Rosen recognizes that the nonlover is rather "base." However, in defense of his lowness, Rosen argues: "It is perfectly reasonable to claim that passion interferes with friendship, as well as with the pursuit of the useful, the just, and the true." The nonlover also praises the cardinal virtues and is eager "to improve the condition of his friend," help him separate pleasure from pain, teach him self-mastery, and show him how to balance justice with mercy. His argument is "a legitimate criticism of the general teaching of the *Symposium*," one reason for its rectitude being that "[t]he erotic man (as the *Symposium* asserts) is the most needy man. If one must gratify the most needy, then one must gratify the worst rather than the best." As for the "concealed lover" of Socrates' first speech, he represents Plato's partial remedy for "the defectiveness of the Platonic position when viewed from a Hegelian perspective." Philosophy is, or ought to be, "vision *and* speech," indeed, "speech of the whole." However, the *Symposium* has "no adequate account of speech." Further, Socrates' second speech in the *Phaedrus* appeals to an erotic madness that is silent. Perhaps it is all well and good that vision should be silent, but there must be speech, and it must be sane: "Philosophical speech requires a detachment from erotic madness." Hence, we may not simply "equate Eros and philosophy, as the *Symposium* apparently does," and, one might add, as Socrates' second speech in the *Phaedrus* does. It is also the case that the philosophic speech, in order to be speech, may not be mythical, this being another "lucid illustration" of the defectiveness of Plato's erotic position. So, there is a great need for a rehabilitation of the nonlover. The concealed lover provides that by treating love with the requisite detachment from erotic madness. Therefore, a "philosophical nature must combine the natures of the lover and the nonlover." This implies that the speeches of Lysias and the shrouded Socrates necessarily belong to Platonic philosophy as something like the first two moments in a Hegelian triad. They are "true" in this sense. Taking the orations as such true moments, we can close all of the speeches in the *Phaedrus* into a circle that has attained to completeness. It is only in this Hegelian way that they may enter public discourse.[37] One could adduce several more defenses of Lysias and the shrouded Socrates, but these suffice to illustrate the main types. I cannot engage in extensive rebuttals, but I shall say a little about Nussbaum and Rosen.

36. Nussbaum, *Fragility of Goodness*, 202–3, 207–10.
37. Rosen, *Quarrel between Philosophy and Poetry*, 78, 90, 93, 97, 93, 91, 98.

First Nussbaum. The Plato of the *Republic* is not so stupid as to make a human being a disembodied reason without passions. Nor does he recommend or demand attacks upon the passions. The Plato of the *Phaedrus* does not recant such a position. Nor does he evict reason from too high a pedestal and raise the passions from too low a place. Plato's view, or, at least, Socrates' idea, of the proper hierarchical relationship between reason and passion is consistent across the two works. There is no evident "development of Plato's ideas."

The differences that Nussbaum thinks she sees are dramatic artifacts. In the *Republic*, Socrates is concerned to take Glaucon's aristocratic tyrannical eros down a few notches, thus necessitating a lengthy dialectical discussion of Glaucon's self-serving concepts of the merits of an unphilosophic reason and the delights of power, wealth, and sex, whereas, in the *Phaedrus*, Socrates is concerned to elevate Phaedrus's base appetites, thus requiring a lengthy examination of his low erotes. The orations of Lysias and the veiled Socrates are not straw men, but this is because they are tempting, not because Plato ever thought them worthwhile. In the *Phaedrus*, the first two speeches are blamed "above all" not for their *naïveté* but for their impiety and mendacity. It is a "real Platonic view" that the *tyrannical* eros is a *diseased* madness but that the *Socratic* eros is a *divine* madness. I am sorry to hear, and hope that it is not true, that "most feminists" would transmit Lysias's advice to a beautiful, talented young woman entering a male-dominated profession, for I think that these hypothetical feminists would be setting their protégée up for victimization, not for intellectual control and freedom from the power of eros, which was the vain dream of Socrates' *sympotai* in the year 416. Freedom from the power of eros does not exist. I also think that they would be educating her to live within the same limited horizons that Phaedrus-Circe-Calypso inhabits.

Nussbaum's "full personal life," "fame," and "autonomy" appear to be psychosomatic pleasure coupled with a quasi-divine domination of all the conditions affecting one's existence. I prefer the *sophrosyne* of Socrates and have been well served by depending on another's love for my fulfillment. It is particularly regrettable in this connection that Nussbaum maintains that "a good part of the time" lovers do love as wolves love lambs. With Socrates, I would reply that lovers *never* love like that. It is sad that Nussbaum thinks she has evidence to the contrary, for she has confused two identities dangerously: It is Lysias's nonlover, not the real lover, who is the wolf to the lamb.

In Rosen's case, we remember that he wants to be a god. He dislikes Diotima's saying that Eros is needy because gods (the "best" men) are supposed to be self-sufficient, not needy (the "worst" men). He insists upon defining philosophy as vision plus nonmythical speech of the whole because a god cannot be a god without being both the idea and the logos.

Like his real teacher, the writer to whom he appeals as the measure of Plato, namely, Hegel, he rejects philosophy that does not dispense with myth, that does not attain to a complete logographic account of the whole, and that does not transform the thinker into a divine idea-logos. His critique of the *Symposium* means that he objects to the dialogue's failures to deify the author. His claim that philosophy cannot be simply identical with eros (qua divine madness) has the same connotation. His reason must be its own ground, its own place, so it must not lack full control of itself, as erotic madness does. This requires him to undertake the project of making the lover into the nonlover and praising the truths of the nonlover. His effort to co-opt Plato for his project forces him to have Plato say the opposite of what he says: the orations of Lysias and the shrouded Socrates contain "nothing healthy or true." As for the notion that it is true that passion interferes with friendship, I repeat that this depends on whether we are discussing tyrannical or Socratic passion. Furthermore, if Rosen really thinks that the nonlover is serious about teaching his friend the cardinal virtues, improving his condition, giving him pleasure without pain, educating him to self-mastery, and balancing justice with mercy, I have a bridge that he might like to buy.

Socrates rises to take his departure from Phaedrus. I intend to follow him, leaving the beautiful Phaedrus-Lysias-Circe-Calypso in the grove with his apologists. However, we must return immediately to Phaedrus as Nausicaa.

8

PHAEDRUS: MUSICAL EROS

Socrates-Odysseus is afraid that he will fall victim to nympholepsy forever. He jumps up, announces his departure, and begins to escape across the Ilissus. Phaedrus-Calypso pleads with him. Phaedrus observes that it is almost noon and begs him to stay so that they can talk over what has been said, waiting until it is cooler before they leave. Phaedrus's intentions are erotic, in two senses. Phaedrus believes, like Calypso in the *Odyssey,* that the magic spell of the promise of immortality might still suffice to keep Socrates as a partner who will revel over the speeches of the alleged nonlovers. The desire for self-deification is an extremely powerful tyrannical eros indeed. Homoerotic sex is probably also on Phaedrus's agenda, just as Calypso has daily lovemaking in mind in Homer's poem. It is not only the weather that is hot when people fall into Corybantic frenzies. It is, though, precisely the combination of sexual lust with the delusion that one can become immortal through clever speech that Socrates-Odysseus fears as spiritually lethal. It is not for nothing that he wants to flee.

As Socrates starts to cross the Ilissus, the dramatic scene is transformed. Spiritually, we have arrived in the land of the Phaeacians. Socrates is the Odysseus who has washed up on the banks of the river. Phaedrus is now Nausicaa, dreaming of a mate. Socrates-Odysseus opens a new conversation by remarking that Phaedrus is simply divine with regard to speeches, just as Odysseus addresses Nausicaa, whose speeches reflect divine wisdom, with the speculation that she could be divine. Socrates expresses amazement that Phaedrus has inspired more speeches than anyone but Simmias of Thebes. He declares that he will speak yet another that Phaedrus has now caused. Phaedrus has been regarding the suddenly truculent Socrates uncertainly, just as Nausicaa stands uncertainly (but courageously) before the wild-looking Odysseus, probably wondering whether she will be offered violence. When Phaedrus learns that another oration is in the offing, he sighs with relief that Socrates is at least not declaring war, just as Nausicaa feels reassured when Odysseus breaks into respectful speech.[1]

As Zvradko Planinc has argued, Plato now begins to refigure the Homeric trope of the meeting of Odysseus and Nausicaa. In the *Odyssey*, the hero blames the gods for his afflictions. He is corrected by Nausicaa.[2] Then he is led by Nausicaa to a sheltered spot on the river to bathe. The bath begins his purification, which continues with the later tales of his adventures recited by Demodocus and himself. It is these narratives that finally move him to tears of contrition. Plato reworks these materials as follows.

In the *Phaedrus*, when Socrates tries to leave, he does not set foot in the stream. He explains that his daimon has stopped him. The daimon always holds him back when it objects to a course of action that he proposes to take. Socrates states further that he thought he heard a voice tell him that he could not leave without cleansing himself of a sin of omission, as if he were guilty of some wrong against the god. He claims that he "really" is a prophet, although not a serious one, being good enough only for his own purposes. He understands his misdeed. The soul is prophetic, for it disturbed him when he was giving the speech of the lying lover, as if he were wronging the gods in exchange for honor from human beings. A few lines later, he concludes that he must purify himself by delivering a palinode. In the course of the palinode, which in part is a mythical odyssey of his psyche, he speaks of having waters of inspiration from Zeus poured over his soul. Hence, Socrates' cleansing reverses the order of Odysseus's purification. In Odysseus's case, the water bath comes first, the stories of his journeys second, and the sorrow third. In Socrates-Odysseus's case, the repentance is first, the story of his soul's adventures second, and the immersion in purifying spiritual waters third. The reversal, with the ascent from physical waters to the waters of Zeus, probably marks Plato's perception that the shaman-philosopher rises higher than the Homeric shaman-poet in their travels along the *axis mundi*. It also seems to represent the judgment that a penitent recognition of guilt is only the beginning of a soul's ascension to its ultimate telos.

We must stress that in the speech just reported, Socrates refers to himself as a prophet (μάντις, 242c4) and to his soul as prophetic (μαντικόν, 242c7). Thus, he openly assumes the role that, in the *Symposium*, he assigns to the probably fictitious Diotima. This is a cue that we should expect Socrates'

1. My account of the dramatic scene is still working within the framework established in the manuscript of the forthcoming book by Planinc, *Plato through Homer.* This paragraph and the next two follow Planinc closely.
2. The correction is not that the gods have no responsibility for Odysseus's trials, but that Zeus gives good fortune to good men and bad, as he wills. The implication is that Odysseus should regard it as a blessing that Zeus has given him this lot. Deserved punishment is good fortune.

palinode to be an equivalent symbolization of Diotima's ascent of the ladder of beauty. This obliges us to face directly a question that we handled summarily in our study of the *Symposium*. In the oration that he is about to deliver, Socrates ranks souls according to merit, that is, according to the degree of truth that they saw in their previous lives as not-yet-embodied spirits struggling to see the hyperuranian realities (248c9–e2). The hierarchy is as follows, from highest to lowest: (1) a philosopher or a lover of beauty, or a musical and erotic individual; (2) a lawful king or warlike ruler; (3) a statesman, household manager, or financier; (4) a lover of gymnastic labor or a doctor for the body; (5) a prophet or celebrant of mysteries; (6) a poet or other mimetic artist; (7) a craftsman or farmer; (8) a sophist or demagogue; and (9) a tyrant. Why does Socrates, a philosopher, assume the guise of an inferior person? Why does he, perhaps, even take on the role of a superstitious believer in revelations that are purely imaginary? Should we not agree with G. W. F. Hegel and Stanley Rosen that this strategy taints his philosophy?

I can reply by saying more fully what I said in my analysis of the *Symposium*. Socrates asserts in his discussion of the ranks that if the souls aloft catch even the barest glimpses of the hyperuranian truths, they become human beings rather than beasts when they fall to earth in newly acquired bodies (248c–d). This means that every person in every rank has at least some access to truth, or that every individual has at least a latent memory of hyperuranian realities, if not an active one. The philosopher Socrates has seen and recalls more of the hyperuranian truths than the people on the levels below him. He knows what these individuals know (or should know) plus more. Consequently, he may speak as a prophet without embarrassment if he confines his pronouncements to the genuine truths to which prophets have access.

This is not all that needs to be said. If the lower ranks have access to real knowledge, their ways of knowing are valid. A philosopher can know philosophically, regally, politically, medically, prophetically, poetically, and so on (but poets, prophets, doctors, statesmen, and kings cannot know philosophically without becoming philosophers). When the philosopher knows realities regally, politically, medically, prophetically, and poetically, he is probably required to know them in these very manners, this well enough for his own aims. When he knows the things of prophecy, for example, he must be and think like a prophet. Socrates is telling the truth about what he "really" is. This explains why, in the *Republic*, Socrates asserts that no one who lives under a bad regime can be saved without "a god's dispensation" (θεοῦ μοῖραν, 493a1–2). Without any evident human teaching or cause, a soul resists evil, as Plato's soul did in the Athens that murdered Socrates (see my analysis of this event in Chapter 3, regarding *Seventh Letter* 324d). Without visible grounds, Socrates' soul opposes the wickedness of his first speech. Socrates, who hears a voice calling for his palinode, undoubtedly attributes this to a god's dispensation and, hence, calls it prophetic. The call that permits him to oppose the evil is mysterious but not superstitious because it is experienced, not conjectured. It does not taint his philosophy as a Hegel, a Kant, or a Rosen claims but, rather, underpins it.

This is still not all that needs to be said. It will be observed below that Socrates speaks his palinode as Stesichorus, who is described as musical. However, a music soul belongs to the first rank of souls. A prophet who is musical is essentially philosophic. Socrates is not the lower type of prophet but the higher. We shall hear a musical view of eros. Hence, we shall expect philosophic insight as we trace Socrates' reaction to his prophetic call, which comes to his soul just before noon, triggering a further ascent that will begin at noon.

Phaedrus wonders what was wrong with Socrates' first speech. Socrates replies that it was terrible, terrible, because it was simpleminded and impious. He asks Phaedrus whether he believes Eros to be the son of Aphrodite and a god. Phaedrus replies evasively: "So it is said." It has been clear for some time that Phaedrus believes not in gods, but in rhetorical references to gods that facilitate his self-deification. Socrates answers that neither Lysias's speech nor his own first oration (which Phaedrus uttered through his mouth that he sent down to the grave with a *pharmakon*) calls Eros a god. However, Eros is, indeed, "a god or something divine" (θεὸς ἤ τι θεῖον, 242e2). The naïveté, or simplemindedness, of Socrates' first speech thus lies not in some notion that human beings can live without passion but in its underrating of the divinity of Eros. I note that Socrates' formula does not directly contradict Diotima's characterization of Eros: a daimon could be less than a god but still "something divine," as the son of a divine father and a mother who is a primordial human nature.[3] Socrates continues by saying that as a god or something divine, Eros could not be bad, but the two previous speeches depicted him as evil. This, again, was of the essence of their simplemindedness: the two orations were quite urbane, but they said "nothing healthy or true" in their effort to get reputation among human beings deceptively by imputing evil to Eros. Therefore, Socrates must deliver a palinode.

Socrates has described the inspiration of his new speech as prophetic. Now he moves to a further delineation of its nature. He claims that there is an ancient purification for those who have erred in the narration of myths.

---

3. The genealogy of Eros is not important in the *Phaedrus*. Socrates drops the subject as soon as he has put his question to Phaedrus. He is simply probing to see whether Phaedrus still takes the same position that he held nine years ago. He does not. He does not even care enough about his earlier argument to insist that Eros is an epiphenomenon of Earth.

The poets Homer and Stesichorus both made the mistake of speaking ill of Helen, with the consequence that both were stricken blind. Homer failed to discern the cause of his problem and did not know the remedy. Stesichorus did grasp what had gone wrong and did know the purification. Apparently unlike Homer, Stesichorus was "musical" (243a6).[4] Therefore, he wrote a palinode, opening with the line "this speech is not true" and denying that Helen went to Troy. His sight was restored immediately.

Socrates will strive to be wiser than the poets. He will give his palinode before evil can befall him. He will speak with his head bare, not veiled for shame as it was earlier. Later, he announces that whereas his original oration was by Phaedrus of Myrrhinus, son of Pythocles, his next one is by Stesichorus, son of Euphemus of Himera. There is important symbolism in these names. The speech will not be the offspring of Eager for Fame (Pythocles) from Myrrh Town. That is, it will not spring from libidos for glory and hedonistic delights that one might associate with myrrh, a resin used in perfumes, cosmetics, and *pharmakons*. Instead, it will be the child of Speaking Well (Euphemus, the Hellenic term for the opposite of blasphemy) from Yearning Town, that is, from a desire *(himeros)* that differs from *epithymia* and that will soon be connected with Zeus. It will be opposite to the first speech in every way. It will also be not only prophetic, but poetic as well. We shall hear a prophetic, poetic account of eros.

This raises a question like the one that we just considered. Why should Socrates take on the guise of a poet? It seems especially strange that Socrates should stoop to this when he says in the *Republic* (607b5) that "there is an old quarrel between philosophy and poetry." May we not now declare certainly that Socrates is adulterating philosophy by mixing it with poetry and its myths? Why does Socrates do this?

To be sure, much has been made of the "quarrel between philosophy and poetry."[5] I do not wish to spend much time on it, however, for I think that the quarrel has been grossly overblown. What I argued about prophecy above stands as well for poetry. In addition, it is necessary to observe—again—that the best souls in Socrates' hierarchy are "a philosopher or a lover of beauty, or a musical and erotic individual" (φιλοσόφου ἢ φιλοκάλου ἢ μουσικοῦ τινὸς καὶ ἐρωτικοῦ, 248d3–4). Socrates has called Stesichorus "musical." Therefore, the poet Stesichorus is on the same level as a philosopher, just as Socrates puts himself in the same rank as a good poet in the *Phaedo* when he surmises that he has always been practicing the "greatest music" by philosophizing (60e6–61a4). Philosophers do not have monopolies on the truth. It is plain that musical poets perceive as much as

---

4. I think that this judgment of Homer is intended to be valid only in the context of the cock-and-bull story that Socrates is feeding Phaedrus.

5. Especially by Rosen in *Quarrel between Philosophy and Poetry,* chap. 1.

philosophers and that the lover of beauty (the *philokalos*) and the erotic person see as much, too. In fact, the three or four types are probably identical. Socrates seems to prefer one or another of the names for them depending on which manifestation of their common nature commands his attention at the moment. After all, it is arguable that Socrates himself is supremely philosophic, beauty-loving, musical, and erotic.[6] It is clear, therefore, that there is not a feud between philosophy and poetry as such but, rather, a dispute between philosophy and unmusical poetry. There is not even a quarrel between Plato and Homer but, perhaps, one between Plato and some unmusical lines in Homer. Those who misapprehend the issue should have heeded Eric Voegelin's words: "The classification shows definitely that the conflict in the *Republic* is not a quarrel between 'philosophy and poetry' in the modern meaning of the words, but the conflict between the poets of the decaying Hellenic society and the true poet of the newly discovered realm of the soul, who is a twin brother of the philosopher, if not identical with him."[7]

As for the reason that Socrates opts to speak as a poet, we do not have to guess what it is. Socrates tells us. In the prayer to Eros with which he ends his speech, Socrates says that it had to be couched in poetic terms because of Phaedrus (257a4–6). This is a pedagogical point. Socrates is interested in improving his friend's soul. Phaedrus is a sophist. Intellectually, the first step in his reform would be to elevate him past the level of a craftsman and up to the rank of a poet. In the *Symposium,* when Socrates wanted to better Agathon, he spoke to this poet from a position one rank above him, that of a prophet. Now, when Socrates hopes to correct Phaedrus, he teaches him from the position to which he hopes to raise him, that of a poet.

Phaedrus-Nausicaa answers Socrates' announcement of his new speech by calling it the most pleasurable thing he has said. Phaedrus is laboring under the same illusion as Nausicaa, that the polite salutations they received from Socrates and Odysseus imply that they are about to win the mates for whom they have yearned. As a comic, corrupt Nausicaa,

---

6. It seems to me that Rosen ignores the equivalence of philosophy, music, love of beauty, and eroticism when he makes Socrates erotically defective and also when he inquires, despairingly, "whether philosophy is possible" (ibid., vii). He envisages a wholly logical, mathematical, unpoetic knowledge that he would like to possess because of its great certainty. He defines this mathematical understanding a priori and un-Platonically as "philosophy." Then, when he discovers "the primary unity between philosophy and poetry" in Plato, he is disappointed and calls it "the triumph of poetry" (xi–xii, 187). He is right about the primary unity. However, he is looking at the triumph of the human spirit in a philosophy that *is* poetry and a poetry that *is* philosophy, not a triumph of poetry that calls philosophy into question. This is a good example of Rosen's tendency to project the aspirations of the Enlightenment back onto Plato anachronistically.

7. Voegelin, *Order and History*, 3:138–39.

Phaedrus is also running a grave risk that the quasi-divine princess did not face. He should not be experiencing pleasure right now, but fear of the retribution that was meted out to Homer and Stesichorus. In fact, he is already suffering that fate spiritually for having thought and spoken evil of Eros. His hedonistic attitude betrays that he does not care about the truth or falsity of the speeches. Like his sophistical instructor, Lysias, he appreciates every well-honed oration for its power to persuade. He probably believes that the speeches of Lysias and the shrouded Socrates already constitute a formidable arsenal of weapons of seduction and that the coming piece by Socrates will complete his collection, being useful for enticing beloveds who are resistant to praises of the non-erosing and denunciations of eros.

Socrates is horrified. He tries to correct Phaedrus. He observes that the two previous discourses were shameless. Then he asks Phaedrus whether a man of "well-born and gentle character" (243c3) who heard those orations would not imagine that he was listening to sailors who had never seen an eros worthy of free men. The question is not so much an expression of class snobbery by Socrates as a reference to the beliefs of the unreformed Odysseus, a sailor. Phaedrus is stirred by the question briefly. He exclaims: "Maybe, by Zeus, O Socrates!" It is hard to tell whether Phaedrus's excitement owes to a sudden prick of shame or the realization that he cannot seduce noblemen with the same appeals that dupe the gullible many. Socrates wants Phaedrus to be ashamed and fearful, like himself. Hence, he reemphasizes these aspects of his new speech. He states that he feels shame before the well-born and gentle character and fear before Eros. Accordingly, he wants to wash away the brine of what they have heard with a fresh logos. He advises Lysias to follow his example. Lysias ought to argue that "in like manners," one must gratify the erosing rather than the non-erosing. Socrates' references to shame, brine, and washing directly parallel Odysseus's shame, his need to be cleansed of brine, and his freshwater bath in Homer's poem.[8]

Phaedrus affirms that when Socrates has praised the lover, he will necessarily compel Lysias to write a speech about the same topic. Socrates replies that he believes this, as long as Phaedrus is who he is. Socrates has undoubtedly answered with his eyes rolling heavenward and with a long sigh. Phaedrus still does not intend to get Lysias to make the right argument. He still believes that Socrates' new oration will be another weapon in his arsenal. He thinks that it would be advantageous to have Lysias supply him with yet another. As the incarnation of the libido of the democratic tyrannical eros, he is sure that he can force Lysias, the logos of the democratic tyrannical eros, to do his bidding. He can, too. It is true that he will compel Lysias to speak "about the same thing" as long as he is who he

8. These essentially are Planinc's insights.

is, but he will induce Lysias to write a speech conducive to his hedonistic advantage. This prospect will hold unless Socrates can convince Phaedrus that there is a good higher than pleasure.

Socrates is ready to start. He asks where his boy is, the one to whom he was speaking. Phaedrus answers that he is right beside Socrates, always there when he wishes. This could be a reference to an imaginary youth. However, some scholars believe that Phaedrus is pointing to himself. I am prepared to accept either alternative. If Phaedrus is referring to himself, he is offering Socrates a love match premised on the false assumption that he can have Socrates on his own sophistical terms. Nausicaa imagines that she can have Odysseus on her terms, too. It was never the case that Phaedrus was always at Socrates' side, however, and it will not be true in the future. Phaedrus and Socrates will part at the end of the dialogue. By then, Phaedrus will have found that he cannot obtain what he wants from Socrates, just as Nausicaa discovers that Odysseus will not be her husband.

Socrates opens with prolegomena that do not belong to his speech proper, namely, the identification of the authors of his two orations, Phaedrus and Stesichorus. Surprisingly, one generally expected thing is missing from these preludes, an invocation of the Muses. Socrates began his first speech with such a prayer. Actually, it is better to say that Phaedrus started out this way, for he was the real speaker. However, why does the new oration lack such an invocation? Is Socrates-Stesichorus less pious than Phaedrus? Do we have here an esoteric indication that philosophy, as represented by Socrates' second speech, silently rejects piety or divine help?

In reply, I agree that Socrates is something of a religious revolutionary. However, it is wrong to infer that his radicalism repudiates piety. On the contrary, it moves toward an even greater piety than that of the poets. Socrates signals his commitment to the superior piety by abandoning the old method of demonstrating piety, the invocation of the Muses, and speaking later of his new manner of showing it. In his fanciful story of the cicadas (258b ff), he asserts that the insects report to the Muses who among the human beings honors them. Some cicadas tell Calliope and Urania of "those who spend their time in philosophy and so honor the music of those two" (259d4–5). Socrates thus indicates that he has no need to invoke the Muses at the beginning of a philosophic myth because his entire way of life honors the philosophic Muses. He consciously intends that his every question and argument should venerate them. This is what it is to be musical. With this, we may turn to the substance of Socrates' second speech.

To analyze Socrates' second oration properly, one must grasp his intention in giving it and work up an accurate outline of it. If one fails either of these tasks, one opens the door to a great deal of exegetical mischief. Understanding Socrates' intention is a simple matter of allowing his speech to be what he says it is. Socrates has stated in advance that his prophetic soul has inspired him to deliver a palinode. He will assert retrospectively that after classifying types of madness, his oration described eros with a likeness that achieved "some truth, perhaps" (265b7), maybe along with some error, thus blending in a measured way "a not wholly incredible logos" (265b8) with "a playfully sung mythic hymn" (265c1). So, the talk is a playful, prophetic-poetic palinode and hymn in which nothing purports to be serious or wholly true. It is not intended as "science" in Enlightened modernity's sense of the word. Socrates means it to be superior to that.

These facts eliminate the possibility of certain esoteric interpretations of the second speech. For example, Seth Benardete argues at length how Socrates "proves" that soul is deathless and self-moving in a manner that suggests that "if the soul is indeed self-moving, Socrates cannot prove that it necessarily moves another." From this he infers, "The good or final cause is silently denied."[9] However, the proof of the soul's immortality and self-moving nature belongs not only to the things that are playfully spoken, but to the part of the speech that is said to be "not entirely incredible," from which we should deduce that it is mostly incredible insofar as it is intended as myth, not literal fact. It is a mock demonstration. As such, this proof provides no foundation for esoteric, nihilistic inferences about final causality and the good.

It is relevant to notice that the Socrates who is not yet a "serious" prophet reminds us of the Plato of the Seventh Letter who has written nothing concerning that about which he is serious because the serious is not a spoken thing (341c1–6). The Socrates of the *Phaedrus* will say soon that he must dare to tell the truth, inasmuch as he is speaking about truth (247c4–5). However, the truth that he proposes to tell will deal with ineffable realities and will be what a philosopher knows when he is prophetic-poetic. It will necessarily be uncertain and playful, even as it is true.

Because Socrates' second oration is a palinode, its structure will be dictated by that of the speech that is being recanted. One could say that the oration of the shrouded Socrates had the following organization: (1) an assumption, supplied by Phaedrus, that madness or unreason is a disease and, hence, an unmitigated evil; (2) an anthropology, or psychology, that analyzed the grounds of madness and of sane happiness in the human soul; (3) a denunciation of eros as madness; (4) an analysis of the evils of gratifying lovers; and (5) a lecture on the advantages of gratifying the nonerosing (undelivered, except for a brief statement that favoring nonlovers yields benefits opposite to the disadvantages of gratifying lovers). Given that the palinode is a recantation, one would expect it to have the following corresponding structure: (1) a denial that madness is always an unrelieved evil and an affirmation that some insanities are great goods; (2) an anthro-

9. Benardete, *Rhetoric of Morality*, 134–36.

pology, or psychology, that elucidates the grounds of felicitous madness and harmful sanity; (3) a definition of a true love that manifests the beneficial madness and a contrasting portrait of a false eros that arises from the injurious sanity; (4) an encomium on the advantages of gratifying true lovers; and (5) a warning about the evils of consorting with the enlightened, hedonistic "nonlovers" who pretend not to be in the grip of *epithymia.*

Socrates does organize his palinode along these lines. However, his prophetic vision requires a somewhat more complicated form than the one just elaborated. Following Plato's customary method, Socrates embeds the needed plan in the text of his speech, remarking at nearly every turn: "Now we must do such and such," or giving other plain indications. One must keep Socrates' outline in mind to prevent disastrous misinterpretations of the twists and turns of the reasoning. Thus, I shall present the plan in its entirety here, as follows.

I. Thesis of the Palinode (244a3–5)
II. The Blessings of Madness (244a4–245c2)
    A. Divinely Inspired Unerotic Manias (244a8–245b1)
        1. Manic prophecy (244a8–244d5)
        2. Manic escape from guilt (244d5–245a1)
        3. The mania sent by the Muses to poets (245a1–8)
    B. Divinely Inspired Erotic Mania (245b1–c2)
        1. What a rational-choice hedonist must prove about love (245b1–6)
        2. What Socrates must prove about erotic madness (245b7–c1)
        3. Who will reject and who will believe Socrates' proof (245c1–2)
III. Proof that Erotic Madness Is a Divine Blessing (245c2–250c6)
    A. The Truth about Soul: How It Is Acted Upon and Its Works (245c2–246a2)
        1. Soul perpetually self-moved, the source of all motion (245c5–246a2)
        2. Soul ungenerated and immortal (245c2–246a5)
    B. The Form of Soul (246a3–b4)
        1. The need for a simile (245a4–6)
        2. Two winged horses and a charioteer (246a6–7)
        3. Divine and human horses (246a7–b4)
    C. Why Living Beings Are Called Mortal and Immortal (246b5–d7)
        1. The task and activity of all soul (246b6–7)
        2. Winged ascent, wingless descent (246b7–c2)
        3. The embodiment of wingless soul as mortality (246c2–6)
        4. How we imagine god (246d1–2)
    D. Why Soul Loses Its Wings (246d2–248d1)
        1. The natural function of wing (246d6–7)

A. Restatement of Intention of the Palinode (257a3–6)
B. Prayer that Socrates' Art of Eros and Sight Will Be Spared (257a6–8)
C. Prayer for the Esteem of the Beautiful (257a8–9)
D. Prayers against Lysias, for Lysias, and for Phaedrus (257b1–6)

It is clear from this outline, and it will become even more plain with an analysis of the argument, that Socrates' second speech is a prophetic correction of the errors of his first one, just as he promises. Its organization is simple and straightforward. Part II on "The Blessings of Madness" is the expected denial of the lying lover's thesis that insanity is an utter disaster. Part III, the "Proof that Erotic Madness Is a Divine Blessing," is the anticipated anthropology, or psychology, that illuminates the grounds of felicitous madness and harmful sanity. However, the anthropology-psychology necessitates a theology and an ethics attuned to the order of being. These three studies further require myths of destiny and memory. Thus, Socrates is forced to expand this section well beyond the narrow confines of the Lysian anthropology. Part IV, on "Unnatural and Natural Loves," is the expected redefinition of erotic love. Parts V and VI are the anticipated reversals of the claims for erosing and non-erosing. Part VI on the nonlover is quite short; it mirrors the brevity of the hooded Socrates' praises of this character. The final prayers to Eros seek the god's mercy and favor.

This analysis of Socrates' plan forecloses additional possibilities of esoteric exegesis of the second speech. For example, Seth Benardete argues that the address is organized as follows: (1) kinds of madness (243e9–245c4); (2) soul as self-motion (245c5–246a2); (3) chariot (246a3–d5); (4) wing (246d6–247c2); (5) hyperuranian beings (247c3–249d3); (6) beauty and wing (249d4–252c2); (7) soul types (252c3–253c6); (8) chariot (253c7–257a2); and (9) the erotic art (257a3–b6).[10] Three remarks about this interpretation and its esoteric strategies are in order.

First, Benardete pays virtually no attention to Socrates' own comments about his plan. This allows him to elevate some subsections of the speech into major parts of it. For instance, the supposed part 2 on "soul as self-motion" is not its own entity at all, but the first segment of a proof to the effect that erotic madness is a divine blessing, as witness the fact that Socrates first proposes to show this and then takes up the analysis of the soul with the words: "Here is the beginning of the proof" (254c4). Benardete ignores this part of the demonstration because he thinks that its thesis is esoterically repudiated by "the very structure of the *Phaedrus*." However, he is appealing to a structure of the *Phaedrus* that he himself is substituting for Socrates' stated plan after having dismissed it as untrustworthy. His reasoning therefore looks suspiciously circular. Benardete's other sections

10. Ibid., chap. 10.

are removed from the contexts in which Socrates places them in similar ways, without argument that Socrates' own headings do not deserve to be treated as the real ones. Benardete also factors sections into the oration that Socrates never envisaged. For example, Socrates does not devote any space at all to "chariot," let alone two parts. Socrates also has no section on "the erotic art," which is mentioned in only one line of the concluding prayer to Eros and not explained. Neither is there a stand-alone section on "wing."

Second, the refusal to accept Socrates' structure enables Benardete to impose his own agenda on the oration by changing it from a prophetic-poetic palinode into a logical-scientific cosmology with meaningful silences about things that should have been in such a cosmology. This parallels Stanley Rosen's method of treating the *Symposium.*

Third, Benardete's outline permits him to assert that the order of sections 7 and 8 reverses the order of sections 2 and 3, thus esoterically creating a duty to wonder about Plato's reasons for the inversion. However, the allegedly reversed sections do not even exist. The remainder of this chapter will follow Socrates' outline.

THESIS OF THE PALINODE

The thesis of the palinode is: "The speech is not true which teaches that, when the *erastēs* is present, one must gratify the non-erosing because the former is mad and the latter is sanely self-controlled" (244a3–5). This thesis jolts Phaedrus, the valetudinarian and rational-choice theorist. Throughout the play, Phaedrus has upheld the proposition that the self-possessed man who can maximize pleasure-pain ratios with precise efficiency should be gratified rather than the man who cannot govern himself. Socrates is propagating the opposite position, a heresy in Phaedrus's eyes, that it is better to take the man who is not self-possessed, self-grounded, and sanely self-controlled (and who is therefore possessed, grounded, and ruled by a maddening force outside himself) as a lover.[11]

Plato's Greek sometimes gives rise to a misunderstanding of the thesis. In English, it appears that Socrates is saying that when a lover is present, he should be preferred to the nonlover, with the implication that when the lover is not around, it is acceptable to gratify a nonlover. I do not see this in the Greek. I think that the English connotation is an artifact of the collision of the Greek idiomatic μὲν . . . δὲ construction with a translator's desire to render texts as literally as possible. I also believe that Socrates' later argument requires the conclusion that gratifying a nonlover would always be

---

11. One can imagine that this thesis is as repugnant to modern individuals who want to be gods as it is to Phaedrus. Gods are supposed to be self-possessed and self-grounded.

injurious to oneself. Philosophically contentious positions ought not to be read into linguistic idioms.

Inasmuch as Socrates' statement of his thesis requires only three lines, this is enough on the subject of the theme. We may proceed to the next step in Socrates' reasoning.

THE BLESSINGS OF MADNESS

To persuade Phaedrus of the truth of his thesis, Socrates first of all must convince him that madness is not an unmitigated evil. He begins with illustrations not evidently associated with the topic of eros, although they might be linked with it in ways that someone will think out someday. He argues that the greatest blessings come to us through madness—when this dementia has been sent to us as a gift of the gods. With an eye on what Socrates will maintain later, we may also say that the greatest goods come to us through madness when the gift of the gods inspires memories of our true home. Obviously, there is another kind of madness that is a fearful evil, touched upon in our previous chapter, namely, the condition of being out of our minds in a manner not caused by gods and resulting in forgetfulness of our true home.

There are three insanities that Socrates can classify as good without exciting Phaedrus's active resistance, even though the argument does probably arouse his skepticism. The first is that of the prophetess at Delphi, the priestesses of Dodona, the Sibyl, and others who received divinely inspired prophecy and foretold the future. These votaries have done many beautiful things for Hellas in public and private when they were mad, but none at all when they were sane. In this connection, one can observe that the ancients approved of madness by defining prophecy as the "manic art." They considered a madness from a divine source superior to sane self-control. The second is that which sometimes has been visited upon people whose families were suffering from ancient curses, releasing the afflicted into a service of the gods that made them safe. Socrates will clarify what he means by this after his speech. The third comes from the Muses to a delicate and pure soul, moving it to a Bacchic frenzy that eventuates in poetry and educates future generations. No would-be poet succeeds if the Muses have not driven him mad. Socrates later forgets exactly what he said about these insanities (265b), proving that he himself was divinely mad when he offered this classification.[12]

12. It should be noted that this prophetic-poetic beginning is entirely mythical in the senses that it (1) involves unverifiable stories of the blessings won for Hellas by prophetic and poetic people and (2) directly appeals to the Muses. Contrary to what some scholars think, we have begun our playful, mythic hymn already. On the three insanities given as examples, cf. Pieper, *Begeisterung* and *Enthusiasm*.

Having suggested the premise that certain types of madness can be beneficial, Socrates must now show that the insanity known as eros belongs to this set. However, he is not ready to shoulder the burden of proof alone. He gives Phaedrus a little pep talk, contending that the existence of good manias should calm us when people try to frighten us by urging us to avoid the mad and befriend the sane. He challenges those who make this argument to demonstrate that eros is not sent by gods to lovers and beloveds for their advantage. He, for his part, must prove that eros is a gift from gods for the greatest good fortune. He adds enigmatically that his demonstration will not be trustworthy to the terribly clever, but it will be believable to the wise. The "terribly clever" are the thinkers whom he previously described as boorishly wise, the partisans of enlightened rationality. Socrates is admitting that his argument will not be sustained by sensory evidence and tight logic. However, the genuinely wise will overlook this and perceive a certain believability in his reasoning. They will see that his myth achieves "some truth, perhaps" and that it is "a not wholly incredible logos." His comments illuminate the nature of philosophy. When we are discussing the relative merits of being self-possessed and being controlled, and arguing that being self-possessed is inferior to being controlled, we are admitting that philosophy cannot be a wisdom founded on sense data and unimpeachable logic, which would be perfect self-possession, and confessing that philosophy will always be a love of wisdom that attains to partial, not wholly incredible, truths, which is to lack absolute control and to be subject to realities higher than oneself.

Proof that Erotic Madness Is a Divine Blessing

So, Socrates wants to prove that eros is a gift from gods for the greatest good fortune. To this end, he says that we must first grasp the truth about soul, divine and human: how it is acted upon, and its works. He will follow this discussion with another on the form of psyche. We should remind ourselves why he abruptly veers into this subject matter. Lysias implicitly, and the shrouded Socrates explicitly, based their erotic teachings on anthropologies that were primarily psychologies. They maintained that two things and two things alone determine the choices of human beings: *epithymia* and rational opinion that leads to "the right," "the best," this defined as the enlightened, rather than the stupid, enjoyment of pleasure. If this axiom were allowed to stand, all our arguments would begin with the assumption that the soul contains nothing but desire for base pleasures and a reason that is the slave of desire, leaving pleasure as our only conceivable telos. It would be impossible to conclude that there are higher goods to which a mad eros could lead us. We would be Typhonic monsters. Socrates also declares that his demonstration begins with this proposition: "All soul is immortal" (245c5). He must persuade Phaedrus of this point, too, for demotic minds immediately revert to base hedonism when they conclude that there is nothing beyond the grave. Socrates extends this meditation into a reflection on soul "divine and human" because our alternative to being Typhonic beasts is to have souls that share a divine fate. Gods are not the highest realities in Socrates' range of vision. This creates an ontological possibility. Although we cannot know gods, Socrates will say that he has anamnestic grounds for supposing that we are close enough to them by nature to be able to participate in their lives to some small degree.

We understand that a demonstration that eros is a divine blessing requires knowledge of the truth about soul, which must be founded on substantiation of the claim that the soul is eternal. However, Socrates' proof of the immortality of the soul is one of the most obscure texts in Plato. It seems to consist in several syllogisms, the definitions, major premises, minor premises, and conclusions of which have been tangled up, thus creating a Gordian knot in which it is hard to see what is supposed to prove what. One pulls at this or that loose end, trying without much success to find a place to start unraveling the jumble. Perhaps Plato does not intend the knot to be unsnarled, for the demonstration is set in the context of a "playfully sung mythic hymn" that contains "not wholly incredible" views and, thus, is almost certainly a philosophic joke. For Socrates' pedagogical purposes, the playful proof does not have to be logically valid. It has to be only as true as Socrates can make it while opening Phaedrus's soul to goods nobler than pleasure. I shall play along with the joke, attempting to reconstitute its syllogisms and observing the reasons it is funny.

I believe that Socrates' demonstration of the immortality of soul commences with two implied definitions and a basic syllogism that underpin parallel chains of deduction, each of which then ends with the same third definition and final syllogism, as follows (244d–246a).

Implied Definitions

To generate all things is a motion, the ruling and strongest motion. (For authority on this definition, see *Laws* 893b–895c.)

To come to be by virtue of being generated is a motion, one different in kind from that of generating all things, a motion determined by and weaker than the motion of generating all things. (Again, see *Laws* 893b–895c.)

Basic Syllogism

All things that come into being must come into being from a beginning, or be moved or generated by a beginning.

The beginning of all things cannot come to be, or be moved, for if it came into being or were moved it would not be a beginning of all things. Therefore, the beginning of all things is not generated but self-moved.

Deductive Chain A: First Syllogism

That which is ungenerated and self-moved does not abandon itself. The beginning of all things is ungenerated and self-moved. Therefore, the beginning of all things does not abandon itself.

Deductive Chain A: Second Syllogism

That which moves and never abandons itself never ceases from moving. The self-moved beginning of all things moves and never abandons itself. Therefore, the self-moved beginning of all things never ceases from moving.

Deductive Chain A: Third Syllogism

That which never stops moving is deathless. The self-moved beginning of all things never ceases from moving. Therefore, the self-moved beginning of all things is deathless.

Concluding Definition

Inasmuch as that which is self-moved has been shown to be immortal, we shall not be ashamed to say that to be self-moved is the being and the logos of soul. Accordingly, soul (by definition) is the deathless self-moved beginning that we have been discussing.

Deductive Chain B: First Syllogism

If the self-moved beginning of all things were destroyed, it would not come into being, for there would be no beginning from which it could come.
All things that come to be must be generated, or moved, by the self-moved beginning of all things.
Therefore, if the self-moved beginning of all things were destroyed, none of the things that come to be could come to be.

Deductive Chain B: Second Syllogism

If the self-moved beginning of all things were destroyed, none of the things that come to be could come to be.

All existing things are constantly changing, or coming to be.

Therefore, if the self-moved beginning of all things were to be destroyed, the heavens and everything else would collapse, stand still, and cease to be movable.

Deductive Chain C: Third Syllogism

If the self-moved beginning of all things were to be destroyed, the heavens and everything else would collapse, stand still, and cease to be movable.

However, this could not happen. (Unstated premise.)

Therefore, the self-moved beginning of all things is incorruptible.

Concluding Definition

Inasmuch as that which is self-moved has been shown to be immortal, we shall not be ashamed to say that to be self-moved is the being and the logos of soul. Accordingly, soul (by definition) is the deathless self-moved beginning that we have been discussing.

Final Syllogism

All body that seems to move itself is ensouled, for self-movement is the nature of soul.

That which is self-moved by nature can be neither generated nor corrupted.

Therefore, soul (including every human soul) is deathless.

This interpretation of the meaning of Socrates' argument is not necessarily the correct one, if there is a correct one. I have seen others that seem equally adequate to the text. None are more satisfactory from a logical standpoint. However one reads it, the reasoning is full of logical holes.

For example, in the version that I have given, the implied definitions make generating and being generated analogues of mechanical motion; all inferences from these definitions that rely on ideas of mechanical motion to win their cases involve the logical fallacy of substituted middle terms. The basic syllogism appears sound. However, then, in the first syllogism of deductive chain A, one cannot see what Socrates means by saying that an ungenerated, self-moved reality does not abandon itself. The claim looks suspiciously like a subterfuge, a screen behind which Socrates smuggles his conclusion into his premises. Socrates takes advantage of this fallacy in the major premise of the second syllogism in chain A. Then, in the major premise of the third syllogism in this chain, he too easily assumes that motion is equivalent to life. The conclusion that the self-moved beginning of all things is deathless has therefore not been established. The first two syllogisms in deductive chain B involve unwarranted logical leaps from the image of an original creation to the notion of sustaining created things in being. Once things have been moved originally by a first mover, they might be able to move other things, thus keeping some things always in being. The transition from the major premise to the implied minor premise in the third syllogism in chain B is a blatant non sequitur. The heavens and earth could well collapse, stand still, and cease to be movable. In fact, the laws of thermodynamics seem to show that the universe is headed in that direction. Therefore, the conclusion that the self-moved beginning of all things is incorruptible is not proved.

Even if I were wrong about the logic so far, Socrates' move to define ungenerated self-movement as the being and logos of soul has no basis in evidence about soul. Socrates asserts that we shall not be ashamed to posit this definition because he *is* probably ashamed to posit the definition and needs to get over the rough spot. Plato knows that the definition reflects no necessity, for he allows both Kleinias and the Athenian Stranger to say that soul has come into being, or that it has a generation, in the *Laws* (896b–c). (We cannot solve the problem of what "Plato's position" on the provenance of soul is.) The last syllogism is a petitio principii. If all this were not enough, Jonathan Barnes rightly points out that the demonstration moves from a definition to an eternal existent, a logically prohibited tactic.[13]

This all-out critique of Socrates' argument does not justify modern shouts of "Aha!" and contempt of Plato as a thinker. The danger in the conceited assumption that one is more sagacious than Plato plus Socrates' warnings that his speech has been sung playfully combine to convince me, as I have said, that the proof of the immortality of soul is a philosophic joke. Socrates' later comment that soul is a subject that only a deity could treat clinches this case. Socrates plays the joke on Phaedrus for pedagogical purposes. I believe that he supposes that the joke will open Phaedrus to the possibility that soul is immortal for an illogical reason: the source of this proof of the deathlessness of psyche was Alcmeon, a physician who dabbled in philosophy.[14] The valetudinarian Phaedrus might accept anything that has been proposed by a doctor. Further, although the proof is logically invalid, it is still credible. It evinces a certain knowledge or awareness that soul is eternal.

On what do I base my claim that the demonstration is plausible? My answer will take me out on a limb, but I have been out there before and do not mind a bit of risk. I believe that human insight into the possible

13. Barnes, *The Presocratic Philosophers*, 1:114–20.
14. Ibid.

deathlessness of soul has nothing to do with logical proofs. In Homer's poem, Odysseus grounds his argument that Nausicaa might be one of the immortals on a logically impossible non sequitur. He declares that he once saw something like her, a young shoot of a palm springing up beside the altar of Apollo in Delos (*Odyssey* 6.160–65). A logician scorns his implicit syllogism. However, he means that Nausicaa inspires the same awe in his soul as the young palm shoot did. The logical sins in Socrates' argument to the beautiful boy correspond to the logical fallacies in Odysseus's statement to the beautiful Nausicaa. The later parts of his myth suggest to me that it is the awe inspired in his soul by the beauty of the beloved that convinces him of the deathlessness of soul.[15] Phaedrus is not ready for this kind of argument yet, so Socrates cannot use it. Socrates must resort to less appropriate logical tricks to get his profoundly irrational scientistic student moving toward genuine rationality. So, let us accept the possibility that psyche is immortal, thus opening ourselves to the prospect that there are goods higher than pleasure, and proceed to the next stage of Socrates' proof that eros is a blessing, that is, the more developed psychology that will eventually show why divine erotic madness fulfills a human being.

Having suggested that self-movement is the being and logos of soul, Socrates turns to a discussion of its form (idea, περὶ δὲ τῆς ἰδέας αὐτῆς, 246a3–4). In part, this is a continuation of the philosophic prank that Socrates has been perpetrating. Socrates has defined the being and logos of soul without having established what soul is. That was comical. Now a good Aristotelian would laugh again, noting that if self-motion is the being and logos of soul, this would seem to preclude the possibility of its having a form.

Regarding the form of psyche, Socrates bluntly tells Phaedrus, "What sort of thing it is, is completely in every way a matter for a long, divine accounting" (246a4–5). Only a god could speak decisively on the topic.[16] This reminds us that in the *Republic*, Socrates prefaces his proof of the tripartite character of soul with the warning that soul cannot be investigated with the

15. Here, it is my intention to follow Cicero, who thought so well of the demonstration that he repeats it in its entirety in both his *Republic* and *Tuscullan Disputations*. While praising the proof in the latter work, and censuring "all the plebeian philosophers" who could "not even understand how subtly it has been derived," he adds something that Socrates does not tell the Phaedrus who still admires the boorish sort of wisdom: "The soul then senses that it is moved itself (*sentit igitur animus se moveri*), and when thus sensing (*quod cum sentit*), it senses at the same time (*illud una sentit*) that it is self-moved by its own power and not by an outside power, and that it cannot ever be abandoned by itself, and this is proof of eternity (*ex quo efficitur aeternitas*) (*Tuscullan Disputations* 1.23.55). I have altered King's translations somewhat.

16. Ferrari, *Listening to the Cicadas,* 120, argues that this formula leaves room for fudging and that Socrates actually feels capable of declaring what soul is. I see no wriggle room. "Completely in every way" does not allow for a "divine man" doing the job because a divine man is not completely and in every way divine. Socrates is not a god.

methods he and the company are currently employing (435d1). It is necessary to go around a longer way. Later in the dialogue, after he has taken the longer way, he repudiates the first demonstration, although Adeimantus calls it "measured" and his other auditors like it, because "a measure in such things, which in any way falls short of what *is*, is no measure at all" (504c1–2). Finally, he argues that soul is simple, not composite (611d–612a; see *Phaedo* 78b–81a). I think that these contradictions reflect Socrates' view that we cannot speak seriously about soul. Given this limitation, Socrates is content to speak playfully of soul as composite for ethical purposes and as simple for metaphysical purposes. On this basis, we must expect the discussion of the form of soul in the *Phaedrus* to be playful, too.

Having confessed to an absolute inability to say what the form of soul is, Socrates adds that to say what its form is like (ἔοικεν, 246a5) is something in our ken. When words fail to capture the essences of ineffable things, we can still use analogies to symbolize our experiences of them. We need such a simile now. Socrates likens soul's form to "a naturally grown together winged pair [of horses] and charioteer" (ξυμφύτῳ δυνάμει ὑποπτέρου ζεύγους τε καὶ ἡνιόχου, 246a6–7). We note that Socrates is restoring to philosophic discourse the Pegasuses for which he previously said he had no time because he was too busy studying himself. The Pegasuses turn out to be major parts of himself. So do the Hippocentaurs of which he formerly declined to speak, for we see winged horses and a charioteer in the picture but no chariot. From some perspectives, at least, the soul could seem to contain a human torso, neck, and head on a winged horse's body.

We should observe that the chariot comes into view only rarely in the myth. In one place, Socrates informs us that it is heavy (246d6), and, in another, he tells us that Zeus drives a winged one (246e5). Given that Socrates does not include the chariot in his original simile of the soul, and given that the divine charioteers can detach themselves and their horses from the chariots (247e), it seems that we may not read the chariots into Socrates' idea of soul. This raises the question of what the chariots represent. Inasmuch as Socrates' image of the soul as composite implies that he is speaking ethically, it is rather hazardous to jump from the myth to ontological inferences. However, we can state that the chariot is not body, for the souls that eventually become human beings have chariots before they get bodies (see 247b1–3, 246c2–3).[17] If we simply must have a metaphysical seat for the charioteer, perhaps we could imagine that the chariots represent two kinds of intangible "prime matter," one for human beings and one for gods, that the souls aloft infuse before the human souls fall

---

17. Therefore, I disagree with Benardete on both the function and the nature of chariot (*Rhetoric of Morality*, 136–37).

into solid-matter bodies. However, this is not important, for Socrates is not doing a serious ontology. What the chariots chiefly represent is humorous counsel that Socrates does not pretend to explain all reality.

Socrates goes on to say that divine souls possess horses and charioteers that are all good and of good descent, but that all other souls are mixed. A human or potentially human soul has one horse that is good and of good descent and another with the opposite qualities (246b). Apparently, it is also possible for the potentially human souls to have good or bad charioteers (248b2). Socrates does not say whether the charioteers are permanently good or bad. As with the chariots, we are curious as to what the horses and charioteers symbolize. Considering the resemblance of the tripartite soul of the *Phaedrus* to that of the *Republic*, and considering also that Socrates is speaking ethically rather than ontologically, we may suppose that for human beings, the good horse, bad horse, and charioteer represent *thymos, epithymia*, and *nous*, and that in the gods, the horses and charioteer stand for *thymos, himeros*, and *nous*. (I change the designation of the human horse *epithymia* to *himeros* in the divine soul because the bad horse in the human must differ in nature from the corresponding good horse in the god somehow and Socrates later associates *himeros* with Zeus.)

Socrates' simile inspires another question. Why should the gods, like human beings, be depicted as having complex souls that are two parts horse *(thymos* and *himeros)* and one part charioteer *(nous)*? Why not portray their souls, as G. R. F. Ferrari inquires, as "all charioteer" (pure reason)?[18] This question requires a threefold answer, as follows.

First, Socrates is no more serious about the complexity of divine beings than he is about the tripartite character of the human soul. In the *Republic*, he refers to gods as simple (ἁπλοῦν, 380d5). Therefore, I assume that his portrait of the gods in the *Phaedrus* has a playful ethical purpose rather than an ontological one.

Second, it will become evident after a certain amount of reflection that our question is anachronistic. Here is the necessary background of this judgment: When Socrates moves to the next section of his proof that erotic madness is a divine blessing, that is, to the short lecture on why living beings are called mortal and immortal, the first thing he says is that all soul cares for that which is soulless. Referring to gods, he then states that perfect and fully winged soul flies upward and "manages the whole cosmos" (246c1–2). To maintain that divine soul is solicitous for the soulless and that it governs the entire universe is to conceive of a providence that directs not just inert matter but all beings that rank below gods. This is

18. Ferrari, *Listening to the Cicadas*, 127. I am impressed, but not persuaded, by Ferrari's answer that the gods of the *Phaedrus* need horses as seats of their desires to care for contingent matter, given that gods who were pure reason could care only for necessary beings (129–30). I see no inherent contradiction in the idea of a god that is pure reason caring for contingent beings.

why Adrasteia will be charged with the task of arranging a system of just deserts for all souls, both those aloft and those embodied on earth (248c). To make divine and human souls similar is to claim that both naturally share in this providential regulation of the cosmos and its justice, to greater and lesser degrees. Once again, the intention of the argument is ethical, not metaphysical.

To postulate that Socrates should have supplied this tale with a providential god who was both a pure reason and a will that cared for contingent being is to imagine that Plato conceived of the transcendent God of the Christians, a simple, unchangeable God for whom to exist, to know universals, to grasp contingent particulars, and to will are the same act (see Augustine, *The City of God,* 8:6; Aquinas, *Summa Theologiae,* 1: q. 14, a. 6, a. 11). If Plato does envisage this God, he never says so. He seems to need to symbolize a providence sensed by his soul at a time when the highest thing in his purview is the Good of the *Republic* (508e–509b), or the Leader Reason *(hegemon nous)* of the *Laws* (εἰς τὸν ἡγεμόνα νοῦν, to which the gods look up, 631d5), or the Essence Really Being of the *Phaedrus* (οὐσία ὄντως οὖσα, 247c7)—all of which might be identical. The Good generates the existence of knowledge and truth while standing beyond being itself. Perhaps it is a pure reason that naturally ponders only itself and the ideas that it generates as necessary beings by thinking them. If Plato does need to symbolize a providence that can care for contingent beings under the auspices of this Good, the only way that he can solve his conceptual problem is to place providence in the hands of beings who are inferior to the supreme reality (the Good) and superior to contingent things, and who mediate between them. The intramundane Olympian gods and daimons of the Homeric tales are nicely suited to this task, so they are kept in Plato's mythical universe. They could perform their function as simple pure reasons that are inferior to the supreme *nous* if Plato chose to make them do so (much as angels do in Christian theology) but, then, human beings could not share ethically in their fates. So, I return to the conclusion that Socrates endows his gods with a charioteer and horses for ethical, not metaphysical, reasons.

Third, if likening the gods to human beings (or vice versa) should cause concern about blasphemy, or if it should occasion esoteric joy in the perception that Socrates is making men into gods, we should notice that it is misleading to emphasize the similarities that Socrates sees between human and divine souls without mentioning their differences. Socrates never argues that the human souls surely have good charioteers, like those of the gods. He never says that the human souls could possess pairs of well-matched, good horses, such as the divine souls enjoy. He never affirms that the human souls will one day ride in winged chariots, like Zeus. As his myth unfolds, he never suggests that human souls could pass entirely outside the roof of heaven into the hyperuranian region, as the psyches of the gods do. If Socrates' story informs us that there is something divine in us, such that we can share in the administration of the cosmos and justice with the gods, it also cautions us not to think that we are or ever will be gods. Thus, Socrates' myth is no more a blasphemy than the Hebrew prophecy that we are created in the image and likeness of God. Neither does it offer esoteric solace to anyone who believes, unaccountably, that the philosophical question of the *Phaedrus* is "how can a human being become a god?"[19] On the contrary, the myth warns such ambitious people against their irrational hybris.

There is one more thing in Socrates' simile that might trouble us. How does it happen that the souls of potential human beings sometimes have bad charioteers and always have one bad horse? Does Socrates suppose that this occurs by nature? If so, should we not say that his image is a contradictory, Manichaean notion of a naturally evil being? I think that this difficulty has the same explanation as the previous ones. It cannot be emphasized enough that Socrates' myth is not an ontology. Here, Socrates does not intend to address the mystery of the metaphysical origins of evil. If he does this in any dialogue, it is in his story of Er the Pamphylian (*Republic* 614b ff), in which human souls of their own free wills paradoxically choose the fates to which they are bound by necessity. In his present myth of the form of soul, he does not say that the human souls have acquired bad charioteers or the bad horses by nature.[20] He only reports what he sees now. Without analyzing how the order of being came to be as it is, he speculates that gods necessarily think and act well because their natures contain nothing that tends toward evil. He also knows from experience that human beings are free to choose good or evil because we are incessantly subject to conflicting pulls in those directions, which he symbolizes with the horses. It is much as if a Christian theologian were to refrain from discussing the causes of Adams's guilt while studying mankind's "fallen nature," observing Paul's two forces contending in his breast or Augustine's struggle between the *amor Dei* and the *amor sui*. Hence, Socrates' point is once again ethical: The human soul cannot attain to the moral perfection of a divine soul. However, it is not fated to a perpetual pursuit of pleasure because it is more than the *epithymia* and rational opinion of the first two speeches. It contains three elements. These parts allow it to choose a good beyond pleasure as well as an evil that wallows in base delights, destroying capacity to rise to the higher good.

The next part of Socrates' proof that erotic madness is a divine blessing spells out the difference between immortals and mortals. Socrates does not

19. Rosen, *Hermeneutics as Politics*, 65.
20. To say that the elements of the soul have grown together naturally is not to say that the elements are bad by nature. They might have been good by nature, one of them subsequently becoming bad, after they had grown together.

bring this topic up for its own sake. He is actually turning from the subject of the form or idea of soul to an explanation of why human beings are not perfectly blessed, so that they stand in need of divine largesse. In doing this, he begins a myth of the fall of mankind, one of Plato's imaginative tales that serve as equivalents, or alternatives, to the story of the expulsion of Adam and Eve from Paradise in Genesis.

The myth opens with the disclosure that all soul cares for that which is soulless. As it does so, it traverses the whole heaven, coming into being at various times in various forms. I assume that what Socrates envisages here is not a contradiction of his statement that soul has no generation or coming into being, but that there is something like a cosmic soul substance that variously lends itself to the formation of divine, daimonic, and human souls.[21] Therefore, human souls by nature participate in the divine fate: they are destined to coresponsibility for the governance of the universe. When soul is "perfect" (presumably meaning possessed of two good horses and a good charioteer, that is, when soul is in divine form) and fully winged, it rises up and governs the entire cosmos. By implication, imperfect (that is, human) soul helps superior, divine psyche with its supreme responsibility for ruling all things. Imperfect soul is not itself sovereign. This is the first element of the distinction between immortal and mortal. Socrates continues to warn against hybris. To repeat, when soul is perfect and fully winged, it ascends and governs the whole cosmos. However, when soul loses its wings, it crashes to earth and takes on a solid-matter body. This never happens to perfect souls but only to lesser ones. The second element of the distinction between immortal and mortal is that the former never risks losing its wings.[22] To continue, the body of the fallen soul appears to be self-moved because it moves by the soul's power. The body and soul joined together are called a living being and "mortal," presumably because the body and psyche are not joined together for all time. "Immortal" is not something for which we have a rational account. We have never seen or properly grasped a god in thought, but we imagine one as a living being with a soul and a body (certainly not a solid-matter body but a protean body, perhaps the prime matter of the chariot) that are joined together forever (probably not in the sense that the gods cannot detach their horses from their chariots but in the sense that they always have the chariots at

---

21. Need I say again that this is not serious metaphysics but poetic ethics?

22. It does not follow from this that "God is wing," as Benardete says (*Rhetoric of Morality,* 138). Three subsequent statements by Socrates show this. First, he asserts at 246d7–8 that wing "partakes" of the divine. To partake in god is not to be god. Second, Socrates states explicitly at 246d8–e1 that the divine is Beauty, Wisdom, Good, and such like, and that wing is nourished by partaking of these. To be nourished by divine attributes is not to be divine. Third, Socrates also declares at 249c5–6 that it is proximity to the hyperuranian realities (and, hence, not wing) that causes god to be god.

their disposal). Socrates means that the last distinction between immortal and mortal is that we, by negative analogy, think that gods lack our capacity to be annihilated by the sundering of their vital constituent parts. However, Socrates adds, let this be spoken in whatever manner is pleasing to god.

The lesson to be drawn from this discourse on immortals and mortals is that mortals need divine blessings primarily because our imperfections cause us to lose our wings so that, like Odysseus, we fall away from our true homes. Proceeding to the next section of his proof that erotic madness is god-sent for our benefit, why soul loses its wings, Socrates expands on this point. His analysis produces some startling lines. Socrates says that the natural function of wing is to carry the heavy (presumably the chariot) up to where the divine race lives. Then he comments about wing that "[i]t participates in the divine more than anything else about the body" (κεκοινώνηκε δέ πη μάλιστα τῶν περὶ τὸ σῶμα τοῦ θείου, 246d7–8). Elaborating on that in which wing participates, he adds: "But the divine is beauty, wisdom, good, and all that is like them" (τὸ δὲ θεῖον καλόν, σοφόν, ἀγαθόν, καὶ πᾶν ὅ τι τοιοῦτον, 246d8–e1). This forces us to ask how a subpart of the soul could be "about the body," especially when the natural work of that subpart is to lift the heavy up and away from material body, and even more especially when it participates in the immaterial qualities of the divine.

We could surmise that Socrates means that wing participates in the divine more than anything else about the body of a psychic horse. This would ease our perplexity, but it would be rather inelegant: Socrates would have to be using language sloppily for this solution of our problem to be the correct one. We could also speculate that the horses, *thymos*, *himeros*, and *epithymia*, exist to facilitate soul's care for the soulless by pulling the charioteer toward inert matter, so that the horses and all their parts pertain to the body. This solution initially looks more suitable than the previous one because *thymos* and *epithymia*, at least, do motivate bodies when the bodies are ensouled. However, these horses motivate bodies only after they have lost their wings. If the horses still had their wings, the wings would be pulling the souls up and away from matter rather than toward it. Therefore, I incline toward a third solution. I think that Socrates slips deliberately here, signaling us that the spiritual wing has a special relationship with a part of the male solid-matter body that is a little winglike, at least insofar as it has a natural upward tendency. The psychic wing and the bodily wing commune in the divine more than anything else about the body because they have particular affinities for, or are especially drawn to, the divine qualities of beauty, wisdom, and good.[23]

23. Here, someone is sure to charge that Plato's philosophy, or my reading, is phallocentric. Let it be so, if it makes anyone happier to utter such clever and philosophically

With this hypothesis advanced, we must recover the thread of the argument. We are inquiring why soul loses its wings. We know now that psychic wings participate in the divine by virtue of their capacity and need to be nourished by the godly qualities of beauty, wisdom, and good. Therefore, Socrates asserts that it is by these qualities that the soul's plumage is most nourished and strengthened. However, the deities *are* beauty, wisdom, and good and all suchlike qualities. Accordingly, the wings of the divine horses are always adequately nourished and at full strength. Beings that are less than divine are not perfectly identical with beauty, wisdom, good, and so on. Consequently, their psychic wings are never strong enough to carry them as high as gods can fly. We shall see that they can get enough sustenance to stay aloft. The potentially human souls do not crash necessarily. The catastrophes occur when, instead of being infused with the divine qualities, the future human souls are filled with their opposites: shamefulness, evil, and, I should think, stupidity. These qualities destroy wing. The souls that assume them come tumbling out of heaven. Socrates does not say how shamefulness and evil are possible up in the ether. However, his myth is consistent with his story of Er. I should say that his myth is even consistent with the tale of Adam and Eve. In all three accounts, choices made in a mythical time and place for no discernible metaphysical reasons land us in our present fixes, with good and evil forces perpetually contending in our breasts. Perhaps it is more germane to Socrates' present enterprise to remark that the tale is also consistent with the *Odyssey,* in which Odysseus's evil choices lie at the root of his loss of Ithaca and Penelope.

If we are curious as to how shamefulness and evil are possible in the heavenly domain, we wonder even more how the gods come to be identical with beauty, wisdom, and good and how divine and human wings come to be nurtured by the qualities. Socrates playfully tutors us on these points. If we follow his story further, pausing to consider his invitations to digress along the way, we shall learn what we want to know.

Continuing his explanation of why soul loses its wings, Socrates takes up the subject of the way of life of the heavenly souls. He reports that Zeus goes first, caring for and ordering all things. Zeus is followed by an army of gods and daimons divided into eleven parts. Of the twelve great gods, only Hestia, the goddess of the hearth, remains home.[24] Each god leads

---

illuminating remarks. This does not mean that women must be excluded from the analysis. There is a part of the female anatomy that could be conceived as winglike, too. The male part has the poetic advantage of being more in evidence.

24. Here there is a possible ambiguity in the Greek. Most translators have eleven gods, led by Zeus and his entourage, coursing around in the ether with ten other Olympian gods and their divisions. However, Kenneth Dorter reads the text as saying that twelve gods are cruising around, thus raising the question of who the twelfth god is if not Hestia. He replies that it must be Dionysus ("Three Disappearing Ladders in

his or her army in the rank assigned. There are many blessed sights and pathways in the heavens, and the gods pass back and forth along them, "minding their own business" (247a6) and, thus, being "just" according to Socrates' early definition of justice in the *Republic* (433b). Whoever wishes to join any of the armies and is qualified may do so, for there is no envy in the ranks. This implies that future human souls volunteer to serve the divine generals and fly along with them. This is as far as we can go without digressing into another question. Why do the deities organize themselves and their followers into "armies" when it seems that they have no one to fight?

One gropes blindly for metaphysical explanations of this oddity until being handed the key that Zdravko Planinc has provided. We begin to understand the militarism of the gods only when we see that Plato is here refiguring another Homeric trope. In Homer, Odysseus is initially bad, makes the choice that deprives him of Ithaca and Penelope, joins an army the leaders of which regularly desert their assigned ranks and perpetrate every kind of injustice, contributes to the failures of the army's business by participating in all manners of jealous intrigues, and wages murderous war. In the *Phaedrus*, Socrates reverses the substance and order of all these events in the heavens. It is the task of an army not to wage murderous war but to tend to the order of the cosmos. There is no jealousy in a heavenly army but, rather, a spirit of kindly cooperation that succeeds in keeping reality orderly. Divine leaders are content to stay in their places. They happily do justice rather than the sorts of injustices committed by Agamemnon and Achilles. The souls of the soldiers of order are initially good, but the imperfect somehow become bad and make the choices that deprive them of their homes. Again, Socrates' point is not metaphysical but moral; we have fallen into an ethically topsy-turvy world.

We return again to the account of how souls lose their wings. Socrates says that there are times when the gods and their followers go up to the feast and the banquet. It is important that Socrates does *not* say that Hestia stays home on such occasions; when the order of the day was tending the cosmic harmonies, she minded her own business at the divine hearth, but now she gets to be nourished as much as any other god.[25] On the festive

---

Plato," 292–93). This is an interesting analysis. However, I am not sure how to resolve the conflict between competing translations.

25. I point this out because Benardete argues: "Hestia is a god even though she never has seen the hyperuranian beings" (*Rhetoric of Morality*, 139). He is referring to Socrates' later point that it is proximity to the hyperuranian beings that causes gods to be gods. Thus, he is striving with might and main to manufacture an esoteric message. However, Socrates says only that Hestia stays home when the gods go about their routine business; he does not assert what Benardete wants him to declare, that she always stays home.

occasions, the gods climb steeply up the underside of the apse of heaven. Their chariots, pulled by good, well-balanced horses that are obedient to the rein, ascend easily, but the others climb with difficulty, for the bad horses that the charioteers have not trained beautifully are heavy and pull the souls down toward the earth, where the utmost toils and troubles await. At the pinnacle of their ascent, the divine psyches pass outside the vault. (Either there is a hole in the apse, the cosmos being built like a temple, or divine souls can pass through walls.) The divine psyches then stand on the ridge of heaven and behold the things outside.

Socrates asserts that the hyperuranian region has never been and will never be hymned worthily by any poet. However, he must try to tell this truth because truth is his subject. We are about to hear a poem by a poet who realizes that his poetry must be inadequate and who nevertheless must indite his poem. As argued above, it is the philosophic poet's duty to speak that which human beings may experience but cannot speak. Therefore, he will try to describe an ineffable reality, the highest truth, with poetic symbols that are not factual propositions.[26]

The poet Socrates-Stesichorus reports that the hyperuranian region is occupied by the colorless, formless, intangible Essence Really Being (οὐσία ὄντως οὖσα, 247c7). All genuine knowledge is concerned with this Essence Really Being, which is visible only to the pilot of the soul, reason, or mind (νῷ, *nous*, 247c8). I should point out here that Socrates has suddenly begun to speak of the gods metaphysically, rather than ethically. He has made it clear that the charioteer is *nous* and that, for the purposes of this part of the tale, a god is *nous*. This is why Socrates can say, a few lines hence (247e), that the gods put their horses up at the manger upon returning home from the feast, which they could not do if the horses were essential to them.

We come next to a critically important statement. Socrates says: "Now, the intellect (διάνοια) of god, together with all the intellect of soul (ἁπάσης ψυχῆς) that can receive what befits it, since it is nourished on *nous* (νῷ) and pure knowledge, rejoices to see reality (τὸ ὄν) for a while, and it is nourished by seeing the truth (τἀληθῆ) until the rotation brings it back around again" (247d1–5). Evidently, the Essence Really Being is simultaneously *nous* (so that it must be identical with the *hegemon nous* of the *Laws*), pure knowledge, reality, and truth. The *nous* of a god, who is a living *nous*, feasts on the Essence Really Being, that is, on the *nous* that is pure knowledge, reality, and truth. The intellects of other souls for which this is fitting do the same. Hence, human minds can behold what divine minds see. This prospect begins to explain how there is something divine in our

26. Thus, Rosen is absolutely right to insist that the viewing of the divine and the good must be "silent" (*Hermeneutics as Politics*, 63–64). However, the reasons for this are not the ones that Rosen imagines.

souls. As they revolve, the divine minds that are feasting on the Essence Really Being also behold "justice in itself (αὐτὴν δικαιοσύνην), sane self-control, and knowledge"—not the knowledge that has a genesis and varies with the things that we name realities, but that which "abides in the Really Being Essence" (ἐν τῷ ὅ ἐστιν ὂν ὄντως ἐπιστήμην οὖσαν). They also see "all the other similar really being things" (τἆλλα ὡσαύτως τὰ ὄντα ὄντως, 247d5–e3). The justice, sane self-control, knowledge, and all other really being things that resemble them are the forms that the *nous* of the Essence Really Being generates by thinking, except that it is wrong to assert that they are generated, for they are coeternal with the *nous* that thinks them. We perceive now that gods can be identical with the various forms (beauty, wisdom, good, justice, sane self-control, and so on) just because they are pure minds that become essentially one with the ideas thought by the Essence Really Being. Lesser souls that lack ability to escape the vault of heaven and contemplate the hyperuranian realities for a whole revolution of the cosmos cannot become divine. We already know that the future human souls lack this ability. Thus, unless we wish to make the *Phaedrus* esoterically say the opposite of what it says, the dialogue is not a treatise on how human beings can become gods.

Those who delight in reading the *Phaedrus* as an esoteric work take another tack here, observing that Socrates does not mention the good as one of the delicacies on which the divine minds feast. Thus, Seth Benardete argues, "The good is not among the hyperuranian beings."[27] If this were true, it would leave a void at the core of Socrates' being. It is legitimate to ask why Socrates' vision of the hyperuranian realities does not list the good among the things seen, but I think that the correct answer differs from Benardete's. When Socrates declares in the *Republic* that the good is "beyond being" (or that it is "beyond essence," ἐπέκεινα τῆς οὐσίας, 509b9), he locates the good in the same region as the Essence Really Being. When he asserts that the good "provides the truth to the things known and gives the power to the one who knows" (508e3–4), he gives the good functions like those of the Essence Really Being. Thus, it seems to me that the good is not absent from the hyperuranian realm: Socrates has merely changed its name. I think that this is confirmed by the fact that a god is essentially "beauty, wisdom, *good*, and all that is like them." Gods are what they are through contemplation of the forms with which they are one. Gods could not be "good" unless the good were in the hyperuranian region.

Finishing his account of the nourishment of divine wing, Socrates asserts that after the feast, the gods return to heaven and put their horses up at the manger, giving them ambrosia and nectar. As distinguished from their

27. Benardete, *Rhetoric of Morality*, 123.

own wings, the horses badly need a square meal, for they had to starve all the time that they were up on the roof, where they could not feed on the Essence Really Being. However, the horses' wings must have a special relationship with *nous,* for we know that the charioteer's nutrition flows into them, making them healthy and strong. The wings of lesser souls (and evidently the wings of the bodies into which some of these souls fall) have the same relationship with *nous.* Thus, we see that Socrates has laid the foundation for his explanation of why soul loses its wings, which now enters its final stages.

Socrates says that nondivine souls fare much less well than divine souls on the journey to the roof of the cosmos. Even the best nondivine psyche, the one that is most like god and best follows god, has all kinds of trouble with its horses. This soul therefore succeeds only in lifting the head of its charioteer into the hyperuranian realm. Because the horses are causing such a rough ride, the charioteer cannot contemplate the hyperuranian realities; he sees all of them but catches only glimpses of them. Another less excellent soul allows its charioteer to see only some of the highest truths. Others whose horses have not been well reared owing to the evil of the charioteers yearn for the upper region but do not get there. Their charioteers are not nourished. Their horses' wings get no sustenance. The result is that the souls career around in the heavens, trampling each other, colliding with each other, and trying to pass each other. Apparently, they no longer belong to the heavenly armies. They have straggled, failing to follow their leaders, and envy has set in among them. In the midst of all the noise, rivalry, and sweat, many wings are lamed or broken. Because these souls cannot feast on reality, they must feed on opinion—which is the only nourishment that the hooded Socrates, speaking under the spell of Phaedrus, offered souls at all. However, being succored only by opinion, the souls fall to earth and acquire solid-matter bodies. Adrasteia (Nemesis) has an ordinance governing this situation. She decrees that a soul that has followed god and beheld the highest truths is free from harm until the next revolution of the cosmos. If such a soul boosts the head of its charioteer into the hyperuranian region every time the cosmos goes around, it will always be safe. However, if through "inability to follow" it fails to behold the realities and is weighed down with forgetfulness and evil—these are the truly sick insanities—and if it crashes, it will fall not into a beast's body but into that of a human being. Like Odysseus outside Scheria, we have washed up nearly dead spiritually, stripped of every shred of noble raiment, hard put to remember our true homes, and desperately in need of divine largesse.

Before leaving this part of Socrates' proof, we should take up an interesting theological question that Benardete poses. Benardete notices that "[d]espite the gods' facility in ascending and descending, they do nothing to prevent accidents in their entourage." From this, he infers, "The gods are not lovers of other souls."[28] We should observe that in the framework of the myth, the gods could not prevent the mishaps by giving the other souls better horses. The teams of good and bad horses are naturally yoked. To do what Benardete envisages, the gods would have to force the other charioteers to train their horses more beautifully.[29] Should the gods do that if they really love the other souls? Again, I acknowledge that it is proper to ask whether gods who loved other souls would prevent them from making evil choices. Again, I differ from Benardete. In the first place, if eros is a madness sent by gods to human beings for their greatest good, the gods obviously could not feel eros for human beings; this would make no sense in the context. However, gods could "love" other souls to the extent that they have *philia* or agape for them. How does it stand with the gods, then? Would *philia* or agape cause a god to prevent a soul from making bad choices? Everyone should recognize that this is one of the classical problems of theodicy. At the same time, everyone should be aware that strong cases have been made for the propositions that a god who loved souls would allow them their freedom to choose and, furthermore, that the loving god would then give errant souls another chance, perhaps even many additional chances. It seems to me that the gods who justly mind their own business in the heavenly life described by Socrates, who refrain from interfering in the decisions of their followers in that existence, and who then finally send Eros to the fallen souls to help them return to the heavenly life ought not to be described as nonlovers of other souls too hastily. Plato is not a Christian, but his symbolization of this particular issue appears to resemble the Christian (or, perhaps, the Orphic) one more than a little.

The next section of the proof that erotic madness is a divine blessing is not introduced by Socrates with an identifying remark. Perhaps Socrates intends it not as a separate part but, rather, as an extension of the discussion of why the mortal souls lose their wings. With some trepidation, I have designated it as an independent section because it obviously takes up a new division of the topic of the loss of spiritual wings, explaining why some people reacquire their wings whereas others do not. Separate subject or not, the argument is moving from the idea of a fall of a soul from its heavenly life to the problem of how the soul can return to its true home. Our gaze is shifting to a new myth of a divinely instituted rescue operation, not dissimilar to Athena's essential role in saving Odysseus. We have come to

---

28. Ibid., 140.

29. It would not be enough to teach the other charioteers how to train their horses. Socrates says that the horses are trained improperly owing to the "evil" of the charioteers. This means that only compulsion would produce the desired results.

the destination of the voyages of the shaman-poet Homer and the shaman-philosopher Plato along the *axis mundi*.

As mentioned above, Adrasteia has decreed that a soul that has seen the hyperuranian realities will never assume the body of a beast when it falls to earth. Rather, it will pass into the body of a human being. I have noted on more than one occasion that there are different ranks of human beings. Adrasteia has ordained that the broken-winged souls become one or another of the human sorts depending on how much each has seen of the hyperuranian truths. Here, once again, is a list of the ranks: (1) a philosopher or a lover of beauty, or a musical and erotic individual; (2) a lawful king or warlike ruler; (3) a statesman, household manager, or financier; (4) a lover of gymnastic labor or a doctor for the body; (5) a prophet or celebrant of mysteries; (6) a poet or other mimetic artist; (7) a craftsman or farmer; (8) a sophist or demagogue; and (9) a tyrant.[30]

This is certainly not intended by Plato as an exhaustive classification of all the possible types of human beings. We meet numerous other kinds of human beings in the other Platonic dialogues. However, Eric Voegelin astutely observes that this list does appear to comprehend the varieties relevant to the political situation with which Plato is dealing here. At the top of the hierarchy, the rank of the manic psyche that includes philosophers, lovers of beauty, musical, and erotic persons, we find the types who have the spiritual authority to restore order to the decaying Athenian polity. The next three levels are composed of the kinds of individuals who could serve the manic leaders who are the sources of order, in supporting roles. We are a little troubled to find "warlike" rulers in this rank, but Socrates is surely not thinking of conquerors like Napoléon: I think that he means "warlike" in the sense of the "armies" aloft, in which one envisages a just use of power to protect right order when the forces of disorder, whatever they are, threaten to run amuck. The next three ranks "are the souls which constitute the decaying Hellenic society." The bottom two levels "are the active element in the decaying society, the carriers of the corruption, the enemies of the manic soul and its supporters."[31] In accord with Plato's present concern with the democratic tyrannical eros, the list does not explicitly place the oligarchs who figure prominently in the *Symposium* in the decadent or destructive ranks: the lower levels of the classification have a distinctly democratic flavor.

---

30. Benardete notes that there are eleven kinds of souls (one type for each of the armies that follows the gods) in the heavens but only nine on earth (ibid., 104). He seems to reckon that this constitutes a difficulty requiring esoteric analysis. However, I think that any of the eleven kinds in the heavens could fall into any of the nine types on earth, depending on how they have behaved aloft. I believe it would be gratuitous to introduce a numerology problem.

31. Voegelin, *Order and History*, 3:139.

Apparently expounding Adrasteia's law further, Socrates promulgates a rule for all the souls in all the ranks, that whoever lives justly receives a better allotment in the next existence and whoever lives unjustly receives a worse allotment. Eschewing a philosophic equivalent of Calvinism, he does not argue that human souls are predestined to lives of justice or injustice.[32] However, it is harder for the lesser souls to do well. Adrasteia's ordinance is that a soul who has been "philosophizing without fraud" (249a1–2) (which lets out Lysias, Phaedrus, anyone who approves of speeches like that given by the shrouded Socrates, and all others who purport to philosophize while implanting the real lie in souls) and a soul who has been "loving boys with philosophy" (παιδεραστήσαντος μετὰ φιλοσοφίας, 249a2) (which lets in the "right pederasts" of the *Symposium*) will regain their wings and fly back to their heavenly homes if they have chosen such lives for three consecutive one thousand–year periods. The other souls meet fates similar to those prophesied in the myth of Er the Pamphylian. When their first lives have ended, they are judged. Then some are sent to places of just punishment, and others go to heavenly places of just rewards for a thousand years. Then they are thrown into a lottery and choose new lives, like Odysseus in the tale, some becoming beasts, others returning to human status. A beastly soul that has never seen the hyperuranian truths will never become human. Phaedrus, who lives in the eighth rank of souls and foolishly aspires to descend into the ninth, has just been warned that he could soon sink further than he wants, becoming an animal or an insect. As we shall be told not long hence, some people pass directly from human bodies into the forms of cicadas (258e–259d).

Like its predecessor, the sixth part of Socrates' demonstration that erotic madness is a divine gift for our benefit is not explicitly marked. Again, it is possible that I have promoted a segment of the fourth section to independent rank, in response to Socrates' move to another branch of the topic of recovery from wing loss. However, I regard it as a new part because it introduces the topic of anamnesis.

Socrates has said that fallen souls that have seen true being become human and that the psyches that have never elevated their charioteers' heads into the hyperuranian region become beasts. Now he explains that the latter cannot become human because they lack the necessary rational power. A human being must grasp what is said about form, that is, that which, going from many perceptions, is gathered into one by reasoning (λογισμῷ, 249b6–c1). However, this is a recollection (ἀνάμνησις, anamnesis, 249c2) of things that the soul beheld when it journeyed with god up to true being, far

32. This would appear to refute the view that Plato or Socrates held out absolutely no hope for the prospects of popular education, at least with respect to each of the many taken singly.

above what we call real things. A soul that has never beheld the hyperuranian beings could not finish the reasoning needful to humanity because it would lack the requisite memory. Not all presently existing human beings do the reasoning that is necessary for human beings. It is just that only the mind of the philosopher is winged, for he, through anamnesis, is always to the best of his ability near that which makes god divine. This is to say that insofar as he is capable, the philosopher can participate in divinity, but not that the philosopher can be a god, for a god would never have fallen from the heavens. Partaking of divinity is the highest privilege to which the philosopher aspires. Those who use memory rightly are always being initiated perfectly into mysteries and alone are perfect. However, the many will criticize them, not realizing that they have literally been "enthused," that is, pervaded by or filled with a god (249c6–d3).

I should like to digress again to note that this story advances our understanding in four ways. First, it ratifies our solution of two puzzles in the Seventh Letter: Why does Plato insist upon the intellectual exercises that yield the knowledge of the fourth level when this science falls short of the only real insight, that of the fifth? On the other hand, why do the four not amount to a method of leaping to genuine knowledge, the fifth? Here, in what seems to be an alternative version of these riddles in the *Phaedrus,* we are taught that discursive investigation of forms is the only avenue to knowledge for beings who must think with words. However, the verbal study does not by itself yield substantive results. If it proceeds without heed to the prior ascent to the supreme reality, it cannot end in the recollection that alone is worthy to be called knowledge. In other words, Socrates' anamnesis is an alternative symbolization of the Seventh Letter's flash of light. In Plato's experience, the science of the four is the sine qua non of the illumination of the fifth, but the leaping spark of the fifth is also the independent sine qua non of the perfection of the fourth. This explains why sophists can reason with great logical cunning without ever attaining to true knowledge. Second, we now see what Socrates means by speculating that he might share in a divine fate without arrogance. We have divinity in our souls that is divine insofar as it receives that which makes god divine. We participate in this fate without arrogance because we cannot receive that which makes god a god so fully as to become perfect gods. After much labor, we still get only glimpses of that which makes god divine. Third, when we notice the oddity that Socrates is demonstrating that eros is a blessed enthusiasm, but that he speaks here only of philosophy as that enthusiasm, we realize that the eros that he has in mind is philosophy, or that philosophy is the highest sort of eros. This is why Socrates claims only to have an art of eros. Philosophy and eros are one as openings of the soul to divine possession. Finally, we now perceive how the philosophic soul is prophetic in a better way than that of the traditional prophets. To have better memories of the realities aloft is to be initiated perfectly into the most real mysteries. To have little memory of the hyperuranian truths, like ordinary prophets, is to be imperfectly initiated.

Socrates now signals that he has come to the conclusion of his proof. He reminds his auditor that all his talk has been about the fourth kind of madness, eros (see 245b1–c1). It is in the nature of this mania that when the philosophic, *philokalic,* and musical or erotic man sees a beauty, he recalls true beauty, feels his wings growing, and yearns to ascend, but cannot do so.[33] (His memory of the true beauty connects the ascent of the *Symposium* with that of the *Phaedrus.* However, the ascent of the *Phaedrus* has surpassed that of the *Symposium,* flying higher than the vision of beauty, all the way up to the Essence Really Being.) The person who recalls the true beauty gazes upward longingly like a bird, caring nothing for what is here below, and is therefore called insane. However, eros is a sharing in "the best enthusiasms" (τῶν ἐνθουσιάσεων ἀρίστη, 249e1). It is a pervasion of our souls by Eros, who is "a god or something divine," an enthusiasm that comes in the form of a salvific anamnesis of our true homes and is identical with philosophy. Whoever communes in this best enthusiasm by loving a beauty is defined as an *erastēs,* a lover.

Now that we know what eros is, at least insofar as we can describe its impact on our souls (we still cannot claim to perceive its essence), we understand why it is a divine blessing. Odysseus's memory of his true home and his plans for returning there, which are stirred up in him and given to him by Athena (see, for example, *Odyssey* 7.70 ff, 13.295 ff), are the only things that pull him through his trials. Our anamnesis of our true home, which is sent to us by gods, is the only thing that will pull us through our trials. It is not easy for souls here below to recall the hyperuranian realities. This is especially difficult for psyches that had only brief glimpses of the supreme truths and also for those who, under the influence of their associations, have been so unlucky as to fall into injustice, so that they have forgotten the realities. Thus, only a few human beings who have the gift of anamnestic eros, or erotic anamnesis, and who thus are favored with philosophy as Odysseus was graced by Athena, recall the hyperuranian beings well enough to get home.

Being one of the few who has the blessing, and hoping to keep his memory as strong as possible in order to be saved, Socrates indulges a reverie,

33. To revisit an issue treated in my *Symposium* chapters, I would say that the lover also loves the beauty for his own sake when he remembers the true beauty. When the soul of the beauty contemplated the form of beauty in the hyperuranian region, insofar as it was able to do this, it became one with the form of beauty, insofar as it was capable of doing this. The true self of the earthly beauty *is* the real beauty. The true identity of all human beings is their grounding in the Essence Really Being. Throughout his palinode, Socrates has continued to obey the command of the Delphi Oracle, "Know thyself."

like the exiled Odysseus dreaming of Penelope. He relates the experience of the erosing souls who remember their homes. When they see an earthly likeness of the things of the other world, they are driven out of their senses and no longer have possession of themselves. They are not sure what they are experiencing, for they cannot see with sufficient clarity. This is partially a function of the disparity between things here and the realities there. The likenesses of virtues such as justice and moderation that we see here do not shine, so that only a few who examine them with the organs of sense can discern that of which they are images. However, in our existence up there, beauty was bright to see when the happy chorus saw the blessed sight and vision, "we with Zeus, others with other gods." In that existence, we accomplished the most blessed rite, celebrating while being whole, perfectly initiated and looking in pure bright light upon happy phenomena, not trapped in our bodies like oysters in their shells as we are now. Let this stand as a tribute to anamnesis, Socrates says, of which he has spoken much through yearning for the things of the other time (250a–c).

Three brief comments are appropriate here. First, we must note the significance of the phrase "we with Zeus." By "we," Socrates means "we philosophers," not "you and I, Phaedrus and Socrates." The phrase is a subtle reference to a line in Hesiod, "kings are from Zeus" (ἐκ δὲ Διὸς βασιλῆες, *Theogony* 96). Eric Voegelin and others argue that between the *Republic* and the *Phaedrus*, the philosopher-king seems to disappear.[34] The philosopher-king has not gone away, however. Socrates has just laid claim to the title, shifting it from poets to philosophers in the process, for the rest of the line reads: "[H]e who is loved by the Muses is happy: sweet speech comes from his mouth" (96–97). Socrates has also portrayed himself as this musical man. Further, he has again aligned himself with Odysseus, a king.

Second, it might seem surprising that Socrates has taken time out to honor anamnesis in a palinode that is supposed to be placating Eros. However, Eros comes to us as anamnesis. (This ultimately explains the anamnestic structure of the *Symposium,* too.)

Third, the conclusion of Socrates' proof has taken on the language, fervor, and tone of the teachings of the Hellenic mystery religions. This is appropriate in a palinode inspired by a prophetic soul. Philosophy is open to any form of genuine truth. It knows the highest truths through anamnestic experiences of the soul that are necessary to complete empirical-logical inquiries.

This concludes Socrates' proof that eros is a madness sent to us by gods for our great good, a demonstration that will be believed by the wise but rejected by the terribly clever.

---

34. Ibid., 138.

UNNATURAL AND NATURAL LOVES

Socrates has arrived at the fourth major part of his palinode, the analysis of unnatural and natural loves that capitalizes on his redefinition of eros as divine madness. He has finished countering the anthropologies of Lysias and the lying lover of his first speech, who saw in the human soul only an innate desire for pleasure and, occasionally, acquired opinion about "the right," that is, the shrewdest means to pleasure. He has envisaged a psyche that contains not only desire, but also *thymos* and, at its core, a higher *nous*, one that seeks its fulfillment by rising above opinion to noetic communion with a real being of which Lysias and Phaedrus, the enchanter of the shrouded Socrates, were wholly unaware. Thus, Socrates has prepared the ground for an argument that the concealed eros of the alleged nonlovers is a false, unnatural love, and that there is a true, natural eros that is good rather than evil, bearing no resemblance to either the eros denounced by the previous speakers or the non-erosing friendship praised by them.

One premise of the new argument will be that both the unnatural and the natural loves are inspired by the same experience, the vision of earthly beauty. Hence, Socrates must examine this stimulus. He remarks that here below, we have found beauty, or more accurately, that which reflects and is named after the genuine beauty (250e2–3), shining through the clearest of our senses, vision. We cannot perceive wisdom or its image with our bodily sight because this would arouse a terrible eros. Wisdom must be a more lovely emanation of the Essence Really Being than beauty. Of all the hyperuranian realities, only beauty, or its reflection, is visible to the eye.

In the case of the false eros, he who is not newly initiated (by whom Socrates seems to mean he who has not recently had anamnesis of the time when we were aloft looking around in the pure bright light) or he who has been corrupted is not able to rise from the sight of an earthly beauty to the eternal reality of beauty. Thus, he does not revere worldly beauty but yields to pleasure and "proceeds like a quadruped to beget children" (παιδοσπορεῖν, 250e5). Befriending hybris, he is neither afraid nor ashamed to pursue pleasure "against nature" (παρὰ φύσιν, 251a1). It startles us to see Socrates suddenly and inexplicably jump out of the context of the homoerotic relationships that have been at issue throughout the play, consign piggish souls to heterosexual reproduction, and call the only possible means of sustaining the human race "unnatural."[35] However, we are reacting to an illusion caused by careless reading. Plato's characters refer to male-female coitus and all *erastēs-erōmenos* bonding as "begetting children," the latter figuratively, for all homoerotic bonding is associated

---

35. Cf. Benardete: "Perhaps the most shocking remark in Socrates' second speech was about the unnaturalness of sexual generation" (*Rhetoric of Morality*, 190; cf. 147).

with begetting the "children" of speeches, virtues, technical abilities, and suchlike. It will be recalled that Diotima regularly spoke this way (see *Symposium* 209c–d). The fact is that both heterosexuals and homosexuals can be piggish and both can beget naturally.[36] Ignoring false problems, we may return directly to what Socrates has just said. I suppose that what he proclaims unnatural is not heterosexual reproduction, but the pursuit of carnal pleasure in sexual intercourse (whether heterosexual or homosexual) without reverence for the beauty upon which one begets, a reverence that must involve rising from the sight of the earthly beauty to the memory of eternal beauty. The act of irreverent begetting is piggish because it is the memory of the real beauty that is the specific difference of human nature.

In the case of natural eros, whoever is newly initiated, having seen much in the other life aloft, can rise from the vision of the earthly beauty to the memory of real beauty. When he sees a godlike face or a bodily form that is a good image of beauty, he shudders. Something of the dreadful things of the earlier time comes over him, meaning, possibly, that he recalls the horrors that cost him his home and, like Odysseus in the presence of the godly Nausicaa and her parents, regrets his errors. However, gazing upon the beauty, he is awed by him as if he were a god. He would sacrifice to the boyfriend as to a statue or a god if he were not afraid of being judged exceedingly mad. He begins to feel hot and to sweat. Beauty flows into his eyes, watering the nature of his wings. Hitherto, the broken wings have not been able to regenerate themselves because they have been stopped up at their sources. However, the heat now opens the clogged orifices, the nourishing beauty surges in, and the wing's quills swell and start to grow from roots all over the soul's form, for the whole soul was once winged. It is clear that Socrates is speaking playfully of something that happens to a lover's spiritual and bodily wings simultaneously. When the lover beholds the beloved, he grows wings of the soul. These lift him from the earthly vision of beauty to the memory of the hyperuranian beauty spiritually. Therefore, he reveres the earthly beauty properly rather than proceeding to beget like a pig. However, Socrates' likenesses are also unmistakable ribald hints that the lover becomes aroused sexually, with a bodily wing swelling and growing from the root.

Continuing his account of the experiences of the natural eros, Socrates declares that the new growth of wings affects the soul in the same way that new teeth affect the gums of a baby. The soul feels itching, irritation, boils, and tickles. When the lover's soul looks upon the lad's beauty and receives particles of that beauty that flow into it, when it is watered and heated, it is relieved of its distress and rejoices. The waters flowing into

---

36. I am attempting to report Socrates' opinion accurately. I am still not certain as to whether he condones gay coitus or envisages only spiritual homoerotic begetting.

the soul as particles are called *himeros* (yearning) by virtue of a punning etymology that does not carry well from Greek into English. *Himeros* is a divine improvement on *epithymia*. When the beloved is absent, the *himeros* does not flow. Then the lover's soul is parched; all the orifices shut down again, choking off the new wing growth; and the entire soul is distressed by goads stinging every one of its pores. However, then the lover remembers or sees the beloved again and rejoices. Alternating between agony and joy in a way that it cannot understand, the lover's soul becomes frenzied and is driven crazy. It cannot sleep at night or hold still by day but runs wherever it hopes to see the beloved. Beholding him, it lets the water of *himeros* pour in, unclogging its pores and winning release from its sufferings, harvesting this "sweetest pleasure" in the present.

Here, Socrates is plainly still speaking of what happens in the lover's soul when he sees the beloved. If we ask whether he envisages sexual acts, too, I answer that I am not sure. We shall see more evidence soon. For now, I can say only that Socrates might want his symbol of an influx of the spiritual waters of *himeros* to make his psychic eroticism a mystical analogue of homoerotic coitus. He is, after all, discussing eros with a gay. Lest Plato's drollery should upset anyone if I dwell on it, I turn directly to another aspect of his humor. W. C. Fields, the great American comedian, once made a movie titled *You Can't Cheat an Honest Man*. The lovable villain of the piece, Larson E. Whipsnade, meets the prospective mother-in-law of his beautiful daughter and finds the pompous, officious woman extremely annoying. Discovering that the woman is deathly afraid of snakes, he begins to tell a tall tale about snakes, causing his antagonist to faint. Every time she wakes up, he shouts the word "snake," causing her to pass out again. In the passage just summarized, Socrates has been taking the same perverse pleasure in torturing his comrade. Phaedrus is a valetudinarian. Pain is his *summum malum*. Socrates has been introducing Phaedrus to the mysteries of natural eros by associating it with images of cutting, irritation, itching, boils, and pain that must be making his comrade's skin creep. Not only that, but every time he has allowed Phaedrus up for a breath, he has also shouted the word "pain" again, undoubtedly driving him into greater hysterics. This has been a good test to determine whether the palinode has helped cure Phaedrus of his will to power. It has been wonderfully funny.

Socrates is not content to torment Phaedrus with images of pain. Having tightened the screws of this torture sufficiently, he begins to harp on slavery, too. He argues that the *erastēs* cannot endure to be separated from his *erōmenos*. The lover forgets family and friends, loses his property through neglect, insanely counts all that as nothing, and volunteers to serve as a slave and sleep wherever he is allowed to lie down near his beloved. He not only reveres the beauty but also finds in him the healer of his afflictions. He concludes: "This is the suffering, O beautiful boy to whom I am speaking, that human beings name eros" (252b1–3). Socrates has horrified Phaedrus by making the lover into the abjectly needy man whom Lysias and he most scorned. Theoretically, Socrates has now established that the natural love is anything but the cool, absolute self-possession to which the valetudinarian Phaedrus aspires. Socrates wants to convert Phaedrus to right pederasty, to the philosophic eros, but he knows that it would be useless to do so under false pretenses.

Socrates brings this section of the palinode to a close with another joke. He quotes the verses of the Homeridae on Eros, which declare that mortals call him "Flying Eros" (Ἔρωτα ποτηνόν), but the immortals name him "Wing-eros" (Πτέρωτα) because he must grow wings. This is a pun that treats the consonant cluster "Pt," the first two letters of "wing" in Greek, as a prefix of "eros," arriving at "Pteros." The pun cleverly shows that wing grows to its fullest extent by absorbing eros, causing aficionados of low humor to love Plato all the more. Although we can believe or not believe the pun as we choose, says Socrates, this nevertheless happens to sum up the cause and the experience of lovers. In natural love, there must be wing that lifts us up to anamnesis of the hyperuranian reality of beauty, causing us to revere its earthly image. The price for developing the wing that ascends to the memory, which is the greatest of divine blessings, is the erotic experience of extreme pain and abject servility, which is a far cry from a personal godhood that can control the order of being.[37]

THE ADVANTAGES OF NATURAL LOVE

The preparations for the fifth part of Socrates' palinode are now finished. Socrates will expound the benefits that a lad can derive from befriending the natural *erastēs,* thus reversing the evil judgments passed on love in the two previous talks. Socrates begins with distressing news. Evidently, it can be dangerous to associate with people possessed by the natural eros. A follower of Zeus (namely, a philosopher-king, Socrates) is not threatening because he can bear more of the maddening winged god than other human beings. However, someone who served in the train of Ares, for example, becomes murderous when he thinks that he is being treated unjustly by his *erōmenos.* This invidious comparison is grandly comical. Previously, Lysias's speech had included a surreptitious advertisement for himself as a suitor, one that maintained that the "previous friend nonlover" was the best choice for a youth confronted with a plethora of loving and nonloving

---

37. In ibid., 146, Benardete makes the pun into an atheist manifesto, arguing that the gods cancel themselves because the consonant cluster "pt" is unpronounceable. This is a rather long stretch.

petitioners for his favor. However, Lysias, the arms manufacturer, would seem to have been a follower of Ares in the former life. Socrates is offering Phaedrus a choice between himself and Lysias, warning that if Phaedrus chooses Lysias, he could get his throat slit by a sociopath, even if Lysias were a natural lover. Phaedrus's eyes must be bulging.

With his self-advertisement broadcast, Socrates next mounts a less grisly defense of true love. In the earlier speeches, the most damaging charge made against eros was that it prompts the lover to ruin his beloved's character. Therefore, Socrates moves immediately to refute this accusation. He remarks that in their first lives on earth, those who are uncorrupted attempt to imitate the gods whom they followed in heaven. Their behavior toward their beloveds and all others is guided by their commitments to honor and emulate their tutelary divinities. Each lover experiences eros for many beauties and then, from among all these, selects as his beloved someone whose character corresponds to that of his leader god. Then he fashions and adorns him like a statue of that god, to honor and worship him. For example, those who are of Zeus (Διὸς) seek a spiritually heavenly (δῖόν, 252e1) erōmenos. They ask whether a prospective beloved is philosophic by nature and capable of leadership. When they have found the youth they want, they do everything in their power to ensure that he has these qualities. It has been pointed out, quite correctly I believe, that Plato's expression in the Greek text, Διὸς δῖόν (the genitive of Zeus paired with the adjective that fundamentally means "Zeus-like" and that needs only to exchange an omicron for an omega to become Dion), is no accident: Plato is writing a love letter to Dion, explaining to his godly erōmenos why he chose him, and telling him his hopes for him.[38]

Be that as it may, the lover realizes that his education of his beloved improves his own character, too, for he grasps the nature of his god in memory, becomes enthused by him, and adopts the god's habits and practices to the extent that a human being can share in the divine.[39] Believing that the beloved is the cause of these benefits, he cherishes him all the more. If he

38. This point about Διὸς δῖόν was first made by Kurt Hildebrandt in *Platon: Der Kampf des Geistes um die Macht*, 289. Next it was taken up by Voegelin in *Order and History*, 3:16–18. Finally, Nussbaum, who cites neither Hildebrandt nor Voegelin, apparently rediscovered the phrase independently and made quite a lot of it (*Fragility of Goodness*, 228–29).

39. Benardete maintains: "The realization of the lover's own nature in the beloved can be done only if there is complete self-knowledge that can divine its own nature in another" (*Rhetoric of Morality*, 148). This ignores the fact that the lover's education of the beloved also educates the lover, who acquires new qualities that he could not have recognized in himself previously because they were not there yet. Indeed, the process raises doubts as to whether complete self-knowledge will ever be possible for human beings. The frequent repetition of the qualifier regarding human participation

draws his waters of inspiration from Zeus, then, just like bacchants pouring water onto their beloveds' souls, he makes the beloved as much as possible like Zeus—no small benefit. There is a tremendous difference between having had one's character ruined, as in the first speech of Socrates, and having had it made Zeus-like. Things go similarly with the followers of other gods. Unlike Phaedrus and Pausanias, these lovers teach without envy or meanness, shaping their charges as much as possible like their gods. The lads become beautiful and happy. However, here is a cautionary note: this is true only in the cases of natural lovers who are uncorrupted.

Still with a view toward elucidating the advantages of taking a natural lover, Socrates decides now to undertake a discussion of the manner in which this *erastēs* captures a beloved. The very manner of having been wooed and won by a natural lover will be beneficial to the youth. In the two previous speeches, it was implied that sick lovers attract their beauties by flattery. It was also demonstrated to the eye that the alleged nonlovers, who are really lying lovers, appeal to their beloveds with a more subtle flattery that addresses them as sophisticates who know the score in the real world. Socrates wishes to argue that the beloveds are caught not by flattery but by overwhelming reverence, and not by a force that seeks to exploit them, a rhetorical violence that is equivalent to rape, but by service. At this juncture, a worldly wise *erōmenos* can be expected to become suspicious. The beloved has been told that the reason his suitor is a human being at all is that he possesses two horses in his soul, one bad and one good, and that the bad horse played a decisive role in the lover's failure in the earlier life, giving his psychic charioteer more trouble than he had the character to handle. Why should the beloved imagine that things will be different in the earthly life? Why should he believe that it will not be the lover's bad horse who calls the shots, endangering beloveds?

This problem compels Socrates to analyze the battle between the lover's horses in this life. The story opens with an account of the goodness and badness of the horses (but not with any information about the natures of the charioteer or the chariot). The good horse stands on the right, in the more beautiful position. He is correct in form, well jointed, disposed to carry his neck high, hook-nosed, white, and dark-eyed. He is an *erastēs* of honor together with sane self-control and modesty, a companion of true opinion, not in need of the whip, and guided solely by command and logos. The bad horse stands on the left. He is crooked in form, large or heavy or complex (all of these being proper translations of πολύς), randomly constructed, strong-necked, short-necked, black, gray-eyed, snub-nosed, and

---

in divinity, "to the greatest extent possible," should be noted. As far as I can determine, the qualifier is never contradicted in the dialogue.

bloodshot. He is a comrade of hybris and boasting, shaggy-eared, hardly obedient to whip and spurs, and dull of hearing or mind (κωφός, here probably meaning deaf to logos, for he can hear perfectly well when his soul mates give him alluring promises).[40]

These traits seem to be apt mythical personifications of *thymos* and *epithymia*. The qualities of the good horse are what one would expect to discover in a good spirited element of good descent that, nevertheless, is still a beast and, hence, in need of the guidance of reason to make it friendly to justice and courage. The qualities of the bad horse are what one would expect to find in pure appetites. I doubt that his attributes have further significance. Many writers do see important implications. They want to identify the black horse as Socrates, who might have been physically crooked, heavy, randomly built, strong- and short-necked, black, gray-eyed, snub-nosed, and bloodshot. However, the comparison fails when we come to spiritual qualities. The Platonic Socrates is not hybristic, except in the accusations of several sophists whom he flusters and in the eyes of esotericists who like the idea of an essentially hybristic philosopher. If we cannot agree on that, Plato's Socrates is manifestly not given to boasting and is even more obviously not unresponsive to the commands of logos. He is not the black horse. Plato is not giving the wise secret clues with his lists of the qualities of the beasts. Of course, I do concede that Socrates is partially the black horse, but only because every human being is part black horse, just as every individual is also part white horse and part charioteer in Socrates' ethical (but not ontological) metaphor.

When the charioteer beholds the erotic eye or face of his beloved and his whole soul is warmed and filled with longing, the horse that obeys the charioteer, restrained by its sense of shame, refrains from rushing the lad. The other horse becomes oblivious of the charioteer's whip and spurs, leaps toward the youth, causes the white horse and charioteer every kind

---

40. Benardete argues that the ten attributes of the white horse and the thirteen attributes of the black horse not only fail to match up as exact opposites but also leave the black horse with three extra traits (ibid., 149). He draws esoteric conclusions from this. His analysis is fatally flawed. First, the white horse has twelve, not ten, traits, and the black horse has fifteen, not thirteen. Next, Benardete, like Hegel, seems to make identifying "opposites" a creative art. For example, it seems to me that "smallish" is not necessarily the opposite of πολύς. If the black horse is desire, πολύς refers to the massive complexity of desire. Its opposite could be "simple," or "light." Also, inasmuch as Socrates has said that only the mind of the charioteer can feed on the hyperuranian vision, and given that the black horse is deaf to logos, it is hard to see how anyone could infer that the opposite of the white horse's spiritedness or association with true opinion is love of knowledge. The proper opposite is more likely love of license. The exegesis seems to be an example of esotericism run amok, probably in aid of the implied argument on the jacket cover of Benardete's book, which depicts two winged horses flying through the heavens, no charioteer, no chariot, and the face of Socrates on the black horse.

of trouble, and proposes the delights of sexual gratification to the lad. The charioteer and white horse resist, on grounds that the black horse is suggesting terrible, unlawful things. Socrates does not tell us why the black horse's intentions are terrible and unlawful. Either he regards homoerotic intercourse as intrinsically wrong or he means that the concupiscence of the black horse is totally lacking in reverence for beauty and, accordingly, unnatural. We shall be able to say more about the correct choice between these alternatives shortly. In the meantime, the charioteer and white horse weaken and agree to do what the black horse wants. The soul of the natural lover is evidently no ethical superhero. Just as it did in the heavenly life, it finds itself too irresolute to avoid being carried in evil directions. Socrates, like Odysseus, is a reed in the moral winds. The beloved was right to suspect his motives. The black horse drags its soul mates all the way up to the boyfriend. The terrible, unlawful seduction is about to begin.

The natural lover's charioteer then looks into the beloved's face. The youth's visage is "flashing like lightning" (254b5). I think that it is precisely at this moment that we most easily understand that prophecy, philosophy, and eros are one. Zeus is the hurler of lightning bolts; the god is communicating with the prophetic core of the lover's soul through the youth's face. The lightning flashing in the boy's eyes drives the *erastēs* back and then carries his anamnesis up to the nature of beauty standing with sane self-control on a chaste pedestal. The dramatic situation replicates the moment in the *Odyssey* when the hero's bad companions have gotten him in trouble and Zeus saves him by striking his ship with a thunderbolt, setting Odysseus on a new route to his rightful salvation.[41] The dramatic situation also replicates the moment in the Seventh Letter when the philosopher, who has been ranging up and down among the four, suddenly receives the flashes of spiritual flame that lift him up to the fifth. However, we are speaking of eros in the present context. Prophecy, philosophy, and genuine, natural eros are the same experience.

When the flashes remind the charioteer of beauty and sane self-control, he is afraid and falls back. His recoil causes him to pull back on his reins, wrenching the horses down to their haunches. His reflex action is the beginning of his salvation from the crime that he was about to commit. The soul acquires its first ordering virtue not through its own devices but through a "divine dispensation" (θεοῦ μοῖραν, *Republic* 493a1–2). The initial divine shock does not complete the soul's formation, either. When the charioteer and the white horse reel away from the boy, stunned, awed, amazed, fearful, and sweaty, the black horse angrily reproaches them for being cowardly and for breaking their agreement. He resumes his troublemaking.

---

41. This analysis, of course, is inspired by the use that Planinc makes of the same Homeric symbol.

His mates weaken again and promise to let him have his way later. He hears and remembers their promise quite well. When the appointed time comes, the charioteer and the white horse pretend that they have forgotten their pledge, but the black horse shamelessly and much more violently forces them to approach the youth again. The effect on the charioteer is the same as before, only stronger. He fearfully falls backward again, pulling on the reins powerfully. The reflex covers the jaws of the black horse with blood and causes him excruciating agony, surely to Phaedrus's extreme dismay. This scene is repeated frequently, until the black horse virtually dies of fright whenever he sees the beloved. From this time forward, the lover's soul follows the lad in reverence and awe. The *erōmenos* can trust the *erastēs* to treat him well not because the lover is born essentially more moderate than other men but because divine interventions have tamed the lover's black horse, making his whole soul eager to serve.

In narrating this myth, Socrates has finally repudiated the most terrifying lie in Lysias's speech, namely, that the lover is in the grip of an iron necessity that constrains him to exploit, demean, and ultimately abandon his beloved. He has argued that the philosophic lover has an intellect that is strengthened by attunement to the highest realities, enabling it to discipline the lowest, most unruly element of his soul and, thus, to avoid doing the greatest evils. Not every so-called lover will achieve this. In every case, the outcome depends upon the interventions of the god and the lover's noetic response to them. However, when things go well, the beloved can expect "all service" from the lover (255a1). Therefore, taking a natural lover who has not been corrupted leads not to massive, irreparable harm but to possession of a devoted friend.

Here, it will be profitable to pursue a digression. One frequently encounters scholarly apologies for the black horse. There is a tradition of sympathy for this horse that goes back for decades, perhaps even centuries. I shall cite two of his most recent defenses.

G. R. F. Ferrari says that "although the charioteer seems to stand for the control of reason and the bad horse for brutish, uninhibited lust, in the struggle between the two it is the bad horse who adopts persuasive language and the methods of reason, while the charioteer maintains control by sheer strength and wordless violence." He contends that the black horse does not force his soul mates to join his lusty campaign by brute strength because they are "persuaded" to help. He calls the sentiment that the black horse expresses in rebuking the charioteer and the white horse for cowardice "lofty." He holds that the bad horse's behavior when he finally whinnies and becomes violence incarnate is understandable because it has been "prompted by a failure to secure his ends through the unquestionably rational means of verbal contract, a failure that in turn derives from an apparent refusal by the voice of reason and his ally in the soul to stick to reason's rules." Ferrari then makes the black horse the myth's hero, claiming that "only through the agency of the bad horse does the charioteer come into full re-possession of his birthright; for he would not otherwise have come close enough to be dazzled."[42]

Seth Benardete agrees: "Without the black horse, the lover would not have approached the beloved, but in shame and awe would have kept his distance and loved in silence. . . . The very possibility that there be a growth of wing depends on the constant concessions the white horse and charioteer have to make to the black horse." Having made the black horse a savior in the tale, Benardete then permits him to grow into the central figure in the entire dialogue. He argues that the real speaker of Socrates' first speech is "the black horse, who has disguised himself to look like the white horse." From this he infers that the white horse "is a complete invention of the black horse." Then he declares that the white horse is Phaedrus displayed to himself through Socrates, with the implication that "Socrates, then, is the black horse, who can be both himself and another."[43]

I think that these arguments are dreadfully wrong. Even so, I believe that there is an important truth in the errors. Therefore, I shall point out what I take the mistakes to be and then say why Ferrari's and Benardete's claims still point toward something right.

As Ferrari is aware, the battle between the black horse and the charioteer commences after the whole soul has been warmed and goaded by the desire stimulated by the sight of the young man. Then Socrates says that the bad horse "leaps violently forward" (σκιρτῶν δὲ βια φέρεται, 254a4), "causing all troubles" (πάντα πράγματα παρέχων, 254a4–5) for his mates, and that he "compels" (ἀναγκάζει, 254a5) them to cooperate in the "terrible and unlawful" (δεινὰ και παράνομα, 254b1) act contemplated. When the charioteer's resistance to the bad horse weakens, the reason is that "the evil has no end" (μηδέν ᾖ πέρας κακοῦ, 254b2). Then, the charioteer and the white horse go along with the black one, "agreeing" (ὁμολογήσαντε, 254b2) to do his bidding.

Thus far, the image that Socrates has presented is scarcely that of a rational philosopher leading an interlocutor to assent to a logical argument by employing the dialectic. To change Socrates' metaphor, the black horse looks more like a bulky adolescent who is pestering his father and brother to help him kidnap and rape a beauty in the family car, and who is bullying them by grabbing the wheel of the moving vehicle, twisting arms, punching, kicking, gouging, shouting, cursing, coaxing, whining, weeping, browbeating, and practicing every other form of savagery included under "causing all troubles." The adolescent should be depicted as using

42. Ferrari, *Listening to the Cicadas,* 186, 188, 192.
43. Benardete, *Rhetoric of Morality,* 150.

"persuasive language and the methods of reason" only if that is a fair reading of this syllogism: "Unless you help me, I'll break your kneecaps and harass you until you die of exhaustion, so it would be prudent for you to do what I demand." When the beleaguered father is "persuaded" by this logic, it is not because he has bowed to "reason's rules," but because he sees "no end of the evil," has grown weary, and believes that he can hold out no longer. He can be viewed as "having entered freely into a contract by unquestionably rational methods" in the same sense that an extortion victim submits voluntarily and wisely, and to the same degree that a subject of torture can execute a binding contract to commit a crime. Socrates' explicit words demand this conclusion and no other. I am astonished and amazed to see Ferrari's construction placed on the passages under consideration.

In fairness to Ferrari, one should note that he admits at one point that the black horse has gained the upper hoof in the first round of the fight not by virtue of his astute reasoning, but by muscle power.[44] Ferrari means to praise the dark steed's conduct not in the first, but in the second round. Therefore, it is necessary to take a closer look at the language with which Socrates describes the next and subsequent stages of the conflict.

Socrates explains that after the charioteer first reneges, the black horse "breaks forth into angry scolding, bitterly reviling (ἐλοιδόρησεν ὀργῇ, πολλὰ κακίζων) his yoke-mate and the charioteer in many ways for their cowardice and lack of manhood in deserting their post and breaking their agreement" (254c7–d1).[45] The bad horse then resumes "compelling" (ἀναγκάζων, 254d1) his comrades to advance and only grudgingly grants their request to postpone the affair. He flies into a rage when they pretend to have forgotten, dragging them forward.

It seems strange to represent this behavior of the black horse as philosophic. It is extremely difficult to see how angry vituperation featuring accusations of cowardice and lack of manhood qualify as "persuasive language and the methods of reason," or how the sentiment in this torrent of abuse is "lofty" rather than hybristic. Perhaps a case could be made for this opinion if the bad horse were legitimately appealing to the ethical principle of the sanctity of contracts, or exhorting soldiers in a just war by shaming them for having betrayed their holy cause. However, he is berating his

44. Ferrari, *Listening to the Cicadas,* 187.
45. For the key words in this translation, I follow Harold North Fowler in the Loeb edition. The verb λοιδορέω signifies abuse of such intensity that when it is applied to the gods, H. G. Liddell and R. Scott translate it as "blaspheme." When Phaedrus twice uses derivatives of this verb to describe how the politicians are abusing Lysias (257c5–6), Ferrari does not suggest that the politicians are using persuasive language and the methods of reason on Lysias. The word ὀργή connotes passionate anger; it is used by Socrates at 257a8 when he implores Eros not to let his anger prompt him to take back his gift of the art of love.

soul mates illegitimately for breaking an extorted promise to be party to an atrocity and, thus, for doing what moral reason requires them to do at this time. Hence, to describe the speech of the black horse accurately, one would have to say that he is mouthing lofty concepts that he heard incidentally from philosophy, using them in total ignorance and disregard of their real meanings, in an attempt to pressure the charioteer. He is adopting not "persuasive language and the methods of reason," but rhetorical violence and the methods of sophistry. This judgment would not be altered if, instead of heaping invective on his mates, the bad horse spoke in the formal syllogisms of Socrates' first oration. It has already been shown that Socrates does not equate reason primarily with logical proofs. *Nous* does not deduce the highest truth from premises; it sees it wordlessly in the hyperuranian region. Logical syllogisms proceed from this vision rather than preceding it, and they must start with its truth to deserve the name of reason. Any sophist can begin with a lie and reason logically from that premise to conclusions that justify his crimes.

Further, besides "reasoning," the black horse reverts to his troublemaking. Near the end of the second round, Socrates declares that this horse starts "compelling" the driver and the other horse forward again (254d1). In saying this, Socrates uses the same term that he had employed in the first round (254a5), when there was no trace of reason in the black horse, and the same word that he will utter again soon (254d5), when this horse becomes pure violence. This implies that the conduct of the bad horse does not change essentially from beginning to end, except insofar as its hybris is intensified by sophistry. Therefore, we must imagine that the second round plays itself out essentially the same way the first one did, with the charioteer caving in to extortion and consenting to help the black horse again, only this time begging to put the crime off until he has rested a bit. The bad horse agrees because he thinks that he will get his way more efficiently if he waits until he can use the charioteer's intelligence to entice the boy, this being the post that he accuses the charioteer of having deserted. Thus, Ferrari's reading is still astonishing, for the new promise extracted from the charioteer is no more a contract reached "through unquestionably rational means" than the previous one.

If this is true, it will be inquired why the charioteer does not subjugate the black horse rationally, by defeating his sophisms with logic. Why should the charioteer maintain control by sheer strength and wordless violence? To put this question is to have missed all the points established previously. Reason consists in the vision of the hyperuranian beings. The vision is silent; anamnesis of it must therefore be silent, too. The charioteer could not relate it to the horses with propositional truths and syllogisms. Also, when the charioteer recalls the vision, he falls back in terror with a strength that is not his, but the power of Zeus. It is doubtful that he could subdue the black horse by himself any more than he could persuade him. *Nous* must control the horses with divine power because it needs that help with a strong brute. We reach the same results when we consider Socrates' previous descriptions of the horses. These steeds have never seen truth and are naturally incapable of appreciating it. By nature, the good horse loves real honor, and this is what allows him to be guided by the word of command and logos. The bad horse is κωφός, that is, deaf to logos. It would be absolutely senseless for the charioteer to reason with the black horse because this steed has no natural ability to perceive the truth or comprehend rational argument, even though he can bandy ideas and mendacious syllogisms, like the courtiers of Dionysius in the Seventh Letter. To attempt a philosophic education of appetite would be much the same as trying to reason with a horse. Accordingly, reason's rule over appetite should be, and only can be, a benevolent tyranny, exercised by sheer wordless strength. Now that reason's wings are broken, the power that it applies to this task must be the god's, not its own. The charioteer is derelict in his duty as master of the psyche when he fails to govern the black horse in this manner. He was a bad charioteer in the ether because he did not train his bad horse well, not because he failed to reason with him (247b2–4). Now the charioteer is getting another chance on earth to pass the tests that he had failed aloft. He had better get the art of governing horses right this time or he might actually become a horse.

As for Benardete, his opinion that the black horse is the inner being of both the white horse and the charioteer collapses *thymos* and reason into appetite, with the implication that the secret truth of love is violence. Benardete thus esoterically arrives at a Socratic dogma that is the direct opposite of what Socrates has labored long and hard to teach exoterically. In the process, he transforms Plato into Hegel, or perhaps Freud. The only answer that I can make to his argument is that it has no foundation in Plato's text. It is true, of course, that the black horse disguises himself when he speaks. However, he strives to look not like the white horse but, rather, like the charioteer, which explains why some believe that he is reasoning. It seems to me that the correct inference to draw from this is not that the black horse is really Socrates but, rather, that it is natural to the black horse to masquerade as what he is not in his struggles to have his own way.

Despite these flaws in the analyses of Ferrari and Benardete, they and their precursors are absolutely right about one thing: the *erastēs* would not have approached his *erōmenos* and, thus, would not have begun to pursue his rewinging if the black horse had not forced him to try to seduce the beauty unlawfully. If the black horse is bad rather than good, and a criminal rather than a hero, he still plays a crucial role in the soul's return to its true home. What are we to make of this? Is evil our salvation?

Before tackling this question, we should notice that we are not dealing with a Platonic anomaly. Kenneth Dorter makes an enormously valuable contribution to our understanding by observing that the argument that we see in the *Phaedrus* is repeated in many different ways in many dialogues. For example, in the *Republic,* the way to the good lies not in an austerity that restricts the city to the necessary appetites but in Socrates' accession to Glaucon's demand for pleasure. "The path to transcendence," says Dorter, "leads through the dangerous fevers of the unnecessary desires, which must later be tamed, in the third city, by the control of reason in the person of the philosopher-ruler."[46] So, I inquire again, what are we to make of this?

I am afraid that my contribution to the solution of this puzzle will be modest. First, I must counsel against a confusion of Socrates' ethical categories. Evil is not good. The black horse is not the white horse or the charioteer. *Epithymia* is not *thymos* or *nous.* The plunge into unlawfulness is not salvation. Next, I must note that the situation that Socrates describes on earth replicates the one that he paints in heaven. In both conditions of the psyche, the bad horse initiates the action. In the *Odyssey,* the worst self of Odysseus has the same function. I conclude that Plato-Socrates is teaching a mystery that might surpass our understanding: In all things human, as I have said previously, the way down is the way up. This is not to argue that down is up but only that we are beings for whom the fall always precedes the ascent. I think that the badness of the black horse symbolizes this fact and not some Manichaean flaw in the original human nature, which tended toward its fall but did not face a metaphysical necessity of falling. The black horse can be trained to revere beauty, which would be impossible if he were fundamentally and permanently bad by nature. Incidentally, the reverence for beauty that resides in the charioteer would have probably guaranteed a reverent approach to the boy had the black horse not interfered. It is not necessarily true that every love must begin with an intended rape. In principle, human lovers *could* approach each other in manners in which reverent reason is impelled by an appetite (black horse) performing its truly natural function: to initiate movements of the whole soul toward its good. The sad empirical truth is that for us, it just does not happen that way, for we always take the way down before we ascend.

We return from our digression to Socrates' palinode. The black horse has been tamed. The lover is ready to offer all service to his beloved. Now Socrates continues the story of how the beloved is caught. Socrates says that the boyfriend sees that he receives all possible service as if he were a god. The beloved also perceives that he has an *erastēs* who is not feigning but

---

46. Dorter, "Three Ladders," 283–85.

who has really been affected this way.[47] He discovers too that by nature, he is a friend to the man who serves him. Previously, under the influence of his schoolmates' warnings, he always repelled the lover, but he now admits the *erastēs* into his company, for it is fate that good will be friend to good. The beloved is amazed at the goodwill that he receives from his "enthused friend" (255b6–7), from the lover who has been pervaded by Zeus. Over time they consort in the gymnasiums, touching one another. Then finally that stream that Zeus named *himeros* when he was in love with Ganymede is directed copiously toward the lover. Part of it enters into him. When he is full, part also flows back out again. (Perhaps gods do not feel human eros for human beings, but they do experience *himeros* for them, which could be a higher sort of eros. Zeus permits this higher type of desire to stream from himself into human lovers, too. The cosmos is awash in divine *himeros*.) The flow of beauty rebounds back into the beloved, through his eyes. From his eyes it goes straight into his soul. Thanks to this watering, his wings begin to grow, just as his lover's wings are sprouting again.

In these lines, Socrates is again speaking of spiritual events. It is the spiritual waters of *himeros* that flow from Zeus into the two lovers, purifying them, and flowing back and forth between them. These waters enter the lovers through their eyes and stream into their souls. The waters do not enter and come to rest at other places. Still, I think that Martha Nussbaum is quite right to maintain: "The complex imagery of Socrates' second speech—in which a flood of liquid entering into the lover brings intense pleasure and the release of his own 'imprisoned waters'—metaphorically expresses a certain type of male homosexual point of view towards sexual experience."[48] It is more clear than ever that Socrates is making the spiritual events of eros a mystical analogue of both sexual and homoerotic intercourse. Socrates-Odysseus is now coupling with his Penelope in the spirit, and Plato is also uniting with his Dion, in the spirit if not yet in the body. Their mutual surrender is animated by spiritual waters of *himeros* that flow from Zeus. For those who might find the imagery offensive, I should point out that this is not the only time in the history of thought that spiritual mysteries have been symbolized as analogues of intercourse. Christianity has its images of the Church as the bride of Christ and its Saint John of the Cross who sings of love between the bridegroom and the soul. The imagery is actually extremely beautiful.[49]

47. That is, the lover has really experienced true eros. This is not just *epithymia* but a desire guided by reason infused with prophetic understanding and strength from Zeus.
48. Nussbaum, *Fragility of Goodness*, 231.
49. Heterosexual Christians would probably relish this image more if we translated the spiritual eros into a mystical analogue of male-female intercourse in which our love of our beloveds streamed into our souls from God. Then, by empathy, we could sense that Plato's metaphor would be most beautiful to a person of gay sensitivity and see

However, what about the body? Socrates finally confronts this question directly. The lover has now caught his beloved. *Himeros* is flowing between them. Their wings and feathers are growing. The beloved is bewildered by all this, not sure what he is experiencing. Much like his lover, he finds that he wants to embrace, kiss, and lie down with his friend. At this point, the lover's black horse speaks up. He has been quiet for a long time, fearing more punishment if he were to demand his unlawful pleasures. However, he now asks for a little consideration. The boyfriend's black horse is sympathetic to the proposition. Nevertheless, the two charioteers and the two white horses resist, with shame and with logos. It seems that when black horses have been tamed, even they can listen to reason.

Unfortunately, we do not hear what logos is telling the horses. Instead, Socrates says that if the better parts of the lovers' minds triumph, leading them to a well-ordered way of life and philosophy, they lead blessed lives here below, mastering themselves, enslaving their bad elements and liberating their sources of virtue. In the end, they become winged and light, having won one of the three wrestling matches that they must win in order to return to the heavens forever. On the other hand, if the lovers befriend honor rather than philosophy, and if they get careless and permit their black horses to carry them away, so that they do things from time to time of which their whole minds have not approved, the two live together as friends, both during and after their period of intimacy. They have given and received from each other pledges of trust that it would be unrighteous to dissolve. In the end, they go forth from their bodies unwinged, yet having striven to acquire wings, so that they win "no small prize" for their erotic madness. What prize? Socrates explains that it is the law that people who have once begun their upward journeys, by which he means not everyone who has fallen from heaven, but those who have begun their return voyages along the *axis mundi,* shall live happily in the light, traveling with each other, and eventually become winged for love's sake.

From this, I infer that Socrates recommends celibacy to homosexual lovers. However, quite unlike the Athenian Stranger in the *Laws,* he has not condemned homoerotic intimacy as wholly unnatural. Instead, after having made spiritual purification the mystical analogue of homoerotic intercourse, he has bestowed "no small prize" upon the homoerotic lovers who do engage in this union. It seems to me that if he regarded homoerotic intimacy as irredeemably evil, or as "terrible and unlawful" (δεινά και παράνομα, 254b1) in itself, beyond all hope of justification, he could not vote them this prize. Nay, he could not depict their deed as a path to rewinging in their future life, on the grounds that they have acted "for

---

how it could be beautiful for us, too. We would understand what Socrates is trying to say and respond to its truth.

love's sake," which implies that they have "begotten" in a manner that reveres beauty rather than like quadrupeds. Nor could he view spiritual eros as a mystical analogue of homoerotic sex, as if the latter were beautiful. Accordingly, in the *Symposium* and *Phaedrus*, his refusal to condone homosexual union is not a denunciation of the act as such. In Christian terms, it is not a judgment that the act is "mortal sin." Rather, the act is a kind of hindrance to perfection (perhaps a "venial sin," with more good than sin in it). Therefore, the Athenian Stranger's rulings in the *Laws* may be less philosophical than political.[50] Meanwhile, Socrates' charioteer must have some as yet unstated reason for choosing homoerotic celibacy. However, what could it be?

In approaching this problem, we must take care not to let our speculations outrun the available information. Thinking back to the story of the souls in the heavenly life, in which these psyches are not naturally intended for embodiment in human form, some are tempted to construe Socrates' commendations of celibacy as the products of a Manichaean hatred of the body. Such loathing would eventuate in demands that souls avoid physical pleasures and that steps be taken to prevent new incarcerations of spirits in bodies through sexual reproduction. However, this does not fit the context. Rejecting this explanation, I see only one other possibility. Plato has experienced his gay orientation as a definite sign of the call to a higher spiritual union. He demands celibacy of himself, for his soul must concentrate on its preparations for the final flight to the heavens.

The discourse on the advantages of taking a natural lover is finished. The benefits are spiritual. They have nothing to do with the wealth and social position desired by Phaedrus. They also completely repudiate the *libido dominandi* of the democratic tyrannical eros.

The Disadvantages of Gratifying Nonlovers

The sixth section of Socrates' palinode is exactly one sentence (of five Stephanus lines) long. It approximately matches the length of Socrates' praises of the benefits of gratifying the non-erosing in his first oration. If the shrouded Socrates refused to eulogize nonlove out of fear, the bareheaded Socrates shortens his denunciation of it out of disdain. He argues simply that the mortal sane self-control (moderation) advocated by Lysias

---

50. If I had space to analyze the *Laws* here, I would go in the direction charted by Randall Baldwin Clark in "Platonic Love in a Colorado Courtroom: Martha Nussbaum, John Finnis, and Plato's *Laws* in *Evans v. Romer.*" This excellent article verifies that it is dangerous to attempt to derive hard-and-fast doctrines from the Platonic corpus.

administers the association of *erastēs* and *erōmenos* in a miserly fashion, producing in the friend's soul the illiberality that is so lauded by the many. Its reward will be even worse than animality. It will cause the soul to roll around mindlessly under the earth for nine thousand years.

A Closing Prayer to Eros

Socrates concludes his recantation with a prayer to Eros. He pleads that he has made his palinode as beautiful as he could, seeing that he was forced to couch it in poetic expressions because of Phaedrus. He asks for pardon, pleads not to be struck blind, and begs Eros not to deprive him of the art of love (τὴν ἐρωτικήν τέχνην, 257a7–8) that the god gave him, but to let his *technē* be honored more than ever by the beautiful. He asks Eros to blame Lysias if anything was said amiss previously. He implores the god to stop Lysias from composing evil speeches and to turn him toward philosophy, as his brother Polemarchus has been turned, so that Phaedrus will also devote himself to Eros and philosophic discourses.

This prayer contains Socrates' first and last reference to his *technē* of love. Inasmuch as the art is identical with philosophy, and eros-philosophy re-wings the soul, one should like to know what the art is. Nothing in Socrates' speech indicates that this art is a science of the type desired by Phaedrus. That is, the art is not a method by which a purely human intellect acquires a knowledge that permits it to dominate the conditions under which it will exist. So far, nothing like modern scientific method has been advocated anywhere. The art is a gift of the god. Continued possession of it depends not on Socrates' expert domination of being, but on the favor of the god. All this is to argue that the art is not a tool for attaining the Hegelian goal of turning philosophy from "mere" love of wisdom into *Wissenschaft*, produced scientific knowledge. Socrates does not believe in the possibility of such a metamorphosis. Later in the *Phaedrus,* he will pointedly reserve the word "wise" for god alone (θεῷ μόνῳ, 278d4), and it has been seen above that he denies that human beings can achieve divine status.[51] If Socrates' recantation indicates anything about the nature of his art at all, it is that this

---

51. Thus, I cannot agree with Benardete: "Socrates' erotic art would thus stand for the possibility of science in general; and inasmuch as the erotic art seems to be the same as philosophy, it would represent the aspiration philosophy must have to transcend itself and become wisdom" (*Rhetoric of Morality,* 103–4). As usual, Benardete is trying to transform Plato into Hegel. His arguments in this regard depend on his conscious and openly stated rejection of what Socrates actually says. No Hegelian interpretation of the art of love could be correct if Socrates meant what he said about the superiority of divine madness.

technē consists in openness to divinely inspired anamnesis and divinely in-stilled awe of real beauty.

THE AFTERMATH

The argument and drama of the *Phaedrus* have arrived at a critical junc-ture. Phaedrus has asked, in effect, whether people should love health de-fined as the painless enjoyment of all pleasures, giving free reign to all their erotes, and whether they should pursue health by means of a rhetoric that violently reduces others to slavery. Socrates has shown that the correct way to look into this hypothesis is not to elaborate an apparatus of definitions, observations, and deductions, as moderns prefer to see scientists do, but to submit the proposition to a psyche of the highest ontological rank, a soul that is philosophic, *philokalic*, erotic, and musical. This soul prophetically rejects Phaedrus's position. Bursting into philosophic song, it teaches that there are unhealthful and healthful erotes. It maintains that the unhealth-ful eros is a sick, egoistic madness. The healthful eros is an enthusiasm, a pervasion by a god, a sharing in a divine madness. This is an alternative symbolization of the account of Eros offered by the prophetess Diotima, in which Eros is a fetus nascent in our nature. For "Stesichorus," Eros is a divine something that is manifest to us as an upward pull exerted on our souls by Zeus. However, it is still an enthusiasm, the essence of which we cannot really state because we do not know what a god is. This Eros teaches human beings that they should love the beauty that emanates from the Essence Really Being; that they ought to embrace the madness and pain that yearning for this unknowable, ineffable good entails; and that they should seek union with this beauty by means of playful, mythical speech that counsels souls freely to open themselves to divinely inspired anamne-sis. Socrates thus lays the basis of the truest and best science of rhetoric that mortals can obtain, one that mythically points to mankind's true object of love (real beauty), that identifies this right object of love as the genuine telos of persuasive speech, and that offers its own presentation of itself as an ex-ample of the sort of rhetoric that best leads to union with the real beauty. If Socrates could capture Phaedrus with this science of rhetoric, the dialogue could close with Socrates' prayer, or with Phaedrus's assent to it. Then we could all breathe a sigh of relief, for Phaedrus, like Socrates, would have been saved from nympholepsy and a fall into the ranks of subterranean things.

Phaedrus professes himself ready to join in Socrates' prayer "if indeed these things are better for us" (257b7–c1). His conditional "if" proves that he is one of the terribly clever who does not believe Socrates' demonstra-tion. A little later, he will declare that one should not live for the sake of pleasures before which one must experience pain in order to be able to feel the pleasure (258e). Socrates' request to Eros to turn Phaedrus to philosophy and to devotion to philosophic speeches proves that Phaedrus has not been spending his life philosophically, as a dear and dedicated student of Socrates. Phaedrus's responses indicate that he will not live this way afterward, either.[52] Socrates must do his best to rescue Phaedrus by employing some other subphilosophic tactics.

52. Thus, with Planinc, I cannot imagine how Nussbaum concludes: "We know that Phaedrus will not long remain a devotee of anti-erotic argument. He will soon, in fact, be deeply moved by a speech that attacks Lysias's condemnation of the lover's madness" (*Fragility of Goodness*, 210).

9

PHAEDRUS: THE RHETORIC OF EROS

Odysseus is carried by a Phaeacian winged ship from Scheria to the outskirts of Ithaca. His homecoming is simultaneously a descent and an ascent. It is a descent because he is forced to face people who are morally inferior to the godly Phaeacians before he can be reunited with the fair Penelope. He must do battle with the suitors. The Phaeacians were wise, good, and generous. The suitors are stupidly clever, evil, greedy for wealth, and ambitious for the power of Odysseus's throne. Owing to these differences, Odysseus must abandon the beautiful, noble methods of dealing with human beings that he used with the Phaeacians and resort to coarser, less agreeable ones. The Phaeacians were open to truthful speech. The only language that the suitors understand is violence. Odysseus must kill them in the banquet hall. This leaves him with a political mess that he can clean up only in a rather unjust fashion. Odysseus also recalls Teiresias's prophecy that he must make another journey to many mortal men, plant his oar in the ground upon meeting a wayfarer who says certain words, and sacrifice to Poseidon before he can rest in Ithaca with Penelope and finally die far from the sea. Thus, his homecoming is a prelude to another descent in the sense that he will recover his Penelope only briefly before being torn away from her again. However, it is also an ascent because it lets him snatch a few moments with Penelope and because he is on the way to his ultimate happiness with her.

When Phaedrus joins Socrates' prayer to Eros conditionally, thus expressing his polite rejection of the idea of eros as a beneficial divine madness, the dramatic setting of the dialogue shifts again. Socrates-Odysseus has been borne away spiritually on the wings of his horses and has landed on the shores of his Ithaca. His homecoming is simultaneously a descent and an ascent. It is a descent because he is forced to confront people who are ethically inferior to his fair lad (the fictitious one, who seems to have usurped Phaedrus's role as Nausicaa at 252b). He must battle men who are the spiritual equivalents of the suitors.

Phaedrus, who has hitherto been permitted to play Circe, Calypso, and Nausicaa, does not get to act Penelope. Thanks to his skepticism about divine erotic mania, he has forfeited any right that he might have had to represent the vision of beauty. Instead, he is drafted to speak for sophistical rhetoricians who have been flocking around the halls of power in Hellas. These orators are the new suitors of tyranny. Unlike the fair lad, they are stupidly cunning, evil, greedy for wealth, and ambitious for the power of the tyrant's seat. Therefore, Socrates-Odysseus must abandon the beautiful, noble methods of dealing with human beings that he used with the fictional boy and resort to coarser, less agreeable ones. The fair youth was open to truthful speech, but the only language that the new suitors can grasp is rhetorical violence. Socrates-Odysseus must "slaughter" them with withering dialectical critique. This will leave him with a political mess that he cannot clean up without the physical carnage with which the *Odyssey* ends. Having enjoyed a restoration of order in his own soul, he will refuse to resort to this sort of injustice. We also know full well that he must make another journey, "plant his oar in the ground" upon meeting someone who says certain words, and sacrifice to Asclepius before he can rest in his spiritual Ithaca with his vision of beauty, having died away from the sea. Accordingly, his homecoming is a prelude to another descent in the sense that he can attain to his vision of beauty only for brief moments before he is torn away from it again. However, it is also an ascent insofar as he can snatch his few minutes with his vision and because he is on the way to his ultimate happiness.

I believe that awareness of these dramatic parallels saves us from a major error. There is a widespread supposition that the concluding half of the *Phaedrus* finally ascends to dialectic and, hence, to real philosophy, replacing the "false" thesis that erotic madness is rational with "sober" argumentation.[1] This gets Plato's intention precisely backward. The transition from Socrates' prophetic poem to the discussion of writing and speaking that Phaedrus initiates is a descent from real philosophy and rationality, qua erotic divine madness, to a subphilosophic rational sobriety. As Zdravko Planinc points out, Phaedrus demonstrates by his reactions to Socrates' second oration that he is incapable of attaining to the highest reaches of philosophy, thereby forcing Socrates to drop the level of the conversation a notch in a last-ditch effort to help him understand at least something in a far less than adequate way.[2] Knowing the plot of the play

---

1. For example, see Benardete, *Rhetoric of Morality*, 103.
2. It should be plain that I am still working within the framework created in the manuscript of Planinc, *Plato through Homer.*

enables us to see that reducing philosophy to dialectic and repudiating erotic madness violates the dialogue's structure. However, we do not need the *Odyssey-Phaedrus* parallel to reach this result. The Seventh Letter leads us to the same determination, for the reception of the illumination and the movement up to the perfect knowledge of the fifth are the equivalent of the erotic madness, whereas the inferior ranging up and down among the four is the dialectic.

BEAUTIFUL SPEECHES, CICADAS, AND KINGS

Phaedrus skeptically affirms Socrates' prayer, declaring that he will join it *if* the things for which his companion has petitioned are better for us. Then he announces that he has been wondering about the second oration for some time, for Socrates made it much more beautiful than his first one. He fears that Lysias will disappoint him if he tries to write another speech to compete with the prophetic poem. Addressing Socrates as "O amazing man," he adds that a politician has lately been criticizing Lysias for "this very thing," calling him a "speechwriter." Therefore, in light of his love of honor, Lysias might decline to write again.

Phaedrus's answer raises some questions. Phaedrus doubts the argument of the second speech but still deems it beautiful. Why does he thus separate truth from beauty? Further, he wonders, but what he wonders about is not the veracity or duplicity of the oration but, again, its beauty. Why? Also, he seems to change the subject without realizing it. What is the link between astonishment at the beauty of Socrates' poem and the statesman's attack on Lysias for being a "speechwriter"? What is "this very thing" that has outraged the politicians? Finally, why does Phaedrus regard the creation of beauty as the affair of a rhetorical competition that involves the love of honor?

I have already indicated sufficiently what Phaedrus's reply about the prayer means. He has understood nothing. He is one of the terribly clever who rejects Socrates' demonstration, not one of the wise who believes it. His separation of truth from beauty is another proof that his soul is closed to philosophy. It will be recalled that Phaedrus was present on the occasion of an earlier conversation about truth and beauty. In the *Symposium*, Socrates was terrified at Agathon's ability to distort truth while achieving a certain verbal beauty. Agathon could do this by transferring the words that generally represent beauty from beautiful realities to ugly realities. His act risked incurring the wrath of Persephone and the permanent entrapment of Socrates-Odysseus in Hades. Phaedrus either does not remember or never accepted Socrates' judgment of this sort of "beautiful" oratory. Rather, he is thrilled by it. He is still much the sophist who cares nothing for truth as long as a speech seems beautiful to those who hear it. He is amazed by what he takes to be Socrates' ability to produce this effect. I believe that this explains his jump from wondering about the beauty of Socrates' oration to the assault on Lysias for being a speechwriter. Phaedrus has not changed the subject. "This very thing" that has infuriated the statesmen is Lysias's insidious practice of detaching truth from beauty in his writings. The politicians might not comprehend that this rhetorical strategy is the thing that exasperates them, but they know that, somehow, sophists always beat them, and they resent it. This is how beauty can be the measure of a competition that involves the love of honor. If a speaker can move his audience to vote his composition the most beautiful, without regard for its truth or falsity, he will bask in thrilling glory. We recall that in the *Symposium*, Phaedrus wanted to be honored for beautiful speeches more than anything else in this life. He has not changed a whit in nine years, despite Socrates' patient efforts with him. I think that if I were Socrates, I would throw up my hands and depart at this juncture. It is to Socrates' credit that he, like Odysseus, desires and strives to save his comrades, who will perish through their own blind folly—fools.

We now see why Socrates is obliged to drop the conversation a level or two if he wants to rescue the hopeless Phaedrus.[3] However, his first problem in this endeavor is to keep his comrade in the conversation. Phaedrus's statement that Lysias would probably refuse to compete is a dismissal, a sign-off, an indication that the discussion is finished. Socrates must prevent Phaedrus from clamming up before he can deal with his errors.

Socrates acts forcefully. He exclaims: "You are stating a ridiculous teaching, young man!"[4] He says that Phaedrus is surely underestimating his comrade if he assumes that Lysias would be frightened off by a little noise. Furthermore, the politician is not serious about reproaching speechwriters. Phaedrus objects. Everyone knows that the powerful men in cities are ashamed to write speeches and leave behind literary deposits, fearing that they will be called sophists. Not so, replies Socrates. Every time a statesman proposes a law, he writes a speech, naming himself as its author and identifying those who have approved of it, that is, the council or the assembly. If he succeeds in getting the law passed, thus becoming an immortal speechwriter, he considers himself equal to a god. Phaedrus would think this great glory. He cannot wriggle out of the conversation by pleading that speech writing in itself is inconsistent with the love of honor. He is compelled to agree.

3. Phaedrus's response alone should suffice to prove that the second half of the dialogue cannot be an ascent to real philosophy. Socrates and Plato always argue that genuine philosophy is for only the capable.

4. This does not mean that Phaedrus is literally a young lad. Although I am in my early sixties at this writing, retired gentlemen in their eighties call me "sonny."

Now Socrates can lead the conversation toward the examination of Phae-drus's mistakes. He suggests that it is not writing in itself that is shameful, but writing in a manner that is "not beautiful," that is, shameful and bad. Phaedrus is again obliged to agree. Then Socrates asks if he and Phaedrus need to inquire into what beautiful and shameful writing is, examining Lysias and all others who have ever written or will ever write. This enor-mous assignment will soon be narrowed down to Lysias and the most fa-mous rhetoricians. The suitors are filing into the banquet hall. In reply to Socrates' question, Phaedrus asks another: "For what, then, would some-one live, if I may speak thus, but for such pleasures? Not, I assume, for those before which one must feel pain in order to enjoy pleasure" (258e1–5). I have mentioned that this reply signifies Phaedrus's total rejection of the argument of Socrates' prophecy, in which both spiritual and bodily eros must be preceded by pain analogous to the irritation of teething. Here, I may append another observation. The answer, which appears to agree to Socrates' proposal, has a subtext. Phaedrus means that he does not really want to talk anymore if the conversation does not produce pleasure with-out pain. He suspects that he is in for another shellacking, so he would actually prefer to lapse into silence. This obliges Socrates to offer another argument for continuing the discussion.

Indeed, declares Socrates, we have leisure. Furthermore, the cicadas singing overhead in the heat are watching us. If they should see the two of us not conversing at high noon but, rather, dozing and bewitched by them, they would laugh at us, thinking that some slaves had come to their resting place to sleep at high noon, like sheep around the well. However, if they see us talking, sailing by them as if past Sirens, not bewitched, perhaps they will bestow upon us the gift that the gods permit them to give to human beings.

This speech requires a short digression. Socrates has emphasized twice within five lines that it is midday, high noon (259a2, 6). Plato wants us to notice this. However, it was also "almost noon" just before Socrates began his second speech (242a4). All through Socrates' long poem, the sun has not moved in the sky, and no time has passed! The prophecy was commu-nicated from the god to Socrates' soul and related by Socrates to Phaedrus in an eternal moment.[5]

To get back to the cicadas, Planinc observes that some scholars have dis-missed this episode as a structural flaw in the dialogue, a weak effort to paper over the juxtaposition of two fragments (one on eros and one on rhetoric) that cannot be forced together as a coherent whole. However, we

5. In this respect, then, we have no good cause for holding the *Phaedrus,* with its mythology, philosophically inferior to the similarly timeless *Republic,* with its math-ematical approach (that is, the proportions in the images of the sun, line, and cave).

have already seen that Phaedrus's response to the prophetic poem is in character and, therefore, dramatically and logically demanded. The parts of the dialogue plainly fit together naturally. Planinc goes on to show that the interlude of the cicadas makes perfect sense in context. It is Plato's refiguration of another Homeric trope. As Plato indicates directly, the cicadas are the Sirens. Socrates-Odysseus is sailing back over a large expanse of ocean that he had navigated earlier because he wishes to save his comrade. Phaedrus desires to hear nothing but song that glorifies him. Socrates is warning Phaedrus that if he sails too close to that song and listens to it, the Sirens will bewitch him, with disastrous consequences. However, if he sails by them, he will receive their gift.

We inquire: What consequences? Phaedrus asks: What gift? Socrates responds that it is quite improper for a lover of the Muses to be ignorant of such matters. Once upon a time, he says, there were human beings before the Muses had come to be. When the Muses came into existence and song was revealed, some of these men were so overcome by pleasure that when they sang, they forgot to eat and drink and died without noticing it. The cicadas arose from them with this gift from the Muses: From birth to death they need no nourishment but sing constantly without food or drink. Then they go to the Muses to report who on earth honors each of them. Some tell Terpsichore of those who honor them in dance. Others commend erotic poets to Erato, and so on. Some fly to Calliope, the oldest Muse, and to Urania, reporting on those who spend their time in philosophy, thus venerating the Muses who are most concerned with the heavens and speech both divine and human, and whose music is most beautiful. So, for these reasons, we ought to talk, not sleep, at noon.

It is obvious that in this response, Socrates is warning Phaedrus that a spiritual death awaits him if he lets the Sirens enchant him or, more tragically, if he bewitches himself with the Siren song of his own glory. As Planinc says, Phaedrus will end up like the husks of men that litter the shore around the Sirens' abode, skeletons that resemble the shells of the cicadas that die off in droves. After that, he will drop out of the ranks of human beings, falling even below tyrants as an insect. However, he can escape this fate if he philosophizes. This will be like tying himself to the mast, for those who philosophize adhere adamantly to the *axis mundi*.

However, this speaks only of the avoidance of punishment. What is the gift that the cicadas can bestow upon the philosophers? Is it simply that they will give good report to the Muses? Or is it that the Muses will favor philosophers with the ability to chant the most beautiful music, thus granting Phaedrus what he has always wanted? I imagine that it is likely that the cicadas will bring these gifts, which are not inconsiderable. However, I think that Socrates has more in mind. His association of philosophy with Calliope is another subtle reference to Hesiod's *Theogony.* Hesiod declares that Calliope is the preeminent Muse. She attends on a reverent king, pouring sweet dew on his tongue, so that gracious words flow from his lips. All people look to this Zeus- and Muse-favored king to settle their causes with true judgments (79–86). In this view, if the cicadas report to Calliope that someone is honoring them by philosophizing, that individual becomes a philosopher-king. This is the second time that Socrates has claimed that rank, transferring it from poets to philosophers, quietly rather than loudly. I believe that Eric Voegelin is right to argue that Plato does not advocate philosopher-kingship as a practical, institutional arrangement in the *Phaedrus*.[6] Thus the understatement of Socrates' claim. However, the philosopher-king remains in the city. His prize is that he functions as a king of the spirit, a man with divine authority who is not a tyrant.

TRUTH, HORSES, AND ASSES

It is established that Socrates and Phaedrus must inquire into the essences of beautiful and shameful speech writing. Socrates now drags Phaedrus's fundamental conviction out into the light. If a speech is to be beautiful, he asks, must not the speaker know the truth about the things of which he speaks? Phaedrus replies that he has heard the opposite: an orator need know not what is really just or good or beautiful but only what seems so to the many, because the most persuasive speaker will be the one who appeals to what the many believe to be true.

Socrates agrees to examine this proposition. Suppose for the sake of argument, he says, that Socrates and Phaedrus are ignorant of horses but that Socrates knows that Phaedrus calls the tame animal with the biggest ears a horse. Suppose also that Socrates seriously attempted to persuade Phaedrus to buy this so-called horse, arguing that the misnamed ass was valuable both as a mount in war and as a beast of burden. Phaedrus replies that this would be absurd. Socrates counters: However, is it not stronger (that is, more persuasive) to be silly than to be clever and hostile (that is, opposed to popular belief)? Socrates is reminding Phaedrus of his endorsement of rhetorical victory gained by false persuasion. Feeling trapped, Phaedrus unwillingly answers: "Apparently." Socrates presses his *reductio* to its conclusion. Noticing that Phaedrus defines the good as the useful, he inquires what the result would be if a rhetorician, ignoring good and bad in themselves, studied the opinions of the many, learned that the many defined the bad as the good, and persuaded the many to do the bad rather than the good. Phaedrus concedes that this would not be well. The admission has been wrung from him. Logically, he should now grant that a speaker ought

6. Voegelin, *Order and History*, 3:133–39.

to know the truth of the matters of which he speaks. His equation of the good with the useful demands this. However, he still resists the inference emotionally. This is because Socrates has not refuted the claim that the most persuasive speaker will be he who appeals to what the many believe to be true. Rather, Socrates has traded on it in order to force Phaedrus into his present logical dilemma.

Socrates moves next to take care of this loose end. He suggests to Phaedrus that they may have treated the *technē* of speaking too boorishly. Perhaps Rhetoric would reply that she forbids no one to know the truth but contends only that a person who has learned what is real should take her up, for this knower will not be able to persuade anybody without her. Well, asks Phaedrus, that is right, is it not? Socrates answers that it would be right if Rhetoric were a *technē*, but he hears some arguments approaching and denying that she is a *technē*. There is no genuine *technē* of speaking without grasping the truth.

The badly shaken Phaedrus wants to hear these arguments. Socrates addresses them as if they were living beings, urging them to persuade Phaedrus that if he does not philosophize adequately, he will never speak adequately about anything. It should go without saying that if Socrates needs to pray (now for the second time) for Phaedrus to be brought to believe that philosophy is necessary, Phaedrus has never been philosophic. Against this background, the inquiry into whether rhetoric is a *technē* begins.

Socrates suggests a definition of Phaedrus's *technē* of rhetoric: it is the art of leading the soul (*psychagogia*) with words, both in public (in law courts and other assemblies) and in private, with regard to both great and small things. Phaedrus objects, swearing by Zeus. Apparently, he is agitated by the inclusion of private gatherings and unimportant objects in the definition. This would be inconsistent with his thesis that rhetoric must appeal to the beliefs of the many, and also with the relationship that he stubbornly insists on seeing between victorious rhetoric and honor. Thus, he argues that rhetoric is an art that pertains to public judicial and political assemblies only. Socrates replies that Phaedrus must have heard only of the rhetorical arts of Nestor and Odysseus and not of that of Palamedes. Phaedrus swears by Zeus again that he has heard of no such *technai*, unless Socrates is equating Nestor with Gorgias and Odysseus with Thrasymachus or Theodorus. Phaedrus has named the three sophists who are the only public speakers whom he thinks worthy of being symbolized as the two greatest orators in the *Iliad*. However, he has misunderstood the allusions. Socrates evasively answers "perhaps" and temporarily falls silent about Nestor and Odysseus, pushing ahead to the topic of Palamedes. He inquires whether the rhetorical art, as practiced in law courts, makes the same thing appear to the same people sometimes as just and sometimes as unjust, as the speaker wishes, and whether it makes the same things seem sometimes good and sometimes bad to the city. Phaedrus takes this for granted, thus betraying his essential commitment to sophistry. Socrates then asks whether the Eleatic Palamedes (Zeno) does not play these tricks (in his private teaching). This is obviously true. Thus, it is established that rhetoric is an art that pertains to all things public and private, great and small, if the *technē* exists. This point might not seem all that important. However, it is significant because it breaks Phaedrus's connection between the genuine rhetoric of which Socrates will speak (one that knows the truth) and allegedly necessary appeals to the beliefs of the many. Plato is nothing if not thorough.

Now Socrates is ready to make another effort to persuade Phaedrus that a speaker must know the truth of the things of which he speaks. The need for such an enterprise has become clear with Phaedrus's evident delight in the sophist's ability to make the repulsive, the unjust, and the evil look like their opposites: Phaedrus simply does not want to be held to the truth. He still wants victory with honor, despite his previous concessions.

The argument that Socrates advances next is not precisely the most inspiring defense of philosophy's commitment to truth that one can find in the history of thought. Rather, it is a rationalization calculated to appeal to Phaedrus's basest instincts, a maneuver to which Socrates resorts because every other approach has failed. It is a statement to the effect that the speaker who knows the truth is able to deceive an audience more effectively than one who is ignorant. Deception arises with regard to things that differ a little rather than much, for the things that differ greatly cannot be mistaken for one another. With respect to two things that differ only a little, a knower can cause the two to be confounded by steering someone away from one to the other by minute, imperceptible steps. Socrates asks Phaedrus whether a speaker who was ignorant of the truth could do this. Phaedrus's answer is no. Socrates then suggests that a man who does not know the truth, trading only in opinions, therefore has a fatuous art of speech. Phaedrus is not convinced, conceding only that "it may be." For once, Phaedrus is right to be skeptical of Socrates' reasoning. Socrates has certainly not proved that knowledge of the truth is necessary to deception. Indeed, his own example of horses and asses has demonstrated that one ignoramus could lead another anywhere. This is to say nothing of the fact that although good differs fundamentally from evil, good and evil are easily confounded by the stupid.

Logographic Necessity, Dialectic, and *Psychagogia*

Socrates asks Phaedrus whether they should now examine Lysias's speech, to determine whether it is artful. Odysseus is about to slay Antinous, the leader of the suitors. Phaedrus is happy about the suggestion. He has been faring poorly in abstract discussion and believes that a substantive example will save Lysias. Little do the suitors know that it is Odysseus who has strung the mighty bow and stripped off his disguise. The argument will continue to proceed on the basis of the premises that the most artful rhetoric is the most deceptive and that he who knows the truth is better able to defraud others than an ignoramus.

As an introduction to the evaluation of Lysias's composition, Socrates remarks that by some chance, his own two speeches furnish an example of how someone who knows the truth can lead audiences astray. As usual, chance is equated with divine action: Socrates asserts that the gods of the place are responsible for the result. Perhaps, also, the cicadas, the prophets of the Muses, have given them this "gift of honor." This is not to say that the gods have been up to deliberate evil. In war, it is beneficial to learn the strategy of the enemy. Socrates is surely thanking the gods for the insights. The first of Socrates' orations illustrates the best deception. The second discloses the truth. Together, the two speeches will serve as the standard against which Lysias's sophistical effort will be measured.

At the behest of Socrates, Phaedrus reads the first lines of Lysias's speech. Socrates then takes up the analysis by distinguishing between essences about which everybody concurs and those about which there is disagreement. For example, everyone recognizes iron as what it is, but there is discord about the just and the good. Socrates argues that it is obviously difficult to hoodwink people about the clear things and easy to delude them about the disputed things. A speaker who would deceive others should divide all things into forms about which the many are necessarily at sea and those with regard to which they are settled. Phaedrus thinks that he who could do this would understand a beautiful form fully. He is incorrigible. Socrates asks whether eros belongs in the category of disputed forms. Phaedrus replies that it plainly does, for otherwise Socrates would not have been able to state in one speech that eros is harmful and in another that it is the greatest blessing. The inference is that the best deceiver must not fail to induce his audience to accept a false definition of the subject that he is expounding.

Having established this standard for assessing Lysias's sophistry, Socrates next declares that his memory has failed because of divine possession and inquires whether he defined eros at the beginning of the speech. We cannot be quite certain whether Socrates is asking about a definition at the start of his first or second oration. We assume that he is referring to the first, but his question is vague. Perhaps this confuses Phaedrus, for he replies: Νὴ Δία ἀμηχάνως γε ὡς σφόδρα (263d4). Now we face a difficulty. Experts disagree about the meaning of this outburst. Here is a sample of their translations: "Yes, indeed, and immensely thorough you were about it" (R. Hackforth). "Yes, indeed; that you did, and make no mistake"

(B. Jowett). "Oh, absolutely, by Zeus, you most certainly did" (Alexander Nehamas and Paul Woodruff). "Yes, by Zeus, and wonderfully well" (Harold North Fowler). "Yes, by Zeus, with a vehemence beyond conception" (James H. Nichols). We are not concerned about the omissions of "by Zeus," an unconscionable practice in which late-nineteenth- and early-twentieth-century translators frequently engaged. What stumps the classicists is what ἀμηχάνως γε ὡς σφόδρα means. Particularly at issue is what ἀμηχάνως means, for γε ὡς σφόδρα is generally recognized as an expression that imparts vehemence to a statement. It is philosophically and dramatically imperative to get the translation right. In this regard, it is impossible that ἀμηχάνως could mean "certainly," "thorough," "wonderfully well," and "beyond conception" simultaneously.[7]

H. G. Liddell and R. Scott offer a wide range of definitions of ἀμηχάνως. It includes "without resource," "inexplicable," and "inconceivable," but not "thorough" or "wonderful." In other Platonic texts (see, for example, *Republic* 509a6 and *Phaedrus* 229e1), the word plainly means "inconceivable." These kinds of evidence indicate that Phaedrus's reply means: "By Zeus, most inconceivably," or, as in Nichols's variation, "Yes, by Zeus, with a vehemence beyond conception," or perhaps, as Zdravko Planinc would have it, "By Zeus, with inexplicable excess." "Certainly" and "absolutely," "thoroughly," and "wonderfully" seem to have little philological basis and less relationship to the context. I think that Phaedrus, who is disturbed enough by what he has heard to swear by Zeus again, is declaring that he cannot conceive of Socrates' combination of two definitions of eros: one that he admired, because it compelled the assent of its addressee with an astonishing power, and another that he hates because it inexplicably resists the self-deification of man and militates against his own honor. Ignoring the insulting implication, Socrates then seizes upon the complimentary half of Phaedrus's answer, saying: "Whew! How much more technically proficient do you say the nymphs, daughters of Achelous, and Pan the son of Hermes are than Lysias the son of Cephalus with regard to speeches." The reference to the nymphs shows that Socrates is arguing that his first oration, which was inspired by nymphs, was technically good, or artful. The invocation of Pan, the speech god who is smooth, divine, and true in his upper parts and rough and false in his lower parts, and who may well be the god in the plane tree, indicates that Socrates is extending his claim to both speeches, taking Phaedrus to admit that Socrates' two orations together were most artful. Phaedrus probably did not intend this at all, but Socrates has now interpreted his reply as the concession that he seeks.

---

7. The Hackforth translation is in the Edith Hamilton and Huntington Cairns anthology. The Nehamas and Woodruff translation is in the John M. Cooper anthology. The Fowler translation is in the Loeb series.

Next, Socrates asks whether Lysias provided a definition that compelled his addressee to assume that Eros was one definite thing, so that all the other assertions in his speech could be related to that thing. Phaedrus reluctantly reads the opening lines of Lysias's oration again. Nothing of the sort is there. I would interject that this is a valid criticism of Lysias: given that his object was to deceive, his speech lacked anything that was guaranteed to compel the mind to succumb to the deceit, even though it contained much calculated to move the emotions in that direction. Thus, Socrates mocks Lysias as a speaker who tries to begin where he should have ended, with things that he might have said after he had established what eros is. Lysias, as it were, attempts to swim upriver through his own speech on his back, from the end to the beginning, like an upside-down Odysseus landing on the isle of the Phaeacians. Furthermore, Lysias throws statements into his speech randomly, as if it did not matter where any particular line of it was located. However, there is a logographic necessity in speech writing. "Every speech, like an animal, must be organized such that it has a certain body of its own, so as not to be headless or footless but to have a middle and extremities, suitably articulated with regard to each other and the whole." Lysias fails this test. Phaedrus complains that Socrates is mocking Lysias, so Socrates leaves off. However, Phaedrus's intervention has been too late. Antinous is dead.

As Planinc has demonstrated, Socrates now returns to the subject of the rhetorical arts of Nestor and Odysseus. Of course, these warriors never wrote treatises on rhetoric. Rather, they delivered speeches in the *Iliad*. Nestor gave one that divided the troops by tribe and clan after Odysseus had given one collecting them. Division and collection are the two functions of dialectic. Socrates is the dialectician who both divides and collects, and who is both Nestor and Odysseus. Indeed, he declares himself a lover of dialectic because it enables him to think. He would follow any man who had the power to see the things that had naturally grown into one or many, as after the footsteps of a god. Many interpret this to mean that dialectic is the highest form of philosophy. However, Planinc has also shown that Socrates' statement refers to lines in Homer in which Odysseus follows in the footsteps of Calypso. The goddess gives Odysseus an ax and an augur so that he can fell trees (divide) and join them together (collect) into the raft on which he can leave her island. Thus, Socrates-Odysseus is returning to a lower stage of his ascent of the *axis mundi* to offer Calypso's tools to a comrade who is still trapped there. The tools do enable one to think well enough to escape imprisonment. However, they are not the wings that one needs for the final ascent to the truth.

This discussion of dialectic begins with Socrates' remark that he will let Lysias alone in order to examine something else proper to speeches. Socrates says that his two speeches were opposites, one arguing for gratification of the lover, the other of the nonlover. He reminds Phaedrus that the two orations were given madly, for eros is madness. There are two forms of madness, one arising from human sickness and the other from divine origins. It is not hard to infer that his first speech represented the sick madness and the second the healthy, divine one.

Now, he says, the second oration divided divine madness into four types: the prophetic inspiration of Apollo, the mystical initiation of Dionysus, the poetic madness of the Muses, and eros, the best madness. Socrates' memories are still defective owing to divine possession. He did not make the original division (244a–245b) exactly in this way, for he never mentioned Apollo or Dionysus explicitly, and he has now forgotten the Zeus served by the prophetesses of Dodona. I assume, however, that this is an illuminating summary of what he meant in his enigmatic first presentation of the division. The madness that relieves people who belong to families that suffer from ancient guilt must be associated with Dionysian cults. Socrates adds that the second speech made an image of erotic experience, perhaps attaining to some truth, perhaps elsewhere being led astray, thus mixing a speech that was not entirely untrustworthy with measured play and a mythical hymn. This was not altogether unpleasant, says Phaedrus. We know that he greatly admired the beauty of the hymn.

These preliminaries out of the way, Socrates remarks that his talks stated two forms by chance. We should keep in mind that chance is equivalent to divine intervention: Socrates is thanking the gods again. The two forms under discussion are division and collection. He says that his two speeches began with the concept of unreason (he means madness) and divided it.[8] They cut one part of eros on the left (thus, a sinister part), justly reviling it (because it was the egoistic love of the professed lover, which was identical with the selfish love of the professed nonlover). They cut another part of eros on the right, discovering something with the same name (eros), something divine that they praised as an extremely great good (because it differed from the evil one, leading us upward). Phaedrus agrees that this was said. Socrates then argues that division and collection enable one to think and that one should follow people who can do this as if they were gods. He calls the art of dividing and collecting dialectic and asks whether it is used by Lysias and Thrasymachus, those wise rhetoricians who offer the gift of speech as if it were a present for kings. Phaedrus insists that these sophists are kingly and agrees to name the art that Socrates has described dialectic, but he denies that Socrates has touched upon anything having to do with rhetoric. That is, he rejects dialectic, ignorantly spurning the lifeline that

8. Here, he does explicitly say that they were two speeches, not one speech with two parts, as some maintain.

Socrates has thrown him. He still believes that sophistry is kingly. He is in grave danger of dying because of his blind folly—a fool. However, Socrates will keep trying to help him.

Socrates acts surprised. He asks whether he has overlooked something beautiful that makes rhetoric a *technē.* Phaedrus responds that he has certainly omitted many such things, namely, all the refinements discussed in the extant books on rhetoric. Phaedrus has unwittingly initiated the slaughter of the rest of the suitors. Inasmuch as we are not familiar with the works that Socrates proceeds to criticize, I shall skip over the arrows and sword thrusts with which he disposes of particular sophistical writers. Instead, I shall concentrate on the element of good rhetoric to which he points. Appealing to the medical *technē* of which Phaedrus is so enamored, Socrates asks whether Eryximachus or Acumenus would agree that someone who indiscriminately administered remedies to sick people was a real physician. Phaedrus thinks that they would call this mad. Socrates seizes upon the admission, saying that to have a true art of rhetoric, a person must know what methods and arguments to use where and when. It will not do to issue blanket prescriptions of fancy techniques for every situation. Phaedrus fears that this might be true and asks where someone might find the power really to persuade. Socrates has caught Phaedrus with a grappling hook. He finally has a means of compelling his interlocutor to value truth.

Socrates answers that genuine power to persuade is found not along the lines followed by Lysias and Thrasymachus, but in the approach of Pericles. He comments that Pericles was perhaps the most perfect orator. This tentative praise contradicts his vehement denunciation of Pericles in the *Gorgias* (515e–516e). We would be startled by this if we had not noticed earlier that Socrates regales Alcibiades with lavish encomiums on the Persian monarchs who are jeered in the *Laws.* Socrates will celebrate Pericles here because Phaedrus regards Pericles as the most successful rhetorical competitor and most kingly man. He will attribute virtues to Pericles not because Pericles had them but because Phaedrus might desire to acquire them if he believes that they accounted for Pericles' achievements.

Socrates shows us, Plato's readers, that he is speaking ironically about Pericles' virtues in order to snare Phaedrus by remarking that all great *technai* require "babbling" about nature and the things aloft. (Phaedrus will appreciate the cynicism of the word "babbling.") Pericles had a good nature and, in addition, acquired what was needed by associating with Anaxagoras (in whom Socrates was disappointed as a youth, and of whom he evidently has a rather poor opinion). Pericles was filled with such high-minded talk. In this respect, his rhetorical *technē* was like the medical art (another inducement to the preposterous Phaedrus to accept Socrates' argument). In both medicine and rhetoric, declares Socrates, it is necessary to divide up nature—the nature of the body in the former case and the nature of the soul in the latter—with a view toward dispensing drugs and nourishment to bodies, and speeches and lawful practices to souls. Phaedrus allows that this is likely.[9] Socrates therefore asks him whether it is possible to understand the nature of soul in a manner worthy of speech without understanding the nature of the whole. He is pushing Phaedrus toward an acceptance of philosophy—that is, toward an acceptance of philosophy at the level of dialectic and, hence, at the inferior level of the four analyzed in the Seventh Letter. Phaedrus remembers that Hippocrates holds that knowledge of the nature of the body requires insight into the whole and seems to accept the analogy. His valetudinarianism is still the grappling hook with which Socrates is pulling him in the right direction.

Accordingly, Socrates seizes his chance to assert that someone who aspires to an art of rhetoric will have to understand the nature of soul, showing whether it is one and uniform or multiple in form, what it naturally does or suffers, and establishing what kinds of speeches do what to the various classes of souls. He is asserting the need for his inquiries into soul in the Typhon passage and his poem. Phaedrus now concedes that this would be beautiful. Socrates answers that anyone who describes rhetoric differently has no *technē* and that the writers to whom Phaedrus appeals have beautiful knowledge of the soul but keep it hidden, so that they cannot be said to discourse artfully about oratory. This statement is obviously ironic: Socrates is still trying to get Phaedrus to accept the necessity of knowing the truth by pretending that the rhetoricians whom he admires know it. Socrates concludes that inasmuch as the power of speech is *psychagogia* (the leading of souls), the rhetorician must discover how many forms of soul there are, what they are, what kinds of people they produce, what kinds of speeches there are, which varieties persuade which types of individuals and why, and how the different sorts of people are recognized when they are present, so that the speaker can act on his knowledge. He must also recognize when to speak, when to be silent, and when to be brief or piteous or intense, and so on. Only then can he be said to have an art of speech. There is a difficulty in all this. Socrates has already proclaimed soul unknowable. Perhaps one can win insights into soul that are not totally untrustworthy, as in Socrates' myth, but this knowledge is inadequate, so that the *technē* of rhetoric here adumbrated seems well-nigh impossible. I am not distressed by this, for I do not presuppose that there must necessarily be an art of rhetoric. We recall that Socrates called its existence into question and that

9. It should be observed that Socrates is not proceeding terribly philosophically here. Rather, he is treating Phaedrus as Phaedrus wishes to treat the many, by appealing not so much to divine madness or logically rigorous dialectic as to what Phaedrus regards as probable. This is why Plato makes Phaedrus answer happily that what Socrates says is "likely."

we have been studying arguments that deny that rhetoric is a *technē.*[10] Now we understand why rhetoric is not and could not be an art. However, Phaedrus has forgotten what the thrust of the reasoning was supposed to be. He has suddenly become quite enthusiastic about investigations of soul that aim at enhancing the power of rhetoric. This is not entirely unfortunate, for Socrates is still trying to pull Phaedrus toward philosophy with his hook.

We should pause here to notice Socrates' reference to silence in this discussion. There are times for speech and times for silence. In this context, Socrates' commendation of silence has nothing to do with either the ineffability of truth, on the one hand, or some necessity of keeping secrets from the many, on the other. Rather, silence is here conceived as one of many sophistical techniques of deception. Some souls can be fooled by it under certain conditions and others not. To opt for silence on these grounds would be to embrace sophistry.

Socrates next asserts that a speaker who falls short on any of the demands that he has just made possesses no genuine art of rhetoric. Phaedrus supposes that some sophistical writer will wonder whether it is really necessary to go to so much trouble. Socrates agrees that we should ask whether it is possible to avoid going the long way around—a clear echo of the *Republic,* in which it proved necessary to take the longer way in quest of the good—when there might be a shorter path to the goal (of effective sophistical deception). Accordingly, he will state the "wolf's" position—another echo of both the *Republic,* in which Thrasymachus burst upon the conversation like a wolf, and Socrates' first speech, in which the wolf lied about who was really the wolf. The beast will still insist that there is no need for a rhetorician to know the truth or to share in justice or goodness—this being a position that Phaedrus has not yet abandoned—for nobody in the law courts cares for such things. All that counts is persuasion. Phaedrus agrees that it is important to consider this claim.

Socrates appoints Tisias as the representative of this view. The sophistical argument—still a technical one—is that persuasive oratory appeals to probability and the probable is that which conforms to the opinion of the many. Socrates' answer is concise. Probability, for the many, is a matter of likenesses to the truth. (I doubt that this is necessarily so. However, it is enough for present purposes if Phaedrus accepts it, and he has been brought to believe it by the comparison of rhetoric with medicine, in which the truth matters greatly.) So, Socrates says, unless a speaker takes the longer way that he has mapped out, comprehending the natures of the people in his audiences and penetrating to the forms of all beings, he will have no *technē.* Artfulness in speech will never be won without long, diligent

10. Socrates has challenged rhetoric's credentials as an art not only in this dialogue but also in the *Gorgias* (462e ff).

study (which would eventually convince Phaedrus that there is no such thing as an art of rhetoric, if his inquiries were carried out philosophically). Therefore, the sanely self-controlled man must contemplate not for the sake of speaking and acting toward human beings but in order to acquire the power to speak what is pleasing to the gods. Phaedrus concedes that Socrates has spoken beautifully. He has not thereby become philosophic. He has merely been persuaded to value philosophic inquiry on the grounds that dialectic might make him a better sophist. Socrates is satisfied, for this is all that he can hope to achieve at the moment. He declares that this is enough on the topic of *technē* and the lack of it in speeches.

Seemly and Unseemly Writing

Socrates now asserts that we still have to treat comeliness and uncomeliness, or fairness and ugliness, or seemliness and unseemliness (εὐπρεπείας, ἀπρεπείας, 274b6) in writing, or how writing can be made beautiful. Phaedrus was so delighted about being taught the quasi-medical secrets of the most powerful deceptive persuasion that he failed to notice that Socrates slipped something by him. I am referring to Socrates' statement that we should study rhetoric not for the sake of its effect on other human beings but, rather, in order to learn how to please the gods. Phaedrus would surely not have approved of this had he been listening, for he does not believe in gods. Socrates has a point that he does not want Phaedrus to miss. Therefore, he asks him: "Do you know how to act or speak about speeches so as to please god best?" (274b9–10).

Phaedrus seems surprised by the question. He admits that he has no idea how to do this and asks Socrates whether he knows. Socrates answers that he has heard something from the first human beings. These people knew the truth (presumably because they were closest to the first things). Socrates adds that we should try to learn the truth, too, and asks whether we should attend any longer to human opinion if we succeed—a question that Phaedrus rejects as ridiculous, not necessarily because he prefers truth to opinion.

What Socrates has heard is a myth. In the story, the ibis-headed Egyptian god Theuth invents numbers, arithmetic, geometry, astronomy, draughts, dice, and letters. He goes to the ram-headed monarch of the Egyptian gods, Thamos, or Ammon, urging him to transmit these *technai* to the Egyptians. Thamos exacts an account of each of the arts from Theuth, praising and blaming each explanation in turn. When Theuth comes to the defense of letters, he claims that they are a *pharmakon* (this time, in the sense of "medicine") that will make the Egyptians wiser and improve their memories. However, Thamos replies that one (deity) can create the *technai* and another

can judge of their harm and benefit. He prophesies that letters will actually cause Egyptians' memories to atrophy for want of exercise. They are
a drug for reminding, not for memory. He also prophesies that letters will
give people the appearance but not the reality of wisdom. Phaedrus objects
that Socrates easily invents stories of Egypt and anyplace he likes. Socrates
answers that the first prophecies at Dodona were delivered by an oak tree,
and that, unlike modern youth, the simple folk of that time were content
to listen to a tree as long as it told the truth.

Naturally, we are curious as to what this myth has to do with speaking
about rhetoric in the manner most pleasing to the gods. We also wonder
why Socrates has switched genres, as it were, telling an Egyptian rather
than a Greek story. I shall start with the latter problem, for its solution
seems to clear up the former.

My analysis takes its cues from G. J. de Vries, who argues that "Thamos"
is probably a corruption of the Egyptian name for Zeus and that the god
or daimon Theuth is the Egyptian equivalent of Prometheus.[11] Socrates is
retelling the Zeus-Prometheus tale to Phaedrus, who, as we recall having
learned from the *Symposium,* has always belonged to a coterie of Titanic,
Promethean revolutionaries with tyrannical aspirations. It is the Egyptians
who are the first human beings and who know the truth. The implication
is that the Hellenes are much further away from the first things than the
Egyptians and therefore do not know the truth. That is to say, the Greek version of the Zeus-Prometheus myth is dead wrong. The god or daimon who
invented the arts and games of chance was no rebel who could outwit Zeus.
Neither was his creation of the *technai* and the games antinomian.[12] Theuth-
Prometheus acted in a time when Thamos-Zeus ruled the universe and the
world directly, the king's word being law. Far from being the "noble" enemy of a tyrant who could inspire modern romances, Theuth-Prometheus
was a loyal technocratic servant of a benevolent monarch and submitted
his inventions to the legislation and judgments of his ruler. The *technai*
and the games of chance themselves are not weapons that can be used
against the god's authority, for both nature and chance are subject to divine governance.[13] This, perhaps, is the most important thing to notice if
we hope to speak of writing or any *technē* in the manner most pleasing to
the gods.

Further, Socrates has shrewdly let Theuth's idea about the utility of letters coincide with that of Phaedrus. When the curtain rose on our play,
Phaedrus was attempting to use a scroll as an aid to memorizing Lysias's
speech—without much success—and imagining that learning Lysias's set

11. de Vries, *Commentary on "Phaedrus,"* 248–49.
12. Cf. Benardete, *Rhetoric of Morality,* 124, 157, 187.
13. Cf. David A. White, *Rhetoric and Reality in Plato's "Phaedrus,"* 253.

piece by heart would make him wise. Thamos's lecture to Theuth informs Phaedrus that he has vainly assigned speech writing imaginary functions and that he himself will attain only to the appearance of wisdom if he persists in acting like an intellectual lackey. Phaedrus is stung. He still wants to overthrow Zeus through his rhetorical art, and he truly desires to be considered wise on account of his memorized speeches. This is why he objects that Socrates' myth is facile.

Socrates' answer to this criticism indicates that he has undergone a transformation, one that has completed the recovery of his Odysseus-soul from its awful fall. At the outset of the dialogue, Socrates was a stranger to the countryside because he did not believe that a tree could teach him anything. Now he accepts a tree's transmission of prophetic truths to the first men. He has discovered that a tree can speak to him when that tree is the *axis mundi*. He ironically mocks Phaedrus for being too "wise" to listen to prophetic myths that come from that source, thus recalling his previous remark that he himself does not disbelieve as the boorish wise do.[14] This reply refigures one last Homeric trope. When Odysseus reveals himself to Penelope, and when she reacts by testing him, it is the olive tree (another *axis mundi* symbol) around which he built his bedstead that establishes the truth of his identity. Socrates has confirmed what is true about his identity with reference to the prophesying oak of Zeus, who has thrown off the Thamos disguise. He is a soul grounded in the truth communicated to human beings through the *axis mundi*. With this, Socrates solves the problem of self-knowledge as well as any person can in this life, truly but with an infinite unknown in his ground.

In his mockery of Phaedrus, Socrates argues that his companion is too concerned about who is speaking and from what country he hails, and insufficiently interested in looking at the truth of the thing under discussion. Phaedrus caves into this criticism. His attachment to the medical *technē* has made it impossible for him to resist appeals to the truth. Accordingly, it is established that one cannot please the gods by speaking about writing as if it were an art that could improve memory and impart wisdom. What, then, should we say that writing is if we want to please the gods? What can it not do, and what benefits should we say that writing confers on mankind? It must do some good, for Thamos did not forbid it entirely, and he did remark that it was useful for reminding.

In reply, Socrates points to the most salient feature of writing. Writing is like painting. The offspring of painting stand like living beings, but if they are questioned, they maintain a solemn silence. Likewise, you might think

14. It seems to me that if we can receive prophecies from trees, we also can accept them from animal-headed or -bodied gods. It would not do to attempt to make more of the shapes of the Egyptian deities than Socrates does merely because we, who do not grasp the Egyptian symbolisms, think such gods ridiculous.

that written speeches talk intelligently. However, if you question them, wishing to clarify their statements, they always repeat the same things. This is to say that written speeches cannot nurture wisdom, for successful instruction entails the possibility of illuminating meanings, that is, getting behind word symbols to the realities that they represent.[15] Further, Socrates continues, every speech, "once it is written, is tossed about, alike among those who understand and those who have no business with it, and it knows not to whom to speak or not to speak" (275d9–e3). In the context of the entire conversation up to this point, this is to maintain that written speeches are poor pedagogical instruments for tailoring their words to the various types of souls. Again in context, this means that writing cannot do what Socrates has been doing with Phaedrus. Socrates has been adapting his speech to Phaedrus's ability to learn. He has been telling Phaedrus the truth, or as much of the truth as he could comprehend, couching the verities in forms that Phaedrus could understand and appreciate. He has been doing this in the broader context of an effort to convince Phaedrus of his great need to learn the truth and to "philosophize without fraud." Accordingly, Socrates' remarks have nothing to do with deliberately deceiving the many in order to keep dangerous secrets from them. They have nothing to do with esotericism, unless it was esotericism as defined by Friedrich Schleiermacher.[16]

Finally, Socrates asserts, the written word, when attacked unjustly, needs its father to help it, for it cannot protect itself. This is a special case of the inability of letters to prevent misunderstandings, one that compounds their failures to impart wisdom by opening doors to the triumph of injustice. So, Socrates concludes a few lines later, someone who has knowledge of the just, the beautiful, and the good will not write about these things, setting them down in speeches that can neither assist themselves in argument nor teach the truth competently (276c). Rather, this man will write playfully, storing up treasures of reminders for himself because he foresees the forgetfulness of his old age (276d).

Socrates' statement is absolute. Writing does not encapsulate the truth about the just, the beautiful, and the good, period. It does not contain the highest truth secretly, transmitting it to the wise few through clever

15. This argument is its own example of itself. I have just expressed my understanding of the meaning of "clarifying meanings." I should like to be able to prove that my usage is the same as Socrates' usage. If I am wrong, I should like to know what Socrates really meant, but the words in the passage always say the same things, never clarifying themselves. Plato could not write the argument that written words are not clear in a way that was clear enough to produce subsequent agreement about what he meant about written words not being clear.

16. In short, I conclude that Strauss and his students interpret the passage quoted out of context, thus distorting it. There simply is nothing in the *Phaedrus* that sustains their reading of the lines.

stratagems. In light of the Seventh Letter, I should say that it does not embody the illuminations that leap like lightning into souls, raising them to the perfect knowledge of the fifth, although it might hold the partial and inadequate truths of dialectic (which are therefore no truths at all) that purify our souls so that we can rise to the fifth. Otherwise, writing is good only for reminding. We can say nothing else about writing that will please the gods.

However, there is more. There is another sort of speech that is the "genuine" brother of the one that we have been examining and, hence, another type of writing about which we must speak fittingly in order to please the gods. This is speech "written with knowledge in the soul of one who learns, capable of defending itself, and knowing to whom it is necessary to speak and to keep silent" (276a5–7). Socrates is referring to metaphorical rather than verbal speech, that is, insight written in the psyches with flashing lightning, yielding such understanding of the highest truths as human beings can enjoy, forming souls in their naturally right order, and giving philosophers the capacity to recognize souls that can bear complex teaching, other souls that need simple instruction, and yet others that are too far sunk in iniquity to be able to hear truth in any form. This spiritual speech is brother to normal inadequate discourse, I assume, because it arises from the union of divine reality with the primordial human nature, symbolized as Penia. The "bastard" speech must be "bastard" because, somehow, it is not the legitimate offspring of this union. Phaedrus, for once catching Socrates' meaning, perhaps because he recalls something from the *Symposium*, guesses that the genuine speech is living and ensouled, implying, I suppose, that it is animated by the divine seed (Eros) stirring in the womb of the human *physis*. Hence, the other speech is bastard because it is not living and ensouled. It is the product of neither the divine reality nor primordial human nature but is an "offspring" of these parents in the same sense that a painting is the offspring of whatever it depicts. It is bastard because it is only an image, not the living, ensouled truth found in the philosopher's *nous*. We must speak suitably about the genuine speech.

The fitting thing to say about this speech is that he who knows the just, the beautiful, and the good will use dialectic to sow the seeds of his knowledge in a suitable soul, in speeches that are able to help themselves. We must inquire what kinds of speeches these might be, for the Seventh Letter informs us that no words suffice to capture the truth. Considering that the sower employs dialectic, I suppose it safe to infer that Socrates is referring to the transmission of necessarily incomplete arguments that stimulate those who can think for themselves with a little guidance. Thus does Socratic education proceed, conducted by those teachers who know the truth of the things of which they speak. Alternatively, Socrates might be referring to the possibility of teaching by driving dialectic to the telos that it seeks, on the basis of definitions that have become perfect and divisions that have gone clear to the uncuttable, in which case he is still trying to entice Phaedrus to approach real philosophy via dialectic. If Phaedrus comes, he will discover soon enough that dialectic cannot lift him as high as he needs to go. It is even more fitting to repeat that Lysias or any other speaker must be blamed for practicing rhetoric without knowledge of the truth, even if the many should praise him, and that no speech has ever been written or spoken in the ordinary way that is worthy of great seriousness. Only that which is written in the soul about the just, the beautiful, and the good is serious. We should pray to have such "genuine sons" in our souls. Phaedrus has been forced to join this prayer. Still, I doubt that he is truly converted. Socrates has been speaking to him in the ordinary way.

Socrates declares that he and Phaedrus have now played in a measured way with regard to speeches. He enjoins Phaedrus to go back to Lysias and tell him that they "went down" to the stream of the nymphs. This indicates to me that in some way, we have repeated the other dialogue in which Socrates went down, the *Republic*. Phaedrus should inform Lysias that he and Socrates heard orations intended for all sophists, rhetoricians, and poets. If any individual has composed something while knowing the truth, being able to defend and examine what is said, and making light of the seriousness of what has been written, that person deserves to be called not wise, an adjective that should be reserved for god alone, but a philosopher. For his part, Socrates will prophesy that his favorite, Isocrates, gives speeches that are truer to nature than any arising from Lysias and his circle, that Isocrates has a nobler character, and that some divine impulse will lead him toward great things, for he has philosophy in him. I think that we may take Socrates seriously about restricting the term "wise" to god alone.

THE PRAYER TO PAN

Socrates concludes the dialogue with his prayer to Pan, the speech god who probably managed his salvation from the plane tree by inspiring the speeches of the drama, sometimes by directing the nymphs and sometimes directly. Socrates prays to be made beautiful in his soul, to have external possessions that are friendly to the things inside him, to be permitted to believe that the wise man is rich, and to be given only so much gold as a sanely self-controlled man could bear. Phaedrus asks to join in this prayer, too, because friends have all things in common. It may be that, against all odds, Socrates has won Phaedrus to true opinion, or to the beginnings of it. Perhaps Phaedrus can eventually be rewinged. However, I would not count on it. Phaedrus is returning to Lysias, and he leans whichever way the last wind blows.

10

Eros, Wisdom, and Silence in the Socratic Art

If we were to ask Plato how he did and did not want us to benefit from his dialogues, he would answer that we should experience their impact wordlessly in our souls and that we should not imagine that we had attained to a science consisting in propositional doctrines of mathematical certainty. The dialogues should move us to open ourselves to the attraction of the eros that is a divine madness, with the result that we commence our ascents of the ladder of beauty and our flights to our true homes. They should not make us suppose that we have learned teachings that make us wise. Nevertheless, we human beings think and communicate verbally, so it is necessary to tie the strands of this inquiry together with some brief closing remarks.

Wisdom, the Socratic Art, and Silence

This investigation began by noticing an apparent contradiction: Socrates proclaims his ignorance and denies being wise while claiming to possess knowledge and a *technē* of eros. It is time to ask how Socrates' seeming inconsistency should be understood. Is Socrates ignorant or wise? Does he know nothing, or does he have a science of eros? Could he possibly be both ignorant and wise, both nescient and scientifically adept? If he is ignorant, wise, or both, or if he is nescient, possessed of an erotic science, or both, how does this relate to his art? We also observed that in the Seventh Letter, Plato denies ever having written anything on that about which he is serious. What is the relationship of Socrates' ignorance, wisdom, or simultaneous ignorance and wisdom, or of his ignorance, science, or simultaneous ignorance and science, to Plato's silence?

It seems to me that compelling demonstrations with regard to these matters are neither within our reach nor legitimate objects of our aspiration. I am willing to settle for judgments that common sense might reach through the careful reading of texts. In the effort to attain to such conclusions, one must prevent the illicit desire for massive certainty from slipping back into one's reflections in the guise of a hermeneutic method that allegedly guarantees its results. There is no way to solve the fundamental problem of writing to which Socrates points: words written about the highest realities cannot convey everything that their author sees or intends. They inevitably raise questions. When we ask them what they mean, they always repeat what they just said, failing to clarify themselves. I can offer nothing but interpretations of Platonic texts that strive to respect Plato's indications about the nature of his writings, and that may or may not achieve superior levels of accuracy for that reason. This being admitted, I follow the Seventh Letter and the dialogues examined in this book to the following results.

Anything to which human experience has at least partial access can receive a name and a definition and be associated with an image. Operating with these elements, we can arrive at propositional knowledge, or science (*episteme*), of the reality that is knowable and true. The dialectic, with its methods of division and collection, works for such knowledge with logical rigor. It develops accounts of its subjects that have varying degrees of validity, depending on how hard Plato tries to make them reliable from one dramatic context to the next. Some of the analyses are good enough to be called "science." However, they are *episteme* only in a limited sense, for words are always inadequate to essences. Name, definition, image, and the knowledge founded upon them can never amount to perfect insight into the knowable and true reality. To the extent that Socrates has the knowledge that is fourth in the series "name, definition, image, knowledge," he knows without knowing absolutely. Therefore, in a way, he knows without knowing at all. This is the first manner in which he can be simultaneously knowledgeable and ignorant.

Plato causes Socrates to spend a great deal of time constructing bodies of science that are not really or perfectly science. One wonders why. I think that the exercises are means to purification. They take opinions to which we are unjustifiably attached, allow us to accept as knowledge only those that survive the most severe tests, and declare even those incomplete. Accordingly, they rid the soul of delusions about what it understands and show us the limits of the logical reason in which we take so much pride.

It is possible to progress beyond the inadequate science that is fourth in the series to a "perfect knowledge of the fifth." This new *episteme* must consist in some access of the soul to the knowable and true reality that does not depend on name, definition, and image. Hence, it is nonpropositional. It is not obtained by the dialectic, although Plato and Socrates expect it to come to persons whose souls have been purified by the dialectic and ethical discipline. The knowledge is evidently not acquired through any initiative of the one who receives it. Plato and Socrates variously symbolize the process by which they attain it as illumination given off by a leaping flame, pervasion of the soul by the daimon Eros that resides in its nature, divine erotic madness, anamnesis, and spiritual ascent to the hyperuranian beings. It seems evident that Plato is a mystic philosopher.

Plato and Socrates mention several realities discerned by the soul in its mystical flights. The highest of these is symbolized variously as nature, the *agathon,* the Essence Really Being, and the *hegemon nous.* The philosophers teach nothing about the nature or essence of nature, the good, the Essence Really Being, and the *hegemon nous.* We hear only that this reality is the ground of the right order or virtue of the soul.[1] If wisdom is illumination, pervasion, divine madness, anamnesis, and spiritual ascent to the highest reality, it is not the transformation of philosophy (love of wisdom) into science, but the opening of the soul to its ordering ground. The reason for this is that mystical noetic union of the soul with its ground is not the identity of the soul with its ground. Wisdom, like science, is therefore incomplete. This is the second manner in which Socrates can be simultaneously wise, or knowledgeable, and ignorant, and this is why Socrates holds that only a god can be wise.

In view of these conclusions, it seems to me that no Platonic dialogue ever intends to impart information, as a treatise would do. Rather, as Kenneth Sayre says in his discussion of Plato's purposes, it appears that "the Platonic dialogues were written to provide occasions for conversations between author and reader of the sort identified in the Seventh Letter as leading to philosophic understanding."[2] That is, the dialogues attempt to purify the reader's soul, thus maneuvering it into positions in which illumination, consciousness of divine pervasion, divine madness, anamnesis, and ascent to the hyperuranian beings can occur. Socrates' erotic *technē* consists entirely in this sort of pedagogy. This inference is confirmed by the dramatic action of all the dialogues examined above. It also agrees with Socrates' statement that writing is a philosopher's reminder. We could inquire: Reminder of what? I think, with Friedrich Schleiermacher, that the answer would be "a reminder of the paths of purification that led to the reception of the illumination."

In keeping with these results, we may say that Plato has a practice of silence. G. W. F. Hegel is wrong to insist that Plato discloses everything he knows. Plato maintains his silence about the highest realities first and foremost because they are ineffable and he does not want to mislead people about their nature, and second because silence is sometimes the most useful pedagogical means of leading students to the mystical visions that

---

1. To describe the reality as the ground of something else is not to say what the reality is in itself.

2. Sayre, *Plato's Literary Garden: How to Read a Platonic Dialogue,* xvi; see also 25–32, 197, where Sayre elaborates upon the point.

order their souls. In this regard, Socratic irony, one of the forms of silence, is best described in Sayre's eminently sensible phrase as "an effective harrow on the roots of false opinion."[3] Therefore, Friedrich Schleiermacher, Søren Kierkegaard, and Eric Voegelin appear to be right about Platonic reticence. Accordingly, we may infer that Plato's silence does not owe to cowardice in the face of an absurd reality or to his intention to deceive people about gods, the secret governance of the demos by noble philosophic tyrants, or some alleged project of self-deification. Friedrich Nietzsche, Leo Strauss, and Stanley Rosen do not seem to be right about that. I believe that my analysis has made a reasonable effort to show that these thinkers reach their conclusions by means of arbitrary readings. In Nietzsche's case, the arbitrariness involves not so much misrepresentation of the contents of Platonic dialogues as attribution of the motive of cowardice to Socrates and Plato, who not only did not dread the uncertainty of the human condition but honestly embraced and proclaimed it as well. In the case of Strauss and his students, the arbitrariness lies first in their insistence on finding thinly concealed propositional truths in Plato, contrary to the philosopher's warning that he has written nothing concerning that about which he is serious, and second in their powerful determination to read all Platonic and other great philosophic texts as secret directives to those who aspire to the ascendancy of human reason, if not to their own divine rulership of the universe.

My view of Platonic silence is not altered by the recent appearance of Seth Benardete's transcription of Leo Strauss's 1959 lectures on the *Symposium*, which came to hand only a day or two before the completion of this book.[4] Strauss suggests that Socrates speaks esoterically (and that Plato writes esoterically) by appealing to a passage in Xenophon's *Memorabilia* (4.6.13–15). I am not entirely satisfied about the legitimacy of this procedure, for Xenophon is not Plato, but I waive the point.

Xenophon declares that whenever someone challenged one of Socrates' statements, Socrates would lead the discussion back to a definition of whatever was in dispute. "By this process of leading back to the premise," Xenophon says in Benardete's translation, "even his opponent came to see the truth clearly." Benardete then makes Xenophon remark: "This was one way." Xenophon continues by reporting that when Socrates himself argued something, he invoked "the most generally agreed upon things," believing that in this consisted the safety of speech." A little later, Xenophon adds

---

3. Ibid., 58.
4. I should have liked to include the Strauss lectures in my long conversation with Plato and his best interlocutors, but, unfortunately, I could interpolate only a few references to them into my argument here and there. Anything more would have involved a substantial rewriting of my entire work. It is a related point that my manuscript went to the publisher before the untimely death of Benardete, who is one of the fine scholars to whom I owe a great deal, even though I disagree with him about virtually everything, and whose replies to my arguments would have been welcome.

that Socrates "said that Homer gave Odysseus the credit of being a safe speaker because he had a way of leading the discussion through those things which appear to be true to human beings." Strauss then comments: "There were two kinds of rhetoric: when Socrates talked to contradictors he chose a way which led to the truth; but when he did not talk to contradictors, . . . he argued only on the basis of accepted premises. . . . This second kind of rhetoric is the Odyssean rhetoric, the rhetoric which Homer allegedly ascribed to Odysseus."[5] Strauss's clear implication is that, according to Xenophon, Socrates had two methods of speaking, one that disclosed the truth and another that preached untrue but generally received opinion for the sake of safety.

It is not perfectly clear to me that Xenophon imputes two kinds of rhetoric to Socrates. When Benardete causes Xenophon to say, "This was one way," he departs from the usual Straussian practice of translating texts as literally as possible. He interpolates a sentence into Xenophon that does not appear in the Greek. He thus factors into Strauss's evidentiary basis more than is really there, slanting the passage in the direction that his teacher wants to drive it. However, we must not criticize this move too harshly, for Benardete is justified to an extent by the fact that Xenophon is definitely talking about two somethings, even if he is not necessarily distinguishing two types of rhetoric. What two things might Xenophon envisage? I think that an excellent argument can be made for the thesis that Xenophon is discussing the application of one kind of rhetoric to two different situations: one in which Socrates answers a person who contradicts him and another in which he lectures people who do not oppose him. In the former situation, Socrates strives for agreement with the individual who has challenged him. In the latter situation, he aims for the general assent of all present. I believe that this is what the text means and says.

Next, when Xenophon's Socrates replies to a contradictor by taking the inquiry back to definitions, Xenophon quotes several queries that Socrates puts to the opponent (this being material that Benardete omits from his translation). For example, "In economic management, then, is not the more useful man he who makes the city more prosperous?" I could list many more such questions, all of which are similar in nature. This one suffices to prove that Xenophon's Socrates speaks to his contradictor, as he leads him to the truth, in the same way that he talks to his docile audience, by invoking rather conventional views. This inspires one to ask why we should assume that the "second way" does not lead to the truth too. It seems clear

---

5. Strauss, *On Plato's "Symposium,"* 179. Here, I have departed from my usual practice of furnishing my own translations and have availed myself of the versions found in Benardete's transcription, which were supplied not by Strauss, but by Benardete. I have done so in order to avoid the appearance of changing Benardete's translations in order to attack him unfairly.

to me that Xenophon's two ways are rhetoric that seeks individual assent to the truth versus that which seeks general assent to the truth, not, as Strauss would have it, rhetoric that discloses the truth versus that which deliberately deceives. It should be observed that although Xenophon does not specifically affirm that the second method leads to the truth, he does not deny it, either. Instead, he delivers an interesting personal remark. Right after finishing the statement that Benardete translates, he continues by inferring that "Socrates frankly disclosed his thought to those with whom he kept company" (4.7.1). To me, this means that Socrates directed both varieties of rhetoric to those who consorted with him, teaching them clearly what he thought. Therefore, the context creates enormous difficulties for Strauss's exegesis, seemingly obvious problems that neither Strauss nor Benardete addresses.

Now that context has been mentioned, we must also inquire what Xenophon means by "safe" speech in this passage. I see no foundation in his text for an a priori assumption that he means "speech that protects philosophers from persecution by implanting real lies in the souls of the many." He might well have in mind "speech that is safe in the sense that it most assuredly leads most auditors to the truth." The allusion to Odysseus does not tilt this consideration in Strauss's favor. The passage in Homer to which Xenophon's Socrates refers (*Odyssey* 8.171) sheds an interesting light on the issue. By "safe" speech, Homer appears to mean speech that a god beautifies, so that people delight to hear it and look upon the speaker as upon a god. Xenophon's Socrates seems to be speculating on how Odysseus managed to be both pleasing to god and persuasive.[6] He is not necessarily confirming that safe speech is wily, as Strauss might wish us to believe. At the end of this inconclusive reflection, it is necessary to move from Xenophon's Socrates back to Plato and his Socrates in order to ascertain the truth about the rhetoric of Plato's Socrates. In the explicit statement of the Seventh Letter, and in the dramatic situations of the dialogues, Plato's silences have to do with the problem that the serious realities are "not spoken things like other lessons" and with the pedagogical strategies that this necessitates, not with "safety." For me, this outweighs anything Xenophon might have meant to ascribe to Socrates.

Eros

For Socrates, Eros is one of the serious realities. Therefore, Plato has written nothing about it. What could this mean when two Platonic dialogues

---

6. That is, Socrates might be making the same kind of point that he establishes in books 2–3 of the *Republic*, that is, that a hero ought not to be portrayed as a liar.

have been devoted to eros? In light of Plato's account of his silence, we must infer that Socrates cannot know or capture the essence of eros in words. Therefore, Plato writes nothing about the nature of eros. In the *Symposium* and the *Phaedrus* primarily, and in other dialogues secondarily, Plato dramatically shows us Socrates practicing his erotic *technē*. Socrates can say things about eros at the level of the four: name, definition, image, and inadequate knowledge. Occasionally, his comments will be good science, as far as they go. More often, they will be remarks intended not to be scientific, not to be literally true, but to maneuver interlocutors (and readers) past the opinions and passions that prevent their ascents of the "ladder of beauty," their "divine madness," and their "flights to the roof of the heavens," expressions that must obviously be understood figuratively, as symbols of spiritual experience, that is, of tensions in the soul in the direction of its divine ground (this symbol also being a metaphor).[7]

Within the framework of these scientific and dramatic possibilities, we may draw the following conclusions from Plato's studies of eros. Socrates discerns two erotes, which can be called the tyrannical and the Socratic, or the left-handed and the right-handed, or, to substitute terms of our own, the evil and the good, or the destructive and the salvific. In Eric Voegelin's words, the tyrannical eros is the Satanic double of the Socratic one. These two erotes should not be understood as metaphysical entities; they are experienced movements in the soul. We may say a little about each, in full consciousness of the limits of our science, starting with the tyrannical eros and ending with the Socratic eros.

It will be instructive to begin the discussion by adverting once again to Xenophon. In his *Memorabilia* (4.6.12), Xenophon makes Socrates define tyranny as rule over unwilling subjects not regulated by laws, but imposed by the ruler's will. This is a definition in terms of institutions, lawlessness, and absence of the consent of the governed. As far as it goes, it is not bad. We still use it today. However, as compared with the portraits of tyranny offered by the Platonic Socrates, it seems flat, colorless, lifeless, and devoid of insight into the real dynamics of tyranny. This is just one of myriads of reasons that many regard Xenophon as respectable but still decidedly inferior to Plato.

Leaving Xenophon behind now and concentrating solely on Plato, we observe that his Socrates cannot capture the essence of the tyrannical eros in words any more than he can catch the nature of the salvific eros in words. The mystery of evil is just as ineffable as the mystery of goodness. Granted, Socrates defines the tyrannical eros as "desire" *(epithymia)*. However, what is desire? Indeed, what is evil, tyrannical desire? Socrates declares that it is a human madness, a disease of the soul. This is helpful, but what is madness?

7. I take the term "tension toward the ground" from many of the works of Voegelin.

We can recognize it when we see it, but this does not imply that we can know or say what it is.

When Socrates comes to the objects of the tyrannical eros, he can do better, describing a broad range of manifestations of the sickness, or tyrannical types. Plato certainly does not intend to make Socrates offer an exhaustive inventory. It is enough that Socrates should study the varieties of tyrannical eros that his empirical observation discerned in Athens.

To repeat conclusions derived earlier, the tyrannical eros is directed simultaneously at individual persons and the would-be tyrant's polity. The diseased eros variously desires to use its beloveds not only as agents of sexual pleasure but as slavish sources of wealth, position, and honor; as slavish witnesses to its godly, creative intelligence; as slavish witnesses to its godlike ability to manipulate human nature by technical means; as slavish alter egos that validate the self-deifying metaphysical rebellions of the "lovers" by ceasing to be others and becoming the mirror-image selves of the "lovers"; as slavish proofs of the eternal divinity of gods who create them as inferior immortal deities; and as slavish means to political power. The sick eros hopes to convert its polity into an instrument of world conquest that improves its domestic status; a guarantee of its illicit sexual and social interests; a tool that facilitates a tyrannical technician's conquest of nature (including the nature of the universe and the natures of the human beings whom it hopes to manipulate); an engine that co-opts all mankind into its metaphysical revolt; a vast association organized to worship the man who incarnates it; and the slavish power base that deifies the tyrant by making him ruler of the world. In all these forms, the diseased eros employs "moving logoi" that transfer the emotional effects of beauty from beautiful realities to itself in order to seduce the intended slaves, charming them into embracing the tyrant and the tyranny as beautiful. Plato's dialogues dramatically show us Socrates administering loving rhetorical therapy to the aspiring tyrants. Socrates rarely or never succeeds in curing them, probably because "some chance" or an "evil demon" has contrived to complicate his situation beyond all hope of remedy: there were too many budding tyrannies in Athens reinforcing one another to allow Socrates to make sufficient headway with any one of them. The *Symposium* illustrates these mutually supporting forces frustrating Socrates' efforts to cure the aristocratic forms of the sickness, and the *Phaedrus* depicts them working to defeat his attempt to heal the democratic prototype of the disease. However, we might be able to apply Socrates' therapies to our own would-be tyrants with better results, if we catch their illnesses in time.

The Socratic, right-handed, good, salvific eros cannot be known or captured in words, as I have said. This is why Socrates permits its definition to float ambiguously from one text to the next. Eros is "something between god and mortal, or a god, or something divine." However, what does that mean, especially when Socrates reminds us that no one has ever seen a god, so that no one can say what a god or something divine is? What we can argue with confidence is that Socrates employs the symbol "eros" to refer to a soul's experiences of divine movements in its interior. The divine reality blends with, or becomes present to, the psyche in ways that cannot be grasped by merely human reason; this is why the experience generates paradoxical expressions. When one takes these symbols literally, let us say as serious metaphysics, it is easy to mistake them for "unintelligible" speech (for example, Strauss's declaration that it is impossible for something to be between mortal and immortal).[8] However, when we understand the phrases as references to the soul's experience of something the being or presence of which it apprehends, without being able to say what it is, Socrates' images become illuminating, not as science, but as analogies that teach us what to expect if we should be so fortunate as to have the experience, too.

The Socratic eros can be known and described more easily with regard to what it does, or its effects on us, than with respect to what it is. It is a divine force that pulls us through all the levels of our being to our proper telos on each plain. It moves our material bodies toward their health. It impels men and women toward the reproduction that sustains the human race. It drives all lovers, heterosexual and homoerotic, toward the rapture with the beauty of bodies that serves human beings both as the foundation of higher friendships and as the first step on the ladder of beauty. It inspires the lovers' ascent of this ladder to the vision of beauty itself, and their flight to the hyperuranian beings and partial visions of these realities, perhaps even including limited insights into the Essence Really Being itself. Thus, it attunes the souls to the grounds of their true order. As Socrates says, everyone should follow this eros.

8. Strauss, On Plato's "Symposium," 189.

BIBLIOGRAPHY

Aelian. *Historical Miscellany.* (Also known as *Varia Historica.*) Ed. and trans. N. G. Wilson. Cambridge: Harvard University Press, 1997.

Aristophanes. *Acharnians. Knights.* Ed. Jeffrey Henderson. Loeb Classical Library. Cambridge: Harvard University Press, 1998.

———. *Birds. Lysistrata. Women at the Thesmophoria.* Ed. Jeffrey Henderson. Loeb Classical Library. Cambridge: Harvard University Press, 2000.

———. *Clouds. Wasps. Peace.* Ed. Jeffrey Henderson. Loeb Classical Library. Cambridge: Harvard University Press, 1998.

———. *The Comedies of Aristophanes.* Trans. Alan H. Somerstein. 11 vols. Warminster, England: Aris and Phillips, 1980–1998.

———. *Frogs. Assemblywomen. Wealth.* Ed. Jeffrey Henderson. Loeb Classical Library. Cambridge: Harvard University Press, 2002.

Aristophanis. *Comoediae.* Ed. F. W. Hall and W. M. Feldart. 2 vols. 1900–1901. Reprint, Oxford: Clarendon Press, 1962–1964.

Aristotelis. *Ars Rhetorica.* Ed. W. D. Ross. Oxford: Clarendon Press, 1959.

———. *Ethica Nicomachea.* Ed. T. Bywater. Oxford: Clarendon Press, 1949.

———. *Metaphysica.* Ed. W. Jaeger. Oxford: Clarendon Press, 1957.

———. *Physica.* Ed. W. D. Ross. Oxford: Clarendon Press, 1960.

———. *Politica.* Ed. W. D. Ross. Oxford: Clarendon Press, 1964.

Aristotle. *Aristotle IV: Physics, Books I–IV.* Trans. P. H. Wicksteed and F. M. Cornford. Ed. G. P. Goold. Loeb Classical Library. 1929. Reprint, Cambridge: Harvard University Press, 1980.

———. *Aristotle V: Physics II, Books V–VIII.* Trans. P. H. Wicksteed and F. M. Cornford. Ed. G. P. Goold. Loeb Classical Library. 1934. Reprint, Cambridge: Harvard University Press, 1980.

———. *Aristotle XVII: Metaphysics I–IX.* Trans. Hugh Tredennick. Ed. G. P. Goold. Loeb Classical Library. 1933. Reprint, Cambridge: Harvard University Press, 1989.

———. *Aristotle XVIII: Metaphysics X–XIV. Oeconomica. Magna Moralia.* Trans. Hugh Tredennick and G. Cyril Armstrong. Ed. G. P. Goold.

Loeb Classical Library. 1935. Reprint, Cambridge: Harvard University Press, 1990.

———. *Aristotle XIX: Nichomachean Ethics*. Rev. ed. trans. H. Rackham. Ed. G. P. Goold. Loeb Classical Library. 1934. Reprint, Cambridge: Harvard University Press, 1990.

———. *Aristotle XXI: Politics*. Trans. H. Rackham. Ed. G. P. Goold. Loeb Classical Library. 1932. Reprint, Cambridge: Harvard University Press, 1990.

———. *Aristotle's De Anima in the Version of William of Moerbeke and the Commentary of St. Thomas Aquinas*. Trans. Kenelm Foster and Silvester Humphries. New Haven: Yale University Press, 1954.

———. *The Complete Works of Aristotle*. Ed. Jonathan Barnes. 2 vols. Rev. Oxford translation. Bollingen Series LXXI.2. Princeton: Princeton University Press, 1984.

Athenaeus of Naucratis. *The Deipnosophists*. Trans. Charles Burton Gulick. Ed. G. P. Goold. Loeb Classical Library. Cambridge: Harvard University Press, 1951.

Augustine, Saint. *The City of God against the Pagans*. Trans. George E. McCracken. Ed. T. E. Page. 7 vols. Loeb Classical Library. Cambridge: Harvard University Press, 1957–1972.

———. *Concerning "The City of God against the Pagans."* Trans. Henry Bettenson. New York: Penguin Books, 1972.

Austin, Norman. *Archery at the Dark of the Moon: Poetic Problems in Homer's "Odyssey."* Berkeley and Los Angeles: University of California Press, 1975.

Barnes, Jonathan. *The Pre-Socratic Philosophers*. Vol. 1, *Thales to Zeno*. London: Routledge and Kegan Paul, 1979.

Benardete, Seth. *On Plato's "Symposium."* Munich: Carl Friedrich von Siemens Stiftung, 1994.

———. *The Rhetoric of Morality and Philosophy: Plato's "Gorgias" and "Phaedrus."* Chicago: University of Chicago Press, 1991.

———. *Socrates' Second Sailing: On Plato's "Republic."* Chicago: University of Chicago Press, 1989.

Berkowitz, Peter. *Nietzsche: The Ethics of an Immoralist*. Cambridge: Harvard University Press, 1995.

Bloom, Allan. *The Closing of the American Mind: How Higher Education Has Failed Democracy and Impoverished the Souls of Today's Students*. New York: Simon and Schuster, 1987.

———. *Love and Friendship*. New York: Simon and Schuster, 1993.

Boeckh, August. *Gesammelte kleine Schriften*. Leipzig: B. G. Tuebner, 1874.

Brandwood, Leonard. *The Chronology of Plato's Dialogues*. Cambridge: Cambridge University Press, 1990.

Brann, Eva. "The Music of the *Republic*. ΑΓΩΝ 1:1 (April 1967): i–vi, 1–117.

Burger, Ronna. *Plato's "Phaedrus": A Defense of a Philosophic Art of Writing.* Chicago: University of Chicago Press, 1980.

Burnyeat, M. F. "Sphinx without a Secret." *New York Review of Books* 32 (1985): 30–35.

Bury, R. G. "Epistle VII: Prefatory Note." In *Plato IX: Timaeus. Critias. Cleitophon. Menexenus. Epistles,* by Plato. Trans. R. G. Bury. Ed. G. P. Goold. Loeb Classical Library. 1929. Reprint, Cambridge: Harvard University Press, 1989.

Catechism of the Catholic Church. San Francisco: Ignatius Press, 1994.

Caven, Brian. *Dionysius I: Warlord of Sicily.* New Haven: Yale University Press, 1990.

Cicero, Marcus Tullius. *Tuscullan Disputations.* Trans. J. E. King. Ed. T. E. Page. Loeb Classical Library. Cambridge: Harvard University Press, 1945.

Clark, Randall Baldwin. "Platonic Love in a Colorado Courtroom: Martha Nussbaum, John Finnis, and Plato's *Laws* in *Evans v. Romer.*" *Yale Journal of Law and the Humanities* 12:1 (winter 2000): 1–38.

Clement of Alexandria. *Stromateis, Books I–III.* Trans. John Ferguson. Washington, D.C.: Catholic University of America Press, 1991.

Cornford, F. M. *"The Unwritten Philosophy" and Other Essays.* Cambridge: Cambridge University Press, 1950. See esp. "The Doctrine of Eros in Plato's *Symposium*."

Cropsey, Joseph. *Political Philosophy and the Issues of Politics.* Chicago: University of Chicago Press, 1977.

Dannhauser, Werner J. *Nietzsche's View of Socrates.* Ithaca: Cornell University Press, 1974.

Davies, J. K. *Athenian Propertied Families, 600–300 B.C.* Oxford: Clarendon Press, 1971.

Deane, Philip. "Stylometrics Do Not Exclude the Seventh Letter." *Mind: A Quarterly Review of Psychology and Philosophy* 82 (January 1973): 113–17.

Derrida, Jacques. *Dissemination.* Trans. Barbara Johnson. Chicago: University of Chicago Press, 1981.

De Vries, G. J. *A Commentary on the "Phaedrus" of Plato.* Amsterdam: Adolf M. Hakkert, 1969.

Diogenes Laertius. *Lives of Eminent Philosophers.* Trans. R. D. Hicks. Ed. G. P. Goold. 2 vols. Loeb Classical Library. New York: G. P. Putnam's Sons, 1925.

Dorter, Kenneth. *Form and Good in Plato's Eleatic Dialogues: The "Parmenides," "Theaetetus," "Sophist," and "Statesman."* Berkeley and Los Angeles: University of California Press, 1994.

———. "Three Disappearing Ladders in Plato." *Philosophy and Rhetoric* 29:3 (1996): 279–99.

Dover, K. J. *Aristophanic Comedy.* Berkeley and Los Angeles: University of California Press, 1972.

———. "The Date of Plato's *Symposium.*" *Phronesis: A Journal of Ancient Philosophy* 10 (1965): 2–20.

———. *Greek Homosexuality.* Cambridge: Harvard University Press, 1978.

Drury, Shadia B. "The Esoteric Philosophy of Leo Strauss." *Political Theory* 13 (1985): 315–37.

———. *Leo Strauss and the American Right.* New York: St. Martin's Press, 1997.

———. *The Political Ideas of Leo Strauss.* New York: St. Martin's Press, 1988.

Eckehart, Meister. *Deutsche Predigten und Traktate.* Ed. Joseph Quint. Munich: Carl Hanser Verlag, 1985.

———. *Sermons and Treatises.* Trans. M. O'C Walshe. 3 vols. Longmead, Shaftesbury, Dorset, England: Element Books, 1987.

Edelstein, Ludwig. *Plato's Seventh Letter.* Leiden, Netherlands: E. J. Brill, 1966.

———. "The Role of Eryximachus in Plato's *Symposium.*" *Transactions and Proceedings* (American Philosophic Association) 76 (1945): 85–103.

Eliade, Mircea. *The Sacred and the Profane: The Nature of Religion.* Trans. Willard R. Trask. New York: Harper Torchbooks, 1961.

Ferrari, G. R. F. *Listening to the Cicadas: A Study of Plato's "Phaedrus."* Cambridge: Cambridge University Press, 1987.

Friedländer, Paul. *Plato.* 2d ed. 3 vols. Bollingen Series. Princeton: Princeton University Press, 1969.

Gadamer, Hans-Georg. "Dialectic and Sophism in Plato's Seventh Letter." In *Dialogue and Dialectic: Eight Hermeneutical Studies on Plato.* Trans. P. Christopher Smith. New Haven: Yale University Press, 1980.

———. "Dialektik und Sophistik im siebenten Platonischen Brief." In *Gesammelte Werke.* Vol. 6, *Griechische Philosophie II.* Tübingen: J. C. B. Mohr, 1985.

———. *The Idea of the Good in Platonic-Aristotelian Philosophy.* Trans. P. Christopher Smith. New Haven: Yale University Press, 1986.

———. "Platos ungeschriebene Dialektik." In *Gesammelte Werke.* Vol. 6, *Griechische Philosophie II.* Tübingen: J. C. B. Mohr, 1985.

———. "Plato's Unwritten Dialectic." In *Dialogue and Dialectic: Eight Hermeneutical Studies on Plato,* trans. P. Christopher Smith. New Haven: Yale University Press, 1980.

Germino, Dante. "Editor's Introduction." In *The Collected Works of Eric Voegelin.* Vol. 16, *Order and History.* Vol. 3, *Plato and Aristotle.* Columbia: University of Missouri Press, 2000.

Goodwin, Doris Kearns. *No Ordinary Time: Franklin and Eleanor Roosevelt, the Homefront in World War II.* New York: Simon and Schuster, Touchstone Books, 1995.

Graeser, Andreas. *Philosophische Erkenntnis und begriffliche Darstellung: Bemerkungen zum erkenntnistheoretischen Exkurs des VII. Briefs.* Wiesbaden: Franz Steiner Verlag, 1989.

Griswold, Charles L., Jr. *Self-Knowledge in Plato's "Phaedrus."* New Haven: Yale University Press, 1986.

Guthrie, W. K. C. *A History of Greek Philosophy.* Vol. 5, *The Later Plato and the Academy.* Cambridge: Cambridge University Press, 1978.

Hackforth, R. *The Authorship of the Platonic Epistles.* Manchester: University Press, 1913.

Hegel, Georg Wilhelm Friedrich. *Lectures on the History of Philosophy.* Trans. E. S. Haldane and Frances H. Simson. 2 vols. London: Routledge and Kegan Paul, 1955.

———. *Vorlesungen über der Geschichte der Philosophie.* Vol. 14 of *Georg Wilhelm Friedrich Hegels Werke: Vollständige Ausgabe.* Ed. Philipp Marheineke. 2d ed. Berlin: Duncker und Humblot, 1842.

———. *Vorlesungen über der Geschichte der Philosophie.* Vol. 2. Vol. 18 of *Sämtliche Werke: Jubiläumsausgabe in zwanzig Bänden,* ed. Hermann Glockner. Stuttgart: Fr. Frommanns Verlag, 1959.

Hesiod. *Homeric Hymns. Epic Cycle. Homerica.* Trans. Hugh G. Evelyn-White. Ed. Jeffrey Henderson. Loeb Classical Library. 1936. Reprint, Cambridge: Harvard University Press, 2000.

Hildebrandt, Kurt. *Platon: Der Kampf des Geistes um die Macht.* Berlin: Georg Bondi, 1933.

Homer. *Homeri Opera.* Ed. David B. Monro and Thomas W. Allen. 3d ed. 5 vols. Oxford: Clarendon Press, 1917–1946.

———. *The Iliad.* Trans. A. T. Murray and William F. Wyatt. 2 vols. Loeb Classical Library. Cambridge: Harvard University Press, 1999.

———. *Odyssey.* Trans. A. T. Murray and George E. Dimock. 2 vols. Loeb Classical Library. Cambridge: Harvard University Press, 1995.

Howland, Jacob. "Re-Reading Plato: The Problem of Platonic Chronology." *Phoenix* 45 (1991): 189–214.

Irigary, Luce. "Sorcerer Love: A Reading of Plato's *Symposium,* Diotima's Speech." Trans. Eleanor H. Kuykendall. *Hypatia* 3 (winter 1989): 32–44.

Isnardi-Parenti, Margherita. *Filosofia e politica nelle lettere di Platone.* Naples: Guida Editori, 1970.

Jefferson, Thomas. *The Life and Selected Writings of Thomas Jefferson.* Ed. Adrienne Koch and William Peden. New York: Modern Library, 1944.

Kagan, Donald. *The Fall of the Athenian Empire.* Ithaca: Cornell University Press, 1987.

Kant, Immanuel. "Von einem neuerdings erhobenen vornehmen Ton in
    der Philosophie." In vol. 3 of *Werke in sechs Bänden,* ed. Wilhelm
    Weischedel. Wiesbaden: Insel Verlag, 1958.

Kierkegaard, Søren. *The Concept of Irony: With Continual Reference to Socrates.*
    Ed. and trans. Howard V. and Edna Hong. Princeton: Princeton Uni-
    versity Press, 1989.

———. *Über den Begriff der Ironie: Mit ständiger Rücksicht auf Sokrates.* Trans.
    Emanuel Hirsch. Düsseldorf and Cologne: Eugen Diederichs Verlag,
    1961.

Klosko, George. *The Development of Plato's Political Theory.* New York:
    Methuen, 1986.

Kojève, Alexandre. *Introduction to the Reading of Hegel: Lectures on "The Phe-
    nomenology of Spirit."* Trans. James H. Nichols. Ed. Allan Bloom. New
    York: Basic Books, 1969.

Lessing, Gotthold. "Leibniz von den ewigen Strafen." In vol. 11 of *Lessings
    Werke.* Stuttgart: G. T. Goeschen'sche Verlagsbuchhandlung, 1890.

———. "Ernst und Falk: Gespräche für Freimaurer." In vol. 12 of *Lessings
    Werke.* Stuttgart: G. T. Goeschen'sche Verlagsbuchhandlung, 1890.

Levison, M., A. Q. Morton, and A. D. Winspear. "The Seventh Letter of
    Plato." *Mind: A Quarterly Review of Psychology and Philosophy* 77 (July
    1968): 309–25.

Liddell, H. G., and R. Scott. *Greek-English Lexicon, with a Revised Supplement.*
    Oxford: Clarendon Press, 1996.

Lutz, Mark J. *Socrates' Education to Virtue: Learning the Love of the Noble.* Al-
    bany: SUNY Press, 1998.

Lysias. *Lysias.* Trans. W. R. M. Lamb. Ed. T. E. Page. Loeb Classical Library.
    1930. Reprint, Cambridge: Harvard University Press, 1943.

Maimonides, Moses. *The Guide of the Perplexed.* Trans. Shlomo Pines. Chi-
    cago: University of Chicago Press, 1963.

Morrison, J. S. "Four Notes on Plato's *Symposium.*" *Classical Quarterly* 14
    (May 1964): 42–55.

Neumann, Harry. "Diotima's Concept of Love." *American Journal of Philol-
    ogy* 86 (1965): 33–59.

Nietzsche, Friedrich. *Basic Writings of Nietzsche.* Trans. and ed. Walter Kauf-
    mann. New York: Modern Library, 1968.

———. *Kritische Studienausgabe.* Ed. Giorgio Colli and Mazzino Montinari.
    New ed. 15 vols. Berlin: Walter de Gruyter, 1999.

———. *Nietzsche Werke: Kritische Gesamtausgabe.* Ed. Giorgio Colli and
    Mazzino Montinari. Berlin: Walter de Gruyter, 1967–.

———. *The Portable Nietzsche.* Trans. and ed. Walter Kaufmann. New York:
    Viking, 1968.

———. *The Will to Power.* Trans. Walter Kaufmann and R. J. Hollingdale.
    Ed. Walter Kaufmann. New York: Vintage Books, 1967.

Nussbaum, Martha. "Aristophanes and Socrates on Learning Practical Wisdom." In *Aristophanes: Essays in Interpretation,* vol. 26 of *Yale Classical Studies,* ed. Jeffrey Henderson. New York: Cambridge University Press, 1980.

———. *The Fragility of Goodness: Luck and Ethics in Greek Tragedy and Philosophy.* Cambridge: Cambridge University Press, 1986.

Nye, Andrea. "The Hidden Host: Irigary and Diotima at Plato's *Symposium.*" *Hypatia* 3 (winter 1989): 45–61.

Pauly, August Friedrich von, and Georg Wissowa. *Pauly's Real-Encyclopädie der classischen Altertumswissenschaft.* 2d ser. Stuttgart: J. B. Metzler, 1914-.

Pieper, Josef. *Begeisterung und göttlicher Wahnsinn: Über den platonischen Dialog "Phaidros."* Munich: Kösel Verlag, 1962.

———. *Enthusiasm and Divine Madness: On the Platonic Dialogue "Phaedrus."* Trans. Richard and Clara Winston. New York: Harcourt, Brace, and World, 1964.

Pindar. *Nemean Odes. Isthmian Odes. Fragments.* Trans. William H. Race. Loeb Classical Library. Cambridge: Harvard University Press, 1997.

———. *The Odes of Pindar.* Trans. Richmond Lattimore. 2d ed. Chicago: University of Chicago Press, 1976.

———. *Olympian Odes. Pythian Odes.* Trans. William H. Race. Loeb Classical Library. Cambridge: Harvard University Press, 1997.

Planinc, Zdravko. *Plato's Political Philosophy: Prudence in the "Republic" and the "Laws."* Columbia: University of Missouri Press, 1991.

———. *Plato through Homer: Poetry and Philosophy in the Cosmological Dialogues.* Forthcoming.

———. *Politics, Philosophy, Writing: Plato's Art of Caring for Souls.* Columbia: University of Missouri Press, 2001.

Plato. *The Collected Dialogues of Plato, Including the Letters.* Ed. Edith Hamilton and Huntington Cairns. Bollingen Series. New York: Random House, 1961.

———. *Complete Works.* Ed. John M. Cooper. Indianapolis: Hackett, 1997.

———. *The Dialogues of Plato.* Trans. B. Jowett. 1892. Reprint, New York: Random House, 1920.

———. *Four Texts on Socrates.* Trans. Thomas G. West and Grace Starry West. 2d ed. Ithaca: Cornell University Press, 1998.

———. *The Laws of Plato.* Trans. Thomas L. Pangle. Chicago: University of Chicago Press, 1980.

———. *Phaedrus.* Trans. James H. Nichols Jr. Ithaca: Cornell University Press, 1998.

———. *Plato.* Ed. G. P. Goold. 12 vols. Loeb Classical Library. 1914–1935. Reprint, Cambridge: Harvard University Press, 1982–1992.

———. *The Republic of Plato*. Trans. Allan Bloom. New York: Basic Books, 1968.

———. *The Roots of Political Philosophy: Ten Forgotten Socratic Dialogues*. Ed. Thomas L. Pangle. Ithaca: Cornell University Press, 1987.

———. *The Symposium of Plato*. Trans. R. G. Bury. Cambridge, England: W. Heffer and Sons, 1932.

Platon. *Werke*. Ed. Friedrich Daniel Ernst Schleiermacher. 6 vols. Berlin: Akademie Verlag, 1984.

Platonis. *Platonis Opera*. Ed. John Burnet. 5 vols. 1901–1907. Reprint, Oxford: Clarendon Press, 1995.

Plutarch. *Lives*. Ed. G. P. Goold. Vols. 4, 6, 7. Loeb Classical Library. 1916–1919. Reprint, Cambridge: Harvard University Press, 1993–2000.

Renault, Mary. *The Mask of Apollo*. New York: Vintage Books, 1966.

Robinson, T. M. Review of *Plato's Seventh Letter*, by Ludwig Edelstein. *Phoenix* 21 (1967): 143.

Rosen, Stanley. *Hermeneutics as Politics*. New York: Oxford University Press, 1987.

———. *The Mask of Enlightenment: Nietzsche's "Zarathustra."* Cambridge: Cambridge University Press, 1995.

———. *Metaphysics in Ordinary Language*. New Haven: Yale University Press, 1999.

———. *Plato's "Symposium."* 2d ed. New Haven: Yale University Press, 1987; reprint, South Bend: St. Augustine's Press, 1999.

———. *The Quarrel between Philosophy and Poetry: Studies in Ancient Thought*. New York: Routledge, 1988.

Sabine, George H. *A History of Political Theory*. 3d ed. New York: Holt, Rinehart, and Winston, 1965.

Saxenhouse, Arlene W. "Eros and the Female in Greek Political Thought: An Interpretation of Plato's *Symposium*." *Political Theory* 12:1 (February 1984): 5–27.

———. "The Net of Hephaestus: Aristophanes' Speech in Plato's *Symposium*." *Interpretation* 13:1 (January 1985): 15–32.

Sayre, Kenneth M. "Plato's Dialogues in Light of the *Seventh Letter*." In *Platonic Writings, Platonic Readings*, ed. Charles L. Griswold Jr. New York: Routledge, 1988.

———. *Plato's Literary Garden: How to Read a Platonic Dialogue*. South Bend: University of Notre Dame Press, 1995.

Schleiermacher, Friedrich Daniel Ernst. *Schleiermacher's Introductions to the Dialogues of Plato*. Trans. William Dobson. New York: Arno Press, 1973.

Sinnett, M. W. "Eric Voegelin and the Essence of the Problem: The Question of Divine-Human Attunement in Plato's *Symposium*." In *Politics, Order, and History: Essays on the Work of Eric Voegelin*, ed. Glenn

Hughes, Stephen A. McKnight, and Geoffrey L. Price. Sheffield, England: Sheffield Academic Press, 2001.

Solzhenitsyn, Alexander. *Cancer Ward.* New York: Modern Library, 1983.

Stone, I. F. *The Trial of Socrates.* Boston: Little, Brown, 1988.

Stone, Robert L., ed. *Essays on "The Closing of the American Mind."* Chicago: Chicago Review Press, 1989.

Strauss, Leo. *The City and Man.* Chicago: University of Chicago Press, 1964.

———. *Liberalism Ancient and Modern.* New York: Basic Books, 1968.

———. "The Mutual Influence of Theology and Philosophy." *Independent Journal of Philosophy* 3 (1979): 111–18.

———. *Natural Right and History.* Chicago: University of Chicago Press, 1953.

———. *On Plato's "Symposium."* Ed. Seth Benardete. Chicago: University of Chicago Press, 2001.

———. *Persecution and the Art of Writing.* Chicago: University of Chicago Press, 1952.

———. *Socrates and Aristophanes.* New York: Basic Books, 1966.

———. *Studies in Platonic Political Philosophy.* Chicago: University of Chicago Press, 1983.

———. *"What Is Political Philosophy?" and Other Studies.* New York: Free Press, 1959.

Strauss, Leo, and Jacob Klein. "A Giving of Accounts." *College* 22:1 (April 1970): 1–5.

Taylor, A. E. *Plato: The Man and His Work.* Cleveland: Meridian Books, 1956.

Tennemann, Wilhelm Gottlieb. *Geschichte der Philosophie.* 11 vols. Leipzig: Johann Ambrosius Barth, 1798–1819.

Thucydides. *The Peloponnesian War.* Trans. Rex Warner. New York: Penguin Books, 1954.

Toobin, Jeffrey. *A Vast Conspiracy: The Real Story of the Sex Scandal that Nearly Brought Down a President.* New York: Random House, 1999.

Vlastos, Gregory. *Platonic Studies.* Princeton: Princeton University Press, 1973.

Voegelin, Eric. *Anamnesis.* Trans. Gerhart Niemeyer. South Bend: University of Notre Dame Press, 1978.

———. *Anamnesis: Zur Theorie der Geschichte und Politik.* Munich: R. Piper, 1966.

———. *The Collected Works of Eric Voegelin.* Vol. 16, *Order and History.* Vol. 3, *Plato and Aristotle.* Columbia: University of Missouri Press, 2000.

———. *The New Science of Politics.* Chicago: University of Chicago Press, 1952.

———. *Order and History.* Vols. 1–3. Baton Rouge: Louisiana State University Press, 1956–1957.

von Fritz, Kurt. *Platon in Sizilien und das Problem der Philosophenherrschaft.* Berlin: Walter de Gruyter, 1968.

White, David A. *Rhetoric and Reality in Plato's "Phaedrus."* Albany: SUNY Press, 1993.

White, Nicholas P. *Plato on Knowledge and Reality.* Indianapolis: Hackett, 1976.

Xenophon. *Hellenica, Books I–IV.* Trans. Carlton L. Brownson. Loeb Classical Library. Cambridge: Harvard University Press, 1997.

———. *Hellenica, Books V–VII.* Trans. Carlton L. Brownson. Loeb Classical Library. Cambridge: Harvard University Press, 1997.

———. *Hellenika.* Ed. Gisela Strasburger. Greek-German ed. Munich: Heimeran, 1970.

———. *Hellenika II.3.11–IV.2.8.* Ed. and trans. by Peter Krentz. Warminster, England: Aris and Philips, 1995.

———. *Memorabilia. Oeconomicus. Symposium. Apology.* Trans. E. C. Marchant and O. J. Todd. Ed. G. P. Goold. Loeb Classical Library. Cambridge: Harvard University Press, 1997.

Xenophontis. *Opera Omnia.* Ed. E. C. Marchant. Vol. 2. Rev. ed. 1901. Reprint, Oxford: Clarendon Press, 1949.

Zuckert, Catherine H. *Postmodern Platos: Nietzsche, Heidegger, Gadamer, Strauss, Derrida.* Chicago: University of Chicago Press, 1996.

Index of Personal Names

Achelous, 411, 419, 435, 528
Achilles, 193n, 214, 288, 345, 405, 488
Acumenus, 422, 422n, 531
Adam and Eve, 484, 485
Adams, John, 86
Adeimantus (brother of Plato), 35, 136, 137, 365, 396, 481
Adeimantus (son of Leukolophides), 414
Adrasteia, 470, 483, 491, 493
Aeschylus, 101
Agamemnon, 201, 288, 384, 488
Agathon (poet), 15, 17, 18, 35, 37, 38, 184–85, 187, 189, 190–91, 193, 234–35, 239, 248, 263, 370–72, 373, 414, 419, 424, 465, 520; his symposium as struggle with Socrates, 194–203, 370; his symposium battle plan and its relationship to drinking ability, 204–7, 226–27, 300; *Symposium* speech of, analyzed, 280–98; treatment as target of Socrates' *Symposium* speech, 300–369 passim; treatment as target of tactical moves of Alcibiades, 383–94, 396, 399, 402, 407–9
Agis, 386, 389
Air (as god imputed to Socrates), 245, 250
Alcestis, 214, 272, 305, 333n, 345
Alcibiades, 3, 4, 13–18, 20, 24, 31, 32, 34, 35, 36, 37, 38, 40, 43, 110, 185, 187, 189, 190–93, 194, 198, 199, 201n, 205n, 207, 246, 254–55, 267, 276, 284n, 335, 337, 346, 349, 350, 351, 353n, 355, 357–58, 370–72, 414–15, 420, 429, 531; as Dionysus in the *Symposium*, 367–69;

consistently portrayed in Plato, Plutarch, and Thucydides, 372–87; *Symposium* speech of, analyzed, 387–410 passim
Alcidamas, 291
Alcmeon, 479
Alexander the Great, 28, 374, 387
Ammon. *See* Thamos
Anacreon, 445
Anaxagoras, 250, 250n, 252, 531
Antenor, 405
Antinous, 526, 529
Antiochus, 386, 415
Aphrodite, 161, 200, 217, 220, 236, 259, 261n, 283, 292, 309, 317n, 319–20, 323, 335, 336, 336n, 337, 338, 339, 350, 354, 356–57, 359, 367, 368, 373, 386, 404, 463
Apollo, 269, 283, 293, 320, 481, 530
Apollodorus of Phalerum, 34, 35, 190–92, 194, 204, 395, 420
Aquinas, Thomas. *See* Thomas Aquinas
Archelaus of Macedon, 387n
Archytas, 148, 164, 166, 168
Ares, 292, 309, 501
Aristodemus of Cydathenaeum, 17, 35, 185, 190, 192, 194, 195, 197n, 198, 199, 200, 201, 203, 204, 207, 248, 284, 285, 287, 368
Aristogiton and Harmodius, 225
Aristophanes, 3, 18, 34, 56, 183, 185, 187, 188, 189, 192n, 194, 200, 201, 204, 205, 206, 207, 226, 227–28, 229, 233, 234, 235, 237, 238, 239, 241–42, 259n, 281, 283, 287, 288, 289, 292, 295, 296, 298, 301, 303, 307, 317, 318, 319,

INDEX OF SUBJECTS

This index is not intended as an exhaustive list of subjects touched upon in the text. Rather, it is offered as a selective guide to the principal problems of understanding Platonic writings and the Platonic arguments, dramas, concepts, myths, and symbols that are most important for this study. The subjects indexed are grouped in analytically coherent clusters.